Compliments of

Cornelius Anderson

On Steel by John Sartain. Phila.

John Smalley.

MEMORIAL.

GENEALOGY,

AND

ECCLESIASTICAL HISTORY.

TO WHICH IS ADDED

AN APPENDIX, WITH EXPLANATORY NOTES,

AND A FULL INDEX.

"The glory of Children are their Fathers."—*Solomon.*

"Those only deserve to be remembered by posterity, who treasure up the history of their Ancestors."—*Burke.*

"There is a *Moral* and *Philosophical* respect for our Ancestors which elevates the character and improves the heart."—*Webster.*

BY ALFRED ANDREWS,

MEMBER OF CONNECTICUT AND WISCONSIN HISTORICAL SOCIETIES.

CHICAGO, ILL.:
PUBLISHED BY A. H. ANDREWS.
1867.

PRINTED BY CASE, LOCKWOOD AND COMPANY,
HARTFORD, CONN.

PREFACE.

When a plain man, more used to the plough than the pen, turns author, and asks to be read, a preface may be used, either to justify, apologize, or explain. This can be taken for either of these purposes, as best suits the reader. I think it was during the Spring of 1850, that a gentleman from Ohio, by the name of Andrews, called on the writer, to inquire after the early settlers of that name, in the State. I could give him no information on the subject, having no history of my ancestors, back of my own grandfather. He passed on, leaving on my mind this reflection. What! lived more than a half century, and know scarce a hundred years of your own family history? I began by looking over old files of deeds and papers, searching family, church, town, and probate records, and the State archives, until I had gathered near four thousand names, and collected several of the branches, into a regular chain of families, from the early settlement of the country, to the child now in the cradle. Some of my friends, knowing what I had done in this line of inquiry, proposed that I take up the subject of an Ecclesiastical History of the First Church and Society of New Britain. The subject was introduced at an annual meeting, by the motion that a committee be appointed, and it was voted at the adjourned annual meeting of the church, held 28th January, 1859, that Alfred Andrews, Noah W. Stanley and Timothy W. Stanley, be a committee to secure, (if they deem it best,) a copy of the records of this church, set in order, and in a form fitted for preservation. This committee have reported progress annually, and been reappointed to carry out more fully the object.

Perhaps no individual then had a thought of doing more than transcribing our incomplete records, scattered in no less than six or seven small books, into one large manuscript volume, with such facts appended, in the form of notes, as would explain and illustrate our history. But after the committee had conferred, and sent a delegation to Goshen, to see an excellent manuscript history of the First Church there, by Deacon Lewis M. Norton, and especially after an examination of a printed history of the First Church in Belchertown, Mass., by Hon. Mark Doolittle, it was thought best to make a book for the public, comprising family genealogy with church history, and what might be found respecting the early settlement of the place.

It was a favorable circumstance for the production of the following pages, that there was a continuous, (though imperfect,) record of the First Church in New Britain, from its first organization, to the present time. This can hardly be said of any other church in this vicinity, whose age exceeds a century. Almost every such church has a break or gap in its history. It is still a mooted question, whether a record voluntarily begun and continued at the pastor's own expense of time, care, and stationery, belongs to him and his heirs, or to the church and their successors. Hence in part the defective church records of Connecticut, and other States. Heirs-at-law have retained them as their property, and carried them to parts unknown. In all the years spent in gathering materials for this work, the compiler acknowledges with gratitude a kind Providence, who has favored him in every weary step. To say nothing of a few *officials*, who have been paid from one to three dollars for a single letter, it is with pleasure he remembers favors from Ex-Governor Pond, of Milford, Deacon Lewis M. Norton, of Goshen, Hon. Tracy Peck, of Bristol, and Rev. Abner Morse, of Boston, (all gone to their final rest during the progress of these researches;) by Doctor D. W. Patterson, of West Winsted, Edwin Stearnes, Esq., of Middletown, A. S. Kellogg, Esq., of Vernon, Ali Andrews, Esq., Bridgeport, and not least, by Gad Andrews, Esq., of Southington. The author takes this opportunity to thank all the clergy in this vicinity, who have kindly given him access to church records, and otherwise aided and encouraged him in the work. He has received kindness and courtesy from society, town, and probate clerks, and especially from Messrs. Trumbull and Hoadley, in giving him access to the State archives, as Secretary of State and State Librarian. By the facilities of correspondence, he he has been aided in this enterprise, in the exchange of more than a thousand letters, some from the remote parts of the country, and some from England. He will never forget the patience of those, (both in this and other towns,) whom he has annoyed with a thousand and one questions. Especially is he under obligation to the old people of this vicinity, not so much for dates, as for connections and locations of the numerous families. It has been found that less than one-third of the families have any record of their children, respecting either births or marriages; and such as are found, are often made from memory, after the family has become so numerous as to trouble the parents in recalling the several dates. It is found that some of the records thus made up do not agree with the public journals nor with the truth.

The compiler has spared no time nor pains to be *correct*, (for correctness is the chief excellence in all history,) yet where there is so much of uncertainty, some errors must be expected.

The most valuable part of this work, and that which will be most appreciated in future years, and which has cost the author the most labor, is its genealogical department. Few know the amount of time, patience, and labor expended on such researches. It has been shrewdly, (if not wisely,) said by a "pedigree hunter," that it was useless to tell antiquaries anything about the cost of such works, for they understood it; and it was equally useless to tell others, for they could not comprehend you. Is there not some danger that families and family religion will be lost sight of, in the shadow of congregations, Sunday Schools, and churches? God, in the days of the *Patriarchs,* made families the depository of his church, and constituted the father the priest of the household, making a covenant with Abraham, which was to be an *everlasting* covenant to him, and his *seed* after him; which covenant was confirmed to Isaac and Jacob, and under the new dispensation to *all*, even as many as the Lord our God should call, who should possess like precious faith with Abraham.*

Hence the author, in the following pages, and in the plan of the work, assumes that the Church of Christ is mainly drawn from families in which God is acknowledged. The fact that over eighty per cent. of the First Church in New Britain, were baptized in infancy, confirms this view of the subject as correct, and that God is far more mindful of his covenant, than his people. We prefer no claim that this work is either complete, or perfect; indeed, from the condition of the records, and other sources of information from which it is compiled, it could not be. If its perusal shall incite one pastor or church, to give greater attention to their own record; if it shall lead one follower of Christ to greater diligence in fulfilling his mission; if it shall inspire one child with more love of home and ancestors; or if it shall expand the contracted brow of a single antiquary in search of lore; just so far the hopes of the compiler will be realized. If, as a book of reference, (and this will be its chief use,) it shall afford those who consult it, a tithe of the satisfaction the author has enjoyed in its construction, he will be gratified. In commenting on the life and character of those who have passed away, the author has aimed in all cases to be impartial. So far as the record of the church extended, it was, of course, made the guide; but where there has been no written history, nor tradition, nor personal acquaintance, the dead are passed in silence. The compiler is very sensible of the delicacy of the subject in this respect, and the difficulty of doing justice to this part of the work, and has aimed to avoid offense on the one hand, and neglect on the other. Should the reader discover want of connection in the events related, or in the different parts of the work, he is reminded that such must necessarily be the case, where so many of the facts and incidents are entirely disconnected of themselves. In closing these prefatory remarks, the subscriber deems it proper to say that he is under great obligations to the committee with whom he is

---

* *Acts* 2, 39. "For the promise is unto you, and to your children, and to all that are afar off, even as many as the Lord our God shall call.

associated, and to the present pastor of the church, for aid and encouragement in his labors, but not in any sense such as to make either of them responsible for any errors or defects that may appear in the work. The author hereby assumes all such responsibilities, and submits the whole to a discerning, yet indulgent public, hoping that generations to come may be benefited by this humble effort to perpetuate the memory of those worthy ancestors of ours, who first settled New Britain and its vicinity.

ALFRED ANDREWS.

NEW BRITAIN, 2d May, 1867.

INTRODUCTION.

The Ecclesiastical history of that territory, or part of ancient Farmington, in Connecticut, lying east of Farmington mountain, bounded east by Wethersfield and Middletown, south by Wallingford, now Meriden, and extending north to what we now call (*Clark Hill,*) is very difficult to understand. Previous to the year 1705, the inhabitants belonged to the parish of Farmington, and attended public worship, and paid their ministerial taxes there only. Hence the early history of the few families that settled on this territory previous to that date, would be mingled with that of their brethren of the church in Farmington, and the parishioners there. A brief sketch of the settlement of that town, and the early history of that church is therefore deemed essential to the right understanding of subsequent events in their proper order. The first settlers in Farmington were from Hartford, being emigrants from Boston, Newtown, and Roxbury, Mass. They began the settlement in 1640, being four years only from the first in Hartford, and were probably attracted by the fine *natural* meadows on the (Tunxis) Farmington river. The town was incorporated in 1645.* The land was purchased of the Tunxis tribe of natives, a very numerous and warlike tribe, by a Comt. and in 1672 divided by eighty-four proprietors, to themselves and their heirs accord-

* Charter of 1645.

John Haynes Esqr., Gov.
Edward Hopkins, Esqr., Dep.
Capt. Mason
Mr Wolcott
Mr Webster
Mr Whiting
Mr Wells
Mr Trott
Mr Olliston
James Boosey
Jno Demon
Mr Hull
Mr Stoughton
Mr Steel
Mr Talcot

December ye first 1645, its ordered that ye plantation called Tunxis shall be called ffarmington, & that the bounds thereof shall be as followeth: The eastern Bounds shall meet with the western of these plantations which are to be five miles on this sid ye Great River, & the Northern Bounds shall be five miles from ye Hill in ye Great Meadow towards Massaco; & the Southern Bounds from ye sd Hill shall be five miles; & they shall have liberty to improve ten miles further than ye sd five, and to hinder others from the like, until the Court see fitt otherwise to dispose of it, and ye s'd plantation are to attend the General Orders, formerly made by this Court, settled by ye Committee to whom the same was referred, & other ocasions, as the rest of ye Plantations upon the River do: & Mr Steel is entreated for the present to be Recorder there, until ye Town have one fitt among themselves; they allso are to have ye like Libertyes as ye other Towns upon ye River

ing to their respective interests or tax lists. The township at the time of incorporation was about fifteen miles square. The early church records were burned,* but the committee subsequently appointed to gather facts say "they have good reason to believe it was organized about 1645, and that Rev Roger Newton was then installed its pastor.

A. D. 1654 he was dismissed, and removed to the church in Milford. Rev. Samuel Hooker, son of the venerable Thomas Hooker, of England, and Hartford, succeeded Mr. Newton, and was ordained probably in 1655. He died in 1695." It was during his ministry that the town voted at their annual meeting, 28th December, 1685, the following "to give £30 for a man to teach Schoole for one year, provided they can have a man that is so accomplished as to teach Children to read and *wright*, and teach the *grammer*, and also *to step into the pulpet* to be helpful *their*, in time of exegenti, and this *Schoole* to be a free *Schoole* for this *toun*." Such were the "accomplishments" required of common school teachers in that day, which shows that our ancestors had a regard for the educational interests of their children.† The town record shows a similar vote at a later date as follows, "18 Dec 1693 at the annual town meeting was chosen a *committy* to agree with a man to teach *Schoole* the first 3 months, January, February and March, and also to treat with a man yt is in capacity to teach *Lattin* and English, and in time of *Exogency* to be help*full* to Mr

---

for making orders among themselves; provided they alter not any fundamental agreements settled by ye s'd Committee hitherto attended.

A True copy of ye Record exam'd
by Hez. Wyllys Secret'y

At a General Assembly held at Hartford May 11th 1671, This Court Confirme unto ffarmington theyer Bounds Ten miles towards ye South from ye Round Hill: provided Capt. Clark injoy his Grant, without those exceptions made in theyer former Grant.

A true copy of Record, exam'd
by Hez. Wyllys Secret'y

* This is happily not true, as supposed, the original record is found, and it gives the date of the organization of the church at Farmington, the 13th of October, 1652.

† "At a meeting of the inhabitants of the town of Farmington held 27th Dec. 1687, it was voted by the town, that they would give 20£ for the maintenance of a Schoole for the year insuing for the instrocting of all such children as shall be sent to it, to learn to read, and wright the English tongue."

"At a meeting of the inhabitants of the town of Farmington held 12th Jany, 1687–8 Whereas the town at a Meeting held 27 Dec 1687 agreed to give twentie pounds, as is their expresst, to teach all such as shall be sent, by vote, the town declare, that "*all such as shall be sent*" is to be understood only *Male Children* that are throw their *korning book*." (Meaning probably to con syllables. Ed.) "At the same Meeting the towne voted that they would have a town hous to keep Schoole in, built this yeare, of 18 foot square, besides the Chimney space, with a suitable height for that servis, which hous is to be built by the touns Charg."

Hooker in the Ministry—and to make return to the select-men of what is attainable in yt matter, yt they may speedily acquaint the town with the same & also in case such a man be not attainable—then to agree with a man to teach *Schoole* the other 3 months of October, November, and December, which *committy* is Lef't Thos Heart, Sargt Saml Wadsworth, & Capt John Hart." It also further appears from the same record of like date, that our forefathers took due care of the manners and morals of the young people. "At the same meeting, to take care, and have inspection over the youth, in ye meeting-house, on the Sabbaths, and other days of *publique Exorcises* their was chosen John Norton junr Stephen Lee, & Thos Bird of James. The following about Indian children in Farmington is from the State archives. "Oct 1733 On a report made by the Rev. Saml Whitman of Farmington, relating to the Indians in sd town. This Assembly do appoint Capt Wm Wadsworth & Capt Josiah Hart of sd town to provide for the Dieting of the Indian lads at 4 Shillings pr week for the time they attend the Schoole in sd town, until the session of the Assembly in May next, and they then make report thereof. Concurred in the Upper House Test Geo. Wyllys, Sec. passed in the lower house Test Jno Russell Clerk."

(*Also May* 1734) "Whereas this Assembly in Oct. last did order that the charges of subsisting certain Indian Children at the Schoole at Far. should be paid out of the public Treas. Whereupon Capt Wm Wadsworth hath laid before this Assembly an acc of the charges which amount to the sum of £33, 6. s. which shall be paid out of the public Treas, unto the sd Wadsworth, who shall answer & pay the several sums to the respective persons mentioned in the acc passed in the Upper House Test. Geo. Wyllys Sec.

Concurred with in the lower house Test. Jno Russell Clerk."

(*Also* 1736) "The Colony of Connecticut indebted to sundry persons in ffarmington for bording Indian boys when at Schoole in Winter seson 1735–1736 to Robert porter 2 boys 18, weaks & 2 days at 4, s. per weak 7–6–0 to Ephraim Smith sen for keeping one boie 13 weaks & a half at 4, s. per weak £2, 14, s. 0, d. To John Wadsworth for bording 2 boise, 18 weaks at 4, s. pr weak £7, 4, s. 0, d. To Thos Cowles for keeping 2 boies 27 weaks each of them at 4, s. per weak £10, 16, 0.—£28, 0.—0—

"Whereas this Assembly in Oct. last did order that the charges of subsisting certain Indian Children at the Schoole at Far. should be paid out of the public Treas. Whereupon Capt Wm Wadsworth hath laid before this Assembly an acc of sd Charges which amount to the sum of £28— which is hereby ordered to be paid out of the public Treas. unto the said Capt Wadsworth, who shall pay the several sums, to the respective persons mentioned with sd acc." passed in the Upper house Test. Geo.

Wyllys Secy *May* 1736. Concurred in the lower house Test. Jno Buckley Clerk.

The above shows that the good people of Farmington were anxious to substitute Puritan civilization for Paganism among the aborigines of the town, and that the General Court of the Colony was willing to aid them. The following farther shows the wise and provident forethought for the children in general. "An Act for the encouragement and better supporting the schools that by Law ought to be kept in the several towns and parishes in the colony, (May 1733.) Be it enacted &c that the seven towns lately laid out in the western lands (as commonly called) shall be disposed of & settled according to such time & regulations as this Assembly shall order, and that the money that shall be given by those that may be allowed to settle in sd towns for the land there, shall be improved for the support of the aforesaid Schooles (viz) those schooles as ought to be kept in those towns that are now settled, and that did make, & complete *Lists* of their Polls & Estates in the year last past, and such towns shall receive sd monies, every town according to the proportion of sd Lists given in as aforesaid the last year, all which money shall be let out & the interest thereof improved for the support of the respective Schooles aforesaid forever, & for no other use, & the committee of each parish (or town where there is but one parish) shall receive the proportion of money arising as aforesaid, & give a receipt, that they have received such a sum of money, to be let out and improved for the support of a school in such town or parish where they are a committee as aforesaid, & that if at any time the sd money, or interest thereof shall be by order of such town or parish, or the committee chosen by them, put to or employed by them for any other use, than for the support of a school there, that then such sum shall be returned into the Treas. of the Colony, & the Treas. of the Colony shall upon refusal thereof, recover the same sum of such town or parish, that have misemployed such money shall forever lose the benefit thereof." past by the upper house Test Hez. Wyllys Sec'y. Concurred in the lower house Test Jno Russell, Clerk. The above is introduced here because in order of time, and will be referred to hereafter.

The ancient church in Farmington was noted for piety, wealth, and influence, and since no list, or catalogue of the original members (to the compiler's knowledge,) has ever appeared in print, he takes the liberty to quote from the original record the following historical facts, only premising that the church, as well as the town records were kept at that early date, by that noted man and recorder, Mr. *John Steele.*

"CHURCH MEMBERS

ANNO DOM 1652 UPON THE 13TH OF OCTOBER.

Mr Roger Newton
Stephen Hart
Thomas Judd
John Bronson
John Coll
Thomas Thompson, and
Robert Porter joined in covenant in Farmington,
About one month after, myself, (meaning John Steele. Ed.) joined with them
About one month after,
Mrs Newton, the
Wife of Stephen Hart, the
Wife of Thomas Judd, the
Wife of John Cole, and the
Wife of Thomas Thompson, did also join with them.
A little before this
John Loomis was joined to this church.
About the 30th of January 1652 (3)
Nathaniel Kellogg and his wife John Steel John Standley
Thomas Newell, and
Thomas Barnes were also joined to the congregation.
Upon February the 7th
John Lankton was joined to the congregation.
July the 12th 1653
Thomas Newell's wife, and
John Standley's wife, and
Robert Porter's wife, were joined to the congregation.
On July 19, 1653
Thomas Porter and his wife, and
Richard Bronson's wife, were joined to the congregation, and
Moses Ventres was joined with them the said 19 July 1653.
Joseph Kellogg and his wife, and
Simon Wrotham, and the
Wife of John Hart, and the
Wife of John Wyatt were joined to the Church October the 9th, 1653.
Upon April the 2d 1654
Richard Bronson, and
John Hart were joined to the church. On that day
Samuel Steele, and his daughter Mary Steele about the age of 16 months were joined to the Church. And on that day
Hannah Woodruff the wife of Matthew Woodruff, and his daughters
Hannah Woodruff age about 5 years, and
Elizabeth Woodruff about the age of 2 years 5 months, were also joined to the Church.
And on that day
Mary Andrews, the wife of John Andrews, and her son
Abraham Andrews, about the age of 6 years, 3 months, and
Daniel Andrews, about the age of 3 years, 10 months, and
Joseph Andrews, about the age of 2 years, 3 months, were joined to the church.

Thomas Orton, and his wife were joined to the Church Dec the 22d, 1656.
John Warner, and
William Smith, and the
Widow Stans, and the
Wife of William Lewis, and the
Wife of John North and the
Wife of Samuel Loomis, were joined to the Ch. 15 Mar 1656-7.
On January the 22d 1657-8.
Anthony Howkins, and
William Lewis, were joined to the Church.
On the 9th May 1658
John Andrews, joined the Church in the covenant.
John Lee, and
William Judd, were joined to the Ch. July the 15th 1660."

Here follows on the record a list of families with children from seventeen years to one day old called "Children of the Church" with dates of baptisms.

We pass over these lists and dates, and come down in the record to 1st March, 1679-80, when we find a full roll of church members in "full communion"* in the church in Farmington. This roll or list seems to be numbered and graded according to rank, standing, or dignity, in the community, beginning with 1, down to 42 heads of families. It is thought our fathers in these nice distinctions took for a basis, "age, list, titles, and whatever else makes a man honorable." Let not the reader be surprised at this practice in the olden time. It was only a necessary preparation for the assignment of seats in the meeting house. If you say such comparisons would not be tolerated in this age, it might be replied, we have no such necessity, for our seats are rented to the highest bidder.

1 Deacon Hart
2 Deacon Judd
3 Thos Newel & his wife
4 Capt Standley & his wife
5 Robert Porter
6 Thos Porter & his wife
7 Richard Bronson & his wife
8 John Lancton & his wife
9 Thomas Barnes & his wife
10 Moses Ventrus
11 Wm Lewis jun & his wife
12 Thos Orton & his wife
13 John North sen & his wife
14 John Andrews sen & his wife
15 Isaac More & his wife
16 John Norton sen & his wife
17 Mr Wrotham
18 Samuel Hooker & his wife
19 John Lee & his wife
20 Wm Judd & his wife
21 John Wadsworth & his wife
22 Matthew Woodruff & his wife
23 Stephen Hart jun
24 Samuel Coales & his wife
35 John Root sen & his wife
26 John Judd & his wife
27 Thomas Hart & his wife
28 John Thompson & his wife
29 John Standley jun & his wife
30 Joseph Bird & his wife
31 John Cole & his wife
32 Benjamen Judd & his wife
33 John Woodruff & his wife
34 John Clark & his wife
35 Thos Porter jun & his wife
36 Thomas Thompson
37 Thos Bull & his wife
38 Wm Lewis sen:

* Implying that others were under the "half way Covenant" as it was called.

39 Jacob Bronson & his wife
40 James Bird & his wife
Mrs Howkins
Samuel Gridley's wife
John Orton's wife
Widow Warner
John Norton jun's wife
Edmund Scott's wife
Mehitabel Smith
John Warner's wife

41 Thos Judd jun & his wife
42 Obadiah Richards & his wife
Samuel North's wife
Richard Seamer's wife
Joseph Woodford's wife
Thomas Warner's wife
Joseph Hiccock's wife
Samuel Hiccock's wife
John Scovil's wife.

DEACONS.

Stephen Hart (d. 1683)
Thomas Judd (removed to Northampton)
John Langdon d. 1689)
Isaac Moore
Thomas Bull (d. 1708)
John Standley (d. 1729)
John Wadsworth (d. 1718)
Samuel Porter (d. 1707)
Lef't Thomas Porter (d. 1718) } elected 19 Nov 1718
John Hart (d. 1753) }
Nathaniel Newell (d. 1753)

6 January 1668–9 It was voted by the Church assembled at Deacon Hart's that with respect to the sacrament, each brother of the Church should send in to the Deacons, a peck of Wheat, or the worth of a shilling in current pay, for the defraying of the next sacrament, and also for the clearing of that little, which according to the Deacons report, was yet due for the sacrament already past.

As also that for the future, every brother of the Church should for each sacrament allow 6, d. except such of the brethren whose wives come not to the Supper, because not members of the Church; and to them it was permitted to pay in 3, d; or 6 d. which they pleased, for each sacrament.

The compiler supposes that most of the families now living in these States bearing the names of the above might trace their pedigree back to these worthy sires and mothers.

It was during the ministry of Mr. Hooker, and the interim to the ordination of Rev. Samuel Whitman, 1706, that the families in the "south-eastern boundary" of Farmington at a place called "Great Swamp," walked with their children in their arms, some eight or ten miles to attend the public worship of God in Farmington village, the men with well loaded guns in front and rear of the company. It shows how much they desired the sincere milk of the word. It affords a striking evidence of their zeal for religion, and that the word and ordinances, were indeed precious in those days.

Richard Seymour and others began this settlement about A. D. 1686, at a place now called "Chrishan Lane." Here stood the Seymour Fort, or Palisades, within which the cabins were constructed, and to which all the settlers repaired at nightfall, for safety against the Indians, and for quiet rest. The well at which they quenched their thirst, still furnishes the best water. It was dug in the center of the fort. Stephen Lee had a grant by the town A. D. 1689, of five roods of land, on the west side of the highway, provided it doth not hinder former grants and the watering place.*

Sergeant Benjamin Judd was located some sixty rods north of Captain Stephen Lee, where now (1862,) Richard Judd owns. Joseph Smith, senior, was a neighbor about half a mile south of Captain Lee, and all on the east street. Isaac Lewis had his house where now, (1862,) stands the house of John Ellis. It was said to be the oldest within the present limits of the town of New Britain, and Robert Boothe, senior, had his home next west where now, (1862,) Enoch Kelsey is located. Deacon Anthony Judd where William Ellis lives; John Woodruff near that little grove east of the alms house, the highway to it long since sold and shut up. Daniel Dewey a few rods south of Deacon Anthony Judd. Thomas North, (ancestor of our North families,) the Seymours and Gilberts clustered about the *Stockade*. Dr. Joseph Steele, the Standleys, Rootes, Harts, Nortons, Cowles or Coles, Nehemiah Porter, Joseph Lankton, Newel, Gridley, Bronsons, were located south of the Palisades, making some fourteen families in all. This valley upon which these pioneers settled was a rich alluvial soil, and might be termed bottom land. The chief objection was its being *too* low, hence its name "Great Swamp." It was part of the hunting grounds of the Mattabesett tribe of Indians, and tradition says their lodge or settlement was at the place called now and has been for many years, "Beckley quarter."† Their *Trail* passed near the "Seamer Fort," past "half-way Hill" to Tunxis, with which tribe they had mutual intercourse.

---

* This location was next north of the present Skinner house, (so called,) and generally known by old people as the "Hinsdale place."

† The first English settler of this locality was Sergeant Richard Beckley, a planter in New Haven Colony, 1639, but moved to this part of Wethersfield, which from his day has been called "*Beckley quarter.*" The following shows his title to the land, and is from the records of lands for Wethersfield, viz., "25 Feb 1680 Lands belonging to Sergt Richard Beckley & to his heirs and assigns forever, lying in Wethersfield, upon Conecticott river, which he purchased of terramoogus (Indian) with the consent of the Court, and town of Wethersfield."

"It is at the south end of sd purchase & grant the whole containing 310 acres, be it more or less, whereon his housing & barn stands, it is bodnded on land not layd out, or not granted South, East, & North, & a highway between the west lots, & the aforesaid land west."

This locality at the "southeastern boundary of ffarmington" called above "Great Swamp," had an early English name, which seems to have been abandoned for this of "Great Swamp," *viz.*, *Meridun*, *Meridan*, or *Meridon*, a name finally given 1725 to the present town of Meriden, to take the place of "Pilgrims Harbor." Rev. George W. Perkins in his History of Meriden, says "When Farmington was settled by the English there was a band of the Mattabesitt tribe, in the southeast part of that town, probably near Kensington." In his Appendix he quotes a deed of Seankett (Indian) of a large tract of Land in the woods towards New Haven, att & about the land now in possession of Mr Jonathan Gilbert, intitled & known by the name *Merideen*, bounded by marked trees & by the land of say'd Jonathan Gilbert, dated 15 Oct 1664.

The same author quotes another deed given as mortgage to John Talcott (which seems to cover the same land,) by *Adam Puit*, Indian, dated 10 Aug 1684, (which is date of record,)in which the land is sd to lie on the road to New Haven, beyond, & next *adjoyneing* to Jonathan Gilbarts farme. But to settle the question of the old name to this locality, I quote from a deed of Captain Daniel Clark, of Windsor, to Jonathan Gilbert, dated 22 Apl 1672, of 300 Acres of land (forty of which was to be meadow, by Grant of the Colony to sd Clark,) lying, situate, and laid out at a place called *Moridam* where Mr Jonathan Gilbert's farm is, & bounded partly on the *Mattabesick River* where it may be allowed of the town of Farmington. Signed by Daniel Clark, and witnessed by Nathnl Bissel, and John Plumbe. This deed is in possession of the Gilbert family, living, 1867, on the same farm said above to be owned by Jonathan Gilbert, previous to 1644.

At a meeting of the inhabitants of the town of Farmington, 23d Dec. 1707, it was voted and agreed that those who inhabit in the limits granted to be a new Society at "Great Swamp," that their dues to the support of a minister here be abated, from March last, provided the selectmen certify who those persons are who have there covenanted to each other, to support the present means they have there. Also at the next annual meeting, 14th Dec—1708 a Committee was appointed to consider of the petition of our neighbors at the "Great Swamp" granted to be a society, they petitioning to be a distinct town, & make report of their opinion in that case to the next town meeting. The next meeting seems to have been held on the 20th Dec. 1708, when the town by vote gave their consent that all those that do or shall personally inhabit within the limits formerly allowed to the Society at the place called the "Great Swamp," that all those, and for what estates they have there, should pay their proportions of charge in setting up, and maintaining the public worship of God there, to that society, as also, all those who shall improve lands within the sd Society limits, shall pay according to law for those lands to sd Society,

2

althoug they personally inhabit elsewhere. The above votes, with what follows of the action of Farmington, as a town, and the special act of the Worshipful General Court of the Colony, show the liberty and authority of these people in a remote "corner of the wilderness" to set up for themselves.

"At a town meeting in Farmington 28 September A. D. 1705, the Town by vote did manifest their consent, that so many of their Inhabitants, that do or shall personally inhabit, at a place called "Great Swamp," and upland belonging thereto, aud in the divisions of land on the East side of the Blow Mountains, and in those lots, called the Batchellor lots, and so much of the division of land against Wethersfield, as shall extend Northward from the "Great Swamp," until it shall include the lot that was William Judd's and no more, so many of them, as see cause (none to be compelled) that they become a Ministerial Society, when they do gain a capable Minister amongst them, and continue so to be, so long as they shall in a compotently constant way, maintain such a Minister amongst them, and whom so long as they shall so do, themselves, and what estate they have there shall be freed from the charge of the Ministry elsewhere, always provided that they shall for their own proportion of labor in the Highways, maintain the passages and highways they have occasion for there amongst themselves, without involving the Town in general therewith, as also that they shall at no time endeavor to surprise their neighbors, by endeavouring to obtain of the General Court other advantages, in which the town in general may be concerned, without first acquainting the Town therewith, nor claim nor chalenge any interest in the sequestered lands, for the maintenance of the Ministry there. A true Copy Test John Hooker Registrar taken this 9 day of Oct A D 1705 Farmington."

"To the Right Honourable and Worshipful General Assembly now sitting at New Haven this 11 day of October A D 1705 Greeting. We the subscribers hereunto, do humbly request this Hon. Assembly to grant unto your humble petitioners a Settlement and confirmation of a Society at a place called the "Great Swamp" within Farmington bounds, having obtained a liberty from said Farmington for that. Your Honours will determine the bounds for said Society accordingly. The principal and only moving cause of this our humble petition, is the remoteness from any town, whereby we are under great disadvantage for our souls good, by the Ministry of the word, and in that your humble petitioners may be under the better advantage to set up and maintain ye worship, & ordinance of Jesus Christ, in that desolate corner of the wilderness, we humbly request that your honors will please to annex into our bounds, for the only use of said Society, all those lands that are between our bounds southward, and Wallingford bounds Northward, for the benefit of the

Taxes of said lands, for ye support, of ye public charge, of said Society, and our unanimous desire is that the Worshipful Capt Thos Hart, will prefer, and declare, this our humble petition, and the circumstances of the case in said court, all which your Honor's petitioners Humbly submit. Dated 16 Oct 1705" signed

John Hart sen	Stephen Lee
Richard Seymour	Daniel Dewey
Stephen Roote	Samuel Seymour
John Lee	Ebenezer Seymour
Daniel Andrus jun	Joseph Lankton
Thos North	Thomas Hart
Nehemiah Porter	Samuel Newel
Jacob Bronson jun	Isaac Norton
Isaac Cowles	John Norton
Samuel Smith	Anthony Judd
John Cole	Benjn Judd
Samuel Cowles	Caleb Cowles
Isaac Lewis	John Stanley
Joseph Smith	Thos Gridley
Nathl Cowles	

This petition was granted. And the parish proceeded to build a Meeting House, but at what precise date is not known; the location is however known to be on the high ground in "Christian Lane," just south of the present Middletown railroad, and back of the dwelling house of Edward Deming, and near his barn, on the east side of the present road. (The road at that time passing further east in front of the meeting house, but in same course.) A portion of the timber used in its construction is still to be seen supporting the cow house of Moses Gilbert. A piece of land was given to the Society by Richard Seymour for a place to bury their dead, (so tradition says, yet it seems doubtful,) near the meeting house, on the west side of the road, which is the oldest cemetery either in Berlin, or New Britain, and contains the bones of most of the signers of the above petition, and their families. The first person interred there was Mr. Richard Seymour, the donor of the land, killed by the fall of a tree,* he was one of the petitioners for the new Society, came from Farmington with others, 1686, and settled in the Great Swamp, and became the keeper of the *Fort* which bore his name, and which stood just back and south of the residence of the late Mr. John Goodrich deceased.† This

* The prudent liberality of the old town of Farmington is shown in voting to Capt Richard Semor, in full town meeting, 1 £ as compensation, or gratuity for planting this Colony. And at a subsequent period a like encouragement to other pioneers, viz., 8 Dec 1718 the town voted and agreed to pay to Dea Anthony Judd & Dea Thos Hart for killing a panther the sum of 6, s.

† This Fort was made of palisades sixteen feet long, sharp at the top, and firmly set in the ground near together. Capt Richard Semor probably died 1710, for the Pro-

new Society (said to be the second "set off" in the State,*) were fortunate in securing an able and intelligent minister in Mr. William Burnham. The words following show when and by whom his services were secured, viz.

"The Inhabitants of the society in the southeastern bounds of the Township of Farmington commonly known by the name of the Great Swamp, in the County of Hartford and Colony of Connecticut in New England, *America, &c*" agreement between said Society and William Burnham respecting his settlement as a Minister of the Gospel, Dated Farmington Village 20 Sep 1709 Signed William Burnham and John Hart sen, and Benjn Judd Comt.

He was Ordained 10 Dec 1712, and a Church was organized the same day. It consisted of ten members the first of which was Rev Mr Burnham, himself.

2d Stephen Lee, 3d Thos Hart, 4th Anthony Judd, 5th Samuel Seymour, 6th Thos North, 7 Caleb Cowles,—these were the 7 pillars. The wife of Stephen Lee, the wife of Saml Seymour, and Sarah the wife of Thos Hart, and these constituted the Church, to which others were soon added. Here follows a copy of their doings as a Church in the matter of Choosing a Deacon. At a meeting of the Church 10 March 1712–13 Anthony Judd was chosen to do the work of a Deacon and to stand as a probationer for the Deacons office. At a meeting of the Church it was agreed that the members of the same should hold conference Meetings on the first days of every Month in the year, to begin about 2 hours before sunset at the Meeting house, the sd meeting shall begin with prayer by one of the Brethren, who also shall propose a Text of Scripture, & a question or questions, on the same, in writing, then to be discoursed on, by his next brother, by House row, by word or by writing, if sd Brother shall see cause. And the Pastor of the Church, and the sd brother from whom an answer is expected at any Meeting, shall at the same meeting lay down the Text of Scripture, and the question or the questions thereon arising to be discoursed on at the next meeting, to his next neighbor successively, till every brother in the Church has taken his turn, then *he* shall begin again who first proposed the question, and so on successively. It was slso agreed that none should be present at sd conference, but those in full communion, but by liberty from the Church. It was agreed that Stephen Lee should begin the first Meeting with Prayer, & lay down the

---

bate record at Hartford says that Administration on the Estate was granted 4 Dec 1710 to Hannah the Widow, & to Samuel a son of Richard Sem or late of Farmington Deceased. An Inventory was presented 27 Nov 1710 of the Estate amounting to £416, 13, s. 3, d. by Thos Seymore, Thos Hart & Thos Curtice.

* The first being East Windsor.

Text, & propose the question or questions to be discoursed on. "The Church in North Middletown sent to our Church in some cases of Difficulty amongst them, in a letter bearing date 15 Feb. 1714–15 wherein they desire of us our aid and assistance in sd cases, upon which occasion, At a meeting of the Church 25d Feb. the same day wherein the Council began, our Church chose Deacon Anthony Judd their Messenger."

"Lord's day afternoon 28 Nov 1714 *Anthony Judd* having been chosen as before mentioned and stood as a probationer for the Deacons office, at the desire of the Church, he was confirmed in, and Ordained to the said office according to the rule of the Gospel, with the following charge. "In the name of our Lord Jesus Christ, I ordain thee, *Anthony* a Deacon of this Church; and I charge thee before God and the Lord Jesus Christ, who shall judge both the quick and the dead at his appearing and kingdom, that thou be faithful to the trust that is committed unto thee, thou art made a steward of the external good things of this Church, and it is required of stewards that they be found faithful, see that thou art grave, not double tongued, not given to much wine, not greedy of filthy lucre, hold the mystery of the faith in a pure conscience, Rule well thine own house, and if thou shalt use the office of a Deacon well, thou shalt purchase to thyself a good degree, and great boldness in the faith which is in Christ Jesus." Another Deacon was early chosen, son of the "Worshipful Captain Thomas Hart" whose home was in Stanley quarter, spoken of in the petition, his *Deacon* Thomas; location was on the present corner, some sixty rods southeast of the Berlin depot, and from his day has been known as the "*Thos Hart place.*" He was a man of great dignity and influence, represented the town of Farmington often in the General Court. The four Deacon Hart's of the church in New Britain, in as many generations, were descendants from him. He lost his wife, Mary, late in life, But m, 2d, Wid, Elizabeth Norton whose age was 79, and his own 84,—they were married before Rev Mr Clark 11 Jan 1764. The Rev. Wm Burnham made a faithful and successful pastor, had a small salary, but accumulated a large estate, and raised a large family; his blood through his descendants, is mingled with our Judds' Norths' Stanleys' Lees' and Wells' families. His residence was at the Norman Porter place. Now just here, and at this period, opens to the mind a wide field for *History*, *Biography*, and *Genealogy*. The author would be glad to enlarge, the materials are ample, the period prolific, but as this is merely an Introduction, as preliminary to the History of the Church in New Britain, which came into being some half century later, he feels constrained to be general in his remarks. It should however be remembered by the old families of New Britain, and their descendants, that the pious zeal of our ancestors for the public worship of God, was peculiar, and their self-denial, and struggles against poverty, bad roads, and "long distances," were great, were difficulties which to less courageous men, would have been insurmountable.

At a meeting of the church, 27th January, 1718–19, upon the desire of Deacon Anthony Judd that another deacon might be chosen, the question was asked whether they would proceed to the choice of another deacon, and it was voted in the affirmative, and Thos Hart, son of Capt Thos Hart, was chosen deacon, (and after some time of probation, was ordained to the office of deacon.)

At a meeting of the Church 20th Nov. 1729, it was agreed by the Church that the Psalm should be sung in the Public, half the time in what is called the old way of singing, and half the time in the New, interchangably, for the space of a year from the fore-mentioned date, and so far beyond that time, till the Pastor shall think there are five more voters for one way, than the other. And they chose Capt Isaac Hart, to set it when it is to be sung in the *New* way, and Mr Nathaniel Hart to set it when it is to be sung in the *old* way.

At a meeting of the Church 17 Feb 1730–31 the Church signified their minds by vote, that the Psalm for the time to come, should be set in the Public Assembly only by *Rule*, or what is called the *New* way.

The reader's attention is now called to the early doings of this settlement as a parish or Ecclesiastical Society. And fortunately we can refer to a manuscript record in a good degree of preservation, and quite full, covering the whole period with the exception of the building the first (Church) meeting-house I should say, for our fathers never used *that* name for the building.

Although no record of definite action of the parish can be found about the place where the building stood, or how or when erected and covered, yet incidental allusions and references to both time and place, confirm tradition, that it stood on land of Dr. Joseph Steele, leased to the Society, for which in after years they voted him compensation, that the building had been erected and covered, and a floor laid, at or before the close of the year 1712.

The church was organized 10th December, 1712, and Mr. Burnham was ordained the same day, and the first month of the next year we find them voting to have a pulpit. It further appears by inference that "peter blin" of Wethersfield, was the carpenter, for the parish some time after seem to be indebted to him some £60 for labor on the meeting-house. We have taken the liberty to quote and make selections from this ancient record, quite extensively, and for several reasons, among which is this. There is no duplicate of them, and in case they should be burned, all would be lost. Besides they are curious and quaint, and some of them unique. To those of us who are descendants, these doings, experiences, and history of our own ancestors, will be peculiarly interesting.

Mr. William Burnham was grandson of Thos, of Hartford, and Ann his wife. Graduated 1702, at Harvard College, Mass.* He was son of Wm., of Wethersfield and Elizabeth his wife, b. about 1684 at Wethersfield. His house and location have already been referred to, but the following in his own words, will show his style of writing, and mode of doing business. The conditions upon which he came are in his own words *viz; First* 5 June 1709 Articles proposed by Wm Burnham of Farmington village as conditions required in order to my continuance in the work of the Ministry in that society; that the land of John North that hath been discoursed of, be made over to me, by a firm conveyance speedily, I paying five pounds in current money to John North, for the exchange, as also that on the North end of Nehemiah Porters lot, as also that the society take care that the 50 Acres of land, that the town of

* Rev Mr Burnham m 18 May 1704 Hannah Wolcott of Wethersfield b. 19 Mar 1684 to Saml & Judith (Appleton) his wife who d. 16 Mar 1747 when he 2d m Wid Buckingham of Hartford who d. soon after, His Children were

Wm b 5 Apl 1705 m 13 Feb 1728-9 Ruth Norton dau of Isaac & Elizabeth (Galpin) had his house next west of his fathers.

Samuel b. 28 May 1707 at Wethersfield died at Farmington 22 Jan 1707-8
Hannah b. 18 Nov 1708 m 7 Jan 1730 Rev Jeremiah Curtiss of Southington
Josiah b. 28 Sep 1716 m Ruth dau of John Norton & Anna (Thompson) his wife
Sarah b. 28 May 1719 d 23 Nov 1726 Ae 8 y.
Mary b. 7 Feb 1721-2 m John Judd No (45)
Appleton b. 28 Apl 1724 m Mary Wolcott of Litchfield
Lucy b m Jacob Root of Hebron
Abigail b. 14 Sep 1713 m Lent Robert Wells of Newington

Substance of the original Will of Rev Wm Burnham dated 15 July 1748 which was accepted by Probate Court first Tues, of Apl 1759 but never recorded—in which he gives his eldest son Wm ⅓ of his real Estate, to Josiah ⅓, and to Appleton ⅓—names his 4 daughters Hannah wife of Rev. Jeremiah Curtis of Southington, Lucy wife of Jacob Root of Hebron, Abigail wife of Lieut Robert Wells of Newington, & Mary wife of John Judd of Farmington. Gives all the remainder of his Estate, viz, Servants, Household stuff, money, plate, Books, horned cattle, Horses, Sheep, Swine, Team Tackling, & any instruments of Husbandry whatsoever, Corn upon the ground, or gathered, linen, wearing clothes of any sort, Horse Tackling, any other tools or instruments besides those of husbandry & all my movable, & personal estate, whatsoever, excepting that concerning my Spanish Indian woman, Maria, my Will is that after my decease she shall have liberty to dwell with any of my children, where she likes best, & if at any time she should not be able to earn a living, that she be comfortably provided for in sickness, and health during life at the cost of all my children, & such as represent them—& concerning my Mulatto Boy James, my will is, that according to my deceased wife's desire, my daughter Abigail may have liberty to take him at the price he shall be valued at.

Item I appoint my eldest son Wm to be my sole Executor.

Signed & sealed by Wm Burnham in presence of

John Root
John Root jun } proved by the witnesses 1st Oct 1750
Eunice Root

Farmington as is reported, propose for my encouragement, be in some suitable manner made sure to me and my heirs, &c upon my settlement.* *Second* That the house begun by 2d society be finished in the manner & to the degree that is ordinary in this country for such sort of houses, be finished by them speedily, that is to say the two "Loer" rooms, at or before the last day of March that shall be in the year 1710, the remainder within twelve months after, I only finding Glass & nails.

Third That for the four first years inclusively of the year past, my Salary be 50, £. per annum in grain, that is to say Wheat, indian corn, or "Ry" such as is Merchantable, at the prices that the General Court shall annually state them at, & from the period of the above mentioned time, 65, £. at the same prices, till such time as the Society shall see cause to raise it.

Fourthly That so much labor be done for me by the Society as may amount to the value of 5, £. per Annum for the four first years inclusively of the year past, & that a Comt be from time to time, during sd term appointed to see to the accomplishment of sd labor for me on that part of the land that I shall esteem most convenient.

Fifth That the Society from time to time procure me a sufficient supply of fire wood for my family use, brought home and made fit for the fire. (Here follows the response of the society five days later.) At a meeting of the society at Great Swamp in the southeastern bounds of "ffarmington" 10 June 1709 it was by vote unanimously agreed, freely and heartily to accept of the above written Articles offered by the much esteemed "Mr william burnham" unto the above sd Society as conditions required in order to his continuance in the work of the Ministry, provided the above sd Mr Burnham, at the confirmation of the lands mentioned in the Articles, do give sufficient security to sd society.*

---

* That the above 50 acres of land was made sure appears by the following from the land records of Farmington.

"At a meeting held in Farmington 23 Dec 1707 At the same meeting there was granted to Mr. Wm Burnham 50 Acres of land to be taken up in our sequestered lands, not prejudicing highways, or former grants and after Mr Whitman hath made his pitch, for what the town hath granted him, this grant is upon conditions that ye said Mr Burnham shall settle a pastor of Church, in ye Society of ye Great Swamp—The above grant was laid out to the Rev. Mr. Wm Burnham Pastor of ye Church at ye Great Swamp upon the plains beyond ye Boggy meadow Southward & lyeth in length 8 Score rods, Butting East on ye highway 160 rods, West on common land, North & South on common land 50 rods.

It is laid out this 10 day of April A D 1713

Signed Thos Hart, Jo'n Wadsworth } Comt.

A true Copy John Hooker Register
Farmington 11 Apl A D 1713.

*Whereas, the inhabitants in the southeastern bounds of the township of Farmington, commonly known by the name of the Great Swamp, in the County of Hart'd &

At a meeting of the Society of Great Swamp ye 11th Jan 1713 Benjn Judd & Stephen Lee were chosen a Committee to provide, & see to the erecting of a Pulpit, & suitable seats in the Meetinghouse. " The pulpit & pews to be built in batten fashion."

Now comes the *Annual meeting* viz. 8*th Dec* 1713 *John* Woodruff was chosen Moderator for the year ensuing—Thos Hart recorder, Issac Hart collector, Nathnl Winchel to take care and get fire wood for Mr Burnham, Isaac Norton & Thos Hart chosen to be Rate makers. At the same meeting there was chosen Benjn Judd, Saml Smith & Thos Hart, to preserve our former records, on loose papers, & transcribe such as they think needful into this book.* Thos North was paid 12, s. for sweeping the Meetinghouse, Nehemiah Porter was chosen to dig graves for such as have occasion from time to time. Another *Annual meeting* viz. 8 *Dec* 1714 *Nathnl* Winchel, Daniel Andrus, & Thos North chosen Moderators for the year ensuing.

Jonathan Lee, chosen Lister for the year ensuing, and Jonathan Lee and Thos. Curtice Rate-makers—John Woodruff "Brandor," and at the same meeting, the Society made choice of John Norton and Wm. Judd

---

Col. of Conn. in New Eng. in America, Have called William Burnham now resident within the bounds of the said Soc. aforementioned, to dispense the word of God amongst them, and for his encouragement unto the work, have according to one of the articles in the agreement bearing date 20 Sept. 1709, confirmed and settled upon him 3 parcels of land within the bounds of said Soc., do further agree as followeth : That provided the said Wm. Burnham shall continue with said Soc. for the space of 9 years to be ended and completed, beginning the account thereof from 11th N. 1707, then the abovesaid House and land shall be and remain in the possession of the said Wm. Burnham and his heirs and assigns forever without any demand of the said Soc. for any retribution to be made by him, or them for the same : But if it so happen that the said Wm. Burnham cannot see it his way to abide in the work the whole time abovementioned, then he shall either relinquish and make over all the right and title he hath unto the house and land to the said Soc. again if he esteem it best, they returning him all his own expenses upon it ; or else he shall pay to said Soc. such a sum of money or other specie as shall by indifferent and able persons be judged sufficient and convenient, the one-half of which arbitrators shall be chosen by the said Soc. or one or more in their behalf; and the other half by the said Wm. Burnham, or such as shall represent him. In virtue whereof, we John Hart, sen. and Benj'n Judd a committee chosen by said Soc. to subscribe this agreement, and the said Wm. Burnham have hereunto set our hands this 20 day of Sep. in the year of our Lord 1709.

Wm. Burnham,
John Hart, Sen.,
Benj'n Judd.

Signed sealed and delivered in presence of us

Stephen Lee,
Thomas Curtice. } Witnesses.

† It was done by Dea Thos Hart 5 Jan 1721–2 on his own responsibility he says, for which service he received 3 shillings.

Smith, to be fence-viewers. *Annual Meeting*, 1*st Dec*., 1715, they agreed by vote to give Mr. Burnham £70 money, or grain, as "as it passeth from one year after another, at the first of May, provided Mr. Burnham will release us from our former obligations, wherein we were bound to provide his fire wood"—also made choice of Sam'l Seymour for Constable, and Sargt. Isaac Hart for Surveyor; also made choice of John Woodruff for brander—made choice of Stephen Lee and Issac Norton to demand and receive of Benj'n Judd* their proportion of Society money, "to be layed out as prudence shall suggest." Agreed by vote to grant to Thos. North 10 s. for sweeping the meeting house, and Thos. Hart made choice of to provide for, and give public Entertainment to travellers and others as the Law directs, and Stephen Lee, and Benj'n Judd chosen to make up the Society's account with Capt. John Hart, and make return to the Society.

"At a meeting of the society at the southeastern bounds of Farmington 20 May, 1715, The question being put whether the sd society did desire that the Southward part of the bounds of the Western Society in the township of Wethersfield should be annexed to the sd southeastern Society in the township of Farmington, and some part of the township of sd Farmington to be annexed to the Western Society of Wethersfield in Lieu thereof, it was voted in the affirmative, and the sd meeting made choice of, Sarg't Benj'n Judd to signify their above written desire, to the Gen. Assembly of this Colony." It is supposed that this is the origin of setting to Newington Ecclesiastical Society, formerly called Wethersfield West Society. *Stanley quarter* (now so called) as far south as the present residence of Henry Pratt, with the exception of Daniel Hart, John Clark and Thos. Standley 2d, with their farms at the extreme North end, who went to Farmington Village for public worship. And also a portion of the south part of Newington, being set (for convenience) to the Great Swamp Society.† This no doubt was a great convenience to these fami-

---

*This implies that Benj'n Judd was at that time Agent or Treasurer of the Colony for Farmington, to hold the *Country* money, [at a later period called excise money] for the encouragement of schools in that town.

†For the better regulating and accommodating those people that do, or may hereafter live upon the lands within the west Division in Wethersfield West Soc. of Wethersfield so called—& those that do now, or shall hereafter live upon several lots in Farmington, butting on Wethersfield West Soc. which lots of Farmington are hereafter described—

Be it enacted by the Gov. & Council & Rep. in Gen. Court sssembled and by the authority thereof, that, that part formerly deemed to be of Wethersfield West Soc. from the North side of Hurlburt's lot, & the North side of Stephen & John Kelsey's lands, to Middletown bounds, including the Beckley land, shall be annexed to the Great Swamp Society, & obliged with all persons & Estates, requirable by law to pay

lies, but made in after years much trouble and perplexity, in making *Rates;* because the Lists of each inhabitant were of course made in the town to which he or she belonged.—6 *Dec.*, 1716. *At the same meeting* it was voted by the Society to give Nath'l Winchell ten shillings for his son's beating the drum on the Sabbath for the year past, to be paid in Mr. Burnham's rate this year—Also granted to Jonathan Hurlbert 19 s. for a journey to New Haven to "cort," and to Hartford and other expenses, as witness our hands.

THOS. NORTH.
THOS. HART.

7 Jan., 1716–17. Thos. North and Thos. Hart were chosen a committee to take a deed of conveyance of the piece of land formerly obtained of the Rev Mr Wm Burnham for a burying place for ye said society in the behalf of said society, and cause it to be entered in the book of records for land at Farmington, that it may be secured to them and their Heirs

---

all Ministerial or parish charges, with the Great Swamp people, to that society, Provided that the said people of that part of the West Soc. of Wethersfield above mentioned shall help, & do their proportionable part with the rest of Wethersfield West Soc. in the finishing the Meeting house in said West Soc., & pay the said West Soc. in Wethersfield £50 according to their agreement under their hand and seal lodged in the Secretaries office.

And be it further enacted, by the authority aforesaid, that the lots in Farmington butting upon Wethersfield West Soc. or township, that is to say, all the lands in the several lots in Farmington bounds, from the south side of John Norton's Lot on Wolf plain, to the North side of the bounds of the Great Swamp, shall be and are hereby annexed to the West Soc. of Wethersfield, & shall pay in propostion with the said West Soc. in Wethersfield, in all Ministerial and parish charges.

Done at New Haven at the session held 13 Oct. 1715.

Tax payers in Farmington part—
Thos. Hart, sen.
Jonathan Smith, sen.
Thos. Bird,
John Thompson,
Thos. Thompson,
Daniel Judd,
Anthony Judd,
Jonathan Smith, Jun.
John Root.

Tax payers in Wethersfield part and in Beckley lands.†
Benj'n Beckley,
Richard Beckley,
Stephen Kelsey,
John Kelsey,
Jonathan Hurlburt,
Sam'l Belding,
Leonard Dix,
Thos. Morton,
Jonathan Buck,
Daniel Andruss,
John Andrus.

†A Gen. Assembly held at Hartford 8 Oct. 1668. This Court grants Serg't Richard Beckley 300 acres of land lying by Mattabeset River, half a mile wide of both sides the river, & to run up from New Haven path so far till it doth contain three hundred Acres—Serg't John Not & Serg't Hugh Wells are desired to lay out the land.

A true copy of record. Examined by

Geo. Wyllys, Sec.

forever, for the above said use.* At the same meeting Insign Isaac Norton was appointed to take care for the obtaining a fashionable and decent "cushing" for the desk of our Meeting house upon the society charge.—17 Nov., 1717, was chosen for a school committee Ins. Isaac Norton, Sergt. Benj. Judd and Mr. Ebenezer Gilbird, to advise and consider what way may be most proper and convenient to order the prudentials of a School in this Society, for the time the Law directs, and offer their advice about it at the next meeting.

7 January 1716–17 This Society finding & considering at this meeting that *all* former methods and acts, taken & recorded in order to a regular seating our Meeting house, being not effectual in order to said end, but many objections being made against them, & much disquietness, & disorder appearing notwithstanding—It was at the same Meeting agreed & voted to seat the Inhabitants of said Society in our Meetinghouse as followeth, viz—In the first "pue" next the Pulpit

1st Benjn Beckley, Lft Steven Lee, Benjn Judd, Mr Ebenezer Gilbird, Samuel Smith, Isaac Norton, Thos Hart.

2d pue John Woodruff, John North, Thos North, Saml Seamer, Hez. Hart.

3d pue, Samuel Bronson Cooper, Joseph Smith, Thos Curtice, Jonath Hurlbut, John Standley, Jonathan Lee.

---

*That this committee attended to their duty, is shown by the following from Farmington town records for lands: 1st Nov. 1718. Rev Wm Burnham for the regard he had for the public welfare of the parish at Great Swamp, in the Southeast part of Farmington & the Southwest part of Wethersfield, & in consideration of the society releasing him from 20 s. he promised to encourage the building the Meeting house, he gave, sold, conveyed & set over to Thos. Hart & Thos. North a committee of said society a piece of land containing by estimation half an Acre more or less, in length 10 rods & in breadth 8 rods. It is part of the same lot that originally was James Bird's, and which I purchaced of Sam'l Semer, and it is understood that it is for the use of said Society, for a possession, for a Burying ground forever—said society is to maintain a good fence at their own cost, and I am not to be taxed for any part of the expense of a division fence as the law in other cases provides, and further until such division fence is made, the said society are not to feed the ground or any way use it except to bury their dead. Said land is situate on a knowl of up land lying a little to the North of a stream called "Gilbert's River," and abutteth east on the highway that passeth Northward from the Meeting House and butts North on land of Nath'l Not, West & South on my own land.

Signed, Wm Burnham.

Stephen Lee,
Ebenezer Gilbert, } Wit.

This time honored Cemetery, so minutely described above, had been sadly neglected for many years previous to 1845, when by the enterprise and liberality of Mr. John Ellis, some few subscriptions were obtained from individuals, and an appropriation of $30 from the parish of Worthington, in which it is located, and a neat white fence, erected on sunk stones with iron braces, at a cost of $160, an undue proportion of which expense was paid by himself.

4 pue East side, Isaac Hart, Samuel Thompson, Joseph "Steale," Isaac Lee, Gersham Hollister, Jonathan "Seamer," Robert "boothe"—

The 1st seat in the square Body, Thos Hancox sen, Nehemiah Porter, Nathl Winchel sen, Saml Bronson, miller, Thos moreton, Richard beckley.

2d seat, Saml peeke, Saml hubbard, daniel andrus, Steven Cellsey (Kelsey,) Jacob deming, Caleb couls. (Cowles.)

3d seat, Geo. Hubbard, John norton, John Cellsie, (Kelsey,) Thos Gridley, Saml Galpin, Ebenezer Seamer.

4th seat, Wm Bronson, Saml Couls, John Gridley, John Roote, John Andrus.

5th seat, daniel beckley, Joseph becly, Joseph harris,* Saml Gridley, Daniel hancox.

In ye pue at the North end East side, John Rue, Saml, hart, Wm hancox, John Gilbird, Saml Bronson jun.

In the fore seat, Widow "becly," goodde "buck," & Widdow "duey," Dea. Judd in the Deacons Seat, & his wife in ye fore "pue."

1st December, 1718, at the Annual Meeting Nathaniel knot was appointed to provide a convenient Lock & "kee" for ye Meeting house "dore" & put it on ye said dore on the charge of the society.

At the same meeting it was voted and agreed that the "sheepe" in this society shall run at large in the common the year in suing—At the same meeting Mr Ebenezer Gilbird was appointed to provide a convenient "cushen" for our meeting house Desk, at the charge of "ye Societie"—And the Comt on Schools report as follows, viz—"This society being so very scattering in distances, & our ways so very difficult, for small Children to pass to a general School in the Society great part of the year, We the Subscribers advice is, that this society be divided into 5 parts or "Squaddams" for the more convenient schooling the children, Advice respecting the establishment of schools in each "squaddam" &c.—That the first part or squaddam be all the Inhabitants south of the river called "betses" "Honhius or Honehas" river (meaning we suppose Mattabesic or Mattabesset) including Middletown neighbors with them—And the Inhabitants in Wethersfield bounds be another part or squaddam—And that all from "betses" River to the River called Gilbirds, Northward be another part,—& that from Gilbirds River Northward, till it includes Dea Judd, & John Woodruff be another part, & that the rest of the society North be another part, & further that the money allowed by the country be divided to each "squaddam" according to the List of the Inhabitants within the limits thereof, & the rest of the charges so arising shall be leaved on ye parents or Masters of ye Children who are "taut"—

* This man moved to Litchfield and was killed there by Indians, August, 1723. He had been appointed town collector there 17th December, 1722. The town record of Hartford says Mary Harris married 16th December, 1725, Stephen Sedgwick; (probably she was then widow of Harris.) Ed.

The following may be of interest to the curious. It purports to be *credits* to Rev. Mr. Burnham's parishioners, entered by the collector, *John Root*, on his rate Bill for 1720 and shows how the Ministers' rates were paid in those days when money was scarce.

	£.	S.	D.
John Standley by 1 bush Wheat,		5	6
Isaac Hart by 1½ bush Corn,		3	9
Samuel Hart by 2 " Wheat,		11	0
Thos Hart by 1 bush. Corn, ½ bush Wheat,		5	3
Jonathan Root by 2½ bush & 1 peck of Wheat his rate, and part of Wm Hancox rate,		11	8
Nathl Hart 1 bush Wheat,		5	6
Saml Smith by 3 bush Wheat,		16	6
Saml Hubbard by 3½ bush wheat wanting 1 pt, 4s of it on Jonathan Nott's ac,		17	9
Benjn Bronson by 3 pecks Wheat,		4	1
Thos Porter by 1½ bush Corn, 3s on his own ac,		3	
and 9d on Thos Harts ac,			9
Jonathan Burnham by 1½ bush Wheat,		8	3
Jacob Deming by ½ bush corn & 1½ pt,		1	2½

NOTE. It is supposed the persons named above were located south of the Meeting house.

But to return from this digression about the "squaddams," to the living activities of this people, and their new Meeting House, so happy in being relieved from their former fatiguing walk to Farmington with their children in their arms. *Now* many of these families could see the place of worship (were it not for the tall and dense forest) from the doors of their dwellings, *Then* they followed the trail of the Tunxis & Mattabesset Indians, traces of which are still supposed to be seen in a direct line from the Stockade to Osgood Hill (or "Half-way-hill," as it was then called.) Now the place becomes attractive, families cluster in and about the locality; a Blacksmith shop and a store and the place is known the state over as "Great Swamp Village." Some years have passed, & the good people feel a little stronger, and greatly encouraged. They talk of putting Galleries into their Meetinghouse, and finishing it up. The following is a copy of an agreement for this purpose:*

"This covenant made this 18 day of Oct. 1720, between Daniel Andrus, of Wethersfield, in the county of Hartford, & colony of Connecticut, in New England, & John Root, son of Stephen, & Samuel Bronson jun.

* This document was kindly furnished by Mr. Timothy Root, a descendant of one of the Committee. It has been wisely preserved by the care of himself and his ancestors, has fallen into the hands of a descendant of another of the Committee and thus is brought to light and use.

of Farmington, in said county, being a Committee for the parish or society in said county, called the *Great Swamp* on the one part, & Richard Austin & Moses Bull both of the town, & county of aforesaid Hartford on the other part witnesses—that the said Richard Austin & Moses Bull have covenanted & agreed, & do hereby covenant & agree to, both jointly and severally to finish the Galleries in the Meetinghouse erected for the public worship of God in said parish or society called the Great swamp, in manner following, viz. to lay the floor of the said Galleries, planing the joice whereupon the said floor is laid,& the under side of the said floor, to build four seats in each of the side Galleries, running through the whole length of them & 8 seats in the front Gallery the foremost of which is to extend the whole length of said Gallery and to raise the high Ground for all the hinder seats in a due proportion, & also to ceil the walls between the said Gallery floor & the plates & beams of said Meetinghouse & to case all the windows that are above said Gallery floor & make fastenings for their casements & to lay the floor double under the three foremost seats in said Gallery, and to put and trim decently 4 pillars to be set under the beams of said Galleries & to set them up in their places, the said committee providing suitable pieces of timber, for the said pillars hewed square. The whole of said work above mentioned to be done workmanlike, & after the manner of the work in the Galleries in Farmington Meetinghouse, & all to be finished & completed at or before the last day of March next ensuing the date hereof. And the said Daniel Andrus, John Root, & Saml Bronson have covenanted & agreed & do hereby covenant & agree both jointly and severally to provide & bring to the said Meetinghouse all needful materials for the said work above mentioned, seasonably, such as nails, boards, slitwork & other timber, & as a reward for the above mentioned, to pay or cause to be paid to the said Richard Austin & Moses Bull or either of them, at or before the 10 day of May next ensuing the date hereof the full sum of £31 in Bills of credit of the aforesaid colony or the Neighboring provences or else in good Mercht Wheat, rye, or Indian Corn, at the price the Merchants generally in Hartford or Wethersfield will accept the said sorts of grain in way of payment of debts due to them, between the first & 10th days of May next ensuing the date hereof—in Witness whereof the said Committee and the said Richard Austin & Moses Bull have hereunto set their hands & seals the day & year above written.

Signed, sealed and delivered in presence of
Wm Burnham, sen.
Wm Burnham, jun.

Daniel Andrus,
John Root,
Samuel Bronson,
Richard Austin,
Moses Bull.

The above instrument so complete in all its parts, I would here observe, seems to be written by the same hand and pen that signed as witness, Wm. Burnham, sen. It shows alike the beauty of his hand writing, the tact and talent he had for business, and the interest he took in the matter in hand. And now a year or two has passed and the village has come to its culminating point, has a finished Meetinghouse with Galleries like Farmington, may be the House painted white, and they are prepared for a better name, probably they asked for it. The State Archives show what and when.

"Resolved by this Assembly that the 2d Society in Farmington, with what of Wethersfield & Middletown is by this Assembly annexed thereto, shall for the future be called and known by the name of *Kensington.*

Passed by both Houses, May, 1722.

It is supposed that the galleries are now done, the carved pillars erected for their support, and the house otherwise much improved. They hold a society meeting 23d May, 1721, where it was voted and agreed that the meeting house should be seated, on these rules, viz. age, list, and whatever else makes a man honorable. They also met again 12th July, 1721, to "dignify" the house. At this meeting it was voted and agreed that the fore seats in the square Body in ye meeting house of this society, shall for the time to come, be equal in dignity with those seats called the fore "pues," and that the pews next to the east door, shall be equal in dignity with those called the middle or second pews. At the same meeting voted to grant Corporal Lee, for the irons to the Communion Table, 3s. The annual meeting 7 Dec. 1724, it was voted & agreed that Thos Hart & Saml Bronson jun should oversee ye Youth on ye Sabbaths in the time of exercise, to Restrain them from unreverent behaviours therein, for the year ensuing. At the same meeting 10 shillings was voted to Wm. Ellis for making a "beere" for the Society. 5 Dec. 1726 was granted to Sargt Benjn Judd 1£ 5s. for a Cloth for the Society. 2 Dec. 1728, Ins Jonathan Lee, Wm Burnham, Ebenezer Hart & John Hinsdale were chosen Rate makers. "At the same meeting it was agreed by vote of the society to be their mind to call in the assistance of some wise, able & indifferent persons, to hear, consider, and determine, the differences there are among them relating to a Meeting house for them."

Let the reader now take a birds-eye view of this apparently happy community. The parish has now had an existence of about twenty years under the title of Great Swamp, and of about ten with the name of Kensington. Its territory extends from Benjamin (now, 1867,) Richard Judd's on the north, far enough south to embrace the Blow Hills, and Blow Mountains, to Wallingford, (Meriden line.) It has the mountainous range of Farmington on the West, Wethersfield and Middletown on the east, yet Middletown then embraced almost the entire locality of the present village of Worthington, (Berlin,) even west to "lower lane," (or Hart street,) and Wethersfield; the east part of that rich valley lying north through which the Hartford and New Haven turnpike passes. The people of Stanley quarter, as far south as Benjamin (now Richard Judd's,) with the exception of three families at the extreme north end, who went to Farmington,) attended public worship at Newington.* The few families located in the present New Britain village and west of it, never did belong to the Great Swamp, or Kensington parish, but to the old society of Farmington, as will fully appear as we advance in our sketches of the history of Kensington. The families had multiplied towards the "Blow Mountain," and the wealth had increased with the Burnham's,† Hart's, Norton's, and Coles' families near the center. By a natural process of reasoning, while passing to and fro, over bad roads, "long distances," and mostly on foot, they had discovered that their meeting house was too small, its locality too far east, and too far north, and another important fact they

* At a General Court held in Hartford, 9th October, 1712, a portion of Wethersfield extending two miles and fifty rods east of Farmington bounds, was made a Ministerial society, bounded north by Hartford bounds, and south by Middletown. It was called "Wethersfield West Society."

A petition was also presented to the town of Wethersfield by the subscribers, who say in their petition that they live in the west part of said town, in which they ask to be set off by themselves as a parish or new society. Dated 24th December, 1712.

Ezekiel Buck,	Nathaniel Hun,
Nathaniel Churchill,	Eliphalet Whittlesey,
Abraham Warren,	Jonathan Wright,
Jonathan Buck,	Stephen Buck,
Richard Boardman,	John Kelsey,
Enoch Buck,	Stephen Kelsey,
Ephraim Whaples,	Daniel Andrus,
John Whaples,	Jonathan Hurlbut,
Joseph Andrus,	Jonathan Buck,
Ephraim Andrus,	Thomas Morton,
Simon Willard,	Richard Beckley,
Benjamin Andrus,	John Deming,
John Stoddar,	Ephraim Deming,
Joseph Camp,	Jabez Whittlesey,
John Camp,	Benjamin Beckley.
Samuel Hun,	

This petition was granted by vote of the town, 24th December, 1712. The General Court sent Mr. Joseph Talcot and Mr. Aaron Cook to fix a location for the meeting house, and they reported as the proper place, on the common, about thirty rods from the house of Dr. Joseph Andrus, May, 1715. They (the west society, now Newington,) got a bonus of £50 for damage of the south part of the parish, when they were annexed to "Great Swamp." Also £100 16s. of Yale College, for relinquishing Mr. Williams, their first minister, to be President of Yale. Also, from those annexed from Farmington £100 towards a settlement of Mr. Williams.

† Capt. William Burnham who died 12th March, 1748, eldest son of Rev. Mr. Burnham, left an estate of £8,246 10s. 11d., old tenor (supposed.)

had also learned by actual experiment, that the south part of the parish could out vote the north part.

At a meeting of the society of Kensington legally warned and held 26th January, 1729–30, it was voted to build a new meeting house in some convenient place, on Sargt John Norton's lot, on the north side of the Mill River,* there being 42 votes in the affirmative, & 36 in the negative, as was then declared. Troubles now multiply from this period rapidly in "poor Kensington," (as our ancestors, the petitioners used to call it.) They had, as appears from the record, still extant and in good condition, been annoyed by the perplexity of making Rate Bills for their neighbors from Wethersfield & Middletown, who belonged to their ecclesiastical society, but not to the town of Farmington, as they did. For several years in succession, they had appointed Committees to negociate with them & to ask the Gen. Court for relief in this matter, but no material relief came until years had passed. The above vote to build a new Meeting house, with so small a majority, & withal to go so far west for a location, (which is supposed to be about where Milo Hotchkiss' new house stands,) kindled a flame of jealousy, passion and prejudice, which seems never to have been quenched, until the final division and incorporation of a separate society. These fathers of ours had a great reverence and love for the honor and worship of God, had a constant care for the education of their children, were sensitive and jealous of their rights to a fault perhaps, were no doubt greatly tempted to be stubborn and self-willed, yet they were patriotic, hospitable, industrious and frugal. They abhorred popery, infidelity, prodigality, laziness and indebtedness. They were patient of labor, persevering and indomitable in energy. Their living was obtained from the products of the soil, in a new country, and in an unsubdued wilderness. With the exception of Mr. Burnham they had but one Mr. in the whole community, viz. Mr. Ebenezer Gilbird (Gilbert,) his inventory 1726, Dec. 17th, amounted to £3,824 12s. 8d., this is less than some of his cotemporaries who died a little later. Saml Bronson, *Miller*, who sawed the timber for both the 1st & 2d Meeting-houses was located on that branch of the "betsis" (Mattabesset) river, later called Mill river,† and owned the Barret place, and

* This Serg. John Norton lived by the well, at the southwest corner of Milo Hotchkiss' house lot, the old house still well remembered by the oldest living. It was on the corner of the main road from Farmington to Middletown, and is said on the record to be opposite the foot crossing on Mill river, (reference doubtless to the locality of the present foot crossing. (Ed.)

† This Mill river had a special interest in the minds of the colonists some half century later, inasmuch as it afforded lead with which to kill the British red coats.

"*Col. Selah Hart* was appointed on a committee, 1775, in May, to provide such stores of lead as they shall judge necessary for the use of the Colony, to contract for & take lead ore that should be raised out of the *Mine* of *Matthew Hart* in Far. & to dig & raise ore in said mine if profitable & necessary for the Colony."

the Mills, which fell to Charles, his youngest son, and after to Asahel, his grandson, known for many years as "Percival's Mills," but (now, 1867,) the site of a large manufacturing establishment of J. T. Hart & Co. The estate of this Samuel Bronson, (miller,) who died 22d April, 1752, amounted to £6,874 8s. 3d, Samuel Thompson and Samuel Lankton appraisers, 5th May, 1752. Among the items of the inventory are one negro man, *Lot*, £400, one negro wench, *Hannah*, £300, eldest boy, *Saul*, £200, youngest boy, *Pharoh*, £130, and he bequeathed by his will to Sarah, his grand-daughter, all his sheep, and an unborn child of Hannah, the wench. I have alluded in another place to the estate of Capt. William Burnham, and will instance but one more, that of Deacon Anthony Judd. He was a large farmer, lived in the north part, was a man of influence, represented the town of Farmington in the General Court many times, from 1717 to 1739, perhaps later, his residence where (now, 1867,) Mr. William Ellis lives, and used the same well—his will made 1750, the inventory of his estate dated 26th November, 1751, amounted to £5,360 old tenor. Did space allow, the author would delight in giving the location and a brief history of each of these worthies. But we return to some farther extracts from the ancient record of the society, since it is one of the principal sources of information. If the reader discovers a strange mixture of Church History, doings of the Ecclesiastical and School Society, with town matters intermingled, it only shows the necessity of the times and circumstances into which they were thrown. Remote from the center of power and influence, (Farmington village,) they felt their own wants and took the responsibility of supplying them the best way they could. If they occasionally chose a surveyor, a constable, a taverner, or voted that their sheep *shall* run on the common, or divided their parish into squaddams, (naturally the legitimate business of the town *only*,) yet they deemed it expedient to help themselves. We find a full record of a yearly appointment of a committee to look after the schools, to demand and receive the "country" money for their encouragement.

At a meeting of the society of Kensington, 7th Dec. 1730, Nathl Cole, John Standley, Sarg. Geo. Hubbard, & Jonathan Lewis, were chosen a committee to order the prudentials for a school for this society for the year ensuing. At the same meeting the society agreed by vote to give to the Rev. Mr. Wm. Burnham for his labor in the Ministry the year past, the sum of £100 in Bills of public Credit, or in grain at the market price in

This *lead mine* is located on this Mill river, (a branch of the Betsis or Mattabesic,) on its west bank, a little distance below Moore's Mills, and the residence of Matthew Hart was the one now, 1863, owned and occupied by Shelden Moore, Esq. These diggings appear on the west bank of the stream at the right hand below the bridge, on the road as you pass from Kensington Church to the Mills. The Moore family have specimens of the ore. (Ed.)

May next. And Jacob Deming & Sarj. John Andrus were chosen prudential comt. in addition to the present comt. for the year ensuing.

A curious document on a matter of conscience we here find on record, dated Kensington 12th February, 1730–1.

We whose names are here unto published, having been desired by fifty nine of the Inhabitants of Kensington in writing subscribed with their names, to give a resolution upon this question, *viz.* "Whether the Lot cast among us as it was, considering how the affairs thereof were managed from first to last, ought to be acounted by the whole society, binding to their *consciences*, there to erect ye Meeting house, viz. where the said Lot fell." And having each of them in ye writing promised that they will act agreeable to the Resolution we shall give of said *Question* under our hands (unles it be manifestly contrary to the rule of God's word,) as by the said writing may appear, We Resolve the said question in the affirmative, that it is our Judgement, that the Lot cast among them, as it was considering how the affairs thereof were managed from first to last, ought to be accounted by ye whole society, *binding to their consciences* there to erect their Meeting house, viz. where the said Lot fell, and do advise that in a tender Regard to the honor of God, & for peace sake, their Meeting house be built there (where the said Lot fell,) by ye said society that they may avoid all danger of being involved in guilt.

As witness our hands (signed)

Nathaniel Chauncey,
Jonathan Marsh,
Samuel Whittlesey,
Samuel Hall.

From other pages of the book of records it appears that these are Rev. Mr. Jonathan Marsh, of Windsor, Rev. Mr. Nathaniel Chauncey, of Durham, Rev. Mr. Samuel Whittlesey, of Wallingford, Rev. Mr. Samuel Hall of Cheshire, and that this is the second council in this matter of the casting the Lot. The *Lot* seems to have been resorted to in order to a settlement of the extremes of a Location for the new Meeting-house. The east point was the southwest corner of John Root's house lot, nearly opposite Rev. Mr. Burnham's (now, 1862,) Mr. Norman Porter's. The other extreme west seems to have been the south-west corner of Sargent John Norton's lot, on the north side of Mill river, against the "Mill foot Bridge," about fourteen or fifteen rods from the highway northward, (as then described.) It appears that the society by vote had previously agreed to decide the controversy by lot, provided it could be done in a reasonable way and before sunset. It seems that Rev. Mr. Burnham was present, and after due caution and solemn invocation to God to give a perfect lot, the first lot was drawn and it fell on the east side, and also the second lot was drawn, and it fell on the southwest corner of John Root's lot. The opposers of the eastern locality claimed that the matter was unreasonable, and done after sunset. In looking over the list of the fifty-nine who agreed to abide the judgment of the council in this matter of the lot, there is the name of but one man from the northern section of the parish.

At a meeting of the Inhabitants of the Society of Kensington 22d Sept. 1731, then convened by order of the worshipful Mr. Nathl Standley, Esq. agreeable to the act of the Gen. Assembly at Hartford, May last, the aforesaid Mr. Standley being present at the meeting, the society made choice of Thos Hart for Clerk, also made choice of Left Isaac Norton, Sargt Hez. Hooker & Stephen Kelsey for a committee to warn & Lead Society meetings for the remainder of the year, also made choice of Nathl Cole, John Standley, Sargt Geo. Hubbard & Jonathan Lewis a committee to order the prudentials of the School for the remainder of the year.

At the same meeting it was tried by vote whether the society would proceed to build a new Meeting house for this Society or no, & it was negatived.

At the same meeting Matthew Hart was chosen Collector of the Ministers' Rate this year.

At a meeting of the society of Kensington 19th Oct. 1731, they voted & agreed to prefer a Memorial to the Gen. Assembly now convened at New Haven, praying them to order, appoint & affix the place, where on, our Meeting house shall be Erected.

At a meeting of the society of Kensington 25th Oct. 1733, a Rate of twelve pence on the pound, was granted for the purpose of building a new Meeting house, & Joseph Porter was chosen collector of the same.

At a meeting of the Society of Kensington, 2d Dec. 1734, Capt. Stephen Lee was chosen Moderator, & Thos Hart Clerk, granted to Joseph Steele for sweeping the old Meeting house for ye year past £1 7s. 6d.

The same meeting made choice of Deacon Anthony Judd, Wm Burnham & Left Isaac Norton to settle account with the Committee for building the new Meeting house, & report.

At the same meeting it was agreed by the society that no vote should be taken after the Sun is set, for the space of 2 years.

At a meeting of the Society of Kensington 3d Dec. 1735, Capt. Stephen Lee Moderator & Thos Hart Clerk, granted to Rev. Mr. Wm Burnham for his services in the Ministry the year past a salary of £140, to be paid in money or good & merchantable grain at the prices following, viz. wheat at 10s. rye at 6s. & Indian Corn at 5s.

Parish of Ken. 1 Dec. 1736, Capt Stephen Lee Moderator, Thos Hart Clerk, Deacon Anthony Judd & Capt Thos Curtiss chosen a Comt, to agree with Thos Hart about the price of the land on which our new Meeting house stands, & to agree about the fence around the Meeting house.

At a society meeting Ken. 7th Dec. 1737, Dea Anthony Judd Moderator, Thos Hart clerk, granted to Ins. Saml Lankton for sweeping the Meeting house, voted that the Comt, of the society, provide a suitable Drum, and procure some meet person to beat it on Sabbath days, for the year ensuing, & also provide an hour glass, with a suitable frame for it, & put them up on the pulpit, in ye Meeting house. Voted that Zebulon Curtice, Josiah Lee, & Daniel Dewy, be the Rate makers for the year ensuing.

At a Society Meeting 6th Dec. 1738, Left Saml Hart Moderator, Thos Hart Clerk, granted Thos Hart £4 for sweeping the meeting house, & to Ins Saml Lankton 5s. for an hour glass, & to Nathl Winchel 30s. for beating the drum the past year, & to John Hinsdil for a frame to the Meeting house glass, 12s.

At the same meeting it was agreed by vote, that Dea. A. Judd & Dea. Thos Hart, be a comt, to seat as speedily as may be, the Inhabitants of this society in the Meeting house at their best discretion.

At the same meeting was granted to Wm Ellis 7s. 6d. & to Allen Goodrich 2s. 6d. for framing a bier to carry the dead. It was also voted & agreed that Elisha Goodrich may take within his own enclosure the burying yard of this society, for five years, provided the said Elisha Goodrich clear, & keep the said yard clear from brush, & keep swine from rooting the same.

Society meeting 9th May, 1739, chose Dea. Thos Hart in their behalf to go before the Gen. Assembly Instantly holden at Hartford, there to show reason if any be why the Memorial of Capt. Stephen Lee & Dea. Judd &c. now depending before said Assembly should not be granted.

Annual meeting of Ken. Soc. 3d Dec. 1740, Capt Stephen Lee Moderator, Thos Hart Clerk, Society granted to Rev. Mr. Wm Burnham* a Salary of £160 to be paid in money or grain at the market price, for his good service in the Ministry the year past.

These ancestors of ours were made of stern stuff; perhaps they *could* bend, but did not accustom themselves to do so very often. And now comes the tug of war. They became restless, and *apparently* contentious and unhappy for a long series of years. Their chief troubles seem to arise from the difficulty in fixing on a location for the new meeting-house. The following shows the sad plight into which they had fallen:

"General Court holden at New Haven, October, 1732.

"Whereas the Inhabitants of the parish of Kensington applied themselves by their Committee to this Assembly at their session in May last, praying that a Committee might be appointed to fix a place for setting a Meeting house in said parish, and whereas the said Assembly did then

* Rev. Wm Burnham was chosen Moderator of the Gen. Association of Ct. at their meeting in Stratford, A. D. 1738; his name is first on the list of Moderators of Gen. Association of Ct.

appoint Capt John Rigs, Capt Isaac Dickerman, & Mr. Ebenezer West to repair to said parish, view the circumstances, & fix the place for building a Meeting House &c. And whereas said Comt, reported to the said Assembly that they in pursuance of the trust reposed in them had affixed the place for building a Meeting house in said parish, and the Assembly thereupon Enacted that a Meeting House in said Society or parish shall be erected in Deacon Thos Hart's home lot, on the north side of the High way but adjoining thereto, to stand about one rod south of an apple-tree which is partly dead, at which place the said Rigs, Dickerman & West have pitched down a stake, and the Inhabitants of said Society are hereby directed & ordered, with all convenient speed to proceed to raise & finish the said house, at the above described place, & Whereas it has been certified to this Court by Mr. Thos Hart, Clerk of said Society, that at a Meeting of the Inhabitants of said Society on the 14th day of June last past, it was Resolved by their vote that they would not appoint suitable & meet persons to be a Committee to set up, build, & finish a house proper & suitable for said Society to attend God's public worship in, on the place the General Assembly hath lately appointed for the same.

"Be it therefore Enacted by the Governor & Council & Representatives at Genl Court Assembled, & by the Authority of the same, that the Treasurer of this Colony shall in his warrant for gathering the next country rate, direct and Command the Constable of the Town of Farmington to collect with the same of the inhabitants of Kensington, Nine pence upon the pound of the Polls & ratable Estate of said Society, & the said Constable is hereby ordered, directed & impowered, to assess & gather the same of said Inhabitants of said Society, & the same being so gathered he shall deliver to the Treasurer, who is hereby ordered & directed upon the receipt thereof, to pay out the same to Capt. John Marsh, Mr. James Church & Capt. Thos Seymour, all of Hartford, who are hereby appointed & impowered to be a Committee or any two of them, to erect & finish a Meeting House at the place aforesaid, for the Society aforesaid. And said Comt, are hereby also ordered & directed to make all convenient speed in the business aforesaid, & give an account to the Assembly of their disbursements of the money aforesaid, & how far they have proceeded therewithal in the business aforesaid, that the Assembly may order what money may be further necessary for the finishing said house to be gathered of the Inhabitants of said Society & to be by said Comt, improved for that end.

We have now come to the autumn of the year 1733, the Committee from Hartford (as will hereafter more fully appear,) have "set up & finished a Meeting house by the appletree in Deacon Thos Hart's home lot;" it is said to be "60×45 ft. & capable of holding 1500 persons."* The

* We are not informed how they were seated, or whether seated at all.

constable is still drawing forth the hard earned coin from the reluctant pockets of the parishioners, and from the northern section it comes forth at last and is laid upon the table for the collector to count, with a kind of will and snap which signifies, "Well, you shall see what comes of this by and by." And yet they make haste slow, for it is some six years before we hear from them in the following petition:

"To the Hon. Gen. Assembly of his Majesties Eng. Colony of Connecticut in New Eng. to be convened at Hartford 10 May 1739 which is to show that we the Subscribers hereunto, Inhabitants of the North part of Kensington parish in Farmington, are under great difficulty to attend the public Worship of God, by reason of the length & badness of travel, especially at some seasons of the year—Whereupon your Memorialists humbly pray that this Hon. Assembly would consider our difficulty & afford us some relief, by granting us the liberty of four Months to meet at some convenient place for the ease of our travel to attend the public worship of God—for the time above specified, we humbly pray that we may be released from paying one third part of the year to our present Minister, provided we procure some suitable person to preach to us the time above specified, or to find some other way as this Hon. Assembly in their great wisdom shall think best for our ease & comfort to attend the public Worship, & we are as our duty is shall ever pray—

Dated at Kensington 9 May 1739—

Stephen Lee	Benjn Judd jun	Ebenezer North
Benjn Judd	John Judd	John Kelsey
Uriah Judd	Phineas Judd	Joseph Smith
James Judd	Anthony Judd	Joseph Smith jun
Zeb. Curtice	Daniel Dewy	Azariah Smith
Thos Curtice	Saml Hollister	Jedediah Smith
Isaac Lee jun	Elijah Bronson	Josiah Lee
Joshua Mather	Joseph Woodruff	Simmons Woodruff
	Jonathan Lewis	Isaac Lee

The parish of Kensington was notified and subpœned to attend and show cause why the above should not be granted. The question was put to the lower house and negatived. The question was put to the upper house and negatived. A single remark is called for just here, viz. the signers to the above petition are supposed to have (at that date) lived at and south of the present house of Richard Judd's, and all east and south of the present village of New Britain, and also within the limits of the present town lines; all other families within the present limits of this town went either to Newington or Farmington for public worship. These petitions not only show the conflicting opinions of the different sections, but also the locality of the subscribers. The oldest living descendants will see that the following petitioners lived near the meeting house referred to in the petition, or central part of the parish.

"To the Hon. Gen. Assembly of his Majesties English Colony of Connecticut, now sitting at Hartford. The humble Memorial of Thos Heart, John Norton, & others subscribers hereunto all Inhabitants of Kensington parish in Farmington in Hartford county humbly showeth—That after a long contention in said parish about a place of Divine service, this Hon. Assembly, did at their session in May 1732 by their committee ascertain the place for the same, but on the Inhabitants neglecting to build a house, though in extreme want thereof, this Assembly at their next session did appoint and authorize a committee to build said house which they speedily and effectually performed of the dimensions of sixty feet in length and 45 in breadth containing in the whole about 1500 persons, this notwithstanding that part of said parish that dwell in the Middletown bounds, have been and are endeavoring now to draw off from us (as your Honors are very sensible) & have parish privileges by themselves elsewhere, although the North corner of their bounds be within ¾ Mile of said Meeting house & the greatest part of the parish is within 2 miles thereof traveling in the highways, & that the Northern part of the Inhabitants of the parish of Kensington, that dwell much farther from the place of public worship than those mentioned in Middletown, & their travel there too in general as bad as the other, did in December last at the annual meeting of the Inhabitants pray that they might all within such & such bounds have leave to obtain of this Assembly, parish privileges for themselves—which prayer aforesaid the Inhabitants granted as followeth viz—Voted that Deacon Anthony Judd be a committee in behalf of said Society to address the Hon. Gen. Assembly at their session in May next, to appoint a committee of able & disinterested persons, at the charge of the parish, to repair to the same, view the circumstances with relation to said prayer, & report to the Assembly of what they think proper to be done in the case, but said Dea. Judd neglecting to move in the affair (for what reason we know not except to help off our south quarter at this time & to break up the whole parish) whereupon with our committee neglecting, or rather refusing to warn a Society meeting at this time, your Honor's Memorialists are obliged in this manner to address this Assembly, humbly praying your Honors once more to take the broken & divided circumstances of "*poor* Kensington" into your wise consideration, & if consistent with your wisdom appoint & authorize a judicious committee (at the Societies charge) to come and view our whole circumstances as to the affairs above mentioned & make return of what they think best to be done for the best good of each quarter of said parish, or some other way prevent the confusion, we are in danger otherwise of falling into, & your Memorialists as in duty bound shall ever pray. Kensington, 17 May, 1742. Signed,

Thos Heart	John Root	John Cowles,
Jacob Deming	Gasham Hollister	Nathl Cole
Joseph Steele	Daniel Cowles	Job Cole
Elisha Goodrich	Jonathan Lee	Saml Cowles
James North	Wm Burnham jun	Saml Thompson
Moses Gilbert	Ebenezer Heart	Allen Goodrich
Samuel Seymour	Isaac North	Joseph Porter
Saml Lankton	Nathl Heart	Saml Bronson

To the Hon. Gen. Assembly of his Majesties Colony in Connecticut now sitting in Hartford, Thos Hart, Saml Seymour, Hezekiah Hart, Saml Lankton, Joseph Porter & many others the major part of the Inhabitants of the parish of Kensington in the town of Farmington Humbly beg leave to show that the Rev. Wm Burnham our worthy Pastor having had long & great bodily infirmity accordingly on the 18th of Inst May signified to our Society Committee his inability longer to discharge his pastoral office among us & thereupon as soon as possible, viz, on the 26 Inst said Society met & agreed & voted if necessary to call some person on probation in order to settle among us in the Ministry, the vote is on record, & also it being put to vote whether they should apply to the Association &c for more special advice it was in fact voted in the affirmative, but yet sundry persons declaring it to be doubtful & moved it might be tried again, the moderator, Capt. Isaac Hart said it was impossible to know whether it was a vote or not, refused any farther trial of it & so no entry thereof was made on the record, thereupon further there being a proposal in writing exhibited to said meeting, whether it was the mind of said Society to apply to the South Association of Hartford County for advice touching their divided & unsettled state, it being read it was voted that the matters in said writing should be tryed by vote of said Society. Immediately whereupon may it please your Honors & before that matter so agreed upon was or could be tried or put to vote, the said moderator stood up and declared he dismissed the said meeting, all respecting the vote above excepted appear on the records of the society. Whereupon we would further observe to your Honors that as the said meeting was dismissed as aforesaid, nothing to purpose being done, so is the said Society under no advantage of having any thing done in the premises till our next annual meeting in December next, our Society Committee neglecting or declining to warn any meeting, before, so that such and so unhappy are our circumstances as not only to be actually destitute of the Gospel Ministry among us, but by any regular means we can use unable to obtain a Man upon probation for the Ministry, or so much as by any public vote or act of the Society to manifest our desire to have or call one. Our humble and earnest request therefore to your Honors is that some one or more of said Society may be specially empowered to warn a Society meeting in said parish to be held on such day as your Honors shall appoint and also to appoint some suitable person to lead, & be the moderator of such meeting in & respecting all such matters as they may act and do, & so we need not be needlessly & unreasonably delayed in a matter of such importance, & we as in duty bound shall ever pray, &c.

Dated at Hartford, this 27th day of May, 1743.

Thos Hart
Saml Seymour
Hezekiah Hart
Saml Lankton
Joseph Porter.

Upon the memorial of Deacon Thomas Hart, Saml Seymour, Hezekiah Hart, and others inhabitants of the parish of Kensington, setting forth the great disorder and confusion in said parish, praying for relief.

Resolved by this Assembly that the said Dea. Thos Hart, Samuel Thompson and Nathaniel Hart, of said Kensington, shall warn all the inhabitants of said society that have a right to vote in parish meeting, to meet on the 6th day of June next, at ten o'clock in the forenoon of said day, at the meeting house in said parish, then and there to transact in such affairs as may relate to said society, and this Assembly do appoint and fully empower Mr. Joseph Buckingham of Hartford, to conduct and lead said meeting as their moderator, and the said moderator is hereby directed to lead said meeting in all such matters and things as he shall think proper, that so peace and order, (if possible,) may be restored to said society and those people conducted in a proper method to the gaining a suitable person to settle with or supply the place of their aged and infirm minister, who hath acquainted that parish that he is not able to serve them longer, to be done at the cost of said parish.

Concurred in ye Lower House, passed in the upper House.

Test James Fowler, Clerk. Test Geo. Wyllys, Sec.

It will be seen that the following petition emanates from "outsiders," for they complain of "long distances" and bad roads.

To the Hon. the Gen. Assembly of his Majesties Colony of Connecticut, to be convened at New Haven on the second Thursday of October next, viz. 1745, the memorial of the subscribers hereto, being inhabitants of the parish of Kensington, in Farmington, in Hartford County, humbly showeth, that your honor's memorialists are some of them, inhabitants of the south part of said parish, are at a great distance from the place of worship in said parish, viz. some three, some four, some six miles therefrom, by which means it comes to pass that your honor's memorialists with great difficulty get to the place of public worship with their families in good weather, and in the winter season have been obliged to hire preaching among themselves, for which they have expended some hundreds of pounds.

Your Honor's Memorialists would also further inform that the said parish are now about to settle a minister among them, and your honor's memorialists think it very hard for them to be obliged to bear their proportion of the extraordinary charge of the same in their present situation, especially when that part of said parish who live near the meeting-house are well able to do the same, and since a part at least of those inhabitants of said parish who live near the meeting-house as aforesaid being convinced of the reasonableness of our being eased of the aforesaid burdens, are willing to have us set off as a parish by ourselves, whereupon your honor's Memorialists humbly pray that as to equity appertains, your Honors, in your wonted wisdom and goodness would take into consideration the case of your Honor's Memorialists, appoint a committee to view said parish, and report to your Honors where and in what manner would be most convenient and proper for your Honor's Memorialists to be set off as a parish by themselves, and that your Honors accordingly grant that your Honor's Memorialists be set off and made a society by themselves, and your Honor's Memorialists as in duty bound shall ever pray.

The question being put to the lower House they concurred.

Joseph Hills,	Amos Judd,	Stephen Lee,
Joseph Hopkins,	John Chivers,	Benjamin Judd, jun.,
Isaac Parsons,	Josiah Lee,	Isaac Lee,
Jonathan Hills,	Watts Hubbard,	Stephen Lee, jun.,
Abraham Hills,	Abijah Peck,	Simmons Woodruff,
Moses Hills,	Daniel Smith,	Jonathan Lewis,
Moses Peck,	Samuel Peck,	John Cole,
Samuel Peck, jun.,	Isaac Peck,	Isaac Norton, jun.,
Timothy Bronson,	Elisha Peck,	Samuel Smith,
John Standley,	Anthony Judd,	John Kelsey,
Aaron Bronson,	Phineas Judd,	Elisha Cole,
Isaac Hart,	Joseph Smith, jun.,	Hezekiah Bronson,
Nathan Cole,	Jedediah Smith	Abraham Parsons,
Stephen Cole,	Benjamin Judd,	George Hubbard,
Amos Peck,	Nathan Judd,	Daniel Dewy,
Matthew Cole,	James Judd,	Aaron Aspinwall.
Noah Smith,	Uriah Judd,	

The question being put to the upper house it was voted Nay.

We have here a sketch of a petition from a few persons in the location of the present village of New Britain, and those living west of it.

April 27th, 1752. Memorial of the subscribers who say they belong to the first Ecclesiastical Society in Farmington, say they are from six to eight miles from the place of public worship in Farmington, say they have heretofore paid Ministerial Taxes to that society, ask now to be set to Kensington.

The Assembly voted Nay.

Nathan Booth,	Moses Andrus,
John Judd,	Job Bronson,
Joshua Mather,	Widow Hannah Root,
Nathaniel Judd,*	Elijah Hart,
James Hosington,*	Ephraim Boardman,*
Judah Hart,	

Six and a half years have now passed and we hear again from the outsiders and about their difficulties.

To the Hon. Gen. Assembly of the Colony of Connecticut, to be convened and holden at Hartford, in the said Colony, on the second Thursday of May, 1752.

The Memorial of us the subscribers, some of us living in the southwest part of the parish of Kensington, in the town of Farmington, in the county of Hartford, and others of us living in the north part of said parish of Kensington, in the town of Farmington, humbly showeth:

That the situation of the said society is such that those inhabitants living in the extreme parts thereof, for a great part of the year can not without the utmost difficulty attend the public worship, where the Meeting house now is, that by reason thereof great difficulties have subsisted in said Society for many years past, and applications have been repeatedly made to this Assembly in order to a division of said society, and Committees have been appointed, and they have reported in favor of such division, and your Memorialists are now assured that no expedient remains that will restore peace, resettle the gospel among us to general satisfaction, and put an end to our expensive and baneful controversy, but to have such division accomplished.

We therefore hereby intreat the interposition of this Hon. Assembly that they will once more employ their wisdom and power to extricate us from our still subsisting troubles, that they will at least grant a Committee to view our circumstances to judge of the expediency of dividing our society, and if they judge that to be expedient and necessary as other Committees heretofore appointed for that purpose have done, that then they be directed to draw the lines for such division and make their report to this Assembly at this present session, or at their session in October next, and as in duty bound ever pray.

Dated 27th day of April, 1752.

This negatived.

Josiah Lee,	Stephen Lee 2d,	James Judd,
Benjamin Judd, jun.,	Nathan Judd,	Uriah Judd,

* Those three with this mark lived at the west part of "Blew Hills" at the south end of the mountain, near the present residence of Gad Andrews, and all lived on the "Reserved lands" of Farmington.

Ezra Belden,
Jedediah Smith,
Joseph Smith, jun.,
Ladwick Hotchkiss,
Matthew Cole,
Elijah Woodruff,
Jonathan Lewis,
Stephen Cole,
Peck,
Isaac Parsons,
Solomon Winchell,
Hez. Winchell, jun.,
Elisha Cole,
David Hills,
Abraham Hills,
Aaron Bronson,
Isaac Lee,
Elijah Bronson,
Amos Judd,
Abraham Parsons,
Robert Booth,
Elisha Booth,
Barnes,
Benjamin Judd,
Stephen Lee,
Joseph Smith,
Joseph Woodruff,
Simmons Woodruff,
Stephen Hollister,
Ebenezer Hart,
John Kelsey,
Al. Grimes,
Daniel Dewy,
Adonijah Lewis,
Phineas Judd,
Hezekiah Winchell.

At a meeting of Ken. Society 2d Dec. 1741, Sar't Samuel Thompson, Wm Burnham, jun. and Ebenezer Hart were chosen a committee, in behalf of the society, to receive into their hands all that estate in bonds and money that is or may be divided to that part of this society that dwell in the bounds of Farmington, as their part or proportion of the money that is or shall be given by the purchasers of the seven townships, called the "western lands," to be loaned out by said committee from time to time, as occasion shall require, always disposing of the interest thereof for the supporting a lawful school in this society, according to the acts and laws of government relating thereto, and be accountable to said society for their doings when required thereto.

At the same meeting upon the motion of Capt. Stephen Lee and others living in the northern part of this parish, praying that they might with the leave of the Hon. Gen. Assembly be released from ministerial charges in this society, and be a society by themselves, it was agreed by vote that Dea. Anthony Judd be a committee in behalf of the society to address the Hon. Gen. Assembly at their session in May next, to appoint a committee of able and disinterested persons, at the charge of the parish, to come into the parish, view its circumstances with relation to said motion, and make report of what they think is proper to be done in the case.

At a meeting of Kensington parish 1st Dec. 1742, Capt. Stephen Lee moderator and Samuel Hart clerk, granted to Rev. Wm Burnham £160 old tenor for his service in the ministry the past year, and to Mr. Judson for his service in the ministry £18 old tenor.

At the same meeting was granted to Joseph Porter for his journey to Stratford for Mr. Judson and entertaining Mr. Judson and his horse, £7 16s. old tenor.

At the same meeting it was voted that the "schoole" committee for the time being, should by their major vote determine the particular place for each schoole in ye several "squadrons,"—(an improvement in spelling,)—in said society.

At the same meeting voted to pay Mr. David Judson for preaching the word among us for the space of four months after the 1st of Dec. inst. in proportion as we paid when he preached before, and that his rate be gathered distinct, by itself.

At a society meeting 26th May, 1743, Capt. Isaac Hart, moderator, a vote was taken whether they thought it necessary to call in some suitable person on probation; voted in the affirmative.

At a meeting of Kensington society lawfully warned, held 26th August, 1743, it was agreed by vote that all male persons over eighteen years of age, and all females from sixteen years old and upward, shall be seated in the meeting-house by the following committee, viz.: Isaac North, David Sage, Moses Peck, Joseph Porter, Joseph Smith, jun., and John Hooker, and Capt. Jonathan Lewis, at their discretion.

At a meeting of Kensington society 13th Sept., 1744, voted to endeavor to call in some suitable person to preach the gospel amongst us, provided Rev. Mr. Wm Burnham will oblige himself to relinquish his salary at or before ye settlement of said person, by 77 votes affirmative, and 43 negative, and at the same meeting it was voted to call the much esteemed Mr. Edward Dorr on probation, provided the Rev. Elders of the South Association advise thereto.

Kensington parish meeting 22d Nov. 1744. Voted to call and settle if it may be Mr. Edward Dorr, (now laboring in the society,) in the work of the ministry, according to gospel order, there being 94 votes in affirmative and 56 in the negative.

At a meeting 3d Wednesday of Dec. 1744, it was voted if Mr. Edward Dorr be ordained to the work of the ministry in this society, he shall have a salary of £50 lawful money for six years, after that £60 lawful money, or grain equivalent thereto.

At the same meeting it was voted to desire and entreat the Rev. Mr. Samuel Whitman of Farmington, the Rev. Mr. Wm Russel and Mr. Edward Eells of Middletown, the Rev. Mr. Ashbel Woodbridge of Glasenbury, and the Rev. Mr. James Lockwood of Wethersfield, as soon as may be to come into this society and hear and consider the circumstances and pleas of the inhabitants thereof in relation to the settlement of a minister among us, and in their wisdom advise us in the two following particulars: viz. first, whether it be for the honor of God and the interest of religion for us under our particular circumstances to endeavor to settle a minister among us over the whole parish, and second, whether it be our duty to proceed in our endeavors to have Mr. Edward Dorr settled in the gospel ministry among us or no. The above council met at Kensington 2d Jan. 1744, Rev. Mr. Samuel Whitman, moderator, and Rev. Mr. Edward Eells, scribe.

We being called by the society of Kensington to advise you with respect to the settlement of a gospel minister among you, and particularly to resolve the two following questions, viz. 1st question, Whether it be for the honor of God and the interest of religion, for us, under our present circumstances, to endeavor to settle a minister among us over the whole parish. Second question, Whether it be our duty to proceed in our endeavors to have Mr. Edward Dorr settled in the gospel ministry among us, or no.

Having heard your pleas, and considered your circumstances, with respect to the first question, we are of opinion you are one entire body under the obligations of maintaining the public worship of God among you so long as he in his Providence continues you so, it is for the honor of God and interest of Religion among you that there be a Pastor over the whole parish. With respect to the second question, considering your divided circumstances, we advise that Mr. Edward Dorr be continued to preach among you till June next, by which time it may be God in his Providence may more open and clear the way of his and your duty with respect to his settlement among you, and that then application be made to the Association for their advice in your further proceeding.

Voted affirmative, Samuel Whitman,
Signed, Wm Russell,
Ashbel Woodbridge,
Edward Eels,
James Lockwood.

A true copy, test Edward Eells, scribe.

At a parish meeting, 6th Feb. 1744–5,

Voted to comply with the advice of council, and also to desire Mr. Dorr to continue his labors with us till June, and Thos Hart appointed to apply to Association on our behalf for advice; said committee waited on the Association and obtained the following advice, viz.:

The Society at Kensington applying to us for advice in respect to Mr. Edward Dorr, we advise them to proceed to his settlement, with the care, deliberation, and caution needful in so weighty an affair, it not appearing to us, there is any sufficient objection against their proceeding to his settlement, in case on a proper examination he appears suitably qualified for the work of the ministry.

Signed Edward Eells, Scribe.

Colchester, 5th June, 1745.

At a meeting 10th Oct. 1745, the society offered Mr. Dorr as a settlement £700, old tenor, and £50 salary for six years, and £60 yearly after six years; also chose at the same meeting Thos Hart on behalf of the society to go to the Gen. Assembly at New Haven, there to answer to the memorial of Capt. Stephen Lee and others, praying for a parish by themselves.

The answer of Mr. Dorr to the offer.

"To the inhabitants of the society of Kensington, with respect to the terms and proposals you have made to me in your votes bearing date 10th Oct. 1745, both for the settlement and annual salary, in case I be ordained and settled among you, my final answer is, that I do hereby accept of each and every of the sums therein granted, according to the time and times therein mentioned as sufficient encouragement, both for settlement and an annual salary, as witness my hand." Edward Dorr.

Dated in Lyme, 30th Oct. 1745.

To cut short the history of this protracted controversy, let me briefly say that the society somewhat changed their position in regard to Mr. Dorr; they reconsidered all former votes about his salary, and offered him by a major vote, 20th August, 1746, a sum equal to one-eighth of the sum of the salaries of the eight neighboring parishes, and called another council to consider and advise in the matter. In the mean time Capt. Stephen Lee and others, of the north part of the parish, were pressing their petitions to the General Court for a separation, and the Rev. Mr. Burnham, whose health had failed somewhat by infirmity, had greatly improved, so that the council upon these considerations discouraged the settlement of Mr. Dorr, and advised the society to sustain Mr. Burnham. Their record shows their regard to the advice, for at the annual meeting, December 3d, 1746, they voted him £190, in bills of public credit, or grain at market price, for his salary for the past year, and in 1747 he was paid £200, old tenor, and in 1748 they granted Rev. Mr. Burnham £350, old tenor.

At the annual meeting of Kensington parish 6th December, 1749, John Hooker, moderator, Thomas Hart, clerk, Samuel Smith and Phineas Judd, collectors of Mr. Burnham's rate that may be granted, the said Phineas Judd to collect that pertaining to Farmington, and the said Samuel Smith to collect that part of the rates that pertain to Middletown and Wethersfield inhabitants to pay; granted to Rev. Mr. William Burnham, for his service in the work of the ministry the past year, as his salary, £300 in money of the old currency, or in wheat at £1 15s. per bushel, or "ry" at £1 50, or Indian corn at 15s. per bushel.

At a meeting of Kensington parish, 18th October, 1750, Capt. Amos Porter, moderator, the inhabitants agreed by vote to address themselves unto the present General Assembly of this government, to send us a committee to view our circumstances, whether we shall divide or continue as we are, and if said committee think fit in their wisdom to divide us, then for said committee to draw lines for said division, and at the same meeting Capt. Joseph Porter and Mr. Daniel Smith were chosen a committee to go to the General Assembly, and endeavor to obtain the above said committee.

At the annual meeting 5th December, 1750, Capt. Amos Porter, moderator, Thomas Hart, clerk, it was voted to raise a rate of £175 to be speedily gathered and paid to the administrator of the estate of Rev. Mr. William Burnham, deceased, for his service in the ministry the year past, to be paid in money, old tenor, or grain at the market price, first of May next.

At the same meeting Capt Samuel Cowles, Capt. Joseph Porter, Elisha Bronson, and Ins. Nathaniel Hart were chosen rate makers. Also agreed that the prudential committee for the year ensuing have full power at the society charge to provide a Minister or Ministers to preach with us until the last day of May next.

At the same meeting it was voted that Elijah Bronson take due care of stray sheep in ffarmington part of the Society.

December 11th, 1751, it was voted to get the advice of the Rev. Association to call some suitable candidate upon probation, there being 82 votes in ye affirmative & 63 in the negative.

At the same meeting it was signified by vote that it was their minds to call in Mr. Ezra Stiles as a candidate, if the Association shall so advise, & Ins. Nathaniel Hart & Joseph Porter were chosen a committee to seek their advice.

On the 19th May, 1752, John Hooker, Esq. was chosen Moderator, being 74 votes in the affirmative & 64 in the negative; question was tried whether the society would appoint any person or persons to go to General Assembly now sitting at Hartford, to show reason why the several Memorials now made to said Assembly relating to the division of this society into several Ecclesiastical societies, & it was voted in the affirmative by 81 to 64 in the negative, & Thomas Hart & John Hooker were chosen a committee to go & Remonstrate against said Memorials by a vote of 77 affirmative & 64 negative; the question was tried whether the society would continue one entire parish & endeavor to settle a Minister for the whole or not. Voted in the affirmative by 81 to 66 negative.

At this meeting the Heirs & Administrator of Rev. Mr. Burnham, deceased, presented a claim for arrearages of salary due the Estate; the Society voted against paying the claim & appointed Sarg. Caleb Galpin, John Hooker, Esq. & Sarg. Moses Peck to do what they may to obstruct the claim, at court.

At an adjourned meeting of the society held 3d Tuesday of Dec. 1752, it was signified by a full major vote, that it was their desire to have the much esteemed Mr. Aaron Brown, called to preach the Gospel among us as a probationer, in order to a settlement, & Ins. Jonathan Lee, Jobe Cole, & Isaac North were chosen a committee to supply the pulpit the year ensuing, at the cost of the society, & to apply to the South Association for their advice as occasion shall call for.

At a meeting 1st March, 1753, Ins. Daniel Dewy, Moderator, it was agreed to call & settle ye much Esteemed Mr. Aaron Brown, and Sarg.

Caleb Galpin, Capt. Joseph Porter & Isaac Lee were appointed a committee to treat with Mr. Brown about his settlement & Salary—the meeting then adjourned to the next Monday, when the said Mr. Brown having informed the Inhabitants that he thought it not convenient so suddenly to propose to the society the said terms, whereupon at the same meeting the society voted to pay to Mr. Brown the full sum of £2000 in money of the old tenor, provided he be settled with us, & it was also voted to give him as a yearly salary for the first two years fifty-five pounds per year in proclamation money, & the third year after his settlement as aforesaid, £65 in proclamation money, and after the expiration of the third year his salary shall be £70 proclamation money, during the whole term of time he shall continue in the Ministry with us, to be paid in silver money or Bills of Credit equivalent thereto, or in grain equivalent to proclamation money.

At a meeting of Kensington society held 8th May, 1753, John Hooker, Esq. Moderator, voted that John Hooker, Esqr. & Sarg't Isaac North be a committee to Remonstrate against the Memorial of Capt. Jonathan Lewis & others of this society that may be preferred or offered to the General Assembly of this government to be convened the 2d Thursday of May Inst.

September 5th, 1753, A society Meeting was held in which the question was tried by vote whether it was their minds to keep together in one entire parish, and the vote was 59 affirmative & 53 Negative.

October 19th, 1753, At a meeting lawfully warned, it was voted to employ John Hooker & Isaac Lee to remonstrate at the Gen. Assembly now sitting at New Haven, against the Memorial of Josiah Burnham,* now depending before said Court.

December 14th, 1753, at a society meeting it was voted that John Hooker & Isaac Lee be a committee to appear before the Gen. Assembly to be holden at Hartford May next, and remonstrate against the petition of Josiah Burnham against this Society on account of arrearages of Mr. Burnham's Salary.

To the Hon. Gen. Assembly of the Colony of Connecticut sitting at Hartford on the 2d Thursday of May, 1754. Whereas this Assembly did at their sessions at New Haven in October last, upon the Memorial of the Inhabitants of the parish of Kensington showing to this Assembly the great difficulty they were under with respect to their settling a Gospel Minister among them by reason of the Inhabitants of said Society being divided in their sentiments with respect to their being divided into several Societies, appointed us the subscribers a Committee & empowered us with

---

* This is the man whom Mrs. Willard, in her beautiful poem entitled "Stealing the Bride," makes the hero of the stealing party, and in a note at the margin, represents him as having murdered and been hung in Haverhill, New Hampshire. Her mistake is, in putting the father for the son, as the murderer, (both having the same name.)

instructions to go into said parish of Kensington & call a Society Meeting or meetings of the Inhabitants of said Society and to lead & Moderate in said meeting or meetings & also to use all proper measures to know the minds, names & number of said Inhabitants that are of the mind to divide said Society into several Societies, and also the forms & lines that those that were for dividing said Society would have drawn to divide said Society, & to view the Society of Kensington & the Inhabitants near to the parish of Kensington & adjoining Kensington, & also to hear the pleas of all parties, & upon the whole to judge & determine whether or no it would be for the best good & welfare & peace of said parish to continue in one entire Society or otherwise, Whether it would be so to divide said parish into several Societies, & if upon the whole we should judge that it might conduce most for the peace & welfare & interest of said Society and the interest of Religion there, to divide said Society, then to divide said Society into so many Societies and draw such lines as we should judge might conduce most to the peace, good & welfare of said Society, & that if we should judge it best that said parish should be divided into two or more Societies, then we should give due attention into such adjoining parishes any part of which we might think best to be added to such Society, by signifying to the committee of said Society our desire that they would call a meeting of such society, if they should think fit & acquaint them, that they might appear by their Committee appointed by such Society & be heard thereon, if they see cause & make our report thereon to this Assembly. Whereupon we take leave to report to this Assembly, that in pursuance to the instructions aforesaid we caused a society meeting to be legally warned in said parish of Kensington to meet on the 27th day of November last past, and they accordingly met, and we attended and moderated in said meeting, and took the number and names of those who were for continuing in one society, and there was the number of 96, and the number and names of those who were for dividing into more societies than one were 31 of the legal voters in said Society, and the two next following days, we viewed the said Society in the circumstances of it and then adjourned to the third Tuesday of April next following, and gave notice unto the parish of Newington and first parish of Farmington, and first Society of Middletown, and the parish of Meriden, to appear in the parish of Kensington on the said third Tuesday of April, by their Committee, to show reasons if they see cause, why there should not be some part of these adjoining parishes taken off from them to be added to accommodate the dividing the parish of Kensington into several parishes and all parties then and there met, by their committee except Meriden, and were fully heard by us in the premises, and upon consideration we judge it would be for the best, and most for the peace of the said parish of Kensington to be divided into three distinct Ecclesiastical societies, with some small additions from other societies, and have drawn the lines for the several societies in the manner and form following, viz: The bounds of the North part or Society, to be a line drawn across the Bridge called the Beach Swamp bridge, and to be on a line due East & West from Wethersfield town line to Southington parish line, and on Wethersfield line Northward until it comes to the North side of Daniel Hart's land, where he now lives, and from Wethersfield line to run on the North side of said Hart's lot to the Northwest corner thereof, and thence to run southerly to the old fulling-mill place, so called, on Pond River, and from thence to a lot of land belonging to the heirs of Timothy Hart, deceased, near Bares hollow, on the east side of the lot, and from thence South until it meets with the North line of Southington parish, then by Southington line as that runs until it meets with the west line afore mentioned.

And the South part or Society we have bounded and described, beginning at the middle of the highway where they cross each other, between the house of Elisha and Stephen Cole, and from thence to run Northwesterly to the Southwest corner of John Coles' lot, where he now dwells, and from thence a west line to Southington parish, thence Southerly by Southington parish line to the Southeast corner thereof, then running Easterly to Farmington Southeast corner bounds, in such form as to include those families in Meriden that are living North of the Mountains, and from Farmington corner to the Southeast corner of that part of Kensington that was taken off from Middletown, then Westerly to the Southwest corner of said Middletown part of Kensington, and then a straight line to the place first mentioned.

And that the middle part of said Kensington between aforesaid two described places or Societies be and remain one entire Society, and that the middle society exclusive of that part annexed from Wethersfield, pay unto the said parish of Newington the sum of £20 a year lawful money three successive years next coming, with the interest arising thereon, and that the improved lands in each parish shall be rated in the parish where it lieth.

And further that the South part or parish have the liberty and privilege of meeting with the Middle Society six months in each year until they shall be accommodated with a Meeting house and Minister among themselves; all which is submitted to this Hon. Assembly by your Honor's humble and obedient servants.

Signed, Jonathan Trumble,
Jonathan Huntington,
Shubel Conont.

Hartford, 16th May, 1754.

The question was put whether this report be accepted and approved. Resolved in the Negative.

May 1754. An Act Limiting the bounds of the Parish of Kensington, and for establishing one other Ecclesiastical Society in Farmington, in the county of Hartford.

Be it enacted by the Governor & Council & Representatives in Gen. Court assembled, and by the authority of the same, That the bounds of the parish of Kensington for the future shall extend no farther North than to an East and West line drawn across the Bridge called the Beach Swamp Bridge from Wethersfield town line to Southington parish line; Easterly by the Ancient line of said Kensington, including those two pieces of land taken off from Wethersfield & Middletown; and from the South West corner of the said Middletown part of Kensington, to run Westerly until it comes into the middle of the highway where they cross each other, between the houses of Elisha Cole & Stephen Cole, from thence Westerly until it comes to the south West corner of John Coles home lot, from thence due west to said Southington Society line, thence Northerly as that line runs, to the line first mentioned, & that the parish Taxes arising, or that shall be levied on the improved lands in said Kensington shall be paid to said Society only.

And it is further enacted by the authority aforesaid, that said parish of Kensington shall have full power & Authority, & full power & authority is hereby granted to said parish, at their legal meetings to tax all such Inhabitants as live South of said Society, & within the ancient bounds of Kensington, equally with themselves for defraying the charge of preaching only, & that their collectors have full power to collect the same until this Assembly shall order otherwise.

And it is further Enacted, by the authority aforesaid, that the said Society of Kensington, exclusive of those Inhabitants that live in the Wethersfield part shall pay to the Society of Newington the sum of £20 lawful money on the 1st day of May, 1755, & £20 more on the 1st May, 1756, & £20 more 1st May, 1757, each payment to be made with the lawful interest arising on such sum, from such sum, from the 1st day of June next, & said Society of Kensington, exclusive of said Wethersfield part, shall have full power at their legal meetings, to tax themselves for the payment of said £60 & interest thereof, & that said Society Committee make a Rate bill accordingly, & that the collector chosen in said Society shall have full power to collect the same as other Society Rates by law are collected, & pay the same to the Society Committee for the use aforesaid.

And the Inhabitants living South of said parish of Kensington shall have free liberty to attend the public worship with the said Society of Kensington, till this Assembly order otherwise.

And be it further Enacted by the Authority aforesaid, that there shall be one other Ecclesiastical Society erected & made & is hereby created & made within the bounds of the town of Farmington, & described as follows, viz: South on the North bounds of Kensington parish, & Easterly on Wethersfield town line as far North as the North side of Daniel Hart's lot, where his Dwelling House now stands, & from thence to run West on the North side of said Hart's lot to the West end of that tier of lots, from thence to run Southerly to the old fulling Mill so called on Pond river, & from thence Southerly to the east side of a Lot of land belonging to the heirs of Timothy Hart late deceased, near "Bares Hollow," & from thence due south until it meets with the North line of Southington parish, thence by said Southington line, as that runs, until it comes to Kensington North line, Excluding Thomas Stanley, Daniel Hart & John Clark & their farms on which they now dwell, lying within the bounds above described, & the same is hereby created & made one distinct Ecclesiastical Society, & shall be known by the name of "New Briton," with all the powers & priviledges that other Ecclesiastical Societies by law have in this Colony, & that all the improved lands in said society, shall be rated in said Society excepting as before excepted.

It is to be regretted that we have no history of the church in Kensington from the pen of Rev. Mr. Burnham himself, and that the catalogue of members is so incomplete. We have to rely on the record and remarks of Rev. Samuel Clark, who succeeded Mr. Burnham 14th July, 1756, and on the testimony of Rev. John Smalley, of New Britain, who began his record 19th April, 1758, of the organization of that Church, by a list of members from Newington Church, and a like list of members from Kensington Church. This last is the only source we have to supply the gap in the record of Mr. Burnham, which was lost or carried away, except the list of Rev. Mr. Clark, of the resident and living members, he says, when he came.

We give here his account of the condition of the record, with a list of his living resident members, and also a list of those who withdrew to help constitute the church in New Britain; (we find no record, but only an intimation by Rev. Mr. Clark that they were ever dismissed from Kensington Church.) We give these lists and this account on the ground that the history of Kensington is a part of the history of those portions that seceded, to the date of their organization, or time of assuming another name.

Rev. Mr. Clark's record and remarks.

Kensington, 14th July, 1756. I was this day set apart to the sacred office of the Gospel Ministry, by the laying on of the hands of the Presbytery, and the Reverend Ministers assisting were,

Ashbel Woodbridge, of Glastenbury.
Daniel Russel, of Stepney.
Grindel Rossen, of Hadlyme.
Edward Eells, of Middletown, upper houses.

Moses Bartlet, of East Middletown.
Samuel Newel, of New Cambridge.
Joshua Belden, of Newington.
James Lockwood, of Wethersfield.
Elijah Latrop, of Gilead.
Timothy Pitkin, of Farmington.

And I took the solemn charge of the church of Christ my Blessed Lord and Master, in this place, (signed) Samuel Clark. And I received the records of the church which were very imperfect and broken, on the 16th day of the above said month; and by those records I find the following relating to the affairs and state of the Church in this place. The Rev. Mr. William Burnham, my predecessor, was ordained in this place on the tenth of December, 1712, and the Reverend Ministers assisting were, Mr. Timothy Woodbridge and Mr. Thomas Buckingham, of Hartford. Mr. Stephen Mix, of Wethersfield, & Mr. Samuel Whitman, of Farmington.

The names of persons taken into the Church since the first forming of; as to those taken in before I came, I can find but an imperfect account; I have their names for a little while at first, and such as were members when I was settled, except a large number which belonged to "New Britton" Society when I was settled, but were not embodied or dismissed from this Church till afterwards.

December 10th, 1712, the Church was formed and consisted of the following members:

Rev. William Burnham, Pastor.
Stephen Lee and his wife.
Anthony Judd, Deacon.
Samuel Seymour and his wife.
Thomas North.
Thomas Hart, Deacon, and his wife.
Caleb Cowles.

March 2d, 1712–13, accepted from other Churches,

Isaac Norton and his wife, Elizabeth.
Benjamin Judd and his wife, Susannah.

February, 1718–19, accepted from other Churches,

Samuel Bronson, sen. and his wife, Abigail, from Farmington.
Daniel Andrus and Samuel Hubbard, from Hartford.
Ebenezer Gilbert, from Hartford.
Samuel Peck and Abigail, his wife, from Hartford.
The wife of Samuel Hubbard, from Hartford.

"Such as were Members when I came."

Supposed to be living and resident. (Ed.) 1756.

Timothy Hubbard and Abiah his wife.
John Beckley and Mary, his wife.

Isaac North and Mary, his wife.
Ann Steele, daughter of Joseph; (she married John Root.)
Ann Burnham, Widow.
Ashbel, (Negro.)
Ebenezer Hart and Elizabeth, his wife.
Isaac Hart and Elizabeth, his wife.
Samuel Thompson and Sarah, his wife.
Martha Norton, Widow.
Jedediah Norton and Acsah, his wife.
Elnathan Norton and Rachel, his wife.
Joseph Deming.
Thomas Goodwin and Sarah, his wife.
John Gridley and Ruth, his wife.
Jonathan Gilbert and Kesia, his wife.
Samuel Peck.
Elisha Peck and Lydia, his wife.
Mary Hooker, wife of Andrew.
Mary Beckley, wife of Benjamin.
Mary Andrus, widow of John.
Eunice Andrus, wife of Daniel.
Jerusha, wife of John Bartholomew, (removed.)
Ann Porter, daughter of John, (married Stephen Mix.)
Samuel Galpin.
Samuel Galpin, jun., and Abigail, his wife.
Lois Peck, widow.
Aaron Bronson.
Samuel Gridley, jun.
Hezekiah Winchel and Mary, his wife; (she married Samuel Lankton.)
Luke Stebbins.
Abigail Bronson, widow.
Elisha Bronson and Sarah, his wife.
Mary, widow of Deacon Jonathan Lee.
Lucy, daughter of Jonathan Lee.
John Lee and Sarah, his wife.
Elijah Peck and Mary, his wife.
Abigail Cowles, widow.
Daniel Cowles and Martha, his wife.
John Gilbert and Eunice, his wife.
Josiah Boardman and Rachel, his wife.
Isaac Norton and Elizabeth, his wife; (she married to Deacon Thomas Hart; age 79.)
Abram Pierson and Sarah, his wife.
Samuel Peck, jun.

Hannah Porter, widow.
Ruth Porter, wife of William.
John Cole and his wife.
Elizabeth Gridley, widow.
Judith Gridley.
Joseph Porter and Hannah, his wife.
Hannah Newel.
Job Norton and Susannah, his wife, (removed.)
John Kisby.
John Squire and Elizabeth, his wife.
Elisha Goodrich and Rebecca, his wife, (removed.)
Abijah Peck and Abigail, his wife.
Elizabeth Galpin, widow.
James Steele and Mercy, his wife.
Daniel Beckley, jun. and Ruth, his wife; (married to Abram Harris.)
Josiah Burnham and Ruth, his wife.
Charles Kelsey and Mehitabel, his wife.
Watts Hubbard and Mary, his wife, (removed.)
David Sage and Bathsheba (Judd,) his wife.
Richard Hubbard.
Roger Norton.
Huit Strong, (chosen Deacon, 1756.)
Ruth Burnham, widow.
Elisha Burnham.
James Hurlbut and his wife.
Ebenezer Gridley.
Amos Gridley.
Nathaniel Winchel.
Nathaniel Winchel, jun.
Moses Deming and Sarah, his wife.
Thomas Standley and Martha, his wife.
Charles Bronson.
Samuel Smith.
Josiah Bronson.
Martha, wife of Daniel Beckley.
Nathaniel Dickinson.
William Allis.

August 8th, 1756, Members to Church from this date.

Jerusha (Lee,) wife of Elisha Burnham.
Lydia, wife of George Hubbard, received from Hartford.
October 3d, Sarah, wife of Richard Hubbard.
September 19th, Servia Allis, wid. of John, (mar. David Webster, Esq.)
Joel Mitchel.

October 10th, Seth Hooker.
December 19th, Job Heart and Eunice, his wife.
Aaron Porter.
Thomas Gridley and Hannah, his wife.
February 6th, 1757, Hezekiah Winchel.
Elizabeth, wife of Joseph Deming.
Azuba (Orvice,) wife of Ebenezer Gridley.
Deborah, wife of Samuel Gridley, jun.
April 10th, Jonathan Lankton.
Daniel Elderkin.
Sarah (Sage,) wife of Ebenezer Steele.
June 19th, Azuba (Eno,) wife of Amos Gridley.
August 28th, Keziah, wife of Elisha Cole.
December 25th, Elijah Heart, of New Britain.

Thus far from Rev. Samuel Clark's record and remarks. (The interlinings by the Editor.)

Here follows a list from the record and remarks of Rev. John Smalley, D. D., in the words and order in which he recorded them, viz:

April 19th, 1758. A Church was gathered in the parish of New Britain, John Smalley being Ordained to the pastoral office in & over the same. From the Church in Kensington, (Rev. Samuel Clark, Pastor.) The widdow Hannah Seymor, the Widdow Mary Andrus, the Widdow Anna Booth, Benjamin Judd & his wife, Widdow Elizabeth Lee, Joseph Smith, Rebecca, wife of Daniel Dewy, Hannah, wife of Gideon Griswold, Martha, wife of Samuel Goodrich, Joseph Smith, jun. & his wife, Jedediah Smith & his wife, Josiah Lee & his wife, Isaac Lee & his wife, Stephen Lee, James Judd, Uriah Judd & his wife, Nathan Judd & his wife, Phineas Judd & his wife, John Judd & his wife, Joshua Mather & his wife, Elijah Hart & his wife, Judah Hart, Elijah Hart, jun., Moses Andrus & his wife, William Patterson, Widdow Hannah Root, John Kelsey & his wife, Joseph Woodruff & his wife, Simmons Woodruff & his wife, Nathan Booth & his wife, Ladwick Hotchkiss & his wife.

The compiler has inserted the above list because the persons originally belonged to the Kensington Church, and the early history of that church is not complete without them, and even with them there will be wanting the names of such as died, or otherwise removed, not only during the interim between Rev. Mr. Burnham and Rev. Mr. Clark, but also from the last entry of Mr. Burnham, February, 1718–19, to the settlement of Mr. Clark, July 14th, 1756, a period of some thirty-seven years. This omission or gap in the record never can be supplied unless Mr. Burnham's record can be found. A few of the names might be supplied, however, by a thorough antiquarian, from neighboring church records, scraps of family history, and incidental notices of individuals, titles of officers, and by tradition.

A century and a half has expired since the organization of this church, and December, 1862, the present pastor, Rev. E. B. Hillard, very appropriately noticed the occasion by a historical sermon to his congregation, the closing reflections of which the compiler has begged leave to quote for this work.

"Mr. Burnham continued to be the minister of the Society till the time of his death, September 23d, 1750. His remains lie buried in the old burying-ground, his gift to the Society, in Christian Lane, the stone that marks his grave bearing the following inscription: "Here lies interred the body of the Rev. William Burnham, Senior, first pastor of the church of Christ in Kensington, who having served his generation according to the will of God fell on sleep September the 23d, 1750, in the sixty-sixth year of his age, and the thirty-eighth of his ministry." The foot-stone is inscribed, "The Rev. Mr. William Burnham, 1750." The grave is near the western end of the ground, the stone an upright slab of freestone, the inscription on the east side facing the road. There, together, in that sacred enclosure, sleep the fathers; the martial leader of the settlement, in his nameless but not forgotten grave; the first pastor surrounded by his flock; the staid and thoughtful men with whom he took serious, manly counsel, their tombstone telling the simple story that they lived and died, "Serving their generation according to the will of God and then falling on sleep," but in that simple inscription telling the whole story of their pious faithfulness, their modest worth; the wives who loved them and helped them by their side; and the little children who came with them into the wilderness, no longer trembling at the wolf's howl or the Indian's yell; there, clustered on the knoll beside the still-flowing river, they lie, their faces to the east, in readiness to greet him whose coming shall be as the coming of the morning; their tombstones lettered on the side towards the road, as though in their old human love still longing to greet with the old words of kindness the passer-by. I visited, a short time since, that sacred spot. I stood beside the ancient graves. I looked around upon the scenes on which the silent sleepers in them used to look. I turned my eyes, as the sun was setting, to the summit of the western mountain, whither, at sunset, their eyes had so often turned when home and friends lay beyond, and all was forest-wild between. In sight and near at hand was the swell on which stood the old meeting-house, in which they first covenanted together to walk with Christ and with each other; where they heard the lessons that took from death its sting, and cheered the gloom of the grave with the light of immortality; within sound of the Sabbath-psalm sung in concert by those, the living, that loved them still, and which, mingling in the stillness of the holy day, with the whispering of the forest foliage and the murmuring of the forest stream, soothed their pious rest. The trees were bare. The snow lay on the ground, as a century and a half before it had lain there on the December day when they first, collecting from their scattered homes, had gathered at the meeting-house to see him whom they had chosen to be their shepherd in the wilderness, set apart to his sacred work, and to covenant with him to be his people. That early covenant they kept with him, and he with them, and now they sleep together near by, in hope of a glorious resurrection. As I stood there and looked around me, these thoughts in my heart, I felt that the ground on which I stood was holy ground. Reverently I trod amid the ashes of the fathers. Silently I prayed that I might be faithful to the charge they had transmitted to me, and that when like them I had done my life's work, I too might die the death of the righteous and my last end be like theirs.

The spot where they sleep seems fit place for their long rest. It is retired and lonely, as is now the history of their lives. The age in which they lived has passed away. The present is new and strange. It is meet that in their final rest they should be withdrawn from it, their slumbers be undisturbed by its tumultuous whirl. And so it is. They sleep in peace. The age is busy around them but it leaves them lonely still. The "desolate corner of the wilderness" in which they planted their lonely settlement, has become the centre of a region of life and activity; their business vexes it; their sounds disturb it; but the scene of their early homes is still almost as quiet as when no sounds were heard there save those of the Indian's footfall or the forest cry. There let us leave them to their sleep, beneath the trees, beside the river.

"Each in his narrow cell forever laid."

Or if we visit their graves let it be to breathe the peace that calmed their souls, and learn the lessons which their virtues teach us."

NEW BRITAIN.

New Britain as an incorporated Ecclesiastical Society. May session, 1754, its name, in honor of Great Britain, given by Col. Isaac Lee.

The etymology of the word is bright, shining, tin or pewter; hence the island of Great Britain was called so from the abundance of tin found in adjacent islands. It is not supposed that our ancestors ever dreamed it was destined to be a village, or even a town. The height of their ambition was to make it an ecclesiastical and school society, where the preaching of the gospel might be sustained, a church organized, its ordinances observed, and convenient schools established for their children. The same lines bound it now, 1867, that bounded it when it took its name, (except a small addition to its northern limit,) embracing a territory only about three and a half miles by four and a half; the surface much broken with moderate hills and corresponding valleys, well watered with springs and small rivulets, but no rivers. It has a much greater elevation than is generally supposed; is the summit of the railroad from Hartford to Plainville; the source of the little river emptying at Hartford; of the Mattabesset, discharging at Middletown, and the Quinnipiac, falling into the Sound, at New Haven. Its natural advantages are not greatly in its favor. Its streams are barely sufficient to turn its grist and saw-mills; its valleys on the eastern portion adjoining the parish of Newington are rich and productive of good hay and grain, and the western portions for good and thrifty wood and grazing. Fruits and grains in great variety have been produced from the soil, from the first settlement of the place, but it has been done with great pains and labor, for the soil in general is hard and gravelly, as is seen by our hard and smooth roads. It occupies a central position in the State, being eight miles west of Connecticut river, and full twenty-five miles north of New Haven. At the date of its incorporation or divorce from Kensington and Newington, the society had about sixty dwellings scattered over its surface; some of them would not be very inviting to the taste of the present generation, mere lodges or huts; yet within were warm hearts and busy hands. The reader will see towards the close of the long introduction to this work, that the incorporating act of the General Court excluded (no doubt from their own choice strenuously urged,) three prominent families at the northern extremity of the parish, with their large farms. This was a grief and trial which we see they soon felt, and strove to remedy by their applications to the General Assembly. Two of the principal patriarchs of this struggling community had now passed away by death; Capt. Stephen Lee and Deacon Anthony Judd. Their names no more appear at the head of petitions for "aid, ease, comfort, or relief of heavy burdens." Capt. Lee's sword now rests in ts scabbard, (unless.

perchance used by his stalwart sons or grand-sons.) Deacon Anthony no more distributes the memorials of the broken body of his Saviour, and the voices of these prominent men are no more heard moderating in church, town or society meetings. But they have left large families, large estates, and what is still more enduring, good examples and name.

They left still living Sergeant Benjamin Judd, active in both church and society, and Capt. Jonathan Lewis, prominent in military, town and society affairs, with a goodly number of younger men, with stout hearts and strong arms. Their first society meeting was held June 13th, 1754, when they voted and agreed that it was necessary to build a house for public worship, and at the same meeting appointed a committee to apply to the County Court to affix the place where to build. Also a committee to procure a suitable candidate to preach the gospel amongst us.

At the same meeting Josiah Lee was chosen clerk, and Isaac Lee, treasurer, and Josiah Lee and others a committee to order the prudentials of the parish.

October 25th, 1754, a committee was appointed to assist the surveyor to make a map of the parish, and find the center of the society, as near as they can. Also the committee directed to endeavor to procure Rev. Stephen Holmes to preach amongst us as a candidate for settlement.

Rev. Stephen Holmes* was first invited to preach as a candidate for settlement; he was paid £10 old tenor per Sabbath; he preached thirteen Sabbaths. For some unknown reason to us, he failed to gain the parish, but he secured a wife in the person of Deacon Patterson's third daughter, Anna, to whom he was united in marriage January 24th, 1759, before Rev. John Smalley, and she had bequeathed to her as part of her portion of her father's estate, Rose, a servant girl.

December 2d, 1754, a meeting of the parish voted that they desire the committee to endeavor to procure the Rev. John Bunnel to preach amongst us as a candidate for settlement in the gospel ministry.

At a society meeting December 16th, 1754, voted to proceed and build a house for religious worship.†

---

* He was settled November, 1757, at Center Brook, in Essex, (Pautapaug,) where he died September, 1773.

† That the parish had religious services previous to having a meeting-house, is shown from the following extracts from the Church Record of Rev. Joshua Belden, Newington: "Elias Hart and wife 'owned the covenant' at New Britain, September, 1754." From the Church Record of Rev. Ebenezer Booge, of Northington: "Baptized, at New Britain, September 22d, 1754, Elizabeth, daughter of Joseph Clark." The reader will observe this last Sabbath service was the next after Rev. Mr. Belden held his. Again, Rev. Mr. Belden, at a later date, "July 27th, 1755: Elijah Smith and Jacob Brandigee 'owned the covenant' at New Britain, and at the same time and place, William Horton owned the covenant' and was baptized." Again, two weeks before New Britain Church was organized, Rev. Ebenezer Booge says in his Church Record: "I baptized at New Britain, April 5th, 1758, Solomon, son of Joseph Clark."

March 17th, 1755, at a meeting of the society of New Britain legally warned, voted to proceed to settle the Rev. John Bunnel, provided we can agree on terms, and also provided the approbation of the Reverend South Association of Hartford county can be obtained.

At the same meeting voted as a settlement £1,200 old tenor, with this proviso, viz. that if he cease to be our minister through his defect, he shall refund his settlement. Also voted as a salary £55 per annum, lawful money. Mr. John Bunnel* declines the call, but at a meeting held May 15th, 1755, a committee is appointed to pray him that he reconsider the request of this society, and that he consider our needy circumstances, and the ill consequences consequent on his denial, and ascertain if there is any way of removing the objections in the way of his settling among us, &c., but if unsuccessful, to procure some other candidate.

December 1st, 1755, at a meeting of the parish it was voted to appoint a committee to apply to the Reverend South Association of Hartford county for their advice, that they recommend some suitable orthodox candidate to preach the gospel amongst us with a view to a settlement.

At the next meeting the committee were instructed to endeavor to procure Rev. Amos Fowler to preach for them as a candidate for settlement. And here the author is constrained, (though reluctantly,) to disclose the fact that we have no authenticated record of the society doings and acts in regard to building the house or supplying the pulpit. That we had, as a society, such a record, kept by the clerk or recorder, is evident, for we copy this early history of the parish from notes purporting to be taken from the record book referred to. The original record, we fear, is irrevocably "lost." The notes are by Doctor Thomas G. Lee, an eminent physician, who had in early life been elevated to the superintendence of the McLane Asylum for the Insane, at Charlestown, Mass., but died 1836, at the age of twenty-eight. While studying with Dr. Todd, of Farmington, and spending some time at his home in this place, having a great taste for antiquarian lore, he gathered these notes, and we are chiefly indebted to his taste and diligence, and to the kindness of his brother, Dr. John R. Lee, for the use of them in the preparation of this work, and thus also for the early history of the parish. We have however a treasurer's record, from 1765 to this date, and a clerk's from November 5th, 1793, to the present time, which will be quoted from as occasion requires. These remarks will show the reader why so many incidentals are introduced to cor-

* His native place, West Haven, was licensed 1738, by New Haven East Association; the church in New Britain had previously applied to Hartford South for advice respecting some proper person to preach to them as a candidate for settlement, as appears from the associational record of a meeting held at Stepney, February 4th, 1755, at the house of Rev. Mr. Daniel Russel, where they say they have advised the society of New Britain to Mr. John Bunnel to preach with them upon probation.

roborate the main history. The following is an instance of incidentals from Farmington town records:

February 1st, 1755, Dr. Isaac Lee, of Middletown, deeded to Farmington, for a highway, three pieces of land in the parish of New Britain, the first piece, one rod wide, and half a mile and six rods long, butted east on the highway that runs by the house where my son Stephen now dwells, south on land lately conveyed to the town by my brother Josiah, north on my own land.* The second piece runs "cross" my said lot, and is butted north on land conveyed to Farmington by Benjamin Judd; east, part on my own land and part on land of Josiah Lee, to be eight rods wide at the north end, and six at the south; butts west on the ledge next west of the place appointed for to build the meeting-house." The third piece begins at the path at the top of the ledge, and runs northerly across the Mill Brook, three rods below the bridge, thence to Benjamin Judd's land, and is in length thirty-five rods.

At a meeting of the society February 29th, 1756, it was voted and agreed that Capt. John Patterson and Isaac Lee be a committee to apply to the General Assembly, moving that those families which were excluded in the north part of our parish, be admitted to the society.

The following in order of time is from the State archives:

At a meeting of the inhabitants of ye parish of New Britain, holden on the 25th day of February, 1756, lawfully warned, at the same meeting Capt. John Patterson and Mr. Ladwick Hotchkiss were chosen a committee to prepare a memorial to the Honorable General Assembly, praying to grant a tax on unimproved lands in the society, to be improved in building a meeting-house, and the settling a gospel minister amongst us.

A true copy of record. Test, Isaac Lee, Society Clerk.

The above appointment and duty of Capt. John Patterson and Mr. Ladwick Hotchkiss was duly attended to, and their petition presented to the Assembly, which granted a tax of one penny an acre on all unimproved lands, for the purpose proposed, for the term of four years next ensuing.

Done at May session, 1756.

We now return to the negotiations of this young society in regard to settling a minister; they have no meeting-house yet to preach in, and their candidates, though numerous, seem coy. Rev. Amos Fowler has been preaching for them as a candidate, and at a meeting of the society April 25th, 1756, they voted and agreed to give Mr. Fowler as a settlement £140, lawful money, and voted to grant him as a salary £50 a year for three years, and £60 as annual salary after that.

At a meeting held June 7th, 1756, voted by almost a unanimous vote that we still desire Mr. Fowler to settle with us. And July 19th, 1756, Mr. Amos Fowler accepts the proposals of the parish, with slight altera-

* This is the north half of "burying yard lane."

tions in respect to salary; and ("provided you continue well united and prosperous, there appears nothing which I shall look upon sufficient to render my settling with you not my duty.) I shall endeavor to do my part in taking the properest steps in order to settle in the work of the ministry with you; though as the work is great and arduous, I choose some length of time before I actually undertake it."

At the same meeting July 19th, 1756, the society agree by vote to comply with the alterations proposed. And a committee appointed to consult about a settlement. And at a meeting August 30th, 1756, it is decided by vote that the society are still desirous that Mr. Fowler* will settle with them. But at a subsequent meeting, viz. November 1st, 1756, a committee is chosen and appointed to endeavor to procure Mr. James Taylor to preach as a candidate; and also to apply to the South Association of Hartford county for advice.

At the annual meeting they continue to pass votes expressive of their satisfaction with Mr. Taylor; and February 7th, 1757, voted to settle Mr. Taylor as soon as may be convenient, and a committee appointed to agree respecting terms, &c.

March 28th, 1757, voted to Mr. James Taylor as a settlement, £270 lawful money, in two several payments. And May 17th, 1757, voted as annual salary £45, to be raised to £60, together with eighteen cords of wood, and also voted to call in Reverend Council for advice.

June 7th, 1757, the parish held a meeting and voted that they desire Mr. Taylor to settle with them, and also voted to call another council for further advice. June 27th, 1757, a committee was appointed to do all things proper for them to do previous to the ordination.†

At the annual meeting December 5th, 1757, voted to apply to the Reverend Association of Hartford South for advice respecting some suitable candidate for the ministry, and a committee was appointed to use their endeavors to procure Rev. John Smalley to preach as a probationer. This seems to be the first mention of his name. He was licensed to preach by the Association of Litchfield South, the same year, 1757. It appears from the votes of the society above referred to, and the deeds of land for highways to accommodate travel, that the location of the "meeting-house" was fixed previous to February 1st, 1755. Whether the county court sent a committee to fix the location and find the center of the parish, don't appear

---

* His native place, North Guilford. He settled June, 1758, over the first Church in Guilford, and died there February, 1800. He was son of Daniel Fowler, of Guilford, a descendant of William, of Guilford, the emigrant.

† Mr. James Taylor settled March, 1758, over the Congregational Church in New Fairfield, Conn., and Fairfield East Association May 29th, 1763, at Bethel, heard a complaint versus him and others, for false doctrine, (Sandemanianism,) and the Consociation silenced him, when he was dismissed June, 1764.

on the court records after diligent search. The record shows, however, numerous instances of the kind in other parishes where there were adverse parties or opposition. In the absence of all record and tradition to the contrary, we conclude our ancestors were harmonious in fixing the location on the ledge near the "Mill Pond" referred to. It stood on the present main road to Hartford from New Britain village, about half a mile, and just north-east of the present "cattle pound" of the town. It had a pleasant front view and was beautified by surrounding oak and hickory trees left of the primitive forest. It is supposed ample provision was made for building, during the year 1756, and that the house was raised and covered the summer of 1757, and yet as late as 1769 and 1770, bills were presented by Timothy Stanley as collector, and also by Capt. Lemuel Hotchkiss, for window springs for *finishing* the "meeting-house." The house was very plain, about eighty by sixty-four feet in size, with steep roof, without bell or belfry, or cupola, and resembled in size and shape, except for the doors and windows, a nice large barn. We have not the means of knowing how it was finished inside, at its first building. It was "built over" outside, and painted, immediately after the great revival of 1784–5, at an expense of some £90 or more. The house had large galleries; the two "high pews," one at each extreme corner to the right and left of the pulpit, in the galleries, were so much raised as to require stairs to ascend and descend, and so high that a tall man could scarcely stand in the pew erect without touching his scalp to the wall over head. The pulpit was built on the side of the house, (opposite a large double front door, with large bull's eyes inserted,) and had a huge "sounding board" impending; the inclosure was small, and had a door each side, with a wood button; and stairs on each side, with railing. The body of the pulpit was ornamented with carved vine, with leaves and grapes,* (a wonder to the children.) A seat for the deacons, directly under the front of the pulpit, between it and the communion table, which table was made by a plain board hung with hinges on the railing of the seat, and when raised was supported with two curiously twisted "iron braces." A large but single door opened at each end of the house, and stairs led to the male side of the gallery, at the extreme right corner of the minister, and a corresponding flight to the female side, on his left hand. The broad aisle, (leading from the broad front door to the pulpit,) in which stood our grand-fathers and mothers, when they entered into covenant with God and the church, was a solemn place. It was not carpeted, but it received many tears of penitence, both from those joining the church, and from such as fell into gross sins, and stood there while their public confession was being read. Then there was a narrow aisle leading quite round the house, leaving one tier of pews

* This was done by subscription, circulated by Capt. Ladwick Hotchkiss, to raise the money.

joining the wall, and leaving inside two squares called the "square body." These pews or pens were made square, with straight backs; top made with open work and banisters inserted some eight inches apart, and seats extending quite round on every side, except barely the door, which was narrow, and fastened with a wood button. The occupants faced inwards, of course some would sit with their backs to the speaker, and hence the habit of standing part of the time during the sermon, which was in the olden time from one to two hours long.* The hour-glass which stood on the pulpit, was turned at the reading of the text, and the audience felt slighted if the sermon ended before the sands had all dropped. The meeting-house was warmed chiefly by the sun, for a chimney, stove, or furnace was unknown for that purpose in those days. A poor substitute, however, was resorted to from necessity, namely, the "foot stove," and the "Sabada house." The matron of each family was careful in the coldest weather to have the foot-stove well prepared with living coals from the home hearth-stone. The Sabba-day† houses were about sixteen feet square, with a small window on three sides, and chimney built of stone, or perhaps part brick, on the outside, with a large fire-place attached. This room was furnished with rough seats, and here the short intermission between the services was spent in mutual greetings, inquiries after health, and perhaps comments on the morning sermon. The sheds to protect the horses, stood near by, and with all these appendages at the right and left wings to the meeting-house, the grand old oaks, (already referred to,) the rocks and boulders cropping out in great profusion, the "meeting-house yard" was a place of great interest. It was the holy "hill of Zion" to the parish; "thither the tribes went up" by five different roads or "lanes" which centred there. It was never called the park, or the green, but the "parade," and was used as a military parade, from the days of the French war of 1762, through the Revolution, and down to the close of the war with England, February, 1815, except occasionally the central park where the fountain has been built. And while we are describing this locality, we must not pass by in silence the "burying yard." This ground was early part of Capt. Stephen Lee's farm, and descended to his grand-sons, Stephen and Isaac, who, tradition says, gave the land to the society of New Britain, for a place to bury their dead.‡ The town record in Farmington

* President Stiles says of Mr. William Robinson's ordination, that himself was "in sermon two hours."

† "At a town-meeting held in Farmington, December 10th, 1759, voted liberty to Thomas Stanley and Noah Stanley, to build a small house in the highway, near the meeting-house in New Britain parish, in the most convenient place for their conveniency on Sabbath days."

‡ At an adjourned meeting of the inhabitants of the town of Farmington, held December 23d, 1771, the town voted that the committee for exchanging highways, be empowered to convey to Isaac Lee, Esq., so much of said highway as may be best

shows how this land came to the parish, by whom, and how he was compensated. It was directly east of the meeting-house, about eighty rods. We have seen that Dr. Isaac Lee, then of Middletown, deeded to Farmington one-half the lane that led to it, while the same year, 1755, his brother, Deacon Josiah Lee, who built the Skinner house, deeded the other half, making two rods wide. The burials began soon after, for the oldest stones found, date 1756. This place designed by our fathers as a city for the dead, was wisely chosen, as to soil and locality. It has been greatly enlarged from time to time, and of late, cared for and beautified, greatly to the credit of the town.

We have supposed the meeting-house was built in 1757, but I find a deed given by Uriah Judd, of a piece of land for a highway to the town of Farmington, dated 1756, in which he says, "to run south from the meeting-house ; said highway to be three rods wide, running through my farm, and past my house."* We have then, 1756, or at the latest, 1757, a plain but decent meeting-house, with surrounding appendages† and approaches, and upon the whole it looks inviting, if not attractive.

We will now return to the doings of the society, for the church is not yet "gathered." At a society meeting held on the 9th day of January, 1758, it was voted unanimously in favor of proceeding to settle Rev. John Smalley, provided the approbation of the Reverend Association can be obtained. Voted as a settlement £150 lawful money. Voted as an annual salary £50 for the three first years, and afterwards £60, and in addition a yearly grant of twenty cords of wood.

This candidate, who became afterwards so rich a blessing to this people, was son of Benjamin Smalley, an Englishman by birth, and a weaver by trade. He married Lydia, sister of Joseph Allen, who was father of Col. Ethan. She died, when second, he married Mary ———, who became the mother of John, June 4th, 1734, at Lebanon Crank, Conn., parish of Co-

---

spared, as shall make him a meet recompense for the burying-place he has found for said society of New Britain."

Another page of the record discloses who this committee were.

"At a town meeting in Farmington, held the 9th day of December, 1771, Noah Stanley, Elijah Francis and David Mather, were chosen for exchanging highways and removing nuisances in New Britain."

* His house stood where Alvin North's house now stands, 1864.

† It should be observed that among the common appendages of a country town or parish, is a prison for unruly cattle. Such a place was provided for this society, at the expense of the town of Farmington, as follows, viz: "At a meeting of the town of Farmington, the 11th April, 1768, voted the society of New Britain have liberty to erect a pound in said society, at the town's cost, and Isaac Lee, Esq. and Capt. Phineas Judd are chosen a committee to appoint a place to erect the same, and Noah Stanley and Ladwick Hotchkiss are appointed to erect it, and Elnathan Smith was appointed keeper, the current year." It was built on the east street, near the residence of Elnathan Smith, now, 1862, the "Rhodes farm." Ed.

lumbia. The parents were esteemed pious, especially the mother, who early gave her only son good instructions, which made a lasting impression, especially his finding her kneeling and praying in a secluded part of the house. When young he was put out to a mechanical trade, but his pastor, Rev. Eleazer Wheelock, perceiving him to be a youth of fair promise, fitted him for college, and he entered Yale at the age of eighteen. While at college his father lost his property, and while the son expected to relinquish his studies, found a patron in Mr. Stiles, who after became the President of that institution. Rev. Mr. Wheelock thought he became pious in early boyhood, but he experienced while in college what he himself called a second conversion. The Smalley family moved to Vermont, where the father died. The son graduated 1756, and studied theology with Rev. Dr. Bellamy, at Bethlehem. Both mother and son became members of the church in Cornwall, Conn., Rev. Mr. Gold, pastor. After the settlement of her son in New Britain, and while living on the Patterson place, she kept house for him a short time, but May 8th, 1759, she married Ensign Samuel Galpin, of Kensington parish, in Farmington, and she was united to that church August 12th, 1759, by letter from church in Cornwall. She died October 23d, 1762, in the sixty-fourth year of her age. She was second wife of Mr. Galpin, and he died December 25th, 1771, aged eighty-five; their head-stones in the old Hill Cemetery, of Berlin. We will now return to the doings of the Ecclesiastical Society, in their efforts to procure a minister.

January 9th, 1758, voted unanimously in favor of proceeding to settle Rev. John Smalley, provided the approbation of the Association can be obtained. Voted to give him £150 lawful money, as a settlement. Voted to give him a salary of £50 per annum for three first years, and afterwards £60 and twenty cords of wood.

March 6th, 1758, Mr. Smalley signifies his acceptance of the terms proposed. We have not been able to find the letter of acceptance, or record of it, but we find on the records of the South Association of Hartford county, the following brief account of the action of that body in the matter of "gathering a church" and ordaining the minister.

At an Ecclesiastical Council convened at New Britain, to gather a church of Christ there, and to ordain Mr. John Smalley to the work of the gospel ministry there, April 18th, 1758, present,

The Rev. Messrs. William Russel, Moderator,
Ashbel Woodbridge,
Moses Bartlet,
Edward Eeels,
James Lockwood, Scribe,
Joshua Belden,
Timothy Pitkin,

Rev. Samuel Clark,
Deacon William Rockwell and Deacon Isaac Lee,
Capt. John Rich,
Mr. Nathaniel Chauncey,
Col. Thomas Wells and Col. Elizur Goodrich,
Deacon Joshua Andrus and Deacon William Wadsworth,
Deacon Thomas Hart and Deacon Hewit Strong.

Voted, that Mr. John Smalley, agreeably to the votes and call of this society, and his acceptance, be ordained to the work of the gospel ministry, according to Saybrook platform, and he was so ordained by this council, this nineteenth day of April, 1758, by the imposition of the hands of the Presbytery, with fasting and prayer.

Test, James Lockwood, Scribe.

Recorded by Benjamin Bowers, Scribe of the Association."

The name of John Smalley next appears on the record of this Association at the bottom of the list, October 3d, 1758, at their meeting in Middle Haddam, (indicating that he was the youngest member, or the latest settled.) October 7th, 1760, "Voted at Marlborough, that Rev. Mr. John Smalley preach the next Association." October 5th, 1762, the record says the Association met at Stepney, at the house of Rev. Mr. Daniel Russel, and Rev. Benjamin Pomroy was moderator, and Rev. Elijah Lathrop, scribe; that Rev. John Smalley preached the sermon, and joined that body, (which it may be observed, consisted of from sixteen to twenty ministers at that date.)

April 1st, 1763, the Ecclesiastical Society voted to increase Mr. Smalley's salary to the sum of £90; but from that time to 1766 the society continues to be annually agitated by the opposition of certain members to the grant, and on account of the uneasiness, Mr. Smalley proposed an abatement of £10 annually.

January 7th, 1768, at a meeting of Hartford County South Association, at the house of the Rev. Mr. James Lockwood, in Wethersfield, Rev. J. Belden, moderator, and Eleazer May, scribe, Rev. John Smalley and Enoch Huntington were appointed delegates to attend the General Convention to be holden at Newark, in "New Jersey," the first Wednesday of October next.

June 6th, 1769, Association met in Kensington, at the house of Rev. Mr. Samuel Clark, Rev. Benjamin Pomroy, moderator, and John Eells, scribe, voted that the Rev. Mr. Smalley prepare a *concio*, to be delivered at the next Association, on the following question, viz: "What kind of profession is required of adult persons in order to admission into the visible church?"*

* Mr. Smalley had discontinued the "half-way covenant," after January 25th, A. D. 1767, in his society.

June 3d, 1777, the South Association of Hartford County met in Middlefield, at the house of Rev. Abner Benedict, Dr. Pomroy, moderator, Rev. Enoch Huntington, scribe. Mr. Smalley was chosen to make a *concio* at the next Association, upon this question, viz: "Whether it is right in any cases, and if in any, in what cases to admit persons of adult years to the enjoyment of one of the sacraments and not to the other?"

In February, 1779, his people voted him an increase to his salary on account of depreciation of paper currency.

June 5th, 1781, Association met at the house of Rev. David Huntington, in Marlborough, Rev. Ephraim Little, moderator, E. Huntington scribe; Association opened with prayer, and a sermon by Rev. Mr. Smalley, and he with three other ministers were appointed a committee to advise on a difficulty in Chatham, where some complained of Mr. Strong for declining to baptize children of parents, neither of whom came to the Lord's Supper.

October 5th, 1784, Association met at New Britain, at the house of Rev. J. Smalley, Rev. E. Huntington, moderator, and Strong, scribe. On motion of New Haven County Association to appoint one of a committee, to join a like committee from that and other Associations, to inspect and assist Mr. Barlow in the new impression of Watts' psalms, the Rev. Mr. Smalley was appointed. It will be observed that this year, 1784, occurred the principal revival of religion during Mr. Smalley's long ministry; some forty or fifty persons were added to the church, as fruits of this work.

The General Association of Connecticut met in New Britain, June 5th, 1787, when Mr. Smalley was appointed moderator, having been previously appointed a delegate to that body.

October 7th, 1788, Association met at Chatham, at the house of Rev. Cyprian Strong, Rev. J. Smalley, moderator, and Mr. Strong, scribe; Mr. Smalley preached the sermon. He was appointed at this meeting a missionary from this Association "into the State of Vermont," agreeable to the recommendation of General Association in June last.

June 1st, 1790, Association met at the house of Rev. John Marsh, in Wethersfield, Rev. Joshua Belden, moderator, E. Huntington, scribe. Mr. Smalley preached the sermon, from John 6, 29. Mr. Smalley and Mr. Fenn chosen delegates to next General Association. Voted to request Mr. Smalley to itinerate, according to the advice of General Association in 1788. He published two sermons on natural and moral inability, 1769. (These were republished in London;) also two sermons on universal salvation, preached at Wallingford, and printed, the one in 1785, the other in 1786, and a sermon delivered in the College chapel, at New Haven, on the Perfection and usefulness of the Divine Law, 1787. His celebrated election sermon, published in 1800. But his principal works were two volumes of sermons, the first published in 1803, the second in 1814. These works are now nearly out of print, and rare to be found. His papers have been borrowed, filched, lost and scattered until little or nothing is left to indicate the style of his writings, or the channel in which his vigorous mind ran. The record he kept of the "gathering" and growth of his church, was in the fewest possible words, (and too many omissions at that;) his letters even to family friends must have been few and far between, and we have been able to find only the brief note following, on file among the church files of Kensington, viz:

"New Britain, September 4th, 1778. Beloved Brethren, these are to certify that Anna Bronson, professing a serious desire to join with the church, and a hope that she has experienced the grace of God in truth, has applied to me to examine her, and that having examined her as to her knowledge, I apprehend she is not so far deficient in that regard but that she may and ought to be admitted to communion, if by her life and conduct she appears to be truly serious and pious. Wishing you grace, mercy and peace, I remain yours in the faith and fellowship of the gospel."

(signed) John Smalley.

The reader will infer that the above named woman was a resident of the parish of Kensington, and during the interim between Rev. Samuel Clark and the ordination and settlement of Mr. Benoni Upson, she made the application to Rev. Mr. Smalley at New Britain, and doubtless was the bearer of the certificate in person to the brethren in Kensington. His object was so to word the paper as to induce the brethren to receive her to their communion, while at the same time, to avoid all flattery to the woman. Hence we perceive the shrewdness and wisdom of the man, in putting into her hands, in a few words, a sermon to herself, and a greeting and blessing to the church with which she sought to be united. We will now return to the doings of the society. The following shows their intention of being prompt and just.

At an annual meeting of the Society of New Britain, in December, 1771, it was agreed by vote that Isaac Lee, jun., Capt. Ladwick Hotchkiss, Dr. Isaac Lee, Mr. Noah Stanley, and John Patterson be a committee to reckon with the several collectors of the Rev. Mr. Smalley's salary, since the year 1763, and settle the same. Also to reckon with the Rev. Mr. Smalley, and settle his salary from the said 1763, according to the several votes, and take his discharge, and if the several rate bills be not sufficient, to order the treasurer to pay the balance to Mr. Smalley, but if there be any overplus, to deliver the same to the treasurer, to be applied for the benefit of the society.*

A true copy of record, examined by Isaac Lee, jun., Society Clerk.

---

* The following found on the town record of Farmington, shows the careful interest our fathers took in the welfare of their pastor.

The above shows the *modus operandi* of paying the minister. A rate bill was put into the hands of a collector, supposed to be sufficient to pay the yearly salary. Abatements on this bill were made from time to time for "Separates," Churchmen, and the poor. It was the duty of the collector to see that the salary was collected and paid to the minister, on or before the expiration of the year, and the balance of his rate bill to pay over to the treasurer of the society. This seems to be a sacred and separate tax bill, called the "Minister's Rate," separated from that of the other expenses of the society, for which they issued yearly what they style on the treasurer's book, a "Society Rate," and had a distinct collector. Some curious transactions appear on this book or record of the treasurer. The debit side is made up of sums paid to individuals per order of the society committee, for school teaching, for repairs to school-houses, for "burying yard" fence, repairs to the meeting-house, for teaching singing, sweeping the meeting-house, for collecting taxes, for boarding the school-master and the "school-dame," to John Stedman, Elihu Burritt, and Lemuel Kilborn, for soldiers' bounty, 1782, &c. The contra side is mostly made up of credits for country money, colony money, salt money, excise money,* grain for the benefit or improvement of highways, and in 1780, at sixty dollars per bushel, (continental;) also credits for the taxes of the society rate bill, and generally a small balance or overplus of the minister's rate bill. Mr. Smalley's salary was fixed at £80, and so continued to the settlement of Mr. Skinner, 1810.

To show who paid these taxes, who composed the male adults of the congregation, and who were the bone and sinew of the parish at the commencement of the Revolution, we insert the following tax list for the year 1772, copied from the Farmington records, for the parish of New Britain. It is premised that the polls were set in the Grand List at that date, at £18, or sixty dollars.

"At a meeting of the inhabitants of the town of Farmington, held the 11th day of December, 1758, upon the memorial of Capt. Jonathan Lewis, Mr. Daniel Dewy, and Deacon Elijah Hart, as agents for the parish of New Britain, the town granted to Rev. Mr. John Smalley about twelve acres of land in the forty rod highway, to be in two pieces, if it may there be had without damaging the road, and also made choice of Left. John Strong, Capt. William Wadsworth, and Mr. Elijah Porter, as a committee to lay out said land, and deed it, so as may be best for said Mr. Smalley, and least damagable to the said highway." This land was sold subsequently to Col. Lee, by Mr. Smalley, and was commonly called Col. Lee's old field; it extended from the foot of Dublin Hill to the present railroad, and adjoined Main street on the west. Col. Lee built a house at the south end for his son Theodore.

* This seems to be a tax of four pence per gallon on imported spirits, 1755, for the benefit of schools.

Tax List of New Britain Parish, 1772.

	£	s.	d.		£	s.	d.
Moses Andrus,	110	17	0	Judah Heart, jun.,	54	8	0
Jacob Andrus,	39	14	0	Lemuel Hotchkiss,	38	0	0
Hezekiah Andrus,	68	12	0	Benj. and Joseph Heart,	115	18	0
Levi Andrus,	66	0	0	Widow Sarah Heart,	27	6	0
Samuel Andrus,	38	12	0	James Hills,	18	0	0
Phineas Andrus,	10	16	0	Gideon Hun,	5	16	0
Ichabod Andrus,	23	0	0	Gideon Hollister,	47	17	0
Seth Arnold,	18	0	0	Capt. Phineas Judd,	129	7	0
Nathan Booth,	172	10	0	James Judd,	76	10	0
Elijah Bronson,	64	16	0	Left. John Judd,	94	16	0
Job Bronson,	66	10	0	John Judd, jun.,	28	0	0
Ezra Belden,	27	18	0	Levi Judd,	58	13	0
Elisha Booth,	121	10	0	John Kilborn,	18	10	0
Leonard Belden,	40	0	0	Timothy Kilborn,	17	4	0
Ezra Belden, jun.,	24	10	0	Josiah Kilborn,	60	16	0
Jonathan Belden,	31	0	0	Joshua Kilborn,	45	15	0
John Clark,	135	18	0	Daniel Kilborn,	6	19	0
Nathaniel Churchill,	48	8	0	Richard Kilborn,	25	7	0
Janna Churchill,	49	1	0	John Root,	1	4	0
John Chester,	2	0	0	Capt. Jonathan Lewis,	30	10	0
Widow Sarah Clark,	21	18	0	Deacon Josiah Lee,	112	18	0
Deacon Daniel Dewy,	43	14	0	Col. Isaac Lee,	136	19	0
Samuel Dickinson,	43	18	0	Ensign John Lankton,	129	8	0
David Dewey,	98	7	0	Stephen Lee,	63	12	0
Cornelius Dunham,	39	0	0	David Lusk,	119	2	0
Moses Deming,	7	5	0	Adonijah Lewis,	54	6	0
Jonathan Eno,	45	8	6	William Lewis,	69	6	0
Elijah Francis,	100	14	0	John Lusk,	43	12	0
Zebulon Goodrich,	58	6	0	Isaac Lankton,	62	3	6
Jedediah Goodrich,	64	4	0	Andrew Lusk,	43	3	0
Gideon Griswold,	149	10	0	Theodore Lee,	46	8	0
Benjamin Goodrich,	9	18	0	Timothy Lee, 2d,	21	0	0
Zebulon Goodrich, jun.,	34	6	0	Ashbel Lee,	27	0	0
Wd. Experience Griswold,	12	0	0	Joshua Mather,	18	2	0
Capt. Ladwick Hotchkiss,	73	3	0	David Mather,	40	18	0
Judah Hart,	49	8	0	Timothy Merrills,	8	16	0
Stephen Hollister,	56	12	0	James North,	43	16	0
Elijah Heart,	64	18	0	Elnathan North,	18	0	0
Thomas Hart,	78	0	0	Jeremiah H. Osgood,	66	0	0
John Heart,	63	8	0	John Patterson,	74	4	0
Jehudah Heart,	50	2	0	Nathaniel Pennfield.	49	10	0

	£	s.	d.		£	s.	d.
John Richards,	78	16	0	Ens. Robert Woodruff,	118	8	0
Elijah Rose,	23	0	0	Judah Wright,	30	15	0
William Smith,	46	10	0	Ezekiel Wright,	48	12	0
Thomas Stanley,	103	6	0	Simeon Wright,	22	0	0
Joseph Smith,	121	8	0	Samuel Wainwright,	31	19	0
Jedediah Smith,	44	19	0	Amos Woodruff,	36	0	0
Noah Stanley,	157	2	0	John Wood,	4	2	0
Elijah Smith,	70	12	0	Joseph Wright,	18	0	0
Timothy Stanley,	170	16	0	Reuben Wright,	18	0	0
Left. Gad Stanley,	172	5	0	Joshua Webster,	18	0	0
Ebenezer Steele,	21	0	0	Levi Warner,	18	0	0
Samuel Smith,	66	10	0	Daniel Heart,	77	14	0
Elnathan Smith,	86	0	0	Ebenezer Porter,	12	5	0
John Stedman,	18	0	0	Fourfold assessment,			
Joseph Woodruff,	78	8	0	Daniel Whaples,	11	2	0

Examined by Solomon Whitman, Town Clerk.

NOTE. The above are supposed to be residents of the parish at that date. ED.

At the annual meeting of the society December 25th, 1779, Col. Lee, Col. Stanley, and Elnathan Smith, were appointed a committee to unite with Kensington, and that part of Worthington in Farmington, to petition the General Assembly for a new town.

In May, 1781, we find the names of Selah Heart, I. Lee, Gad Stanley, Mathew Cole, and Elnathan Smith, signed as agents to a petition addressed to the General Assembly, (then sitting at Hartford,) for a new town, the name to be Kensington. The subject was pressed and agitated until the spring of 1785, when the object was obtained, and a part of Wethersfield and Middletown added, and the whole called Berlin. Several bills of expense were paid by the society to Col. Lee and Col. Gad Stanley, for "procuring the new town."

When the war of the Revolution broke out, Mr. Smalley's people discovered that his sympathies were inclined to the side of royalty. An incident has come down, not only by tradition, but in writing, to illustrate and show the state of feeling. Two British vessels appeared off New London, and an express was sent to alarm the people of the colony. It arrived in New Britain on the Sabbath, just before the close of the afternoon service. As soon as the blessing was pronounced, Capt. Gad Stanley gave notice to his company to appear on the parade the next morning, and when Mr. Smalley passed out at the front door, from his pulpit, many of his people had gathered there in great excitement, when he (imprudently) made the following remark: "What! will you fight your king?" The people were offended, and some few here, and more in the old society of Farmington, threatened violence; but Col. Lee (who had unbounded influence,) came to the rescue of both parties, and the tempest was hushed and passed off without any serious outbreak. Mr. Smalley's views were somewhat modified, and the final results of the great struggle happily satisfied all parties.

That the talents and acquirements of Mr. Smalley were appreciated by his cotemporaries in this vicinity, appears by the records of the South Association of Hartford County, already quoted to some extent on the foregoing pages, where his appointments to preach were numerous, as well as to write on knotty and practical questions. He was twice chosen moderator of the General Association of Connecticut, at Windham, 1797, and at New Britain, 1787.

We find in Sprague's Annals of the American Pulpit, an article from the pen of Professor Park, of Andover, in which he says, speaking of Dr. Emmons, that he placed himself under the instruction of Rev. John Smalley, who had then, (1769,) the reputation of being one of the ablest divines in New England. We confess our surprise at this remark, so early in his career, only eleven years of experience in the ministry, and before he had published any of his efforts, except his two sermons on Natural and Moral Inability. If it was an appropriate remark of his popularity at that early period of his history, how much more so after the great awakening of 1784, when the General Association of Connecticut invited him to labor as a missionary in Vermont, and when his theological researches had been elaborated and perfected at a later date. Probably his palmiest days were from 1780 to 1795, when his talents, piety, and character were most fully developed. In 1800, he had conferred upon him, by the College in New Jersey, the title of D. D.; his friend, Rev. Mr. Strong, of Hartford, rallied him on the title as of little worth; but the same College the next year, conferred the like honor upon Mr. Strong. The first time Dr. Smalley met his friend afterwards was on the side walk in Hartford, when he took him by the hand with the remark, "I congratulate you, Dr. Strong, on the title which a short time since you so much affected to despise."

During the revival of 1784, Father Mills, of Torringford, was invited to spend some time in this parish, and did so, to great profit; his efforts are still remembered by a very few who have survived the ravages of time. He was a revival preacher, and was early sent as a missionary from Connecticut to Vermont. It has already been stated that Mr. Smalley had been invited to labor in Vermont, as a missionary, and requested to itinerate as late as 1790. All these itinerate labors looked towards the later organization of the Connecticut Missionary Society, and other kindred institutions,* though unconsciously to the actors. Mr. Smalley was not

* The "Missionary Society of Connecticut" was first the General Association, which adopted a constitution as a Missionary Society, 1798, incorporated, 1802, but

attractive as a preacher, although tall and large, with a dignified and commanding appearance, yet destitute of that easy and graceful manner so desirable in a public speaker.* His voice was nasal and harsh, his manner stiff, and his gestures awkward. Yet notwithstanding these natural disadvantages, the acuteness and discrimination of his mind, would show in every sermon, and sound reasoning and rich instruction rewarded every hearer.

Concerning the people of the parish during the last quarter of the eighteenth century, it may be said no people were more constant in attendance on public worship, and none better fed and instructed. He was very sensitive and jealous of any neglect, remissness or wandering of his people, and they were very proud of his talents and celebrity. In his social and domestic relations he was somewhat reserved and uncongenial; so naturally, and constitutionally, as well as from close study and constant research.

Either from the smallness of his salary, or from the love of imparting knowledge, (probably from both,) he took from time to time, a few students in theology into his family to board, and into his study to recite. Doubtless this was a source of some income to his family, and literary satisfaction to himself. Some of these divinity students made a mark in the world, and with a hope of adding some little to the common stock of general history, we venture to make a list of some of those known to be under his tutelage.

Oliver Ellsworth, of Windsor, Conn., son of David and his wife, Jemimah, born April 29th, 1745, graduated 1766, at Nassau Hall, began the study of divinity with Mr. Smalley, 1767; he left the next year, however, the study of theology for the study of law, and became, 1784, Judge of the Superior Court of his native State, and March 4th, 1796, Chief Justice of the United States. He died at Windsor, Conn., November 26th, 1807, in the sixty-third year of his age. He was one of the stars of Connecticut.

Nathaniel Emmons, born April 12th, (O. S.,) 1745, at East Haddam, Conn., to Samuel and his wife, Ruth (Cone,) graduated at Yale College, 1767, became a theological student of Rev. Mr. Smalley, 1768, licensed to preach by Hartford County South Association, October 3d, 1769, at

---

began to act by committee and otherwise, 1792, and is the oldest in the country. See Rev. Horace Hooker's Contribution to Ecclesiastical History of Connecticut.

* Dr. Upson, of Kensington, was fond of a joke, and often exchanged with Dr. Smalley. When old Mr. Eldad Peck, of "Blue Hills," a section of Mr. Upson's parish, paid his silver coin to the parish collector, for Dr. Upson's rate, he said to him, "Tell Dr. Upson that no part of that is for the preaching of Mr. Smalley, for I don't like him." When Mr. Upson heard of it, he made up his mind to enjoy the joke on Dr. Smalley, the first fit opportunity. "Ah!" (was the quick reply,) "Ah! brother Upson, evidence that your people think more of the *manner* than the *matter*."

New Britain, Conn., was settled in Franklin, a parish of Wrentham, Mass., 1773. Dartmouth College gave him the title of D. D., 1798. He died September 23d, 1840, aged ninety-five years and five months. It is wholly unnecessary to speak of the standing of Dr. Emmons. He says, "When I first went as a pupil to Dr. Smalley's I was full of old Calvinism, and thought I was prepared to meet the Doctor on all points of his new divinity. For some time all things went on smoothly. At length he began to advance some sentiments which were new to me, and opposed to my former views. I contended with him, but he quietly tripped up my heels, and there I lay at his mercy. But I had no thought of giving up so. I arose and commenced the struggle anew, but before I was aware of it I was floored again. Thus matters proceeded for some time; he gradually leading me along to the place of light, and I struggling to remain in darkness. At length he gained the victory; I began to see a little light; it was a new point and seemed distant; by degrees it grew and came nearer. From that time to this the light has been increasing, and I feel assured that the great doctrines of grace which I have preached for fifty years, are in strict accordance with the law and the testimony." His published works were about one hundred and fifty volumes.

Nathan Fenn, of Milford, graduated at Yale, 1775, ordained and installed over the church and society in Worthington parish, Berlin, May, 1780, was a divinity student of Mr. Smalley about 1776, licensed to preach by New Haven East, 1776. He died in the midst of his usefulness, April 21st, 1799, in his fiftieth year, and nineteenth of his ministry in Berlin, Conn. His widow, Eunice, died August 12th, 1807, aged fifty-five. Their graves are shown side by side in the hill cemetery in Berlin.

Ebenezer Porter, son of Ebenezer, born October 5th, 1772, at Cornwall, Conn., graduated at Dartmouth, 1792, was a divinity student of Mr. Smalley, 1793–4; he was licensed to preach at Meriden, Conn., by Hartford South Association, June 3d, 1794, said at that time to be from Tinmouth, Vermont. He was ordained September 6th, 1796, and installed over the church and society in Washington, Conn., dismissed December 18th, 1811. In 1814, the degree of D. D. was conferred upon him by Dartmouth College. In 1827, he became President of Andover Theological Seminary. He died April 8th, 1834, at Andover, aged sixty-two. Few men on the American Continent ever attained to higher usefulness or eminence as a theologian, or in correct and elegant writing.

Oliver D. Cook, see No. (227.)

Gad Newell, of Southington, son of Isaac and his wife, Rachel Pomroy, of Northampton. He was baptized September 11th, 1763, at Southington, by Rev. B. Chapman, pastor. He married Sophia Clapp. He was licensed to preach June 2d, 1789, at Marlborough, by the Hartford County South Association; graduated at Yale, 1786; was a divinity student of

Mr. Smalley, A. D. 1787. He died February 26th, 1859, aged ninety-six, at Nelson, New Hampshire.

Isaac Porter, son of Timothy, born August 1st, 1766, at Farmington, graduated at Yale, 1788, was a theology student with Mr. Smalley, 1789; he was examined, approbated and licensed to preach June 1st, 1790, at Wethersfield, by Hartford South. He was settled in Granby, Conn. He married Mary, daughter of Rev. Mr. Smalley, October 20th, 1794. He died April 14th, 1844, aged seventy-eight, at Granby, Conn.

Joseph Eleazer Camp, born April 6th, 1766, at Bethlehem, Conn., to David and his wife, Margary (Johnson,) of Guilford. He graduated at Yale, September, 1787; commenced the study of theology, June, 1789, with Mr. Smalley. He was examined, approbated and licensed to preach, October 6th, 1789, at the house of Rev. James Eells, in Eastbury, by Hartford South; ordained and installed February 17th, 1795, over the church and society in Northfield, Litchfield county, Conn. Salary £80 and thirty cords of wood per annum. He was dismissed June 27th, 1837. He died May 27th, 1838, aged seventy-two, at Northfield. The maiden name of his wife was Rhoda Turner, daughter of Titus and Sarah (Blakesley) Turner. See No. (229.)

Timothy Langdon, son of Capt. John, of New Britain, born December 4th, 1757, graduated at Yale, 1781, studied divinity with Rev. Mr. Smalley; ordained and installed August 31st, 1786, over the church and society at Danbury, Conn., and Rev. Mr. Smalley preached the sermon from 1st Cor. 1, 21. Mr. Langdon, the first minister raised in New Britain. He died February 10th, 1801, aged forty-four, at Danbury. He had married Lucy Trumbull, who died, when second, he married Elizabeth P. Perkins, of Hartford. He left several children, and his son John became a pastor of the church in Bethlehem, Conn., and died 1830.

Israel B. Woodward, son of Israel, of Watertown, and his wife, Abigail (Stoddard,) born 1767, graduated at Yale, 1789, was a divinity student at Rev. Mr. Smalley's, 1790; was examined, approbated and licensed to preach, June 7th, 1791, at the house of Rev. John Lewis, of (Stepney,) Rocky Hill, Conn., by Hartford South. He was settled at (Farmingbury,) Wolcott, June, 1792. He married October 22d, 1792, Sarah, the fifth daughter of his instructor in divinity. He died October, 1810, aged forty-three, leaving no posterity.

Isaac Maltby, see No. (228.)

Bezaleel Pinneo, born July 28th, 1769, at Lebanon Crank, Conn., graduated at Dartmouth, 1791, studied divinity with Rev. Mr. Smalley, 1792 and 1793, was examined, approbated and licensed by Hartford South, October 1st, 1793, at the house of Rev. Mr. Miner, of Westfield, Conn.; ordained pastor of the church in Milford, Conn., 1796. He died September 18th, 1849.

Jeremiah Mason, born April 27th, 1768, at Lebanon, Conn., graduated at Yale, 1788, studied theology with Rev. Mr. Smalley for a time, but like Oliver Wolcott thought the science of law would be more congenial to his taste. His legal knowledge he obtained partly in Connecticut, and partly in Vermont; his residence, 1797, was at Portsmouth, New Hampshire. He became one of the most eminent American lawyers of his time; was appointed attorney-general of New Hampshire, 1802; he was elected United States Senator, 1813, but in 1817, he resigned his seat. In 1832, he removed to Boston, where the opportunities for the lucrative practice of his profession were more numerous. Mr. Webster ascribed much of his own success to the discipline he received by being brought in contact with him, and by witnessing his system of practice, and he said of Mr. Mason, that he became great by the exercise of strong sense and sound judgment, by the comprehensive views which he took of things, and by the pursuit of high and elevated purposes. He was physically as well as mentally great, being almost a giant in stature. Jeremiah Mason, LL. D. died at Boston, November 14th, 1848, being then over eighty years of age.

William Hart, son of Thomas, of New Britain, the second minister raised in the parish, see No. (208.)

Thomas Rich, see No. (305.)

James Kasson Garnsey, see No. (230.)

Pitkin Cowles, see No. (304.)

Abijah Carrington, see No. (303.)

Mark Mead, born November 6th, 1782, to Jonas, of Greenwich, Conn., and his wife, Sarah (Howe.) Mr. Mead graduated at Yale, September, 1802, studied divinity, 1803, with Rev. John Smalley, D. D., taught district school in Stanley quarter, one season, was examined, approbated and licensed to preach June 5th, 1804, at the house of Rev. Calvin Chapin, at (Stepney,) Rocky Hill, by Hartford South; was for a time a Domestic Missionary in the State of New York. He was ordained and installed pastor of the church in Middlebury, New Haven county, November 1809; dismissed, March, 1830; is now, 1862, residing in his native town of Greenwich, from which he says in a letter to the compiler, "I shall not probably remove until I am called to my everlasting home." He is a half-century minister.

Andrew Rawson, born March 10th, 1773, at Mendon, Mass., to Perne and his wife, Mary (Aldrich,) licensed to preach, 1804, by New Haven East, at Cheshire, Conn., having graduated at Brown University, Rhode Island, and studied theology for a time with Rev. Mr. Smalley, in this place, and he is still remembered by a few old members of this church, as an ardent revival preacher. It was his custom to invite the people here to hold small meetings in the evening in different sections of the parish, where and when he exercised his talents in prayer and exhortation. Some are still living who date their first religious impressions to his earnest appeals.* He married January 21st, 1807, Jerusha, daughter of Deacon Skinner, of Hartford, Conn., by whom he had four children, viz:

Mary, born July 31st, 1809, married 1827, Alvah Lewis, of Ohio, son of Deacon John.

Samuel A., born August 23d, 1811, at Pompey, N. Y., now Rev. Samuel A. Rawson, of Jasper, Steuben county, New York; married 1839, Susan Hubbard, of New York city.

Lydia E., born September 28th, 1813, residing at Oberlin, Ohio, now, 1862, with her mother.

Martha W., born April 16th, 1825, at Barre; married 1849, George W. Congdon, of Peru, and resides at Oberlin.

The father died March 28th, 1835, at Barre, Orleans county, New York.

His widow married second, Elisha Parish, Esq., of Ohio, and is still, 1862, living at Oberlin, Ohio, aged seventy-six, from whom the above facts are derived. Rev. Andrew Rawson was ordained and first settled at Pompey, Onondaga county, New York, 1805. He was subsequently appointed by the Philadelphia Board of Missions, a missionary among the destitute churches in western New York, in which service he continued twenty-one years. From an obituary notice published in the village of Albion, N. Y., and written by Rev. G. Crawford, we make the following extracts, viz: "He preached Christ and him crucified in almost every town west of Utica; assisted in the organization of many now large and flourishing churches, and fed many feeble ones with the bread of life. He preached the first gospel sermon ever delivered in Albion, and for three months labored in his sacred calling in a barn. Mr. Rawson was a revival preacher, whose labors were blessed of the Holy Spirit extensively, at an early day, when revivals were but little known in this State. His mind was clear and discriminating; he loved to contemplate divine truth in the simple grandeur of God's sovereignty and electing love; as a consequence his piety was calm, uniform and active. He carried his religion into all the walks of life, and thus adorned the Christian profession. With a sweet and holy submission to the divine will, the natural consequence of such "most holy faith," this Christian minister received the fatal shaft without surprise, bowed to the high decree, and quit the sorrows and sufferings of this mortal state for the world of bliss."

* An uncommon degree of zeal and excitement sprang up in these meetings, and Mr. Smalley (as was his custom in the cure of all irregularities in his parish,) introduced the subject in one of his sermons, and lectured the young man for his unwarranted zeal and extravagance in a severe manner, and cautioned those that were excited, of danger. This incident is well remembered by the oldest people, to this day, for Mr. Rawson (as was the custom for students,) sat in the pulpit during service, and in the application of the sermon Mr. Smalley turned upon his pupil his scathing remarks.

Since the above was written a letter from his son, Rev. Samuel Rawson, of Jasper, Steuben county, N. Y., has been received, from which the following condensed extracts are made: "My father, Andrew Rawson, early consecrated himself to God, and feeling that he was called of God to the work of the ministry, he prepared himself for college with his pastor, Rev. Caleb Alexander, and graduated at Brown University, 1800, spent three years in teaching a "Grammar School" and studying theology, part of the time with Mr. Goff, of Sutton, and part with Dr. Emmons, of Franklin. While on a visit to Durham, Conn., he was invited by Rev. David Smith to preach for him. He spoke three times on the Sabbath, although he had not been licensed. Before the next morning both he and Mr. Smith were called from their beds to lead inquiring sinners to Christ. A revival followed. Mr. Rawson had adopted the "exercise scheme," and the doctrine of natural ability, and hence when he applied for license at Cheshire, a strong opposition was manifested. After a debate of three days,* he was licensed on condition that he should study a year with Dr. Smalley. He ever spoke of Dr. Smalley with great interest and affection. In revivals he often used to read a printed sermon published by Dr. Smalley from the text, "The law of the Lord is perfect." While a student at New Britain, he prepared a sermon from the text, "Where art thou?" From the fly-leaf we learn that it was preached at New Britain, Rocky Hill, Middletown, and Durham. This sermon has a history which will not be fully known till the judgment; it was the means, under God, of the conversion of hundreds if not of thousands. He often quoted Dr. Smalley's remarks thus: "If you wish to have a revival begin, preach the law; if your revival begins to wane, preach the law; if you wish to secure sound conversions, preach the law." Deacon Owen Brown of Hudson,

---

* This may be partly tradition, yet the copy of record indicates something of the kind. It is in substance as follows: "May 29th, 1804, the East Association at Cheshire, Conn., Mr. Andrew Rawson, of Mendon, Mass., presented himself for examination as a candidate for the gospel ministry, and was examined, whereupon the Association voted as follows, viz: this Association license Mr. Andrew Rawson as a preacher of the gospel, subject to the following advice; that he apply himself diligently to the pursuits of theological knowledge, under the direction of some able divine of his own choosing; that he do not offer himself as a candidate for settlement in the ministry, but wait for the advice of this Association, at their next stated session in September next; that he cautiously avoid the discussion of intricate, mysterious points of disputatious theology, and particularly the doctrine of the immediate and efficient agency of God in the production of sinful volitions." At a meeting of Association held October 9th, 1804, at the house of Rev. John Eliot, D. D., in "East Guilford," now Madison, is this entry: "Andrew Rawson, A. B., of Mendon, Mass., presented himself for examination as a candidate for the gospel ministry, was approved, licensed, and recommended to the Christian churches, according to the rules of the Association." It seems then, that Mr. Rawson, under these circumstances, put himself under the instruction of Dr. Smalley, who had been a guide of Dr. Emmons. (Ed.)

Ohio, (the father of the celebrated John Brown, of Kansas and Harper's Ferry,) said of Rev. Andrew Rawson, "I remember him well, for he led me to Christ; he came to my house in Hudson, in September, 1814. He had a kind of ragged way of preaching, but he was the most wonderful man to promote a revival that I ever knew; his first sermon was from the text, "Where art thou?" In the course of the sermon he stated that he had left his wife and children in the State of New York, to come here, to tell you how you may be saved. In coming here I have staid in the woods, sometimes spending half the night in fighting wolves, to keep them from killing my horse; but what is all that compared to what Christ has done for you. Almost the whole congregation were in tears; our college grew out of the revival that followed." (Thus from Deacon Brown.) In 1820, he removed to Barre, Orleans county, N. Y., where he preached three or four years. While residing in Barre, he preached in neighboring towns. In 1831, he found a company of women in a house in Shelby, (a town adjoining to Barre,) and he engaged them all to pray fifteen minutes a day for a deeper work of grace in their own hearts. A revival of great power followed, and sixty-four were added to the church; meanwhile he circulated a subscription for a house of worship, and when it was dedicated he commenced a protracted meeting, during which he went to Medina, about four miles distant, and asked a merchant by the name of Coan, if he had not sold goods about long enough with a wicked heart. The merchant became maddened and enraged, but at length attended the meeting and consecrated himself to God, and then through the influence of Mr. Rawson, entered Auburn Seminary. While at Auburn Mr. Coan was accustomed to spend a part of each year in assisting Mr. Rawson, in holding protracted meetings. When Mr. Coan went to the Sandwich Islands as a missionary, he at once disapproved of the manner in which the missionary enterprise wasconducted. "This idea," said he, "of letting the old folks die and go to hell, while you by your slow means educate the rising generation, I do not approve. I believe these old pagans may be reached now as well as in the time of Paul." When discouraged by his brethren, he said, "Give me an interpreter and I will try my experiment." So mounting a box in the street, he called a company around him, and preached to them Christ and Him crucified. In a few weeks a great many had professed to have found the Saviour. Thus commenced the great revivals at the Sandwich Islands.

We see by the foregoing that several of Dr. Smalley's students have occupied high positions; that two of them married into his family, and that he was reckoned among the progressive or "new divinity" men of his age, and stood high as a theologian. We discover three reasons for the eminence he attained; first, he was set right on the start in his career; by Dr. Bellamy; second, he had native talent, especially an acute and discriminating mind; and third, and most to his credit, a determined and close application of all the powers God had given him. It has excited some surprise that Dr. Smalley, from his small salary, should accumulate so much property as to be called one of the rich ministers of the State.* Doubtless he was indebted for his success in this direction, to the rigid economy of his wife, and especially to her prudent forethought. The plain and simple habits in the mode of dress and living, had also much to do with the point of expense in those days. The exemption of the clergy from all taxes of person or property, was no unimportant item of relief, and twenty cords of wood (I think generally made ready for the fire by a "wood bee,") must have been very convenient, to say the least. And then, too, the butter and cheese, and the clothing of the family, were nearly all made in the house. The farm furnished the flax, wool and milk, and the inmates of the house had the skill, industry and tools to manufacture them. The society records, already referred to, show that the daughters of Dr. Smalley, Col. Stanley, Elnathan Smith, Deacon Noah Stanley, and Capt. Belden, with many other prominent families, engaged cheerfully in teaching the district common schools of the parish, in the summer season. Thus Dr. Smalley's family (which by the way were all daughters,) were for a time self-supporting. They were, at length, suitably and agreeably married, though the early affections of one,† were crossed by the sternness of the father.

We of the present age can have but meagre ideas of the amount of dignity and reverence which surrounded the minister and magistrate. When Dr. Smalley or Col. Lee were approached, it was with hat in hand, and when either of them passed on the road, men at work in the fields, even at some distance, raised their hats. Their will generally became equivalent to the best good of society, and soon culminated in a rule or law. Their influence was, however, in the direction of conservatism. Innovations and extravagances were frowned down. But two laymen of his church, Col. Lee and Ensign Mather, were ever heard to pray in public. The encroachments of the "Anabaptists" were a grief to Dr. Smalley, and if any of his flock ran after them, (as was sometimes the case,) they were very likely to hear from him soon. We should remember that it was natural for Mr. Smalley to consider the people *his* parishioners; probably they were so, at his settlement, without an exception, for in 1772, there were but three Churchmen, and perhaps not a greater number of Baptists, or as they were usually termed " Separates." The first immer-

* President Stiles' Itinerary. He calls him so, and says he had one hundred and fifty head of cattle. I think his flock of sheep were embraced in the enumeration. (Ed.)

† The object of her predilections was a young physician of great promise, Doctor Jesse Andrews, son of Sergeant Moses, who in the language of a cotemporary, "pined away and died in early manhood, of a broken heart."

sion in the place was Mr. Jeremiah H. Osgood, (familiarly known as "Grandfather Osgood.") He was from Westfield parish, in Middletown, and came here with predilections for that denomination. He was a member of Mr. Smalley's congregation, but not a member of his church. He was baptized by immersion, in the valley west of Samuel Smith's house, about A. D. 1776, by a man by the name of Shepherd. Sufficient water had been expressly provided for that occasion by damming up the rivulet that passes through that valley. Father Osgood was a man eminent for piety and holy living, greatly gifted in prayer, and universally respected for his honesty. Either that year or the next, No. (79) of Mr. Smalley's church left and joined the Baptists, by immersion in the Mill pond of Benjamin Adkins, the place known for many years as Churchill's Mill. The next was probably No. (91,) a man constitutionally insane at intervals, and who hung himself at last. He was also immersed at the Mill pond, at a later date. Their meetings were at first held at Mr. Smith's house; he had taken offense at some remark of Mr. Smalley's, and so opened his doors to the "Separates," although he never joined their church. From this small beginning, after long and severe struggles, a church was formed, which, from occasional revivals, has become one of the prominent Baptist churches of the State.

We come down now in the history of Dr. Smalley, to 1804, when he was three score and ten.* He had often told his brethren in the ministry that a man should retire at that age, and true to his convictions, he proposed it to his people, but they were quite well satisfied, and wished him to continue his ministry still longer. He consented, but was evidently in his wane, for he had occasional ill turns when in public, and lost all consciousness, but after sitting in his pulpit a short time would recover, and ask where he was, and what he was doing; being told, he would resume his prayer or sermon and finish the service as if nothing had occurred to interrupt. It is, however, distinctly remembered, that intense anxiety was depicted on the countenances of his hearers. He continued his active duties as pastor until the fall of 1809, a term of more than fifty-one years from his settlement, and fifty-two from his first effort in the place, when he was relieved by the church and society calling to his aid Mr. Newton Skinner, of Granby, as colleague pastor. He, however, continued to preach occasionally, until September 26th, 1813, when he delivered his last sermon. The next year, 1814, he put his last volume of sermons to press. The balance of his days were spent mostly at his pleasant home, with books and friends, with many happy reflections on the past, and

* The compiler was then seven years old, and remembers his appearance and dress. He wore a three-cornered "cocked-up" hat, short clothes, with knee-buckles, and very large shoe-buckles, in the Puritan style, after the old English fashion, but without wig, and was a good equestrian.

bright anticipations of the future. His earthly career was closed by a fit of apoplexy, which deprived him of reason except at some lucid intervals, in which he expressed his submission to the will of God, and a humble hope of an interest in Christ. He died the first day of June, 1820, when he had almost completed his eighty-sixth year. His friend, Rev. Dr. Perkins, of West Hartford, preached his funeral sermon, but the manuscript seems to have been lost. From the scanty materials we have been able to find of Dr. Smalley's distinctive characteristics, we conclude his preaching was mostly doctrinal, and chiefly upon his favorite themes. The burden of his prophecy as an ambassador for Christ, seems to have been to "justify the ways of God to men," especially in the sterner attributes of His character as a holy and just Being. He addressed himself not to the sympathies or passions of his hearers, but to their understanding and cool judgment. In looking after truth he cautioned his students not to stretch their vision beyond its locality, (or to use his favorite expression,) not to go "below the bottom of things." He himself directed his telescopic, (or rather we should say,) his microscopic vision with so steady a hand, that where common minds were beclouded with mists and fogs, he saw with the clearness of noonday. And just here, I think his great strength lay, in an acute discrimination of the parts, and at the same time a comprehensive view of the whole system of God's dealings with men. In reviewing his published works, it would probably be conceded that his first effort was his best, or most distinctive and useful, viz: "Natural and Moral Inability." The light he was enabled, with God's blessing, to throw around this previously obscure subject, was looked upon with great favor. Hence the celebrity of an obscure parson of a country parish, in one of the British colonies in America, in the year 1769, extended not only through New England but to Old England, where his work was republished. The halo that then gathered about his name was not of that ephemeral kind that is blown away with the first wind, but remains, with nearly the same brightness with which it radiated nearly a century ago. The present inhabitants of New Britain in their haste, but poorly realize how much honor and notoriety have incidentally clustered about the town, from the fact of its being the home of Dr. Smalley, and the locality of his distinguished labors. May the blessings of the Abrahamic covenant which he held up to the faith of the fathers, descend and rest upon the children.

We now come to the call and settlement of Mr. Newton Skinner, as a colleague with Dr. Smalley, December 2d, 1809.

"At a meeting of the church in New Britain, warned for the purpose, it was voted unanimously to give Mr. Newton Skinner a call and invitation to settle in the office of a pastor and teacher of this church and people.

At the same meeting the following members were chosen a committee to wait upon Mr. Skinner with the above vote, and request his answer:

Col. Gad Stanley, Deacon Benjamin Wright, Mr. Levi Andrews, James North, Esq., Deacon Elijah Hart, and Deacon David Whittlesey.

Test, John Smalley, Pastor.

January 7th, 1810, the same committee was appointed to call an ordaining council, and transact other business of the church relative to ordination, should there be one. John Smalley.

At a legal meeting of the inhabitants of New Britain Ecclesiastical Society in Berlin, held by adjournment the 12th December, 1809,

Voted, that this Society, having some acquaintance with Mr. Newton Skinner, and from sufficient experience of his ministerial gifts and qualifications, are satisfied that he is eminently qualified for the work of the gospel ministry, we do now call and invite him to settle with, and take the charge of the people of this Society in that important work.

Voted, that this Society do grant to Mr. Newton Skinner, on his accepting the call of this Society, as expressed in the foregoing vote, and on his being ordained and set apart to the work of the gospel ministry here, as an annual salary, and compensation for his service in that work, during his continuance therein amongst us, six hundred dollars, to be on interest in two months after due. Also, as a settlement, the sum of three hundred dollars, one-half to be paid in one, and the other half within six months after ordained.

Voted, that Messrs. Gad Stanley, James North, Levi Andrews, and Andrew Pratt, be appointed a committee to present to Mr. Newton Skinner a copy of the votes of this meeting, inviting him to settle here, in the work of the gospel ministry, and request him to take the subject into consideration, and give his answer as soon as may be convenient.

Attest, Thomas Lee, Clerk.

Berlin, January 10th, 1810.

To the second Church and Society in Berlin:

Fathers and Brethren, With gratitude I now acknowledge the receipt of your call and invitation, which has been communicated to me by your committee, to settle among you in the work of the gospel ministry, and through them desire you to accept my answer.

Having attentively and seriously considered your invitation, and weighed well your proposals, having heard with pleasure of the unanimity which has appeared in this important transaction, and been assured of the present prospect of future peace and harmony, having consulted friends and asked the counsel of Heaven, I am led to regard your invitation as a call in Providence to settle with you in the gospel ministry.

Sensible, in some measure, of my unworthiness to be inducted into this sacred office, and of my insufficiency to perform its important duties, and at the same time, relying upon God for direction, assistance and success, and under him upon your friendship, candor, united efforts and prayers, I now humbly and cordially accept your invitation.

I do also fervently beseech the great Head of the Church, if he shall see fit to honor me by putting me into the ministry, to furnish me more and more to the work, and make me faithful and successful in my labors. I likewise earnestly solicit the prayers of this church and congregation, that if the important relation which is contemplated be formed between us, it may be permanent and happy.

Signed, Newton Skinner.

At an Ecclesiastical Council convened by letters missive from the church and society in this place, at the house of Rev. John Smalley, D. D., February 13th, 1810, for the purpose of ordaining Mr. Newton Skinner as colleague pastor,

Present, Rev. Messrs. John Smalley, D. D.,
Nathan Perkins, D. D.,
Benoni Upson,
Ebenezer Gay,
Isaac Porter,
Israel B. Woodward,
Joab Brace,
Noah Porter.

Delegates.

Deacon Elijah Hart, New Britain,
Deacon Abijah Colton, West Hartford,
Deacon Noah Cowles, Kensington,
Deacon Gad Taylor, Suffield,
Granby,
Deacon Isaac Bronson, Wolcott,
Deacon James Wells, Newington,
Deacon Martin Bull, Farmington,
Deacon Benjamin Dutton, Southington,
Deacon Jedediah Sage, Worthington.
Dr. Smalley, chosen Moderator.
Mr. Woodward, Scribe.

The council was opened with prayer by the Moderator.

All necessary documents were then received, expressing the invitation of the church and society to Mr. Skinner to settle among them in the gospel ministry, and his acceptance of their invitation. The council then proceeded to a critical and thorough examination of the candidate respecting his various qualifications for the sacred office, and being satisfactorily ascertained of his literary talents and experimental acquaintance with the religion of Jesus Christ,

Voted, unanimously, that we proceed to the ordination of Mr. Skinner,—

that the scribe introduce the public exercises by reading the doings of the council,—that Mr. Isaac Porter make the introductory prayer,—that Mr. Gay preach the sermon,—that Dr. Perkins make the consecrating prayer, and Dr. Smalley, Dr. Perkins, Messrs. Upson and Gay, impose hands,—that Mr. Upson give the charge, and Mr. Brace the right hand of fellowship, and Mr. Noah Porter make the concluding prayer.

Voted to adjourn to ten o'clock to-morrow morning.

Wednesday morning, February 14th, the council convened agreeable to the adjournment. The minutes being read, were accepted, and the council adjourned to the meeting-house.

Test, Israel B. Woodward, Scribe."

(The ordination and installation of Mr. Skinner took place agreeably to the above programme. Ed.)

He was born in East Granby, Conn., October 10th, 1782; he graduated at Yale, 1804; studied theology with Rev. E. Gay, of Suffield, Conn. Mr. Skinner spent his early days on a farm; had a strong and rugged constitution. He was son of Mr. Roswell Skinner, of Turkey Hills, and his wife, Mary (Gay.) He had a vigorous and active mind; was a man of medium height and size, with very penetrating, black eyes. He, like his predecessor, made no pretentions to the graces of oratory, or the flowers of rhetoric. His sermons were without much illustration or ornament, but he made strong points, and forcible applications. He was an earnest, business-like man, abounded more in the sterner, rigid virtues, than in the softer and social. He was rather repulsive than attractive, in his manners, and performed the duties of his calling in a business-like way. He bought the farm on the corner of East and Smalley streets, and the house still retains his name. He was a good farmer, and accumulated a snug little property, which he left to his wife, No. (391,) and his three children. In his public prayers he was gifted and comprehensive, and some thought more edifying than in his sermons. But the great revival of 1821 was as rich a blessing to him as to his people. From the commencement of that work of God's power and grace, he became more spiritual-minded, more devoted to his calling, and more affectionate to his people. Having his whole soul enlisted, he did an incredible amount of ministerial labor, broke loose from accustomed shackles of form, and went far beyond himself. He had an interesting field of labor; there were many young people; the population had greatly increased; the whole aspect of things was changed; from the staid, farming community of 1800, it had become a busy, thriving, manufacturing village, not indeed like the present, but compared with the past. The congregation was straitened for room in the old meeting-house. After the revival had subsided in the fall of 1821, the subject of building new, began to be agitated. The question of a new location was discussed, and a place decided upon after much talk, where the present building stands now, 1862, called the Strickland Hall. No. (168) gave the lot to the society, but the ground being exceedingly uneven, it cost a vast deal of labor to prepare it. This, however, was done cheerfully, and the house erected 1822, at a cost of something over $6,000, besides what was saved of the old one. It being built with such harmony, cheerfulness and zeal, it has generally been spoken of as one of the fruits of the revival of the preceding year. Mr. Skinner was very happy in the unanimity and zeal of his people, and dedicated the house with solemn services, and with the only sermon he ever published. We thought it wonderful in the delivery, and requested a copy for the press, but to read it now, without considering the joy and excitement of the hearers at the time, it would probably appear tame.

Mr. Skinner was greatly interested in our common schools, and did much to raise their standard. A Sunday school society, the first in Hartford county, was formed in his parish, the spring of 1816, and he was appointed its president. He was a warm advocate of the missionary cause, and labored to instil into the hearts of his people a true spirit of benevolence. The literary attainments of Mr. Skinner (if we are permitted to judge,) were respectable, but not of the highest order; his judgment was sound, and his common sense excellent. The last four years of his ministry was a culmination of all that is happy and desirable, in the relation of pastor and people. But the tenderest ties are sundered, and the strongest attachments are broken; his last sermon was preached in Middletown, Upper Houses, on an exchange with Rev. Mr. Williams; he was ill when he went, and returned to his home still more so, and the same week, 31st March, 1825, died of a malignant fever, aged forty-two years, five months, twenty-one days, and from his installation fifteen years, one month, seventeen days. This death was so sudden, and seemed withal so untimely, that both his family and people were for a time overwhelmed with distress. His parishioners awoke as from a dream, to the consciousness of his worth, and their loss, not before being sensible of the strength of their attachment.

The inventory of his estate amounted to about $10,000. Mr. Skinner came to this town without funds; boarded at first with the family of Mr. Gad Stanley, in Stanley quarter, and afterwards for some four or five years, with Deacon Whittlesey's family, at the home of Dr. Smalley. Indeed he lived there when he married. The second purchase he made of real estate was the Abner Clark place, now, 1862, the house of Charles M. Lewis. This was sold to William B. North, at an advance. He first bought at a good rate, the farm now, 1862, belonging to O. B. North, at the corner of East and Smalley streets, where he died. His funeral sermon was preached by Rev. Joab Brace, of Newington, who was a classmate of his in college, and with whom he was very intimate during his ministry. They often exchanged pulpits on the Sabbath and "Lecture-days." Although Mr. Skinner was a vigorous, active, strong-minded man, yet his sermons (it is said,) cost him much continued hard study and labor. The Association of Hartford South held Mr. Skinner in high repute, and treated him with marked attention from the first, as is seen by their appointing him scribe and preacher to their own body, and delegate to General Association of this and other States. The last year of his life he was appointed delegate to the General Association of Massachusetts, to be held in 1825, but he died too prematurely to attend it.

We come down now in the history of the parish of New Britain to a period when a great step was taken in advance, in the direction of progress. Hitherto the only accommodation for mails was for the manufacturers each to take his turn in riding to the Berlin post-office once a week, for the New Britain letters; and like means were adopted to fetch the newspapers from Hartford once per week. But the spring of 1825, Thomas Lee, Esq., by his sagacity and political influence obtained the establishment of a post-office in the place, and for post-master his son, L. P. Lee, who hired John Francis to carry the mail from New Britain to Hartford twice a week. The office was granted as a doubtful experiment, and on condition that it should cost the government nothing; nor would the government claim for the time being any revenue. The whole proceeds for the first quarter was about nineteen dollars, a few dollars less than cost of carrying. But this never happened again. The office was kept a few years in the "stone store," but soon after in a small building directly west, and opposite the meeting-house, now, 1862, called "Strickland's Hall." Now there are five mails each day to arrive and depart, and the proceeds per quarter ending April, 1864, (being the highest ever taken,) was $1,425.46, an evidence of a great increase of population and business.

We will now introduce to the reader as a candidate for the ministry, Mr. Henry Jones, of Hartford, recommended to our people by Joel Hawes, D. D., of that city.

"August 9th, 1825, at a meeting of the members of the church, legally warned and held this day, it was voted unanimously to give Mr. Henry Jones an invitation and call to settle in the office of a pastor and teacher of this church and people.

Voted, that the following persons be a committee to wait on Mr. Jones with the above vote, viz:

Elijah Francis, Adna Stanley, Thomas Lee, Seth J. North, Alfred Andrews, and David Whittlesey.

Voted to adjourn without day.

Attest, David Whittlesey, Clerk.

September 27th, at a legal meeting of the church, voted that Elijah

Francis, Adna Stanley, Thomas Lee, and David Whittlesey, be a committee to transact all business respecting the ordination which is expected.

D. Whittlesey.

Berlin, August 15th, 1825. At a special meeting of the second Ecclesiastical Society in the town of Berlin, legally warned and held this day, Dr. Adna Stanley was chosen moderator.

1st. Voted unanimously, that this society give Mr. Henry Jones a call to settle with us in the work of the gospel ministry.

2d. Voted unanimously, that this society give Mr. Henry Jones as a compensation for his services, if he settle with us, the sum of five hundred dollars annually, the same to be on interest in two months after due.

3d. Voted, that this society give to Mr. Henry Jones as a settlement, if he settle with us, the sum of three hundred dollars, to be paid within one year from the day he is ordained pastor of the church and minister of the people here, conditioned as follows, to wit: if Mr. Jones shall not continue to perform the duties of his office of pastor and teacher more than one year, then he, the said Mr. Jones, is to refund the sum of two hundred dollars; if he continue to perform said duties two years and no more, then he is to refund the sum of one hundred dollars, otherwise to retain and possess the whole of the said sum of three hundred dollars.

4th. Voted to appoint Elijah Francis, Noah Stanley, Adna Stanley, Seth J. North, Thomas Lee, Esq., Alfred Andrews, Ira E. Smith, and David Whittlesey, a committee to wait on Mr. Jones with the above votes, and request his answer as soon as convenient.

5th. Voted that Elijah Francis and David Whittlesey, be a committee to supply the pulpit. Attest, David Whittlesey, Clerk.

Hartford, August 31st, 1825. To the second Church and Ecclesiastical Society in Berlin:

Respected Friends, Your several committees have communicated to me the result of your meetings held on the 9th and 15th of the current month, and permit me here to express my gratitude for your favorable opinion thus publicly manifested. By your concurrent votes you have submitted to my decision a question of no small moment, and under a sense of this I have taken time for the consultation of friends, and for mature deliberation. The work of the gospel ministry, always arduous beyond the strength of unassisted man, has appeared to me almost overwhelming in view of my own youth and inexperience. When again I have thought of the wise and devoted servants of Christ, whose labors you have heretofore enjoyed, I have felt that an increased responsibility must rest on him who ventures to succeed them.

On the other hand, there are considerations which have given me much encouragement. Time and experience may, with the blessing of God, in some measure supply these personal deficiencies, which now I can not but feel so sensibly, and if your former pastors have by their faithfulness rendered the work of their successor in some respects more arduous, yet he will have occasion to thank them, under God, for a congregation at once enlightened and attentive. Above all, I have reflected with the utmost pleasure, on the uncommon degree of unanimity which has characterized your movements in this affair.

Considerations like these have, I say, given me encouragement. I have been led at length to conclude that it is the will of Providence that I become your pastor, and where God directs I may not refuse to follow. I come to this decision, indeed, not without fearfulness and hesitation, when I remember my own weakness. But I find a refuge in the hope of your prayers and Christian candor, and I can ever look forward with confidence when I remember the promised aid of Him whom I call my Master and Lord.

You will please to accept this as an affectionate answer to the call with which you have presented me.

With the strongest wishes for your spiritual prosperity, I subscribe myself yours in the bonds of Christian love, Henry Jones."

At an Ecclesiastical Council convened in Berlin, October 11th, 1825, by letters missive from the second church and society in that town, for the purpose of ordaining Mr. Henry Jones to the work of the gospel ministry, and of installing him as the pastor of said church,

Present, Rev. Nathan Perkins, D. D.,
Rev. Benoni Upson, D. D.,
Rev. Samuel Goodrich,
Rev. Noah Porter,
Rev. Joab Brace,
Rev. Royal Robbins,
Rev. Joel Hawes,
Rev. Charles A. Goodrich,
Rev. David L. Ogden,
Rev. Leonard Bacon.

Delegates.

Rev. Roderick Colton,
Deacon Daniel Galpin,
Brother Samuel H. Cowles,
Brother William Deming,
Deacon Samuel Peck,
Brother Joseph Trumbull,
Deacon Phineas Pardee,
Deacon Simeon Butler,
Deacon William Willard.

Dr. Perkins was chosen moderator, and Mr. Brace, scribe.

The council was opened with prayer by the moderator. Rev. Ebenezer Porter, D. D., and Rev. Isaac Porter, being present, were invited to sit with the council.

Several documents were exhibited to the council by the committee of the church and society, showing that Mr. Henry Jones had been regularly and unanimously invited to take the oversight of this church and people, in the work of the gospel ministry, as pastor and teacher, and that he had accepted the invitation.

Mr. Jones having produced satisfactory testimonials of his good standing in the church of Christ, and of his license as a Christian preacher,

Voted, that the council are ready to enter on an examination of Mr. Jones, with a view of his ordination, and that the moderator take the lead in the examination. After a full examination of the pastor elect, in natural and revealed religion, in Christian experience, and in his motives in desiring the office of a bishop:

Voted unanimously, that the council are satisfied with his qualifications for the Christian ministry, and that the way is prepared to set him over this people in the Lord.

Voted, that the solemnities of the ordination be attended to-morrow, the exercises to commence at eleven A. M., and that the several parts be performed by the following members of the council, viz: the record of the council to be read by the scribe, the first prayer to be offered by Mr. Robbins, the sermon to be preached by Dr. Porter, the ordaining prayer to be offered by Mr. Goodrich, senior, during which Messrs. Perkins, Goodrich, and Porter, lay on hands, the charge to be delivered by Dr. Perkins, the right hand of fellowship to be given by Mr. Brace, the concluding prayer to be offered by Mr. Hawes.

The council was adjourned to meet again to-morrow at a quarter before ten. Wednesday morning met according to adjournment. Rev. Calvin Chapin, D. D., appeared and took his place in the council.

Voted the foregoing as a true record of council; the ordination was performed accordingly. Attest, Joab Brace, scribe.

At the time of the foregoing transactions the deacons of the church were David Whittlesey and Elijah Francis. The standing committee of the church were Messrs. James North, David Whittlesey, Elijah Francis, Alvin North, William Smith, Amon Stanley, and Alfred Andrews.

Thus far the record in the hand-writing of Rev. Mr. Jones, transcribed from the doings of the council, and from the documents placed before them. He was a good penman, kept a correct record, spelled well, and was an easy and graceful writer, as appears from his answer to the call as above. He was born October 15th, 1801, at Hartford, Conn., to Major Daniel Jones, of that city, and his wife, Rhoda (Mather,) daughter of Dr. Charles Mather; was baptized in infancy, by Dr. Strong; admitted to the first church in Hartford, February 6th, 1814; entered Yale College, 1816; graduated there, 1820, A. B. and 1823, A. M.; studied theology at Andover, Mass., four years, and graduated there, 1824; ordained and installed in New Britain, as above. He married September 5th, 1825, Eliza S., daughter of Noah Webster, LL. D., of New Haven, (see No. 588, for herself and family.) He and family occupied the house of Professor E. A. Andrews, in Stanley quarter, made vacant by his removal to North Carolina. For about one year and a half the pastoral relation of Mr. Jones seemed prosperous and happy. He introduced the present system of Sunday schools, in the spring of 1826. An interesting revival of religion was enjoyed, and a large number of young people were admitted to the church, February, 1827, and several during the summer, 1826, so that in all, during his ministry of two years, three months, eight days, there were sixty-three additions to the church, fifty-eight of them on profession. During the last half of the second year of his pastorate, his health began to fail; and that kind of prostration and despondency so common to young ministers the second or third year, came upon him; a portion of his people became impatient, and the result was, a mutual council was called, and the connection dissolved, December 19th, 1827. Mr. Jones opened a high school for young ladies, at Greenfield, Mass., October 1st, 1828, and ten years after, viz., December 1st, 1838, opened the Cottage School, on Golden Hill, in Bridgeport, Conn. He accepted, also, the office of deacon in the first Congregational church in the same town, February 26, 1858, thus making himself useful to the church and the rising generation at the same time. It is proper here to observe, that Mr. Jones, with seven others of his successors, are still living, and therefore a just sense of propriety forbids any formal history or criticisms, farther than merely the statistics of their settlement and dismission, together with some brief notice of their origin, families, employment and location.

That a single parish should have so many ex-ministers still living, seems strange, but we consider it more our misfortune than our fault. Circumstances have appeared to demand these results; some have been called to higher fields of usefulness; others dismissed for want of health. If the people have differed in opinion on some of these results, or on the precedents that led to them, yet they have invariably returned to their accustomed harmony, when the momentary excitement had passed away. Not a single instance of permanent disaffection or alienation has occurred in the settlement or dismission of ministers (numerous as they have been,) among this people. And this is said just here, partly to their credit, and partly to rebut some calumnies from abroad.

After the dismission of Mr. Jones, the pulpit was supplied by Mr. Jason Atwater, then a member of the Theological Seminary at New Haven. He was a native of Hamden, Mount Carmel Society; graduated at Yale,

1825; licensed to preach, 1827. During the year 1828, a powerful work of grace was experienced under the joint labors of Mr. Atwater and Rev. Samuel Griswold, of Lyme, Conn., as the fruits of which seventy-one were added to the church, in the early part of 1829. Mr. Atwater settled in Middlebury; was installed October 31st, 1830, where he labored successfully some fifteen years. He also spent some ten years in the ministry at Newtown, to the great comfort and edification of that church. He died April 1st, 1860, at West Haven, aged fifty-nine. He had become connected by his third marriage, with the Principal of the West Haven Female Seminary, Mrs. S. E. Wright, and removed to that place about one year previous to his death. A funeral sermon was delivered by the pastor of that church, Rev. George A. Bryan, from Proverbs 10, 7. "The memory of the just is blessed." We have felt it but right thus to give one page of this work to the memory of that just man, through whose abundant labors very many of our people have derived such rich blessings in former years. "He that winneth souls is wise, and they who turn many to righteousness shall shine as the stars forever and ever."

We come now to the call of Rev. Jonathan Cogswell. At an adjourned meeting of the church held in the conference room April 7th, 1829,

Voted, unanimously, to give Rev. Jonathan Cogswell an invitation and a call to settle in the office of a pastor and teacher of this church and people.

Voted, that Messrs. David Whittlesey, Thomas Lee, and Seth J. North, be a committee to wait on Mr. Cogswell with the above vote, and to request his answer.

Voted, to adjourn this meeting until next Tuesday at four o'clock P. M.

Attest, Thomas Lee, Clerk.

At an adjourned meeting of the church held the 14th day of April, 1829, at the Conference Hall, the following communication from Rev. J. Cogswell was received and read.

To the Congregational Church of Christ in New Britain Society, Berlin:

Fathers and brethren, your votes of the 7th inst. have been communicated to me by your committee, and have been seriously and prayerfully considered. The unusual harmony and unexpected unanimity which appear to prevail among you, connected with other circumstances which seem clearly to indicate the mind of God, fully convinces me that I ought to accept your invitation to settle among you in the ministry. The work before me appears to be great, but my dependence is on Him in whom is infinite fulness. Your assistance and prayers I most earnestly request. Looking to the great Head of the Church for all needed grace, your highest happiness will be the chief object of my daily pursuit. Wishing you grace, mercy and peace from God the Father, and from our Lord Jesus

Christ, permit me to subscribe myself yours in the fellowship of the gospel.

Dated at Berlin, April 13th, 1829. Jonathan Cogswell.

To Messrs. David Whittlesey, Thomas Lee and Seth J. North, committee of the Church:

Voted, that Messrs. David Whittlesey, Thomas Lee, Seth J. North and Elijah Francis, be a committee to transact all business respecting the installment of Rev. J. Cogswell.

At an Ecclesiastical Council convened in New Britain, the second Congregational Society in Berlin, by letters missive from the Church and Society in that place, April 28th, 1829, for the purpose of installing Rev. Jonathan Cogswell as Pastor of the Church and people in New Britain. Present, Rev. Nathan Perkins, Pastor of the Church in West Hartford, Deacon Moses Goodwin, delegate; Rev. Samuel Goodrich, Pastor of the Church in Worthington, Deacon Samuel Galpin, delegate; Rev. Noah Porter, Pastor of the Church in Farmington, Rev. Joab Brace, Pastor of the Church in Newington, Deacon Levi Deming, delegate; Rev. Charles A. Goodrich, Mr. Jason Atwater, licentiate; Deacon Ebenezer Stillman, delegate from Wethersfield; Brother Israel Williams, delegate of the Church in Rocky Hill. Dr. Perkins was chosen Moderator, and Mr. Brace, Scribe.

The Council was opened with prayer by the Moderator. Papers were laid before the Council by the Committee of the Church and Society, and by Mr. Cogswell, from which it appeared that the Church and people of New Britain had, in a regular way, given him a call to be their Pastor, and that he had accepted their invitation; that Mr. Cogswell had been regularly dismissed from his former charge in Saco, in the State of Maine, and been highly recommended by that council, as a good and beloved minister of Jesus Christ. Whereupon,

Voted, that the way is prepared for the examination of Mr. Cogswell, with a view to his installation. The council having examined the pastor elect in the doctrines of natural and revealed religion, in his personal acquaintance with Christ, and his views of the pastoral office, and having obtained satisfaction of his qualifications for the ministry,

Voted, unanimously, to install him as the pastor and teacher of this church and people, the services to commence at half an hour after ten o'clock to-morrow morning, the parts of the solemnity to be performed as follows, viz: Rev. Charles A. Goodrich to make the introductory prayer; Rev. Caleb J. Tenney to preach the sermon, and Rev. J. Brace, his substitute; Dr. Perkins to offer the installing prayer, and Rev. Samuel Goodrich to deliver the charge; Rev. Royal Robbins to give the right hand of fellowship; Dr. Porter to make the concluding prayer. The council adjourned to meet at nine o'clock to-morrow morning.

Wednesday morning met according to adjournment; Rev. C. J. Tenney, pastor of the church in Wethersfield, and Rev. Royal Robbins, pastor of the church in Kensington, and Deacon Simeon Hart, delegate of the church in Farmington, appeared and took their seats in the council. The council engaged in a season of prayer, imploring the presence and direction of God in the transactions of the day, and the outpouring of the Holy Spirit upon the people, and upon the whole church of God. The installation was performed according to the above arrangement.

Attest, Joab Brace, Scribe.

Mr. Cogswell was born in the town of Rowley, Mass., September 3d, 1782, to Dr. Nathaniel Cogswell and his wife, Lois (Searle.) He graduated 1806, at Harvard. He settled first in Saco, Maine, October 24th, 1810, and was dismissed October 16th, 1828. He passed a few months in the city of New York, when he was called as above to New Britain. He married for his first wife, Elizabeth, (daughter of Joel Abbot and his wife, Lydia,) born about 1790, in Westford, Mass. She was early left an orphan, when her uncle, Samuel Abbot, Esq., (the original founder of Andover Theological Seminary, and of the Abbot Professorship there,) adopted her into his own family. (For some brief history of her and their children see No. (714.) Mr. Cogswell having been appointed on the 21st day of January, 1834, by the Directors of the Theological Institute of Connecticut, to the office of Professor of Ecclesiastical History in that Institution, was, at the expiration of his five years' pastorate in New Britain, dismissed by a mutual council called for that purpose, April 29th, 1834. He had occupied the house of Professor E. A. Andrews, during his stay in this place, from which he removed to East Windsor Hill. His wife, Elizabeth, died there April 30th, 1837, a lady of high literary and Christian attainments. In December, 1837, Professor Cogswell, for his second wife, married Miss Jane G., daughter of Chief Justice Andrew Kirkpatrick, of New Jersey, by whom he had one son and one daughter. In 1840, the Union Theological Seminary, of New York city, conferred on him the title of D. D. Drawing towards the wane of life he resigned his office at East Windsor, 1844, and retired to New Brunswick, New Jersey, where he died August 1st, 1864, in his eighty-second year. He was a man of much general knowledge and observation, very social and cheerful, and possessed a charitable and liberal disposition. He was above the medium size, large and portly, went about with an open hand, an open purse, and a warm heart. During his ministry in this place of five years, fifty-five were added to the church, twenty-nine by profession, and twenty-six by letter. He wrote his sermons rapidly and profusely, and sometimes without due regard to connection or unity; but they were full of instruction, variety and interest.

Call and settlement of Mr. Seward.

At a meeting of the church held December 7th, 1835, voted unanimously that we give Mr. Dwight M. Seward a call to settle with us in the gospel ministry.

Voted, that the Deacons inform the Ecclesiastical Society of our vote, and ask their concurrence.

Voted, that Seth J. North, E. H. Burritt, Alfred Andrews and Samuel Booth, be a joint committee with those of the Society, to present this call to Mr. Seward and ask his acceptance.

Signed, E. H. Burritt, Moderator, William B. North, Clerk.

At a meeting of New Britain Ecclesiastical Society, held December 7th, 1835, E. H. Burritt, Moderator, and Norman Hart, Secretary *pro tem.*, voted unanimously to unite with the church in giving Mr. Seward a call.

Voted, that this Society pay Mr. Seward annually, on the first day of February, a salary of seven hundred and fifty dollars, so long as he continues to be our minister.

Voted, that Curtiss Whaples, Norman Hart, William B. North, and F. T. Stanley, be a committee to unite with that of the church to communicate the call and votes to Mr. Seward, and ask his acceptance.

A true copy, attest, J. R. Lee, Clerk of Ecclesiastical Society.

Mr. Seward's reply dated December 24th, 1835, at Durham, Conn.

Brethren and friends, the question presented by your recent vote, I have made the subject of deep, prayerful reflection. The result is a determination to accept of the call you have given me, to settle among you in the ministry. To this decision I have not come without anguish of feeling and deep solicitude for the future, the objection arising from my own conscious weakness, I could not easily dispose of; but the ardor of youth bids me to try; the love of souls prompted a wish to try. Friends who had long prayed for my usefulness said you may try, and a voice from Heaven seemed to add, "I am thy shield and thy exceeding great reward." And with the hope of such support I am willing to make the desired effort. I have a motive for thus speaking to you of my fears. Methinks a people should know the state of feeling with which their servant enters into his new relation. I wish you not to expect too much. I desire you to remember that you will receive an untried and earthen vessel. I can adopt prospectively the sentiment of Paul, "I shall be with you in weakness, in fear, and in much trembling." And now permit me to say, in conclusion, that I shall claim your sympathies, your prayers, and your assistance. With these the office is one of fearful responsibility,—without them, an angel might shrink from the work.

Yours affectionately, Dwight M. Seward.

At an Ecclesiastical Council convened in New Britain, February 2d, 1836, by letters from the Church and Society in that place, for the purpose of ordaining Mr. Dwight M. Seward as Pastor and Minister of the Church and people, in the Gospel of Jesus Christ:

Present, Noah Porter, D. D., and Deacon Edward Hooker, from the church in Farmington.

Rev. Joab Brace, and Brother Roger Wells, from the church in Newington.

Rev. Jonathan Cogswell, Theological Institute, East Windsor.

Rev. John R. Crane, and Brother E. B. Thompkins, first church in Middletown.

Joel Hawes, D. D., and Brother Barzillai Hudson, first church in Hartford.

Rev. David L. Ogden, and Brother Julius Barnes, from church in Southington.

Rev. Charles A. Goodrich, from Worthington.

Rev. Horace Bushnell, and Brother B. B. Barber, Hartford North.

Rev. Zebulon Crocker, and Brother Richard Warner, Upper Middletown.

Rev. James M. McDonald, and Dr. Horatio Gridley, Worthington, and Deacon I. Botsford, Kensington.

The council was organized by the appointment of Noah Porter, D. D., Moderator, and Rev. Joab Brace, Scribe, and was opened with prayer by the Moderator. The Committee of Church and Society exhibited the record of the transactions, showing the regular and unanimous call of Mr. Seward to the work of the Christian ministry among this people, and his acceptance of the call. After a particular examination of the candidate in doctrine, knowledge and experience, the council having obtained full satisfaction,

Voted, unanimously that Mr. Seward be ordained and installed as the pastor and minister of this church and people, according to their request, and that the ordination be attended Wednesday, February 3d, at eleven o'clock, A. M. The following ministers were appointed by the council to perform the public services at the ordination, viz:

Rev. J. R. Crane, introductory prayer.

Rev. Joel Hawes, D. D., sermon.

Rev. J. Brace, ordaining prayer.

Noah Porter, D. D., and J. Hawes, D. D., laying on of hands.

Jonathan Cogswell, D. D., charge.

Rev. James M. McDonald, right hand of fellowship.

Rev. D. L. Ogden, concluding prayer.

Adjourned to Wednesday, February 3d, ten o'clock A. M., when the ordination and installation was performed according to the above arrangement.

J. Brace, Scribe.

Mr. Seward was born at Durham, Conn., July 31st, 1811, to Deacon Seth Seward, of that town, and his wife, Rhoda (Picket.) He graduated at Yale College, 1831. He studied theology at the Seminary in New Haven, Conn., and married March 2d, 1836, No. (887,) which see for a brief sketch of Mrs. Seward and their children. On the 4th October, 1836, he joined the South Association of Hartford county, and June 4th, 1839, he was appointed to superintend the interests of the Home Missionary Society within the bounds of the Association. The church was blessed with two revivals during his ministry, one in the year 1837, when eighty-one persons were added to their number; the other in 1841, when they received an accession of thirty-six. The whole number gathered into the church during his ministry was 194, of whom 136 by profession and 58 by letter. He was often interrupted in his labors here from much bodily pain and debility, and yet upon the whole the connection was happy and successful. It was towards the close of his ministry when the subject of dividing the church and society was agitated, and Mr. Seward made up his mind to retire. He accordingly, on the 22d of May, 1842, made the following communication to the church and society:

Brethren and friends, it is with reluctance and pain that I now perform the duty which in the providence of God devolves upon me. The relation between us has existed a little more than six years. During that period we have twice enjoyed the special influences of the Spirit of God. Your continued kindness, confidence and affection, I have abundant occasion to acknowledge, and although my labors have been frequently interrupted by ill health, I do gratefully record that the harmony of the relation remains undisturbed. Within this period however as you are aware, very trying events have occurred. Contentions, it is true, have prevailed among this people for many years, but the subjects to which they formerly pertained have in a great measure given place to others; while in one spot the wounds have appeared to be rapidly healing, they have violently broken out in another. In order to the adjustment of difficulties, meetings have been held, committees for consultation appointed, and plans of compromise suggested, but no permanent good result has been achieved. The issue to which events are now rapidly tending, must be perceived by all. You, beloved friends, who have mingled your songs and prayers in the same sanctuary, expect soon to be gathered into different places of worship. The necessity now occurs of having the pastoral relation dissolved. Though I contemplate the bearing of this state of things upon the interests of piety with trembling solicitude; though my attachment towards you is undiminished; though I would gladly spend and be spent for you, yet my usefulness, should I longer remain, would be greatly abridged; not so much from the diminished size of the field as from the peculiar position which I should occupy. Moreover, my health, as you know, has been much impaired by the animosities which have prevailed, and though it has materially improved, yet it is my full conviction that I should be unable to labor with vigor and success in circumstances so trying as those in which I should be placed.

In view of these facts and considerations, I respectfully request you to unite with me in calling a council, to dissolve, if they deem it expedient, the pastoral relation. Your affectionate pastor, D. M. Seward.

The church and society consented to the call of a mutual council, and Mr. Seward was dismissed June 15th, 1842. The principal reason of the dismission, the council say, is "the contemplated division of the church and society;" "a division owing entirely to other causes than the character or services of the minister."

The "contentions and animosities" to which Mr. Seward refers above, are probably the conflicting opinions the people entertained, at the time, on the subject of temperance, anti-slavery, and new and old school divinity. From the manner in which these subjects were presented and pressed, (at that time,) on the public mind, they were called *agitating* subjects. The public were extremely sensitive at that period, and almost every parish and community was more or less agitated by them. The flight of twenty-five years has happily carried with it much that was unpleasant, and left in return a similarity of views; so that we look back with wonder, that so slight causes should have produced so great a breach. Indeed we are forced to look for other and more potent causes, and on the above as mere occasions for greater causes to operate. About one-half the church and society withdrew and built anew, leaving their interest in the old house to those that remained.

On the 5th July, 1842, one hundred and nineteen of the members of the church withdrew, and were organized by the South Consociation of Hartford county as the "South Congregational Church in New Britain." Many disinterested persons thought and said at the time that this division would be disastrous to both societies, but from the active business habits of the people, the result has proved quite otherwise. The population has increased so rapidly that very respectable congregations have been secured in both parishes, notwithstanding the rapid growth of other denominations in the mean time. The yearly contributions to general benevolence may have been somewhat lessened, from the double expense of maintaining two societies in place of one, yet even this does not necessarily follow, for (strange as it may seem,) the ability of a community to give is in the proportion they are in the habit of giving. Over-grown churches, like overstocked bee-hives, with many drones, need sometimes to swarm, for a full development of their working power. Some may say, why not pass these scenes in silence? Our reply is, we are writing partly for future generations, and should be recreant in duty to them to have said less; and lest we injure the feelings of some one living person, or do injustice to the dead, we refrain from saying more.

Mr. Seward retired to his native home in Durham, but was called to a new field in West Hartford, where he was installed January 14th, 1845, and dismissed December 18th, 1850.

He was called to the oversight of a church in Yonkers, New York, 1851, where he is now, 1867, zealously engaged in the work of the ministry. The Union Theological Seminary of New York conferred the title of D. D. upon him 1862.

We find the following upon the records of the church upon the subject of the division.

At a meeting of the church held on Tuesday, June 14th, 1842, Deacon Chauncey Cornwall was chosen Moderator. The following petition, signed by Elijah Francis and others, was presented to the meeting:

Reverend and beloved: whereas we the subscribers, being desirous of forming a new church in this place, and having nearly completed a suitable edifice for our accommodation, request you to permit us peaceably to withdraw ourselves from our particular connection with you, and to give us an equal share in the property of the church, and Sabbath school library.

Signed, Elijah Francis and others.

Voted, to appoint a committee to report upon the petition, one week from this day, and David Whittlesey, Matthew Clark, Amon Stanley, Samuel Booth, Ira Stanley, Eli Smith, William Ellis, Ira Stanley, jun., William A. Churchill, Dan Clark, Alfred Andrews, Timothy W. Stanley, John Stanley, Horace Wells, Adna Hart, and Noah W. Stanley, were chosen that committee, when the meeting adjourned one week.

At the adjourned meeting of the church June 21st, 1842, the following report and resolution was presented:

To the Congregational Church in New Britain: Dear brethren, your committee to whom was referred the petition of Deacon Elijah Francis and others, praying for liberty to withdraw themselves from this church, and share equally in the property of the Church and Sabbath school books, having taken the important subject into serious consideration, beg leave respectfully to report.

Your committee are very sensible that as a church and society we have come to a crisis which is perplexing in the extreme; just on the point of taking a step which will be deeply deplored in all future time; making a breach which neither we, our children, nor our children's children will be able to heal. We would meet it with all brotherly kindness and affection. We are among those who believe in the right of petition, and although it is our fixed opinion that we ought not to separate families and beloved brethren and friends, your petitioners have the same right to think and say, "we can enjoy ourselves better apart, and we wish you to let us go in peace." We would call on our dear brethren and sisters in the petition, to pause and inquire, are there any good and substantial reasons why a division should be made in this church? Many of us have walked together in the fellowship of the gospel, and in brotherly love for years; some almost to the end of our pilgrimage, and not a jar in our affections has disturbed our peace. Your committee can not discover any just cause for granting the request of the petitioners at this time, and especially in its present form, but would exhort all of our beloved sisters and brethren in the Lord, to stand still and hope unto the end. We remember the difficulties and trouble in former years, and would also call on our souls and all within us to bless and praise the Lord for His goodness, and for His wonderful works, in pouring out upon us His Holy Spirit, especially in the year 1821, and in subsequent years, thus reviving us when we were "minished and brought low," and delivering us from all our distresses. Now, dear brethren, viewing with anxious solicitude our present condition, and contemplating our future prospects, which so deeply affect us all, we are united in our opinion, and do recommend the passage of the following resolution, viz:

Resolved, that the petitioners have leave to withdraw their petition, or if they prefer, we consent that the whole case, all matters and things, with all its load of consequences, be referred to the decision of the consociation, provided our friends, the petitioners, will relinquish all claim to the property of the church, and pay their share of the debts contracted for their benefit as well as ours.

David Whittlesey, Chairman of Committee.

Dated at New Britain, this 21st day of June, 1842.

The report was accepted, and the resolution passed, and the meeting adjourned without day. William H. Smith, Clerk.

At a meeting of the church held the 28th day of June, 1842, Dr. Samuel Hart was appointed Moderator; after the doings of the last meeting were read, the following vote was passed:

Voted, that this church unite in calling a meeting of the Hartford South Consociation, to assemble in this village on Tuesday, the 5th day of July next, at nine o'clock A. M. in reference to forming and organizing a new Congregational church in this parish, provided they deem it expedient.

Voted, to appoint a committee to carry the above vote into effect, and the following persons were appointed: Seth J. North, Elnathan Peck, Augustus Stanley, and William A. Churchill.

Voted to adjourn without day. William H Smith, Clerk.

According to the vote of the church, on Tuesday, June 28th, 1842, the Consociation assembled July 5th, 1842, at nine o'clock A. M. Prayer by the Moderator, Dr. Chapin.

The petitioners and remonstrants were heard by counsel and otherwise, and after due deliberation the Consociation announced their readiness to form a new church, and the following persons were organized into a new church, to be known by the name of the "South Congregational Church of New Britain."

Elijah Francis,
Chauncey Cornwell,
Seth J. North,
Alvin North,
Samuel Hart,
Norman Woodruff,
Henry North,
Ozias Hart,
Dennis Sweet,
Andrew P. Potter,
Josiah Dewey,
Elijah Hart,
John Judd,
Abijah Flagg,
Alonzo Stanley,
Aaron C. Andrews,
George Hart,
William Bassett,
William H. Smith,
Chester Hart,
George L. Tibbals,
Edmund Steele,
Sarah North,
Ann W. Burritt,
Mary G. Cornwell,
Sarah G. Cornwell,
Maria Seymour,
Julia A. North,
Mary Peck,
Esther Dewey,
Mary Cordelia North,
Sarah E. North,
Abigail Woodruff,
Louisa Hart,
Lois E. Bassett,
Mary S. Bassett,
Lucretia M. Smith,
Sarah M. Loomis,
Harriet S. Smith,
Elizabeth A. Smith,
Theodore A. Belknap,
Samuel W. Hart,
Salmon Hart,
Horace Butler,
Joshua Carpenter,
Robert G. Williams,
James Judd,
Eliza A. Marshall,
Ezekiel Andrews, jun.,
Elnathan Peck,
Henry Stanley,
Catharine A. Stanley,
Curtiss Whaples,
Esther L. Lee,
Abigail Seymour,
Mary Ann Seymour,
Dorothy Francis,
Edmund Warner,
Elizabeth W. Warner,
Francis Hart,
William B. Stanley,
Charles M. Lewis,
Betsey Judd,
Betsey Carpenter,
Alma Woodruff,
Honor Flagg,
Melvina C. Stanley,
Chloe A. Stanley,
Abigail L. Stanley,
Maria N. Erwin,
Electa Andrews,
Harriet A. Stanley,
Elizabeth F. Hart,
Marilla Callender,
Hannah Root,
Selina Churchill,

Elvey W. Hart,
Lucy N. Steele,
Matilda C. Warner,
Almira W. Warren,
Polly Clark,
Romeo Francis,
Catharine Francis,
Catharine A. Francis,
Nancy M. Eddy,
Matilda Slater,
Dolly S. Hart,
Nathan R. Cook,
Lucy B. Cook,
Jane Francis,
Orpha Hart,
Lauretta S. North,
Amelia S. Williams,
Orpha H. Butler,
Charlotte N. Stanley,
Sarah B. North,
Georgianna M. North,
Louisa B. North,
Lucinda H. Smith,
Lydia S. Dewy,
Clarissa B. North,
Betsey North,
Rosetta Hart,
Maria Steele,
Mehitabel Hart,
Louisa Hart,
Eliza Judd,
Gunilda Judd,
Sarah E. Andrews,
Sarah Whiting,
Sarah Hart,
Mary Gridley,
Lucy Winchell,
Mary Curtiss,
Julia A. Curtiss,
Lucy Wright,
Sylvia Hart,
Charles A. Warner,
Caroline U. Sweet,
Olive B. Wright.

My object in putting these names on this book is to give the church information that they may know who are members of the church remaining.

William H. Smith, Clerk.

It is proper here to remark that the number who remained in the first church was 207. The first meeting of the church for business after the division, was held in the conference room, July 12th, 1842, when Deacon David Whittlesey was appointed Clerk, and they voted to hold their annual meeting on the first Wednesday of January yearly, then to appoint their clerk, committee, and do all necessary business.

Voted to hold a church prayer meeting on Thursday afternoon weekly.

Adjourned. Attest, D. Whittlesey, Clerk.

The pulpit was supplied for some months chiefly by Dr. Taylor, of New Haven, when at a legal meeting of the church warned for the purpose, and held 13th December, 1842,

Voted, that this church give Chester S. Lyman a call to settle over them in the gospel ministry.

Voted, that Amon Stanley communicate this act of the church to the Ecclesiastical Society, and request their concurrence in the same.

Voted, that David Whittlesey, N. W. Stanley, and William Whittlesey, be a committee to unite with such as the society shall appoint for the same purpose, in presenting to Mr. Lyman the call now voted, and solicit his acceptance of the same. Adjourned. D. Whittlesey, Clerk.

The society concurred in voting a salary of six hundred dollars, and appointed William Ellis, Norman Hart, and Samuel Booth, to unite with those on the part of the church to present the call to Mr. Lyman.

His reply to the above call.

New Haven, December 29th, 1842. To the committee of the first Congregational Church and Society in New Britain: The invitation which you recently communicated to me in the name of the first Congregational Church and Society to become their pastor, I consider it my duty, after careful and prayerful consideration, to accept. In thus deciding, I have acted not only according to the advice of those in whose judgment I put confidence, but also I trust from a sincere desire to follow the leadings of Providence. I hope, therefore, the steps I have taken will meet with the divine approval. The relation which, if ordained, I thus assume to the church and society is one, I am aware, of great responsibility; and conscious as I am of my own deficiences, I feel that it is also one in sustaining which I shall need your cordial co-operation and prayers, as well as the special blessing of our common Master. That this relation in consequence of our mutual faithfulness, may result both in our own spiritual well-being, and in the glory of God's name, is my most earnest prayer, and will be made the object of my constant efforts.

Yours in the fellowship of the gospel, C. S. Lyman.

Proceedings of the Council.

An Ecclesiastical Council called by letters missive from the first Congregational Church in New Britain, for the purpose of ordaining Mr. Chester S. Lyman to the work of the gospel ministry, convened on the 14th of February, 1843, at the academy, at half past six P. M.

Rev. B. F. Northrop was chosen Moderator; prayer was offered by the Moderator. There were present from the church in Farmington,

Bishop Noah Porter, D. D.
Rev. William W. Woodworth, from Worthington.
Rev. Samuel Rockwell, from New Britain South.
Rev. B. F. Northrop, from Manchester.
Rev. Royal Robbins, from Kensington.

Delegates.

Brother A. F. Williams, Farmington.
Brother Edward Wilcox, Worthington.
Deacon Elijah Francis, New Britain South.
Brother Thomas Stowe, Middletown North.
Brother M. W. Keeney, Manchester.
Deacon Cyprian Goodrich, Kensington.

Rev. Messrs. Herrick, Whittlesey, and Hull, being present, were invited to sit with the council. Documents respecting the call of the church and society to Mr. Lyman, and his acceptance of the same; also respecting his licensure were presented and deemed satisfactory by the council; also satisfactory evidence of his church-membership was given. The council proceeded to examine Mr. Lyman respecting his knowledge of natural and revealed theology, his Christian experience and motives for entering the ministry, after which it was unanimously voted that we proceed to the ordination of Mr. Lyman the following day.

The parts were assigned as follows:

Invocation and reading the Scriptures, by Rev. Mr. Herrick.

Introductory prayer by Rev. Mr. Rockwell.

The sermon by Rev. Dr. Porter.

Ordaining prayer by Rev. Mr. Robbins.

The charge by Rev. Mr. Northrop.

Right hand of fellowship, by Rev. Mr. Woodworth.

The concluding prayer by Rev. Mr. Northrop, and

Benediction by the pastor.

The council met February 15th, according to adjournment; the minutes were read and approved, and the public services were performed according to the above arrangement.

Signed, B. F. Northrop, Moderator.

Attest, William W. Woodworth, Scribe.

Mr. Lyman was born January 13th, 1814, at Manchester, Conn., (then Orford, a parish of East Hartford,) to Chester Lyman and his wife, Mary (Smith.) He graduated at Yale, 1837, and at Yale Theological Seminary, 1842; settled in New Britain as above. The church enjoyed a revival, 1843, under his ministry, as fruits of which twenty-two united with the church. His health failed and he was dismissed April 23d, 1845, making a term of a little more than two years, during which forty were added to the church, thirty-one by profession and nine by letter. He went to the Sandwich Islands for health, October, 1845, and landed May, 1846; from thence to California, 1847, and returned home 1850. He married, June 20th, A. D. 1850, Miss Delia Williams Wood, daughter of Hon. Joseph Wood, of New Haven, and his wife, Frances (Ellsworth,) daughter of Chief Justice Ellsworth, and grand-daughter of Chief Justice Oliver Ellsworth, of Windsor, Conn. She was born September 13th, 1820, at Stamford, Conn. Their children:

1. An infant, born April 11th, 1851, died young.
2. Elizabeth Ellsworth, born November 11th, 1852.
3. William Chester, born March 15th, 1855, died May 24th, 1855.
4. Oliver Ellsworth, born May 10th, 1856.
5. Delia Wood, born October 3d, 1858.
6. Chester Wolcott, born May 25th, 1861.

Mr. Lyman is now, 1862, a resident of New Haven, and was appointed, July, 1859, Professor of Industrial Mechanics and Physics, at Yale College. This people remember him as their former pastor with high regard.

The following relates the call and settlement of his successor:

At a meeting of the church duly warned and held on the first day of May, 1845, David Whittlesey was chosen Moderator, and I. N. Lee, Clerk. It was unanimously voted to call and invite the Rev. Charles S. Sherman to become our pastor.

Voted, that this act of the church be communicated to the society, and request their concurrence.

Voted, that David Whittlesey, Norman Hart, and Doctor Woodruff, be a committee to unite with such as the society shall appoint for the same purpose, in presenting the doings of this meeting to Rev. Mr. Sherman, and solicit his acceptance of the same. The Ecclesiastical Society concurred, and the first day of May, 1845, voted a salary of six hundred dollars.

Mr. Sherman's Answer.

Rockville, May 12th, 1845.

To the committee of the first Congregational Church and Society of New Britain: Dear brethren, your letter in behalf of the first Congregational Church and Society, inviting me to become their pastor, was received on the 3d inst., and with a view to acting with careful and prayerful deliberation upon a matter of such importance, I have refrained giving an earlier answer. The solemnity of assuming, no less than dissolving the relation of pastor to a people, I can not view with indifference, nor can I be insensible to the duty which in all ordinary cases is urged upon a Christian minister to assume that relation, when invited to it by the united and friendly wishes of a people who are, and who are worthy to be by him respected and beloved. These being my views and feelings, I have endeavored carefully and with prayer to weigh the considerations bearing upon my duty in the case, and as the result of my deliberations have concluded to accept, and do hereby accept the invitation of your church and society to become their pastor. In the mean time let me bespeak your prayers that the blessing of the great Head of the Church may rest upon the decision to which we have been mutually led; especially, that my anticipated ministry among you may be a revival ministry, crowned with the Holy Spirit's greatest work. If such be your daily prayers, I am sure that when I come unto you, I shall come in the fulness of the blessing of the gospel of Christ. The Lord bless you and keep you; the Lord make His face to shine upon you, and be gracious unto you; the Lord lift up His countenance upon you and give you peace.

I am with sincere respect and affection, C. S. Sherman.

Probably Mr. Sherman was never furnished with a copy of the doings of the council at his installation, hence we have no record on our books;

but he writes that it occurred July 2d, 1845, and also that he was dismissed September 5th, 1849. He was born April 26th, 1810, at Albany, N. Y., to Josiah Sherman, (brother of Roger Minot Sherman, late of Fairfield, Conn.,) and his wife, Hannah (Jones,) daughter of Daniel, of Hartford; graduated at Yale, 1835, and at Andover Theological Seminary, Mass., 1838. He married, June 11th, 1839, Martha E., daughter of Cyrus Williams and his wife, Martha (Wheeler.) They embarked July 17th, 1839, as missionaries to Palestine, from the port of Boston, Mass. They remained at Jerusalem until April, 1842, when loss of health compelled them to return to this country; when he was settled and dismissed as above. He was soon called and was settled in Naugatuck, over a Congregational Church, where he now, 1867, resides. For his family see No. (995;) also No. (1,026.) Mr. Sherman greatly improved our Sunday school, by introducing the children to the Monthly Concert, and giving them an opportunity to sing, and repeat verses of scripture.

We now come to the call of Rev. E. B. Andrews, of Cornwall, Conn.

At a meeting of the first Ecclesiastical Society of New Britain, held May 6th, 1850, voted to unite with the church in extending an invitation to Rev. E. B. Andrews to become our pastor.

Voted, to give him a salary of seven hundred and fifty dollars.

Voted, that I. N. Lee, O. C. Stanley, and William A. Churchill, be a committee to unite with that of the church in presenting him their united call.

Action of the Council.

An Ecclesiastical Council regularly convened by letters missive from the first Congregational church and society in New Britain, for the purpose of installing Rev. E. B. Andrews as their pastor, was held June 26th, 1850, in the lecture room of said church and society.

The following pastors and delegates were present, viz:

From the church in Farmington, Rev. N. Porter, D. D. and Brother John E. Cowles, delegate.

Newington, Rev. Joab Brace, and Deacon Jeremiah Seymour, delegate.

Kensington, Rev. Royal Robbins, and Brother Jabez Langdon, delegate.

Wethersfield, Rev. Mark Tucker, D. D., and Brother E. T. Cook, delegate.

New Britain South, Rev. Samuel Rockwell, and Brother E. A. Andrews, delegate.

Plainville, Rev. William Wright, and Brother J. C. Hart, delegate.

East Windsor, Rev. Samuel J. Andrews, and Brother N. S. Osborn, delegate.

Worthington, Rev. W. W. Woodworth, and Deacon Joseph Savage, delegate.

West Hartford, Rev. D. M. Seward, and Brother Charles S. Mills, delegate.

Hartford South, Brother John H. Goodwin, delegate.

Meriden, Brother H. Foster, delegate.

New Britain, first church, Brother I. N. Lee, delegate.

Rev. E. W. Andrews, Rev. Charles S. Sherman, Rev. W. G. Jones, Rev. Joel Grant, and Rev. John S. Whittlesey being present, were invited to sit with us, as corresponding members.

Dr. Porter was chosen Moderator, and Rev. W. W. Woodworth, Scribe. Prayer by the Moderator. Documents were then presented showing that the church and society had proceeded regularly in the call, and that Mr. Andrews had been regularly dismissed from the church and society of which he was formerly pastor, and that he is a member in good and regular standing, of Berkshire Association, in Massachusetts. The council then proceeded to examine Mr. Andrews in respect to his knowledge of natural and revealed religion, his religious experience, and his reason for entering the ministry. Whereupon it was unanimously voted, that we approve of the examination of Mr. Andrews, and will proceed to his installation this afternoon, at two o'clock. The parts of the installation service were assigned as follows, viz:

Introductory prayer by Rev. S. Rockwell, of New Britain South.

The Sermon by Rev. Samuel J. Andrews, of East Windsor.

Installing prayer by Rev. Joab Brace, of Newington.

Charge to the pastor by Dr. Tucker, of Wethersfield.

Right hand of fellowship by Rev. W. W. Woodworth, of Worthington.

Charge to the people by Rev. Mr. Robbins, of Kensington.

Concluding prayer by Rev. Mr. Sherman.

Benediction by the Pastor.

And the installation took place accordingly.

W. W. Woodworth, Scribe.

Rev. Ebenezer Baldwin Andrews was son of Rev. William, of Ellington, Windham, Danbury and Cornwall, and his wife, Sarah (Parkhill,) of Benson, Vermont. He was born April 29th, 1821, at Danbury, Conn.; graduated at Marietta College, Ohio, 1842; he was licensed to preach June 4th, 1845, by Litchfield North; he was ordained and installed pastor of the church at Housatonicville, April 29th, 1846, and dismissed April 4th, 1849. He then engaged for a year in the "Alger Institute," at South Cornwall, Conn., where he also supplied the pulpit and received a call to settle. He married December 25th, 1850, Catharine Francis Laflin, born at North Adams, Mass., June 16th, 1831. His health being impaired he left New Britain, to take the chair of Natural Science and Natural Theology Marietta College, Ohio. He enlisted 1861, into the thirty-sixth Regiment Ohio Volunteers as Major under Colonel Crook; was at the battle of Louisburg, Virginia; at the South Mountain and Antietam battles, where the regiment won honorsat the battle of Antietam. He was made Colonel, and returned to his professorship after spending about two years in the army.

Their Children.

1. Clara Laflin, born in Westfield, Mass., April 18th, 1852.
2. Catharine Francis, born in Marietta, Ohio, October 16th, 1854.
3. Cutler Watson, born in Marietta, Ohio, February 2d, 1856.

The following will best show the reasons of his early dismission:

At a church meeting held November 4th, 1851, the following letter was read:

To the first Congregational Church, New Britain: Beloved friends, you have been called together to-day to receive a communication from your pastor. The nature of this communication you have doubtless anticipated. It is my request that the peculiar and official relation which I now hold with this church be dissolved, and that you, by your committee, unite with me in calling an ecclesiastical council for the purpose of effecting such dissolution. This is a step which I have taken after long and prayerful deliberation. For many weeks my mind has been in a state of very deep and painful anxiety to know what the Head of the Church would have me do. Settled pleasantly over a large and important parish, I have not wished nor dared to leave my position, unless it should be clearly revealed to me as my duty so to do. The arduous labors of the station (and they are far more arduous than any one not a minister can understand,) I have endeavored cheerfully to perform in the hope that they might be blessed to your highest good; but such is the present condition of my health that I can no longer meet the engagements and responsibilities of my office, and the prospect of greater ability in the future seems remote and uncertain. For more than five months I have been struggling with an increasing bronchial disease. During these months I have been absent at one time six weeks, in the hope that I might be improved by rest; and when at home I have availed myself of all the occasional assistance I could obtain, so that I have probably not preached more than half of the time; yet notwithstanding the disease has been constantly gaining ground, and now I am almost entirely unable to speak in public. Had I complied with the advice of my physician I should have given up preaching some months ago. Of the future I know nothing; it is in the Lord's hands, and he will do with me and with us all what seemeth him good. I hope and pray that he has yet work for me to do as a preacher of the gospel of his dear Son. One of my predecessors, whose disease he assured me was much like my own, has never yet been able to resume the work of the ministry. It may not be improper for me to state that I am not the only one of my father's family who has suffered from the same difficulty. Two brothers have been prevented by it from preaching, one for nearly two years at one time, and the other for the last ten months. Still another brother is now disabled from preaching by a disease somewhat similar, but more pulmonic in its nature; but the fact that my father died of a bronchial disease in the midst of his usefulness, is the most disheartening consideration of all.

I have thus briefly stated to you my present condition. Now in view of it, what ought I to do? In endeavoring to answer this question I am conscious that I have not for a moment forgotten the interests of this church and people. I would do nothing that would in any way prove injurious to the cause of our common Redeemer among you. You need for your pastor a man of firm health and much physical vigor, to meet the full demands which are made upon him. It may therefore be deemed best that I in my illness and necessary inefficiency, should give place to one more vigorous, and consequently more able to perform the labors of the station. I have also consulted friends and esteemed judicious clergymen, respecting my duty in regard to the whole matter, and my request today is in entire harmony with their advice. I therefore, dear brethren, now ask you to unite with me in calling an ecclesiastical council for the purpose of considering this matter, and if deemed best, to dissolve the relation now subsisting between us. But I can not close this communication without referring to the unusually pleasant relations which have always existed between us. I came among you an entire stranger, but I have always received kind and Christian treatment. You have ever given a friendly hearing on the Sabbath, (never showing the slightest disposition to prescribe the themes of my discourse, nor the modes of presenting them,) and also you have treated me with kindness and courteous respect in all my private intercourse with you. It has been the friendly relation which should ever exist between a Christian pastor and a Christian people. This fact is an encouragement for the future; indeed it seems to me prophetic, that with another pastor you will live in mutual love, and grow in all the gentle graces of the Christian life.

Wishing you manifold blessings here, and eternal life hereafter, I am your friend and pastor, E. B. Andrews.

New Britain, November 4th, 1851. Upon receiving the foregoing the church passed the following:

"Whereas we have this day received a communication from our pastor, Rev. E. B. Andrews, asking us to unite with him in calling a Council to dissolve his pastoral relation with us, and whereas the circumstances under which the request is made, render it painfully necessary for us as a church to assent, therefore,—

Resolved, that although our connection has been so brief, it has been exceeding pleasant and happy, and it is with emotions of deep regret that we consent to its termination. Our Pastor has been in and out among us in such Christian kindness and faithfulness, in such tender sympathy and charity, as to win our confidence and affection; his fine feelings and tender sensibilities will be held by us in enduring remembrance. We commend him to the Grace of God, and the sympathy of the Church, wherever he may be located.

N. W. Stanley, Henry Walter and Dan Clark, were appointed to unite with the pastor and the committee on the part of the society, in calling the proposed council.

Mr. Andrews was dismissed November 12th, 1851.

We continue our extracts from the church and society records.

"At a meeting of the church held the 11th October, 1852, Deacon Alfred Andrews was chosen moderator; the following resolve was passed unanimously, viz:

Having heard the Rev. Horace Winslow, of Rockville, in our pulpit and conference room with satisfaction, and otherwise learned somewhat of his character and good standing as a gospel minister, therefore,

Resolved, that we cheerfully and cordially extend to him a call to become our pastor.

Voted, that Dr. Hawley be a committee to unite with such person as the society may appoint to present the doings of this meeting to Rev. Mr. Winslow, and solicit his acceptance of the call now voted.

Morton Judd, Clerk.

Mr. Winslow's Answer.

Dear Brethren, the invitation extended to me to become your Pastor, I have taken into prayerful, and I trust careful and candid consideration, and I am not aware that a further delay would discover to me any more clearly the path of duty than now. I feel that it is a delicate matter to leave a people whom I love, and by whom I have the assurance that I am myself beloved; but even with such a fact circumstances may make it a a duty for me to change this field of labor. Such seem to be the circumstances that now surround me. It is with a desire to be in the way of duty, and with a feeling that I am following the providence of God, that I now accept the call to become your pastor. I expect this life to be one of labor, and wherever I may be, I desire to be useful, and this is my expectation and desire if God shall consummate the invitation and make me your minister, but if we are prospered the Lord must smile upon us; let me with your co-operation, bespeak for myself your prayers upon my anticipated labors among you.

Yours in Christian bonds, Horace Winslow.

Rockville, November 6th, 1852.

It should here be stated that the Ecclesiastical Society had concurred in the call and voted a salary of one thousand dollars, and appointed James Stanley a committee to unite with Dr. Hawley, appointed on the part of the church, in presenting the call.

At an Ecclesiastical council convened at the lecture-room of the first Congregational Church of New Britain, December 29th, 1852, by letters missive from said church:

Present from the church in Farmington,

Rev. Noah Porter, D. D., Deacon Simeon Hart, delegate.

Newington, Rev. Joab Brace, Brother Marcus Stoddard, delegate.

New Britain South, Rev. Sam'l Rockwell, Dr. Lucius Woodruff, delegate.

New Britain First, Rev. William Whittlesey.

Springfield, Mass., North, Rev. R. H. Seeley.

Brooklyn, New York, Second, Rev. Nathaniel H. Eggleston.

Meriden, Rev. George W. Perkins.

The council, after being called to order, was organized by the choice of Rev. Joab Brace, moderator, and Rev. George W. Perkins, scribe.

After prayer by the moderator, the following documents were presented: the invitation from the church to the Rev. Horace Winslow to become their pastor; the vote of the society concurring in the call, with the pledge of a suitable support; the letter of acceptance from the Rev. Mr. Winslow; the result of council whereby the previous pastoral relation of Mr. Winslow was dissolved, whereupon,—

Resolved, that the documents now presented are satisfactory, and that we proceed to the customary examination of the candidate for installation. The examination was then conducted by the moderator and council, whereupon,

Resolved, that being satisfied with the examination, we will proceed to install Rev. Horace Winslow as pastor over the first Congregational church in New Britain.

That Rev. Dr. Porter, Rev. William Whittlesey, and Rev. Mr. Winslow, be a committee to arrange the installation services. The committee reported a recommendation that the services should be as follows:

Introductory prayer by the Rev. Mr. Rockwell.

Sermon by the Rev. Mr. Seeley.

Installing prayer by Rev. Mr. Brace.

Charge to the pastor, by Dr. Porter.

Right hand of fellowship by Rev. George W. Perkins.

Concluding prayer by Rev. Mr. Eggleston.

Which recommendation was accepted, and the council took a recess.

After recess the council met and with appropriate services installed Rev. Horace Winslow as pastor of this church.

Signed, G. W. Perkins, Scribe. J. Brace, Moderator.

The subject of building a new meeting-house began to be agitated soon after Mr. Winslow came into the place.

February 7th, 1853, the society appointed a committee to inquire as to the expense of enlarging and repairing the old house, and also to inquire for a location for a new one, and report.

They reported February 21st, 1853, in favor of building a new house, and April 20th, 1853, the society, by vote, instructed their committee to buy the place of Ira Stanley, jun., for a location, and voted to build with brick. The place consisted of a substantial dwelling-house and out-buildings, with four acres of land, and cost the Ecclesiastical Society, $7,000. The house was moved and is now, 1867, the one owned and occupied by Dr. Comings.

The house of worship was dedicated August 23d, 1855; is in the Romanesque style of architecture, one hundred and thirty-eight feet long by sixty-three feet wide, including the chapel, with a spire one hundred and ninety feet high. The audience-room is seventy-five feet long by sixty-three wide. The chapel is directly in the rear of the audience-room, thirty-eight feet long by thirty-six feet wide, having two smaller rooms or parlors connected with it.

The church was blessed with two seasons of revival during the pastorate of Mr. Winslow, 1854, the first, and the second, 1857; as the result, seventy-nine were received to communion on profession. There were also other additions by letter, to the number of forty-four, making in all during his ministry, one hundred and twenty-three. Finding his salary inadequate to his support, and having a call from the church in Great Barrington, Mass., with a remuneration better adapted to his necessities, on the 23d November, 1857, he communicated his resignation to the church, at a meeting held for the purpose, and requested them to unite with him in calling a council to dissolve the relation, if the council should advise.

A council was held December 2d, 1857, and the connection was dissolved, to take effect on and after the 20th of that month.

Rev. Horace Winslow was born May 18th, 1814, at Enfield, Mass., to John H. Winslow and his wife, Elizabeth (Mills;) graduated at Hamilton College, N. Y.; studied theology at Union Seminary, New York city; settled first at Lansingburg, N. Y.; second, at Rockville, Conn., October, 1845, and dismissed, November, 1852; third, installed and dismissed as above in New Britain; fourth, installed, 1858, at Great Barrington, Mass.; and in 1862, accepted an appointment as chaplain to the fifth regiment of Connecticut Volunteers, under the command of General Banks, at Virginia. After serving several months as chaplain, he resigned and was installed, December 1st, 1863, at Binghamton, N. Y. He married May 8th, 1850, No. (1,090,) which (for brief sketch of his family,) see.

We come now to the call and installation of the present pastor of the first church.

At a meeting of the church held the 18th day of January, 1858, Noah W. Stanley was chosen moderator; prayer was offered by Deacon Alfred Andrews, when the following resolve was passed unanimously, viz:

Whereas, we have enjoyed the ministrations of the Rev. Lavelette Perrin for two Sabbaths, and otherwise learned something of his antecedents, and thus having good reason to believe his piety and talents are well suited to our necessities as a church and people, therefore,

Resolved, that we hereby unanimously extend to him a cordial invitation to become the pastor of this church, and minister to our congregation.

Resolved, that Deacon Alfred Andrews be a committee to present this call to Mr. Perrin, with our respectful solicitation for its acceptance, and report his answer, if practicable, at our next meeting.

Attest, M. Judd, Clerk.

At a legally warned meeting of the first Ecclesiastical society of New Britain, held January 18th, 1858, voted to concur with the call of Rev. L. Perrin by the church, and voted him a salary of twelve hundred dollars, to be paid quarterly, and appoined William A. Churchill a committee to unite with the church committee in presenting the call.

Rev. Mr. Perrin's Reply.

Dear Brethren, I have received and prayerfully considered the call you were pleased to extend to me on the 18th instant, and hereby accept the same. In doing so I humbly crave your prayers that the great Head of the church will smile upon this relation when consummated, and make it the source of enduring profit to all whom it specially affects. May the Lord enable me to come to you in all the fullness of the gospel, and give me acceptance and success among you, in the work of the ministry.

Yours in Christian bonds, Lavelette Perrin.

Goshen, January 26th, 1858.

Pursuant to letters missive, an Ecclesiastical Council was convened in the lecture-room of the first Congregational Church and Society in New Britain, on Wednesday morning, February 3d, 1858, at ten o'clock, to counsel and advise with regard to the installation of the Rev. Lavalette Perrin, to whom said church and society had extended a call to become their pastor.

The churches represented on the occasion were as follows:

Church in Farmington, Rev. Noah Porter, D. D., pastor, and Brother Chauncey D. Cowles, delegate.

First church in Hartford, Rev. Joel Hawes, D. D., pastor.

Church in West Meriden, Rev. George Thacher, pastor, and Brother Roswell Hawley, delegate.

South church in New Britain, Rev. Samuel Rockwell, pastor, and Brother William H. Smith, delegate.

Church in West Hartford, Rev. M. N. Morris, pastor, and Brother Charles S. Mills, delegate.

Church in Newington, Rev. William P. Aikin, jun., pastor, and Brother Edwin Wells, delegate.

Church in Rocky Hill, Rev. L. B. Rockwood, pastor, and Brother Allen A. Robbins, delegate.

Church in Kensington, Brother Samuel Upson, delegate.

Great Barrington, Mass., Rev. Horace Winslow, pastor.

The council was organized by the choice of Rev. Dr. Hawes, moderator, and Rev. William P. Aikin, as scribe. Prayer was offered by the moderator. Rev. Frederick Gridley, Rev. Messrs. Orcutt, Jewett and Bond, being present, were invited to sit with the council. Papers were exhibited showing the action of the church and society, by which it appeared that the Rev. Mr. Perrin had been regularly called to become their pastor, and had accepted the same.

The council then proceeded to the examination of the candidate, as to his views of religious truth, his Christian experience, and motives for entering upon the work of the ministry. After a full hearing, it was unanimously voted, that the council approve the examination, and will proceed to the services of the installation at two o'clock in the afternoon.

The several parts in the public services were assigned as follows:

Reading the minutes by the scribe.

Introductory prayer and reading the scriptures by Rev. Mr. Aikin.

Sermon by Rev. Mr. Thacher.

Installing prayer by Rev. Dr. Hawes.

Charge to the pastor by Rev. Mr. Morris.

Right hand of fellowship by Rev. Mr. Rockwell.

Concluding prayer by Rev. Mr. Winslow.

Benediction by the pastor.

A true copy of the minutes.

Attest, William P. Aikin, Scribe.

The installation was performed in accordance with the above arrangement. Attest, William P. Aikin, Scribe.

Mr. Perrin now, July, 1867, has been faithfully and successfully laboring in this field; the church has enjoyed two special seasons of revival, in 1858,* and in 1866, and one hundred and eight were in consequence added to the church on profession. The whole number added, both by profession

* The 19th April of this year, 1858, being the completion of one century from the organization of the first church in the town, it was observed and celebrated by holding in the Center Church a general gathering of the citizens of the town, especially of Congregational churches, when Messrs. Elihu Burritt, N. W. Stanley, and Rev. William

and letter during this period, a little more than nine years, is two hundred and fifty-six.*

We propose here to recapitulate, giving the names of the foregoing ministers, with the addition of such other ministers and licentiates as were employed in supplying the pulpit during the revival and interims, (not however, embracing those who have only preached one or two Sabbaths.) The object is to give the reader at one view, and on a single page, a list of those who have been the principal preachers to the first church from its first.

Organization to the present time, it being one hundred and nine years.

Rev. Stephen Holmes, first preacher, thirteen Sabbaths, A. D. 1754, died 1773.

Rev. John Bunnel, called 1755, but declined.

Rev. Amos Fowler, called 1756, but declined, then settled in Guilford, died 1800.

Rev. James Taylor, called 1757, but declined, was silenced 1764, for Sandemanianism.

Rev. John Smalley, called 1758, ordained and installed April 19th, 1758, died 1820.

Rev. Samuel J. Mills, of Torringford, preached a short time in the revival of 1784, died 1833.

Rev. Jonathan Bird, preached when Dr. Smalley was ill, occasionally, died 1813.

Rev. Horatio Waldo, called 1809, declined for want of harmony in the parish.

Rev. Newton Skinner, called 1810, ordained and installed as colleague of Dr. Smalley, 1810, died 1825.

Whittlesey, greatly entertained the audience by reading sketches of our history from the early settlement of Old Farmington, the colony at Kensington, and the habits and customs of our ancestors, thus occupying the afternoon; when the evening was improved, first, by a like essay from the compiler of this work, and closed by a historical sermon by the pastor, Rev. L. Perrin. It was on this occasion that the people discovered that we had a history, and have ever since been waiting to have it brought out. The result is this book, which partakes largely of an ecclesiastical form, because the nucleus from which it emanated was such.

* And it ought to be said just here, to the enduring credit and praise of the parish, that as the year 1862 was drawing to its close, and during the second year of the great rebellion of the slave-holders, and while the appalling gloom of civil war hung over the country, they unitedly and simultaneously extinguished a debt of some $13,000, contracted in building their church edifice, 1854–5. About one-third of this debt was paid by the Wells family, and the balance by members of the congregation, with the exception of $500 by Mr. Norman L. Hart, of Philadelphia, formerly a member of this church and society.

Rev. Henry Jones, called 1825, ordained and installed, 1825, now, 1862, school in Bridgeport, dismissed from this church, 1827.

Rev. Jason Atwater, preached in revival of 1828–9, settled at Middlebury, Newtown, Southbury, died 1860.

Rev. Samuel Griswold, labored here with Mr. Atwater, during the revival of 1828–9.

Rev. Charles A. Goodrich, supplied the pulpit at various times for years, died 1862.

Rev. Jonathan Cogswell, called 1829, became Professor at Theological Institute, East Windsor Hill, dismissed from this church, 1834, died 1864.

Rev. Asahel Nettleton, supplied after the dismission of Mr. Cogswell, died 1844.

Rev. Horatio N. Brinsmade, supplied after the dismission of Mr. Cogswell.

Rev. Alfred Newton, (supply,) settled at Norwalk, Ohio.

Rev. Thomas H. Gallaudet, (supply,) Superintendent of Deaf and Dumb Asylum, Hartford, died 1851.

Rev. Martyn Tupper, preached a few Sabbaths in 1835, settled in Hardwick, Mass.

Rev. Dwight M. Seward, called 1835, ordained and installed the 3d of February, 1836, dismissed from this church, 1842.

Rev. William Whittlesey, supplied the pulpit directly and indirectly occasionally.

Rev. James L. Wright, supplied during the illness of Mr. Seward.

Rev. Jared R. Avery, supplied summer of 1837, settled after in Groton, and dismissed.

Rev. Nathaniel W. Taylor, D. D., supplied after the dismission of Mr. Seward, some time, died 1858.

Rev. Noah Porter, jun., D. D., supplied after the dismission of Mr. Seward, now, 1862, Professor Theological Seminary, New Haven.

Rev. Nathaniel H. Eggleston, supplied at different dates, 1863, at Stockbridge, Mass.

Rev. Chester S. Lyman, called 1842, ordained and installed, February 15th, 1843, dismissed from this church, 1845.

Rev. William W. Backus, preached in the revival of 1842–3.

Rev. Oliver E. Daggett, preached after the dismission of Mr. Lyman.

Rev. Charles S. Sherman, called 1845, now, 1863, at Naugatuck, Conn., dismissed from this church, 1849.

Rev. Eliphalet Whittlesey, supplied the pulpit several times, 1849–50.

Rev. Ebenezer Baldwin Andrews, called 1850, dismissed from this church, 1851, now, 1862, in the army as Major, but returned to his Professorship in Marietta College, Ohio.

Rev. John S. Whittlesey, preached after the dismission of Mr. Andrews, died 1862.

Rev. Charles H. Bullard, preached after the dismission of Mr. Andrews.

Rev. William Aichinson, preached after the dismission of Mr. Andrews.

Rev. Horace Winslow, called October, 1852, installed December 29th, 1852, dismissed from this church, 1857.

Rev. Timothy F. Clary, supplied at Mr. Winslow's vacation.

Rev. Alvan Underwood, preached in the revival of 1857.

Rev. Lavalette Perrin, called January, 1858, installed February 3d, 1858.

As no record has been kept of the supply of the pulpit, some may have officiated more than three Sabbaths, not included in this list.

We purpose here to give a list of the Deacons of the Church, in the order of appointment, and the Standing Committee, with some reference to their No. ( ).

Deacons.	Chosen.	Died.	Age.	No. ( )
John Patterson,	1758	1762	54	No. (2)
1st Elijah Hart, sen.,	1758	1772	61	No. (49)
Josiah Lee,	1772	1797	86	No. (33)
Isaac Lee,	1772	1802	86	No. (35)
Daniel Dewy,	1772	1786	80	No. (85)
Noah Stanley, about	1774	1778	54	No. (14)
2d Elijah Hart,	1780	1800	66	No. (52)
Timothy Stanley,	1795	1817	90	No. (113
Benjamin Wright,	1801	1813	76	No. (274)
3d Elijah Hart,	1805	1827	68	No. (181)
David Whittlesey,	1807	1851	76	No. (321)
Elijah Francis,	1822	*1846	87	No. (413)
Chauncey Cornwell,	1837	*1863	68	No. (401)
Norman Hart,	1843	resigned,		No. (954)
Morton Judd,	1851	resigned,		No. (918)
Alfred Andrews,	1851			No. (478)
Roswell Hawley, M. D.,	1851	resigned,		No. (1,068)
Albert D. Judd,	1859†			No. (1,028)
Lemuel R. Wells,	1859†	1867	40	No. (943)
Henry P. Strong,	1865			No. (1,148)
Elijah F. Blake,	1867			No. (1,442)

* Withdrew to South Church, 1842.

† Elected for two years, but August 25th, 1861, they, by ballot, were re-elected indefinitely, and August 30th, were consecrated as Deacons by laying on of hands, and by prayer, the pastor being assisted by Rev. Erastus Ripley; this service in connection with the lecture before communion, Friday afternoon.

November 9th, A. D. 1843, the Church adopted the rule that the Standing Committee shall consist of three members, besides the Deacons, and that these members go out in rotation, and the vacancy be supplied annually.

Standing Committees other than Deacons at the time of Election.

	Chosen.	No. ( )
Josiah Lee, - - - -	1761	(33)
Daniel Dewy, - - -	1761	(85)
Isaac Lee, - - - -	1761	(35)
Ladwick Hotchkiss, - - -	1761	(67)
Noah Standley, - - - -	1761	(14)
Col. Gad Standly, - - -	1779	(115)
Capt. John Lankton, - - -	1779	(107)
David Mather, - - -	1779	(138)
Elijah Hart, - - - -	1779	(52)
Thomas Hart, - - -	1795	(93)
Capt. James North, - - -	1795	(149)
Levi Andrews, - - -	1807	(122)
David Whittlesey, - - -	1807	(321)
Joseph Mather,* no record, - - -	-	(217)
Levi Wells,* no record, - - -	-	(299)
William Smith, - - -	1823	(337)
Amon Stanley, - - - -	1823	(550)
Alfred Andrews, - - -	1823	(478)
Dan Clark, - - - -	1843	(679)
Ira Stanley, jun., - - -	1843	(921)
Samuel Booth, - - - -	1843	(370)
Noah W. Stanley, - - -	1845	(849)
Morton Judd, - - - -	1846	(918)
Thomas Stanley, - - -	1847	(680)
William A. Churchill, - - -	1848	(695)
Julius Parker, - - -	1849	(864)
Gilman Hinsdale, - - -	1850	(1,015)
Benjamin F. Pierce, - - -	1851	(1,045)
Henry Walter, - - - -	1852	(1,066)
Ira Stanley, jun., - - -	1853	(921)
Norman Hart, - - - -	1854	(954)
Thomas Stanley, - - -	1855	(680)
Timothy W. Stanley, - - -	1856	(915)

* Dr. Smalley omitted the record of their appointment, but Mr. Skinner says at his first record, 1810, they were members of the Standing Committee then.

	Chosen.	No. ( )
Noah W. Stanley, - - -	1857	(849)
Lemuel R. Wells, - - -	1858	(943)
Omri M. North, - - -	1859	(1,061)
John B. Minor, - - - -	1860	(1,143)
Sylvanus Stone, - - -	1861	(776)
Charles Northend, - - -	1862	(1,144)
William A. Churchill, - -	1863	(695)
Jacob W. Biglow, - - -	1864	(1,202)
Julius Parker, - - -	1865	(864)
John N. Bartlett, - - -	1866	(1,282)
William A. Churchill, - -	1867	(695)

EXPLANATORY.

Members of the first Church in New Britain arranged in the same order in which they were admitted, whether by profession in public, or by letter from other churches. There are a few unavoidable exceptions to this rule of chronologic order, however, and such cases are noted in the history of the individual.

Dr. Smalley (the first pastor,) kept no record of dismissions to other churches, hence the few noted in this list as being removed were found on the records of other churches, where they thus located. Rev. Mr. Skinner began a list of dismissions with his ministry, but for the first ten years merely said such a person was dismissed, not designating to what church.

Abbreviations and contractions.

b. for born, d. for died, bap. for baptized, m. for married, dis. for dismissed, rec. for recommended, to ch. for being admitted either by profession or letter, Ken. for Kensington, Far. for Farmington, Hart. for Hartford, Weth. for Wethersfield, Mid. for Middletown, Wm. for William, Thos. for Thomas, Tim. for Timothy, æ. for age, leg. for legislature, rep. for representative. For index of members of the church and corresponding numbers, see the last pages of the book.

Names of members of the church will be found as originally entered on the record, hence females uniting with the church before marriage, must be looked after by the maiden name. No individual, with two exceptions, is entered as a member but once, however often dismissed to other churches and received back, but these removals and return are noted in the person's history.

A few females will stand as members only, like the original entry on the record, as the "wife of" such an one; in all such cases, the compiler, after diligent search, has failed to find a former or family name.

"OWNED THE COVENANT."

I. "HEZEKIAH ANDRUS," May 14th, 1758, see No. (112.)

II. "DAVID MATHER," June 11, 1758, see No. (138.)

III. "JOHN KILBOURN," July 30th, 1758, see No. (86.)

IV. "WIFE OF JOHN KILBOURN," July 30th, 1758, her maiden name Jemima Neal, daughter of William of Southington, and his wife, Anne (Barnes,) b. , bap. July 17th, 1737, at Southington, m. , No. (III.) he d. 1781, and she m. second, 1783, No. (II.) she d. Sept. 20th, 1813, æ. 76, they lived at the foot of "Half-way Hill."

V. "NOAH FULLER, owned the covenant, July 30th, 1758, b. to , m. June 3d, 1757, No. (VI.), they lived back of Dublin Hill. His estate was £31 17s. 6d. and administration was granted February 3d, 1767, and Janna Churchill gave bond to court with the widow, Alice. Isaac Lee, Noah Stanley and Elijah Francis were commissioners on the estate.

VI. WIFE OF NOAH FULLER, owned covenant July 30th, 1758; her maiden name Alice Brown; tradition says that their eldest son, Gad, died in the army, of starvation, which report almost killed the mother, yet she so far recovered as to m. a Mr. Smith, of Sandisfield, Mass.

THEIR CHILDREN.

1. Gad, b. , bap. June 3d, 1759, d. Dec. 2d, 1776, in captivity at New York.
2. Noah, b. Sept. 26th, 1761, bap. Oct., 1761, see No. (186.)
3. Lydia, b. , bap. March 31st, 1765, m. Martin Kent, in Dorset, Vt.

VII. SAMUEL SMITH, owned the covenant October 8th, 1758, b. Sept. 7th, 1732, to Wm. and his first wife, Rebecca (Hun,) of Weth.; he m. Dec. 6th, 1759, Mary Goodrich, daughter of Zebulon and Anne (Francis,) his wife, b. Aug. 23d, 1737. He inherited his father's home in Stanley quarter; was an extensive farmer; for further history and family, see No. (89.)

VIII. EBENEZER DICKINSON, owned the covenant October 8th, 1758, b. Feb. 25th, 1734, to Elihu and his second wife, Lucy (Deming,) m. June 2d, 1757, No. (IX.) He was a soldier of the Revolution, had his poll-tax abated on list of 1775, by the legislature of 1777.

IX. "WIFE OF EBENEZER DICKINSON," owned the covenant Oct. 8th, 1758; her maiden name Mabel Whaples; m. June 2d, 1757, No. (VIII.)

She was from Newington. They owned land together near "Osgood, or Half-way Hill," 1761. It is supposed they then lived in Newington.

THEIR CHILDREN.

1. Hopestill, b. July 2d, 1758, bap. Oct. 8th, 1758, by Dr. Smalley, and he called the child a daughter, but the same child is called Waitstill, on Farmington town record, and called a son.
2. Hannah, b. , bap. Oct. 11th, 1761, by Rev. J. Belden, Newington.
3. Ebenezer, b. June 9th, 1771.
4. Orran, born June 10th, 1779; perhaps others.

X. "THOMAS HART," owned the covenant Dec. 3d, 1758, see No. (93.)

XI. "ROBERT BOOTH," owned the covenant March 18th, 1759, b. Aug. 20th, 1730, to Robert, sen., from Stratford, and his wife, Ann (Hollister,) from Glastenbury. He m. May 9th, 1757, Ruth, daughter of Josiah Kilbourn, of Weth., and his wife, Ruth (Warner,) daughter of John. She d. when he m. second, May 5th, 1774, Anna Bronson, daughter of Joseph and his wife, Jemima, No. (218.) This family moved to Southington.

THEIR CHILDREN.

1. David, b. Feb. 23d, 1759, bap. March 18th, 1759, m. Hannah Mather, daughter of Joseph.
2. John, b. , bap. Nov. 8th, 1761, m. Oct. 6th, 1791, Almira Barnes, m. second, Naomi Case.
3. Stephen, b. , bap. Aug. 5th, 1764, m. April 15th, 1790, Lucy Booth, of Nathan.
4. Ziba, b. Jan. 17th, 1775, m. Sept. 14th, 1820, Hannah Granniss, of Southington; he then of Kingston, Upper Canada.
5. Johnson, b. Feb. 16th, 1777.
6. Orrin, b. , d. Sept. 3d, 1818, æ. 53.
7. Abner, b.
8. Amos, b. June 2d, 1779, m. Nov. 26th, 1807, Phebe Case, sister of John's wife, see above.

XII. "THOMAS LUSK," owned the covenant Oct. 7th, 1759, m. Nov. 1758, No. (90,) which see for history and family.

XIII. "MARY, wife of Adonijah Lewis," owned the covenant Oct. 18th, 1761, see No. (111.)

XIV. "EUNICE, wife of Ezekiel Wright," March 14th, 1762, see No. (143.)

XV. "AMOS WRIGHT," Feb. 13th, 1763, son of Judah, m. Oct. 15th, 1761, No. (XVI.)

XVI. "Wife of Amos Wright," owned the covenant Feb. 13th, 1763; her maiden name Deborah Neal, daughter of Wm. of Southington, and his wife, Anne (Barnes,) bap. Sept. 25th, 1743.

THEIR CHILDREN.

1. Daniel, b. March 22d, 1763, bap. May 1st, 1763.
2. Judah, b. June 13th, 1767.
3. Isabel, b. Dec. 11th, 1769.
4. Lydia, b. Jan. 19th, 1777.
5. Oliver, b. Feb. 25th, 1779.

XVII. "JOSHUA KILBOURN," owned the covenant Feb. 26th, 1764, b. March 9th, 1742, at New Britain, to George, of Weth., and his wife, Abigail, daughter of Benjamin Judd. He m. July 14th, 1763, No. (XVIII.)

XVIII. "Wife of Joshua Kilbourn," owned the covenant Feb. 26th, 1764, b. April 2d, 1742, to Joseph Mather, sen., and his wife, Anna (Booth,) daughter of Robert, sen.; her maiden name Mehitabel Mather; her husband d. Jan. 25th, 1776, in the thirty-fourth year of his age, when she married second, James Lusk, of Farmington. She d. 1820, æ. 86.

THEIR CHILDREN.

1. Mehitable, b. April 23d, 1764, see No. (157.)
2. Elizabeth, b. Sept. 24th, 1765, m. Reuben Hart, of Far., moved to Whitestown.
3. George, b. Nov. 19th, 1769, m. Almira Wilcox, of Simsbury, lived in Hudson, O.
4. William, b. Jan. 22d, 1772, m. Susan Bidwell, lived in Avon, Conn.
5. Joshua, b. June 3d, 1775, was a tanner and shoemaker, lived in Far , but moved to West Avon, where de died 1837, aged 63.

XIX. "ANDREW LUSK," April 15th, 1764, b. , m. July 1st, 1763, No. (XX.) He was a drummer in Capt. Patterson's company, at the Havanna, 1762.

XX. "Wife of Andrew Lusk," owned the covenant April 15th, 1764, b. ; her maiden name Mary Smith.

THEIR CHILDREN.

1. Selah, b. March 25th, 1764, bap. April 15th, 1764.
2. Bela, b. March 23d, 1766.

XXI. "LEMUEL HOTCHKISS," owned the covenant July 15th, 1764, see No. (121.)

XXII. "Wife of Lemuel Hotchkiss," July 15th, 1764, see No. (188.)

XXIII. "JOHN LUSK," Sept. 2d, 1764. He was a one-eyed man, lost one eye by sickness, in childhood. He m. August, 1763, No. (276,) which for further history, see. In 1762, he bought of Judah Wright, for £94, his house, barn and home lot, lying in Farmington, seventeen acres; it was bounded east, west and north on highway, and south on Elijah Francis. He d. June 8th, 1797, æ. 67. This was afterwards the Ira Andrews place.

XXIV. "JONATHAN ENO," owned the covenant April 14th, 1765, son of David and his wife, Mary (Gillet,) of Windsor, b. 1739, m. Jan. 7th, 1765, No. (XXV.) He built the house in Hart quarter, owned and occupied by Thomas Gridley, by Capt. Eleazer Curtiss, and then by Ira Stanley, sen.; is in good condition now, 1862; it stood between the house of Capt. John Langdon and that of Deacon Elijah Hart, the second. Mr. Eno sold to Thomas Gridley, and moved to Simsbury, where he d. Dec. 4th, 1813, aged 74.

XXV. "Wife of Jonathan Eno," owned the covenant April 14th, 1765, b. Dec. 26th, 1744, in Hart quarter, to No. (49) and his wife, No. (50;)

her maiden name Mary Hart; she d. Oct. 8th, 1834, æ. 90, at Simsbury. She was an only daughter of her parents.

THEIR CHILDREN.

1. Polly, b. Dec. 21st, 1764, bap. April 14th, 1765, m. Elijah Tuller, of Simsbury.
2. Rhoda, b. Aug. 12th, 1766, m. Daniel Phelps, of Simsbury.
3. Jonathan, b. March 15th, 1769, m. Theodocia Case, of Simsbury.
4. Lucretia, b. Feb. 13th, 1771, m. David Humphrey, of Simsbury.
5. Elizabeth, b. Aug. 9th, 1773, at New Britain, m. Dec. 12th, 1793, Alexander Phelps, of Simsbury.
6. Sintha, b. May 28th, 1777, m. Hezekiah Case, of Simsbury.
7. Salmon, b. Dec. 13th, 1779, m. June 2d, 1805, Polly Richards, daughter of Amos, of John. She now, 1867, living in New Britain.
8. Chauncey, b. Dec. 19th, 1782, m. Amarilla Case, of Simsbury.
9. Abigail, b. Feb. 28th, 1785, m. Oct. 2d, 1805, John Viets, of Simsbury and Granby. She died Dec. 20th, 1863, in her 79th year, at East Granby.

XXVI. "JOHN PATTERSON," owned the covenant Jan. 25th, 1767, b. (about 1744,) to No. (2) and his wife, No. (3,) m. June 2d, 1766, No. (XXVII.) He graduated at Yale College, 1762. He taught school, and was also a practicing attorney and justice of the peace in this place. He lived at his father's old homestead, (where Henry M. Pratt lives, on East street,) until about 1774, when he moved with his wife's father, Deacon Josiah Lee, to Lenox, Mass. From there he moved subsequently to the town of Binghampton, Broome county, New York, where he became chief justice of the court of that county. He was a member of the legislature of that State four years, and a representative to Congress from that State from 1803 to 1805. He was a brigadier-general in the American army during the Revolutionary war.* He was a member of the council that tried "Major Andre." He was a member of the convention to amend the constitution of the State of New York, A. D, 1801. He was one of the proprietors of the Boston purchase in Broome and Tioga counties, New York, containing 230,000 acres, called the "Free township." He d. July 19th, 1808, aged 64, at his residence in Lisle, Broome county, New York. We should judge from the number and variety of the offices and trusts bestowed on Gen. Patterson, that he was in these respects the most distinguished man ever raised in New Britain. His removing from the place so early in life is the reason probably, why our oldest people know so little of his history.

XXVII. "Wife of John Patterson, owned the covenant January 25th,

* The following is from "Storer's Record of Free Masonry," page 12: A petition was presented Oct. 6th, 1779, of a number of brethren, officers of the American army, praying that the Grand Lodge would grant them a charter to hold a traveling Lodge, was read, and Gen. John Patterson, Col. Benjamin Tupper, and Major William Hull, being nominated as Master and Wardens, voted, that a dispensation be granted them under the title of "Washington Lodge," to make masons, pass fellow craft, &c.

1767; her maiden name Elizabeth Lee, only child of No. (33) and his wife, No. (34,) m. June 2d, 1766, No. (XXVI.)

CHILDREN.

1. Josiah Lee, b. Oct. 8th, 1766, bap. Feb. 1st, 1767, m. Jan., 1788, Clarissa, daughter of Gen. Caleb Hyde.
2. Hannah, b. , m. Eggleston.
3. Polly, b. at Lenox, Mass., d. at South Carolina, unmarried.
4. Ruth, b. Aug., 1774, at Lenox, Mass., m. Nov. 14th, 1797, Ira Seymour of Lisle, New York.
5. Betsey, born She died unmarried; no dates.
6. John Pierce, b. May 5th, 1787, at Lenox, m. Sept. 16th, 1809, Sally Osborn, at Lisle, N. Y.
7. Maria, born 1789, at Lenox, m. April, 1808, to Samuel Kilborn, living, 1864, at Spencerport, N. Y.

The following persons "owned the covenant" previous to the organization of the church, and although not embraced in the list of Dr. Smalley's "half-way covenant" members, yet are inserted here, and it is thought with propriety, under this note.

XXVIII. "Elias Hart," owned the covenant Sept. 15th, 1754, before Rev. Joshua Belden, of Newington, officiating in New Britain. He b. Feb. 25th, 1735–6, to (No. 51) and his wife, Ann (Norton,) m. Oct. 17th, 1753, (No XXIX.) He lived in and owned one-sixth part of his father's house, (now that of Widow Henry Williams, in fourth district.) He died 1756; the inventory of his estate was £333 11s., taken Jan. 14th, 1757, by Judah Wright and Isaac Lee. Administrators, the Widow Hope, and John Judd.

XXIX. "Wife of Elias Hart," owned the covenant Sept. 15th, 1754; her maiden name Hope Whaples, of Newington; m. Oct. 17th, 1753, (No. XXVIII,) who died 1756, when she m. second, Aug. 18th, 1760, Josiah Wright, jun. They soon after removed to Williamstown, Mass., and 1794, she deeded all her interest to her first husband's estate in Berlin to Elijah Hart, jun., for £17.

CHILDREN OF ELIAS HART AND HOPE, HIS WIFE.

1. Jacob, b. May 2d, 1754.
2. Rose, b. Jan. 8th, 1756, and Feb. 8th, 1758, Nehemiah Gates, of Middletown, was appointed her guardian, by Probate Court of Hartford.

XXX. "Elijah Smith," owned the covenant July 27th, 1755, b. Oct. 29th, 1721, to Joseph, No. (25,) and Mary (Royce,) his wife; lived next door south of Landlord Smith, his brother, No. (29;) was a farmer; m. April 6th, 1752, Sarah Grimes. It is a tradition that Rev. William Burnham held the first religious meeting or service in the place, at his house. He died July 12th, 1777, aged 56.

THEIR CHILDREN.

1. Elijah, b. May 30th, 1753, m. July 7th, 1774, Susannah, No. (223.)
2. Sarah, b. Sept. 1st, 1755, m. Feb. 9th, 1775, No. (161.)

3. Joel, b. Aug. 5th, 1757, m. Hannah Griswold, of Gid., m. second, Lydia Stanley, of Deacon Timothy.

4. Elizabeth, b. March 2d, 1760, bap. March 23d, 1760, m. June 3d, 1784, No. (434.)

5. Solomon, b. Sept. 2d, 1767, bap. Dec. 6th, 1767, m. Jan. 1789. No. (206.)

XXXI. "Jacob Brandigee," July 27th, 1755, before Rev. J. Belden, of Newington, officiating at the time in New Britain. It is said the name was originally Brundige, and that he came from Nine Partners, N. Y., when only thirteen years old. The Newington record of marriages says Jacob Brandigat m. Oct. 11th, 1753, Abigail Dunham. His mother's maiden name was Brock, and he was b. 1729; was a weaver by trade, but kept a store in Great Swamp village, at first near the present residence of Moses Gilbert, and afterwards opposite the present residence of Norman Porter. He was engaged in the West India trade, and run vessels from Rocky Hill. He died March, 1765, at sea, aged 36. He was 22, and Abigail 16, when married, (so says the family Bible,) but if born 1729, he must have been older. She m. second, Rev. Edward Eells, of Upper Middletown. She died Jan. 25th, 1825.

CHILDREN OF JACOB BRANDIGEE AND ABIGAIL, HIS WIFE.

1. Elishama, b. April 17th, 1754, m. March 10th, 1778, Widow Lucy Weston, widow of Jeremiah.

2. Rhoda, b. Oct. 5th, 1756, bap. Jan. 2d, 1757, at Ken., d. April 16th, 1781.

3. Persis, b. Aug. 31st, 1758, bap. Oct. 1st, 1758, at Ken., m. Rev. Mr. Brace.

4. Abigail, b. Aug. 31st, 1760, bap. Oct. 12th, 1760, d. Sept. 26th, 1823.

5. Mary, b. Dec. 18th, 1763, d. Dec., 1764.

6. Jacob, b. Jan. 4th, 1765, d. Jan., 1786.

The mother had a daughter by her second marriage, Sarah Eels, who m. first a Sage, and second a Morrison. She d. March 7th, 1838, at Berlin. The mother is supposed to be sister to No. (76.) Jacob Brandigee, sen., was the progenitor of all of the name in Conn. He had two brothers, one named David, the other Joseph, all b. at Nine Partners.

XXXII. "Wm. Horton," owned the covenant at the same time, July 27th, 1755, and was bap. at New Britain, (so says the Newington record,) by Rev. Joshua Belden, who officiated.

XXXIII. "David Lusk," owned the covenant in Newington, with his wife, No. (XXXIV.,) Aug. 17th, 1755, before Rev. J. Belden, which act was acknowledged here by Rev. Mr. Smalley, inasmuch as he baptized their second child, David Lusk, jun. Mr. Lusk was a man of considerable property; built the house occupied many years by Chauncey Merrills, back of "Dublin Hill." His taxable estate, 1772, was set in the list at £119 2s., and at that date there were but nine men in the parish who had larger estates. He m. May 29th, 1753, No. (XXXIV.) He died July 6th, 1793.

XXXIV. "Wife of David Lusk," owned the covenant August 17th, 1755, with her husband, at Newington. She was b. Nov. 26th, 1730; her maiden name, Prudence Hurlbert; m. May 29th, 1753, before Rev. J. Belden, at Newington, to No. (XXXIII.)

THEIR CHILDREN.

1. Seth, b. 1755, bap. Sept. 6th, 1755, at Newington, m. Sept. 6th, 1781, No. (242.)
2. David, b. , bap. Oct., 1760, at New Britain, m. No. (386.)
3. Solomon, b. , m. Nov. 25th, 1784, No. (226.)
4. Rhoda, b. , m. John Whaples, of Newington.

CONFESSION OF FAITH AND COVENANT.

THE following is a true copy of the original Confession of Faith and the Covenant, owned and assented to by the constituent members of the first Church in New Britain, at their "embodying," on the 19th day of April, 1758.

"We believe that there is one only living and true God, the Almighty maker and constant preserver of Heaven and Earth, and the rightful Supreme Lord over all: that in God there are three persons, the Father, the Son, and the Holy Ghost, who are the same in substance, equal in power and in glory: that the Scriptures of the Old and New Testaments are the Word of God, and a complete rule of faith and practice: we believe the original holy and happy state of man, as he first came from the hand of God, and that all mankind by their apostacy from, and rebellion against God, have exposed themselves to his wrath and curse, and that being utterly unable to deliver and save themselves, God, out of the infinite riches of his free Grace, sent his only begotten Son into the world to be a Saviour, to die, the just for the unjust, that he might bring them to God; and that he hath graciously made a promise of pardon and eternal life, and all the saving benefits of the Redeemer's purchase, to all that sincerely repent of their sins, and humbly receive and rest upon him for Salvation, as he is offered in the Gospel: and from the merciful encouragements, the condescending gracious offers and invitations of the Gospel, together with a sense of our own sinfulness and unworthiness, we do as far as in us lies, make choice of the living God for our God, of God the Father for our Father, and the original spring of all life and Grace; of Christ, the Son of God, for our Saviour, of the Holy Ghost for our Comforter and Sanctifier, and of the Word of God for the rule of our belief and manners, and we do now solemnly dedicate and give up ourselves to God, to be wholly and forever his: to be guided by his Spirit, to be ruled by his Laws, disposed of by his Providence, and to be eternally saved in the Gospel way, promising by the help of Christ, without which we can do nothing, that we will live soberly, righteously and Godly all the days of our lives: and as we are now called by the Providence of God, to unite and incorporate in Church state, we do likewise freely covenant and bind ourselves to walk together as becomes a particular visible church of Christ, in all the holy ways of Gospel worship and ordinances, watching over one another as members of the same body, with all brotherly tenderness and love, submitting ourselves to the discipline and government that Christ hath instituted in his house: that we will make it our great concern in our several places and relations, to please and honor God—to approve ourselves to Him, and to grow up here on earth to a meetness for an other and better world."

MEMBERS OF FIRST CHURCH OF NEW BRITAIN.

THE following list comprises the names, with their chronological numbers, of those who have been communicants of the first Church of Christ in New Britain, from its organization, April 19th, 1758, to 1867, a period of one hundred and nine years.

1. JOHN SMALLEY, son of Benjamin, of Lebanon, Conn., and his second wife, Mary. He was an only son of his mother, born June 4th, 1734, at Lebanon. His father was English, and a weaver, whose first wife was Lydia Allen, sister of Joseph, who was father of Col. Ethan. Mr. Smalley was fitted for college by his pastor, Rev. Eleazer Wheelock, and entered Yale at eighteen years of age; graduated 1756, made a profession of religion at college, studied divinity with Dr. Bellamy, of Bethlehem, Conn., invited to preach in New Britain, Nov., 1757, was recommended from the church in Cornwall, to the church in New Britain, Rev. Hezekiah Gold, pastor, was ordained at the gathering of the church, April 19th, 1758; he m. April 24th, 1764, No. (96;) he bought of William Patterson, 1759, the Elnathan Smith place, now, 1862, the Rhodes place, on East street, for £300, and resided there until 1788, when he bought the house and lot of Lemuel Smith, for £168, where he lived and where he died, June 1st, 1820, aged 86; see page 87.

CHILDREN.

1. Sarah, b. Feb. 22d, 1765, bap. Feb. 24th, 1765, d. May 5th, 1770, aged 5.
2. Mary, b. Dec. 20th, 1766, bap. Feb. 1st, 1767, m. Oct. 20th, 1794, Rev. Isaac Porter. She died Dec. 19th, 1846, aged 80. He d. April 14th, 1844, in his 78th year.
3. Anna, b. Feb. 24th, 1768, bap. April 10th, 1768, m. Oct. 6th, 1793, Roger Whittlesey, Esq. She died Feb. 5th, 1806, aged 38.
4. Phebe, b. Sept. 7th, 1770, bap. Sept. 8th, 1770, died same day.
5. Sarah, second of name, see No. (393.)
6. Rebecca, see No. (315.)

2. "Major JOHN PATTERSON," son of James, of Wethersfield, and Mary Talcot, alias Widow (Talcot,) his wife, born Feb. 14th, 1707–8; he m. Jan. 28th, 1730–31, No. (3;) was chosen and appointed to the office of deacon soon after the incorporation of the church, (so says the record;) his residence where (now, 1863,) Henry Pratt lives; was a large landholder, a military man, and held some slaves, as appears from a short sketch of his will, viz: "May 11th, 1759; Being called of God to serve

my country in the present intended expedition against our northern enemies, the French!! calling to mind the danger of martial life, &c. *Imprimis,* to my dear wife, Ruth, I give half my lot I bought of Serg. Ebenezer Smith, all my right in common and undivided land in Farmington, and all my personal estate, except my negro girl, Rose! and also the use of all I shall give my son John in this will, until he arrive at twenty-one years, and half during her life, but she is to give my son John Patterson, a college education. Item, to my daughter Anna, wife of Rev. Stephen Holmes, I give my negro girl, Rose!" His slaves, when they died, were buried on the high ground back of his house, where, 1849, at the construction of the railroad, two graves were opened and one skull disinterred. It is said he was a liberally educated man. He held a captain's commission under the king, in the taking of Havanna, 1762; had in his company nearly one hundred men, mostly from Wethersfield and Farmington, among whom was his faithful negro servant, "London." Deacon Patterson seems to have anticipated his fate in his will, for he fell with more than one-third of his company, victims to the yellow fever, at Havanna, where he d. Sept. 5th, 1762, aged 54.

THEIR CHILDREN.

1. Mary, born Dec. 5th, 1731, m. April 18th, 1751, John Pierce, of Litchfield.
2. Sarah, born June 13th, 1734, m. Dec. 30th, 1754, James Lusk.
3. Anna, see No. (80.)
4. Ruth, see No. (81.)
5. John, see list of those who owned "the covenant." (XXVII.)

3. "Wife of Major John Patterson," daughter of Joseph Bird, jun., of Farmington, and his wife, Mary Steele, b. , m. Jan. 28th, 1730–31, (No. 2.) Her maiden name, Ruth Bird.

4. ' Thomas Richards," son of Thomas, of Hartford, and Mary (Parsons,) who was daughter of Deacon Benjamin Parsons, of Springfield, Mass., his wife, b. April 3d, 1694, at Hartford, m. June 16th, 1717, Abigail Turner, of Hartford; they lived in Southington, 1728 to 1750, when the family moved to Stanley quarter, in New Britain, and located on the corner west of the former school-house; his wife, Abigail, died Sept. 24th, 1736, when he married second, Dec. 28th, 1738, No. (5;) he was to church in Newington, Sept. 23d, 1750, by letter from Southington; a blacksmith by occupation.

CHILDREN.

1. Susannah, born May 12th, 1718, at Hartford, m. June 5th, 1735, Jonathan Andrews, of Benjamin.
2. Abigail, b. , bap. May 4th, 1718, died young.
3. Abigail, b. Feb. 2d, 1721–2, to church in Southington, 1737, m. Oct. 9th, 1742, Thomas Lankton.
4. John, b. , bap. Aug. 20th, 1724, at Hartford, died young.
5. Samuel, see No. (12.)

6. Elizabeth, b. Nov. 22d, 1728, bap. Nov. 24th, 1728, to church in Southington, 1749, m. Dec. 24th, 1750, James Horsington.
7. John, b. March 31st, 1730-1, see No. (95.)
8. Lydia, b. March 23d, 1732-3, bap. March 25th, 1732-3, at Southington.
9. Experience, b. , bap. May 4th, 1736, at Southington.

5. "Wife of Thomas Richards," Widow Rachel Orvice; this is his second wife, daughter of Thomas Andrus, and Rebecca Carrington, his wife, b. July 11th, 1686, and when she m. No. (4,) was the widow of Samuel Orvice; she to church in Southington, 1744, and to Newington, by letter, Sept. 23d, 1750.

6. WILLIAM SMITH, son of Jonathan and his wife, Sarah , born March 30th, 1699, m. July 22d, 1725, No. (7;) he was a farmer by occupation, remarkably conscientious; he lived on Stanley street, at the head of that street called "Spiritual Lane;" his farm has been kept in the name through several generations, down to the late Samuel Smith, deceased. He and his brother, Ebenezer, first built and owned what is called Churchill's Mills. His wife, Rebecca, died Feb. 23d, 1771, aged 74, when he married second, July 11th, 1771, Widow Mary Wells, of Newington, who had been the mother of Joshua Wells, who m. Mercy, the daughter of Jedediah Goodrich; she d. June 30th, 1774, aged 60; he d. Jan. 9th, 1779, in his 80th year.

7. "Wife of William Smith," Rebecca Hunn, born Aug. 26th, 1697, to Samuel and his wife, Sarah (Dix,) daughter of John. She m. No. (6.) before David Goodrich, justice of the peace at Wethersfield, July 22d, 1725.

HIS CHILDREN BY REBECCA, HIS FIRST WIFE.

1. Elijah, born May 1st, 1726.
2. Sarah, born March 2d, 1727-8.
3. Abijah, born Sept. 2d, 1728, died Sept. 12th, 1728.
4. Lydia, born Sept. 18th, 1729, m. Steele.
5. Samuel, born Sept. 7th, 1732, m. Dec. 6th, 1759, No. (89.)
6. Moses, born Sept. 21st, 1735, died Oct. 19th, 1756, in the French war.

8. "EBENEZER SMITH," son of Ebenezer, sen. and Mary (Whittlesey,) his wife, born July 1st, 1725, m. Oct. 18th, 1750, No. (9;) they both "owned the covenant" in Newington, April 14th, 1751; lived near to and owned Churchill's Mills, near Newington bounds, inherited from his father; he was grandson of Jonathan Smith. His will dated 1767, gives two-thirds the mill to Elisha, his eldest son, and the other third to Lemuel; amount of inventory £455; says in his will that the mill place is in Wethersfield, about thirty rods east from his new dwelling-house; names three daughters, Frances, Abigail and Elizabeth; he made Elijah Francis sole executor; he died 1767, aged 42; the witnesses to his will were Jonathan Griswold, Zeb. Goodrich and Noah Stanley.

9. Wife of Ebenezer Smith, Mehitable Buck, daughter of Pelatiah, of Newington, and sister of No. (13,) and also of No. (93,) b. d.

CHILDREN.

1. Elisha, b. Aug. 14th, 1751, bap. Aug. 18th, 1751, in Newington, m. Lucy Loomis, of Torringford; he lived and died there.
2. Frances, b. March 3d, 1753, bap. March 4th, 1753, at Newington, m. June 24th, 1773, Nathan Booth, jun.
3. Abigail, b. March 10th, 1755, bap. March 30th, 1755, at Newington, m. Feb. 13th, 1777, Giles Hooker; second, Joseph Woodruff.
4. Elizabeth, b. Feb. 4th, 1757, m. Sept. 11th, 1777, Samuel Bronson; she d. May 20th, 1820, aged 62.
5. Lemuel, b. Mar. 11th, 1759, bap. Mar. 11th, 1759, m. Oct. 10th, 1790, No. (437.)
6. Ezekiel, b. 1761, bap. March 8th, 1761.
7. Bela, born 1763, bap. May 27th, 1763; went to Pennsylvania, and Hartford Probate Record says, April 7th, 1767, Elijah Francis was made guardian to Timothy Smith, aged six years, and Bela Smith, aged four years, sons of Ebenezer Smith.

10. THOMAS LUSK was a member of Newington church when Mr. Belden was settled, 1747. He had a brother, John, who was a merchant in Newington; also a brother William, who with his wife, came from Meriden to Newington church, by letter, Aug. 13th, 1749. These brothers were of Scotch origin, and settled in the north of Ireland for a time, and came to America early in the eighteenth century, and from them descended all of the name in Connecticut; it is said Gen. Levi Lusk, of martial spirit and revolutionary memory was a son of William, from Meriden. It is thought Thomas, the subject of this notice, settled in that part of New Britain called "Strip-lane," where some of his descendants became large land-holders.

11. "Wife of Thomas Lusk;" she was also a member of Newington church when Mr. Belden first settled there, 1747, and no other record is found of either of these persons.

THEIR CHILDREN.

1. John, born , married August, 1763, No. (276.)
2. Andrew, born , married July 1st, 1763, Mary Smith; he was the drummer
3. Thomas, born , married Nov. 23d, 1758, No. (90.)
4. David, b. , married May 29th, 1753, Prudence Hurlbert, of Wethersfield.

12. SAMUEL RICHARDS, son of No. (4) and his first wife, Abigail Turner, b. Oct. 22d, 1726, bap. Oct. 23d, 1726, m. Dec. 8th, 1747, No. (13;) he was in the old French war, as a servant to a surgeon, at Cape Breton; thus obtained his knowledge of physic and surgery, which he practiced in after life. He lived with his father in Southington, then a parish of Farmington; joined the church there June 5th, 1748; removed by letter to Newington church, Sept. 23d, 1750; lived five years at Newington, but 1755, moved to Canaan, then after three years returned to Newington, near the meeting-house, until 1778, when he went to New Hartford for some three years; then to Plainville; he lived near "Redstone Hill," south part of Farmington, and died Nov. 10th, 1793, aged 66; a red sand-stone in Plainville cemetery heads his grave.

13. Wife of Samuel Richards, Lydia (Buck,) daughter of Pelatiah and "Lydia, daughter of John Stoddart," his wife, all of Newington, b. April 22d, 1725, at Newington parish, in Wethersfield, to church in Newington, April 10th, 1748; she died March 25th, 1807, at the house of her son, Deacon Selah Richards, in the limits of Bristol, aged 82.

CHILDREN.

1. Aaron, b. May 20th, 1748, bap. May 21st, 1748, at Newington, m. 1778, Dorcas Adams; m. second, Polly Dickinson, of Torringford.
2. Eliphalet, born Feb. 28th, 1751, bap. March 23d, 1751, at Newington, m. Steele; resided at Natches.
3. Samuel, jun., born Oct. 18th, 1753, m. Sarah Gridley; chosen deacon, 1808; he died Dec. 31st, 1842, Pennsylvania.
4. William, born Oct. 9th, 1755, bap. Nov. 19th, 1755, at Newington, m. Sarah Shepherd.
5. Pelatiah, born Jan. 9th, 1758, died Nov. 19th, 1758.
6. Pelatiah 2d, b. Sept. 5th, 1759, bap. Oct. 7th, 1759, at New Britain, m. Abigail Barber, daughter of Thomas, of Canton; he died 1826, aged 67.
7. Lucretia, born June 4th, 1762, m. Deacon John Barnes, of Southington.
8. Seth, born Oct. 5th, 1764, m. Salome Carrington.
9. Selah, b. Sept. 17th, 1767, m. 1792, Esther Cowles; 1796, Helena Lewis; 1812, Candice Winchell; he was chosen deacon in Farmington church, 1822; he d. May 3d, 1857, greatly beloved and lamented; remarkable for piety, intelligence and usefulness.

14. NOAH STANDLEY, son of Thomas 2d and Esther (Cowles,) his wife, b. Jan. 16th, 1724, m. Nov. 2d, 1749–50, Ruth Norton, daughter of Thomas, jun. and Elizabeth (Macon,) of Stratford, his wife, born March 11th, 1725–6. They lived where his grandson, N. W. Stanley, now, (1862,) does, and there kept a tavern; he was lieutenant of the king's troops in the French war; was chosen deacon (it is supposed,) to supply the place of Deacon Josiah Lee, about 1774, (when he moved to Lenox, Mass.;) no record appears of the exact date; he left a large Bible, with the names, births and baptisms of his children, in a beautiful hand, with the number of times he had read the Bible through; he died May 5th, 1778, of palsy, aged 54.*

CHILDREN.

1. Seth, born March 18th, 1751, bap. March 24th, 1751, at Newington, m. Jan. 6th, 1774, Ruth Clark, daughter of John.

---

* The following lines are on his "head stone:"

Now I am dead and out of mind,
Upon this stone my name you'll find,
And when my name you plainly see,
You can no less than think of me.

His widow, Mrs. Ruth Stanley, died Dec. 8th, 1811, aged 87. He was grandson of Thomas Stanley 1st, and his wife, Anna, daughter of Rev. Jeremiah Peck, and he was great grandson of Capt. John Stanley, of Farmington, and his wife, Sarah (Scott,) who were among the first settlers of Tunxis. This Capt. John was born in England; was ten years old at emigration; lost his father, John, on the passage; lived a few

2. Sylvia, b. Oct. 24th, new style, 1753, bap. Oct. 28th, 1753, at Newington, m. Nov. 12th, 1780, James Francis.

3. Ruth, b. July 11th, 1756, bap. July 18th, 1756, at Newington.

4. Noah, b. April 16th, 1759, bap. April 19th, 1759, m. first, Lucy Lewis; second, 1786, Experience Wells; third, see No. (202.)

5. Adna, born Jan. 28th, 1763, see No. (438.)

6. Asa, born Dec. 6th, 1766, bap. next day, and died the 12th, aged six days.

7. Cynthia, b. Dec. 29th, 1767, bap. Jan. 17th, 1768, m. Jan. 16th, 1810, Asa Butts, of Canterbury.

15. "Ruth Kilbourn," widow of Josiah, and daughter of John Warner, m. Nov. 27th, 1726, before Capt. Joshua Robbins, of Wethersfield, justice of the peace; moved soon after marriage into the limits of New Britain, where he died.

THEIR CHILDREN.

1. David, b. Dec. 21st, 1727; was a soldier in the old French war; died at Litchfield.

2. Ruth, b. 1729, m. May 9th, 1757, Robert Booth, son of Robert.

3. Josiah, b. 1731, see No. (200.)

4. John, b. 1733, see No. (86.)

5. Richard, b. 1735, m. Dec. 8th, 1763, Mercy Bronson, daughter of Elijah, sen.

6. Elizabeth, b. , bap. Nov. 15th, 1747, at Newington, m. Nov. 7th, 1771, Jedediah Norton.

16. "Wife of Jonathan Griswold;" this was his second wife; her maiden name, Experience Warren, daughter of Abraham, of Wethersfield, and Experience (Stephens,) his wife, born June 9th, 1712; was sister of old Will Warren, who was the hermit, and had his den on "Rattlesnake Hill," so often referred to, even to this day. She became the second wife of No. 83,) on the 6th Oct., 1748; she long outlived her husband; they lived just over the "Peede* bridge," east of George Francis, it being named from her, a contraction of Experience, common in those days; she was familiarly called "Aunt Peede;" she died at the house of Nathan Booth, at the advanced age of 86, on the 24th May, 1797.

17. "Ruth, wife of Robert Woodruff," daughter of , m. ; they lived where Horatio A. Pratt (now, 1863,) does; owned a large farm; he was son of Samuel Woodruff, the cordwainer, and was born Oct. 8th, 1710; he deeded, 1755, a portion of his farm to Farmington, for a highway, beginning at the north end of a ledge, and from thence to extend south across his land, three rods wide; this is supposed to be part of a new highway to pass to the new meeting-house, when it should be built, "at the place appointed for it," where the present "pound" stands. She to church in Newington, before 1747.

---

years in Hartford, with his uncles, Thomas and Timothy; went to Farmington when about twenty, and became prominent and greatly useful there. His will is dated 1705; amount of inventory, £360 7s. 1d. He died Dec. 19th, 1706.

* The level tract of land stretching from this locality northeast, towards West Hartford, is called on the early land records of Farmington, "Wolf Plain."

CHILDREN OF ROBERT AND RUTH WOODRUFF.

1. Seth, b. 1744, was deaf, and lived a bachelor; died Nov. 30th, 1823, aged 79.

2. Amos, b, 1745, m. Oct. 27th, 1768, No. (565;) they moved to Lenox, Mass.

3. Sarah, b. Oct. 6th, 1749, bap. Oct. 8th, 1749, at Newington, m. Dec. 31st, 1777, Capt. William Walker, of Lenox.

4. Ruth, b. April 10th, 1751, bap. April 14th, 1751, at Newington, m. Elizur Whaples; she died May 27th, 1794.

18. "Wife of Daniel Kilbourn;" she was received to Newington church June 28th, 1752, then called Widow Mary Cushing, by letter from the church of Christ at Killingworth, Conn. See No. (70;) maiden name, Stephens.

Thus far, with the exception of No. (1,) came from Newington church, but no mention of the fact appears on the record of that church.

"*From the church in Kensington, Rev. Samuel Clark, Pastor.*"

19. "The Widow Hannah Seymor," she, daughter of Thomas North and Hannah (Newel,) his wife, the widow of Samuel Seymor, son of Richard, the captain of the fort; she was a constituent member of the church, 1712, in "Great Swamp," and lived to become also a constituent member of this new church; she m. Samuel Seymor, May 10th, 1706; she was grand-daughter of John North, the settler, from England.

THEIR CHILDREN.

1. Hannah, b. March 28th, 1706-7, m. Dec. 10th, 1729, Allen Goodrich, the blacksmith, of "Great Swamp village."

2. Mary, born Nov. 13th, 1708.

3. Eliakim, b. , m. Susanna, daughter of Deacon Anthony Judd; second, Mary Hooker.

4. Rebecca, b. June 25th, 1711, m. Nov. 21st, 1734, Elisha Goodrich.

5. Mercy, b. Sept. 11th, 1715, m. Feb. 19th, 1747, Uriah Judd; was his second wife; went to Lenox.

20. "The Widow Mary Andrus," daughter of Jacob Goffe, of Wethersfield, and Margarie (Ingersol,) his wife, b. Nov. 15th, 1693, at Wethersfield, near Kensington line, m. June 17th, 1712, John Andrus, of Farmington, son of Daniel; her husband died June 16th, 1740; his inventory amounted to £676 4s. 4d.; the society record of Newington shows that he signed, 1720, a £50 note payable to that society, with Daniel Andrus and others, for being annexed to Farmington; she probably spent the remainder of her life with her son, Moses, at the old house (now, 1867,) still standing on West Main street, near Deacon Milton Andrews; she d. Sept. 7th, 1769, aged 75, and her grave-stone is south side of New Britain cemetery.

THEIR CHILDREN.

1. David, b. Jan. 28th, 1718, m. Margaret ; lived in Waterbury, Conn., and Egremont, Mass.

2. Moses, b. May 12th, 1722, m. Nov. 10th, 1748, No. (54.)

3. Mary, b. 1728, probably m. Samuel Dickinson, sen.; house on Russell's corner, at Woodruff Hill.

4. Abraham, b. ; he chose, 1744, his brother Moses, for guardian.

5. Esther, b. 1732; she chose, 1744, her mother for guardian; m. April 27th, 1757, Daniel Root, of Kensington; she d. Feb. 27th, 1758, and buried in Blue Hills cemetery.

21. The Widow Anna Booth, daughter of Capt. Stephen Hollister, of Glastenbury, and Abigail, his wife, b. 1690, m. Nov. 27th, 1712, Robert Booth, from Stratford, a descendant of Sir Richard; their house stood where (now, 1867,) that of Enoch Kelsey stands; used the same well by the fence in the valley; she had a brother, Gershom, at the Blinn house, east, and brother, Stephen, settled on the road next west. Mr. Booth probably located here soon after marriage, for he held office in "Great Swamp" society as early as 1715; he died Dec. 17th, 1750, aged 61; his grave in "Christian Lane" cemetery; his estate settled 1750–51; inventory, £591; Nathan, the eldest son, gave bond with Widow Ann, to court, and Widow Ann made guardian to Elisha, who is, 1750–51, nineteen years old; probably she m. second, Doct. James Harvey Hurlbut, of Kensington.

THEIR CHILDREN.

1. Hannah, b. July 22d, 1716, m. Joshua Mather. See No. (47) and (48.)
2. Anna, b. Sept. 16th, 1718, m. Joseph Mather, sen. She d. Sept. 13th, 1798, æ. 80.
3. Nathan. See No. (65.)
4. James, b. May 25th, 1723.
5. Robert, b. Aug. 20th, 1730; "owned the covenant." See that list, No. (XI.)
6. Elisha, b. May 20th, 1732, m. Dec. 5th, 1751, Esther Hollister; second, Widow Mary Gilbert.

22. "BENJAMIN JUDD," son of first Benjamin, and grandson of Deacon Thomas, the emigrant; his mother, Mary (Lewis,) daughter of Capt. William, of Farmington; he born 1671, m. Jan. 18th, 1694, No. (23;) his residence at the present home of Richard Judd; his title, Sargeant, seldom omitted; he was one of the patriarchs of the "Great Swamp Society," greatly useful in church and civil affairs; was a large land-holder; made no will; died March 9th, 1764, aged 94.

The Kensington church record (by note says) that Benjamin Judd and wife dismissed to New Britain, 1757.

23. "Wife of Benjamin Judd;" she daughter of John North and Susanna (Francis,) his wife, born 1676, died April 23d, 1764, aged 88.

THEIR CHILDREN.

1. Benjamin, b. March 2d, 1697, m. Nov. 9th, 1727, Sarah Hollister, of Glastenbury; lived and died there.
2. Susannah, b. Aug. 12th, 1699, m. July 1st, 1756, David Bronson.
3. Mary, b. Feb. 6th, 1702, m. 1723, Joseph Beckley, grandson of Serg. Richard, of Wethersfield.
4. Abigail, b. Sept. 5th, 1703, m. May 20th, 1746, George Kilbourn; he died 1763.
5. Kezia, b. Sept. 14th, 1705, m. June 12th, 1729, Amos Judd, son of Deacon Anthony; she died May 2d, 1791.

6. Bathsheba, b. Aug. 20th, 1707, m. 1728, David Sage, of Middletown and Berlin.
7. Joanna, b. Oct. 16th, 1709, m. 1731, Samuel Hubbard, jun., of Middletown.
8. Catharine, b. Oct. 26th, 1711.
9. Uriah, see No. (39.)
10. James, see No. (38.)
11. Nathan, see No. (41.)
12. Hezekiah, b. June 19th, 1722, d. Sept. 9th, 1727.

24. "Widow ELIZABETH LEE;" she was Elizabeth Royce, of Wallingford, m. Oct. 1st, 1690, Stephen Lee, son of John, the settler, and Mary (Hart,) his wife, b. 1668, d. June 7th, 1753, aged 87; they were both constituent members of the church at "Great Swamp," both to church in old Farmington, Oct. 5th, 1707; he was located on East street; built the old Hinsdale house, now gone, (1863,) and has been for many years; owned the land from East to Main street.* He was buried in "Christian Lane" cemetery, but she in New Britain, with the following epitaph: "Here lies the body of Mrs. Elizabeth Lee, (the relict of Capt. Stephen Lee, deceased,) who served in the office of midwife forty-five years, until she was ninety years of age; deceased ye 2d of May, 1760, in ye 91st year of her age." She daughter of Isaac Royce, of New London, and Elizabeth (Lathrop,) his wife.†

THEIR CHILDREN.

1. Isaac, b. Sept. 5th, 1691, a physician, m. Dec. 8th, 1713, Mary Hubbard; second, Susanna Wolcott.
2. Child, no name, b. April 18th, 1693, d. in infancy, same day.
3. Elizabeth, b. July 12th, 1694, m. Dec. 28th, 1721, Samuel, son of Joseph Langdon.
4. Sarah, b. Nov. 8th, 1696, m. Jan. 18th, 1721, John Lankton, father of No. (107.)
5. Stephen, b. April 18th, 1700, d. Sept. 17th, 1718.
6. Martha, b. Feb. 17th, 1701, m. Nathaniel Hart; second, m. Joseph Francis.

---

* Will of Capt. Stephen Lee was made Nov. 26th, 1747, and gave his wife, Elizabeth, one-third of his movable estate, and one-half his house, one-third of barn and cow-house, and the service of my negro Richard, so long as she remains my widow, and bears my name, during her life, after which my youngest son, Josiah, shall have liberty to purchase said negro, at his appraised value. Item, I give my eldest son, the north half my lot on which my house stands. Item, I give my second son, above named, Josiah, the south half of my house, and half my home lot, and half of all my lands. Item, I give my daughter, Hannah, so much in bills of credit as to be equal to seventy-four ounces of silver. Item, I give my grandson, Stephen Root, £3. Item, I give my four surviving daughters, viz., to Sarah, wife of John Lankton, the wife of Nathaniel Hart, of Wallingford, Martha; to Mercy, wife of Benjamin Beckley; he calls Hannah above a single woman, and he appointed his wife, Elizabeth, and his son, Isaac, executors of the will.

William Burnham, } Witnesses.
Isaac Norton, }

† The will of Widow Elizabeth Lee, exhibited July 15th, 1760, gives to Isaac, (this is Dr. Isaac,) 5s., to Josiah, 5s., to the heirs of Martha Francis, one-third for the children she had by her first husband, Nathaniel Hart; to my daughter, Mary Beckley, her children, one-third; to the heirs of Hannah Barber, (this is No. 84,) one third, and I ordain my son, Josiah, my executor. Inventory, £60, taken June 6th, 1760.

7. Mary, b. Sept., 1704, m. Benjamin Beckley, of "Beckley quarter."
8. Ebenezer, b. Sept. 14th, 1706, d. Aug. 28th, 1725.
9. Hannah, b. Oct. 15th, 1708, m. Nathaniel North; second, William Barber, see No. (84.)
10. Josiah, b. Aug. 13th, 1711, see No. (33.)

25. "JOSEPH SMITH," son of Joseph, sen. and Lydia, his wife, born probably, 1682, baptized at Farmington, Aug. 10th, 1684; was one of the petitioners for the "Great Swamp Society," 1705, m. Jan. 19th, 1707–8, Mary Royce, daughter of Isaac, of Wallingford, and Elizabeth (Lathrop,) his wife. He lived on East street, the old home of the Smiths, in which were five Josephs, in as many generations. He owned the covenant in Farmington, Sept. 24th, 1710.

THEIR CHILDREN.

1. Joseph, b. July 13th, 1710, bap. Sept. 24th, 1710, in old Farmington, see No. (29.)
2. Azariah, b. Dec. 28th, 1712, m. Aug. 14th, 1740, Mary, daughter of Joseph Root, of "Great Swamp Society."
3. Jedediah, b. Feb. 12th, 1715–16, see No. (31.)
4. Esther, b. , d. May 18th, 1725.
5. Elijah, b. Oct. 29th, 1721, see No. (XXX) of half-way covenant.

26. "REBECCA, wife of Daniel Dewy;" this is Rebecca Curtiss, daughter of Thomas "Curtice" and Mary (Goodrich,) his wife, born 1705, m. Jan. 27th, 1731; her father was an early settler of Great Swamp; was, 1716, seated in the third "pue," with Joseph Smith and John Standley and others; for location, see No. (85;) she died March 6th, 1781, æ. 76; head-stone in old part of cemetery in New Britain.

27. "HANNAH, wife of Gideon Griswold," daughter of Joseph Root, of "Great Swamp Society," and his wife, Hannah (Kellogg,) of Hartford, b. July 13th, 1719. She was sister of No. (54,) and m ; they lived near where Horatio Waldo (now, 1863, does;) he was son of David Griswold and Severance , his wife, born Oct. 2d, 1717; was a large land-holder, and driving farmer; he "owned the covenant" in Newington, Jan. 27th, 1754; he died Sept. 3d, 1807, aged 90; she died June 19th, 1814, aged 95; she was born July 13th, 1719, at Newington, near Kensington line.

THEIR CHILDREN.

1. Elijah, b. , bap. Aug. 23d, 1752, at Newington, died , aged 16; stone in New Britain.
2. Samuel, b. Jan. 15th, 1754, bap. Jan. 27th, 1754, at Newington, died Sept. 2d, 1776, Revolutionary Army at New York.
3. Ashbel, b. May 12th, 1757, m. Elizabeth Woodruff, daughter of Noah.
4. Hannah, b. April 3d, 1760, bap. April 13th, 1760, m. Joel Smith; she d. March 31st, 1786, aged 26.
5. Lydia, b. Nov. 24th, 1765, m. Sept. 15th, 1788, Michael De Recor, a French soldier, who was taken a prisoner from Burgoyne's army.

28. "MARTHA, wife of Samuel Goodrich;" this was Martha Lankton,

daughter of John, and his wife, Sarah (Lee,) b. Dec. 31st, 1724, m. Sept. 24th, 1747, No. (69;) they were both dismissed and recommended to Kensington by letter, and received there Dec. 23d, 1764; she died Feb. 22d, 1810, aged 76, at Luther Stocking's, in Kensington.

29. "JOSEPH SMITH, jun.," son of No. (25) and Mary (Ryce,) his wife, b. July 13th, 1710, m. March 2d, 1737, No. (30;) she d. May 21st, 1764, aged 45, when he m. second, Sept. 1766, Widow Esther Deming, No. (167;) he kept a tavern on East street, probably the homestead of his father; he went by the title of *landlord* many years; he left an estate of £1,146 13s.; he d. March 25th, 1792, aged 82; Capt. Jonathan Belden, executor; his second wife, Esther, No. (167,) died June 21st, 1804, aged 82.

30. "Wife of Joseph Smith, jun;" this was Thankful Hubbard, of Middletown, daughter of George and Marcy (Seymour,) his wife, daughter of Capt. Richard, b. July 23d, 1719, m. March 2d, 1737, No. (29.)

THEIR CHILDREN.

1. Elnathan, b. Nov. 3d, O. S. 1738, m. July 9th, 1767, No. (156.)
2. Gideon b. Dec. 1st, 1740, d. Nov. 30th, 1762, at Havanna, in the French war, Capt. Patterson's company.
3. Joseph b. Oct. 11th, 1744; was in the war of Revolution; m. an only daughter of Dr. White, of Philadelphia.
4. Thankful, b. Nov. 17th, 1746, m. 1st, 1766, Isaac Langdon, before Rev. Samuel Clark.
5. Gordon, b. Aug. 12th, 1749, m. Oct. 11th, 1772, Ruth Judd, daughter of Capt. Phineas; he died in the army of the Revolution.
6. Abigail, b. April 15th, 1752, m. Dec. 17th, 1769, No. (124.)
7. Rhoda, b. Sept. 15th, 1753, m. John Doge, of Boston; descendants in Vermont.
8. Dolly, born 1762, bap. April 29th, 1764, m. Oct. 10th, 1790, Lemuel Smith, of Ebenezer, jun., see No. (437.)

31. "JEDEDIAH SMITH," son of Joseph and his wife, Mary (Royce,) born Feb. 12th, 1715–16, m. Jan. 1st, 1740–1, No. (32;) he lived near his brother, No. (29;) he probably m. second, Elizabeth Kellogg, Oct. 29th, 1777; she of Newington.

32. Wife of Jedediah Smith; she daughter of Joseph Cogswell and Anna (Orvice,) his wife; her name Susanna, born Aug. 10th, 1720, in Far. South Farms, alias Southington.

THEIR CHILDREN.

1. Mary, b. Jan. 28th, 1741–2.
2. Anna, b. Nov. 1st, 1744.
3. Huldah, b. Jan. 4th, 1749, m. Nov. 5th, 1772, Joseph, son of first Elijah Hart.

33. "JOSIAH LEE," the youngest son of Capt. Stephen and his wife, No. (24,) b. Aug. 13th, 1711, m. Nov. 3d, 1737, No. (34;) he was chosen deacon April 1st, 1763, to supply the loss of Deacon Patterson, at the Havanna, 1762. He too was a military man, as appears from the follow-

ing: "I Stephen Lee, for parental love to my son, Josiah, and his wife, Hannah, do give them the north half of my dwelling-house, and also half my barn, garden and orchard, with use of cellar; it is understood that my son is bound on the present expedition against our northern enemies, the French!! if any accident befall him that he return no more, his wife is to have free liberty to use, occupy and enjoy the premises as above, so long as she remains his widow.

Dated April 15th, 1747."

He, like his father before him, was captain of the militia company of Farmington. About the year 1774, he with his son-in-law, John Patterson, Esq., moved to Lenox, Mass., and subsequently to Chenango county, New York, where he died, 1797. He had built what is now called the "Skinner house," and sold it with his barn and his farm of sixty acres, with half the irons of the saw-mill, by the meeting house, and half of five and a half acres of land there, to John Richards, for £555, March 16th, 1776. His ratable estate, 1763, stood in the list of that year, £121. The house probably built soon after the decease of his father, 1753, and the distribution of his estate.

34. "Wife of Josiah Lee," Hannah Warren, of Glastenbury, probably daughter of Abraham and his wife, Experience (Stephens,) b. Oct. 19th, 1714, m. Nov. 3d, 1737, No. (33;) she was sister of "Will Warren, the hermit," and sister of the mother of No. (91.)

THEIR CHILDREN.

1. Elizabeth, b. , the only child they had to live to adult years; she m. June 2d, 1766, John Patterson, Esq., son of Deacon John, and they both "owned the covenant" Jan. 25th, 1767; moved to Lenox, 1774. See Covenant list, No. (XXVII.)

35. "Isaac Lee," the second son of Doctor Isaac and Mary (Hubbard,) of Middletown, his wife, b. Jan. 17th, 1716, m. July 10th, 1740, No. (36;) he was chosen one of the standing committee of the church, at its first meeting, and a deacon Sept. 3d, 1772, to supply the loss of Deacon Elijah Hart. He is known as Colonel Lee, and was a marked character, strong, physically, mentally and morally. As a magistrate some thirty years, he was a "terror to evil doers," and a "praise to them that do well." He was a farmer by occupation, and was of Herculean strength. He was the leader of the "ring" in athletic sports and gymnastics, especially in wrestling, so common in his age. He is the man to whom Mrs. Willard alludes in her poem of "Stealing the Bride," and No. (36) was the bride. Many anecdotes are related of him, such as throwing barrels of cider into his cart, as common men would pumpkins; throwing to the ground the big bull; and thrice throwing the big Indian, in Farmington street. He lost, however, the bride he so exultingly carried off, for she died Nov. 2d, 1770, with a cancer, when he married second, Dec. 30th, 1772, No. (170;) his residence is still standing, 1867, near the foot of Dublin Hill, east side of

Main street. He was one of the two men in New Britain who were treated with the utmost reverence. When Dr. Smalley or he were approaching or passing, all hats were doffed, even by men laboring in the field some distance from the road. His second wife died May 17th, 1782, of small pox, when he married third, Oct. 9th, 1783, No. (175.) He was active in securing the incorporation of the society, in building the first house of worship, and after, viz., 1784–5, in securing the incorporation of the town of Berlin, with our share in the school fund. He died Dec. 13th, 1802, aged 86; his head-stone, very truly, and according to the custom of that age, gives him two titles, Colonel and Esquire. Col. Isaac Lee and Gen. Selah Hart, were delegates to the State Convention, held at Hartford, Jan. 3d, 1788, for the adoption or rejection of the Constitution for the United States.

36. "Wife of Isaac Lee," daughter of Isaac Norton and his wife, Elizabeth (Galpin,) of Stratford, born Dec. 20th, 1718, at Kensington; name Tabitha (Norton;) she was the mother of his children, the baptisms of whom are lost with the loss of the records of Rev. William Burnham, of Kensington, and the like of other families.

1. Theodore, b. May 21st, 1741, d. March 5th, 1742.
2. Theodore, b. Sept., 26th, 1743, m. Nov. 10th, 1768, Olive Boardman, settled in Torringford.
3. Chloe, b. Jan. 15th, 1746, m. July 9th, 1767, Elnathan Smith, son of Joseph.
4. Isaac, b. Jan. 11th, 1749, d. March 16th, 1749.
5. Isaac, b. March 29th, 1752, m. May 25th, 1773, No. (154.)
6. Asahel, b. Feb. 22d, 1759, bap. March 4th, 1759, m. April 30th, 1772, Sarah Hun; he died 1776, in army of Revolution, at Scheensborough, New York, aged 27.

37. "Stephen Lee," son of Dr. Isaac Lee and his wife, Mary (Hubbard,) b. March 16th, 1723, m. Feb. 6th, 1746, No. (73;) he inherited from his father the old homestead of his grandfather, Capt. Stephen Lee, called later the "Hinsdale house," at the south corner of East and Smalley streets. He died Sept. 14th, 1783, aged 60½ years, at Lenox, Mass., to which place he moved about 1777. He sold to Elijah Hinsdale, Feb. 12th, 1777, for £208, (except the incumbrance of his father,) his home lot of two acres, and house, his barn lot of twenty-four acres, and his lot next east of the meeting-house, containing eight acres.

CHILDREN OF STEPHEN AND KATA LEE.

1. Ashbel, b. Feb. 28th, 1747; lived in Lee, Mass.; m. April 30th, 1772, Sarah Hun.
2. Timothy, b. Oct. 19th, 1748, m. April 23d, 1772, Lucy Camp; settled in Pittsfield, Mass.
3. Mabel, b. Feb. 19th, 1750, m. April 22d, 1773, Daniel Luddington.
4. Kata, b. Nov. 25th, 1751, bap. Nov. 27th, 1751, at Newington.
5. Martha, b. Nov. 25th, 1754, m. May 17th, 1773, Ladwick Hotchkiss, No. (278.)
6. Anna, b. June 22d, 1756, m. Feb. 1st, 1781, Abel Hubbard.
7. Sarah, b. Aug. 22d, 1758, bap. Aug. 27th, 1758.

38. JAMES JUDD, son of No. (22) and No. (23,) m. 1749, Hannah (Andrus,) daughter of Daniel, jun. and Mabel (Goff,) his wife, b. Sept. 8th, 1723, near Wethersfield line, at the "Great Swamp." They lived on the old homestead of his father; owned the saw-mill long known as "Judd's Mill;" he d. Feb. 15th, 1783, aged 66; his widow d. Dec. 29th, 1789, aged 67, with the following on her head-stone: "Blessed and happy are those who die in the Lord." His will was proved in court Feb. 17th, 1783; names in it two sons and four daughters.

THEIR CHILDREN.

1. Hannah, b. Sept. 27th, 1750, m Jan. 4th, 1770, Leonard Belden, son of Ezra; she died Sept. 10th, 1780, aged 30.

2 Abigail, b. June 5th, 1752, m. Jan. 6th, 1774, Abel Clark, son of John; she died April 27th, 1829.

3. Lydia, b. Oct. 6th, 1754, m. Feb. 6th, 1777, Joseph Andrews, son of No. (53;) she died April 21st, 1804.

4. James, b. April 22d, 1755, d. July 13th, 1755, aged three months, nine days.

5. James, b. Jan. 27th, 1757, bap. Jan. 30th, 1757, m. 1779, No. (318;) he bap. in Kensington.

6. Asahel, b. May 24th, 1759, bap. May 27th, 1759, d. Oct. 13th, 1777, aged 19.

7. Daniel, b. Aug. 14th, 1761, bap. Aug. 23d, 1761, m. Irene Hitchcock, see No. (435.)

8. Anne, b. March 19th, 1764, d. Oct. 31st, 1775, in her 12th year.

9. Sarah, b. 1768, m. Oct. 31st, 1794, Moses Smith, son of Samuel; she died Aug. 24th, 1833, aged 66.

39. URIAH JUDD, son of No. (22) and No. (23,) b. Dec. 28th, 1713, m. Dec. 20th, 1744, Mabel Bidwell; she d. Aug. 25th, 1745, when he m. second, Feb. 19th, 1747, No. (40;) he lived just south of the first church, probably where Alvin North does now, (1861;) he deeded, 1756, land for a highway through his farm and past his house, three rods wide; he removed to Pittsfield, Mass., May, 1769, and to Lenox, 1774, where both died, leaving six children.

40. Wife of URIAH JUDD, Mercy Seymor, daughter of Samuel Seymor, and his wife, Hannah (North,) daughter of Thomas, b. Nov. 13th, 1708, grand-daughter of "Capt. Richard Seamer," of the stockade.

CHILDREN.

1. Uriah, b. Dec. 20t, 1745, m. 1772, Lucy Miller; m. second, Elizabeth Brattle.
2. Mehitable, b. , m. Benjamin Bush, of Sheffield.
3. Samuel, m. 1774, Naomi Noble, of Pittsfield, daughter of Luke.
4. Benjamin, b. July 3d, 1755, m. 1776, Keziah Jacobs, of Northbury parish, Conn.
5. Mercy, b. , m. Rufus Parker, of Lenox; she d. May 13th, 1837.
6. Molly, b. May 7th, 1761, m. Titus Parker, of Lenox; she was living, 1850.

41. NATHAN JUDD, son of No. (22) and No. (23,) b. Aug. 24th, 1719, m. Feb. 3d, 1743, No. (42;) they lived on the corner of East Main and East street, the north side; his estate settled 1764; amount £442; James and Uriah, his brothers, administrators; Ladwick Hotchkiss, Daniel Dewy

and Noah Stanley, appraisers; done Oct. 9th, 1764; he died Sept. 1st, 1764, aged 45.

42. Wife of Nathan Judd, Thankful Wright; she d. Aug. 25th, 1764.

THEIR CHILDREN.

1. Anna, b. 1744, m. 1771, Daniel North, of Daniel; she died 1805, aged 60.
2. Thankful, b. 1747.
3. Levi, b. 1749.
4. Susanna, b. 1752.
5. Mary, b. 1754.
6. Rosanna, b. 1756.
7. Nathan, b. 1758, bap. April 5th, 1758, by Rev. E. Booge, of Northington, at New Britain; "his church record;" this was just two weeks before the ordination of Mr. Smalley.

43. PHINEAS JUDD, son of Deacon Anthony, b. Feb. 4th, 1715, was a captain; m. No. (44;) he inherited the homestead of his father, (now, 1862,) owned and occupied by William Ellis. His father, for parental love, 1748, gave him five pieces of land and half his house; A. D. 1763, he became guardian for his nephew, James North, son of James, deceased, and John Hooker, Esq. certified that the boy was fourteen years old the 18th day of Jan., 1763. His will was proved Jan. 4th, 1791. Capt. Judd died Dec. 22d, 1790, aged 75; he enlisted into the army of the Revolution during the war, Feb. 24th, 1777; had a bounty of £10.

44. Wife of Phineas Judd; this was Ruth (Seymour,) daughter of , and sister of Sarah (Seymour,) mother of James North, Esq.; she was born 1724. Widow Ruth Judd died Nov. 23d, 1799, aged 75.

THEIR CHILDREN.

1. Phineas, jun., b. Dec. 13th, 1750, m. Dec. 17th, 1780, Elizabeth Mazuzen; he died 1784, when she m. second, No. (118.)
2. Anthony, b. Aug. 1st, 1752, m. Aug. 29th, 1782, Rebecca Belden, of Ezra; they moved to Owego.
3. Ruth, b. March 31st, 1754, m. Oct. 11th, 1772, Gordon Smith; m. second, Elijah Root, of Plainville.
4. Susanna, b. Feb. 7th, 1756, m. July 7th, 1774, Elijah Smith, jun.; moved to Owego, N. Y.
5. Job, b. Oct. 21st, 1757, m. Andrus, of Glastenbury, sister of Daniel; went to Owego, N. Y.
6. Isaac, b. ; removed to Owego, N. Y.
7. Hannah, b. March 15th, 1761, bap. March 15th, 1761, at New Britain, m. March 17th, 1785, Martin Hooker.
8. Selah, b. July 17th, 1763, bap. July 17th, 1763, at New Britain, m. Elizabeth Andrews, of Hezekiah; he died 1788, and she m. second, Dec. 16th, 1790, Roger Francis, of Newington and West Hartford.

45. JOHN JUDD, son of Deacon Anthony and his first wife, Susannah (Woodford,) b. April 25th, 1718, m. No. (46;) they lived near where their descendants (now, 1863,) do Deacon Morton and Oliver Judd. He one of the early settlers of New Britain village, perhaps next after Nathan

Booth and Joshua Mather. Tradition says that he boarded the candidates for settlement over the new parish; that among them (for there were several,) was one overcome by the temptation of a nice imported "case" that stood open in a closet next his room, indulged too freely, and the fact having in more senses than one leaked out, he for a farewell sermon shrewdly took the text, 1st Thess. ii. 18. "Wherefore we would have come unto you (even I Paul) once and again; but Satan hindered us." Left. John Judd died Oct. 16th, 1781, aged 64; his inventory, £466.

46. "Wife of John Judd;" her maiden name, Mary Burnham, b. Feb. 7th, 1721–22, to Rev. William and his first wife, Hannah, daughter of Mrs. Judith Wolcott, of Wethersfield. She is said to have been a woman of great beauty and accomplishments. Mary, the widow of Left. John Judd, died May 22d, 1801, aged 80.

THEIR CHILDREN.

1. John, b. Feb. 14th, 1746, m. No. (135.)
2. Mary, b. Aug. 31st, 1748, m. No. (115.)
3. Seth, b. April 8th, 1751, m. Oct., 1772, Lydia Richards, of John; he died 1777, killed by the accidental discharge of a gun, in the Revolutionary army.
4. Rhoda, b. Jan. 9th, 1754, m. No. (149.)

47. "Joshua Mather," son of Ensign Atherton Mather, of Windsor and Suffield, and Mary, his second wife, b. Nov. 26th, 1706, at Windsor, Conn., a descendant of Rev. Richard; the emigrant, lived at the "Sugden house," near the present site of Frederick North's mansion; he m. No. (48.) Tradition says, while he was upon a journey, and stopping at a village over the Sabbath, where the pulpit was vacant, the people learning his name, and observing his black coat, invited him to preach, nothing doubting his authority or ability. He, (probably hoping to do good,) accepted the invitation, and delivered the only sermon he had with him; but at the intermission of services, he fell into a great quandary, for being only a plain farmer, and no second sermon with him, the hour for the second service at hand, and no expedient yet devised, the people very opportunely sent a deputation, which at once relieved his distress, saying they were so greatly interested in his discourse, they wished him to repeat it in the afternoon. He died May 16th, 1777, aged 71.

48. "Wife of Joshua Mather," Hannah (Booth,) daughter of Robert, sen. and Ann (Hollister,) his wife, b. July 22d, 1716, sister of No. (65,) and near neighbor for life; she died April 8th, 1777, aged 61.

THEIR CHILDREN.

1. Cotton, born Sept. 19th, 1737.
2. David, born Oct. 7th, 1738, m. June 1st, 1767, No. (139.)
3. Thomas, born Sept. 7th, 1741, married March 12th, 1764, Huldah Bull, sister of Deacon Bull, of Farmington; he settled in Farmington, as a physician, and died there Aug. 10th, 1766, aged 25.
4. Hannah, born Jan. 25th, 1745, m. Oct. 1st, 1767, William Lewis, son of Capt. Jonathan.

5. Elenor, born Sept. 27th, 174 , record illegible.
6. Elisha, born April 19th, 1749.
7. Joshua, jun., b.

49. "ELIJAH HART," son of Deacon Thomas of Kensington, and Sarah (Thompson, of Farmington, his wife, b. June 15th, 1711, bap. Aug. 12th, 1711, at old Farmington, m. Dec. 26th, 1734, No. (50;) settled in "Hart quarter," at the southwest portion of the society, a near neighbor to Judah Hart, sen., and from these came the name to this section; his house was near the one now called the "State house;" he was a very economical and industrious farmer, greatly athletic, yet in carrying a stick of fencing timber on his shoulder, he stepped into a hole in the ground, and the weight crushed him; he died in consequence, and the following epitaph: "In memory of the justly esteemed and much lamented Deacon Elijah Hart, who provided for his own and served his generation with great diligence and fidelity, even to the last day of his life, was taken suddenly to the inheritance above, on the third day of August, 1772, in the 61st year of his age." The record says Sergeant Elijah Hart was chosen and appointed deacon at a meeting of the church soon after its incorporation. From the death of Deacon Hart, Dr. Smalley kept a record of deaths in his parish, which unfortunately had been before neglected. He was grandson of Capt. Thomas Hart and his wife, Ruth (Howkins,) who located in Stanley quarter, and belonged to Newington Society. *He* was son of Deacon Stephen, the first settler of the name, first at Cambridge, Mass., then at Hartford, and last at (Tunxis,) Farmington; he was a deacon in each of these places. Capt. Thomas stood high in military rank in Farmington, and was buried 1723, with military honors. His will, dated 1721, in which he gives his children over 2,000 acres of land.

50. "Wife of Elijah Hart," Abigail (Goodrich,) daughter of Allen and Elizabeth, his wife, daughter of David Goodrich, Esq., of Wethersfield; she, Abigail, born Dec. 14th, 1714; she was a woman of great force of character; she died Jan. 21st, 1809, at Simsbury, (with her only daughter, Mary, who m. Jonathan Eno,) at the advanced age of 95 years. She was sister of No. (69) and No. (63.)

THEIR CHILDREN.

1. Elijah, born Sept. 26th, 1735, see No. (52.)
2. Thomas, born Jan. 12th, 1738, see No. (94.)
3. Jehudi, born Dec. 12th, 1739, see No. (118.)
4. Josiah, born April 28th, 1742, see No. (127.)
5. Mary, born Dec. 26th, 1744, see list that "owned the covenant."
6. Benjamin, b. Oct. 16th, 1747, see No. (131.)
7. Joseph, born May 17th, 1750, see No. (210.)
8. Elizur, born Dec. 25th, 1752, see No. (231.)
9. Aaron, born Oct. 1st, 1756, bap. Oct. 31st, 1756, in Kensington, died Feb. 12th, 1761, aged five years. Abedmelech, a servant of Deacon Hart, was baptized at the

same time with his youngest son, Aaron, by Rev. Samuel Clark of Kensington. The family record of this father, (the first Elijah,) was in his own hand on a leaf of a Bible printed in London, 1696, and can be seen at Dr. Hart's, in Southington, 1863.

51. "JUDAH HART," grandson of John, sen., the man who headed the first petition A. D. 1705, for a new parish at the southeast corner of Farmington. He was son of John, jun. and Esther (Gridley,) his wife, born Oct. 25th, 1709, m. Feb. 20th, 1734–5, Anne Norton, daughter of Sergeant John, of Kensington, and his wife, Anna (Thompson,) b. Jan. 15th, 1718; he probably settled in "Hart quarter" soon after his marriage, which occurred the same year with that of his neighbor and kinsman, Deacon Elijah Hart, the first. His house is still standing, and in good condition, opposite the school-house in District No. 4. He was a man of more than ordinary intelligence, of much force of character, often employed in public matters. Anne, his wife, was cousin to Tabitha, the wife of Col. Lee, and these families were intimate; she died, and he married second, Sept. 27th, 1759, Widow Sarah (Seymour) North, the widow of James North, sen., and the mother of his son, James North, Esq. Mr. Judah Hart died Sept. 14th, 1784, aged 75. Neither of his wives' names appear on the church records. Sarah, consort of Mr. Judah Hart, died Aug. 20th, 1781, aged 61. His will was dated Sept. 6th, 1784, in which he gives his son, Judah, jun., all his estate on condition he pay all his debts, funeral charges, tomb stones, and the following legacies, viz: to the heirs of son, Elias Hart, deceased, 20s.; to the heirs of my daughter, Ann, late deceased; to my daughter, Esther, the wife of Eliphaz Alvord, Esq.; to the heirs of my son, John, deceased, 10s.; and I appoint my son, Judah, jun., my sole executor. The will was exhibited and proved in Probate Court at Farmington, Dec. 6th, 1784.

Isaac Andrus,
Thomas Booth,
Lemuel Hotchkiss, } Witnesses.

THEIR CHILDREN.

1. Elias, born Feb. 25th, 1735-6, m. Oct. 17th, 1753, Hope Whaples, (No. (XXIX.)
2. Judah, born Sept. 5th, 1737, died Nov. 3d, 1745, aged 8.
3. Anna, b. May 22d, 1739, m.
4. Esther, } twins, b. April 4th, 1742, { m. Nov. 29th, 1764, Eliphaz Alvord, Esq., [of Winchester.
5. Lois, } twins, b. April 4th, 1742, { died at birth.
6. John, born Jan. 20th, 1743, m. Oct., 1764, Anna Deming; he No. (101.)
7. Roger, born May 10th, 1745.
8. Ruth, born Jan. 19th, 1748.
9. Judah, second of name, born Sept. 10th, 1750, (see No. (140.)

52. "ELIJAH HART," jun., son of No. (49) and his wife, No. (50,) born Sept. 26th, 1735, m. Sarah Gilbert, daughter of Ebenezer and his wife, Marcy (Cowles,) born May 11th, 1737. He first located in Hart quarter, near the present residence, 1867, of Levi O. Smith; but at middle life he built near the mills, and lived in the north part, and deeded, Sept. 10th,

1793, the south part to his son, Elijah, third of the name. He was a man of puritanical habits, stern virtue, and of great diligence and economy. He was a plain farmer, with a large family, and large property. He was chosen deacon June 1st, 1780; his business was all laid aside by four o'clock Saturday afternoon, by himself, workmen and servants, his face shaved, his long boots brushed, his cows milked before sunset; his best boots would last him seven years, and his best surtout coat, twenty years. He led the singing in church, many years, having a grand voice, and good musical taste for that age, (not operatic.) He was deacon twenty years, and died Dec. 10th, 1800, aged 66; his widow died Sept. 22d, 1809, aged 73. He was admitted to Kensington church Dec. 25th, 1757, only four months before this church was organized. No evidence appears that his wife was ever a member.

THEIR CHILDREN.

1. Elijah, born May 7th, 1759, bap. May 13th, 1759, see No. (181.)
2. Aaron, born Oct. 16th, 1761, bap. Oct. 25th, 1761, see No. (247.)
3. Ozias, born Aug. 8th, 1768, see No. (281.)
4. Sarah, born Feb. 21st, 1765, bap. Feb. 24th, 1765, m. March 3d, 1785, No. (296.)
5. Selina, born Aug. 30th, 1770, bap. Aug. 30th, 1770, m. Dec. 30th, 1790, No. (240.)
6. Olive, born 1775, bap. Aug. 27th, 1775, m. Aug. 8th, 1803, Seth Merill, son of Allyn and his wife, Mary (Andrews.) They lived in the yellow house on Dublin Hill. The father, Allyn Merill was killed raising Farmington meeting-house, July 11th, 1771, aged 37, at one o'clock P. M.

53. "MOSES ANDREWS," son of John, of Newington, and Mary (Goffe,) his wife, born May 12th, 1722, m. Nov. 10th, 1748, No. (54;) they came to this place soon after marriage, and occupied the house still standing on West Main street, one mile west of the village; the house and barn, with the home lot was given to Mrs. Andrews by her brother, Joseph Root, jun., who had built the house for his own use, but was suddenly taken away by death, 1748, aged 28; the lady to whom he was betrothed having suddenly died before him. Mr. Andrews was a short thick set man, of the kindest natural disposition, a carpenter by trade, and he was greatly respected for piety and benevolence; he was chosen one of the church committee Sept. 3d, 1772; his military title was Sergeant, and seldom if ever omitted in writing or speaking his name; he died May 17th, 1806, aged 85.

54. "Wife of Moses Andrews;" she was Lydia (Root,) daughter of Joseph, sen. and his wife, No. (56,) born Oct. 5th, 1725; a woman of great Christian patience and meekness; she fitted out for the Revolutionary Army, six of her nine sons, by her own industry; she died July 6th, 1806, aged 82.

THEIR CHILDREN.

1. Samuel, born Nov. 2d, 1749, see No. (124.)
2. Moses, born Dec. 15th, 1750, died Dec., 1752, buried in Christian Lane cemetery.

3. Joseph, born Dec. 23d, 1751, m. Feb. 6th, 1777, Lydia Judd; m. second, Amy Cowles.

4. Moses, second of name, born April 7th, 1755, see No. (191.)

5. Isaac, born Jan. 31st, 1757, m. No. (298;) he a physician.

6. John, born Nov. 29th, 1758, bap. Dec. 3d, 1758, m. May 10th, 1792, No. (249.)

7. Jesse, born Dec. 19th, 1760, bap. Jan. 11th, 1761, a physician, died April 4th, 1790, unmarried.

8. Nathaniel, born Oct. 15th, 1762, m. 1786, No. (184;) m. second, Oct. 3d, 1790, Jerusha Sage.

9. Seth, born Aug. 19th, 1765, bap. Aug. 25th, 1765, died Nov. 18th, 1766, in the second year of his age.

55. "WILLIAM PATTERSON," brother of Edward, the tinman, of Berlin; they had a sister, Ann, all born at Dungannon, county Tyrone, Ireland, (the seat of the O'Neal's, the great enemies of England.) He was in Wethersfield, 1747; his wife, sister of Solomon Dunham, Esq., see No. (82;) he lived in the present Rhodes house, for in 1759, he deeded for £300, twenty-six acres, bounded east on Wethersfield line, north and west on highway, with my dwelling-house and all the buildings thereon standing, except the shop of Ladwick Hotchkiss, and the land it stands on, to Rev. John Smalley. It seems probable they left the place soon after, for the Ken. church record says, Wm. Patterson and his wife were received April 11th, 1762, to our communion, from New Britain, by letter of recommendation. He deeded, 1777, to Jedediah Norton, (of the present limits of Berlin,) 130 acres, with house, barn, &c. for £800. He is supposed to have been of Scottish origin, and of the sturdy Presbyterians, who settled in the north of Ireland.

THEIR CHILDREN.

1. Esther, b. July 26th, 1752, m. Oct. 10th, 1769, Gershom Graham, at Kensington.
2. John, b. , supposed to have moved to Piermont, N. H.
3. Elizabeth, b. Jan. 18th, 1757.
4. Sarah, } twins, b. Nov. 21st, 1758, bap. Nov. 26th, 1758, m. May, 1801, Moses Foster, of Newington.
5. Susanna, } supposed to have died young.
6. William, b. Nov. 14th, 1760, bap. Nov. 16th, 1760, m. Jan. 17th, 1788, Wealthy Dorrance.
7. Thomas, b. March 7th, 1762, bap. March 7th, 1762, m. March 25th, 1784, Prudence Williams.
8. David, b. Aug. 7th, 1763, with but one ear, bap. in Kensington, Aug. 14th, 1763.
9. George, b. Jan. 7th, 1765, bap. in Kensington, Jan. 13th, 1765.

56. "Widow Hannah Root," her maiden name, Hannah Kellogg, said to be of Hartford, m. Oct. 20th, 1715, Joseph Root, son of John and Mary (Woodruff,) his wife, bap. March 19th, 1693; they lived in Wethersfield, near Kensington; she spent the close of life with her daughter, Lydia, wife of Moses Andrus, for she signed the petition to the General Assembly, 1752, with those then living in the limits of New Britain, and directly west of it. She died March 19th, 1771, aged 84; the head-stone to her

grave near the front fence in the old part of the cemetery in New Britain. He died Oct. 15th, 1747, aged 56, leaving an estate of £1,988 11s. 7d. He was buried in the old cemetery at "Christian Lane," with his sons, Samuel and Joseph. This family lived early in Hartford.

THEIR CHILDREN.

From Hartford Town Record.

1. Samuel, born June 28th, 1716; made his will Oct. 12th, 1747; gave all to three sisters and brother, Joseph; he died Oct. 27th, 1747, aged 32.
2. Thankful, born July 15th, 1717, m. 1736, Nathaniel North, son of Nathaniel, of Thomas; she died 1747.
3. Hannah, born July 13th, 1719, see No. (27.)
4. Joseph, born June 4th, 1720; will dated 1748; gave all to sisters and cousins; died May 29th, 1748, aged 28.
5. Mary, born April 16th, 1722, m. Aug. 14th, 1740, Azariah, son of Joseph Smith.
6. Lydia, born Oct. 5th, 1725, see No. (54.)
7. Benjamin, born July 9th, 1733.
8. Temperance, born 1734, m. Oct. 8th, 1752, Job, son of Samuel Bronson; she died May 19th, 1778, aged 45; they lived at the corner west of "Burritt Hill;" hence the name, "Job's corner."
9. Sara, born , m. Peck.

57. "John Kelsey," son of John, sen. and his wife, Mary (Buck,) daughter of Ezekiel, all of Wethersfield, born Nov. 22d, 1706, m. April 26th, 1739, No. (58;) he lived in a house long since gone, which stood west and opposite the present school-house, in the south-east district; he was brother to Enoch Kelsey, sen., who lived near David Webster, towards Beckley quarter. They had,

Amos, born April 11th, 1743, and perhaps others.

58. "Wife of John Kelsey;" she was Martha Bronson, born Oct. 18th, 1711, to William and his wife, Eunice (Barnes;) she was aided by the town late in life; she was remarkable for punctuality and good season at church; when asked why she went so early, replied, "to have time to pray;" she died in the autumn of 1800, at the house of James Booth, sen., aged 89.

59. "Joseph Woodruff," son of Joseph and Elizabeth (Curtice,) of Wethersfield, his wife, born July 7th, 1716, m. May 29th, 1735, No. (60;) they lived on a road running east and west between the "Bachelor lots," east of the present town-house; the highway long since sold and shut up; the location of these houses of Woodruff, some two or three families, is indicated by the brickbats that plough up; he died Feb. 5th, 1777, aged 61, of small-pox. He was a captain.

60. "Wife of Joseph Woodruff," her name, Margaret (North,) daughter of Nathaniel, of (Northington,) Avon, and Margaret (Holcomb,) of Simsbury, his wife, born Jan. 2d, 1713; she was sister of No. (68.)

THEIR CHILDREN.

1. Margaret, born April 11th, 1736, m. Jonathan Whaples; m. second, Left. Elijah Porter, of Farmington.
2. Dorcas, born April 8th, 1739, m. Cornelius Dunham.
3. Sarah, born 1744, m. May, 1775, Asahel Goodrich, son of Allen.
4. Joseph, jun., born Sept. 4th, 1753, m. Sept. 5th, 1771, Rhoda Hollister, daughter of Stephen; he m. second, Feb. 17th, 1785, Abigail, the widow of Giles Hooker, and daughter of No. (8;) she died, when he m. third, Widow Wright, whose maiden name was Prudence Spellman, of Granville; among his large family was Erastus, now, 1863, of Hartford.

61. "SIMMONS WOODRUFF," son of John, born Jan. 5th, 1710–11, bap. July 31st, 1711, in old Farmington, m. No. (62;) lived near No. (59) He inherited his father's homestead. His will dated March 17th, 1767, made his wife, Sarah, and his son, Asa, executors. In the settlement of his estate, he is said to be of Hartford, late deceased. The following from Farmington town records shows where his location once was, viz: Thomas Hart and Jonathan Lewis, town committee, sold on the first day of April, 1746, to Joseph and Simmons Woodruff, two acres of the east end of a highway that runs east and west between the "Bacheldor lots," so called, butted east on Wethersfield line, and west on the remainder of the highway. He died 1767, at Hartford, aged 57.

62. "Wife of Simmons Woodruff," her name, Sarah.

THEIR CHILDREN.

1. Asa, born Dec. 10th, 1745.
2. Mary, born Jan. 5th, 1750–1.
3. Sarah, born June 26th, 1753.
4. Guardian, born July 14th, 1755.
5. Martin, born Oct. 19th, 1757.
6. Huldah, born , bap. Sept. 3d, 1758.

63. "JEDEDIAH GOODRICH," son of Allen and Elizabeth, his wife, b. July 24th, 1717, m. No. (64,) lived at the corner on East street, next east of the present school-house of south-east district. He is spoken of by the few who remember him, as a kind, "clever" man, and good neighbor; he died Oct. 13th, 1803, in his 87th year, at the house of his son-in-law, No. (168.)

64. "Wife of Jedediah Goodrich," she was Mercy Hooker, daughter of Samuel and his wife, Marcy Leet, of Guilford, born Oct. 22d, 1719, at Kensington; she died June 13th, 1800, aged 81, of a cancer on one side of her head, of enormous size. She was great-grand-daughter of Rev. Samuel Hooker, of Farmington.

THEIR CHILDREN.

1. Mercy, born Jan. 1st, 1751, see No. (120.)
2. Abigail, born Oct. 30th, 1753, see No. (154.)
3. Thomas, born June 20th, 1762, died July 1st, 1764, in third year of age.

65. "NATHAN BOOTH," eldest son of Robert, from Stratford, and his wife, Ann (Hollister,) from Glastenbury. He was born Aug. 6th, 1721, m. No. (66;) he is called the first settler within the limits of the borough of New Britain, and to have cut the first tree; he was about the age of John Judd, sen. and probably located about 1746, near the present Methodist church, some four rods south-east, where Arch street was opened nearly a century later. He was a large farmer and landholder, and died Dec. 31st, 1802, aged 82, on the same month and year in which his cotemporary, Col. Lee died. His house, after owned and occupied by his son, Robert, and his grandson, Samuel, is, (1861,) in good condition, and occupied by Henry Andrews. A. D. 1775, he had the largest tax-list of any one man in the parish.

66. "Wife of Nathan Booth;" this was Abigail (Steele,) daughter of Dr. Joseph, of "Great Swamp," and his wife, Elizabeth (Hollister,) from Glastenbury, born Jan. 5th, 1720; she died Dec. 3d, 1789, aged 69.

THEIR CHILDREN.

1. James, born March, 1747-8, m. Nov. 23d, 1775, No. (166)
2. Abigail, born Oct. 3d, 1748, m. March 24th, 1773, Joshua Webster; m. second Sylvanus Dunham, see No. (171.)
3. Nathan, jun., b. March 1st, 1749, m. June 24th, 1773, Frances Smith, of Ebenezer.
4. Joseph, born Oct. 1st, 1751, m. Dec. 18th, 1777, No. (155.)
5. Anna, born 1754, m. Sept. 6th, 1781, Seth Lusk, son of David, see No. (42)
6. Robert, b. June 20th, 1758, bap. June 25th, 1758, m. May 30th, 1782, see No. (194.)
7. Lucy, born March, 1760, bap. March 16th, 1760, m. April 15th, 1790, Stephen Booth, (cousins.)
8. Chloe, born 1763, bap. Jan. 1st, 1864, m. Jan. 11th, 1804, No. (174.)

67. "LADWICK HOTCHKISS," son of Josiah and Abigail Parker, born Jan. 18th, 1723, at Wallingford; came to this town from New Haven; he was a blacksmith, had his shop on the east side of east street, near the Elnathan and Ira E. Smith house; he lived on the west side. When William Patterson, A. D. 1759, sold to Rev. John Smalley, he reserved the shop of Ladwick Hotchkiss, and the ground it stood on. He built with his son, Lemuel, a house and saw-mill on and near the road to Horse plain. The house built by Eli B. Smith, a few years since, stood on the same spot. He was a captain and had his title invariably. He moved to (Farmington Plains,) Plainville, and united with Farmington church, 1780. He m. Dec. 23d, 1743, No. (68;) she died Feb. 21st, 1775, aged 57, when he m. second, Aug. 9th, 1775, Widow Mercy Hills, widow of Moses Hills; she died Feb. 7th, 1777, aged 49, when he m. third, Sept., 1777, Lydia (Hotchkiss,) the widow of Thomas Hart, of Bristol, who died Aug. 27th, 1798, in her 66th year; he moved with his son, Lemuel, to New Durham, N. Y., where he died March 7th, 1803, aged 81. He was a man much in public affairs, of strong mind and great influence; was appointed one of the church committee, 1761.

68. "Wife of Ladwick Hotchkiss," her maiden name, Molly North, daughter of Nathaniel, of (Northington,) Avon, and his wife, Margaret (Holcomb,) of Simsbury. She was born March 18th, 1716–17, was a woman of superior mind, imparted much of herself to her children, viz.

1. Lemuel, born Nov. 8th, 1741, m. March 26th, 1764, No. (188.)
2. Molly, born July 21st, 1747, m. Dec. 17th, 1769, John Stedman; moved to New Durham, N. Y.
3. Ladwick, born May 25th, 1752, m. May 17th, 1773, No. (278.)
4. Josiah, born Nov. 7th, 1757, bap. Nov. 10th, 1757, in Kensington, Rev. Samuel Clark, m. Feb. 22d, 1781, Mary Root, daughter of John; m. second, Widow Esther Carrington; he blacksmith, lived and died at (Farmington Plains,) Plainville; he died April 14th, 1832, a kind and honest man.

Thus far, beginning with No. (19,) from Kensington church, and these sixty-eight persons constituted the first church of New Britain parish, to which were added from time to time in the following order:

69. "Samuel Goodrich," to church May 14th, 1758, by letter from the church in Wethersfield; to the church there, 1748. He was born April 23d, 1720, in Wethersfield, to Allen and his wife, Elizabeth, daughter of Col. David Goodrich, m. Sept. 24th, 1747, No. (28;) they were dismissed to the church in Kensington, by letter, and received there Dec. 23d, 1764; they lived on "West Lane," in Kensington, near the farm of Frederick North. He died there May 30th, 1789, aged 69.

THEIR CHILDREN.

1. Samuel, born Dec. 17th, 1747, died Dec. 6th, 1750, aged three years.
2. Asa, born June 26th, 1750, m. Dec. 16th, 1779, Lydia Bronson; lived in Canaan, Conn. He died Sept. 28th, 1794, aged 44 years.
3. Sarah, born July 6th, 1753, m. July 17th, 1775, Luther Stocking, of Kensington. She died March 22d, 1829, aged 76.
4. Martha, born Nov., 1756, m. Dec. 21st, 1780, No. (238.)
5. Rhoda, born Jan. 3d, 1760, bap. Jan 10th, 1760, m. April 3d, 1786, Selah Stanley, of Thomas, of Kensington; lived in Farmington.
6. Samuel, born Feb. 19th, 1762, m. Aug. 1783, Mary, daughter of Bela Strong, of Kensington.

70. "Daniel Kilbourn," son of Left. Ebenezer and Eunice (Hale,) of Thomas, of Glastenbury, his wife, born May 5th, 1705, m. No. (18;) they lived in a log-hut, which stood in the home-lot of Hiram Smith, and back of his house. They had no posterity. He was received to this church May 14th, 1758, by letter from Newington church. He wasted his property and had, 1766, William Smith, his neighbor, appointed to oversee him. He was suspended from special ordinances, Oct. 1st, 1760.

71. "Jemima Lamb," to church May 14th, 1758, by letter from Newington church; she "owned the covenant" there May 25th, 1755, and was

received to full communion there June 6th, 1756.* She deeded, 1763, to John Lusk, five acres of land, lying north-west of the meeting-house, butts partly on the Mill pond, south on the highway, west on her own land, and 1765, she deeded the balance, eight acres, to Josiah Lee, and made her mark to the deed. She had living, one, at least, of her parents, for June 4th, 1762, she was suspended by the church for breach of the fifth commandment; on confession in July, 1762, she was restored.

72. "ZEBULON GOODRICH," to church May 21st, 1758, by letter from church in Newington, born Nov. 22d, 1713, to Col. David, of Wethersfield, and his second wife, Prudence Churchill; lived near "Churchill's Mills," m. Jan. 8th, 1735–6, Anne Francis, daughter of James and his first wife, Elizabeth (Howard,) born Aug. 23d, 1714. She was sister of No. (91.)

THEIR CHILDREN.

1. Mary, born Aug. 23d, 1737, see No. (89.)
2. Elizabeth, born June 4th, 1739, m. Nov. 23d, 1758, Thomas Lusk, see No. (90.)
3. Phebe, born July 9th, 1741.
4. Zebulon, jun., born June 11th, 1744, m. Oct. 5th, 1759, Oner Whaples; he moved to Lebanon, and became a Quaker.
5. Ann, born Nov. 23d, 1746, bap. Nov. 24th, 1751, at Newington, m. Heman Judd, of Farmington.
6. Millicent, born Jan. 24th, 1752, bap. Jan. 26th, 1752, at Newington, m. Solomon Hollister.
7. Elijah, born June 3d, 1755, bap. July 13th, 1755, at Newington.
8. David, born Dec. 14th, 1757, m. Sept. 25th, 1783, Huldah Booth.

73. "Kata, wife of Stephen Lee;" she was the first added to the church on profession of faith, after its organization; to church May 21st, 1758; her maiden name, Catharine Furbs, (Farmington records,) m. Feb. 6th, 1746, No. (37.) This family moved to Lenox, Mass., about 1775.

74. "JOHN COLEMAN," (son of John, of Wethersfield, and his wife, Comfort Robins,) born July 27th, 1729, m. No. (75;) they both "owned the covenant" in Kensington, Sept. 15th, 1755, Rev. Joshua Belden, of Newington, officiating, and both to this church on profession of faith, Aug. 20th, 1758.

75. Experience, wife of John Coleman, see No. (74.) They lost a child, buried in "Blew Hills," June 17th, 1757.

76. "SOLOMON DUNHAM;" he is said to have come from "Martha's Vineyard," born Sept. 20th, 1732; was a tinner by trade; m. March 2d, 1758, No. (77;) they both to this church Oct. 8th, 1758; they were both

* She and her sister, Marcy, both of Wethersfield, Jan. 9th, 1756, bought out the farm of Benjamin Judd, jun., for £8,200, old tenor, 118 acres, with his house, barn, shop, saw and fulling mill, standing thereon, butted east on Wethersfield line, west on highway, north on James Judd, and south on lands belonging to the heirs of Capt. Stephen Lee; in 1765, she sold to Isaac Lankton, for £235, her house and barn, with 27 acres of land on the west of highway, and three acres on the east of said highway, and made her mark to the deed.

dismissed and received by letter to Kensington church; they were admitted there June, 1759; they were afterwards constituent members of Worthington church, 1775; they were parents of Capt. Reuben Dunham, and there they located from here at the north end of Worthington village, then in Wethersfield bounds. He was many years a magistrate and a prominent man; he died Jan. 22d, 1811, aged 78.

77. "ELIZABETH, wife of Solomon Dunham," see No. (76;) her maiden name, Elizabeth Ives, of Wallingford, born July 24th, 1734; she died Aug. 9th, 1793, aged 60; their bodies lie in the Bridge cemetery, Berlin, indicated by head stones.

THEIR CHILDREN.

1. Elizabeth, born Dec. 3d, 1758, in Farmington, m. Abel Porter; she died May 10th, 1783.

2. Warner, born Dec. 4th, 1759, bap. Dec. 14th, 1759, at Kensington, m. second, Mary (Wolcott,) widow of Elisha Andrus.

3. Solomon, jun., born Jan. 18th, 1762, bap. March 1st, 1762, at Kensington, died Aug., 1786, at Point Peter, Gaudaloupe.

4. Elishama, born Feb. 17th, 1764, bap. April 8th, 1764, at Kensington.

5. Lucy, born March 5th, 1766, bap. March 23d, 1766, at Kensington.

6. Mary, born Oct. 25th, 1768, bap. Nov. 6th, 1768, at Kensington, m. Lardner Deming.

7. Reuben, born Feb. 13th, 1773, m. Dec. 14th, 1797, Betsey Norton, daughter of Roger, jun. and Hannah (Rice.) Capt. Reuben Dunham died April 5th, 1829, aged 56.

78. "ANNA, the wife of Josiah Kilbourn;" she m. May 3d, 1754, No. (200;) both "owned the covenant," Dec. 7th, 1755, at Newington; she to this church Oct. 8th, 1758; her maiden name, Anna Neal, daughter of William, of Southington, and Anne (Barns,) his wife, born July 27th, 1734, bap. Aug. 4th, 1734, at Southington; she was sister of Jemima, wife of No. (86;) she was member of Farmington church, April 19th, 1796, when they occupied the "Brown place," west of "Dead Swamp." She died January, 1812, aged 78, at the Berlin "Alms-house," (in Kensington, at that date.)

79. "SARAH, wife of Stephen Hollister," daughter of Joseph Cogswell, of Southington, and Johannah Andrus, his wife, born May 10th, 1726; she to this church Dec. 10th, 1758; a woman remarkable for prayer and piety; she gave in old age, a bible to her daughter, Anna, wife of David Daniels, sen., with good advice in her own hand, with her family records in it. She left this church for the Baptist, 1777, and 1778, the church withdrew their watch; she died May 6th, 1814, aged 88, see No. (169) for her husband and family.

80. "ANNA PATTERSON," daughter of Deacon John and Ruth (Bird,) his wife, born Dec. 27th, 1736, m. Jan. 24th, 1759, Rev. Stephen Holmes; she to church Dec. 10th, 1758. He was the first candidate employed to preach in the parish; he preached thirteen Sabbaths, at £10 per Sabbath, old tenor.

81. "RUTH PATTERSON," sister of No. (80,) born June 10th, 1739; she was, on the 11th of May, 1759, unmarried, for her father, in his will of that date, gave her all that lot he bought of David Curtiss, and if she remained single, one-quarter of his dwelling-house and barn; she to church Dec. 10th, 1758.

82. "SARAH, wife of William Patterson," by letter from the church in Meriden to this church, April 1st, 1759; Sarah Dunham, probably sister of No. (76;) William Patterson and his wife received to Kensington church from New Britain, April 11th, 1762, see No. (55.)

83. "JONATHAN GRISWOLD," to church April 16th, 1759, m. Feb. 3d, 1725–6, Mary Willard, of Wethersfield; she died April 30th, 1741; was the mother of his children; he m. second, Oct. 6th, 1748, No. (16;) his house stood next east of George Francis' place, in Stanley quarter, on the east side of the brook, where is a pleasant locality, and where several families lived. He born 1695; he died Feb. 26th, 1771, aged 76 years.

THEIR CHILDREN.

1. Mary, born Nov. 27th, 1726.
2. Jonathan, born April 25th, 1731.
3. Rhoda, born April 4th, 1733; she died Aug. 23d, 1733.
4. Ashbel, born Sept. 8th, 1735, died Feb. 13th, 1557, aged 22.

84. "HANNAH, wife of William Barber;" she was daughter of Capt. Stephen Lee, and widow of Nathaniel North, born Oct. 15th, 1708, bap. May 8th, 1709, in old Farmington; she to this church April 1st, 1759; she probably died before May, 1760, for the grandmother of her children, No. (24,) calls them in her will, the heirs of Hannah Barber, and William Barber m. Nov. 8th, 1764, Abigail Cole, of Kensington, born June 25th, 1735. to Stephen; she died Aug. 15th, 1766, and was buried in Beckley quarter. Hannah's father, in his will dated 1747, calls her a single woman, and gave her in bills of credit, so much as to be equal to seventy-four ounces of silver.

85. "DANIEL DEWY," son of Daniel and "Catharon" (Beckley,) his wife, daughter of John, and grand-daughter of Sergeant Richard, born Aug. 24th, 1707, m. Jan. 27th, 1731, Rebecca, daughter of Thomas Curtice and Mary (Goodrich,) his wife, see No. (26.) He to church 1760; was chosen deacon Sept. 3d, 1772; he lived next house south of Deacon Anthony Judd, and Capt. Phineas Judd, south end of Stanley street, and inherited the old homestead of his father, Daniel, who died in the midst of life, for his mother, "Catharon," m. Aug. 12th, 1731, Deacon John Deming, of Wethersfield, before Rev. William Burnham. He was appointed one of the standing committee July 30th, 1761. He was mild and amiable in his temper and deportment. He died Oct. 28th, 1786, aged 80.

THEIR CHILDREN.

1. David, born March 16th, 1732, m. Feb. 12th, 1755, Esther Dunham.
2. Rhoda, born Nov. 24th, 1736, died Oct., 1748, aged 11 years and 10 months; lies in "Christian lane."
3. Josiah, born July 7th, 1737, m. Aug. 11th, 1756, Experience Smith.
4. Hannah, born March 9th, 1740, m. April 7th, 1757, John Goodrich.
5. Lucy, born Nov. 1st, 1742, died Oct. 22d, 1748, aged 5 years and 11 months; grave in "Christian lane."

86. "JOHN KILBOURN," to church Nov. 9th, 1760, son of Josiah, sen. and Ruth (Warner,) his wife, born April 23d, 1733, m. Jemima Neal; they both "owned the covenant," July 30th, 1758; he lived at the foot of "Half-way Hill;" they had three sons, but all died young; he died 1781, aged 48; his widow m. 1783, No. (138;) she sister of No. (78,) bap. July 17th, 1737, at Southington.

87. "HEPZIBAH, wife of John Woods," to church March 9th, 1761, maiden name, Hepzibah Beckley, born April 16th, 1735, at Beckley quarter, to Joseph and his wife, Mary, daughter of Benjamin Judd, m. Jan. 18th, 1753; they lived in a log-house near where John Henry Andrews (now, 1864,) does; he was born Oct. 15th, 1728, to Elixoder, (an Englishman,) and was a clothier, and had great skill in his art; he died Oct., 1798, aged 70, at Bristol. She was a member of the church in Bristol when she died, 1793, aged 58; he bought his land to build on of Uriah Judd, who was brother to Mrs. Wood's mother.

THEIR CHILDREN.

1. Eli, born Oct. 23d, 1753.
2. Huldah, born Oct. 13th, 1754.
3. Hepzibah, born Jan. 8th, 1756, m. Nov. 3d, 1774, Judah Barns.
4. Ruth, born March 13th, 1757.
5. Silas, born Feb. 7th, 1759, bap. March 25th, 1759, died June 15th, 1760.
6. Charlotte, born April 21st, 1763, bap. May 1st, 1763.
7. Silence, born Oct. 10th, 1764, bap. Oct. 21st, 1764.
8. Abigail, born Oct. 10th, 1766, brought up at Ensign Levi Andrews, m. Benoni Johnson, of Harwinton.
9. John b. April 1st, 1768, bap. June 19th, 1768, d. Aug. 22d, 1769, in his 2d year.
10. Thankful, born , bap. Nov. 18th, 1770; lived at Lot Stanley's.
11. Zadoc, born , bap. April 26th, 1772, m. Huldah (Winchel,) widow of Mark Mildrum.

88. "ADONIJAH LEWIS," to church Oct. 18th, 1761, son of Capt. Jonathan and his wife, Elizabeth (Newel,) of Thomas, born July 12th, 1722, m. July 31st, 1760, at Southington, No. (111;) he inherited lands of his father, and had his house where (now, 1862,) John Ellis lives; his name is on the public records as a man of public spirit and business; he was a blacksmith by trade and occupation; he died Dec. 22d, 1799, at the house of Dr. John Andrews, aged 78. The first wife of Dr. Andrews was a daughter of his.

THEIR CHILDREN.

1. Lucy born Dec. 18th, 1761, m. Noah Stanley.
2. Lydia, born 1763, m. March 23d, 1780, Amos Richards.
3. Polly, born Nov., 1765, m. 1786, No. (251.)
4. Phebe, born , bap. May 15th, 1768, m. May 10th, 1792, No. (197.)
5. Elizabeth, born , bap. July 1st, 1770, d. unmarried, partially insane.
6. Seth, born May 3d, 1772, m. Feb. 15th, 1795, No. (440.)
7. Erastus, born June, 1774, bap. July 31st, 1774, m. May 28th, 1801, No. (568.)
8. Sally, born Sept. 15th, 1776, bap. Jan. 12th, 1777, m. Nov. 6th, 1796, No. (337.)
9. Gad, born , bap. July 9th, 1779.
10. Isaac, born , bap. Aug. 13th, 1780, died young.
11. Isaac, born , bap. Oct. 13th, 1782, m. Oct. 28th, 1804, No. (957.)
12. Abi, born , bap. March 20th, 1785, m Nov. 5th, 1802, Thomas Eddy; she died May 6th. 1814.

89. "MARY, wife of Samuel Smith," to church April 11th, 1762, daughter of Zebulon Goodrich and Anne Francis, his wife, born Aug. 23d, 1737, m. Dec. 6th, 1759; he "owned the covenant" Oct. 8th, 1758; he inherited the home of his father No. (6,) south part of Stanley quarter, at the head of "Spiritual lane," so called. He died May 16th, 1802, aged 70; she died Feb. 13th, 1819 aged 81½ years.

THEIR CHILDREN.

1. Sarah, born April 5th, 1761, m. April 21st, 1791, Francis Cosslett, see No. (636.)
2. Chloe, born , m. Cornelius Bassett, who died Nov. 20th, 1806.
3. Moses, born Jan. 1st, 1766, m. Oct. 31st, 1779, Sally Judd, of James; he died Oct. 9th, 1828.
4. Abijah, born Nov. 14th, 1767, bap. Nov. 15th, 1767, m. Jan. 18th, 1792, No. (520,) which see.
5. William, born Sept. 2d, 1771, m. Nov. 6th, 1796, No. (295;) he m. second, Feb. 10th, 1812, No. (472.)
6. Levi, born Sept. 29th, 1773, bap. Nov. 14th, 1773, m. Mary Olmsted, of James, of East Hartford.
7. Mary, born Sept. 9th, 1777, bap. Oct. 19th, 1777, m. Roger Hurlburt, of Levi, of Newington; they moved to York State; she died at Homer, aged 84.

90. "ELIZABETH, wife of Thomas Lusk," to church April 11th 1762; she daughter of No. (72,) sister of No. (89,) born June 4th, 1739, m. Nov. 23d, 1758, before Rev. John Smalley, the first on his record of marriages. He "owned the covenant," Oct. 7th, 1759; was son of No. 10 and his wife, No. 11; had a tax-list in the town, 1763, of £22; owned no real estate, and moved to West Stockbridge, Mass., and March 6th, 1789, she sold her interest in her father's estate, one and one-quarter acres of land, for £3 12s.; she made her mark, and is called a weaver. He signed the deed also, at West Stockbridge, and is called a carpenter, and Elizur, their son, signed as witness to the deed; the land was sold to Samuel Smith, who had married her sister, Mary, No. (89.) She to church in West Stockbridge, 1784. The family moved to Bloomfield, New York.

THEIR CHILDREN.

1. Elizabeth, born , bap. Oct. 7th, 1759.
2. Sylvia, born , bap. Dec. 6th, 1761.
3. Asahel, born , bap. June, 1764.
4. Elizur, born
5. Amos, born , was a member of Stockbridge church, and excommunicated.

91. "ELIJAH FRANCIS," to church May 23d, 1762, son of James of Newington, and his 2d wife, Abigail (Warren,) of Wethersfield, born Feb. 25th, 1752-3, m. April 22d, 1755, No. (92 ;) his title was Lieut.; he lived in the south part of Stanley quarter; bought his house and farm of Josiah Kilbourn, 1773. Towards the close of life he lived with his son, Deacon Elijah, near " Osgood Hill, where from despondency or insanity he hung himself, Aug. 18th, 1812, aged 81.* In 1757, he was guardian to James, son of James Francis, of Wethersfield, then eighteen years old.

92. " Wife of Elijah Francis," to church May 23d, 1762 ; name, Hannah Buck, daughter of Pelatiah and Jemima (Andrus,) his wife, sister to No. (9) and No. (13,) a woman with strong mind, said to be the only person in the parish who dare tell Dr. Smalley his faults. She died May 14th, 1811, aged 80, one year before the sad death of her husband. Dr. Smalley held her memory in high regard, for he said at the funeral of Lieut. Francis, that probably his insanity was induced by the loss of his excellent wife.

THEIR CHILDREN.

1. Elizabeth, born Dec. 12th, 1755, m. Dec. 18th, 1777, Joseph Booth, of Nathan.
2. James, born Oct. 24th, 1757, m. Nov. 12th, 1780, (No. 355.)
3. Elijah, jun., born Jan. 6th, 1760, m. Dec. 21st, 1785, No. (221.)
4. Justus, born Jan. 25th, 1762, m. March 10th, 1785, Abi, daughter of Deacon Timothy Stanley.
5. Sylvia, born Dec. 12th, 1763, bap. Dec. 18th, 1763, see No. (205.)
6. Hannah, born Nov. 20th, 1765, died Aug. 1st, 1784, at the old house near " Half-way Hill."
7. Selah, born April 5th, 1768, bap. May 15th, 1768, m. Roxy Buckley, of Rocky Hill, moved to York State.
8. Orange, born April 21st, 1771, bap. June 16th, 1771, died Aug. 28th, 1781, aged 10 years.

93. "THOMAS HART," to church June 4th, 1762, son of No. (49) and No. (50,) born Jan. 12th, 1738, m. Feb. 2d, 1758, No. (209;) was a farmer and shoe-maker ; lived on West Main street, the same house now, (1862,) owned and occupied by Ira Steele. He was a man of great industry and economy ; was noted for prayer and piety. He first built at the east corner of his home-lot, but found no water, and just as his house

* This insanity might have been constitutional or hereditary from his mother, who was insane the last of her days, restless nights, disturbing the household, called on the neighbors with a note-book to have them write something about her son, James, who died in early manhood, and broke her heart.

was finishing, the joiners left for dinner, it took fire from shavings, and it burned down. He died Jan. 7th, 1830, aged 93.

THEIR CHILDREN.

1. Ruth, born Nov. 10th, 1758, bap. Dec. 3d, 1758; her father "owned the cove nant" same date.

2. Abigail, born Oct. 27th, 1761, bap. Nov. 1st, 1761, m. Feb. 15th, 1781, Jonathan Seymour.

3. Abijah, born April 7th, 1764, m. Sept. 22d, 1794, No. (211.)

4. Ismena, born , bap. July 17th, 1768, never married, see No. (216.)

5. William, born 1772, bap. March 16th, 1772, see No. (208.)

94. "ELIJAH THOMPSON," to church Nov. 13th, 1763, by letter from the church in Kent; son of Daniel, born Dec. 21st, 1732, m. No. (100.)

THEIR CHILDREN.

1. Samuel, born , bap. Sept. 7th, 1766, at Kensington.
2. Daniel, born , bap. Feb. 19th, 1769, at Kensington.
3. Aaron, born , bap. Dec. 8th, 1771, at Kensington.

A child buried in "Blew Hills," Dec. 24th, 1773.

95. "JOHN RICHARDS," to church Aug. 5th, 1764, son of No. (4) and No. (5,) born March 31st, 1730–31, m. April 14th, 1752, Mary French; he was by trade and occupation a blacksmith; had his house and shop in Stanley quarter, opposite the former school-house, on the corner, where James North learned his trade. Mary, his wife died , when he married second, Dec. 26th, 1776, Elizabeth Dickinson, daughter of Elihu and Lucy Deming, his second wife. He bought A. D. 1776, March 16th, for £555, of Deacon Josiah Lee, the Skinner house and farm of sixty acres, and lived there a few years; built and occupied the Smith shop, subsequently occupied by Elijah Hinsdale. He sold to Capt. John Hinsdale, 1781, for £900, and moved to Piermont, New Hampshire, where he had a splendid farm on Connecticut River. At Piermont he was chosen deacon of the church. His wife, Elizabeth, died about 1800, when he married third, Jan. 31st, 1802, Hannah Bear, of Hopkinton, New Hampshire, she being six feet in height, and 70 years old, while he was 72. He died 1821, aged 90. He and his son, Amos, signed the deed March 3d, 1781, of seventy acres, with house and other buildings to Capt. John Hinsdale.

THEIR CHILDREN.

1. Lydia, born April 10th, 1754, bap. April 21st, 1754, at Newington, m. Oct., 1772, Seth Judd; he was accidentally shot in the army, when she married second, Samuel Huggins, of New Hampshire; she died Aug. 30th, 1841, aged 87.

2. Elijah, born July 10th, 1756, bap. July 18th, 1756, died in the army, at Skeensboro, 1776.

3. Amos, born April 7th, 1759, m. March 20th, 1780, No. (277.)

4. Esther, born May 15th, 1764, bap. May 20th, 1764, at New Britain, m. Deacon Joseph Ford, of Piermont.

SECOND WIFE'S CHILDREN.

5. Elijah, second of name, born Nov. 11th, 1777, bap. Nov. 16th, 1777, graduated at Dartmouth College, 1799.

6. John, jun., born , m. Dec. 9th, 1809, Polly Burton; he died 1855, aged 67.

7. Lucy, b , died young.

96. "SARAH, wife of John Smalley," to church Aug. 11th, 1765, daughter of Peter Garnsey and his wife, Anne (Gunn,) born about 1740, at Milford, Conn.; her father and family removed to Bethlehem, Conn. A woman of remarkable skill and economy in household matters; relieved her husband from much of the anxiety incident to the care of a farm and parish at the same time. Dr. Smalley was numbered among the "rich ministers of Hartford county," and for this success, was doubtless much indebted to her forethought. She died Oct. 10th, 1808, aged 68. She had a brother, Richard, from whom her grandson, Richard S. Porter, the present clerk of the town, 1867, took his name; also a brother Solomon, who married Sarah Kasson, of Bethlehem, Conn.

97. "JANNA CHURCHILL," to church Aug. 11th 1765, son of Nathaniel, of Westfield, in Middletown, and his wife, Rebecca (Griswold,) born Feb. 20th, 1738, m. No. (98;) he was a farmer, and lived on the present Holcomb farm, which he owned, together with five-elevenths of the saw-mill, land and appurtenances, called Capt. Hotchkiss' mill, on "Pond River," alias Quinipiac. His first wife, No. (98,) died, leaving no children. In 1774, he fell under church censure for intemperance in strong drink. He married second, the widow of Thomas Foster, of Essex, Mass; her maiden name, Sarah Mix. He moved to Hubbardston, Vermont; he died June, 1815, at Georgia, Vermont, aged 77.

98. "Wife of Janna Churchill," to church Aug. 11th, 1765; this his first wife.

THE CHILDREN BY SECOND WIFE.

1. Sarah J., born , m. Isaac Allen, of Peru, Vermont.

2. Thomas Foster, born Feb. 26th, 1780, m. Sept. 1st, 1808, Mary Strong; he drowned Feb. 17th, 1820, in Lake Champlain.

3. Josiah, born

4. Janna, born , m. Betsey Pierson, of Fairfax, Vermont.

5. Olive, born , m. Walker Rumsey, of Hubbardston, Vermont.

6. Rachel, born , m. March 26th, 1811, Elisha Lincoln.

7. Lucy, born , m. 1813, Samuel Brigham; she died 1814, of consumption.

8. Laura, born , died 1829, of fever.

99. "LOIS BLINN," to church 1766, supposed to be daughter of Peter, of Wethersfield, and his wife, Martha (Collins,) born May 13th, 1745, at Wethersfield.

100. "SARAH, wife of Elijah Thompson," about 1766 to church, as appears from the Kensington church record, which says that Elijah Thompson and his wife, Sarah, received to this church from New Britain, June 21st, 1767, m. No. (94.)

101. "JOHN HART," to church June 8th, 1766, son of Judah, sen. and Anna (Norton,) his wife, see No. (51,) born Jan. 20th, 1743, m. Oct. 17th, 1764, Anna Deming, daughter of Zebulon, of Southington, and his wife, Esther (Adkins;) her mother became the second wife of "Landlord Smith," No. (29.) He lived near his father, in Hart quarter, where now, (1862,) Harlowe Eddy does; he was a farmer and large land-holder; he died Sept. 13th, 1776, aged 33, and his widow married second, Aug. 28th, 1777, David Hills; she died Oct. 30th, 1804, aged 63 years.

CHILDREN OF JOHN AND ANNA HART.

1. Roger, born 1765, m. Sibil Robinson, daughter of John and Mary (Strickland,) his wife; she born 1764, at Middletown. He inherited a large farm; married second, No. (266.)
2. John, born 1772, bap. July 12th, 1772, died Sept. 10th, 1776, aged 4 years 3 mo's.
3. Roswell, born 1775, bap. Aug. 13th, 1775, died Sept. 10th, 1776, aged 14 months.

102. "DAVID DEWY," to church May 24th, 1767, son of No. (85,) lived with his father, was a farmer, born March 16th, 1732, m. Feb. 12th, 1755, No. (103,) before Rev. Joshua Belden. The family, after some years, moved to Harwinton, where he died 1814, aged 82; he married second, Widow Johnson, of New Hartford.

103. "Wife of David Dewy," to church May 24th, 1767; maiden name, Esther Dunham, sister of No. (76) and No. (139;) she died May 24th, 1799, aged 70.

THEIR CHILDREN.

1. Josiah, born Jan. 6th, 1756, m. Nov. 24th, 1785, No. (157.)
2. Rhoda, born Feb. 14th, 1758.
3. Oliver, born Oct. 3d, 1766, m. Nov. 2d, 1792, Mary, daughter of No. (115.)
4. Asahel, born Oct. 24th, 1768, bap. Oct. 30th, 1768.
5. Daniel, born May 6th, 1771, bap. May 19th, 1771.
6. Elishama, born April 6th, 1774, bap. May 8th, 1774.

104. "NATHANIEL CHURCHILL," to church June 28th, 1767, son of Nathaniel, of (Westfield,) Middletown, consequently a brother of No. (97,) and of Lucy, the first wife of Jeremiah H. Osgood, familiarly known as grandfather Osgood. He was in the army of the Revolution; was a captain; very fond of hunting; lived near Osgood, alias "Half-way Hill;" he was born June 25th, 1731, at Westfield, m. Sept. 25th, 1755, Elizabeth Sage; she died ; he married second, Feb. 16th, 1761, No. (105;) the family moved, 1802, to New Canaan, New York.

105. "Wife of Nathaniel Churchill," to church June 28th, 1767; this was his second wife; her maiden name, Jane Bushnell, daughter of , of Saybrook.

THE CHILDREN.

1. Nathaniel, jun., born March 2d, 1756, at Middletown, m. April 2d, 1783, Lydia Osgood, widow of Jeremiah Osgood, and daughter of Nathaniel Penfield, sen.

2. Bette, born Nov. 18th, 1757, at Middletown; she m. 1780, Stephen Williams, of Middletown.

3. Abigail, born Dec. 5th, 1759, m. Ward, of Westfield, in Middletown.

SECOND WIFE'S CHILDREN.

4. Stephen, born Nov, 19th, 1761, m. Sept. 17th, 1787, Polly De Wolf, of Stephen; went to New Canaan.

5. Sage, born Dec. 13th, 1763, m. Elizabeth Mather, of David, see No. (254.)

6. John, born March 20th, 1765.

7. Solomon, } twins, born April 24th, 1767, bap. June 28th, 1767, m. Dec. 30th, 1790, No. (241.)

8. Sarah, } twins, born April 24th, 1767, bap. June 28th, 1767, m. Reuben Peck, died 1846, aged 80, in Vermont.

9. Jane, born Jan. 17th, 1769, m. Oct. 21st, 1790, William Stedman.

10. Mehitable, born Jan. 30th, 1773, bap. March 14th, 1773, m. Dec. 24th, 1792, Appleton Woodruff.

11. Almira, born April 28th, 1776, bap. May 26th, 1776, m. Dec. 9th, 1795, Jason Warner.

12. Anna, born April 14th, 1778, bap. May 10th, 1778, m. April 10th, 1798, Jesse Nickerson.

106. "JACOB ANDRUS," by letter from Kensington, July 4th, 1767, son of Daniel, jun., of Newington, and Mabel (Goff,) his wife, born Jan. 24th, 1729, m. Feb. 2d, 1758, Eunice Emmons, of Litchfield. He to church in Kensington, March 23d, 1760. He lived on the mountain, west of Roswell Steele. He inherited ten acres of his farm from his father, and from his grand-father, Daniel, sen., of Farmington, one of the eighty-four proprietors; it was "reserved land," so called. He, brother of No. (112,) was illiterate, like many others of his age, for 1788, when he deeded his farm to Dr. Smalley, he made only his mark. He with his family, moved to New Durham, New York, with the Hotchkiss families.

THEIR CHILDREN.

1. Jacob, jun., born Jan. 20th, 1760, bap. March 23d, 1760, at Kensington, m. Jane Payne.

2. Caroline, born Oct. 20th, 1762, bap. Nov. 28th, 1762, at Kensington.

3. Sarah, born Jan. 7th, 1765, bap. March 31st, 1765, at Kensington.

4. Rhoda, born April 2d, 1767, m. Nov. 23d, 1786, Phineas Hamblin; she to church in Farmington, 1795.

5. Leaming, born , bap. July 21st, 1771, at New Britain, m. Phebe Case, of Simsbury; he was drowned in Tunxis river, at Hitchcockville, found at Farmington, and buried there, 1804.

6. Luther, born , bap. June 5th, 1774.

7. Ira, born , bap. May 2d, 1779; went to Barkhamsted, with Leaming.

8. Rachel, born , bap. June 20th, 1784.

9. Ard, born

10. Laban, born

107. "JOHN LANKTON," to church July 12th, 1767, son of John and Sarah (Lee,) daughter of Capt. Stephen, his wife, born 1729, m. Dec. 12th, 1754, No. (108;) they lived in Hart quarter. He was a captain, always known by his title, a farmer and a man of property and influence; he died Jan. 5th, 1791, aged 62.

108. "Wife of John Lankton," to church July 12th, 1767; maiden name, Mercy Eno, daughter of David Eno, of Simsbury, and Mary Gillet, his wife; she died Nov. 3d, 1806, aged 72.

THEIR CHILDREN.

1. Asa, born Sept. 14th, 1755.

2. Sarah, born Dec. 9th, 1756, m. Jan. 1st, 1778, Elizur Hart, of first Elijah, see No. (232.)

3. Timothy, born Dec. 4th, 1758, bap. Dec. 10th, 1758, graduated at Yale, 1781, m. Lucy Trumbull, daughter of Rev. John and Sarah, his wife. He studied divinity with Dr. Smalley, who preached his ordination sermon at Danbury, where Mr. Langdon settled, Aug. 31st, 1786; he continued there in the ministry fourteen years, five months, and died Feb. 10th, 1801; his first wife died March 7th, 1794, aged 35, when he married second, Elizabeth Pitkin Perkins, of Hartford.

4. Mercy, born Sept. 6th, 1761, bap. Sept. 13th, 1761, m. No. (172.)

5. John, born , bap. July 12th, 1767, died Nov. 18th, 1789, aged 22.

6. Hannah, born Nov. 1st, 1771, bap. Nov. 3d, 1771, m. Jan., 1790, Asahel, son of Jehudi Hart.

7. Huldah, born , bap. Nov. 28th, 1773, m. Samuel Whaples; he died Dec. 2d, 1833, aged 72.

8. Abi, born , bap. July 30th, 1775, m. No. (442.)

9. Mary, born , bap. May 2d, 1779.

109. "William Lewis," to church June 26th, 1768, son of Capt. Jonathan, brother of No. (88,) m. Oct. 1st, 1767, No. (110;) lived on the old homestead of his father, just south of the town-house, on the west side of East street, said to be the oldest place in New Britain; built near the present house erected by Edwin Belden. Hannah, his wife, died when he married second,

110. "Wife of William Lewis," to church June 26th, 1768; Hannah (Mather,) daughter of No. (47) and (48;) she born Jan. 25th, 1745, m. Oct. 1st, 1767, No. (109,) died Feb. 15th, 1773, aged 29.

HIS CHILDREN.

1. Thomas, born July 20th, 1768, bap. July 24th, 1768, m. Hannah Belden, daughter of Leonard.

2. Ammah, born , bap. March 17th, 1771.

SECOND WIFE'S CHILDREN.

3. Hannah, born , bap. Aug. 20th, 1775, died 1776, aged two years.

4. Elizabeth Newell, born , bap. July 20th, 1777.

5. Abner, born , bap. Feb. 10th, 1782.

6. William, born , bap. April 11th, 1784.

111. "Mary, wife of Adonijah Lewis," to church July 3d, 1768, born Feb. 8th, 1742–3, to James Bronson and his wife, Hannah Peck, of Southington. She married at Southington, July 31st, 1760, No. (88.) She was some twenty years younger than her husband. She died Feb. 8th, 1790, in her 48th year. The head-stones of both about the center of the old part of New Britain cemetery.

112. "HEZEKIAH ANDRUS," to church Aug. 7th, 1768, "owned the covenant" May 14th, 1758, the first on that list. He was son of Daniel, jun., son of Daniel, sen., son of John, the settler, of (Tunxis,) Farmington, born Aug. 14th, 1731, m. May 26th, 1757, No. (312;) came to this place soon after, built on West Main street, two miles from the village, the same house his grand-son, Ezekiel, now, (1867,) lives in; built also a saw-mill on the Quinnipiac. He was a man of mild temper, kind disposition, of good Christian deportment; he died April 19th, 1796, aged 65.

THEIR CHILDREN.

1. Hezekiah, born Jan. 22d, 1758, bap. May 14th, 1758, m. June 25th, 1787, No. (721.)
2. Anna, born Sept. 6th, 1760, bap. Oct. 1760, m. Dec. 21st, 1780, No. (181.)
3. Lois, born Dec. 1st, 1763, bap. Jan. 1st, 1764, m. Nov. 9th, 1786, Justus Francis, of Newington.
4. Elizabeth, born June 8th, 1766, see No. (222.)
5. Hannah, born June 11th, 1768, bap. Aug. 7th, 1768, m. June 12th, 1796, (No. (345.)
6. Bethankful, born April 7th, 1771, bap. May 26th, 1771, m. June 6th, 1793, Jonathan Wells, of Wethersfield.
7. Rebecca, born March 21st 1773, bap. May 9th, 1773, m. Jan. 12th, 1801, Amzi Porter, of Farmington.
8. Ezekiel, born May 25th, 1775, bap. June 25th, 1775, m. Dec. 11th, 1796, No. (314.)

113. "TIMOTHY STANDLY," to church Aug. 28th, 1768, son of Thomas, 2d, and his wife, Esther (Cowles,) born Aug. 13th, 1727, m. May 5th, 1757, No. (114;) he was tanner and shoe-maker by trade; his house opposite the home of his father, north part of Stanley street, on the east side of the road, subsequently owned and occupied by his son, Oliver. He was elected deacon 1795. Late in life he was somewhat deaf, and stood in the pulpit, the better to hear. His hair then white, and he used an ear-horn. His habits were strictly puritanical, a careful observer of holy time; his wife shaved his face Saturday afternoon invariably, and all preparations made for the due observance of the Sabbath; he died April 28th, 1817, aged 89 years 10 months.

114. "Wife of Timothy Standly," to church Aug. 28th, 1768; maiden name, Lydia Newell, daughter of Capt. John, of Farmington, and his wife, Elizabeth (Hawley.) She was a woman noted for energy and piety; she died Dec. 17th, 1826, aged 89.

THEIR CHILDREN.

1. Oliver, born July 5th, 1758, died Aug. 3d, 1758.
2. Rachel, born March 20th, 1761, m. Eleazer Curtiss; m. second, No. (402.)
3. Lydia, born April 26th, 1763, m. Dec. 9th, 1787, Joel Smith, son of Elijah.
4. Abi, born Aug. 9th, 1765, m. March 10th, 1785, Justus Francis; m. second, No. (149.)
5. Timothy, born June 29th, 1771, bap. July 14th, 1771, m. Abigail Robins, daughter of Uni, of Newington.

6. Oliver, born May 1st, 1775, bap. June 17th, 1775, m. May 10th, 1797, Frances Booth.

7. Jesse, born Oct. 26th, 1779, bap. Dec. 26th, 1779, m. Sept. 27th, 1801, Almira Lee; she died Sept. 29th, 1815, aged 35, when he married May 1st, 1816, No. (403.)

115. "GAD STANLEY," to church Aug. 28th, 1768, son of Thomas 2d,* and Esther (Cowles,) his wife, born March 21st, 1735, m. Oct. 29th, 1767, No. (125;) lived where William F. Raymond now, (1862,) does; this was the old site of his father's home. He was a large farmer, a man well qualified for public business, in both civil and military life. He was a captain in the war of the Revolution; was at Washington's retreat from Long Island, and led (it is said,) a regiment off safely past the British forces. He was active in school and society affairs, especially in procuring the incorporation of the town of Berlin, 1785, and in securing our share of the school fund, in conjunction with Col. Lee. He was a civil magistrate many years; had the title of Colonel from the year 1779, always prefixed; held other important offices, and was a man of courtly address and bearing, yet courteous and affable; he died Jan. 10th, 1815, aged 79.

THEIR CHILDREN.

1. Esther, born Sept. 21st, 1768, m. March 26th, 1789, William S. Judd, son of Major William, of Farmington.

2. Amzi, born Oct. 23, 1770, bap. Oct. 28th, 1770, m. Sept. 27th, 1801, Lucy Webster, daughter of Joshua.

---

* This Thomas 2d, died Oct. 13th, 1755; his will was made 1747, in which he gives his dearly beloved wife, Esther, the use of one-third of his real estate, during her life. and one-third the personal, to be her own forever, and she is to take my negro woman, Priscilla, for part of said dowry; also the service of my negro girl, Katharine, during her life; also the service of my negro boy, named Richard, until my son, Gad, shall be twenty-one, provided she lives my widow; and furthermore, I do give my dearly beloved wife, my great Bible, and one silver spoon during her life, and at her decease, I give the Bible to my son, Thomas, and the spoon to my grand-daughter, Anna. Imprimus, I give to my son, Thomas, and his heirs, the house he now lives in, and the barn, and six acres of land, they stand on, the east side of the highway, and my silver-headed cane. Item, I give to my sons, Noah and Timothy, the house I now live in, and the barn on the west side of the highway, and five acres on which they stand, in a square piece, the south bounds to be an ash tree about three rods south of said house. Item, I give Abigail, a front chamber in my house, &c. Item, I give my son, Gad, lands in New Cambridge, and my negro, Richard, when he, Gad, is of age, and ten sheep. Item, I give to my children, Thomas, Noah, Timothy, Abigail and Gad, all my right in the reserved lands in Farmington, which was my grand-father's, John Stanley. Item, my will is that my three eldest sons, Thomas, Noah and Timothy, shall build a house on the four acre orchard, in New Cambridge, (this is now Bristol, ED.) for my son, Gad, where he shall choose to sit it on, on the land given him in this instrument; all the great timber to be good white oak, and the house to be 38 by 20 feet, covered and glazed like the house given to my son, Thomas, and must be finished when Gad is twenty-two.

3. Mary, born Aug. 2d, 1772, bap. Oct. 4th, 1772, m. Nov. 2d, 1792, Oliver Dewy, of David.

4. Abigail, born Aug. 18th, 1774, m. July 25th, 1796, Stephen W. Cornwell, of Timothy, of Middletown.

5. Gad, born Aug. 13th, 1776, bap. Oct. 6th, 1776, m. Nov. 3d, 1799, No. (589.)

6. Phebe, born Aug. 28th, 1778, bap. Oct. 25th, 1778, m. Sept. 28th, 1800, Thomas Stow, of Zebulon, of Middletown.

7. Elizabeth, born July 17th, 1780, bap. Aug. 20th, 1780, m. Sept. 27th, 1801, No. (449.)

8. Anna, born Jan. 15th, 1783, bap. March 30th, 1783, m. July 15th, 1804, No. (330.)

9. Orrin, born Nov. 6th, 1784, bap. Dec. 26th, 1784, died Mar. 2d, 1786, aged 2 years.

10. Cyrus, born July 29th, 1787, bap. Sept., 1787, m. Sept. 7th, 1806, No. (422.)

11. Emily, born Aug. 31st, 1791, bap. Nov. 6th, 1791, d. May 7th, 1792, aged 1 year.

116. "NATHANIEL PENNFIELD," to church 1768, by letter from Mr. Whittlesey's church, New Haven; he was probably son of Nathaniel, of Meriden Society, Wallingford, and his wife, Hannah. He built the house on Main street, west side, and about sixty rods south of "Osgood Hill," which is still standing, (1864;) he was a farmer; has a numerous race of descendants; he died May 18th, 1777, of small-pox, in Meriden. His father had died in Meriden, Jan., 1776.

117. "Wife of Nathaniel Pennfield," to church 1768, by letter from the church in New Haven, Mr. Whittlesey, pastor; her maiden mame, Lydia Barnes, m. No. (116,) Jan. 9th, 1755; after the death of her husband, No. (116,) she m. April 23d, 1778, her next neighbor, Jeremiah H. Osgood, son of Jeremiah, of Haverhill, Essex county, Mass.; she died Jan. 31st, 1811, aged 76.

THEIR CHILDREN.

1. Phineas, born June 6th, 1756, m. April 9th, 1778, Lucy Osgood, daughter of Jeremiah H.

2. Lydia, born Aug. 19th, 1758, m. April 9th, 1778, Jeremiah Osgood; second, Nathaniel Churchill, jun.

3. Nathaniel, jun., born Nov. 14th, 1760, m. Oct. 22d, 1780, Eunice Kelsey, daughter of Enoch, sen.

4. Rebecca Rena, born May 9th, 1763, m. Oct. 26th, 1780, William Steele, son of Ebenezer, sen.

5. Milla, or Amelia, born May 26th, 1766, m. Nov. 16th, 1786, Samuel Dickinson, jun.; second, m. Thompson, of Farmington.

6. Phebe, born , bap. Aug. 19th, 1772, m. Samuel Gladden, son of Azariah.

7. Sylvia, born June, 1774, bap. July 31st, 1774, m. James Hart; second, John Wyard.

8. Elizabeth, born , m. Oct. 29th, 1789, Elisha Savage, of Berlin.

Each of these were heirs to the father's estate, Feb. 10th, 1779, £6 11s. 5¼d. being set to them by the distributors, Elijah Francis and Lemuel Hotchkiss.

118. "JEHUDI HART," to church Sept., 1769, son of No. (49,) born Dec. 12th, 1739, m. July 9th, 1767, No. (119;) he was a farmer; settled and built some twenty rods south of his father, in Hart quarter; an honest,

inoffensive man, retiring in his manners, with such fondness for home that it is said he never saw the city of Hartford, although living to old age, within twelve miles. He married second, the widow of Phineas Judd, jun., Elizabeth (Mezuzen;) she died April 26th, 1825, aged 73; he died Aug. 25th, 1825, aged 86. She was daughter of Mark Mezuzen, and had brothers, Orian and Mark. This was a French family.

119. "Wife of Jehudi Hart," to church Sept., 1769; her maiden name, Mary Munson, daughter of Reuben, born 1751, bap. April 14th, 1751, at Southington, and parents originally from Wallingford. She died in child-bed, Oct. 28th, 1786, aged 36.

THEIR CHILDREN.

1. Mary, born Aug. 5th, 1769, bap. Sept. 17th, 1769, m. Dec. 24th, 1806, Eliphelet Wadsworth, of Farmington.
2. Asahel, born May 24th, 1771, bap. June 23d, 1771, m. 1790, Hannah Langdon.
3. James, born May 22d, 1773, m. Sylvia Pennfield; he d Mar. 29th, 1813, aged 40.
4. Sylvia, born Aug. 15th, 1774, bap. June 11th, 1775, died Nov. 19th, 1776.
5. Sylvia, born April 15th, 1777, bap. June 1st, 1777; single and living Jan., 1863, No. (335.)
6. Joel, born June 14th, 1779, bap. Aug. 1st, 1779, m. Sept. 17th, 1800, Lydia North.
7. Benjamin, born Nov. 20th, 1781, bap. Feb. 10th, 1782, m. Honor Deming.
8. Abigail, born Oct. 28th, 1786, m. Jan. 29th, 1807, No. (420.)

SECOND WIFE'S CHILDREN.

9. Oliver, born Dec. 13th, 1788, bap. April 19th, 1789, m. Jan. 3d, 1838, Deborah E. Hurlburt; m. second, Lurancy Osborn.
10. Laura, born , bap. Aug. 4th, 1791, died young.
11. Elizur, born Oct. 9th, 1794, bap. Dec. 28th, 1794, m. Sept. 11th, 1832, Sophronia Jerome, of Bristol; frozen in a snow-storm in Ohio, Feb. 16th, 1842, aged 48.

HER CHILDREN BY FIRST HUSBAND, PHINEAS JUDD.

1. Betsy, born March 11th, 1785, bap. Sept. 11th, 1791, m. Moses Ellis, of Owego; she died 1850.
2. Polly, born April 11th, 1787, bap. Sept. 11th, 1791, m. Nov. 24th, 1814, Jesse, son of Charles Eddy and Eunice (Kelsey,) his wife, born July 16th, 1788; lived in Berlin; she remarkable for great energy; she died at Berlin, July 2d, 1860, aged 74.

120. "Mercy, daughter of Jedediah Goodrich," to church Dec. 3d, 1769; her mother, No. (64;) she m. Nov. 29th, 1790, Joshua Wells, of Newington, son of Mary, the second wife of No. (6,) and her former husband; she lived on the old homestead of her father, and died in a fit, April 22d, 1804, aged 53.

121. "Lemuel Hotchkiss," to church Dec. 17th, 1769, son of Capt. Ladwick and No. (68,) m. March 26th, 1764, No. (188;) he was, like his father, a blacksmith; was a man of great force of character; was at Horse Neck in the Revolution; had a horse shot under him; was with Col. Stanley at the retreat from Long Island, as lieutenant. He lived a few years on East street, with his father, when he built on Horse Plain, where Eli B. Smith lately built a house; he had a saw-mill on "Pond River,"

Quinnipiac; had iron works there; brought ore from Bristol, "New Cambridge;" made wrought nails quite extensively, by hand. He taught school in early manhood, winter seasons, and was for many years a school visitor. His title was Capt. Lemuel, to distinguish him from Capt. Ladwick, his father. He moved to New Durham, New York, where he died Feb. 18th, 1802, aged 58.

THEIR CHILDREN.

1. Lemuel, born July 11th, 1764, bap. July 15th, 1764, died July 13th, 1766.
2. Chloe, born April 24th, 1767, m. Jan. 18th, 1792, Abijah Smith, son of Samuel, see No. (520.)
3. Lydia, born March 15th, 1769, bap. Dec. 17th, 1769, m. Jan. 18th, 1791, Harvey Peck, of Kensington.
4. Penelope, born June 25th, 1771, bap. Sept. 1st, 1771, m. Joseph Crane; she died Nov. 6th, 1830.
5. Lemuel, b. Nov. 30, 1773, bap. Feb. 7th, 1774, m. Abigail Ellis, of Hudson, N. Y.
6. Joseph, b. Oct. 28th, 1775, bap. Dec. 10th, 1775, d. May 24th, 1786, aged 11 years.
7. Nancy, born Feb. 16th, 1778, bap. April 5th, 1778, d. June 16th, 1786, æ. 9 years.
8. Jason, b. Nov. 30th, 1779, bap. Feb. 13th, 1780, m. Nancy Parker; he died 1828.
9. Anna, born June 22d, 1782, bap. July 28th, 1782.
10. Henry, born Aug. 9th, 1785, bap. Oct. 9th, 1785.
11th. Nancy, born Feb. 18th, 1788, bap. April 6th, 1788, m. Rev. John B. Whittlesey, York, N. Y.
12. Joseph, born July 24th, 1791, bap. Sept. 11th, 1791, died Sept. 13th, 1794.

122. "Levi Andrus," to church May 5th, 1771, son of Joseph, of Newington, and Sarah (Wells,) his wife, born Feb. 23d, 1747, m. Dec. 20th, 1770, No. (123;) he was executor of his father's will and estate in Newington, 1775; the house in which he was born is still, 1862, standing; he located in the south part of Stanley quarter; his house where the late Professor E. A. Andrews' stands. He was clerk and treasurer of the society several years. He obtained the title of Ensign in the militia, and ever after was known by it. In December, 1807, he was chosen one of the standing committee of the church, which office formerly, among us, was for life, or good behavior, or ability to serve. He resigned 1823. He was a very successful farmer, of kind and cheerful disposition, and a great lover and promoter of peace. He was great-great-grand-son of John, the settler on Tunxis river, and was a fine, social and genial specimen of his race. He died May 8th, 1826, aged 80. He was son of Joseph, of Newington, who was son of Benjamin, who was son of Joseph, of John, the settler and his wife, Mary. He had a sister, Sarah, who married Deacon Jedediah Mills, of West Hartford.

123. "Wife of Levi Andrus," to church May 5th, 1771, by letter from Newington church; her maiden name, Chloe Wells, daughter of Capt. Robert and Abigail (Burnham,) his wife, born May 31st, 1746, at Newington. She was a quiet, unassuming woman, a great lover of order and

home, and a devoted Christian. She died Jan. 11th, 1837, aged 92. Her father, Capt. Robert Wells, died Feb. 3d, 1786.

THEIR CHILDREN.

1. Levi, born Oct. 8th, 1771, bap. Oct. 13th, 1771, died March 10th, 1795, at Newbern, N. C.
2. Chloe, born Nov. 16th, 1774, died Sept. 19th, 1775, aged one year.
3. Chloe, born Aug. 29th, 1777, bap. Aug. 31st, 1777, m. Nov. 3d, 1799, Gad Stanley, jun.
4. Ethan Allen, born April 7th, 1787, bap. May 20th, 1787, m. Dec. 19th, 1810, No. (392.)

124. "Samuel Andrus," to church Nov. 17th, 1771, son of No. (53) and No. (54,) born Nov. 2d, 1749, m. Dec. 17th, 1769, Abigail Smith, daughter of No. (29) and No. (30;) his house on the corner next east of Alfred Andrews, two miles west of the village. He was in the war of the Revolution, and died Sept. 20th, 1776, in the service, aged 27 years; his widow married second, Nov. 9th, 1780, No. (176.)

THEIR CHILDREN.

1. Seth, born May 4th, 1770, bap. Dec. 8th, 1771.
2. Samuel, jun., born March 7th, 1772, bap. April 12th, 1772, m. Nov. 14th, 1796, No. (447.)
3. Lydia, born Feb. 18th, 1774, bap. Feb. 20th, 1774, m. Nov. 8th, 1797, Oliver Richards, son of Joseph who had married her mother, (after the death of Ephraim Rice;) she died Jan. 8th, 1861, aged 87, at Newington; was the mother of Amon, Samuel, Oliver.

125. "Mary, wife of Gad Stanley," to church Nov. 17th, 1771; she daughter of No. (45) and No. (46;) she was both "well born and well bred;" became the mother of a large and respectable family, to whom she imparted much of herself; she died Jan. 8th, 1818, aged 70.

126. "Ichabod Andrus," to church Nov. 8th, 1772, eldest son of Gideon, of Southington, and Abigail (Potter,) his wife, born July 15th, 1745, bap. March 24th, 1751, at Southington, m. Nov. 17th, 1763, Lydia Smith, of Southington; he was a soldier of the Revolution; had his poll-tax of £18 on list of 1775, abated by the legislature, 1777; she died Sept. 19th, 1772, of consumption, when he returned to Southington for a time. He is next heard from as collector in (West Britain,) Burlington, 1782.

THEIR CHILDREN.

1. Clement, born March 22d, 1764.
2. David, born April 14th, 1766.
3. Hosea, born , bap. Nov. 8th, 1772, at New Britain.

127. "Doctor Josiah Hart," to church July 25th, 1773, from the first church in Wethersfield. This was son of No. (49) and No. (50,) born April 28th, 1742; graduated at Yale College, 1762, became a physician, was surgeon in the army of the Revolution; he prepared for college under Rev. Dr. Norris, studied medicine with Dr. Potter, of Wallingford, m.

1765, No. (128;) she died June 4th, 1777, of small-pox, when he married second, March 25th, 1778, Abigail Harris, of Wethersfield. He lived in that town, and represented it in the legislature several times; he was chosen a deacon there April 17th, 1793. His second wife died Aug. 8th, 1796, at Wethersfield, when he removed to Ohio, near Marietta, where his two sons were early in life settled. He was chosen deacon of the Congregational church there at its first formation. He had a third wife, who was Miss Anna (Moulton,) of Newburyport, Mass. In 1811, he moved to a farm ten miles from Marietta, where he died Aug., 1812, aged 74; his wife died a few hours after him, and both were buried the same day. Doctor Hart was of high repute as a physician, surgeon, scholar, and Christian; doubtless one of the brightest stars that New Britain has yet raised.

128. "Wife of Dr. Josiah Hart," to church July 25th, 1773, by letter from Wethersfield; her maiden name, Abigail Sluman; she was from Stonington; with her husband at Wethersfield, "owned the covenant" April 20th, 1766, and also, Dec. 4th, 1768; she died June 4th, 1777, at Wethersfield, of small-pox.

THEIR CHILDREN.

1. Abigail, born Feb. 3d, 1766, m. Thomas Wells.
2. Josiah, born Dec. 10th, 1768, died Jan. 15th, 1769, aged one year.
3. Hannah, born 24th, 1769, m. Joshua Robbins; she died May 28th, 1862, aged 94, at Avon.
4. Emily, born Feb. 3d, 1771, m. Gideon Wells.
5. Josiah Sluman, born Jan. 10th, 1773, bap. Feb. 7th, 1773, by Dr. Smalley, at New Britain.
6. William, born March 4th, 1775, m. Wolcott.
7. Thomas, born Dec. 14th, 1776, m. in Ohio.

SECOND WIFE'S CHILDREN.

8. Betsey, born Dec. 22d, 1778, m. Titus Buck.
9. Clarissa, born , m. in Ohio.
10. Cynthia, born , m. in Ohio.

129. "ISAAC PARSONS," to church Nov. 6th, 1773, son of Isaac, born March 12th, 174 , m. , he m. second, July 17th, 1766, No. (130;) we find by Southington church record that both he and his wife, Mary, were dismissed from this church to that, and received there, July 9th, 1780; he had a previous wife, who died April 7th, 1766, at Southington.

130. "Wife of Isaac Parsons," to church Nov. 6th, 1773; maiden name, Mary Atkins; was his second wife.

THEIR CHILDREN.

1. Isaac, born March 3d, 1769, died Sept. 1st, 1776, in "Blue Hills," Kensington.
2. Lemuel, born , bap. Nov. 21st, 1773, died Sept. 8th, 1776, in "Blue Hills."
3. Mary, born , bap. Dec. 10th, 1775.
4. General, born , bap. June 16th, 1782, in Southington.

131. "BENJAMIN HART," to church Dec. 12th, 1773, son of No. (49) and (50,) born Oct. 10th 1747, m. Aug. 19th, 1772, No. 132,) before Rev. Samuel Clark, of Kensington. His house and farm at the head of the mill pond of Ozias Hart, now, (1867,) Henry North's. He was a tall, bony man, of industrious and regular habits, a successful farmer, and walked orderly in his Christian life. He raised a large family to respectability, and died Feb. 21st, 1827, aged 80.

132. "Wife of Benjamin Hart," to church Dec. 12th, 1773, daughter of Ephraim Fuller, of Berlin, and Mary (Dunham,) his wife, bap. Jan. 2d, 1757, in Kensington, by Rev. Samuel Clark; her mother, sister of No. (76.) She named Mary after her mother. She died Oct. 22d, 1834, aged 79.

THEIR CHILDREN.

1. Benjamin, born Feb. 7th, 1773, m. Jan. 30th, 1800, Hannah Kellogg, of Martin; second, Almina Carter.
2. Mary, born 1775, died July 6th, 1790, aged 15.
3. Rhoda, born Jan. 10th, 1778, died May 9th, 1786, in her ninth year.
4. Roxana, born June 21st, 1780, bap. Aug. 13th, 1780, m. Nov. 9th, 1797, Leonard Belden, jun., No. (324.)
5. Theron, born Dec. 29th, 1782, bap. Feb. 9th, 1783, m. Abia Warner; second, Lydia Hart; he died Jan. 16th, 1859, in his 77th year.
6. Fanny, born Feb. 17th, 1785, m. Dr. Chauncey Andrews; she died Feb. 7th, 1860; he died Oct. 14th, 1863.
7. Rhoda, born Feb. 8th, 1788, bap. March 30th, 1788, m. March 28th, 1839, Asa Tuller, of Simsbury.
8. Ephraim, born Nov. 4th, 1790, bap. Nov. 4th, 1790, died young.
9. Polly, born May 2d, 1792, bap. June 10th, 1792, m. David Walkley, of Haddam.
10. Cyrus, born July 19th, 1795, bap. Sept. 6th, 1795, m. March 31st, 1819, Betsey Clark.
11. Esther, born March 5th, 1798, bap. June 10th, 1798, m. March 16th, 1819, Edwin Gridley, of Southington.

133. "CATHARINE, wife of Joseph Wright," to church March, 1774, daughter of William, of Hudson, N. Y., an Englishman. Mr. Wright was a soldier of the Revolution, and found his wife during his service on the Hudson River. They raised a large family on small means; lived on the corner opposite the David Steele house, on Main street, back of Dublin Hill. She was a sedate, pious woman; he a stirring, jovial man; she died Aug. 27th, 1817, aged 71; he died Feb. 26th, 1825, aged 84.

THEIR CHILDREN.

1. John, born , bap. March 20th, 1774.
2. David, born , m. May 4th, 1795, Abigail Wadsworth; second, widow Hart, (alias) Clarissa (Hopkins.)
3. Dan, born , bap. March 19th, 1777, died March, 1777.
4. Dan, born , bap. Aug. 2d, 1778, m. Oct. 20th, 1800, Roxy Daniels, daughter of David.
5. Crujah, born , bap. Sept. 17th, 1780, m. Nabby Goodrich, of John, of Newington.

6. Joseph, jun., born , bap. April 6th, 1783, m. May 31st, 1802, Esther Kelsey, of Enoch.

7. Lois, born , bap. March 23d, 1788, killed carelessly by Sage Churchill, with gun.

8. Anson, born , bap. Aug. 24th, 1790.

9. Solon, born

10. Chauncey, born Jan. 21st, 1788, m. Dec. 23d, 1812, Elizabeth Warner, daughter of Daniel, of Kensington, and Elizabeth (Kellogg,) his wife, no children.

134. "JOHN JUDD, jun.," to church May 29th, 1774, son of John, sen., and No. (46,) born Feb. 14th, 1746, m. Nov. 23d, 1769, No. (135 ;) lived near the site of Deacon Morton Judd's residence now, (1862,) and was his grandfather. He made his will 1795, and his property was distributed 1798. He died Jan. 6th, 1796, aged 50.

135. "Wife of John Judd, jun.," to church May 29th, 1774, name Lydia (Mather,) daughter of Joseph, sen., and Anna (Booth,) his wife, born Jan. 17th, 1744, one of a numerous family, born and brought up near the old red store of Elnathan Smith, which place Joseph, her father, owned and occupied many years. The well and grounds back a little still show the spot.

THEIR CHILDREN.

1. Bela, born Aug. 4th, 1770, bap. June 5th, 1774, m. Rachel Lusk, daughter of John.

2. John, born May 8th, 1772, bap. June 5th, 1774, m. May, 1792, Ursula Stanley, of Lot, No. (637.)

3. Alvin, born June 24th, 1774, bap. July 10th, 1774, died Nov. 7th, 1776.

4. Anna, born July 17th, 1776, died Oct. 1st, 1777, aged two years.

5. Lydia, born Jan. 7th, 1779, said to have become a beautiful woman, m. Seth Smith.

6. Oliver, born June 9th, 1782, m. March 11th, 1804, Elizabeth Belden, of Capt. Jonathan.

136. "PHINEAS SMITH," to church July 24th, 1774, by letter from the church in West Springfield. He m. May, 1767, No. (137,) before Dr. Smalley.

137. "Wife of Phineas Smith," to church July 24th, 1774, by letter from the church in West Springfield. Her maiden name, Hannah Smith.

138. "DAVID MATHER," to church June 26th, 1774, son of No. (47) and No. (48,) born Oct. 7th, 1738, m. June 2d, 1757, No. (139 ;) he was a farmer by occupation; lived on Main street, just south of, and at the foot of "Osgood Hill." He was a man of great muscular and mental power; had only a common school education, but was one of those few that Dr. Smalley ever called upon to pray in public. He was for many years one of the school visitors. On the 2d of December, 1779, he was chosen one of the standing committee of the church. His wife died, and he m. second, 1783, widow of John Kilbourn, Jemima (Neal ;) she sister of No. (78.) Mr. Mather was in the war of the Revolution, at Horse Neck; had a title, Ensign, by which he was ever after known. He "owned the cov-

enant" June 11th, 1758. His second wife, Jemima, died Sept. 20th, 1813, aged 76; he died May 27th, 1817, aged 77. He was chosen selectman at the first meeting of the new town of Berlin, June 13th, 1785.

139. "Wife of David Mather," to church June 26th, 1774; her maiden name Hannah Dunham, sister of No. (76) and No. (103.)

THEIR CHILDREN.

1. Elenor, born March 14th, 1758, bap June 11th, 1758.
2. Percia, born Jan. 2d, 1760, bap. Jan. 17th, 1760, m. Dec. 7th, 1780, Thomas Sugden, English, a deserter from the British army of the Revolutionary War; came to New Britain 1777; had several children; moved to Simsbury, and in 1802 to Canton.
3. Cotton, born Aug. 3d, 1764, bap. Aug. 5th, 1764, died Sept. 7th, 1779.
4. Mary Ann, born , m. Libeus Hungerford; m. second, David Hills.
5. Elizabeth, born Nov. 20th, 1767, m. No. (254.)
6. Hannah, born Aug. 10th, 1769, bap. July 10th, 1769, m. March 30th, 1794, Seth Hungerford.
7. Cotton, born Sept. 2d, 1771, bap. July 10th, 1774, m. June 19th, 1791, No. (375.)
8. Thomas, born Dec. 10th, 1773, died same day.
9. Rhoda, born Oct. 27th, 1776, bap. Nov. 10th, 1776, m. Orrin Goodrich, of Asahel.
10. Polly, born Dec. 27th, 1778, bap. Feb. 21st, 1779, m. April 23d, 1800, Ebenezer Gridley, of Seth.

140. "Judah Hart, jun.," to church July 24th, 1774, son of No. (51,) born Sept. 10th, 1750, m. April 19th, 1770, No. (141;) was a farmer; inherited his father's homestead, opposite the school-house in South-west district. He had a frail constitution. He was brother of No. (101,) and the large estate of their father was divided to them equally, after deducting for their sisters' share. The amount of his inventory was taken A. D. 1795, at £1,149 4s. 7d.; he died April 28th, 1795, aged 45. His wife was daughter of his step-mother, and was sister of James North, Esq.

141. "Wife of Judah Hart, jun.," to church July 24th, 1774, maiden name, Sarah North; was daughter of James, sen. and Sarah (Seymour,) his wife, born Feb. 22d, 1749; she died Sept. 15th, 1822, aged 74. She was a woman of great diligence and economy.

THEIR CHILDREN.

1. Sarah, born Nov. 7th, 1770, bap. July 31st, 1774, m. July 30th, 1793, Asahel Hart, of Jehudi.
2. Anna, born May 3d, 1773, bap. July 31st, 1774, died Sept. 17th, 1776, aged 3 years, 4 months.
3. Salmon, born May 20th, 1775, bap. June 25th, 1775, m. May 2d, 1796, No. (347.)
4. Judah, jun., born Dec. 16th, 1777, bap. Feb. 8th, 1778, m. May 1st, 1800, Abigail Belden, of Bildad.
5. Anna, 2d, born March 17th, 1780, bap. April 30th, 1780, m. Sept. 17th, 1804, Truman Woodruff; she died Nov. 20th, 1857, in her 78th year.
6. Roxana, born Oct. 23d, 1784, bap. Dec. 12th, 1784, m. Nov. 22d, 1803, Albert Meriman, of Southington; m. second, James Beecher; she d. Nov. 26th, 1859, aged 75.
7. Henry, born , bap. Feb. 11th, 1787.
8. Amzi, born July 10th, 1792, bap. Aug. 19th, 1792, drowned in a well, Sept. 27th, 1795.

9. Lydia, born Dec. 14th, 1786, m. June 20th, 1805, Samuel Porter, of Southington.

10. Eliphaz, born June 28th, 1789, m. Eliza Armstrong, of Franklin, Conn. He was a jeweller.

142. "EZEKIEL WRIGHT," to church August, 1774; Dr. Smalley's record says he was baptized March 14th, 1762, an adult. He m. Jan. 26th, 1761, at Southington, No. (143.) He built a new house on the south branch of Bass River, near Reuben Wright's, and sold it 1785, to Elisha Hart, with two acres of land, butted east on highway, and north on Justus Francis; this location on the road over the mountain to Farmington; probably moved to New Hartford, New York State.

143. "Wife of Ezekiel Wright," to church August, 1774; her maiden name, Eunice Neal, daughter of William, of Southington; baptized there June 22d, 1740; she "owned the covenant" March 14th, 1762, in New Britain; she sister of No. (78) and No. (XVI.)

THEIR CHILDREN.

1. Lucy, born March 25th, 1763, bap. March 27th, 1763, m. Ebenezer Steele, jun.
2. Rachel, born , bap. May 30th, 1779.

144. "Widow MARGARET WHAPLES," to church Nov. 6th, 1774; she was widow of Jonathan Whaples, (son of Jonathan and his wife, Sarah;) was daughter of Joseph Woodruff, No. (59) and No. (60;) probably her husband died at Claverack, N. Y. She married second, Dec. 22d, 1774, Lieut. Elijah Porter, of Farmington; this was his third wife. She and her first husband "owned the covenant" at Newington, May 5th, 1754; she to church in Farmington, 1777. After the death of Lieut. Porter, in Farmington, she returned to this place, and died Nov. 6th, 1810, aged 75, at the house of Selah Steele, sen.

HER CHILDREN.

1. Samuel Whaples, born , bap. May 5th, 1754, at Newington, m. Huldah Langdon.
2. Elizur Whaples, born , bap. Dec. 28th, 1755, at Newington, m. Ruth Woodruff, of Robert.
3. John Whaples, born , m. Rhoda Lusk, daughter of David.
4. Sally Whaples, born Jan., 1758, bap. Jan. 15th, 1758, at Farmington, by Rev. Mr. Booge, of Northington, m. Seth Porter, son of her mother's second husband.
5. Mary Ann Whaples, born , bap. Sept. 2d, 1774.
6. Amzi Porter, born Nov. 17th, 1775, m. Jan. 12th, 1801, Rebecca Andrews, of Hezekiah; Amzi Porter to church in Farmington, 1799; Rebecca, his wife, 1821. They moved to Oswego, N. Y., where they died.

145. "Widow LUCINA STEDMAN," to church March 16th, 1777, the widow of Theodore Stedman, who was a soldier of the Revolution; was taken prisoner and died January, 1777, in this place, soon after his return from captivity in New York. He seems to have resided in Kensington, for his tax for building the meeting-house there was abated by vote of that society Dec. 4th, 1777.

THEIR CHILDREN.

1. Ashbel, born , bap. April 6th, 1777.

2. Betsey, born , bap. April 6th, 1777; her mother appointed guardian June 14th, 1784, by Probate Court at Farmington.

3. Theodorus, born bap. April 6th, 1777.

4. Henry, born , posthumous, bap. July 4th, 1779.

146. "LYDIA NORTH," to church Aug. 10, 1777, daughter of James, sen. and his wife, Sarah (Seymour,) sister of No. (148;) she died April 18th, 1814, aged 68.

147. "SOLOMON RUGG," to church Aug. 10th, 1777, by letter from church in Kensington; he was dismissed by letter, 1813; no reference had to the place. He was a miller by occupation; lived east of Deacon Hart's mill-pond, and attended his mill. He had united with Kensington church by profession March 15th, 1772. His wife was Margaret (Hudson,) born June 13th, 1738, to Thomas; she died Nov. 21st, 1807, aged 69. He died near Ballston Springs, N. Y., 1817.

THEIR CHILDREN.

1. Solomon, born , bap. Sept. 24th, 1777, m. Phebe Hitchcock, March 23d, 1786; she to church in Southington; a widow, 1804; she died 1835.

2. Matthew, born 1767, bap. Sept. 24th, 1777, m. Polly Webb, daughter of David, of Salem; was a cooper by trade; lived in District No. 4, by Harlowe Eddy's; he died April 29th, 1819, aged 52; was a quiet, inoffensive man.

3. Phebe, born , bap. Sept. 24th, 1777, m. April, 1791, Submit Bailey, of Kensington.

4. Sylvanus, born , bap. Sept. 24th, 1777, m. Polly

5. Seth, born , bap. Sept. 24th, 1777, m. Sabra and moved to New Marlboro, Mass.; he a cabinet maker; learned of Aaron Roberts.

148. "Wife of Ebenezer Steele," to church from Kensington church, 1777; her maiden name, Sarah Sage, daughter of David and his wife, Bathsheba Judd, "of Great Swamp Society;" she was admitted to Kensington church April 10th, 1757, m. Aug. 10th, 1749. He was born May 12th, 1727, to Doctor Joseph Steele and his wife, Elizabeth (Hollister,) of Glastenbury, who lived in "Great Swamp," near the first meeting-house. She was the mother of thirteen children, from eight of whom, at the time of her death, had descended seventy grand-children, one hundred and seventy-one great-grand-children, and twenty-four great-great-grand-children, making then in all, 278. She served in this place as midwife many years. She died March 16th, 1823, aged 94, having lived about seventy-two years with her husband, in Kensington, until their children had been born and baptized, when they moved on to "Osgood Hill," next door south of "Grand-father Osgood." He died Jan. 22d, 1821, aged 94. He never united with the church, but thought he experienced a saving change late in life. He was a soldier of the Revolutionary War.

THEIR CHILDREN.

1. Ebenezer, jun., born 1749, m. Lucy Wright, of Ezekiel; second, Hannah Brewer, No. (225.)
2. Sarah, born March 26th, 1750, m. Ezra Belden; second, Lewis Seymour, a French soldier.
3. Mary, born Sept. 7th, 1754, m. Aug. 19th, 1773, Elisha Booth; she died Nov. 1st, 1742, at Colebrook.
4. William, born 1757, m. Oct. 26th, 1780, No. (246.)
5. Josiah, born 1758, bap. June 11th, 1758, at Kensington, m. No. (377.)
6. Charles, born 1760, bap. July 6th, 1760, at Kensington.
7. Allen, born 1762, bap. Jan. 3d, 1762.
8. Selah, born April 19th, 1764, bap. May 6th, 1764, married April 14th, 1786, No. (853.)
9. Huldah, born 1768, bap. Jan. 3d, 1768, at Kensington, m. June 24th, 1784, No. (183.)
10. Rebecca, born May 30th, 1769, bap. July 7th, 1769, at Kensington, m. June 19th, 1781, Cotton Mather.
11. Salmon, born 1771, bap. March 17th, 1771, at Kensington.

It is thought two other children not in this list died young.

149. "JAMES NORTH," to church Sept. 14th, 1777, son of James, of "Great Swamp," and Canaan, where he died, 1758, and his wife, Sarah (Seymor,) born Jan. 18th, 1748, (his own record,) see No. (43,) m. Sept. 29th, 1774, No. (150;) he had before this learned his trade of blacksmith of John Richards, at Stanley quarter; he had his shop at first on the site of his grand-son, Henry North's, opposite the present Episcopal church, but moved it opposite his house, the same where his son, Henry, lived and died. He was a man of enterprise and influence; was in public offices and employment; of good understanding and judgment, and was popular; was captain, magistrate, representative; was on the 6th Sept., 1795, chosen one of the standing committee of the church, and Dr. Smalley then entered his name as Capt. James North. He wrote a fair hand and was treasurer and clerk of the school and ecclesiastical societies, after the resignation of Col. Lee. Having a sound body, a good trade, and a handsome property by his wife, he began his career in life with fair prospects, which by the great diligence and economy of both, proved a success. His wife, Rhoda, died March 15th, 1824, aged 70, when he married second, Feb. 26th, 1828, Abi, the widow of Capt. Justus Francis, and the daughter of Deacon Timothy Stanley. James North, Esq. died May 14th, 1833, aged 85; his widow, Abi, died Oct. 3d, 1852, at West Avon, aged 87, but buried in New Britain cemetery. He was son of James, of Thomas, son of Thomas, who was son of John, the settler.

150. "Wife of James North," to church Sept. 14th, 1777; her maiden name, Rhoda Judd, daughter of No. (45) and No. (46,) born Jan. 9th, 1754, see No. (149.)

THEIR CHILDREN.

1. Rhoda, born Feb. 10th, 1776, bap. Nov. 9th, 1777, m. No. (645.)

2. James, jun., born Dec, 19th, 1777, bap. Feb. 8th, 1778, m. May 1st, 1800, Rhoda Belden, daughter of Capt. Jonathan.

3. Seth Judd, born Aug. 13th, 1779, bap. Sept. 19th, 1779, m. Sept. 27th, 1801, No. (396.)

4. Alvin, born Aug. 13th, 1781, bap. Oct. 7th, 1781, m. July 15th, 1804, No. (331;) married second, No. (411.)

5. Henry, born Nov. 3d, 1783, bap. Dec. 7th, 1783, died young.

6. Abi, born Nov. 21st, 1784, bap. Dec. 26th, 1784, m. Oct. 10th, 1802, No. (550.)

7. Nancy, born Jan. 11th, 1787, bap. Feb. 18th, 1787, m. Oct. 11th, 1807, Cyrus Booth, son of Joseph.

8. Henry, 2d, born Sept. 24th, 1789, bap. Nov. 8th, 1789, m. 1810, Sarah Cosslett; married second, No. (744.)

9. Orpha, born Aug. 12th, 1793, bap. Sept. 15th, 1793, m. 1812, No. (311.)

10. William Burnham, born Dec. 6th, 1797, bap. Feb. 4th, 1798, m. Aug. 16th, 1824, No. (651.)

151. "The wife of Seth Judd," to church Sept. 14th, 1777; her maiden name, Lydia Richards, daughter of John, the blacksmith, and Mary (French,) his wife, born April 10th, 1754, bap. April 21st, 1754, at Newington, m. Oct., 1772, Seth Judd, son of No. (45) and No. (46;) he was accidentally shot in camp in time of the Revolution, when she m. second, Samuel Huggins, of New Hampshire, to which State she had moved with her father; she died Aug. 30th, 1841, aged 87.

152. Widow Mary Gilbert," to church March 15th, 1778, from the church in Worthington, by letter; to church there 1777. Her maiden name, Mary Butrick; she m. May 27th, 1762, Ebenezer Gilbert; their house was opposite John Ellis' place. He was killed in the army, Feb. 15th, 1776, when she married second, Nov. 19th, 1778, Lieut. Elisha Booth, who built the Colonel Wright house, (now, 1867, Goodwin's,) about 1761, as indicated by the carpenter's mark on the barn. He sold this place the spring of 1795, to Deacon Benjamin Wright, and moved to Hartland, where he died; she took a letter to that church, but after the settlement of Lieut. Booth's estate, at Hartland, she returned, (so says Dr. Smalley's record,) Aug. 3d, 1800, and spent the remnant of life at the old Gilbert house, and died March 30th, 1831, aged 86, and was buried in New Britain cemetery. Elisha Booth was the youngest son of Robert, and had married Dec. 5th, 1751, before Rev. Joshua Belden, Esther Hollister, by whom he had seven children, when she died Aug. 25th, 1776, aged 44.

CHILDREN.

1. Thomas, born Sept. 6th, 1750, m. Eunice (Hurlbert,) widow of Jonathan Gilbert.

2. Elisha, born Nov. 8th, 1753, m. Aug. 19th, 1773, Mary Steele, of Ebenezer, sen.; he died Nov. 16th, 1804, aged 51.

3. Esther, born Sept. 1st, 1755; never married; kept house for Thomas; she died July 15th, 1826.

4. Huldah, born Oct. 28th, 1760, bap. Nov. 16th, 1760, m. Sept. 25th, 1783, David Goodrich.

5. Sylvanus, born Feb. 10th, 1763, bap. Feb. 27th, 1763, died in the army of the Revolution.

6. Nancy, born Aug. 18th, 1768, m. May 15th, 1797, No. (279.)

7. Sally, born July 25th, 1770, died Aug. 4th, 1776, aged four, of camp distemper.

SECOND WIFE'S CHILDREN.

8. Hannah, born Aug. 17th, 1779, bap. Sept. 19th, 1779.

9. Lois, born Jan. 14th, 1782, bap. Feb. 17th, 1782, m. Jan. 5th, 1812, Joseph Taylor.

10. Abi, born May 30th, 1784, bap. July 18th, 1784, m. Aug. 31st, 1800, Sylvester Mygatt.

153. "MERCY NORTH," to church Aug. 2d, 1778, sister of No. (149,) m. July 18th, 1782, Samuel Bass; they lived on West Main street, near where Norman Hough has his residence. She was an active, industrious woman. Mr. Bass died Nov. 29th, 1802, aged 50, of a cancer; she died Aug. 6th, 1819, aged 66.

THEIR CHILDREN.

1. Her daughter Asenath, born , bap. Aug. 2d, 1778, m. Nov. 29th, 1798, Charles Eddy.

1. Daniel, born , bap. July 6th, 1783.
2. Bethia, born , bap. Dec. 12th, 1784, m. Dec. 31st, 1804, Darius Woodford.
3. Henry, born Dec. 9th, 1786, m. Amelia M. Love; he died 1860, aged 74, of cancer, at Cokesbury, S. C.; he a Methodist minister.
4. Lydia, born , bap. Feb. 11th, 1787, died young.
5. Samuel, born , bap. June 14th, 1789.
6. Lydia, born , bap. June 10th, 1792, see No. (474.)
7. Gunilda, born Oct. 3d, 1795, bap. Nov. 15th, 1795, m. No. (459.)
8. Infant, no name, died young.

154. "ABIGAIL, wife of Isaac Lee, 3d," to church May 2d, 1779, daughter of No. (63) and No. (64,) born Oct. 30th, 1754, m. May 25th, 1773, No. (168;) she died April 9th, 1811, aged 58.

155. ELIZABETH, wife of Joseph Booth," to church May 2d, 1779, daughter of No. (91) and No. (92,) born Dec. 12th, 1755, m. Dec. 18th, 1777, Joseph Booth, son of No. (65) and No. (66;) they lived on Dublin Hill, the only house there for many years; it is still standing; his son, Joseph, went with James North, jun. and Joseph Shipman, to Stockbridge, Mass., and learned the trade of brass-founder. The family moved to Charlotte, N. Y. She died May 18th, 1819, aged 64. He died June 10th, 1835, aged 84.

THEIR CHILDREN.

1. Joseph, jun., born June 10th, 1778, bap. May 23d, 1779, m. Charlotte Bowman, New York.
2. Abigail, born Aug. 21st, 1779, bap. Sept. 19th, 1779, m. Charles Spoor, N. Y.
3. Orange Francis, born March 5th, 1782, bap. April 7th, 1782, m. Lucy Hart, of Candor, N. Y.

4. Elizabeth, born Aug. 29th, 1783, m. June 21st, 1801, John R. Lincoln; m. second, No. (442.)

5. Hannah, born April 15th, 1785, bap. June 5th, 1785, m. May 18th, 1807, Hermas Carter; she died Aug. 29th, 1867, at the residence of her son, Newton, in Hartford.

6. Cyrus, born Oct. 10th, 1786, bap. Jan. 29th, 1787, m. Oct. 11th, 1807, No. (340.)

7. Jesse, born Aug. 29th, 1790, bap. Nov. 7th, 1790, m. Roxy Francis; lives in Wisconsin, 1861.

8. Selah, born April 1st, 1792, bap. June 10th, 1792, m. Fuller; lives in Wisconsin, 1861.

9. Francis, born June 10th, 1795, bap. Sept. 6th, 1795, died March, 1835, in N. Y.

10. Jane Clark, born Oct. 8th, 1797, bap. April 1st, 1798, m. Hiram Fuller, brother of Selah's wife.

156. "CHLOE, wife of Elnathan Smith," to church May 16th, 1779, only daughter of No. (35) and No. (36,) born Jan. 15th, 1746, m. July 9th, 1767; she had a lady-like appearance, and bore a good Christian character. He lived in the house on East street, known (now, 1861,) as the Rhodes house. He was a man of wealth, standing and influence in public affairs. He kept the first store of goods to retail in the parish, (with the exception of Joseph Clark, who had done a little in that way.) He was in the old French war, and acted as commissary in the Revolution. He taught district school, in the winter season, in early life. He was a man of large proportions and strong passions. He bought his place of Dr. Smalley, 1788, for £400. He died March 6th, 1826, aged 88. She died Sept. 26th, 1825, aged 80, having lived together nearly 60 years.

THEIR CHILDREN.

1. Elnathan, born May 6th, 1768, bap. May 23d, 1779, m. Lois Beckley, of Berlin, daughter of Elias Beckley and Lois (Parsons,) his wife; he died at Berlin, Feb. 22d, 1801, aged 33.

2. Nancy, born March 17th, 1770, bap. May 23d, 1779, m. Benjamin D. Galpin; m. second, Simeon Lincoln.

3. Sylvia, born May 23d, 1772, died April 26th, 1773, aged one year.

4. Sylvia, born April 5th, 1774, bap. May 23d, 1779, m. Oliver Goodrich, of Rocky Hill.

5. Chloe, born May 23d, 1776, bap. May 23d, 1779.

6. Joseph Lee, born May 28th, 1779, bap. Aug. 1st, 1779, m. Francis M. Kirby, of Litchfield. Col. Joseph L. Smith, died May 27th, 1846, aged 67, at St. Augustine; had been U. S. Judge of Florida.

7. Lydia, born March 28th, 1782, bap. May 26th, 1782, never married.

8. Mary, born July 1st, 1784; never married; died April 4th, 1859, at New Haven, aged 75.

9. Ira Elliot, born Dec. 21st, 1786, bap. Feb. 11th, 1787; never married; died Sept. 5th, 1849, aged 63; he was a lawyer of considerable ability, Judge of County and Probate Courts, and was a leader of the Democratic party for many years in town.

157. "MEHITABEL KILBOURN," to church Jan. 30th, 1780, daughter of Joshua and Mehitabel (Mather,) his wife, born April 23d, 1764, bap. Aug. 29th, 1764, m. Nov. 24th, 1785, No. (179.)

158. "JONATHAN BELDEN," to church Nov. 12th, 1780, son of Ezra and Rebecca (Dix,) his wife, born Jan. 11th, 1750, m. Dec. 29th, 1774, No. (159;) was a carpenter by trade, but followed farming; was a man of great firmness of purpose; a self-made man of much intelligence. He was an ardent politician of the Jefferson school. He was engaged much in public business, and was very capable. He was patriotic, public-spirited and liberal. His residence was that now, (1862,) owned by Edmund Steele, on Stanley street. He owned much of the present village land, and was apparently prosperous for many years. He was a captain, and so called. At length he became involved in debt, fell under censure of the church, became disheartened, and died Sept. 10th, 1824, aged 73. He died at the house of David Steele, where his daughter, Polly (Clark,) was then living. He was naturally a fine specimen of the "old Roman character," and was in his day considered a prodigy of learning. It was said of Elizur Hart, the great school-master, that he (Hart,) knew *every thing*, he knew almost as much as Capt. Belden. The action of the church in the discipline of Capt. Belden, was noted; it was pending a long time, and created great excitement. The church took action A. D. 1812, and an appeal to Consociation was had 1813.

159. "Wife of Jonathan Belden," to church Nov. 12th, 1780; maiden name, Mary Allen, sister of No. (318,) sister also of No. (708.) She was a woman that looked well to her household. "Her children arise up and call her blessed." She daughter of Ephraim, of Wallingford, Plymouth and Southington, and his wife, Hannah Williams; she died Aug. 16th, 1823, aged 72, at the present house of Harlowe Eddy, in District No. 4.

THEIR CHILDREN.

1. Polly, born , d. Sept. 9th, 1780.
2. Jonathan, born , died Sept. 12th, 1780.
3. Polly, born April 9th, 1780, bap. Nov. 26th, 1780, m. Feb. 14th, 1800, Abner Clark, see No. (639.)
4. Rhoda, born Dec. 22d, 1781, bap. March 24th, 1782, m. No. (443.)
5. Elizabeth, born April 3d, 1784, bap. May 2d, 1784, m. March 11th, 1804, Oliver Judd, of John.
6. Jonathan, born 1786, bap. March 26th, 1786, m. May 1st, 1803, Catharine Andrus, of Phineas.
7. Infant, born , bap. April 16th, 1788, died young.
8. Nancy, born Aug. 31st, 1792, bap. Oct. 7th, 1792, m. May 5th, 1812, No. (370.)

160. "SIBBEL, wife of Noadiah Brownson," to church, Nov. 26th, 1780; her maiden name, Horsington, daughter of John, of Southington, and his wife, Sarah (Templar,) of Wallingford, born 1745, m. June 5th, 1766, Noadiah, son of Elijah Bronson and Abigail (Winchel,) his wife; he born Sept. 18th, 1740; he died July 11th, 1803, aged 63, at Kensington, the same year his grand-son, Orestes A. was born. They had no permanent

location; lived several years at the Nathan Judd house, on the corner east of Dr. Smalley's, and south of the Skinner house.

THEIR CHILDREN.

1. Sylvester, born June 7th, 1772, bap. Dec. 3d, 1780, became the father of Orestes A., the philosopher.
2. Sibbil, born March 29th, 1775, bap. Dec. 3d, 1780.

161. "COLLINS LUDINGTON," to church Dec. 31st, 1780, son of Daniel, of East Haven, and Susan (Clark,) his second wife, born about 1749, m. Feb. 9th, 1775, Sarah Smith, daughter of Elijah, sen. and his wife, Sarah (Grimes.) He built the Whipple house, formerly the only house between Alvin North's and Capt. Belden's. He moved to Owego, N. Y., at the time our people had the "Wago fever," as it was called. He moved his family in the Spring, and came to the Hudson River in the sleigh. The people there told him not to cross, for the ice was old and brittle. The family walked over and all arrived safe on the opposite bank, where they eat their dinner in the sleigh, and while doing so, the ice parted just above, and all the river where they had just crossed was clear. They cried for joy at their narrow escape. He settled in Candor, where his name, 1814, was on their church catalogue. He had a bad corn on one of his toes, and cut the toe off with a chisel, and came near dying in consequence. He used the first two-horse wagon in New Britain, it is said. He died 1821, at Candor, N. Y. He was in the war of the Revolution, from Farmington.

THEIR CHILDREN.

1. Sally, born Feb. 5th, 1777, died July, 1780.
2. Anna, born March 20th, 1781, bap. Aug. 22d, 1781, died young.
3. Anna, 2d, born March 20th, 1783, bap. June 15th, 1783.
4. Sophia, born , bap. May 29th, 1791.
5. Sarah, born , bap. Sept. 14th, 1794.

162. "JOHN HINSDALE," to church 1780, son of Barnabas, jun. and his wife, Martha (Smith,) of Hartford, born Aug. 13th, 1706, at Hartford; was a blacksmith; had his shop near his house, opposite the present Methodist church, in Berlin street. He was a constituent member of Worthington church, 1775; was moderator of the second church meeting in their new meeting-house. He came to this place about 1780, having been dismissed and received from Worthington church. He m. Nov. 8th, 1733, No. (163,) and both were received to Kensington church soon after. He was one of the standing committee in Kensington church, 1766. He bought the Deacon Josiah Lee farm, (alias) the Skinner place, and owned a large part of that square. He sold 1788, to Dr. Smalley, ten acres and sixty-two rods of land. His will is dated July 26th, 1792, names Theodore, John, Elizabeth, Lucy, Lydia and Elijah. He died Dec. 2d, 1792, aged 86. He had made his son-in-law, Samuel Hart, executor of his will.

163. "ELIZABETH, wife of Capt. John Hinsdale," to church 1780; her maiden name, (Cole,) born at Hartford, probably March 18th, 1709–10, to Nathaniel and his wife, Elizabeth (Knight;) she died July 1st, 1782, in her 74th year; her grave at cemetery, Worthington South.

THEIR CHILDREN.

1. John, born Aug. 19th, 1734; he died young, Oct. 13th, 1743, aged nine years; grave in "Christian Lane."

2. Elizabeth, born June 29th, 1736, m. April 28th, 1758, David Atkins, of Middletown, Conn.

3. Theodore, born Nov. 25th, 1738, graduated at Yale, m. Anna Bissell; settled a minister at Windsor, Conn., North Society, April 30th, 1766.

4. Lucy, born July 16th, 1741, m. Jan. 27th, 1763, Samuel Plumb, of Middletown, Conn.; she died Feb., 1791.

5. Elijah, born April 1st, 1744, m. Ruth Bidwell; owned the Stephen Lee farm, (alias,) the Hinsdale place; extended west to meeting house yard, except the "burying-ground;" he a blacksmith; also made silk from the mulberry orchard next west of the cemetery; he died June 26th, 1797, aged 54.

6. Lydia, born Aug. 11th, 1747, m. Oct. 4th, 1770, Samuel Hart; she mother of "Mrs. Willard and Mrs. Phelps."

7. John, born Aug. 21st, 1749, m. Philomela, daughter of Dr. James Hurlburt. He father of Col. Hosea Hinsdale, of Winsted. The father buried at Berlin, died Dec. 9th, 1795, grave at cemetery, Worthington South. Col. Hinsdale died 1866, aged 91.

164. "SARAH FISHER," to church March 11th, 1781, by letter from West Hartford; her maiden name, probably Sally Bibbins, or Bevans; to church there Oct. 14th, 1775, and baptized. She married Jan. 20th, 1778, Eleazer Fisher, who was a soldier of the Revolution; had his poll tax abated by the legislature, 1777, on list of 1775, £18, and then resided in this place.

THEIR CHILD.

Jonathan, born , bap. March 11th, 1781.

165. "JAMES BOOTH," to church Sept. 9th, 1781, son of No. (65) and No. (66,) born March, 1748, m. Nov. 23d, 1775, No. (166;) his house stood where that of John Stanley's does; his farm bounded north by land of Col. Lee, west by Thomas Hart, and south by John Judd, and east by highway; his house was built by Col. Lee, for his son, Theodore. Mr. Booth was a plain farmer, and an honest, conscientious, Christian man. He died Sept. 18th, 1830, aged 66.

166. "Wife of James Booth," to church Sept. 9th, 1781; maiden name, Thankful Winchel, daughter of Ebenezer, of Torringford, and his wife, Thankful (Loomis,) of Westfield, Mass., born about 1756; is remembered as a woman of energy and character; she died Oct. 26th, 1820, aged 64.

THEIR CHILDREN.

1. James, born Sept. 11th, 1776, bap. Oct. 7th, 1781, m. Dec. 22d, 1800, No. (338.)

2. Ebenezer Winchel, born July 3d, 1778, bap. Oct. 7th, 1781, m. June 14th, 1802, Betsey Benham.

3. Aurelia, born 1781, bap. Oct. 7th, 1781, m. Dec. 8th, 1801, Timothy Percival; m. second, No. (425.)

4. Osmyn, born 1796, bap. July 31st, 1796, m. Dec. 22d, 1819, No. (431.)

167. "ESTHER, wife of Joseph Smith," to church 1781; this was his second wife, m. Sept., 1766, No. (29,) before Dr. Smalley, and was called at her marriage to him, Widow Esther Deming, born June 1st, 1720, at Wallingford, to Benoni and Esther Adkins; she died June 21st, 1804, aged 84; she died at the old tavern stand of her husband, (Seth Lewis having bought out the heirs to the estate previous to her decease.) She was the widow of Zebulon Deming, of Southington, who was drowned May 17th, 1762, (tradition says in the Hudson River.) Her maiden name, Esther Adkins, to church in Southington, June 26th, 1737; she m. Deming about 1740; they lived in the north part of Southington.

HER CHILDREN BY FIRST HUSBAND, ZEBULON DEMING.

1. Anna, born , bap. Feb. 21st, 1742, at Southington, by Rev. Jeremiah Curtiss, m. Oct., 1764, at Southington, before Rev. B. Chapman, No. (101.)

2. Zealous, born , bap. Feb. 9th, 1746, at Southington, by Rev. J. Curtiss.

3. Samuel, born , bap. July 11th, 1756, at Southington, by Rev. B. Chapman; he died Sept. 14th, 1775, in his 20th year; his grave in New Britain cemetery; probably died with his mother, at "Landlord Smith's." Zebulon Deming, the father, was uncle to John and Chauncey, of Farmington.

168. "ISAAC LEE, jun.," to church Sept. 30th, 1781, son of No. (35) and No. (36,) born March 23d, 1752; No. (154,) his wife, m. May 25th, 1773. He was a farmer, and inherited his father's homestead, still called the old Lee house. He was a pious, good man, greatly interested in the welfare of the church and society. He owned a large part of the land on which has been built the present village of New Britain; his wife, Abigail, died April 9th, 1811, aged 58, when he married second, No. (386.) He gave the land on which the second church edifice was built, now called "Strickland Hall," and in other ways showed his liberality. He died April 11th, 1828, aged 76.

THEIR CHILDREN.

1. Isaac, jun., born April 13th, 1775, bap. May 9th, 1779, m. Sept. 27th, 1799, No. (348.)

2. Thomas, born Nov. 28th, 1776, bap. May 9th, 1779, married Oct. 10th, 1797, No. (357.)

3. Almira, born July 17th, 1780, bap. Aug. 20th, 1780, m. Sept. 27th, 1801, Jesse Stanley.

4. Polly, born Dec. 22d, 1783, bap. Feb. 8th, 1784, m. July 11th, 1802, No. (461.)

5. Josiah, born Aug. 6th, 1786, bap. Sept. 10th, 1786, died Nov. 29th, 1788.

6. Abigail, born May 14th, 1788, bap. June 15th, 1788, m. Sept. 7th, 1806, Cyrus Stanley.

7. Josiah, 2d, born Sept. 21st, 1791, bap. Oct. 8th, 1791, died Oct. 9th, 1791.

8. Chloe, born July 24th, 1793, bap. Sept. 15th, 1793, m. Oct. 8th, 1820, Treat Deming, of Wethersfield.

9. Lorenzo, born Dec. 23d, 1795, bap. Feb. 7th, 1796, died Nov. 7th, 1798, by burn.

169. "STEPHEN HOLLISTER," to church 1781, born Aug. 6th, 1729 to Gershom; lived at the south end of Stanley street, near the brick-kiln, just north, on the east corner, m. No. (79;) he died Aug. 31st, 1800, aged 73.

THEIR CHILDREN.

1. Rhoda, born May 10th, 1756, m. Sept. 5th, 1771, Joseph Woodruff, jun.
2. Anna, born June 23d, 1758, bap. July 2d, 1758, m. David Daniels.
3. Thomas, born Sept. 10th, 1762, married March 9th, 1786, Sarah Hurlburt, of Wethersfield.
4. Charlotte, born June 21st, 1766, m. May 30th, 1787, Edward Patterson, of Berlin.
5. Stephen, jun., born Jan. 1st, 1769, bap. Jan. 1st, 1769, m. Flowers.
6. Sarah, born , m. April 19th, 1772, Simeon, son of Job Bronson.

170. "ELIZABETH, wife of Col. Isaac Lee," to church Dec. 30th, 1781; her maiden name, (Grant,) from East Windsor, m. Dec. 30th, 1772, see No. (35;) she died May 17th, 1782, of small-pox.

171. "ABIGAIL, wife of Joshua Webster," to church June 23d, 1782, daughter of Nathan Booth and Abigail (Steele,) his wife, born Oct. 3d, 1748, m. March 24th, 1773; they lived on West Main street, and the house he built gave place to the present residence of Edmund R. Swift. He died June 10th, 1798, aged 49, when she married second, March 15th, 1813, Sylvanus Dunham, who lived at the head of Shuttle Meadow. She was received to Southington church, 1814, by letter from this church; she returned after the death of Mr. Dunham, to this church, June 6th, 1824, and died May, 1829, aged 81, at the alms-house, at Berlin.

WEBSTER CHILDREN.

1. Leonard, born , bap. July 14th, 1782, went west unmarried.
2. Abigail, born , bap. March 2d, 1783, m. March 22d, 1802, Abner Webster; she died July 9th, 1823, aged 40 years.
3. Lucy, born , bap. Oct. 24th, 1784, m. Sept. 27th, 1801, Amzi Stanley, son of Col. Gad; she died Aug. 8th, 1823, and he Aug. 4th, 1823, at Marietta, Ohio; the parents of Maria, wife of Deacon Orson Seymour, of south church, see No. (656.)

172. "DANIEL AMES," to church Sept. 15th, 1782, son of John, of Rocky Hill, and his wife, Abigail (Butler,) born Feb. 1st, 1751; he m. Sept. 7th, 1780, No. (173.) He learned his trade, cabinet-maker and joiner, (as was common in those days, to have them combined,) at Rocky Hill; he built the Aaron Robert's house, and owned the place which he sold to Mr. Roberts, he being a fellow craftsman, having served their time as apprentices together. He afterwards built the house in Hart quarter, now occupied by Waldo Hayden. He lost one arm by the bursting of a gun, 1788, after which he kept school. He had a kind of vice to hold the quill, while he made the pen with one hand. He moved to Southington, and lived also in Simsbury; had a second wife, Lucina (North,) of Simsbury. He died Nov. 19th, 1822, aged 71, at Southington.

173. "Wife of Daniel Ames," to church Sept. 15th, 1782, Mercy, daughter of Capt. John Langdon, and No. (108,) born Sept. 6th, 1761; she died Sept. 12th, 1817, at Southington, aged 56.

THEIR CHILDREN.

1. John, born Jan. 24th, 1781, bap. Oct. 20th, 1782, died Aug. 30th, 1784, aged three and a half years.
2. Laura, born Feb. 23d, 1784, m. March 25th, 1807, Timothy C. Cressey, of Southington.
3. Anne, born April 23d, 1786, died April 24th, 1786, aged one day.
4. Horace, born July 21st, 1788, m. Sophia Loyd; he a physician at Granville.
5. John, 2d, born June 10th, 1790, bap. July 11th, 1790, died May 11th, 1806, aged 16.
6. Amon Langdon, born Aug. 16th, 1798, bap. Oct. 14th, 1798, m. Feb. 17th, 1825, Rosanna Hart.
7. Ira, born May 7th, 1800, bap. Aug. 17th, 1800, m. May 23d, 1822, Hannah Clark, of Southington.

174. "Asahel Hart," to church Jan. 26th, 1783, son of Joseph, of Northington, now Avon, and Anna Barnes, of Thomas, of Southington, his wife, born May 12th, 1754, bap. May 25th, 1754, Rev. E. Booge, officiating, at Northington. He bought of Elisha Hart, 1791, his new house which Ezekiel Wright built, on Farmington road, near Bass River, with two acres and ten rods of land, where he lived some years; he m. No. (224.) He was a brick-mason by trade and occupation, a stirring, lively man, naturally impulsive. After some years he moved to the foot of "Osgood Hill," on the same road. His wife died Feb. 22d, 1803, when he m. second, Jan. 11th, 1804, Chloe Booth, daughter of Nathan, sen.; she died Feb. 10th, 1807, aged 44; when he m. third, July 29th, 1807, Widow Prudence Gridley, of Avon, widow of Stephen; her maiden name, Park. Mr. Hart died at North Granby. Gridley, her former husband, was drowned at the whirlpool below Farmington bridge; he had swam the river once safely, when a bet was offered that he could not do it again, and he was drowned in the attempt.

THE HART CHILDREN.

1. Anna, born , bap. May 18th, 1783, m. Samuel Cossett, of Granby.
2. Beula, born , bap. May 18th, 1783, never married, died at Simsbury.
3. Asahel, jun., born , bap. Oct. 3d, 1784, m. in Ohio; returned and drowned in Farmington.
4. Joseph, born , bap. Oct. 28th, 1787, m. Sophrona Hart; second, Laura Buel.
5. Eunice, born , bap. Jan. 3d, 1790, m. Sept. 15th, 1818, Chauncey Clark.
6. Azuba, born , bap. Sept. 16th, 1792, m. Apheck Woodruff, Nov. 9th, 1809.
7. Elizabeth Norton, born , bap. May 14th, 1795, m. Wakeman Stanley.
8. Adna Thompson, born 1796, bap. May 28th, 1797, m. Lydia Woodruff.
9. Hannah Day, born March 20th, 1799, bap. May 19th, 1799, m. Ozem Woodruff, of Avon.
10. Ezra, born , bap. May 17th, 1801, unmarried, occasionally insane.

175. "Phineas Pennfield," to church April 6th, 1783, son of No. (116) and No. (117,) born June 6th, 1756, m. April 9th, 1778, No. (190;) he was a farmer, and sometimes cooper; house on Farmington road, still standing, (owned by Thomas Hicks,) supposed to be the house of his father. It shows the primitive style of architecture, as well as the action of time. He is well remembered as a simple-hearted, honest man, large reverence, and strictly conscientious. He died March 28th, 1834, aged 77. His posterity numerous and mostly pious.

THEIR CHILDREN.

1. Lucy, born Jan. 26th, 1777, bap. April 13th, 1783, m. April 7th, 1800, Elijah Hull, of Farmington.
2. Abel, born June 3d, 1782, bap. April 13th, 1783, m. Lydia Slater; second, Sally Richards; he m. third, April 11th, 1813, Betsey Squire; m. fourth, Mindwell Norton.
3. Nancy, born July 20th, 1783, No. (457.)
4. Phineas, jun., born Oct. 18th, 1785, m. Nov. 25th, 1812, No. (526.)
5. Salome, born Sept. 2d, 1788, bap. Oct. 5th, 1788, m. May 13th, 1807, No. (462.)
6. Minerva, born Oct. 22d, 1798, bap. Feb. 24th, 1799, see No. (527.)

176. "Ephraim Royce," to church April 6th, 1783, from (Northbury church, i. e. Plymouth,) son of Ephraim, of Meriden, baptized there, July 15th, 1744, m. Oct. 4th, 1764, Abigail Fox, of Cheshire, both to church in Meriden, June 23d, 1765, in Northbury, 1773, by letter. He m. Nov. 9th, 1780, Widow Abigail Andrews, of this place, widow of Samuel Andrews, and daughter of "Landlord Joseph Smith." Mr. Royce was a cooper; lived at the house of his second wife, Abigail, opposite Alfred Andrews' present place. He made cedar tubs and pails; procured his stock from the cedar swamp in Wolcott. He was a pious, good man; he died Jan. 5th, 1790, aged 46; his grave in the west and old part of our cemetery.

HIS CHILDREN BY HIS SECOND WIFE, ABIGAIL.

1. Chauncey, born Oct. 28th, 1781.
2. Abigail, born Jan. 24th, 1783, bap. April 6th, 1783.
3. Mary, born May 25th, 1789, bap. July 26th, 1789, m. Nov. 3d, 1807, Amos A. Webster; she died Nov. 30th, 1853, at Enfield, Conn., aged 65.

177. "Mrs. Mary Lee, wife of Col. Isaac Lee," to church Jan. 25th, 1784, "not by letter of recommendation merely, but upon a particular profession of her religious sentiments, &c." Her maiden name, Mary Johnson, daughter of Ephraim, of Wallingford. When she married Col. Lee, she was the widow of Amos Hall, who kept the great tavern in Wallingford, in the time of the Revolutionary War. She m. Oct. 9th, 1783, Col. Lee, and after his decease she returned to her old home, where she died, Dec. 22d, 1810, aged 73.

178. "Anthony Judd," to church Oct. 3d, 1784, one of the converts of the principal revival in Dr. Smalley's ministry; son of No. (43) and

No. (44,) born Aug. 1st, 1752, m. Aug. 29th, 1792, Rebecca Belden, daughter of Ezra and Rebecca Dix, his wife, born March 23d, 1757. He was a joiner by trade; lived in the Thomas Hooker house for a time; then built the Alvin North house, now moved and occupied by Orrin S. North. He moved about 1801, to Owego, N. Y. The parish library was kept at his house while the meeting-house was "built over," A. D. 1787. He is spoken of as a kind and worthy man.

THEIR CHILDREN.

1. Jesse, born , bap. Nov. 13th, 1785.
2. Alvin, born , bap. Aug. 1st, 1790.
3. Jason, born , bap. Sept. 8th, 1793.
4. Almira, born , bap. May 28th, 1797, see No. (500.)
5. Selah, born , bap. Nov. 9th, 1800.

179. "JOSIAH DEWY," to church Oct. 3d, 1784, son of No. (102) and No. (103,) born Jan. 6th, 1756, m. Nov. 24th, 1785, No. (157;) he taught school in early life three winters in succession, in South-east district. He lived at the old Dewy house, south of William Ellis. He was a man of eminent Christian graces, especially meekness and kindness. He died April 17th, 1838, aged 82.

THEIR CHILDREN.

1. Daniel, born 1787, bap. Feb. 18th, 1787, m. Fanny Shepherd, of Hartford, daughter of Capt. Charles.
2. Esther, born , bap. March 30th, 1788, single, died March 7th, 1852, aged 64, No. (398.)
3. Franklin, born 1790, bap. Oct. 17th, 1790, died south, aged 25.
4. Josiah, born Aug. 11th, 1792, bap. Oct. 7th, 1792, m. March 2d, 1814, Betsey Recor; second, No. (488.)
5. Asahel, born Nov. 14th, 1794, bap. April 19th, 1795; lives in Dorchester, Mass.
6. Mehitable, born Jan. 28th, 1797, bap. May 28th, 1797, m. June 2d, 1824, Edmund Hart.
7. Seth, born 1799, bap. June 16th, 1799, m. Harriet Sacket, of Westfield, Mass.
8. Rebecca, born Aug. 26th, 1801, bap. Oct. 25th, 1801, m. April 21st, 1824, Isaac Catlin.
9. Mary, born July 2d, 1804, bap. Oct. 21st, 1804, see No. (597.)

180. "Widow COMFORT HART," to church about 1784, widow of Daniel Hart, of Stephen and Sarah Cowles, his wife, born March 21st, 1708, and who lived at the northermost house in the parish, at the foot of "Clark Hill;" she was his second wife; his first was Abigail Thompson, whom he married July 18th, 1734, daughter of Thomas and his wife, Abigail (Woodruff;) she born Sept. 3d, 1710, died, when he m. second, No. (180,) the widow of Benjamin Stephens, and the daughter of ; her maiden name, Comfort Kelsey; she m. Benjamin Stephens, Oct. 20th, 1740, see Farmington town record.

CHILDREN OF DANIEL HART AND HIS FIRST WIFE, ABIGAIL.

1. Eldad, born June 6th, 1735, died May 17th, 1736.

2. Eldad, 2d, born March 22d, 1736, m. July 8th, 1761,   Stephens, daughter of Benjamin.

Sarah, born May 18th, 1742.

Stephen, born Dec. 8th, 1744, m. No. (563.)

181. "ELIJAH HART, jun.," to church Oct. 3d, 1784, son of No. (52) and Sarah (Gilbert,) his wife, born May 7th, 1759, bap. May 13th, 1759, m. Dec. 21st, 1780, No. (182;) he lived at the south part of the parish, and owned the mills; was a large farmer and extensive manufacturer of corn-meal for West India trade. "Nov. 26th, A. D. 1805, Capt. Elijah Hart declared his acceptance of the office of a deacon in this church, to which he had been chosen by the brethren, at a previous meeting duly warned," and 1807 he was added to the standing committee of the church. In 1824, he and his wife took letters of dismission and recommendation to the church at Mount Carmel, in Hamden, where he had built a house and mill, and where he lived several years. He however returned, and died Aug. 4th, 1827, aged 68, by the sting of a bee. He enlisted into the Revolutionary army, March 18th, 1778, for three years; was at the taking of Burgoyne.

182. "Wife of Elijah Hart, jun.," to church Oct. 3d, 1784, daughter of No. (112) and No. (312,) born Sept. 6th, 1760, bap. Oct., 1760, m. Dec. 21st, 1780, No. (181.) A modest, quiet woman, of great industry and economy; died Dec. 2d, 1835, aged 75.

THEIR CHILDREN.

1. Elijah, born Feb. 11th, 1782, bap. Oct. 3d, 1784, died May 13th, 1802, aged 20.
2. Selah, born Nov. 6th, 1784, bap. Dec. 12th, 1784, m. Oct. 5th, 1805, No. (454.)
3. Samuel, born April 7th, 1786, bap. June 18th, 1786, married March 18th, 1812, No. (366.)
4. Jesse, born April 20th, 1789, bap. June 7th, 1789, m. April 5th, 1810, No. (397.)
5. Jonathan, born Feb. 20th, 1792, bap. April 1st, 1792, see No. (483.)
6. Norman, born Aug. 5th, 1794, bap. Sept. 14th, 1794, m. Sept. 8th, 1818, No. (385.)
7. Anna, born Dec. 5th, 1796, died young.
8. Ira, born July 22d, 1798, m. May 3d, 1820, No. (485.)
9. Anna, 2d, born Nov. 17th, 1801, died Aug. 8th, 1817, aged 6.
10. Elijah, 2d, born Sept. 11th, 1804, m. March 15th, 1826, No. (723.)

183. "BETHEL HART," to church Oct. 3d, 1784, son of Joseph, of Avon, brother of No. (174,) born Nov. 1762, bap. Nov. 28th, 1762, at Avon, by Rev. E. Booge, m. June 24th, 1784, No. (243;) was a farmer, and later in life a peddler; his house stood opposite of the present house of Elam Slater's. He was much gifted in prayer, and was esteemed a pious, good man; was lame late in life, which led him to sell for a living, pewter and tin ware. His wife, Huldah, died Sept. 28th, 1810, aged 44, when he m. second, May 16th, 1811, Widow Nancy Seely, of Rocky Hill, see No. (361;) he died Dec. 25th, 1824, aged 62.

THEIR CHILDREN.

1. Huldah, born Oct. 18th, 1786, bap. Dec. 3d, 1786, m. March 1st, 1804, Silas Pennfield.

2. Nancy, born Jan. 2d, 1790, bap. Feb. 14th, 1790, m. April 26th, 1809, No. (450.)

3. Sarah Sage, born , bap. July 27th, 1794, m. Feb. 25th, 1816, Henry, son of Seth Root.

4. Betsey, born Sept. 28th, 1797, m. May 11th, 1813, Romanta Woodford, of Avon and Berlin.

5. Lavinia, born Dec. 1st, 1798, bap. Feb. 24th, 1799, m. Dec. 5th, 1819, Silas Goff, jun., of West Springfield.

6. Salome, born Aug. 14th, 1801, bap. Oct. 25th, 1801, m. Jan. 30th, 1832, Henry, son of James Judd.

7. Adna, born Jan. 28th, 1804, bap. April 15th, 1804, m. March 20th, 1825, No. (509.)

8. Daniel, born , bap. June 3d, 1806, died June 4th, 1806.

9. Rosanna, born May 3d, 1807, bap. July 19th, 1807, m. Joseph Yemans; married second, No. (1,001.)

10. Caroline Upson, born Sept. 16th, 1809, bap. April 29th, 1810, m. July 3d, 1828, No. (912.)

184. "Polly Lewis," to church Oct. 3d, 1784, daughter of No. (88) and No. (111,) born Nov., 1765, m. 1786, No. (251;) she bare to her husband one daughter, and died of consumption, Jan. 1st, 1789, aged 24.

185. "Widow Elizabeth Clark," to church Nov. 28th, 1784, by letter from the first church in Farmington, daughter of Capt. John Newel, of Farmington, and his wife, Elizabeth (Hawley;) she was the widow of Mr. John Clark, who lived where Omri North does now, A. D. 1864; sister of No. (114,) and were next door neighbors. She m. Sept. 2d, 1742, John Clark, son of Matthew. This family was one of the three set off, or rather excepted in the incorporation of the parish. They chose to go to Farmington, where it appears they had always belonged. Mrs. Clark came here after the death of her husband; she was partially deaf, and was accustomed to stand in the pulpit to hear. She died Feb. 2d, 1791, aged 70. He died June 10th, 1782, aged 70.

THEIR CHILDREN.

1. Mercy, born 1742-3, m. Dec. 1766, William Wadsworth, of Farmington; she died July, 1813, aged 71.

2. Mary, born Feb. 23d, 1745, see No. (272.)

3. Marvin, born Nov. 26th, 1746, m. Jan. 18th, 1773, Sarah Woodruff, daughter of Abraham, of Farmington Farms.

4. Dan, born Aug. 11th, 1748, m. Jan. 24th, 1771, Lucy Stanley, daughter of Thomas, 3d.

5. Abel, born 1751, m. Jan. 6th, 1774, Abigail Judd, daughter of James, No. (38.)

6. Ruth, born March 19th, 1752, m. Jan. 6th, 1774, Seth Stanley, son of Deacon Noah.

7. John, born March 18th, 1754; went to Canandaigua; died 1819.

8. Huldah, born 1756, m. Caleb Richard Walker; went to Lenox.

9. Elizabeth, born May 14th, 1758, m. Moses Andrews, jun.; she died 1840, at Montague, Mass.

10. Jane, born Nov. 20th, 1763, m. Dec. 21st, 1785, No. (221.)

186. "NOAH FULLER," to church Dec. 5th, 1784, from church in Kensington, son of No. (V.) and his wife, No. (VI.) bap. in infancy, Oct. 4th, 1761, A. D. 1785; he bought one and a quarter acres, with house and barn, of No. (29,) on the corner directly west of the present school-house in South-east district, and the same year he bought of No. (63,) one and a quarter acres where now, 1865, stands the barn of James P. Moore, which land, with a "tan-works and pump," he sold to David Wetherell, 1788, and then called himself of Dorset, Bennington county, Vermont. He m. Jan. 20th, 1792, at Dorset, Vermont, Lucy Wilson, of Coventry, Conn. He died Feb. 19th, 1846, at Dorset, Vermont, in his 84th year. She died March 16th, 1855, at Clarkson, N. Y., in her 84th year.

CHILDREN.

1. John W., born Dec. 14th, 1792, m. Aug. 20th, 1825, Amelia Teryl, at Salina, New York.
2. Alice S., born Sept. 16th, 1795, m. Dec., 1824, George Brace, at Dorset, Vt.
3. Sarah, born Sept. 17th, 1797, m. Jan. 25th, 1815, Horace Johnson, of Rupert, Vt.
4. Orson, born Nov. 28th, 1799, m. Sept. 5th, 1822, Eunice P. Smith, at Dorset, Vt.
5. Alvin, born Feb. 8th, 1802, m. Sept., 1840, Emily White, at Alden, N. Y.
6. Lucy, born Feb. 21st, 1804, died June, 1820.
7. Noah, jun., born March 9th, 1806, m. Jan. 12th, 1845, Margaret Hand, in Va.
8. Gurdon T., born Feb. 12th, 1810, died June, 1819.
9. Mehitable Y., born May 1st, 1815, m. Sept. 14th, 1842, at Lancaster, N. Y., Austin Pinney, of Buffalo, N. Y.

187. "Wife of Samuel Wainwright," to church Dec. 5th, 1784, daughter of Doctor Isaac Lee and his second wife, Susanna, born April 27th, 1746, m. Aug. 23d, 1768, before Dr. Smalley; her name, Mary. Their house stood about thirty rods south-east from the residence of John Judd, in Hart quarter, and the east side of the house was in the east line of District No. (4.) Her mother was probably Susanna Cornwell, of Middletown, and widow of Peter Wolcott, when she married Dr. Lee. She (i. e. Mary,) died at Middletown, 1832, aged 86.

188. "Wife of Capt. Hotchkiss," to church Dec. 5th, 1784; her maiden name, Penelope Mather, daughter of Joseph, sen. and Anna (Booth,) his wife, born May 27th, 174–, m. March 26th, 1764, No. (121;) she kept house for Dr. Smalley, before her marriage; her father's location was opposite the William Patterson house, or the first residence of Dr. Smalley.

189. "Wife of Seth Stanley," to church Dec. 5th, 1784; Ruth, daughter of John Clark and No. (185,) which see. He built, 1773, the house of Martin Brown, (which burned down, 1860,) where they lived until Feb., 1796, when they moved to Ontario county, N. Y. He played the

bassoon in church choir, and composed some pieces of music. His grandson, John Mix Stanley, son of Seth, jun., is the author of the great Indian Gallery of Paintings, which has attracted so much attention in the country; about 1860, located at Washington, D. C., now, 1863, at Buffalo, N. Y. He died May 5th, 1823, aged 72, at Stanley Corners, N. Y. She died Sept. 13th, 1796, aged 44.

THEIR CHILDREN.

1. Asa, born Nov. 21st, 1774, bap. Jan. 9th, 1785, m. Tirza Hayden.
2. Cruger, born Nov. 19th, 1775, bap. Jan. 9th, 1785, m. Sally Reed.
3. Erastus, born Oct. 22d, 1776, bap. Jan. 9th, 1785, m. Temperance Smith.
4. Horatio, born Nov. 24th, 1777, bap. Jan. 9th, 1785, never married, died at sea, buried at New Haven.
5. Salma, born Oct. 10th, 1779, bap. Jan. 9th, 1785, m. Sally Welch; second, Lois Whitman; third, Rachel Smith.
6. Nancy, born Jan. 2d, 1781, bap. Jan. 9th, 1785.
7. Kata, born Jan. 15th, 1782, bap. Jan. 9th, 1785.
8. Janna,* born March 7th, 1783, bap. Jan. 9th, 1785, m. Sophrona
9. Seth, born June 6th, 1784, bap. Jan. 9th, 1785, m. Sally
10. Ruth, born Nov. 14th, 1785, bap. Jan. 9th, 1785.
11. Cyrus, born April 8th, 1787.
12. Huldah, born March 26th, 1788, bap. June. 1st, 1788.
13. Caleb Walker, born Nov. 20th, 1790, bap. Jan. 23d, 1791.
14. Infant, no name, born March 25th, 1792.
15. Lucius, born April 5th, 1793, bap. July 7th, 1793, m. Sally Runyan; second, Polly Whedon.
16. Elizabeth, born Nov. 18th, 1794, bap. May 17th, 1795, m. John McKnight.

190. "Wife of Phineas Pennfield," to church Dec. 5th, 1784, Lucy, daughter of Jeremiah H. Osgood, from Middletown, and Lucy (Churchill,) his wife, born May 5th, 1757, m. April 9th, 1778; for locality and family see No. (175;) she died Nov. 4th, 1832, aged 75.

191. "Moses Andrews, jun.," to church Dec. 5th, 1784, son of No. (53) and No. (54,) born April 7th, 1755, m. No. (192;) lived on West Main street, two miles from the village; the same house William Wright (now, A. D. 1862,) owns and occupies. He lived one year in the Demas Warner house, on the hill, north-west of where he built his new one on the Quinnipiac, by the bridge. He removed to Montague, Mass., on Connecticut River, about 1800, where he died July 20th, 1848, aged 93; his obituary notice says "one of nine sons, seven of whom were in the Revolutionary army."

192. "Wife of Moses Andrews, jun.," to church Dec. 5th, 1784; her maiden name, Elizabeth Clark, daughter of John and No. (185,) born May 14th, 1758; she a resolute, spirited woman, with much force of character, She died at Montague, Mass., Dec. 8th, 1840, aged 82. She once came

* Written by himself and family, Jonathan, but by Rev. Mr. Smalley, at baptism, Janna.

under the censure of the church for assaulting an officer who was arresting her husband; on confession, restored, 1807.

THEIR CHILDREN.

1. Sidney, born March 8th, 1780, bap. Dec. 5th, 1784, m. Oct. 24th, 1804, Mary Clark. He a printer by trade.

2. Noah, born March 19th, 1782, bap. Dec. 5th, 1784, m. Feb. 22d, 1807, Ruth Griswold; lived in Ohio.

3. Buly, born April 6th, 1784, bap. Dec. 5th, 1784, m. Dr. J. H. Hills, of Farmington; lived in Ohio.

4. Betsey, born June 22d, 1786, bap. Aug. 7th, 1786, m. Wallace; second, Handley, in Ohio.

5. Cynthia, born Feb. 20th, 1788, bap. March 30th, 1788, m. Barber; second, Phinney, in Ohio.

6. Kata, born June 8th, 1790, m. Nov. 24th, 1813, No. (470.)

7. Jesse, born Oct. 28th, 1792, bap. Jan 6th, 1793, m. Jan. 11th, 1818, S. Alvord, of Greenfield.

8. Nancy, born Feb. 4th, 1796, bap. May 1st, 1796, m. Thomas Russel; second, John Ortt, of Greenfield.

193. "ROBERT BOOTH," to church Dec. 5th, 1784, son of No. (65) and No. (66,) born June 20th, 1758, m. May 30th, 1782, No. (194,) inherited the home of his father, near the present Methodist church; spoken of as a devout Christian and worthy man; was a large farmer, and died suddenly of colic, May 8th, 1796, aged 38.

194. "Wife of Robert Booth," to church Dec. 5th, 1784, Abigail, daughter of William Barton and Abigail (Sage,) of Kensington, his wife; she baptized on admission to church; she married second, Jan. 7th, 1817, Constant Welch, of Chatham and Bristol; she died Jan. 31st, 1831, aged 64, in this place.

THE CHILDREN OF ROBERT AND ABIGAIL.

1. Salome, born March 15th, 1785, bap. May 29th, 1785, married May 28th, 1801, No. (568.)

2. Rhoda, born Oct., 1787, m. July 5th, 1810, Ira Strong, of Northampton.

3. Samuel, born Jan. 23d, 1790, bap. Feb. 28th, 1790, m. May 5th, 1812, No. (365.)

4. Abigail, born July 5th, 1792, bap. Aug. 19th, 1792, m. March 17th, 1813, No. (557.)

5. Robert, born Dec. 8th, 1794, bap. Feb. 1st, 1795, died, aged one year.

6. Robert, 2d, born Aug. 1st, 1796, bap. Aug. 31st, 1796, m. Nov. 26th, 1818, Sally Whaples; he died Oct. 23d, 1823, aged 27.

195. "JAMES JUDD," to church Dec. 5th, 1784, son of No. (38) and Hannah (Andrus,) his wife, born Jan. 27th, 1757, m. 1779, No. (318.) He brother of No. (435.) His house, built 1779, still (A. D. 1864,) standing, owned and occupied by Henry Judd; he with his brother, Daniel, owned and run the saw-mill so long known as "Judd's Mill," which they sold to J. Shipman and sons, now near the site of O. B. North's factory. He died Nov. 10th, 1822, aged 66.

THEIR CHILDREN.

1. Anna, born 1781, bap. Dec. 12th, 1784, m. Nov. 25th, 1802, Joseph Churchill.
2. Esther, born July 22d, 1782, bap. Dec. 12th, 1784, m. William Steele, jun.
3. James, born March 12th, 1785, bap. June 5th, 1785, m. Salome Lusk; second, Gunilda Bass.
4. Asahel, born Feb. 1st, 1787, bap. May 6th, 1787; lived in Avon, N. Y., 1839.
5. Samuel, born Jan. 25th, 1789, bap. May 3d, 1789, April 23d, 1822, No. (560.)
6. Amzi, born May 15th, 1791, bap. Aug. 7th, 1791, m. Jan. 10th, 1816, Susanna Hamblin; he died Jan. 13th, 1863, aged 71½.
7. Hannah, born 1793, bap. June 2d, 1793, died unmarried, June 6th, 1835 aged 42.
8. Allen, born Sept. 15th, 1795, m. June 10th, 1819, Harriet E. Johnson; second, Sarah Kilby; third, Rhoda Deming.
9. Ethan, born March 25th, 1798, bap. Aug. 26th, 1798, m. Nov. 18th, 1828, Melissa Collins.
10. Henry, born Jan. 15th, 1801, bap. Aug. 2d, 1801, m. Jan. 30th, 1822, No. (498.)

196. "ISAAC ANDREWS," to church Dec. 5th, 1784, son of No. (53) and No. (54,) born Jan. 31st, 1757. He was a physician, located in Hart quarter, about thirty rods south-east of the residence of John Judd; the old road which ran past the house, closed up, and the house long since gone. He m. No. (298;) he died Jan. 11th, 1799, aged 42.

THEIR CHILDREN.

1. Isaac, jun., born bap. May 17th, 1795, died at New York.
2. Elizabeth, born May, 1797, died Aug. 24th, 1798, aged fifteen months.
3. Jesse, born bap. May 25th, 1800, died at Berlin, 1824, Oct. 8th, aged 25; his grave in cemetery south part Worthington.

197. "JOHN ANDREWS," to church Dec. 5th, 1784, a brother of No. (196;) was a physician; taught school in early life; located near his father's; house still owned and occupied by his son, Deacon Milton Andrews, on West Main street, one mile west of the village. He was a kind-hearted man, and a conscientious Christian. He married May 10th, 1792, No. (249,) who died Nov. 13th, 1797, when he married second, March 16th, 1800, No. (378.) He was of slender frame and constitution, yet lived to June 19th, 1839, when he died, aged 82.

THEIR CHILDREN.

1. Phebe Lewis, born Oct. 28th, 1797, bap. Feb. 4th, 1798, m. March 18th, 1823, Asa Cowdry, see No. (497.)
2. Milton, born Nov. 12th, 1801, bap. April 4th, 1802, m. May 3d, 1827, Charlotte Osgood.
3. John, born Oct. 10th, 1803, see No. (539.)
4. Abigail Bronson, born May 16th, 1806, bap. July 6th, 1806, see No. (532.)
5. Hiram, born April 7th, 1808, bap. June 26th, 1808, died Oct. 10th, 1815.
6. Caroline Porter, born Sept. 21st, 1812, bap. Oct. 25th, 1812, died Oct. 4th, 1819.

198. "AARON ROBERTS," to church Dec. 5th, 1784, son of Dr. Aaron and Hepzibah (Shepherd,) his wife, born April 20th, 1758, a twin with Molly, who died young, born at Middletown. He served his time at

Rocky Hill, to learn his trade of joiner and cabinet making. He owned the farm (now, A. D. 1861,) belonging to and occupied by O. B. Bassett, Esq., and lived in the old house near, still standing, which he bought of Daniel Ames, a fellow-apprentice with him. He was a kind neighbor, a good citizen, a liberal man; had no children. He married Feb. 17th, 1785, No. (220,) who died Feb. 18th, 1828, aged 70; he married second, May 20th, 1829, No. (292.) He gave thirty dollars towards our communion service, and was otherwise liberal in sustaining church and society. He died Sept. 27th, 1831, aged 73. His father and mother lie by his side in the old part of our cemetery.

199. "Selah Judd," to church Dec. 5th, 1784, son of No. (43) and No. (44,) born July, 1763, m. No. (222;) he died 1788, aged 25.

200. "Josiah Kilbourn," to church about 1784, son of Josiah and Ruth, daughter of John Warner, of Wethersfield, his wife; born there, July 29th, 1730, came to New Britain with his parents in childhood, married May 3d, 1754, No. (78.) It appears from land records that he lived with his father, who built the house where Elijah Francis, sen. lived, and sold him the farm; he, Josiah, jun., had after this a small hut where now Hiram Smith's barn stands. He then built the Slater house, near Dead Swamp, after owned by Joel Smith. He also built a house south-west of this, on the Brown place, near the line of the parish. His house was in the bounds of Farmington, and both their names appear on the church record there, at that date, about 1796. He was an honest, laborious man; raised a large family on small means. He lost his property in the war of the Revolution; struggled hard to buffet the storms of adversity. He died 1812, at the alms-house in Berlin, aged 81.

THEIR CHILDREN.

1. Josiah, born Feb. 15th, 1756, bap. Feb. 22d, 1756, was in the army at 19, became a captain, m. Dec. 13th, 1780, Isabella Whaples, daughter of Daniel.

2. William, born Jan. 12th, 1758, by trade a clothier, married Sarah, daughter of Jedediah Sage.

3. Anna, born Dec. 24th, 1759, bap. Dec. 30th, 1759, m. No. (174.)

4. Eunice, born July 7th, 1762, died Aug. 28th, 1776, in her 15th year, of camp distemper.

5. Lemuel, born Oct. 7th, 1764, bap. Oct. 14th, 1764, m. Sarah Hastings, of Southington.

6. Urania, born Oct. 17th, 1767, m. Sylvester Higley; second, Shubel Hoskins, Esq., of Simsbury.

7. James, born Oct. 19th, 1770, bap. Nov. 4th, 1770; learned the clothier's trade, and became an Episcopal minister, and a member of Congress from Ohio, from 1813 to 1817. He married Nov. 8th, 1789, Lucy Fitch, daughter of John, of steamboat celebrity. He became wealthy; had the title of colonel, and in several respects the most distinguished man New Britain ever raised. He was self-made, having with the advice of his father left his home, Sept. 23d, 1786, to seek his fortune in the wide world. He had a second wife, Cynthia (Goodale,) married 1808; he died April 24th, 1850, aged 80, in Ohio.

8. Azubah, born Nov. 16th, 1772, bap. Nov. 22d, 1772, died Aug. 17th, 1776, aged 4.
9. Deborah, born , died in infancy.
10. Amasa, born 1780, went to Vermont, thence to Lower Canada; died 1805.

201. "HULDAH COUCH," to church Dec. 5th, 1784, sister of No. (336;) never married; she was kind and inoffensive and useful. She died Feb. 15th, 1829, aged 78, daughter of Thomas, of Southington, and baptized there, April 14th, 1751.

202. "NAOMI BURRITT," to church Dec. 5th, 1784, daughter of Elihu, of Stratford, and Eunice (Wakeman,) his wife; she taught school several years before her marriage to Noah Stanley, as his third wife. She was social and intelligent, possessing a discriminating mind. Their home had been that of Deacon Noah Stanley, and (now, A. D. 1862,) is owned and occupied by their son, N. W. Stanley. She probably born 1761, at Stratford, and married in the fall of 1790, before Col. Lee. He was a light-horseman in the war of the Revolution; became a substantial farmer; a man of scrupulous honesty, and firm integrity. He died May 4th, 1829, aged 70; she died Jan. 12th, 1853, aged 92. Mr. Stanley had married Lucy Lewis, daughter of No. (88) and No. (111;) she died July 24th, 1784, aged 23. He married second, Oct. 26th, 1786, Experience, daughter of Joshua Wells, of Wethersfield, and Experience (Dickinson,) his wife, born Aug. 14th, 1758; she died Aug. 9th, 1789, aged 31.

CHILD BY HIS FIRST WIFE.

1. Noah, born March 26th, 1782, died April 2d, 1782, aged eight days.

SECOND WIFE'S CHILDREN.

2. Lucy Lewis, born Sept., 1787, bap. March 4th, 1792, see No. (342.)
3. Pede Wells, born bap. March 4th, 1792, died March 9th, 1794.

THIRD WIFE'S CHILDREN.

4. Naomi Burritt, born Sept. 24th, 1791, bap. March 4th, 1792, see No. (810.)
5. Wakeman Norton, born March 9th, 1793, bap. June 2d, 1793, see No. (475.)
6. Noah Wells, born Nov. 19th, 1794, bap. May 24th, 1795, see No. (849.)
7. Jason, born Aug. 12th, 1796, bap. Nov. 13th, 1796, died Sept. 12th, 1803, aged seven years, one month.
8. Pede, 2d, born , died Aug. 23d, 1803, aged five years.
9. Horatio, born , bap. July 5th, 1801, died Aug. 19th, 1803, aged two years.

203. "ABIGAIL HART," to church Dec. 5th, 1784, daughter of No. (93) and No. (209,) born Oct. 27th, 1761, m. Feb. 15th, 1781, Jonathan Seymour, of Kensington, son of Eliakim and Susanna (Judd,) his wife, born Oct., 1757; was a blacksmith; built the Saxy Hooker house, in Kensington; had his shop opposite. She was received to Kensington church May 5th, 1788, her husband uniting at the same date; they moved west, and she died Jan. 1st, 1833, aged 72, at Harford, Pa. He became a deacon at Otsego, where he located, and where he died July 26th, 1819. These are the grand-parents of Professor Tyler, of Amherst College. Jonathan

Seymour was great-grand-son of Capt. Richard, of the Seymour Fort, in "Great Swamp."

204. "MARY ANN MATHER," to church Dec. 5th, 1784, daughter of No. (138) and No. (139,) m. Lebbeus Hungerford; married second, Aug. 3d, 1807, David Hills, who had first married Aug. 28th, 1777, Anna, widow of John Hart, who died Oct. 30th, 1804. David Hills once owned the Lincoln house, where now, 1862, William Harlowe Eddy lives; he then bought the "State house," so called, and last he lived and died at the old house of Chester Hart's; all these in Hart quarter. Mrs. Mary Ann Hills was dismissed and recommended, March 3d, 1816, (record of Rev. N. Skinner;) she went West to her friends. David Hills died June 3d, 1813, aged 65.

205. "SYLVIA FRANCIS," to church Dec. 5th, 1784, daughter of No. (91) and No. (92,) born Dec. 12th, 1763, bap. Dec. 18th, 1763, married Hull; he died, when she married second, Scovil; she died 1847, at Charlotte Creek, New York, aged about 84.

206. "LUCY CARTER," to church Dec. 5th, 1784, daughter of Thaddeus, of Wallingford and Lucy (Andrus,) his wife, born 1768; she was given to Mrs. Mary Hall, who became the third wife of Col. Lee, and thus came to this place; she married Solomon Smith, son of Elijah, sen. and Sarah (Grimes,) his wife, born Dec. 6th, 1767; learned the blacksmith trade of James North, Esq.; they moved to Kensington, where she was received to that church, by letter from this, Jan., 1790; she died June 13th, 1831, aged 63, at Wallingford; he died Sept. 1st, 1844, aged 76. Their marriage was solemnized by Col. Lee.

THEIR CHILDREN.

1. Laura, born April 17th, 1790, bap. Aug. 8th, 1790, at Kensington, m. Erastus P. Parmelee, Broadalbin, N. Y.
2. Amos Hall, born April 11th, 1792, bap. June 11th, 1792, at Kensington, m. Philena Benham.
3. Solomon, born Sept. 26th, 1794, bap. Nov. 2d, 1794, at Kensington, m. Sarah R. Ryan, of Woodbury, Conn.
4. Mary Johnson, born Oct. 11th, 1796, bap. Nov., 1796, at Kensington, married Dec. 22d, 1824, Chauncey Clark.
5. Willis, born July 13th, 1798, m. Olive Smith.

207. "Wife of Joseph Mather," to church Dec. 5th, 1784, daughter of Elihu Burritt, of Stratford, and Eunice (Wakeman,) his wife, born 1750, name, Polly; she married at sixteen, No. (217.) A woman of exemplary life and Christian deportment. She died Nov. 3d, 1823, aged 70; sister of N. W. Stanley's mother.

208. "BILLY HART," so the record, meaning William, (ED.) to church Dec. 5th, 1784, son of No. (93) and No. (209,) born 1772, bap. March 16th, 1772, graduated at Yale, 1792, m. 1798, Hannah Bridge Campe, at Shoreditch church, Wapping, London, England; she born 1765, at Lon-

don. He prepared for college with Dr. Smalley; licensed to preach the gospel by Hartford South Association, at Southington, June 3d, 1800. His wife died April 30th, 1817, aged 52, at Hartford, Conn. It will be observed that he was but twelve years old when received to church, very young for that period, and for the usages of that age. He was of feeble health and constitution; of the kindest disposition; maintained a devoted Christian life. He preached only occasionally; not settled. He had a second wife, Widow Joanna Hand, (alias) Joanna Meigs, sister of Return J. Meigs, at Madison, Conn. He died Aug. 2d, 1836, aged 64, at Candor, N. Y., with his son, Jonathan.

THEIR CHILDREN.

1. Hannah Bridge, born Feb. 11th, 1799, m. March 25th, 1818, Henry M. Pratt; she died Aug. 15th, 1823, at Marietta, Ohio.
2. Jonathan Bird, born Aug. 25th, 1800, m. March, 1823, Elvira Humiston, of Plymouth.
3. Mehitabel, born Jan. 11th, 1806, at Middletown, Conn., m. March 20th, 1844, Peter J. Krom, of Candor, N. Y., and lives there, 1862, near her brother, Jonathan.

209. "Wife of Thomas Hart," to church Jan. 9th, 1785; her maiden name, Mehitabel Bird, daughter of Jonathan, sen. and Hannah (Thompson,) his wife, born July 15th, 1738, m. Feb. 2d, 1758, No. (93.) She was well adapted to the age in which she lived; industrious, economical, and self-sacrificing, Christian habits and deportment; she died March 18th, 1825, aged 87. She was a sister of Jonathan Bird, M. D., and who was also a minister of the gospel; she was likewise sister of "Zurviah," who married Daniel Whaples, and late in life known familiarly as "Aunt Viah," and lived in the old school-house she bought and moved from opposite the present William Woodruff house, to near the barn of O. C. Stanley. Her correct name, Zeruiah. She was born March 30th, 1734, at Farmington; died at the house of Joseph Mather, May 4th, 1818, aged 84.

210. "JOSEPH HART," to church Jan. 9th, 1785, son of No. (49) and No. (50,) born May 17th, 1750, married Nov. 5th, 1772, Huldah Smith, daughter of Jedediah, and Susanna (Cogswell,) his wife, born Jan. 4th, 1749. He built in Hart quarter, next north of his father, the same house now owned and occupied by Edwin Francis, which he sold to Oliver Gridley, and moved to New Durham, N. Y.

THEIR CHILDREN.

1. Joseph, jun., born , bap. Sept. 11th, 1785, m. Sept. 7th, 1800, Lydia North, of Jedediah.
2. Luther, born , bap. Sept. 11th, 1785.
3. Huldah, born , bap. Sept. 11th, 1785.
4. Selah, born , bap. Sept. 11th, 1785.

211. "ABIJAH HART," to church Jan. 9th, 1785, son of No. (93) and No. (209,) born April 7th, 1764; he took an honorary degree at Yale,

1795; taught school several years; married Sept. 22d, 1794, at Middletown, before Rev. E. Huntington, No. (326.) He became extensively engaged in merchandize and commerce in New York city, firm of Hicks, Vanderbilt & Hart; lost all by French spoliations, and returned to the old home of his father, about 1808, where he followed farming. He was a man of science and taste, but was called somewhat visionary in practical affairs. He lost his first wife, and married second, Oct. 26th, 1826, Widow Lucy Dunham, widow of Samuel, see No. (634.) He died May 3d, 1829, aged 65.

THEIR CHILDREN.

1. Julia Ann, born Sept. 1st, 1795, m. Dec. 16th, 1818, Seth Lewis; second, Oakley, see No. (765.)

2. Caroline Bird, born April 15th, 1798, in New York city, married Dec. 16th, 1818, No. (478.)

3. Thomas Giles, born Dec. 2d, 1800; never married; educated a merchant; died July 26th, 1825, at Raleigh, N. C.

4. Henry Abijah, born Aug. 9th, 1805; a physician; m. April 24th, 1827, No. (607.)

5. Samuel Mansfield, born August 30th, 1807; never married; died 1838, see No. (686.)

212. "LOIS ANDRUS," to church Jan. 9th, 1785, daughter of No. (112) and No. (312,) born Dec. 1st, 1763, bap. Jan. 1st, 1764, m. Nov. 9th, 1786, Major Justus Francis, of Newington, died 1813, aged 49. She was received to Newington church, March 4th, 1777, by letter from New Britain. She was the third wife of Major Francis, the mother of a large family, and gave place in the midst of her usefulness to his fourth wife, who was Widow Ruth Barber, of (Wintonbury,) Bloomfield; her maiden name, Ruth Pettibone, and married Aug. 15th, 1815, Major Francis. His first wife was Keturah Andrus, of Newington, whom he married May 2d, 1773; she died Aug. 14th, 1780, aged 28, when he married second, July 3d, 1783, Mary, daughter of Rev. Joshua Belden, who died March 5th, 1785, when he married third and fourth as above. He died Jan. 8th, 1827, aged 76.

HIS CHILD BY FIRST WIFE, KETURAH, DAUGHTER OF PHINEAS.

1. Appleton Andrus, born August 9th, 1778, m. Charlotte Webster, daughter of David, Nov. 18th, 1805.

HIS CHILD BY SECOND WIFE, MARY.

2. Keturah Andrus, born March 19th, 1784, died April 9th, 1784, aged one month.

HIS CHILDREN BY LOIS, HIS THIRD WIFE.

3. Harvey, born Jan. 27th, 1789, m. Abigail Kilborn, Nov. 29th, 1828.

4. Anson, born Nov. 4th, 1790, m. Almira Owen.

5. Newman, born June 25th, 1793, m. Octavia Strickland.

6. Alfred, born Nov. 2d, 1795, m. Nancy Deming, Aug. 25th, 1818.

7. Cyrus, born Dec. 16th, 1797, m. Sabra Blin; second, Nancy D. Pratt, No. (493.)

8. Laura, born Jan. 23d, 1800, m. Grandison Barber, of Wintonbury, Nov. 20th, 1816.

9. Erastus, born Nov. 16th, 1802, m. Birtha Stoddard, July 17th, 1825, and married second, Caroline Stoddard.

10. Mary, born June 28th, 1808, m. Orange C. Butler, of Hartford, Mar. 31st, 1831.

213. "MILLA PENNFIELD," to church Feb. 6th, 1785, daughter of No. (116) and No. (117,) born May 26th, 1766, at New Haven, m. Nov. 16th, 1786, Samuel Dickinson, jun., son of Samuel, sen. and Mary (Andrus,) his wife; he was a joiner and cabinet-maker; lived at the turn of the road, next north of Edwin Francis; he was injured seriously by a cart-wheel, seven years before his death; he died Dec. 16th, 1793, when she married second, Jan. 23d, 1804, Eben Thompson, of Farmington; she was received to that church June 3d, 1804, by letter from Dr. Smalley, (so Farmington church record;) she is called on the church record of New Haven, Emelia, and was baptized there June 1st, 1766.

THEIR CHILDREN.

1. Milla, born Aug. 30th, 1787, bap. Oct. 14th, 1787, m. May 19th, 1814, Sylvester Hills, son of Chauncey, of Plainville.

2. Samuel, born Aug. 9th, 1789, m. Sept. 23d, 1812, Sukey Porter, daughter of Shubael, of Farmington.

3. Elihu, born Dec., 1791, bap. March 4th, 1792, m. Dec., 1813, Thirza B. Thompson, of Farmington.

214. "ELIZABETH PENNFIELD," to church Feb. 6th, 1785, daughter of No. (116) and No. (117,) sister of No. (213,) m. Oct. 29th, 1789, Elisha Savage, of Berlin, who learned his trade of joiner and cabinet-making of Aaron Roberts. She was dismissed by letter to Worthington church, 1789. They removed to Western New York; had sons and daughters.

215. "ISABEL CORNWELL," to church Feb. 6th, 1785, daughter of Capt. Timothy, of Middletown, and Mary (Warner,) his wife; she married Ithuel Hill, of Long Island; she dismissed and recommended to Newington church by letter, Nov. 4th, 1787, where she was received. She was sister to Stephen Cornwell, and No. (296,) of this place.

216. "ISMENA HART," to church Feb. 6th, 1785, daughter of No. (93) and No. (209,) born 1768, bap. July 17th, 1768; never married; lived and died on the old premises of her father, where (now, 1862, Ira Steele lives;) she was remarkably devoted and conscientious as a Christian; gave the residue of her property by will to the Home Missionary Society, prized at $750. She died Feb. 20th, 1854, aged 86.

217. "JOSEPH MATHER," to church Feb. 26th, 1785, son of Joseph and Anna (Booth,) his wife, m. No. (207.) He served in the war of the Revolution, both in land and naval forces; he was a tanner and shoemaker; learned in Wethersfield; located on West Main street, one and a half miles west of the village, (where now is Arma Jerome, A. D. 1863.) He was in early life a sailor, in West India voyages. He married second

July 10th, 1825, Widow Hannah Sage, of Wethersfield, widow of Solomon Sage. He was later in life an exemplary man; by industry obtained an honest living, and raised a large and respectable family. He died July 10th, 1833, aged 83. He was a member of the standing committee of the church, 1810.

THEIR CHILDREN.

1. Stephen, born 1773, m. Oct. 12th, 1794, Mehitabel Loomis; he born in Stratford; died an elder of the church in Utica, 1856.

2. Eunice, born May 12th, 1775, m. 1797, Asahel Pennfield; she born at Stratford; he born July 6th, 1770, to Samuel, of Branford, and Rebecca Scovil, of Meriden, Conn.

3. Polly, born , bap. Feb. 26th, 1785, died Feb. 3d, 1791; born in this place.

4. Phebe, born July 30th, 1780, bap. Feb. 26th, 1785, m. Aug. 31st, 1809, No. (756.)

5. Betsey, born Feb. 17th, 1783, bap. Feb. 26th, 1785, m. No. (299;) also married second, No. (747.)

6. Naomi, born , bap. Oct. 9th, 1785.

7. Polly, 2d, born , bap. July 6th, 1788.

8. William C., born July 19th, 1790, m. March 20th, 1820, Julia M. Vandusen; he died June 13th, 1863, aged 73, at Lyden, near Chicago.

9. Azuba, born , bap. July 21st, 1793.

10. Jerusha, born May 10th, 1793, see No. (379.)

11. Chauncey, born 1796, bap. June 5th, 1796; never married; died Feb. 13th, 1819, aged 22.

NOTE. The father's second wife was Hannah Treat, of Berlin, when she married Solomon Sage. Mrs. Hannah Mather died March 4th, 1831, aged 70; grave-stone south part of New Britain cemetery.

218. "JEMIMA, wife of Joseph Bronson," to church Feb. 26th, 1785, daughter of Cornelius Dunham and Dorcas (Woodruff,) his wife, born March 5th, 1760; he son of Job, who lived at "Job's Corner," west of "Burritt Hill," and from whom that corner took its name. His will is dated Jan. 30th, 1783, in which he gives his daughter, Esther Munson, six sheep, and twenty shillings. He also gives his daughter, Anna Booth. The appraisers to the estate were Ladwick Hotchkiss and Ichabod Andrus; the witnesses to the will were Ladwick Hotchkiss, Mary Smith, and John Booth; his inventory amounted to £72 4s. 8d.

219. "AZARIAH GLADDING," to church June 12th, 1785, from church in Farmington, son of Azariah, of Norwich and Kensington, and his wife, Anna (Hudson,) daughter of Thomas, m. March 25th, 1792, No. (269;) she died; he married second, Sophia Stone.

220. "RUTH, wife of Aaron Roberts," to church Aug. 7th, 1785, daughter of No. (93) and No. (209,) born Nov. 10th, 1758, bap. Dec. 3d, 1758, m. Feb. 17th, 1785, No. (198;) she had no children, but adopted others; she died Feb. 18th, 1828, aged 70.

221. "JANE CLARK," to church Aug. 7th, 1785, daughter of John and his wife, Elizabeth (Newel,) i. e. No. (185,) m. Dec. 21st, 1785, No. (413;) was a woman of vigorous intellect, and kind feelings; a nice house-keeper,

and greatly respected; she died Feb. 16th, 1849, aged 85; she had no children.

222. "ELIZABETH ANDRUS," to church Nov. 24th, 1785, daughter of No. (112) and No. (312,) born June 8th, 1766, m. No. (199;) he died 1788, when she married second, Dec. 16th, 1790, Roger Francis, of Newington, New Britain and West Hartford, son of Josiah, of Newington, and Milly (Stoddard,) his wife. He was a blacksmith in New Britain; bought the house (now, 1862, Edwin Francis,) and had his shop opposite. After a few years he exchanged his farm with his brother, Allen, and removed back to Newington, to which church she was received by letter, Sept. 4th, 1791. He subsequently went to West Hartford, and became a wealthy farmer. He died Sept. 16th, 1839, aged 76. She died Sept. 1st, 1845, aged 79.

CHILDREN OF ROGER FRANCIS AND HIS WIFE, ELIZABETH.

1. Charles, born Aug. 12th, 1792, died Oct. 17th, 1835; never married.
2. Amzi, born July 31st, 1794; became a minister of the gospel; settled in Long Island; married March 10th, 1824, Eliza Talcott, of West Hartford; she died, when he married second, Feb. 15th, 1832, Mary L. Hedges, of Long Island.
3. Julia Ann, born June 1st, 1807, died April 17th, 1810.
4. Chester, born Feb. 21st, 1812, m. Sept. 4th, 1834, Lucy Halsey, of Long Island; he inherits the old homestead of his father, in West Hartford; is a successful farmer, and has been superintendent of their Sunday school.

223. "SUSANNA, wife of Elijah Smith," to church Feb. 5th, 1786, daughter of No. (43) and No. (44,) born Feb. 7th, 1756, m. July 7th, 1774; they lived with his father, and cultivated his farm until they moved to Owego, N. Y. The house stood on East street, next north of Leonard Belden's, and the same house is now the house of Samuel Kelsey, deceased, having been bought when Smith moved west, and moved by Mr. Kelsey, in 1814, and fitted up. Elijah Smith, jun., was son of Elijah, sen. and Sarah (Grimes,) his wife, born May 30th, 1753; he died Dec. 31st, 1824, aged 71½ years, at Candor, N. Y. He was a soldier in the "Army of the Revolution;" was at the battle of Yorktown, and a witness of the surrender of Cornwallis. He kept a diary of these events, which is still extant.

THEIR CHILDREN.

1. Lydia, born Jan., 1776, and died Aug. 24th, 1776.
2. Elijah, born April 28th, 1777, bap. July 16th, 1786, died June 3d, 1827; was insane.
3. Jesse, born Jan. 31st, 1782, bap. July 16th, 1786, m. Feb. 2d, 1815, Esther Hart; married second, Betsey Bacon.
4. Sarah, born April 7th, 1775, bap. July 16th, 1786, died June 12th, 1786.
5. Selah Judd, born Oct. 18th, 1788, bap. Jan. 18th, 1789, m. Sept. 12th, 1812, Rhoda Potter.
6. James, born April 20th, 1791, bap. Sept. 11th, 1791, m. Dec. 31st, 1818, Eunice Colburn.
7. Amzi, born July 16th, 1797, m. Sept. 8th, 1819; he died Nov. 22d, 1850.

224. "ANNA, wife of Asahel Hart," to church April 1st, 1787, daughter of No. (200) and No. (78,) born 1759, bap. Dec. 30th, 1759, m. No. (174;) she died Feb. 22d, 1803, aged 44.

225. "HANNAH BREWER," to church June 2d, 1787, daughter of David, of Chatham, and his wife, Hannah (Eddy;) she became the second wife of Ebenezer Steele, jun., about 1789; she born June 1st, 1766, at East Haddam; they lived on "Horse Plain," at the corner east of Elam Slater's present location. She was neice to Charles Eddy, sen., her mother being his sister. He was a feeble consumptive; lived by peddling pewter and tin ware, and raised a large family on small means. His first wife was Lucy (Wright,) probably daughter of Ezekiel and Eunice (Neal,) his wife, born March 25th, 1763, bap. March 27th, 1763, and probably married about 1775; she died, when he married as above. Mr. Steele died July 27th, 1812, aged 61, widow Hannah died April, 1842, aged 76, in Troy, N. Y.

FIRST WIFE'S CHILDREN.

1. Lucy, born March 3d, 1776, m. Feb. 16th, 1796, Truman Andrus, see No. (265.)
2. Sally, born , m. March 20th, 1796, John Belden, son of Ezra.
3. Salmon, born , m. Nelly Williams, see No. (406.)
4. Ebenezer, jun., born m. in Hartford, and died 1813, at Hartford, Conn.
5. Polly, born , bap. May 29th, 1791, on account of her grand-mother, Sarah, to whom she was given.
6. Keziah, born , m. Oct. 16th, 1814, Elisha S. Lewis, see No. (394.)

SECOND WIFE'S CHILDREN.

7. Jason, born Jan. 15th, 1790, bap. June 26th, 1791, died as a soldier, in the U. S. Army, at Sackett's Harbor, in the war of 1812.
8. Hannah, born June 1st, 1792, m. Feb. 20th, 1809, Elias Curtiss, son of Amos.
9. Chauncey, born , bap. Aug. 31st, 1794, died unmarried in Philadelphia.
10. Anna, born , bap. May 28th, 1797, m. Judd Eggleston, of Westfield, Mass.
11. Marinda, born , bap. April 14th, 1799, died Jan. 25th, 1815, aged 16.
12. Eliza, born Sept. 27th, 1802, m. Roswell Hart, son of Roger, Feb. 13th, 1826; live in Michigan.
13. Edmund, born Oct. 9th, 1804, bap. Dec. 30th, 1804, m. Oct. 10th, 1830, Lucy Newel, No. (689.)
14. Infant, born , died Oct. 1st, 1806.
15. Anna, born April 15th, 1808, bap. Sept. 11th, 1808, m. Peter Miller, of Troy, N. Y., May 12th, 1831.

226. "Widow ELECTA LUSK," to church Dec. 7th, 1788, daughter of Stephen De Wolf, of Berlin, and Mary (Whaples,) of Newington, his wife; she married Nov. 25th, 1784, Solomon, son of David Lusk, sen. and Prudence (Hurlburt,) his wife; they lived on the Farmington road, north of "Dublin Hill." In bringing from the mountain a load of wood on a sled, in the evening of the 8th of February, 1788, he was caught between the load and a tree, where he was found frozen stiff, with his arms up, as if protecting himself, or holding the load from turning over on to him. He had said the previous morning that the Bible was not true, for it de-

clared that the "wicked should not live out half their days," but he had more. His widow taught school at the North-west district, for three seasons next after the death of her husband. She married second, Aug. 29th, 1793, No. (253,) and moved to Nelson, New York; she died Aug. 27th, 1858.

CHILDREN OF SOLOMON AND ELECTA (DE WOLF) LUSK.

1. } twins. { Saphrone, born Nov. 20th, 1785, bap. Jan. 18th, 1789, m. Feb. 12th, 1804, John Francis.
2. } twins. { Salome, born Nov. 20th, 1785, bap. Jan. 18th, 1789, m. May, 7th, 1805, No. (459.)

227. "OLIVER D. COOK," to church July 12th, 1789. He was a divinity student of Dr. Smalley; son of Aaron, of Northford, in New Haven county, and Lucretia (Dudley,) his wife; graduated at Yale, 1786; licensed to preach 1789, by New Haven East; he settled in the ministry at New Fairfield, Conn., May, 1792, but was dismissed for bad health, Nov., 1793; he then engaged successfully in the book-trade in Hartford, where he died 1833, aged 65. He was a man of a good spirit, and was greatly respected.

THEIR CHILDREN.

1. Oliver Dudley, born , m. Sarah Belknap.
2. Edward Pratt, born , m. Anna Kissam, New York.
3. Laura Sophia, born , m. William J. Hamersley, New York and Hartford.
4. Julia Maria, born , m. Richard Kissam, New York.

228. "ISAAC MALTBY," to church July 12th, 1789. He was a divinity student of Dr. Smalley; son of Deacon Benjamin, of Northford, and Elizabeth (Fowler,) his wife, born 1767; graduated at Yale, 1786; licensed to preach 1789, by New Haven East, m. Nov., 1790, Hatfield, Mass., Lucinda Murray, only child of Gen. Seth, and he settled on his farm. He was twice elector of President; was made brigadier-general in 1813, and soon after removed to Waterloo, N. Y., with six children, whither he was preceded by two of his sons and eldest daughter, as the wife of Rev. Ephraim Chapin. A. D. 1860, eight of his children were living and had families. He died Sept. 9th, 1819, aged 52, at Waterloo, N. Y.; his widow died June 9th, 1844, aged 73, at Buffalo, N. Y.

229. "JOSEPH E. CAMP," to church Aug., 1789, a divinity student of Dr. Smalley; son of David, of Durham, Conn., and Margery (Johnson,) of Guilford, Conn., his wife, born April 6th, 1766, at Bethlehem, Conn.; graduated at Yale, 1787; licensed to preach 1789, by Hartford South Association; ordained 1795, and installed over the church at Northfield, Litchfield county; salary £80 and thirty cords of wood; married Dec. 3d, 1795, Rhoda Turner, of the same place, daughter of Titus and Sarah (Blakesley,) his wife. He died May 27th, 1838, aged 72, at Northfield.

THEIR CHILDREN.

1. Albert Barlow, born Feb. 16th, 1797, m. Feb. 3d, 1829, Mary Ann Wilder, of Rindge; she died 1830; he married second, Frances Ann Stearns, of Boston; live, 1860, in Bristol; title Rev.

2. Ralph Garwood, born June 14th, 1799, m. Oct. 29th, 1845, Louisa Ann Clark, of Northfield, who died 1848; he married second, Jane Fidelia Norton; live in Baraboo, Wisconsin; Colonel, Judge, Esquire.

3. David Bushrod Washington, born Feb. 8th, 1804, married Fanny J. Fox; his title M. D.

4. Elizabeth S., born March 3d, 1807, m. Nehemiah Kimberly, West Haven.

5. Joseph W., born March 12th, 1809, m. Lucy A. Brewster; live in Baraboo, Wisconsin.

6. Jabez McCall, born June 26th, 1811, m. Mary Heaton; lives at Campville, Conn.

230. "JAMES KASSON GARNSEY," to church Sept. 5th, 1790, a theological student of Dr. Smalley; born Dec. 31st, 1769, at Bethlehem, Conn., to Solomon and his wife, Sarah (Kasson.) He was licensed to preach Oct. 8th, 1790, at Newington, by Hartford South, at the house of Rev. J. Belden, and was then said to be from Castleton, Vermont. He is said to have preached the second sermon in the village of Canandaigua, N. Y. He seems to have left the ministry, for he was chosen sheriff of Ontario county, 1806, to succeed Phineas P. Bates. He married April 27th, 1807, Hannah Trowbridge, of Albany; she died April 7th, 1816, when he married second, April 29th, 1821, Electa Howes. He died March 6th, 1841, in his 72d year, at Pittsford.

THEIR CHILDREN.

1. Sarah Elizabeth, born April 27th, 1808, m. at Pittsford, by Rev. Mr. Mahan, Jan. 31st, 1831, Mortimer F. Delano.

2. Julia Norton, born Aug. 20th, 1809.

3. James Augustus, born Nov. 2d, 1811, died 1848.

4. Frances Dickinson, born Feb. 17th, 1815, m. Oct. 15th, 1839, Simon Traver.

SECOND WIFE'S CHILDREN.

5. George Elliot, born Feb. 11th, 1822.

6. Godfrey, born Oct. 8th, 1823, died Jan. 1st, 1834.

7. Catharine, born March 20th, 1825, died March 15th, 1848.

8. Lucy Ellen, born Aug. 12th, 1826; she is the authoress of "Irish Amy," &c.

9. Clara Florida, born Oct. 1st, 1836; these two last live with their widowed mother, at Rochester, N. Y., now, 1864.

The father was chosen a director in Livingston County Bank, N. Y., July, 1830.

231. "ELIZUR HART," to church Nov. 21st, 1790, son of No. (49) and No. (59,) born Dec. 25th, 1752, m. Jan. 1st, 1778, No. (232;) he was a noted school-teacher; had taught seventeen seasons, and it was said of him that he knew *almost* as much as "Capt. Belden." He was called "Landlord Hart," from his keeping a tavern in Hart quarter, now called the "State house," in which was a dancing-hall, occupied for that purpose very extensively. It was, however, during the revival of A. D. 1821,

used as ardently for a praying and preaching hall. Mr. Hart went, A. D. 1794, to the West Indies for his health, and died at Kingston, Jamaica, aged 42.

232. "Wife of Elizur Hart," to church Nov. 21st, 1790; her maiden name, Sarah Langdon, daughter of No. (107) and No. (108,) born Dec. 9th, 1756; her husband having died 1794, she married second, Seth Wadsworth, of Farmington; she was dismissed and recommended by letter to that church, 1817; she died June 14th, 1822, aged 65, at Farmington.

THEIR CHILDREN.

1. Sally, born Nov. 9th, 1778, bap. July 10th, 1791, m. Manly Clark; second, Martin Lee.

2. Polly, born Oct. 5th, 1781, bap. July 10th, 1791, m. Sept. 8th, 1800, John Hills, of David.

3. Sophia, born Sept. 3d, 1785, bap. July 10th, 1791, m. Franklin Hitchcock, of Southington.

4. Erastus L., born May 8th, 1787, bap. July 10th, 1791, m. Mary Parmelee, of Goshen; he M. D.; began practice in Wolcott; went to Goshen, but settled in Elmira, N. Y., where he is an elder in the Presbyterian church, and has an extensive practice as physician.

233. "ANNA, wife of Leonard Belden," to church May 1st, 1791; she was the second wife, and her maiden name, Anna Buck, from Newington, m. Nov. 21st, 1782; she had no children, and died March 16th, 1840, aged 94. His first wife was Hannah Judd, daughter of No. (38) and Hannah (Andrus,) his wife, born Sept. 27th, 1750, m. Jan. 4th, 1770; she died Sept. 10th, 1780, aged 30. She was the mother of his children. He was son of Ezra and his wife, Rebecca (Dix,) born Feb. 22d, 1749; lived at the old home of his father, on East street; his grand-father's name was also Ezra, and belonged in Wethersfield; his wife, Elizabeth. His will, dated Aug. 10th, 1770; he made Ezra, jun., sole executor; he also gave, 1749, for love to his son, Ezra, jun., in Kensington, Farmington, sixty acres of land, and the dwelling-house and barn thereon standing. This Leonard died March 18th, 1809, aged 60.

THEIR CHILDREN.

1. Leonard, jun., born Jan. 4th, 1770, died young.
2. Hannah, born July 26th, 1770, m. Thomas Lewis, son of William.
3. Lydia, born Nov. 3d, 1772, m. June 22d, 1794, Luther Porter; she died 1847, aged 75.
4. Olive, born Aug. 18th, 1775, m. Uni Wright, see No. (547.)
5. Leonard, 2d, born July 13th, 1778, m. Roxy Hart, No. (324.)
6. Ezra, born Aug. 13th, 1780, died young.

234. "Widow RUTH GRIDLEY," to church May 1st, 1791, daughter of Deacon John Lee, of Kensington and Berlin, the widow of John Gridley, of Kensington; she came here with No. (238,) her son, and No. (235,) her daughter; they both removed to Bristol about 1799, and the record of

that church says they were received by letters from New Britain church. Widow Ruth Gridley died Aug. 12th, 1811, aged 91, at Bristol.

235. "Betsey Gridley," to church May 1st, 1791, daughter of John and Ruth (Lee,) his wife; she was baptized Aug. 28th, 1757, in infancy, at Kensington; her father died July 2d, 1784, aged 63, at Kensington; she was sister of No. (238;) she died Sept. 29th, 1826, aged 69, at Bristol.

236. "Hannah, wife of Elisha Hart," to church Feb. 5th, 1792; they lived in a house he bought of Ezekiel Wright, near the south branch of Bass river, on the road to Farmington, and at the head of the road running west from Stanley quarter school-house. They moved out of town about A. D. 1791, having sold their home to No. (174.)

THEIR CHILDREN.

1. Truman, born , bap. May 10th, 1791.
2. Sarah, born , bap. May 10th, 1791.
3. Phebe, born , bap. May 10th, 1791.
4. Hannah, born , bap. May 10th, 1791.
5. Rhoda, born , bap. May 10th, 1791.
6. Elisha, born , bap. May 10th, 1791.

237. "Nathaniel Pennfield," to church Feb. 5th, 1792, son of No. (116) and No. (117,) born Nov. 14th, 1760, at New Haven, and there baptized Jan. 25th, 1761, (New Haven church record,) married Oct. 22d, 1780, Eunice Kelsey, daughter of Enoch, sen. and Mary (Bidwell,) his wife, born Aug. 22d, 1757, bap. Aug. 28th, 1757. He was a cooper by trade and occupation, and also a farmer; lived on "Horse Plain," next west of "Job's Corner;" was a kind, peaceable man, and very industrious. His wife, Eunice, died Jan. 23d, 1822, aged 64, when he married second, Oct. 3d, 1822, Widow Polly Rugg, the widow of Matthew; her maiden name, Webb, daughter of David, of Salem, Conn. He was in the Revolutionary war, at "Horse Neck and White Plains." He died Feb. 6th, 1838, aged 77.

THEIR CHILDREN.

1. Nathaniel, jun., born Feb., 1781, bap. July 1st, 1792, m. Nov. 5th, 1798, No. (549.)
2. Silas, born , bap. July 1st, 1792, m. March 1st, 1804, No. (341.)
3. Polly, born Sept. 4th, 1786, bap. July 1st, 1792, m. Aug. 11th, 1801, Shubel Curtiss, of Amos.
4. Eunice, born May 12th, 1789, bap. July 1st, 1792, m. May 22d, 1808, William Pennfield, of Jesse.
5. John, born Oct. 18th, 1791, bap. July 1st, 1792, m. March 12th, 1815, No. (432.)
6. Betsey, born April 13th, 1793, bap. July 7th, 1793, m. Feb. 6th, 1820, Enos Pennfield, of Jesse; he died, and she married second, April, 1835, Deacon Joseph Langdon, of Sugar Grove, Pa.
7. Chester, born Jan. 23d, 1796, bap. May 15th, 1796, m. June 4th, 1820, No. (528.)
8. Sally, born Nov. 8th, 1800, bap. May 17th, 1801, see No. (496.)

238. "OLIVER GRIDLEY," to church March 25th, 1792, son of John and No. (234,) born Nov. 16th, 1751, in Kensington, on the spot where Frederic North's farm-house stands. He bought out Joseph Hart, in Hart quarter, (now, A. D. 1862,) Edwin Francis. He married Dec. 21st, 1780, No. (239;) was a gentlemanly man, of good deportment and excellent Christian character. He moved to Bristol, about 1799, removing his connection to that church, where he died Nov. 16th, 1831, aged 80; a farmer by occupation.

239. "Wife of Oliver Gridley," to church March 25th, 1792; she was daughter of No. (69) and No. (28,) born 1757; her maiden name, Martha Goodrich; was dismissed with her husband to church at Bristol, and died there, Feb. 11th, 1820, aged 63.

THEIR CHILDREN.

1. Alva, born Sept. 18th, 1783, bap. July 22d, 1792, m. Oct. 29th, 1814, Clarissa Goodrich, of Kensington.
2. Laura, born Oct. 25th, 1787, bap. July 22d, 1792; she died Feb. 16th, 1849, aged 62.
3. Huldah, born Jan. 17th, 1790, bap. July 22d, 1792, died Dec. 8th, 1808, aged 19.
4. Lucy, born April 10th, 1794, bap. April 25th, 1794; living, 1863, in Bristol.
5. Cyrus, born Oct. 25th, 1797, m. Mary, daughter of Samuel Root, of Plainville; lives in Ohio.

240. "SOLOMON CHURCHILL," to church March 25th, 1792, son of No. (104) and No. (105,) born April 24th, 1767, bap. June 28th, 1767, m. Dec. 30th, 1790, No. (241;) had a twin sister, Sarah. He turned his hand to various employments, and lived in various localities; raised a large family on small means. Late in life united with the Episcopal church. He died April 27th, 1841, aged 81.

241. "Wife of Solomon Churchill," to church March 25th, 1792; her maiden name, Selina Hart, daughter of No. (52) and Sarah Gilbert, his wife, born Aug. 30th, 1770; she died Nov. 22d, 1845, aged 75.

THE CHILDREN.

1. Solomon, jun., born Oct. 20th, 1791, bap. April 8th, 1792, m. Dec. 1st, 1812, No. (388.)
2. Amzi, born Dec. 11th, 1793, bap. Feb. 2d, 1794, m. Maria White, of Long Island.
3. Prudentia, born 1795, bap. May 15th, 1796, died Sept. 24th, 1798, aged three.
4. Cyrus, born Dec. 15th, 1797, bap. April 1st, 1798, m. Clarissa Bradley, of Guilford.
5. Infant, born 1799, bap. Selina Hart, died Nov. 17th, 1799.
6. Selina Hart, born March 5th, 1801, bap. May 31st, 1801, m. Andrew Rapelye.
7. Prudentia, 2d, born July 15th, 1804, bap. Oct. 6th, 1805, m. 1820, Albert Webster.
8. Louisa, born Nov. 20th, 1807, bap. Nov. 31st, 1807, died Jan. 5th, 1808, aged 1.
9. Louisa, 2d, born Feb. 8th, 1809, bap. April 30th, 1809, m. 1833, Ebenezer Evans; she died Dec. 18th, 1862.
10. Jane Bushnel, born May 20th, 1810, m. Ebenezer Evans, of Southington; she died Sept. 11th, 1866, aged 56.

11. John, born Aug. 10th, 1813, m. Emeline Cleavland; married second, Lucy French, and has one son, Henry Hart, born Jan. 22d, 1834; he is living, 1863, in New Hartford.

242. "ANNA, wife of Seth Lusk," to church April 7th, 1793, daughter of No. (65) and No. (66,) m. Sept. 6th, 1781; he son of David and Prudence (Hurlburt,) his wife, bap. Sept. 6th, 1755, at Newington; lived at the "old Lusk house," (half of which, with twenty acres of land, was given him, 1788, by his father,) back of "Dublin Hill," on the Farmington road; he was a farmer; a large man; he died Sept. 19th, 1823, aged 68; she died Jan. 28th, 1822, aged 68.

THEIR CHILDREN.

1. Nancy, born 1783, bap. June 2d, 1793, m. Sept. 27th, 1799, No. (348.)

2. Adna, born , bap. June 2d, 1793, unmarried; subject to fits; died May 10th, 1826, aged 43.

3. Seth, jun., born April 6th, 1786, bap. June 2d, 1793, m. July 6th, 1806, Roxy Recor, of Michael; he died Jan. 3d, 1857, in New York; his widow lives, 1862, at McCornel's Grove, Illinois.

243. "HULDAH, wife of Bethel Hart," to church April 7th, 1793, daughter of Ebenezer Steele and No. (148,) his wife, born 1768, see No. (183;) she baptized Jan. 3d, 1768, in Kensington; she died Sept. 28th, 1810, aged 44.

244. "REUBEN WRIGHT," to church May 26th, 1793, son of Judah and his wife, Mary (Judd,) bap. July 9th, 1749, at Newington. He a carpenter and joiner; learned of his father; married March 12th, 1780, Martha Gridley, daughter of Ebenezer, of Kensington and Farmington Plains, and Zubah Orvice, his wife; she born April 10th, 1756. He built on the Farmington road, north of "Half-way," or "Osgood Hill;" his house burned in the fall of 1790, when he built again. His joiner shop stood opposite his house, and has been moved east to the next corner, and is the house of Philip Recor. Mr. Wright moved west, to Redfield, Oneida county, New York, with his family, in 1803; he died April 17th, 1841, aged 93.

THEIR CHILDREN.

1. Gad, born Sept. 30th, 1780, bap. July 7th, 1793, died in Virginia.

2. Martin, born Sept. 5th, 1782, bap. July 7th, 1793, m. Feb. 22d, 1812, Mary Tryon; he died Sept. 23d, 1865, aged 83.

3. Reuben, jun., born Nov. 17th, 1784, bap. July 7th, 1793, m. March 10th, 1811, Betsey Seymour.

4. Hannah, born Jan. 23d, 1787, bap. July 7th, 1793, m. Henry Brooks, Jan. 25th, 1807.

5. Lois, born July 28th, 1789, bap. July 7th, 1793, m. Feb. 5th, 1812, Michael Hinman.

6. James, born Oct. 25th, 1791, bap. July 7th, 1793, m. Jan. 16th, 1823, Julia Strong.

7. Mary, born Feb. 13th, 1794, bap. April 6th, 1794, m. April 28th, 1819, James Bacon; she died July 29th, 1864, aged 70.

8. Nancy, born April 21st, 1796, bap. May 22d, 1796, died Aug. 22d, 1839, unmarried.

9. John, born , married, and now, 1865, living in DeSoto, Kansas.

245. "ELIJAH ANDRUS," to church May 26th, 1793, son of Elijah, of Newington, and his wife, Phebe (Hurlburt,) born Oct. 16th, 1752, married March 2d, 1775, No. (252;) he a shoe maker and tanner; learned his trade of No. (113;) lived on the road from Stanley quarter school-house, west to Farmington road. He was a man greatly beloved for his kind and courteous disposition; is well remembered for his piety; he died Nov. 24th, 1839, aged 87.

THEIR CHILDREN.

1. Truman, born Jan. 23d, 1776, bap. July 7th, 1793, m. Feb. 16th, 1796, No. (265.)

2. Ebenezer, born Dec. 24th, 1778, bap. July 7th, 1793, m. Oct. 26th, 1800, Mary Griswold.

3. Josiah, born June 29th, 1781.

4. Phebe Hurlburt, born June 17th, 1783, bap. July 7th, 1793, m. Sept. 1st, 1822, Harvey Curtiss.

5. Ira, born Dec. 8th, 1785, bap. July 7th. 1793, m. May 28th, 1807, Amy Steele, No. (642.)

6. Rachel, born Feb. 6th, 1789, bap. July 7th, 1793, see No. (344.)

7. Azuba Orvice, born March 20th, 1791, bap. July 7th, 1793, m. May 10th, 1815, Otis Robinson.

8. Dinah, born Aug. 21st, 1793, bap. Oct. 6th, 1793; is deaf and unmarried.

9. Abi, born Aug. 28th, 1795, bap. Sept. 1st, 1795; is blind and nearly deaf.

10. Benjamin, born Jan. 8th, 1799, bap. June 16th, 1799, m. June 16th, 1823, Sallie Innis, of Philadelphia.

246. "BECCARENA, wife of William Steele," to church May 26th, 1793, daughter of No. (116) and No. (117,) born May 9th, 1763, at New Haven, and the town record has her name Rebecca Rena, married Oct. 26th, 1780. He was son of Ebenezer, sen. and his wife, No. (148,) born 1757; he lived in part of his father's house, made up of the old school-house of the North-west district, which he bought. He was in the war of the Revolution, and a noted fifer; was a short thick set man; he died March 28th, 1825, aged 68; she died April 26th, 1838, aged 75; she was baptized in New Haven, May 9th, 1763, and is called on their church record Rebecca Rhena.

THEIR CHILDREN.

1. Lydia, born , bap. July 7th, 1793, m. July 12th, 1801, Elisha Vaughn.

2. Billy, born July 8th, 1787, bap. July 7th, 1793, m. Esther Judd.

3. Samuel, born , bap. July 7th, 1793.

4. Rena, born Feb. 2d, 1794, bap. May, 1794, m. Sept. 25th, 1814, Moses Gilbert, see No. (751.)

5. Cynthia, born April 8th, 1796, bap. May 22d, 1796, m. Aug. 24th, 1818, No. (646.)

6. "Jemmy," } twins. { born , bap. May 19th, 1799, m. Dec. 2d, 1819, Rosetta Hunter; he died Jan. 31st, 1849, aged 50.

7. Nancy, } twins. { born , bap. May 19th, 1799, m. Nov. 4th, 1819, No. (955.)

8. John, born Feb. 13th, 1801, bap. May 17th, 1801, m. Dec. 2d, 1822, No. (571.)
9. Jefferson, born , bap. March 1st, 1804, m. Feb. 16th, 1823, Betsey Goff.
10. Henry, born April 5th, 1806, bap. June 15th, 1806, m. Nov. 19th, 1827, No. (528.)

247. "AARON HART," to church May 26th, 1793, son of No. (52) and his wife, Sarah Gilbert, born Oct. 16th, 1761, m. March 4th, 1790, No. (248;) was a captain and a farmer; inherited the old home of his father, in the south-west corner of the parish, (now, A. D. 1861,) owned and occupied by his son, Horace, but 1862, owned and occupied by Levi O. Smith. He was a large, portly man, of stern virtue and integrity. He made weaver's reeds, with tools used by his father, and inherited by him from *his* grandfather, Deacon Thomas Hart, of the "Great Swamp" Society. The will or deed conveying the tools, is dated March 14th, 1760, by which he gives them to his grand-son, Elijah Hart, jun.

248. "Wife of Aaron Hart," to church May 26th, 1793; maiden name, Sarah Francis, daughter of Josiah Francis, of Newington, and his wife, Milly (Stoddard,) born April 6th, 1769; possessed a social, genial spirit, active and quick, even in old age; she died Jan. 1st, 1847, aged 78; he died July 2d, 1829, aged 68.

THEIR CHILDREN.

1. Francis, born Dec. 18th, 1791, bap. June 23d, 1793, married Dec. 30th, 1812, No. (343.)
2. Chester, born Feb. 7th, 1793, bap. June 23d, 1793, m. No. (489,) and married second, No. (490.)
3. Sarah, born 1798, bap. April 29th, 1798, died June 24th, 1814, aged 16.
4. Anson, born , bap. Aug. 24th, 1800, died May 13th, 1850, aged 50, unmarried.
5. Betsey, born 1795, bap. Oct. 18th, 1795, died Sept. 5th, 1798, aged three years and a few days.
6. Betsey, 2d, born Feb. 26th, 1803, bap. June 12th, 1803, m. April 10th, 1822, No. (674.)
7. Aaron, jun., born Nov. 25th, 1805, bap. April 20th, 1806, m. Nov. 27th, 1827, No. (532.)
8. Horace, born July 29th, 1808, m. Dec. 2d, 1831, Harriet J. Church, daughter of James, of Haddam.
9. Walter, born , by trade a silver-plater; died Sept. 10th, 1847, aged 40, unmarried.

249. "PHEBE, wife of John Andrus," to church May 26th, 1793, daughter of No. (88) and No. (111,) born , bap. May 15th, 1768, m. May 10th, 1792, No. (197,) died Nov. 13th, 1797, aged 29.

250. "Wife of Nathaniel Andrus," to church May 26th, 1793; maiden name, Jerusha Sage, daughter of Deacon Jedediah, of Berlin, and Sarah (Marcy,) his wife, born Aug. 15th, 1771; was his second wife, his first being No. (184;) his widow, Jerusha, died Dec. 9th, 1857, at Flint, Michigan, aged 86.

251. "NATHANIEL ANDRUS," to church June 23d, 1793, son of No.

(53) and No. (54,) born Oct. 15th, 1762, m. 1786, No. (184;) married second, Oct. 3d, 1790, No. (250;) he was a farmer; was in the army of the Revolution, at the age of sixteen years; was above common height, well-proportioned, of kind and conciliatory spirit, greatly beloved and respected. He lived with his father, in the same house, still, (A. D. 1867,) standing, when about A. D. 1805, and after the decease of his parents, who were very aged, he moved with his family to Whitestown, N. Y.; he died Aug. 27th, 1845, at Flint, Michigan, aged 83.

THEIR CHILDREN.

1. Polly, born Jan. 13th, 1787, bap. April 15th, 1787, m. 1820, Ambrose Cone, and died A. D. 1848.
2. Orpha Sage, born Aug. 12th, 1791, bap. June 30th, 1793, married Major James Delibar, 1813.
3. George, born Dec. 2d, 1793, bap. Feb. 2d, 1794, m. 1817, Polly Walker, and lives, A. D. 1863, in Troy.
4. Philip, born March 16th, 1796, bap. May 8th, 1796; is a machinist, in Chemung, Michigan.
5. Clarissa Sage, born Feb. 5th, 1798, bap. April 15th, 1798, unmarried, died Oct. 24th, 1828.
6. Samuel, born July 21st, 1800, bap. March 16th, 1800; lives in West Bloomfield, Michigan.
7. Sarah Marcy, born Feb. 11th, 1802, bap. April 25th, 1802, m. 1820, John Beebe.
8. Lydia Root, born March 8th, 1804, bap. April 15th, 1804, m. 1824, Rev. Charles G. Finney, of Oberlin.
9. Mary Ann, born March 21st, 1806, m. Thomas Beebe, 1826; she died Oct. 24th, 1829.
10. Edward W., born Oct. 29th, 1808; a gunsmith by trade and occupation; lives in Oberlin, Ohio; married Margaret McMillen; married second, Delia

252. "RACHEL, wife of Elijah Andrus," to church June 23d, 1793, daughter of Ebenezer Gridley, of Kensington and Farmington Plains, and his wife, Azuba Orvice, born Nov. 10th, 1753, m. March 2d, 1775, No. (245;) she died Oct. 20th, 1836, aged 83.

253. "ISAAC GOODRICH," to church July 14th, 1793, son of Asahel and Abigail (Gilbert,) his wife, born Feb. 2d, 1765, bap. April 21st, 1765, in Kensington; he was a blacksmith; married March 14th, 1790, Polly Wright; she died March 24th, 1793, aged 26, when he married second, Aug. 29th, 1793, No. (226.) He first established his business in Hart quarter, District No. 4, near the school-house, but when the shop of Elijah Hinsdale was left vacant by his death, he moved there; after a few years he built a new house and shop on Horse Plain, and subsequently went to Avon, and last to Nelson, New York. He died April 19th, 1847, at Georgetown, Madison county, New York. He united with the Baptists, and became a preacher in that denomination, in the later years of life; he is spoken of as a conscientious, good man.

THEIR CHILDREN.

1. James, born April 20th, 1791, died May 10th, 1791, aged twenty days.
2. Polly, born April 12th, 1792, died , aged three hours.
3. Polly, born Aug. 28th, 1795, bap. Aug. 30th, 1795, m. May 17th, 1817, Deacon Anson Chidsey, of Avon.
4. Laura, born May 8th, 1796, bap. Oct. 2d, 1796, m. June 8th, 1813, Anson Kellogg.
5. Betsey, born Sept. 21st, 1798, bap. April 7th, 1799.

254. "ELIZABETH, wife of Sage Churchill," to church Aug. 4th, 1793, daughter of No. (138) and No. (139,) born Nov. 20th, 1767, m. No. (257;) she married second,

255. "DAVID CLARK," to church Feb. 5th, 1759, bap. same time; his name not on list of members, but is on list of baptisms, as an adult, with two of his sons, as his children. He is out of chronologic order from the fact that proof of his membership did not appear until this work had thus far progressed. He son of . , born , married Christian; she died July 30th, 1766, when he married second, March 8th, 1770, Lois Andrus, of Wethersfield.

HIS CHILDREN BY FIRST WIFE.

1. Martha, born Feb. 27th, 1746.
2. David, born , bap. Feb. 5th, 1759.
3. Bildad, born , bap. Feb. 5th, 1759.
4. Huldah, born , bap. March 18th, 1759.
5. Christian, born , bap. Sept. 13th, 1761.

256. "Widow WRIGHT," to church Sept. 3d, 1793; her maiden name, (probably,) Keziah Loveland, when married, Aug. 15th, 1770, to "Master Judah Wright;" she was the widow of Joseph Crofoot, of Kensington; she died March 20th, 1806, aged 72; she was his second wife, the first probably, Mary Judd, of Northampton, Mass., who was the mother of his children. He lived where his son, Reuben, built, north of Half-way Hill. A. D. 1775, his taxable estate was £30 15s. In 1752, he bought of Thomas Stanley, at Half-way Hill, a pitch of eight acres, called the "Flagg Swamp," and lies south-west of the house. He was probably son of Judah and Mary Hoyt, his wife, of Deerfield, married April 4th, 1707.

CHILDREN OF JUDAH WRIGHT AND HIS FIRST WIFE, MARY JUDD.

1. Daniel, born , died in the old French war.
2. Amos, born 25th, see No. (XV.)
3. Simeon, born , m. March 25th, 1766, Ann Whaples, of Newington.
4. Joseph, born Oct. 11th, 1741, see No. (133.)
5. Lois, born Sept. 17th, 1744.
6. Reuben, born , bap. July 9th, 1749, see No. (244.)
7. Asahel, born , bap. Sept. 22d, 1751, at Newington.

257. "SAGE CHURCHILL," to church Sept. 3d, 1793, son of No. (104) and No. (105,) born Dec. 13th, 1763, m. No. (254.) He when a lad,

carelessly killed the only daughter of Joseph Wright, with a gun; she a school-girl. He died Feb. 27th, 1813, aged 50, at Lake Champlain; she married second,

THEIR CHILDREN.

1. Aaron, born , bap. Oct. 6th, 1793.
2. Bushnel, born , bap. Oct. 6th, 1793.
3. Betsey, born , bap. Oct. 6th, 1793.
4. Roxan, born , bap. Oct. 6th, 1793.

258. "Lois, wife of Zenas Goodrich," to church Sept. 3d, 1793, daughter of Peat. Galpin, of Berlin, and his wife, Lois (Beckley,) born Dec. 10th, 1758, bap. Dec. 10th, 1758, at Kensington. He was son of John and Hannah (Dewy,) his wife, born Nov. 6th, 1763, bap. Nov. 13th, 1763, in Kensington; was a blacksmith; learned of his father; lived and had his shop on the corner west of John Ellis' house; he and family moved to New Durham, New York.

THEIR CHILDREN.

1. Salome, born , bap. Oct. 27th, 1793.
2. Chauncey, born , bap. Oct. 27th, 1793.
3. Billy, born , bap. Oct. 27th, 1793.
4. Hannah, born , bap. Oct. 27th, 1793.
5. Lois, born , bap. Oct. 27th, 1793.

259. "Asher North," to church Dec. 1st, 1793, son of James, sen. and Sarah (Seymour,) his wife, born 1741, m. April 29th, 1773, No. (260.) He was brother of No. (149;) was a very small man, but active and quick; lived west of "Clark Hill," hence "Asher corner," to this day; lived in various localities; raised a large family on small means. He died Feb. 29th, 1816, aged 75. Was a light-horseman in the Revolutionary war.

260. "Wife of Asher North," to church Dec. 1st, 1793; her maiden name, Betsey Foster, probably of Kensington; the Widow Betsey North was by letter dismissed and recommended Sept. 12th, 1819.

THEIR CHILDREN.

1. Samuel, born , went south.
2. Thomas, born , bap. June 8th, 1788, on account of Thomas Hart; was a mariner, in New York.
3. Asher, born , bap. June 8th, 1788, on account of Daniel Ames; lived in New York.
4. Betsey, born , bap. June 8th, 1788, on account of Elijah Hart, jun., married Samuel Carter.
5. Edward, born ; a mariner, died at sea.
6. Mary, born Jan. 6th, 1785, m. July 10th, 1804, Elisha Stone; married second, David Buel.
7. Sally, born July 29th, 1787, m. Ira Buel, of Litchfield, see No. (1427.)
8. James, born , died at Harwinton.

They had a child buried in Beckley quarter, Dec. 5th, 1773, (the eldest, probably,) and not embraced in this list.

261. "FANNY, wife of Nathan Booth," to church Dec. 1st, 1793, daughter of No. (8) and No. (9,) born March 3d, 1753, m. June 24th, 1773; she died Sept. 14th, 1828, aged 74, at Springfield, Mass., and buried there. He was son of No. (65) and No. (66,) born March 1st, 1749; he owned and occupied the Joseph Shipman place, on Stanley street, in Shipman district, and sold it to Mr. Shipman, when he moved to Granville, Mass., where he died Feb. 19th, 1825, aged 76.

THEIR CHILDREN.

1. Sylvester, born , bap. April 6th, 1794, married a widow in Canada.
2. Fanny, born Dec. 27th, 1776, bap. April 6th, 1794, m. May 10th, 1797, Oliver Stanley, of Timothy.
3. Nathan, jun., born May 3d, 1782, bap. April 6th, 1794, m. April 5th, 1805, Ruth Bates, of David.
4. Horace, born , bap. April 6th, 1794, m. Martha Lewis; he died, aged 24, in Cherry Valley, N. Y.
5. Aziel, born , bap. April 6th, 1794; never married; died at New Britain, April 9th, 1853, aged 68.
6. Mehitabel, born Jan. 13th, 1790, bap. April 6th, 1794, m. Benjamin P. Stiles.
7. Elisha Smith, born June 8th, 1794, bap. Aug. 17th, 1794, m. No. (648.)
8. Jeptha, born , bap. April 7th, 1799, married in the State of New York; lived and died there.

262. "POLLY OSGOOD," to church July 6th, 1794, daughter of Jeremiah H. Osgood, and Lucy (Churchill,) his wife, born June 5th, 1776; she married Josiah Beeman, of Fairfax, Vermont.

263. Widow SARAH FLAGG," to church about 1794; her name not on Dr. Smalley's list of members, but on the Deacon's tax-list, for the supply of the table, (as was the case with several other known members.) She was born at Cheshire, 1724; married June 3d, 1744, Joseph Bill, who by a former wife had a son, Joseph; Joseph Bill and Sarah Clark had a daughter, Mollee, born Nov. 27th, 1747, when the father died, and Sarah, the widow, married July 4th, 1754, Abijah Flagg, from Sudbury, Mass., (who had a former wife, Mary Stone, by whom he had Eunice.) Abijah and Sarah, his wife, lived in Bristol, where she owned the covenant. She was received to Kensington church from Bristol, Sept. 7th, 1766; from Kensington to West Hartford, Jan. 7th, 1781; from there, here, as above. She died Jan. 15th, 1812, aged 88 years, at the house of Josiah Andrews, on Horse Plain.

CHILDREN OF ABIJAH AND SARAH FLAGG.

1. Abijah, jun., born May 5th, 1755, at Bristol; learned tanner's trade; married Feb. 7th, 1782, Thankful Seymour; he married second, Thankful Woodhouse; he died Nov. 22d, 1842.
2. Abigail, born 1757, m. March 18th, 1784, Josiah Andrews, see No. (329.)
3. Solomon, born 1758, m. Olive, daughter of Zachariah Hart and Abigail Beckley, his wife.
4. Dimond, born July 16th, 1761, m. Sarah Carrington, of Southington; was a clothier; raised a large family in Cheshire, and died there, June 22d, 1797, aged 36.

5. Sarah, born , bap. Sept. 7th, 1766, at Kensington, married Joseph Bill, son of Joseph.

6. Martha, born , bap. Sept. 7th, 1766, at Kensington, married Asahel Holcomb, of East Granby.

7. Allen, born Jan. 5th, 1771, bap. April 29th, 1771, at Kensington, married Jemima Bidwell; married second, Sally Taylor. He made spinning-wheels in Berlin.

264. "ABIGAIL WOODS," to church July 27th, 1794, daughter of No. (87,) and her husband, John Woods. She was brought up at Ensign Levi Andrews, and she married Benoni Johnson, of Harwinton; she died 1848, aged 82.

265. "LUCY STEELE," to church July 31st, 1794, and baptized an adult same time, daughter of Ebenezer and Lucy (Wright,) his wife, born March 3d, 1776, m. Feb. 16th, 1796, Truman Andrus, son of Elijah; she died Dec. 19th, 1820, aged 45. He lived in the old home of his father, see No. (245.) He died June 18th, 1849, aged 73. He had a second wife, married Feb. 17th, 1822, Sally Barnes, by whom he had Benjamin.

THEIR CHILDREN.

1. Elijah, born Feb. 9th, 1797, bap. May 28th, 1797, m. Oct. 1st, 1817, Nancy Bronson; he died 1843.

2. Miran, born Jan. 18th, 1799, m. Lois Barnes; he died April 30th, 1845, aged 46.

3. Amzi, born Dec. 15th, 1800, bap. May 17th, 1801; lives in Chester, Randolph county, Illinois.

4. Curtiss, born May 16th, 1803, m. Almira Barnes, see No. (581.)

5. Keziah, born Dec. 6th, 1805, m. May 5th, 1825, Lyman Booth, see No. (555.)

6. Lucy Maria, born Aug. 29th, 1808, bap. Aug. 13th, 1809, m. March 8th, 1830, William Rugg, of Matthew.

7. Dinah, born Dec. 20th, 1810, bap. June 2d, 1811, m. Henry Dunbar.

8. Almira, born Feb. 22d, 1813, bap. March 5th, 1813, died March 7th, 1813.

9. Truman Erastus, born Aug. 18th, 1814, bap. June 18th, 1814, m. Aug. 19th, 1839, Mary Montroy.

SECOND WIFE'S CHILD.

10. Benjamin, born Nov. 1st, 1822.

266. "PHEBE, wife of Samuel Gladden," to church Aug. 31st, 1794, daughter of No. (116) and No. (117,) baptized Aug. 19th, 1772, m. He son of Azariah and Anna (Hudson,) of Saybrook, his wife. They lived on the road leading to the mountain, from near the school-house, in District No. 4, or South-west. He was a stout, heavy-built man, a farmer by occupation, but was cut down suddenly by spotted fever, an epidemic fatal to many of our people that year. He died Aug. 14th, 1823, aged 56. His widow married second, Oct. 24th, 1824, Roger Hart, her next neighbor. He was son of No. (101) and his wife, Anna (Deming,) born 1765, married Sibil Robinson, daughter of John, of Middletown, and Mary (Strickland,) his wife; she baptized Dec. 18th, 1763; died Jan. 15th, 1817, aged 53, when he married second, the widow of Joel Tryon; (her maiden name, Lavinia Frisbee;) she died Nov. 22d, 1822, when he mar-

ried third, Oct. 24th, 1824, No. (266;) he died July 31st, 1828, aged 63. Mr. Hart inherited a large farm from his father, but by mismanagement it wasted away soon after his first marriage, when his friends helped him move a small house from "Strip Lane," which is the one now, 1862, occupied by Solomon Hamblin. He raised a large family to respectability on small means, by industry and economy.

HIS CHILDREN BY HIS FIRST WIFE, SIBIL.

1. Azuba, born July 7th, 1789, m. Allen Goodrich, of Farmington, son of Elias, Dec. 13th, 1807.

2. Betsey, born Sept. 17th, 1791, see No. (432.)

3. Polly, born June 5th, 1793, m. Nov. 27th, 1828, George Cook, son of John and his wife, Lucina (Lewis.)

4. Chauncey, born Oct. 5th, 1795, m. May 3d, 1821, Polly Markum, of Kensington; he a carriage-maker.

5. John, born March, 1798, m. Polly Stephens, of New Haven; he a cabinet-maker.

6. Ann, born Sept. 6th, 1800, m. Curtiss M. Doolittle, of New Haven, an engraver.

7. Roswell, born Sept. 1st, 1802, m. Feb. 13th, 1826, Eliza, daughter of Ebenezer Steele, jun.; she born 1802. [Roswell Hart learned the trade of harness-maker, of A. Bodwell, of Farmington, and lives now, 1862, in Plymouth, Michigan.]

8. William, born Oct. 14th, 1805, m. Sarah, daughter of Theodore Barnes; married second, Sept. 19th, 1859, Widow Harriet Dagget.

CHILD OF ROGER HART AND HIS SECOND WIFE, LAVINIA.

9. Levi, born , went to Illinois.

HER CHILDREN BY HER FIRST HUSBAND.

1. Anna, born , bap. Sept. 21st, 1794, m. Jamin Goodrich.
2. Phebe, born , bap. June 18th, 1795.
3. Samuel, born , bap. April 11th, 1798, died May, 1798.
4. Leva, born , bap. July 11th, 1802.
5. Samuel Hudson, born , bap. July 23d, 1809, died Sept. 23d, 1810, aged 2.
6. Riley Ward, born , bap. May 10th, 1812.

267. "ELIZABETH, wife of Reuben Wright," to church Sept. 28th, 1794, see No. (244,) for her husband and family.

268. "SARAH, wife of Lewis Seymour," to church Nov. 16th, 1794, daughter of Ebenezer Steele, senior, and No. (148,) born March 26th, 1750, married first, Ezra Belden; she married second, Sept. 1st, 1788, as above; he was a Frenchman, taken prisoner of war, with Michael DeRecor, and while held as such in Hartford, Mr. Gideon Griswold, one of the principal farmers then of this place, paid some debts they had contracted, and brought them home with him. They both made industrious citizens. She and her first husband lived in Rocky Hill, but for some cause unknown to us, he left and went to New York State, where he died, when she returned to her father's home. She had one son, "John Belden," but no child by Seymour. He, Seymour, died Sept. 6th, 1810, aged 60.

269. "ELIZABETH, wife of Azariah Gladden," to church Nov. 16th, 1794; her maiden name, Alderman, of Simsbury, married March 25th,

1792, before Dr. Smalley, No. (219 ;) she dismissed and recommended to Kensington church, July, 1796.

270. "ASENATH BASS," to church Nov. 16th, 1794, daughter of No. (153,) bap. Aug. 2d, 1778, m. Nov. 29th, 1798, Charles Eddy, son of Charles and Hannah (Kelsey,) his wife, born March 26th, 1773; he lived in the house on West Main street, owned (now, 1866,) by Mrs. Tolles, which was built by Elijah Dickinson. Mr. Eddy was a stout, tall and athletic man; he died Sept. 1st, 1826, aged 53, when she married second, Jan. 1st, 1850, James Fortune, of Wethersfield; she died April 8th, 1852, aged 74, and he died Aug. 8th, 1855. She was a devout woman.

THEIR CHILDREN.

1. Rebecca Bass, born Oct. 3d, 1799, bap. Nov. 17th, 1799, m. June 28th, 1825, Albert Norton, of Kensington.

2. Emeline, born Feb. 22d, 1802, bap. April 25th, 1802, m. Oct. 12th, Ralph S. Cornwell; married second,

3. William Harlowe, born Feb. 4th, 1805, bap. May 19th, 1805, m. Sept. 23d, 1827, Mary Dobson, of John.

4. Levi, born June 9th, 1809, bap. Aug. 20th, 1809, died Oct. 3d, 1828, aged 19.

5. Caroline, born Aug. 30th, 1811, bap. Oct. 27th, 1811, m. James H. Webb.

6. Samuel Henry, born July 15th, 1815, bap. Oct. 15th, 1815, died May 7th, 1828, aged 13.

271. "ELIZABETH, wife of Andrew Pratt," to church April 29th, 1795, daughter of Daniel Whaples' former wife, (Mrs. Mary Hunn,) was baptized on admission to church; had her two children, Lydia and Daniel, baptized May 4th, 1795, and she died on the 15th of the same month. Her step-father owned and occupied the Pratt, alias Patterson farm. She married June 1st, 1787, No. (345.) She inherited one-half of her step-father's estate, by will made Aug. 30th, 1780, and her sister, Isabel, who married Josiah Kilborn, jun., the other half, abating the use of one-third, (alias the jointure,) Mr. Daniel Whaples made, with his last wife, viz. Zeruiah (Bird,) before marriage, and one-third part* he gave Mary, the wife of Timothy Lee, and daughter of Widow Mary Hunn, deceased. His estate amounted to £889 14s. 2d. He says these heirs by his will were called Elizabeth (alias) Betty Whaples and Isabel Whaples, and that they were daughters of Mrs. Mary Hunn, alias Widow Mary Hunn, deceased, and in this will he says, Betty was the youngest daughter of Mrs. Mary Hunn; the executors to the will were Col. Gad Stanley and Lieut. Elijah Francis; the distributors were Isaac Lee, Lemuel Hotchkiss, and Levi Andrus; they set to Betty, the Ruth lot, the Green Swamp lot, the north dwelling-house and the barn, and made her to share equally with Isabel, in the rest of the estate.

272. "MARY CLARK," to church March 22d, 1795, daughter of No.

---

* This one-third part of the household goods he received of said Widow Mary Hunn.

(185) and John Clark, her husband, born Feb. 23d, 1745; she was a school-teacher; had a private school, the first known in the place, on East street, in the old Thomas Hooker house, which stood on the west side of the road, on the site of Amzi Judd's. She had scholars from Hartford, and other places. She was dismissed and recommended to Farmington church, 1803; she died Feb., 1814, aged 70; never married.

273. "HULDAH, wife of Simeon Lincoln," to church Aug. 2d, 1795, daughter of Gideon Porter and Huldah (Hart,) his wife, and widow of John Riley, when she married Mr. Lincoln. She had by her first husband, to whom she was married April 1st, 1773, two children, when he was killed or otherwise fell in the war of the Revolution, at Northampton, Mass.; she returned to Kensington with her two children, and married Mr. Lincoln, who is supposed to have come from near Boston, Mass. In his deed of four and a half acres by David Hills, he is said to be of Wethersfield. He was a brick-mason by trade, but chiefly farmer; built the house on West Main street, now occupied and owned by Timothy Loomis, and Mr. Revoir in 1863. He after bought the place where Harlowe Eddy owns and occupies, near the school-house, District No. 4, and subsequently built opposite, the house owned and occupied by Oris Tolles. He went to Demerara, West Indies, for a patrimony, but never was heard from after. She died Jan. 24th, 1812, aged 59.

THEIR CHILDREN.

1. Theodore Riley, born April 7th, 1775, m. Jan. 18th, 1808, No. (427.)
2. Electa Riley, born Dec. 13th, 1776, m. Oct. 10th, 1797, No. (356.)

CHILDREN BY HER SECOND HUSBAND.

1. John Riley Lincoln, born , bap. Sept. 27th, 1795, m. June 21st, 1801, No. (319.)
2. Roxana Lincoln, born , bap. Sept. 27th, 1795, m. June 6th, 1809, Moses Peck.
3. Simeon Lincoln, jun., born April 2d, 1790, bap. Sept. 27th, 1795, m. Oct. 5th, 1817, Almira Hart, daughter of Capt. Samuel Hart, of Hart street, in Berlin, and his second wife, Lydia (Hinsdale;) she was the seventeenth child of her father, and younger sister of the celebrated Mrs. Emma Willard, of Troy. Mr. Lincoln, her first husband, was a printer by trade, and died Oct. 4th, 1823, when she married second, Phelps, and now, 1863, resides at the Eutaw place, near Baltimore, in Maryland.
4. Porter Lincoln, born , bap. Nov. 8th, 1801, died Oct. 4th, 1802.

274. "BENJAMIN WRIGHT," to church Oct. 4th, 1795, by letter from the church in Stepney, son of Deacon Benjamin and Hannah (Holmes,) his wife, born July 25th, 1737, at Stepney, m. No. (275;) they came to this place March, 1795; bought the farm of Lieut. Elisha Booth, (now, A. D. 1861,) owned and occupied by David Osborne, and by a mark on the barn, "T. L. 1761, B.," probably indicates the date and builder or carpenter. He had been a captain of militia in the war of the Revolution; also a deacon of the church in Stepney, (alias) Rocky Hill. He was

chosen to and accepted the deacon's office in this church, Feb. 1st, 1801; was a retiring, inoffensive man, and a plain farmer. He died Sept. 23d, 1813, aged 76.

275. "Wife of Benjamin Wright," to church by letter from the church in Stepney, Oct. 4th, 1795; her maiden name, Elizabeth Culver; was of Long Island, and driven off by the war of the Revolution, and took refuge in Stepney, where she became acquainted with and married Mr. Wright. She died Jan. 21st, 1814, aged 69.

THEIR CHILDREN.

1. Joseph, born Oct. 7th, 1779, m. Feb. 3d, 1814, No. (559.)
2. Huldah, born , married Isaac Jones, of Hartford.
3. Rhuhamah, born , died in infancy.
4. Rhuhamah, 2d, born , m. June 20th, 1804, Eleazer Wheeler, of Vermont.

276. "Mary, wife of John Lusk," to church Jan. 10th, 1796, daughter of Ebenezer Smith, sen. and Mary (Whittlesey,) of Newington, his wife; she married Aug., 1763. He had but one eye, the other lost in childhood, by sickness; they lived north of "Dublin Hill." He died June 8th, 1797, aged 67; she died Dec. 30th, 1819, aged 93. He "owned the covenant," Sept. 2d, 1764. No. (XXIII.)

THEIR CHILDREN.

1. Mary, born Feb. 22d, 1768, bap. Aug. 28th, 1768, married Samuel Stedman, see No. (333.)
2. Eliphalet, born , a brick-mason; learned of Asahel Hart; went west.
3. Rachel, born , married Bela Judd, son of John, jun.; she died A. D. 1848, in Albany, at the house of her son, Franklin.

277. "Lydia, wife of Amos Richards," to church Aug. 7th, 1796, daughter of No. (88) and No. (111,) born 1763, married March 23d, 1780; he son of No. (95) and Mary (French,) his wife, born April 7th, 1759, and died at Lyme, Jefferson county, New York, near Lake Ontario. She was probably admitted to church on a sick bed, at the house of Thomas Hooker, where now stands the house of Amzi Judd, for she died Aug. 11th, 1796, aged 33, of consumption, only four days after the baptism of two of her children, and her admission to church. She had taught school at Unionville, and was brought home sick. She had taught school in the summer of 1794, in the South-east District.

THEIR CHILDREN.

1. Adna, born , bap. Aug. 7th, 1796, m. Anna Douglas, of New York State.
2. Mary, born Sept. 29th, 1785, bap. May 1st, 1791, on account of Aaron Roberts, by whom she had been adopted; married June 2d, 1805, Salmon Eno, of Simsbury, son of Jonathan and Mary (Hart,) his wife, born Dec. 13th, 1779; lived in Simsbury, but built in New Britain, on Washington street; he died April 3d, 1842, aged 62.
3. John, born , bap. Aug. 7th, 1796; learned tin making, of Seth Lewis; he married Mary Britton, of New York State.

278. "MARTHA, wife of Ladwick Hotchkiss," to church Oct. 2d, 1796, daughter of No. (37) and No. (73,) born Nov. 25th, 1754, m. May 17th, 1773; he son of No. (67) and No. (68,) born May 25th, 1752; they lived in various localities; he was a soldier of the Revolution; she died Feb. 20th, 1813, aged 59. He was a large man, of quick and comprehensive mind; he died Dec. 1st, 1823, aged 72.

THEIR CHILDREN.

1. Ladwick, born Dec. 6th, 1773; learned the blacksmith trade of Jonathan Seymour, at Kensington, and went west with him, when he moved.
2. Seth, born June 3d, 1775, m. Temperance Kelly, of Yarmouth, Mass.
3. Orren, born Feb. 26th, 1778.
4. Jesse, born Dec. 4th, 1780.
5. Sally, born Aug. 26th, 1782, bap. June 4th, 1797, m. No. (522.)
6. Abi, born Aug. 15th, 1784, bap. June 4th, 1797, m. Dec. 1st, 1805, No. (425.)
7. Levi, born June 12th, 1786, m. Abigail Jones, of Newburyport, Mass.
8. Alvin, born May 1st, 1788, bap. June 4th, 1797, m. Jan. 31st, 1810, Sally Williams; second, married No. (1,094.)
9. Mabel, born Dec. 11th, 1791, bap. June 4th, 1797, m. June, 1813, Ira, son of Luke Bronson; called later in life, Mehitable; she died Jan. 13th, 1859, aged 68, at Kensington.
10. Daniel, born Aug. 22d, 1794, bap. June 4th, 1797, died 1821, at Kensington.

279. "ELEAZER MERRILL," to church Dec. 4th, 1796, from the church in Newington; he married May 15th, 1797, No. (280;) was dismissed and recommended back to Newington the next year, and yet had a taxable estate in the list of 1799, of $77, in New Britain parish.

280. "Wife of Eleazer Merrill," to church from Newington, Dec. 4th, 1796; her maiden name, Nancy Booth, daughter of Lieut. Elisha and Esther (Hollister,) his wife, born Aug. 18th, 1768, dismissed and recommended back to Newington, with her husband, by letter, June 2d, 1797.

281. "OZIAS HART," to church June 4th, 1797, son of No. (52) and Sarah (Gilbert,) his wife, born Aug. 8th, 1768, m. No. (282.) He was by occupation a farmer, yet built and run a saw-mill, on the North branch of the Mattabesset River, at the south end of the parish. His residence is now owned by Henry North. He had an active, but somewhat erratic mind; a man of stern virtue and integrity; he died February 6th, 1845, aged 77.

282. "Wife of Ozias Hart," to church June 4th, 1797; her maiden name, Sarah Lee, daughter of Deacon John Lee, of Worthington, and his wife, Sarah Cole, baptized Aug. 16th, 1761; she died Oct. 19th, 1829, at Holland Patent, New York State. She was grand-daughter of Deacon Jonathan Lee, the blacksmith of "Great Swamp" memory.

THEIR CHILDREN.

1. Ozias, jun., born Dec. 9th, 1793, bap. June 4th, 1797, m. Nov. 15th, 1816, No. (410.)

2. John Lee, born , died in infancy.
3. Emily, born , bap. April 1st, 1798, died April 3d, 1813, aged 15.
4. Otis, born Feb., 1800, bap. April 20th, 1800, died July 1st, 1819, aged 19, No. (408.)
5. Sarah Cole, born , bap. April 3d, 1803, died Jan. 12th, 1804, aged one year and ten months.
6. Sarah Cole, born March 27th, 1805, bap. June 16th, 1805; lives in New Britain, unmarried, 1867.
7. Eliza Ann, born 1808, bap. April 21st, 1808, died May 8th, 1808, aged 3 months.

283. "ELEAZER BROWN," to church June 2d, 1799, by letter from Newington church, married No. (284,) and these persons to Newington church, 1798, by letter from church in New London; he to church there, 1795; he probably (says Miss Caulkins,) came to New London from Stonington.

284. "ANNA, wife of Eleazer Brown," to church June 2d, 1799, from Newington, m. No. (283;) she to church in New London, 1794, and had their children baptized there in the Congregational church, see New London church record.

CHILDREN OF ELEAZER BROWN AND ANNA, HIS WIFE.

1. Esther, born , bap. July 22d, 1794, at New London, Congregational church.
2. Ebenezer, born , " " " "
3. Thomas, born , " " " "
4. Isaac, born , " " " "
5. Anna, born , " " " "
6. Sarah, born , " " " "

285. "Widow PHEBE BRONSON," to church Sept. 22d, 1799, daughter of Joseph Mather, senior, and his wife, Anna (Booth,) born Jan. 6th, 1748, m. Roger Bronson, of Kensington, and moved to New Durham, with Capt. Hotchkiss, where he was frozen to death, when she returned and married second, Nov. 28th, 1814, Josiah Andrus; he lived several years on Dr. Smalley's farm, on the South Mountain, afterwards on the Capt. Lemuel Hotchkiss farm, on the Horse Plain road. She in a fit fell into the fire, in an old-fashioned large fire-place, and burned to death, Feb. 21st, 1824, aged 76. He had a previous wife, Abigail (Flagg,) whom he married March 18th, 1784; he died Oct. 16th, 1824, aged 74. He was a light-horseman in the Revolution, and body-guard to Gen. Pulaski, and related in after life, many feats of valor. He was a thick-set robust man, but left no posterity. He was a brother of No. (245.) His first wife is No. (329.)

286. "STEPHEN GLADDEN," to church Feb. 2d, 1800, son of Azariah and Anna (Hudson,) his wife, m. July 4th, 1796, No. (287.) He was brother of No. (219.) He died in a fit of apoplexy, in the store of Elnathan Smith, Aug. 23d, 1803, aged 31.

287. "Wife of Stephen Gladden," to church Feb. 2d, 1800; her maiden

name, Azuba Warner, born Oct. 4th, 1778, to Demas and his wife, Rhoda (Gridley ;) she was baptized on admission to church.

THEIR CHILDREN.

1. Infant, born , died Oct. 23d, 1799, aged five months.
2. Azariah, born , bap. Feb. 16th, 1800, died June 7th, 1800.
3. Sophronia, born , bap. July 12th, 1801.
4. Lois Warner, born , bap. April 24th, 1803.

288. "Wife of Chauncey Merrill," to church Feb. 2d, 1800; maiden name, Polly Hart, born June 25th, 1770, to Stephen and his wife, No. (563,) m. Aug. 1st, 1793; he son of Abraham, of West Hartford; they lived north of "Dublin Hill," in a house vacated by David Lusk. She died March 12th, 1825, aged 55.

THEIR CHILDREN.

1. Rhoda Hart, born , bap. March 2d, 1800, married Jan. 22d, 1822, Jerry D. Goodrich.
2. Mary Hart, born Dec. 30th, 1802, bap. April 24th, 1803, m. Dec. 1st, 1819, John Bunce; married second, April 15th, 1827, Augustus Robinson, son of Amos.
3. Judith Brace, born , bap. June 16th, 1805, m. Sept. 21st, 1826, Austin Moshier.
4. William Walter, born , bap. June 26th, 1808, died, aged two years and six months.

289. "Wife of Levi Smith," to church Feb. 2d, 1800; maiden name, Mary Olmsted, daughter of James, of East Hartford, and his wife, Mary (Beaumont;) he was son of Samuel and his wife, No. (89,) baptized Nov. 14th, 1773; he lived in the house by the bridge, next south of Martin Brown, in Stanley quarter; they moved, Sept., 1804, to Sangersfield, where he was killed by the rolling of a log, Feb., 1806. She was recommended to the church there, and married second, 1808, Pliny Nims; she died Sept., 1813, aged 36.

THEIR CHILDREN.

1. Maria Mercia, born May 1st, 1798, bap. May 25th, 1800, m. Nov. 23d, 1815, Sylvester P. Herick.
2. Norman Olmsted, born March 15th, 1800, bap. May 25th, 1800, m. May 13th, 1832, Rebecca Mather.
3. Julietta, born Oct. 9th, 1802, bap. April 24th, 1803, m. 1826, Benjamin Anderson.
4. Mary Beaumont, born Feb. 9th, 1805, m. 1830, Henry D. Smead.

CHILDREN BY SECOND HUSBAND.

5. Abigail Nims, born Dec. 9th, 1809, to Pliny Nims and his wife, Mary O. (Smith;) she married, 1839, Phineas R. Hunt, and sailed for Madras, as a missionary, July 30th, 1839.

290. "Wife of Elihu Burritt," to church Feb. 16th, 1800; maiden name, Elizabeth Hinsdale, daughter of Elijah and Ruth (Bidwell,) his wife, daughter of James, of Hartford, born Feb. 6th, 1775, m. July 20th, 1793; he was son of Elihu, of Stratford, and Eunice (Wakeman,) his

wife, born Dec. 13th, 1765; was in the war of the Revolution; was a man of an active and speculative mind, scrupulously honest and moral; a shoemaker by trade; learned of No. (217 ;) had his residence at first on Main street, where now, 1863, is the house of Mrs. O. C. Stanley; the building is still standing, at the foot of "Dublin Hill;" he lived in various other localities; raised a large family on small means. Her father owned the lot west of the "Burying Ground;" had on it a mulberry orchard, and a "Silk-house," where the worms were fed and grown, and where the silk was reeled and manufactured to such an extent that he obtained a yearly bounty from the State for many years. This "Silk-house" was occupied by Mr. Burritt and his family until its destruction by fire, when another house was built on the north-west corner of the lot, where he died, Jan. 29th, 1827, aged 63. She was equally well versed in the Bible as in the silk business; was a woman of strong faith and prayer, and died Aug. 27th, 1843, aged 68, at the house of Stephen L. Strickland, her son-in-law.

THEIR CHILDREN.

1. Elijah Hinsdale, born April 20th, 1794, bap. Nov. 2d, 1800, m. Oct. 28th, 1819, No. (755.)
2. Betsey Hinsdale, born July 22d, 1796, bap. Nov. 2d, 1800, m. Aug. 24th, 1829, Hezekiah Seymour, of Hartford.
3. Emily, born Aug. 12th, 1798, bap. Nov. 2d, 1800, m. 1838, Capt. Taylor, of Texas, see No. (418.)
4. George, born Dec. 5th, 1800, bap. Nov. 29th, 1801, died Aug. 22d, 1822, in Georgia, aged 22.
5. Mary, born Feb. 18th, 1803, bap. May 20th, 1804, m. May 26th, 1825, William Williams, of Kensington.
6. William, born July 8th, 1805, bap. Dec. 1st, 1805, m. May 5th, 1826, Clarissa Cole, of Kensington.
7. Isaac, born May 31st, 1808, bap. Oct. 23d, 1808, m. Oct. 16th, 1832, Nancy Barnes, see No. (598.)
8. Elihu, born Dec. 8th, 1810, bap. Dec. 1st, 1811, see No. (584.)
9. Eunice Wakeman, born May 2d, 1813, bap. Nov. 30th, 1817, see No. (599.)
10. Almira Bidwell, born July 27th, 1816, bap. Nov. 30th, 1817, see No. (855.)

291. "POLLY CRANDALL," to church Feb. 16th, 1800, daughter of Crandall, of Norwich, and Molly (Bill,) who was half-sister of Abigail Flagg, who married Josiah Andrus. She, Polly, taught school several seasons, in the South-west district of New Britain, A. D. 1795, and later. She married Michael Gillet, of New Hartford, and they moved to Prattsburgh, New York, where they died childless.

292. "MARY HART," to church March 30th, 1800, daughter of No. (118) and No. (119,) born Aug. 5th, 1769, married Dec. 24th, 1806, Eliphalet Wadsworth, of Farmington; he died Jan. 21st, 1823, aged 75, when she married second, May 20th, 1829, No. (198 ;) she removed her connection from this to Farmington church, April 5th, 1807, but was recommended back by letter Oct. 4th, 1829; she was a very discreet,

patient and good woman; was removed again to Farmington church, by letter Aug., 1834; she died Nov. 11th, 1847, aged 78; grave in Farmington, old cemetery, on the hill.

293. "JAMES HART," to church March 30th, 1800, son of No. (118) and (119,) born May 22d, 1773, married June, 1793, No. (294;) he built opposite his father, in Hart quarter; a farmer by occupation; his house disappeared, and his family was scattered; he died March 29th, 1813, aged 40; had fallen under censure of the church, for intemperate habits.

294. "Wife of James Hart," to church March 30th, 1800; her maiden name was Sylvia, daughter of No. (116) and No. (117,) married June, 1793, No. (293;) he died March 29th, 1813, when she married second, Jan. 7th, 1818, John Wyard, of Wolcott, and she was recommended by letter to that church.

THE HART FAMILY CHILDREN.

1. Lydia, born May 13th, 1796, bap. May 25th, 1800, m. Nov. 25th, 1818, John C. Root, of Farmington.

2. Ethan, born Sept., 1799, bap. May 25th, 1800, m. Nov. 3d, 1819, Martha Wyard.

3. Clarissa, born Feb. 22d, 1803, bap. June 12th, 1803, m. June, 1822, Enos Beckwith.

4. Harriet, born Oct. 6th, 1806, bap. May 31st, 1807, m. April, 1821, William McCreary.

5. Mary, born Jan., 1810, bap. Oct. 7th, 1810, m. June, 1831, George McLaughlin.

6. James, born March, 1812, bap. June 27th, 1813, as son of Widow Sylvia Hart, died Nov., 1819, aged 7.

295. "Wife of William Smith," to church March 30th, 1800, daughter of No. (88) and No. (111,) married Nov. 6th, 1796, No. (337;) she died Feb. 4th, 1810, aged 34, of consumption; a disease common and fatal to the Lewis family, with some few exceptions; she was attractive in person and deportment.

296. "ROBERT CORNWALL," to church April 20th, 1800, son of Capt. Timothy, of Middletown, and his wife, Mary (Warner,) born Aug. 30th, 1757, married March 3d, 1785, No. (297;) he was brother of No. (215;) was a cooper by trade; his house, that (now, A. D. 1862,) owned and occupied by Charles L. Baldwin, in Hart quarter, where he had his shop, opposite his house, and where he kept a tavern several years, after the Middletown and Berlin turnpike was constructed, in A. D. 1810. He was a plain, honest man, of common size; maintained a consistent, Christian life, and died Oct. 5th, 1819, aged 62; latter part of life, somewhat deaf.

297. "Wife of Robert Cornwall," to church April 20th, 1800, daughter of No. (52) and Sarah (Gilbert,) his wife, born Feb. 21st, 1765, married March 3d, 1785, No. (296;) was a discreet, worthy woman, and died Sept. 15th, 1846, aged 81.

THEIR CHILDREN.

1. Sally Gilbert, born June 2d, 1786, bap. May 25th, 1800, m. Oct. 1st, 1812, Erastus Storrs, a jeweller.

2. Robert, born Oct. 7th, 1788, died Aug. 30th, 1798, aged 10.

3. George, born Nov. 7th, 1791, bap. May 25th, 1800, m. Aug. 24th, 1815, Hannah Hooker, of William.

4. Chauncey, born Sept. 22d, 1795, bap. May 25th, 1800, m. July 15th, 1819, No. (404.)

5. Mary, born July 12th, 1798, bap. May 25th, 1800, m. April 4th, 1816, Moses W. Beckley.

6. Robert, born Aug. 16th, 1801, bap. Oct. 18th, 1801, see No. (798.)

7. Julia Ann, born Feb. 16th, 1804, m. Oct. 3d, 1821, Harvey Dunham, jun., of Southington.

298. "BETSEY, widow of Dr. Isaac Andrews," to church April 20th, 1800; maiden name, Talbot; she had a sister, Hope; was the wife of No. (196,) but after his death married second, on the 26th of April, 1806, Elijah Loveland, of Berlin, a tavern-keeper; probably dismissed and recommended to Berlin church, 1806, but no record of either church shows the date; her maiden name is on Berlin church catalogue, incorrectly called Percival.

299. "LEVI WELLS," to church Aug. 3d, 1800, by letter from the church in Newington, son of Elisha and Lydia (Deming,) his wife, born 1764, at Hartford Rocky Hill, married Dec. 9th, 1790, No. (300;) they both to Newington church, Dec. 9th, 1797. He bought out the farm of Timothy Kilbourn, and moved to New Britain, in the spring of 1800; the house stood opposite the present residence of his son, Horace; he was an industrious farmer; his wife, Hannah, died March 1st, 1809, aged 39, when he married second, Nov. 21st, 1813, No. (334;) he died Oct. 23d, 1823, in his 59th year, of spotted fever, a disease that year fatal to many of our people.

300. "Wife of Levi Wells," to church Aug. 3d, 1800; her maiden name, Hannah Wells, daughter of Capt. Robert, jun. of Newington, and his wife, Abigail (Hurlburt;) she died March 1st, 1809, aged 39; born 1770, at Newington.

THEIR CHILDREN.

1. Lydia, born Oct. 24th, 1792, bap. June 12th, 1797, at Newington, see No. (368.)

2. Levi, born Sept. 7th, 1793, bap. June 12th, 1797, married Ann Ames; lived in Illinois; died there.

3. Horace, born Aug. 11th, 1795, bap. June 12th, 1797, see No. (511.)

4. Hannah, born Aug. 1797, bap. May 27th, 1798, m. Sept. 19th, 1821, No. (481,) in Newington.

5. Elva, born Sept. 11th, 1800, bap. Nov. 9th, 1800, m. May 12th, 1824, No. (481.)

6. Lemuel Watts, born July 4th, 1803, bap. Sept. 25th, 1803, see No. (512.)

7. Marilla, born Sept. 26th, 1805, bap. Aug. 17th, 1806, see No. (491.)

301. "Widow EUNICE BURRITT," to church Oct. 5th, 1800; she was the mother of Elihu, the widow of Elihu, sen.; her maiden name, Wake-

man, daughter of Stephen and Sarah, of Green's Farms, and a descendant of Ezborn; she was the mother of No. (202) and No. (207;) she died Jan. 29th, 1802, aged 62, at the house of Joseph Mather.

302. "MABEL, wife of Daniel Luddington," to church Nov. 16th, 1800, daughter of No. (37) and No. (73,) born Feb. 19th, 1750, m. April 22d, 1773; he son of Daniel, of East Haven, and Susan (Clark,) his second wife, born May 9th, 1744, at East Haven. They lived on the hill, opposite "Judd's mill;" house built by Elijah Bronson; he was a joiner by trade; they had no children; he had a brother, No. (161;) he died May 8th, 1820, aged 78; she died Oct. 10th, 1822, aged 74.

303. "ABIJAH CARRINGTON," to church April 11th, 1802, son of Dr. Elias, of Woodbridge, and Esther (Northrop,) of Milford, his wife, born Nov. 22d, 1778; graduated at Yale, 1800; studied theology with Dr. Smalley; was licensed and began to preach, but speaking publicly affected his lungs unfavorably, and he went into trade; had a store in Milford; was State Senator; was Comptroller, Judge of Probate, &c.; married Amanda (Tyler,) of Wallingford; second, Ann (Austin;) third, Sarah Gunn, both of Milford; he died March 15th, 1851; on his monument of granite is this: "Honored and esteemed by his fellow-citizens, he filled with ability and integrity many important offices; fondly attached to his family, he was an affectionate husband and father; he was an able counsellor, and a faithful Christian." He had two children by his first wife, and two by his second wife; his third is, 1860, still living.

304. "PITKIN COWLES," to church April 11th, 1802, born April 7th, 1777, to Ashbel, of Southington, and his wife, Rhoda (Lee;) graduated at Yale, 1800; gave an oration at Southington, 1800, on Washington's death; studied divinity with Dr. Smalley, 1802; settled over the Congregational church in North Canaan, Aug. 29th, 1805; he continued in the pastoral office until January, 1833; he died in Southington, in the same room where born, while on a visit, Feb. 8th, 1833; buried in Canaan. He married May 25th, 1808, Fanny Smith, born June 2d, 1784, to Ebenezer Smith, an officer of the Revolutionary war, and resident of New Marlboro, Mass.; she was sister of Rev. Dr. David, of Durham, Conn.

THEIR CHILDREN.

1. Frances A., born April 19th, 1809, m. Dr. Albert A. Wright, of Goshen, May 17th, 1831.
2. Sarah Lee, born Nov. 18th, 1811, m. Jan. 12th, 1853, Gen. Thomas Harvey, of New York; he died in 1854.
3. Catharine R., born Oct. 25th, 1813.
4. Edward P., born Jan. 19th, 1815, married Nov. 25th, 1851, Sarah E. Boies, of Northampton, Mass.; he a judge and lawyer.
5. David S., born Feb. 25th, 1817; a lawyer, settled in Hudson, New York.
6. Walter S., born Feb. 25th, 1819; a lawyer, married Mary Thompson, and settled in Syracuse, New York.

7. Almira Canning, born Aug. 26th, 1826, married Rev. Elisha Whittlesey; settled in Leroy, New York.

305. "THOMAS RICH," to church April 19th, 1802, son of Capt. Cyrus, and Abigail (Field,) his wife, born Feb. 9th, 1775, in Weston, now Warren, Mass.; graduated at Dartmouth, 1799; studied theology with Dr. Smalley; ordained in Westbrook, Conn., June 13th, 1804; was a delegate to General Association of Connecticut, June, 1808; dismissed Sept. 5th, 1810; installed at Columbia, Conn., March 6th, 1811; dismissed June 13th, 1817; preached at Sharon, and Salisbury, Mass. His wife, Mary (Field.) He died at Amesbury, Mass., Sept., 1836, aged 61; a heavy built man, with powerful voice; a good preacher, and greatly respected. While here he taught a school in the North-east District, to great acceptance.

THEIR CHILDREN WERE

1. Abby. 2. Charles. 3. Thomas. 4. Mary Field, baptized, Sept., 1811. 5. Robert, baptized, May, 1814. 6. George Cutler, baptized, 1817.

306. "ALLEN STEELE," to church Aug. 1st, 1802, son of Josiah, sen. and his wife, No. (377,) born Nov. 23d, 1779, married July 29th, 1799, No. (307;) they lived in a small house next north of Deacon Francis; his wife died Nov. 24th, 1820, aged 48, when he married second, Feb. 5th, 1821, Ruth Hinsdale, daughter of Elijah and Sarah (Daniels,) his second wife, who was a worthy member of the Baptist church, and died April 30th, 1858, aged73; he died May 9th, 1828, aged 49; a man of kind disposition, correct habits, of slender constitution; he was a farmer by occupation.

HIS CHILDREN.

1. Naboth Lewis, born Oct. 17th, 1800, bap. May 22d, 1803, married Aug. 18th, 1819, Sarah Hunter.

2. Ebenezer Hart, born Nov. 17th, 1802, bap. May 22d, 1803, married Marilla Richards, of Oliver.

3. Lyman Jerome, born Aug. 16th, 1805, bap. Nov. 3d, 1805, married Jan. 8th, 1828, Mary Wescott.

4. Allen, born May 24th, 1808, married first, Sabra Dorman; second, Clarissa Wright; he a Methodist preacher.

5. } twins. { Emily, born May 12th, 1811, married Miles Peck; second, Abner Ray; she died Feb. 6th, 1867, aged 55.
6. } { Emeline, born May 12th, 1811, married Moses Wilson; she a distinguished scholar and teacher.

307. "Wife of Allen Steele," to church Aug. 1st, 1802; maiden name, Lucy Jerome, daughter of Andrew, of Bristol, and Chloe (Sage,) his wife, born Feb. 6th, 1773; she learned to weave of Timothy Hart's family, at the Jesse Stanley house; she was brought up at Rev. Samuel Newel's, in Bristol; married Oct. 2d, 1791, Ebenezer Hart, son of Stephen; he died on his passage from the West Indies, of yellow fever, May 30th, 1798,

when she married second, No. (306;) she died Nov. 24th, 1820, aged 48. In 1808, she joined the Baptist church, and in the year 1820, united with the Methodist church.

THE HART FAMILY.

1. Emily, born April 27th, 1792, died April 20th, 1796, aged 4.

2. Albert, born Nov. 18th, 1793, died Feb. 29th, 1795, aged fifteen months.

3. Dorothy, born Sept. 16th, 1795, bap. May 22d, 1803, married Feb. 3d, 1814, Col. Joseph Wright.

4. Ebenezer, born May 21st, 1798, killed by the kick of a horse, Feb. 3d, 1802, aged four years.

308. "MOSES THOMPSON," to church Aug. 1st, 1802; said to have come from Vermont; was a day-laborer; lived in various localities; made himself useful; was inoffensive and kind; he married No. (309;) he died Jan. 2d, 1826, aged 63; he fell under church censure Jan. 26th, 1824.

309. "Wife of Moses Thompson," to church Aug. 1st, 1802; Susan Steele, daughter of Josiah, senior, and No. (377,) married No. (308;) and married second, Oct. 16th, 1828, George Daniels, the blacksmith. She fell under church censure, A. D. 1832.

THEIR CHILDREN.

1. Emeline, born Dec. 12th, 1803, bap. April 15th, 1804, married Aug. 22d, 1824, Leander S. Hart; she died at Hubbardston, Vermont, Nov. 1st, 1840.

2. Milo, born 1807, bap. April 3d, 1808, married July 22d, 1829, Amelia Squire, of Solomon.

3. James Harvey, born 1810, bap. April 29th, 1810, died Feb. 27th, 1811, aged 1 yr.

4. Porter S., born Oct. 7th, 1822, married June 10th, 1851, Rosey McCartney.

310. "The Widow DORCAS DUNHAM," to church Aug. 22d, 1802; her maiden name, Dorcas Woodruff, daughter of Capt. Joseph, of the "Great Swamp" parish, and his wife, Margaret (North,) of Northington, now Avon, born April 8th, 1739, married Cornelius Dunham, senior. He had an estate "taxable," A. D. 1775, of £39; he enlisted in the army of the Revolution, Feb. 6th, 1778, during the war, and had £10 bounty. She died of a cancer, at the house of Moses Andrews, April 9th, 1803, aged 64.

SOME OF THEIR CHILDREN.

1. Cornelius, jun., born April 25th, 1756; he enlisted into the same company with his father, but two years previous, viz. Feb. 24th, 1777; had £10 bounty.

2. Jemima, born March 5th, 1760, married Joseph Bronson, see No. (218.)

3. Samuel, born July 26th, 1763.

4. Dorcas, born , died Jan. 27th, 1777.

311. "SAMUEL HART," to church Oct., 1802, son of No. (181) and No. (182,) born April 7th, 1786, married March 18th, 1812, No. (366;) was the principal physician for many years in this place; an active and laborious man; built his house on the west side of Central Park; successful in farming, as well as physic; of slender form and constitution, for

many of his last years unable to walk, from rheumatic affection and paralysis; to South church, 1842; he died June 20th, 1863, aged 77; his voice was seldom if ever heard in public, yet his influence in town and society matters was very controlling; he was for more than sixty years a member of the church.

THEIR CHILDREN.

1. Anna, born Sept. 9th, 1813, bap. Oct. 31st, 1813, died July 23d, 1819, aged 6 y'rs.
2. Samuel B., born Sept. 23d, 1818, died, aged seventeen days.
3. Lucinda, born Aug. 30th, 1820, bap. Nov. 5th, 1820, married 1842, No. (652.)
4. Samuel Waldo, born May 22d, 1825, bap. Aug. 7th, 1825, see No. (815.)
5. Louisa, born Oct. 5th, 1828, bap. Nov. 23d, 1828, see No. (896.)

312. "The Widow ANNA ANDREWS," to church Dec. 5th, 1802, the widow of No. (112,) daughter of Thomas Stedman, of Wethersfield, and Mary (Sage,) his wife, born June 20th, 1736, on "Stedman Hill," in Wethersfield; of fine form and features; of a proud and indomitable spirit and will, but was subdued by the grace of God, late in life; she died Sept. 17th, 1809, aged 73.

313. "EZEKIEL ANDREWS," to church Sept. 11th, 1803, son of No. (112) and No. (312,) born May 25th, 1775; inherited his father's homestead and mill; a man of full common size, of nearly perfect form and features, possessing his mother's spirit, yet of some noble impulses; was patriotic and public spirited; was in the war of 1812, as a captain; drew part of his land bounty during his own life, and his widow the balance. He was a successful farmer; had much military taste and spirit, but his early training and education deficient. He married Dec. 11th, 1796, No. (314;) she died Jan. 4th, 1832, aged 54, when he married second, Oct. 20th, 1833, No. (762;) he died Sept. 3d, 1852, aged 77, leaving an estate of some $16,000.

314. "Wife of Ezekiel Andrews," to church Sept. 11th, 1803; maiden name, Roxana Hinsdale, daughter of Elijah and Ruth (Bidwell,) daughter of James, of Hartford, his first wife, born June 10th, 1778, bap. Sept. 11th, 1803, on admission to church; a woman of prayer and piety; she died Jan. 4th, 1832, aged 54; left some interesting written reminiscences of religious experiences.

THEIR CHILDREN.

1. Alfred, born Oct. 16th, 1797, bap. Oct. 30th, 1803, married Dec. 16th, 1818, No. (479;) married second, No. (657.)
2. Thesta, born Dec. 16th, 1798, bap. Oct. 30th, 1803, married Nov. 27th, 1823, Bryan Porter, of Samuel.
3. Allura, born April 16th, 1801, bap. Oct. 30th, 1803, died single, hopefully pious, May 30th, 1831, aged 30.
4. Infant, born March 8th, 1803, died March 10th, 1803.
5. Edwin Norton, born June 27th, 1804, died single of fever, Aug. 25th, 1825, aged 21.

6. Mary Bidwell, born April 13th, 1807, bap. June 7th, 1807, married April 21st, 1830, Samuel E. Curtiss.
7. Ezekiel, born July 19th, 1809, bap. Oct. 22d, 1809, married Aug. 7th, 1833, No. (690.)
8. Nathan Hosmer, born June 23d, 1812, bap. Aug. 30th, 1812, died single, in Texas, Oct. 27th, 1837.
9. Roxana, born April 6th, 1815, bap. Sept. 3d, 1815, see No. (672.)
10. Jane Louisa, born Feb. 2d, 1818, bap. April 26th, 1818, No. (784.)
11. Elijah Hinsdale, born Aug. 11th, 1820, bap. Oct. 8th, 1820, died Oct. 30th, 1821, of croup.
12. Ellen Maria, born Sept. 18th, 1824, bap. March 20th, 1825, No. (976.)

315. "Rebecca Smalley," to church Nov. 27th, 1803, daughter of No. (1) and No. (96,) born Dec. 3d, 1778, married Oct. 15th, 1804, No. (321;) she was deranged for some years late in life, but in passing a bridge on the Western Canal, was hit on the head and restored to reason. She was a woman of fine social qualities, and very industrious; she died Jan. 8th, 1838, aged 59.

316. "Sabrina Steele," to church Jan. 6th, 1805, daughter of Josiah and his wife, No. (377;) the family write the name Sabra; she married April 12th, 1805, Uriah Carrington, son of Jesse and (Hungerford,) his wife; a Methodist preacher and went west.

317. "Nancy Hart," to church Jan. 6th, 1805, daughter of No. (183) and No. (243,) born Jan. 2d, 1790, married April 26th, 1809, No. (450;) he died March 4th, 1838, and she was dismissed to the church in West Meriden, 1840, where she now, A. D. 1867, lives.

318. "Esther, wife of James Judd," to church Feb. 3d, 1805, married 1779, No. (195;) she sister of No. (159) and No. (708,) daughter of Ephraim Allen and his wife, Hannah Williams, of Wallingford and Plymouth; she died Sept. 28th, 1847, aged 87.

319. "Elizabeth Lincoln," to church April 7th, 1805, the widow of John Riley Lincoln, son of Simeon, and Huldah (Porter Riley,) his wife, see No. (273;) he died Feb. 15th, 1803, aged 22, when she married sec ond, Nov. 25th, 1807, No. (442;) her maiden name, Booth, daughter of Joseph and his wife, No. (155,) born Aug. 29th, 1783; a woman faithful in all her relations and duties in life.

CHILD OF JOHN RILEY LINCOLN AND NO. (319.)

Eliza Riley, born Oct. 19th, 1801, bap. May 26th, 1805, see No. (529.)

320. "Salome Pennfield," to church Oct. 6th, 1805, daughter of No. (175) and No. (190,) born Sept. 2d, 1788, married May 13th, 1807, No. (462;) he died June 14th, 1836, aged 50; she was dismissed and recommended to the Congregational church in West Meriden, 1841, where A. D. 1867, she still lives with her daughter, Fowler; a modest, retiring woman, but of sterling worth.

321. "DAVID WHITTLESEY," to church Oct. 13th, 1805, son of Eliphalet, of Stockbridge, Mass. and Comfort (Waller,) his wife, born Feb. 14th, 1775; a farmer and school-teacher; married Oct. 15th, 1804, No. (315;) he occupied the home of Dr. Smalley, as he had no sons, and was chosen deacon, 1807; led the church singing many years; was the first Sunday school superintendent in the place or county, organized May, 1816; represented the town; was magistrate, school visitor, &c.; he was a man of stern integrity, and a reformer; headed the list of temperance and anti-slavery societies in the place; intelligent and public-spirited; was a successful farmer; raised and educated a large and respectable family; he died July 21st, 1851, aged 76, of cancer.

THEIR CHILDREN.

1. William born Sept. 19th, 1805, bap. Oct. 20th, 1805, see No. (541.)
2. Nancy Smalley, born Feb. 19th, 1807, bap. May 24th, 1807, married No. (680.)
3. Sarah Guernsey, born Sept. 15th, 1808, bap. Oct. 22d, 1808, see No. (534.)
4. Mary, born Sept. 2d, 1809, bap. Dec. 3d, 1809, married No. (679.)
5. John Smalley, born Jan. 8th, 1811, bap. Aug. 4th, 1811, died Oct. 4th, 1811, aged nine months.
6. John Smalley, born Oct. 2d, 1812, bap. Nov. 8th, 1812, married No. (611.)
7. Rebecca Smalley, born June 26th, 1814, bap. July 24th, 1814, married Deacon Daniel Fairchild, of Stockbridge, Mass.
8. David Waller, born March 31st, 1816, bap. Nov. 17th, 1816, see No. (767.)
9. Calista Curtiss, born Nov. 7th, 1818, bap. Jan. 17th, 1819, married Oct. 10th, 1843, Amos M. Ebersol.
10. Eliphalet, born May 14th, 1821, bap. June 17th, 1821, married Oct. 31st, 1854, Ann A. Patten.
11. Elizabeth Pamela, born Nov. 1st, 1822, bap. April 27th, 1823, married Oct. 27th, 1847, Rev. Charles W. Camp.

322. "STEPHEN WEBSTER," to church July 5th, 1807, by letter from the church in West Hartford, son of Isaac and Amy (White,) his wife, married May 9th, 1765, Anne McCloud, of Wethersfield, who died March 10th, 1805, when he married second, June 1st, 1806, Hannah, the widow of Seth Kilborn, and lived on her farm, where now, 1867, Levi S. Wells, owns and occupies; her maiden name, Churchill; he was a farmer, and the family moved west.

HIS CHILDREN BY HIS WIFE, ANNE.

1. Norman, born,
2. Polly, born , married Cook, of Plymouth.
3. Theodore, born April 15th, 1769, married Feb. 12th, 1795, Chestina, daughter of Stephen Hart; he died Aug. 2d, 1851, aged 83; she died April 26th, 1828, aged 55; he born in West Hartford, and died there.
4. Stephen, born , bap. Sept. 9th, 1770, in West Hartford, married Prudence Butler, of Gershom.
5. William, born , married Nabby Johnson, of East Berlin.
6. Allen, born , married Polly Hurlburt, of Newington.
7. Anne, born , married Shapley.
8. McCloud, born , married Lucina Townsend, of Bolton.

323. "Widow Eunice Bartholomew," to church Dec. 6th, 1807; maiden name, Orvice; was the widow of Abraham Bartholomew, of Bristol. His estate was settled 1777; it amounted to £202 8s. 11d. She was the mother of No. (436,) and spent the last of life with her on East street, at the old home of that family of Judds. She died May 13th, 1825, aged 85.

324. "Widow Roxy Belden," to church April 3d, 1808; daughter of No. (131) and No. (132,) born June 21st, 1780, married Nov. 9th, 1797, Leonard Belden, jun., son of Leonard and Hannah (Judd) his wife, born July 13th, 1778; lived on the home of his father and grandfather Ezra, on East street, near the former school house. He was a farmer, and died March 8, 1807, aged 29. She took a letter to the church at East Windham, N. Y., living, A. D. 1861, at Big Hollow, Green county, N. Y., but died Feb. 12th, 1864, in her 84th year, at Big Hollow, N. Y.

THEIR CHILDREN.

1. Emily Hart, born Sept. 12th, 1798, bap. June 26th, 1808, married May 16th, 1820, Lee M. Watrous.
2. Hannah Judd, born July 23d, 1800, bap. June 26th, 1808, see No. (499.)
3. Rhoda Roxalina, born Aug. 24th, 1802, bap. June 26th, 1808, see No (556.)
4. George Dunham, born Feb. 7th, 1805, bap. June 26th, 1808, married July 17th, 1826, Elizabeth Sanger.
5. Leonard Dix, born Jan. 29th, 1807, bap. June 26th, 1808, married Nov. 6th, 1836, Mary C. Smith, of Southington; he married 2d, Aug. 11th, 1844, Emily Avery, daughter of Asa, and lives on the old home of his great grandfather on East street.

325. "Rhoda Hart," to church April 3d, 1808, daughter of No. (131) and No. (132,) born Feb. 8th, 1788, married March 28th, 1839, Asa Tuller, of Simsbury, lived there until her husband died, Nov. 7th, 1853; she attended the Methodist church in Simsbury, and does so here since her return; has never been dismissed from this church; had no children; lived, A. D. 1861, on Arch street; taught school in early life.

326. "Anna, wife of Abijah Hart," from New York city, June 5th, 1808, to church; maiden name, Hall, daughter of Capt Giles, of Middletown, and his wife, Anna (Lord,) born Aug. 24th, 1765, married Sept. 22d, 1794, No. (211.) She was a noble looking woman, of elegant manners, kind disposition, and a warm Christian heart; died Jan. 15th, 1824, aged 58.

327. "Daniel Taylor," to church Sept. 1st, 1808, by letter from church at Thompson; son of Othniel, born March 24th, 1778, at Worcester, Mass., married Dec. 28th, 1802, No. (328;) he, by occupation a miller, came here to run Deacon Hart's mill, lived on the east side of the mill pond; was a man of great kindness and charity, and distinguished for piety; left this town 1815, with a letter to the church at Canton, Ct. He died there Sept. 14th, 1845, aged 67.

328. "Wife of DANIEL TAYLOR," to church, Sept. 1st, 1808 by letter from Thompson, Ct.; maiden name, Phebe Upham, daughter of Luke, of Thompson; she was born Feb. 24th, 1778, married No. (327,) and with him dismissed and recommended to church in Canton, where they were received, May 7th, 1815. She died March 24th, 1842, aged 66.

THEIR CHILDREN.

1. Sabin, born Oct. 21st, 1803, at Thompson, married April 12th, 1827, Diodama C. Stockwell.

2. Eliza, born Nov. 27th, 1805, at Thompson, married Jan., 1827, Ebenezer Hamblin.

3. Mary Gaines, born Jan. 26th, 1808, at Palmer, Mass., bap. at New Britain Aug. 21st, 1808, and died Sept. 22d, 1809.

4. Maria, born Sept. 11th, 1810, died Jan. 22d, 1811.

5. Nancy, born Aug. 9th, 1812, bap. Nov. 8th, 1812.

6. Mary Ann, born Sept. 17th, 1815, at Canton, Ct., married Jan., 1834, Green Taylor.

7. Lucinda, born June 5th, 1818, at Canton, married Aug. 23d, 1842, Rev. Luther Barber.

8. Emeline, born July 26th, 1822, at Canton, bap. Feb. 10th, 1823, died Feb. 12th, 1823.

329. "ABIGAIL, wife of JOSIAH ANDREWS," to church July 9th, 1809, daughter of Abijah Flagg, sen., of Berlin, and No. (263,) his wife; married March 18th, 1784, Josiah Andrews, brother of No. (245;) was his first wife, a tall woman of kind disposition. She adopted a daughter named Abigail Bills, (daughter of her sister Sarah,) after her marriage to Josiah Andrews, who died April 21st, 1805, aged 22, of consumption. Abigail, the wife of Josiah Andrews, died April 2d, 1814, aged 57. For further history, see No. (285.)

330. "ALVIN NORTH," to church Oct. 1st, 1809, son of No. (149) and his wife, No. 150;) born Sept. 4th, 1781, learned trade of cabinet maker, in Hartford, of John I. Wells, located on the corner of East Main and Stanley Streets, house built by Anthony Judd, but in 1830 gave place to a new one. He married July 15th, 1804, No. (331.) She died, when, 2d, he married, May 1, 1816, No. (411.) He was an extensive manufacturer of various kinds of hardware, and was so active in old age as to make, after he was 79 years old, a well made and handsomely finished bureau for his wife, and one for each of his children. Honest in his dealings, successful in his business, and liberal in his public benefactions. He, with his 2d wife, to South church, 1842. He died Sept. 1st, 1865, aged 84.

THEIR CHILDREN.

1. Orrin Stanley, born July 13th, 1805, bap. Oct. 8th, 1809, married Feb. 3d, 1831, No. (712.)

2. Harriet A., born March 5th, 1807, died March 4, 1809, aged 2; scalded.

3. Henrietta, born August 16th, 1809, bap. Oct. 8th, 1809, died Oct. 5th, 1810, aged 1.

SECOND WIFE'S CHILDREN.

4. Oliver Burnham, born March 13th, 1817, bap. June 29th, 1817, married, 1843, Martha E. Post, of Glastenbury.

5. Harriet A., born Sept. 28th, 1818, bap. Nov. 22d, 1818, see No. (769.)

6. Sarah Rogers, born Aug. 28th, 1820, bap. Nov. 5th, 1820, see No. (830.)

7. Hubert Franklin, born Nov. 13th, 1822, bap. April 27th, 1823, see No. (831.)

8. Mary Cordelia, born July 1st, 1825, bap. Oct. 16th, 1825, see No. (934.)

9. Henrietta Clarissa, born Sept. 16th, 1829, married July 18th, 1855, Josiah Shepherd, N. O., but 1867, of New Britain.

331. "ANNA, wife of Alvin North," to church, Oct. 1st, 1809; born January 15th, 1783, to No. (115) and his wife, No. (125,) married July 15th, 1804, No. (330.) She died June 26th, 1815, aged 32.

332. "EUNICE, wife of Asahel Pennfield," to church Oct. 1st, 1809, daughter of No. (217) and his wife, No. (207;) born at Stratford, married He was son of Jesse, of Plymouth, Ct., and his wife, Mary (Upson.) They lived where Albert Williams now (A. D. 1861) does, near the school house in the Southwest district. They moved to N. Y., about 1810.

THEIR CHILDREN BORN AT NEW BRITAIN.

1. Edward, born , bap. Oct. 22d, 1809.
2. Almira, born , bap. Oct. 22d, 1809.
3. Horatio, born , bap. Oct. 22d, 1809.
4. Asahel, born , bap. Oct. 22d, 1809.
5. Eliza, born , bap. Oct. 22d, 1809.

333. "MARY, wife of Samuel Stedman," to church Oct. 1st, 1809, daughter of John Lusk and his wife, No. (276;) born Feb. 22d 1768, married 1790, lived at the Slater house, near "Dead Swamp," and in West Hartford, then in Southwest district, where now, 1861, Gideon Deming does. He was son of Charles, and his wife Jemima (Gaines,) of Wethersfield, born 1760, died Aug. 31st, 1825, aged 66, of a bad foot. She was dismissed and recommended by letter to church in Southington, August, 1834, and from that to Farmington church, 1848, where she became partially paralyzed, and died there Jan. 30th 1861, aged 93. She knit for years when she could not walk, and thus saved some funds to pay her funeral charges and for a headstone at her grave in Farmington, and yet she had been helped by the kindness of friends and the church there. She was a woman of courage and fortitude, struggled bravely with poverty and calamity, and we trust won a crown at last by the grace of God.

THEIR CHILDREN.

1. Laura, born July 12th, 1791, not married, had a daughter who married Charles Bradley, and married, second, Charles Cowles.

2. Fanny, born Jan. 31st, 1793, married Nov. 29th, 1820, Willys Bradley, son of Ichabod, of Southington.

3. Jennette, born May 1st, 1795, bap. Oct. 19th, 1809, to church at Farmington April 5th, 1858, not married.

4. Eliphalet, born Nov. 15th, 1797, bap. Oct. 19th, 1809, died young.

5. Rhoda, born Nov. 13th, 1798, bap. Oct. 19th, 1809, very squint eyed, died April 26th, 1828, aged 30.

6. Henry, born Nov. 20th, 1799, bap. Oct. 19th, 1809, married Emeline Clark, of Meriden.

7. Franklin, born March 7th, 1802, bap. Oct. 19th, 1809, married widow Mary Lyon (alias) Banks.

8. John Lusk, born Oct 25th, 1804, bap. Oct. 19th, 1809, see No. (544.)

9. Horace, born April 17th, 1806, bap. Oct. 19th, 1809, died Dec. 13th, 1832, at Milledgeville, Ga.

334. "Betsey Mather," to church Oct. 1st, 1809, daughter of No. (217) and No. (207,) born Feb. 17th, 1783, married Nov. 21st, 1813, Levi Wells, No. (299;) he died Oct. 23d, 1823, when she married, second, Oct. 23d, 1835, Eli Smith, No. (747.) She had a discriminating mind, had been in early life a school teacher. After the death of her first husband, she used her dower in fitting up her father's old home on West Main street, where she spent the remnant of her life; she had no posterity. She died July 20th, 1864, in her 81st year.

335. "Sylvia Hart," to church Oct. 1st, 1809, daughter of No. (118) and No. (119,) born April 15th, 1777, lived at the home of her father, during his life, then in various families, having no certain dwelling place; never married; retained her faculties to old age, epecially memory. She died May 9th, 1864, aged 87 years and 24 days, at the old house of Chester Hart; to South church, 1842—was supported in old age by the church and by the town, but chiefly by Deacon O. Seymour, her nephew.

[Here ends Dr. Smalley's record and that of Rev. Newton Skinner begins.]

---

336 "Ebenezer Couch," to church Aug. 5th, 1810, son of Thomas, of Southington, and baptized there May 21st, 1749; he was a grandson of Ebenezer, of Wethersfield. He was brother of No. (201,) both distinguished for honesty, humility and homeliness. He married, Aug. 8th, 1786, Hannah, daughter of Moses Barnes, sen., and his wife Blakesley, . She had a daughter Nancy before her marriage to Mr. Couch; she was sister to Blakesley Barnes of Berlin, who, from a boy, without a penny, became a man of wealth by his tact, energy and industry. She died Aug. 5th, 1813, of consumption. He died July 6th, 1826, aged 77. He left no posterity. They lived in various localities. Her father was located on the hill near Mr. Revoir, 1½ miles west of

of New Britain village, where is a spring in the rocks bearing his name on the old land records. This spring was his well.

337. "WILLIAM SMITH," to church, Oct. 7th, 1810, son of Samuel and his wife No. (89;) born Sept. 2d, 1771, married Nov. 6th, 1796, No. (295;) she died Feb. 4th, 1810, agee 34, when he mar., second, Feb. 10th, 1812, No. (472.) He was a farmer and bought the farm on West Main street, embracing all Walnut Hill at that time and the present location of Mr. Swift. He was a successful business man, engaged sometime in manufacturing tin ware. He was chosen, Dec. 30th, 1823, one of the standing committee of the church in place of Levi Wells, deceased. He represented the town, was justice of the peace, and held other town offices; was active in every duty and relation of life, possessing an ardent, sanguine temperament. He died Nov. 2d, 1838, aged 67.

THEIR CHILDREN.

1. Betsey Lewis, born Nov. 24th, 1797, bap. May 25th, 1800, not married, died Jan. 30th, 1836, aged 38.
2. William Henry, born Oct. 22d, 1800, bap. Jan. 11th, 1801, married Aug. 7th, 1825, No. (633,) second, No (770.)
3. Lauretta, born Sept. 24th, 1802, bap. April 24th, 1803, married Jan. 24th, 1821, No. (743.)
4. Samuel Walter, born May 15th, 1805, bap. Sept. 1st, 1805, married.
5. Sally Maria, born April 11th, 1816, bap. Oct. 19th, 1817, see No. (841.)
6. Levi Olmsted, born March 25th, 1818, bap. Sept. 12th, 1819, married Oct. 26th, 1847, Sarah E. Whiting.
7. Harriet Strong, born Sept. 29th, 1820, bap. June 3d, 1821, married May 14th, 1845, Horace Brown.
8. } twins. { Elizur Newton, born Dec. 13th, 1822, bap. June 1st, 1823, married Dec. 22d, 1846, Laura L. Clark.
9. } twins. { Elizabeth Augusta, born Dec. 13th, 1822, bap. June 1st, 1823, see No. (938.)

338. "JAMES BOOTH, jun.," to church Oct. 7th, 1810, son of No. (165) and (166;) born Sept. 11th, 1776, married Dec. 22d, 1800, No. (358.) He was by trade a tanner and shoe maker; had his tannery where now, 1861, Hall & Stanley's store stands, (alias) Elizur N. Smith's building. His house, that now owned and occupied by his son Horace. He was a man much given and gifted in prayer and exhortation, but somewhat erratic. He kept a boarding house and hotel several years. He removed his church connection from the First to the South, June 8th, 1856. He died January 2d, 1859, aged 82.

THEIR CHILDREN.

1. Aurelia, born Feb. 10th, 1802, died March 19th, 1809, aged 7.
2. Lyman Wilcox, born Feb. 9th, 1804, bap. Oct. 21st, 1810, married May 5th, 1825, No. (555.)
3. George W., born Jan. 30th, 1806, bap. Oct. 21st, 1810, see No. (519.)
4. Ralph, born April 29th, 1811, bap. June 16th, 1811, died March 3d, 1818, aged 7.

5. Lucetta, born Aug. 6th, 1814, bap. Oct. 2d, 1814, see No. (671.)
6. Ralph, born May 25th, 1818, bap. Aug. 2d, 1818, married Jan. 26th, 1846, Julia Daily of Providence.
7. Horace, born Nov. 6th, 1821, bap. April 1st, 1822, see No. (793.)

339. "ABI, the wife of Amon Stanley," to church Dec. 2d, 1810, daughter of No. (149) and No. (150;) born Nov. 21st, 1784, married Oct. 10th, 1802, No. (550.) A kind and watchful mother and a devout Christian woman. "Her children arise up and call her blessed, her husband also and he praiseth her."

340. "NANCY, the wife of Cyrus Booth," to church Dec. 2d, 1810, daughter of No. (149) and No. (150,) born Jan. 11th, 1787, married Oct. 11th, 1807, Cyrus Booth, son of Joseph and No. (155,) his wife, born Oct. 10th, 1786, a brass founder by trade, and well skilled in the art. They lived in the house on Main street lately owned by Grove Loomis, now deceased, but he lived in various localities, and his wife Nancy having died, June 18th, 1818, aged 31, he married, second, July 1st, 1825, Myrta Loper, moved to Manchester, Ill., makes lime and drives farming.

THEIR CHILDREN.

1. Mary Burnham, born April 18th, 1808, bap. June 2d, 1811, married June 1st, 1826, Edmund F. Booth, of Joseph.
2. Maria, born April 15th, 1809, bap. June 2d, 1811, married July 1st, 1827, Theodore C. Bronson.
3. William, born Sept. 10th, 1810, died young.
4. Elizabeth Frances, born Oct. 31st, 1811, bap. Dec. 22d, 1811, mar. Sept. 11th, 1832, No. (812.)
5. Cyrus, born Oct. 12th, 1813, bap. Dec. 19th, 1813, died 1839, in Texas.
6. Nancy North, born Oct. 26th, 1814, bap. April 16th, 1815, married David P. Hughes.
7. Henry North, born Dec. 2d, 1816, bap. Jan. 16th, 1817.

SECOND WIFE'S CHILD.

8. Helen Mary, born , bap. Nov. 17th, 1830.

341. "HULDAH, wife of Silas Pennfield," to church Jan. 6th, 1811, daughter of No. (183) and No. (243,) born Oct. 18th, 1786, married March 1st, 1804, Silas Pennfield, son of No. (237,) and his wife Eunice (Kelsey,) born , bap. July 1st, 1792. He built next west of his father, on Horse Plain, where Mr. Hunter now lives; was a farmer, and died Nov. 29th, 1812, aged 28. She married, second, Jan. 18th, 1814, No. (463.) She died June 23d, 1852, aged 67.

THEIR CHILDREN.

1. Caroline, born 1805, died Aug. 23d, 1809, aged 4.
2. Caroline, born , bap. April 7th, 1811.

3. Elvira, born June 18th, 1807, bap. April 7th, 1811, married, Dec. 9th, 1824, No. (515.)

4. William, born April 22d, 1809, bap. April 7th, 1811, married Nov. 8th, 1828, Jane Smith, of New Haven.

342. "LUCY L. STANLEY," to church, Jan. 6th, 1811, daughter of Noah Stanley and his second wife Experience (Wells,) of Wethersfield, born Sept. , 1787, never married; of a quiet, retiring and kind disposition, she exemplified a good Christian character, and died Feb. 3d, 1859, aged 72.

343. "DOLLY STANLEY," to church Jan. 6th, 1811, daughter of Lot Stanley (son of Thomas 3d,) and his wife Rhoda (Wadsworth,) of Farmington, born Feb. 15th, 1794, married Dec. 30th, 1812, No. (353;) had no children to live. He died June 27th, 1845, aged 54. She married, second, Oct. 22d, 1860, Solomon D. Gridley, of Southington, son of Joel, and Amanda (Woodruff,) his wife, born July 14th, 1805. They now, 1867, live in her house on Arch street. She was baptized on admission to church. She became, 1842, a constituent member of the South church.

344 "RACHEL ANDREWS," to church January 6th, 1811, daughter of No. (245) and No. (252,) born Feb. 6th, 1789; never married, but lived with her father near Bass river, on the road to Farmington, took kind care of him during his long life, where she died May 20th, 1840, aged 51.

345. "ANDREW PRATT," to church March 17th, 1811, son of Humphrey, of Saybrook, and his wife, Lydia (Tulley,) born Nov. 8th, 1756; was a farmer and shoe maker, a man of intelligence, with an active mind, was a warm politician, and represented the town of Berlin in 1817 and 1818; was a magistrate, and active in the care of the public library. He married, March 1st, 1780, Nancy Dorrance, of Rhode Island. She died, Feb. 2d, 1785, aged 28, when he married, second, June 1st, 1787, No. (271,) who died, May 15th, 1795, when he married, third, June 12th, 1796, No. (346.) They lived on East street, first in the old house of Deacon Patterson's. He built new on the same site, which is now, A. D. 1862, owned and occupied by Henry his son. He was short, thick set and robust. He died Jan. 2d, 1830, aged 73.

346. "Wife of Andrew Pratt," to church, March 17th, 1811; she was his third wife, and the daughter of No. (112) and No. (312,) born June 11th, 1768, married June 12th, 1796, No. (345;) was a woman of a strong masculine mind, of great energy and force of character, of generous impulses, and very industrious; she died Dec. 28th, 1841, aged 74.

FIRST WIFE'S CHILDREN.

1. Sally, born Dec. 3d, 1781, died , aged 16 months.
2. Tully, born March 25th, 1784, died , aged 14 months.

SECOND WIFE'S CHILDREN.

3. Lydia, born Nov. 16th, 1788, bap. May 4th, 1795, married Nov. 10th, 1811, Hiland Parker, second, Benjamin Taggart.

4. Daniel Humphrey, born Sept. 20th, 1793, bap. May 4th, 1795, died January 28th, 1823, aged 30.

THIRD WIFE'S CHILDREN.

5. } twins, { Betsey Whaples, born February 23d, 1797, bap. June 16th, 1811, see No. (492.)

6. Henry Morgan, born February 23d, 1797, bap. June 16th, 1811, married March 25th, 1818, daughter of No. (208;) she died Aug. 15th, 1823, at Marietta, Ohio; he married, second, June 18th, 1826, Mary S. Loveland, who died May 23d, 1863, aged 61; she was daughter of Elijah, of Kensington, and his wife Azubah (Scovell.)

7. William Tully, born March 27th, 1801, bap. June 16th, 1811, married May 6th, 1825, Eliza Steele, of Horace, of Berlin.

8. Nancy Dorrance, born March 25th, 1803, bap. June 16th, 1811, see No. (493.)

9. Horatio Andrews, born June 27th, 1808, bap. June 16th, 1811, married Sept. 24th, 1832, Charlotte Francis, daughter of Appleton, of Kensington, and his wife Charlotte (Webster,) of David, of Berlin.

347. "SARAH, wife of Salmon Hart," to church, April 7th, 1811, daughter of Asahel Goodrich and Sarah (Woodruff,) his second wife, born May 2d, 1777, married May 2d, 1796, No. (441;) she died Aug. 2d, 1815, aged 38.

348. "NANCY, wife of Isaac Lee, jun.," to church April 7th, 1811, daughter of Seth Lusk and No. (242,) born , 1783, baptized June 2d, 1793, married Sept. 27th, 1799, No. (351.) Widow Nancy Lee died May 9th, 1825, aged 42, of dropsy of the heart.

349. "MARY, the wife of Joseph Shipman," to church April 7th, 1811, daughter of No. (168) and No. (154,) born Dec. 22d, 1783, married July 11th, 1802, No. (461.) She died Nov. 2d, 1838, aged 55. I quote part of an obituary notice of her from the New York Evangelist: "She exemplified in her last sickness, the patience, the faith, and the hope of the Christian in a remarkable degree. Social Society is thus deprived of one of its brightest ornaments, the church one of its corner stones, polished after the similitude of a palace."

350. "JESSE BROWN," to church April 7th, 1811, was brother of No. (548,) taught school in the Southeast district one winter; went to Little Rock, Arkansas, and married and died there.

351. "ISAAC LEE, jun.," to church, June 2d, 1811, son of No. (168) and No. (154,) born April 13th, 1775, married Sept. 27th, 1799, No. (348;) of frail constitution, he taught school several winters, was in company with his brother Thomas in merchandize, went south for his health. He was gentlemanly in his address and manners. He lived in part of his father's house, which is still (1867) standing. He died April 16th, 1818, aged 43, of consumption.

THEIR CHILDREN.

1. Henry, born , bap. June 2d, 1811, died on his passage to the West Indies, Dec. 22d, 1819, aged 20.

2. Phillip, born May 6th, 1802, bap. June 2d, 1811, married Dec. 28th, 1823, No. (655.)

3. Betsey, born March 27th, 1804, bap. June 2d, 1811, married June 12th, 1827, No. (858.)

4. Harriet, born 1806, died April 10th, 1811, aged 5.

5. Nancy, born 1807, bap. June 2d, 1811, married Sept. 27th, 1826, Henry Belden, of Jonathan, jun.; she died Dec. 17th, 1854, aged 47.

6. Maria, born 1809, died April 11th, 1811, aged 2.

7. Charles, born , bap. Aug. 1st, 1813, drowned in a well April 28th, 1817.

8. Isaac Newton, born Nov. 18th, 1810, bap. June 2d, 1811, married Oct. 20th, 1833, No. (734.)

9. Harriet, born 1812, bap. May 24th, 1812, died of consumption Aug. 15th, 1828, aged 16.

352. "Ezra Carter," to church June 2d, 1811, son of Ithiel, of Kensington, and his wife Lois (Deming,) married Sept. 29th, 1811, Mary Stanley, daughter of Lot, and Rhoda (Wadsworth,) his wife born Feb. 13th, 1791. He was a tanner and shoe maker, learned of Oliver Stanley, at the old tannery of Deacon Timothy Stanley. He was baptized on admission to church; was dismissed and recommended to church in Leyden, N. Y., Jan. 28th, 1821. She died there May 27th, 1846, aged 55. He married, second,

THEIR CHILDREN.

1. Loyal Wadsworth, born , bap. Nov. 8th 1812, married Jan. 6th, 1839, Lucy Rose, of Farmington.

2. Ezra, born , bap. April 16th, 1815, died June 14th, 1815.

3. Francis Hart, born Jan. 20th, 1822, at Leyden, N. Y., married Oct. 19th, 1848, No. (1022.)

353. "Francis Hart," to church Aug. 4th, 1811, son of No. (247) and No. (248,) born Dec. 18th, 1791, married Dec. 30th, 1812, No. (343.) He was a tanner and shoe maker, learned of Treadway, of Torringford. He lived in Hart quarter, the place formerly owned and occupied by Asahel Hart, on the corner near the Shuttle Meadow road. He was active as a citizen and as a Christian; to South church, 1842. He died June 27th, 1845, aged 54. He had often been entrusted with both civil and military offices, and was a colonel. He left no posterity.

354, "James Francis," to church Oct. 6th, 1811, son of No. (91) and No. (92,) born Oct. 24th, 1757, married Nov. 12th, 1780, No (355.) He was a farmer and lived in south part of Stanley quarter; a substantial man, of good understanding and judgment, was in the war of the Revolution, and often called to do public business. His wife died, when he married, second, Oct. 22d, 1827, widow Sarah Clark, of Wethersfield. He died, April 13th, 1839, aged 82.

355. "Wife of James Francis," to church October 6th, 1811, maiden name, Sylvia Stanley, daughter of No. (14) and his wife, Ruth (Norton,) born Oct. 24th, 1753. She died Jan. 21st, 1822, aged 68.

THEIR CHILDREN.

1. Ursula, born Jan. 18th, 1781, married Oct. 28th, 1804, No. (458.)
2. Laura, born Nov. 16th, 1782, married April 26, 1811, Daniel Willard, of Newington.
3. James, jun., born July 21st, 1786, married Feb. 28th, 1820, No. (473.)
4. Romeo, born May 30th, 1790, married Nov. 24th, 1813, No. (471.)

356. "Thomas Lee," to church Oct. 6th, 1811, son of No. (168) and No. (154,) born Nov. 28th, 1776, married Oct. 10th, 1797, No. (357.) Soon after marriage set up tin making at the present house of Mr. Pettis, on West Main street, then with his brother, No. (351,) set up a store of goods on Main street, where now stands the house of Henry North. This was the second store in town, but the first in the village. He was also engaged in various manufactures. He represented the town of Berlin, was magistrate, judge of probate, postmaster, and was an active politician. His wife having died, he married, second, Feb. 2d, 1831, widow Laura Whittlesey, of Newington, No. (740.) She died Feb. 9th, 1837, when he married, 3d, Jan. 3d, 1838, No. (880.) His house he built on the site of Elihu Burritt's, and is now (1861) occupied by Mrs. O. C. Stanley. He died Aug. 20th, 1840, aged 64.

357. "Wife of Thomas Lee," to church Oct. 6th, 1811, baptized same time ; her maiden name, Electa Riley, daughter of John, of Northampton, and his wife, Huldah (Porter,) of Kensington, No. (273 ;) born Dec. 13th, 1776, married Oct. 10th, 1797, No. (356.) She was a superior woman of great decision of character. She died Dec. 5th, 1826, aged 50.

THEIR CHILDREN.

1. Minerva, born April 22d, 1798, bap. Nov. 3d, 1811, married Sept. 8th, 1818, No. (954.)
2. Lorenzo Porter, born April 12th, 1800, bap. Nov. 3d, 1811, married Nov. 3d, 1828, Jennette Hills.
3. Thirza, born Nov. 19th, 1801, bap. Nov. 3d, 1811, married Sept. 20th, 1849, Rev. David Tilton.
4. John Riley, born April 22d, 1804, bap. Nov. 3d, 1811, graduated at Yale College 1826, No. (900.)
5. Electa, born March 24th, 1806, bap. Nov. 3d, 1811, married Aug. 20th, 1826. Wells Hubbard.
6. Thomas Goodrich, born Sept. 1st, 1808, bap. Nov. 3d, 1811, see No (545.)
7. Caroline, born Nov. 8th, 1810, bap. Nov. 3d, 1811, No. (609.)
8. Almira Stanley, born Aug. 9th, 1812, bap. Oct. 18th, 1812, No. (825.)
9. William Henry, born Feb. 10th, 1816, bap. June 2d, 1816, died Dec. 27th, 1816, aged 11 months.
10. William Henry, born May 19th, 1818, bap. Aug. 30th, 1818, married Jan. 6th, 1849, Louisa Northam.
11. Angeline, born January 4th, 1824, bap. April 4th, 1824, married No. (826.)

358. "OLIVE, the wife of James Booth, jun.," to church, Oct. 6th, 1811, daughter of Josiah Wilcox, of Berlin, and his wife, Huldah (Savage,) born Jan. 14th, 1778, baptized May 24th, 1778, at Worthington, by Rev. Mr. Strong, of Hartford, married Dec. 22d, 1800, No. (338.) She was a woman of strong mind and good sense, very large and fleshy. She died Feb. 16th, 1847, aged 69.

359. "EBENEZER ANDREWS," to church Oct. 6th, 1811, son of No. (245) and No. (252,) born Dec. 24th, 1778, married Oct. 26th, 1800, Mary Griswold, daughter of Ashbel, and his wife, Elizabeth (Woodruff,) born 1783. She died Oct. 18th, 1858, aged 75, at Rochester, N. Y. He was a carpenter by trade, learned of Deacon John Osgood; lived on the road to Farmington, in the house built by her father. He was a fine looking man, with kind and amiable disposition. He died Aug. 5th, 1827, aged 49.

THEIR CHILDREN.

1. Adna Gridley, born May 22d, 1801, bap. Dec. 15th, 1811, married April 19th, 1825, Maria Andrews, of Elisha, of Canaan; he married, second, July 29th, 1849, Jane Evarts of Rochester.
2. Aaron Cadwell, born Feb. 25th, 1804, bap. Dec. 15th, 1811, married Sept. 6th, 1830, No. (684.)
3. Philo, born May 8th, 1806, bap. Dec. 15th, 1811, married Nov. 27th, 1828, Amelia Kelsey.
4. Walter, born June 14th, 1811, bap. Dec. 15th 1811, married Oct. 10th, 1831, Emily Beckley; live in Wisconsin.
5. Mary Griswold, born , bap. Dec. 15th, 1811, see No. (713.)
6. Orpha, born May 13th, 1813, bap. Aug. 1st, 1813, married Sept. 6th, 1830, Thomas Burrill.
7. Henry Woodruff, born April 10th, 1819, bap Aug. 29, 1819, married Nov. 29th, 1843, No. (1076.)
8. Sophia, born July 24th, 1821, bap. Dec. 16th, 1821, married Oct. 13th, 1844, Samuel Stanley.
9. Charles, born , died Feb. 9th, 1827, aged 3 years.
10. Ebenezer Newton, born , married Ann Hunter, of Rochester, N. Y.

360. "NANCY JUDD," to church Oct. 6th, 1811, daughter of John, jun., and No. (637,) born Sept. 17th, 1793, married Dec. 12th, 1813, Austin Woodford, of Vermont. She was dismissed and recommended, 1814, to She was baptized on admission to church. She died Oct. 24th, 1814, in Vermont, aged 21. Her sister, No. (369.)

361. "NANCY, wife of Bethel Hart," to church Dec. 1st, 1811, by letter from the Third church in Wethersfield. She was his second wife, called widow Nancy Seely, m. May 16th, 1811. He died Dec. 25th, 1824, when she married Elias Brown, of Farmington, son of Ephraim, jun., of Windsor, and Mercy (Wesland) his wife, born March 15th, 1758. She died June 8th, 1850, aged 85. He was fife major in the Revolution and drew a pension late in life.

362. "POLLY, wife of Shubel Curtiss," to church Feb. 2d, 1812, daughter of No. (237,) born Sept. 4th, 1786, married Aug. 11th, 1801, son of Amos, and Mabel (Squire) his wife. He was a cooper by trade, learned of his father Pennfield; lived in the old place of Josiah Steele, on "Horse Plain," but late in life built near "Job's Corner," where his widow still (1866) lives. He died Oct. 3d, 1845, aged 64. She is a woman of great patience and industry; to South church, 1842.

THEIR CHILDREN.

1. Mary, born July 31st, 1802, bap. June 21st, 1812, married Oct. 4th, 1819, John Eaton; married, second, Daniel Cook; married, third, Pliny Richardson.
2. Andrew, born Nov. 3d, 1804, bap. June 21st, 1812, married Aug. 7th, 1825, Laura Dunham.
3. Charlotte, born , bap. June 21st, 1812, married Pliny Sanders.
4. Eunice, born , bap. June 21st, 1812, married Horatio Webster.
5. William, born March 7th, 1812, bap. June 21st, 1812, died August 25th, 1812, aged 6 months.
6. Adaline, born 1813, bap. Jan. 30th, 1814, married Thomas Butler, of Hartford.
7. Harriet, born 1816, married Joel Cook, she died Dec. 5th, 1839, aged 23.
8. William, born, Oct. 16th, 1819, married Sept. 1st, 1840, Lucy Ann Pennfield, of Nathaniel, jun.
9. Julia Ann, born March 16th, 1824, married Aug. 24th, 1852, Jarvis Hall, see No (800.)
10. Emeline L., born 1825, married, Nov. 4th, 1849, Benjamin F. Eddy, of Thomas.
11. Electa, born Dec. 16th, 1829, married Oct. 17th, 1845, Augustus Hinman.

363. "HETTY CONE," to church Feb. 2d, 1812, daughter of Joshua, of Daniel, of Middletown, who lived on Main street, at the extreme south end of the parish, and his wife Mehitable (Blinn,) of Wethersfield. She was a tailoress by trade, social and kind, but became insane. She was baptised on admission to church. She died April 16th, 1858, aged 74, at the alms house; never married.

364. "ADELIA GRIDLEY," to church, Feb. 2d, 1812, baptised same time, daughter of Alexander, of Farmington, and Chloe (Bidwell,) his wife. She is still remembered by some of our people as a lovely girl; married Feb. 10th, 1812, No. (371.) She was born Oct. 18th, 1790, at Farmington; now, 1862, living with her daughter, Delia La Foy, of Madison, New Jersey.

365. "NANCY BELDEN," to church Feb. 2d, 1812, daughter of No. (158) and No. (159,) born Aug. 31st, 1792, married May 5th, 1812, No. (370.) She was greatly gifted by nature and grace, possessed a strong, discriminating mind, had a leading voice in church music, was ready for every good work, and engaged in public reforms, with modest and becoming zeal. She and her husband were dismissed and recommended, March, 1816, to church in Cherry Valley, N. Y., but received back in 1817. After the death of her husband she was dismissed and recommended to

the North church in Hartford. She died in Canada, July 4th, 1852, aged 62; brought home for interment. During the vicissitudes of an eventful life she manifested a calm trust in God, and doubtless sings the song of victory with the hundred and forty-four thousand.

366. "ORPHA NORTH," to church Feb. 2d, 1812, daughter of No. (149) and No. (150,) born Aug. 12th, 1793, married March 18th, 1812, No. (311.) She was scrupulously devoted to the cause of Christ and his church; to South church, 1842. She died Jan. 12th, 1847, aged 53.

367. "PERCES ROOT," to church, Feb. 2d, 1812, baptized same time; she lived in the family of Amzi Stanley on the new "Highway" road, and married, Sept. 20th, 1813, Rice Wells, son of Eli. They moved to the west the same year, and she took a letter of dismissal and recommendation.

368. "LYDIA WELLS," to church Feb. 2d, 1812, daughter of No. (299) and No. (300,) born Oct. 24th, 1792, married Jan. 20th, 1814, Augustus Flagg, of West Hartford, son of Abijah, and his wife, Thankful (Seymour.) He was a shoe-maker and tanner by trade. She was dismissed and recommended to church in West Hartford, July 28th, 1816, and in 1845 she removed her church connection to Yonkers, N. Y., where now (1866) she resides; a woman of sterling qualities, genial, social and happy. He died Jan. 21st, 1842; he was born March 19th, 1784.

THEIR CHILDREN.

1. Marcia M., born May 31st, 1815, at New Britain, bap. Aug. 27th, 1815, died Aug. 27th, 1851, at Yonkers, N. Y.

2. Levi W., born Feb. 14th, 1817, at West Hartford, married June, 1848, Charlotte S. Whitman.

3. Newton, born Dec. 17th, 1819, at West Hartford, married June, 1854, Ellen H. Goodwin, of Illinois.

4. Ethan, born July 20th, 1820, at West Hartford, married Jan. 30th, 1850, Marietta Wells, daughter of Lemuel Wells, No. (512.) She died, when he married, second, March 7th, 1855, Julia Baldwin.

5. Lucy A., born February 17th, 1822, married John Olmsted, 1855, died June 7th, 1858.

369. "AURORA JUDD," to church Feb. 2d, 1812, baptized same time, daughter of John, jun., and No. (637,) born March 20th, 1795; never married. She died April 20th, 1816, aged 21, of consumption; sister of No. (360.)

370. "SAMUEL BOOTH," to church Feb. 2d, 1812, son of Robert, 2d, and his wife, Abigail (Barton,) born Aug. 31st, 1792; was by trade a blacksmith; learned of James North, Esq.; he inherited the home of his father and grand-father, Nathan, senior, the old red house at the south end of the "Green," has been removed and remodeled, and (now, 1863,) is on Arch street, and occupied by Henry Andrews. Mr. Booth was a man of prayer and piety; could hear "the sound of a going in the tops of the

mulberry trees," as early as any other one in the church; was greatly useful in social prayer meetings; a constant laborer in the Sabbath school, and active in the various reforms and benevolent objects of the age. He became one of the standing committee of the church, 1843. He lost one leg by amputation, from a bad knee, and bore the operation with such Christian fortitude that it astonished beholders. He had various losses and successes in business, experienced much joy and sorrow in life, and died in hope of a glorious resurrection, May 11th, 1846, of dropsy, aged 56; wife, No. (365.)

THEIR CHILDREN.

1. William Belden, born April 13th, 1813, bap. June 27th, 1813, married March 31st, 1837, Betsey Blin; he married second, Jan. 1st, 1846, Maria A. Keach; he married third, May 29th, 1855, Widow Mary C. Reid.
2. Mary Ann, born March 24th, 1815, bap. March 27th, 1815, died March 27th, 1815, aged three days.
3. Walter Henry, born Dec. 26th, 1816, bap. June 29th, 1817, died Nov. 16th, 1822, aged six years.
4. Nancy, born July 28th, 1819, died same day.
5. Nancy, born Aug. 28th, 1821, bap. Oct. 28th, 1821, see No. (792.)
6. Hubert Henry, born Dec. 12th, 1823, bap. March 28th, 1824, see No. (791.)
7. Albert, born July 13th, 1828, died Oct. 15th, 1829, aged fifteen months.
8. Samuel Albert, born June 29th, 1830, bap. Oct. 17th, 1830, died Aug. 5th, 1831.
9. Mary Allen, born June 1st, 1833, bap. Sept. 15th, 1833; is a sweet singer; married 1866, George Gladwin, the artist.

371. "Erastus Cone," to church Feb. 2d, 1812, baptized same time, son of Joshua and his wife, Mehitable (Blinn,) of Wethersfield. He was a saddler and harness-maker; learned of Abner Clark; married Feb. 10th, 1812, No. (364,) both dismissed by letter of recommendation, A. D. 1813, to church in Simsbury; lived in Newark, New Jersey, now, 1862, living with his daughter, Delia La Foy, at Madison, New Jersey. He was born Jan. 25th, 1790, at New Britain.

THEIR CHILDREN.

1. Thomas, born Jan. 3d, 1813, at Simsbury, died Sept., 1815.
2. Thomas B., born Aug. 26th, 1814, at Simsbury.
3. Sophia, born Aug. 25th, 1816, at Simsbury.
4. Harriet N., born May 6th, 1819, at Middletown.
5. Adelia, born March 17th, 1821, at Middletown, married La Foy.
6. Walter North, born Oct. 13th, 1822, at Middletown.
7. Julia Bidwell, born July 30th, 1824, at Newark, New Jersey.
8. Alexander Gridley, born Dec. 16th, 1825, at Newark, New Jersey.
9. Margaret Douglass, born Oct. 16th, 1827, at Newark, New Jersey.
10. Edward Tuttle, born March 11th, 1830, at Newark, New Jersey.
11. William, born April 20th, 1832, at Newark, New Jersey, died March, 1836.

372. "Jason Steele," to church Feb. 2d, 1812, son of Ebenezer, jun. and his wife, No. (225.) He was her eldest son, baptized June 26th,

1791, soon after birth; was an interesting young man and Christian. He died 1812, as a soldier of the United States, in the war of that year.

373. "JOHN PENNFIELD," to church Feb. 2d, 1812, son of No. (237) and Eunice (Kelsey,) his wife, born Oct. 18th, 1791, married March 12th, 1815, No. (432;) was a farmer; lived and died on the place vacated by the death of his brother, Silas; was a Christian of much prayer and strong faith; was illiterate but honest and earnest; he lost one leg by the fall of a tree, endured much pain and suffering of body, but was joyful in spirit. He had removed his connection from the first church to the Methodist, about 1830, and our watch was withdrawn Dec. 1st, 1831. No doubt the Methodist church was more agreeable to his tastes and sympathies. He died July 15th, 1846, aged 55.

THEIR CHILDREN.

1. Eliza Ann, born Jan. 16th, 1816, bap. May 19th, 1816; never married; eminently pious.
2. Jane Maria, born Sept. 25th, 1818, bap. Nov. 15th, 1818, married Aug. 28th, 1842, George Williams.
3. Burnham H., born April 3d, 1824, bap. Aug. 8th, 1824, married May 10th, 1846, Annette Judd, daughter of Amon. He was killed Jan. 25th, 1847, aged 23, by running against a clothes line.
4. Chester, born Aug. 21st, 1831, married Dec. 22d, 1850, Sarah Hamilton, of Hartford.

374. "KILBOURN BATES," to church Feb. 2d, 1812, son of David, of Granville, Mass. and his wife, Abigail (Burt,) born Jan. 12th, 1793; was an apprentice to Oliver Stanley, in the tanning and shoe-making business; married May 4th, 1814, Rhoda Booth, daughter of Elisha, jun. and Mary (Steele,) his wife, born Oct. 17th, 1792, died July 28th, 1818, by drowning in a pool of water, aged 26. He married second, Isabel Hall, of Blanford, Mass.

THEIR CHILDREN.

1. David, born , married Elizabeth Ripley.
2. Catharine, born , died Jan. 14th, 1856, aged 38.

375. "Widow REBECCA MATHER," to church April 5th, 1812, born May 30th, 1769, to Ebenezer Steele and his wife, No. (148,) married June 19th, 1781, Cotton Mather, son of No. (138) and No. (139,) born Sept. 2d, 1771. He was a heavy, robust man, but of dissipated habits. He lived near his father, at the foot of "Osgood Hill;" died July 25th, 1807, aged 43. At the funeral, while the body was being conveyed with a bier on men's shoulders, the frame or bier broke, the coffin parted as it fell, and the body rolled out upon the ground. She died June 3d, 1813, aged 38, of consumption.

THEIR CHILDREN.

1. Cyprian, born May 30th, 1792, married Jan. 18th, 1814, No. (341.)
2. Elenor, born July 9th, 1794.

3. Hannah, born Aug. 1st, 1796, married Sept. 14th, 1818, William Morgan; she died May 16th, 1851.

4. Rebecca, born Feb. 16th, 1799, married May 13th, 1822, Norman O. Smith.

5. Thomas, born June 5th, 1800, married Aug. 14th, 1820, Susanna Hungerford, of Harwinton, daughter of Tertius and Ruth (Cook,) his wife, born Aug. 12th, 1801.

6. Alonzo, born May 9th, 1802, died May 10th, 1802, aged one day.

376. "WILLIAM BASSETT," to church April 5th, 1812, baptized same time, son of Cornelius and his wife, Chloe (Smith,) daughter of Samuel, born Jan. 19th, 1795, married April 23d, 1823, Polly Judd, daughter of No. (435) and No. (436,) born Dec. 15th, 1795; she died June 26th, 1837, aged 42, when he married second, June 3d, 1838, No. (882.) He was a wagon-maker by trade; learned of Henry North; built on the site of William A. Churchill's residence; had his shop where Churchill and Stanley's jewelry shop stands. He sold to Churchill, and built on West Main street, the house now, 1866, owned and occupied by A. P. Collins. He sold out and moved to Simsbury, where he died Dec. 21st, 1860; he to South church, 1842.

THEIR CHILDREN.

1. Charles, born Feb. 26th, 1824.

2. Mary Smith, born Dec. 13th, 1825, see No. (941.)

3. Jennie Maria, born Dec. 10th, 1832, married June 2d, 1857, Frederic Hart, of Salmon.

SECOND WIFE'S CHILDREN.

4. Dwight Evans, born April 17th, 1839, married July, 1861, Susan Hutchins, of Canton.

5. Marcelon Cornelius, born Aug. 20th, 1844.

6. Eugene Selden, born Oct. 2d, 1846, died, aged sixteen months.

7. William Clark, born June 29th, 1850, died Nov. 21st, 1850, aged five months.

8. Walter Clark, born Aug. 19th, 1852.

377. "SUSANNA, wife of Josiah Steele," to church June 7th, 1812; her maiden name, Lewis; she was from Oxford, Conn.; they lived on "Horse Plain," near Capt. Lemuel Hotchkiss' saw-mill and iron works; he was a blacksmith; was in hard service in the war of the Revolution; compactly built and of great endurance, he enlisted into the Revolutionary army April 20th, 1777, for three years; had £10 bounty; he died March 25th, 1825, aged 68. She was a kind-hearted, good woman; buffeted the storms of adversity bravely, and died July 31st, 1821.

THEIR CHILDREN.

1. Josiah, jun., born Feb. 9th, 1778, married Nov. 5th, 1798, No. (445.)

2. Allen, born Nov. 23d, 1779, married July 29th, 1799, No. (307.)

3. Susanna, born , married No. (308,) and married second, Oct. 16th, 1828, George Daniels.

4. Sybil, born Oct. 21st, 1782, married April 9th, 1799, Nathaniel Carrington, of Farmington, son of David.

5. Avery, born , married Polly Rugg; married second, Jerusha Williams.

6. Levi, born , married Nov. 23d, 1811, Betsey Gilbert; he died Aug. 5th, 1829, by suicide.

7. Sabra, born , married April 12th, 1805, see No. (316.)

8. Amon, born , married Electa Curtiss, daughter of Amos.

9. Cynthia, born , married Feb. 23d, 1817, James Hull, of Isaac and Eunice (Carrington.)

10. George, born , bap. June 21st, 1812, married Jan. 11th, 1824, Lucina Belden, of John; he died July 8th, 1837, when she married second, Noble Andrus, of Farmington and Bristol.

378. "CAROLINE, wife of John Andrews," to church June 7th, 1812, baptized same time, born Feb. 1st, 1769, to Jesse Bronson, of Kensington, and his wife, Abigail (Allen,) married March 16th, 1800, No. (197;) she possessed a happy turn of mind, took great delight in the ordinances of the gospel, and means of grace; died Dec. 25th, 1846, aged 77; her mother is No. (708.)

379. "JERUSHA MATHER," to church June 7th, 1812, daughter of No. (217) and No. (207,) born May 10th, 1793, married May 15th, 1827, No. (773;) she was a tailoress by trade, very industrious, intelligent and discreet; died Oct. 17th, 1838, aged 45; left no posterity.

380. "BULAH HART," to church Aug. 2d, 1812, by letter from the church in Simsbury, baptized May 18th, 1783; never married; died at Simsbury; she was daughter of No. (174) and No. (224.)

381. "NORMAN WOODRUFF," to church Oct. 4th, 1812, baptized same time, son of Gad and his wife, Sarah (Loomis,) born Nov. 6th, 1790, married March 19th, 1813, No. (557;) a brass-founder by trade; his house stood where now, 1861, Dr. L. Woodruff's stands, on Main street; his shop back of the house, where he was largely engaged in manufacturing brass goods. His present residence, 1866, is in Plainville, with his son, John. He was dismissed July 23d, 1815, to the church in Lenox, Mass., but subsequently returned viz. Feb. 2d, 1823, by letter of recommendation from that church, with his wife. He was a tall man, of serious turn, and sober demeanor, but honest and generous. He and wife South church, 1842.

THEIR CHILDREN.

1. Sarah, born Dec. 21st, 1813, bap. March 20th, 1814, see No. (670.)

2. Almira, born Feb. 2d, 1816, see No. (927.)

3. Betsey, born May 19th, 1818, married Oct. 8th, 1838, No. (861.)

4. Maria, born May 5th, 1820, married June 3d, 1842, No. (862.)

5. John, born May 11th, 1823, bap. Aug. 24th, 1823, married Sept. 23d, 1851, Sarah Stowe.

6. James, born April 26th, 1827, bap. Sept. 16th, 1827, married Dec. 14th, 1854, Clara R. Clapp.

7. Mary, born March 14th, 1830, died April 2d, 1830.

8. Norman, born Feb. 7th, 1834, bap. July 11th, 1834, died Aug. 12th, 1834.

382. "BENJAMIN CADWELL," to church Oct. 4th, 1812, baptized same time; he was an apprentice of James Booth, jun., at the bnsiness of tan-

ning and shoe-making; came from the town of Durham, Conn.; kept the turnpike gate on the Middletown and Berlin road, on the west side of the parish, where he died, of consumption, Jan. 9th, 1818, aged 27. He married Feb. 15th, 1813, Roxana Hamblin, of Farmington, daughter of Phineas and his wife, Rhoda (Andrus,) born Oct. 3d, 1793; she died March 3d, 1849, aged 56, at Wethersfield. He adorned his profession by a lowly walk.

THEIR CHILDREN.

1. Adelia, born May 24th, 1814, bap. July 10th, 1814, married Feb. 14th, 1836, William Taylor, a machinist and instructor of convicts at Connecticut State Prison, at Wethersfield; he died May 1st, 1853; she resides in Hartford, 1860.

2. Benjamin, born June, 1817, bap. Sept. 23d, 1817, died March 23d, 1818, aged nine months.

383. "OLIVE, wife of Cyprian Hart," to church Dec. 6th, 1812, daughter of James Whedon and his wife, Dinah, of North Branford, born June 20th, 1765; he came into this place to run Deacon Hart's mill, and lived near it; he was son of Lieut. Noadiah and Lucy (Hurlbut,) his wife, born May 23d, 1772, at Kensington; they lived several years where now, 1862, Silas Wright does, on the "Mountain Lake road;" he died July 5th, 1843; she died June 17th, 1846; she was dismissed by letter from this church Sept. 5th, 1819, but our records previous and up to that date never say where dismissed to.

THEIR CHILDREN.

1. Truman, born June 11th, 1793, married July 4th, 1815, Laura Lewis Steele, daughter of Josiah, jun.

2. Noadiah, born April 16th, 1795.

3. Bera, born March 31st, 1797, married May 6th, 1819, Mary, daughter of Samuel Whaples; live in St. Lawrence county, New York.

4. James Griffing, born April 19th, 1799.

5. Leander Sidney, born Aug. 10th, 1801, m. Aug. 23d, 1824, Emeline Thompson; married second, Electa, daughter of Solomon Humphrey.

6. Percy, born June 17th, 1805, died April 3d, 1809, aged four years.

7. Ordelia, born Jan. 17th, 1808, died April 4th, 1809, and both buried in one grave.

384. "PRUDENCE, wife of John Clark," to church Feb. 7th, 1813, by letter from the first church in Farmington, daughter of Joshua Woodruff, of Farmington, and his wife, Prudence (Curtiss,) born Aug. 3d, 1793, married Aug. 26th, 1812; he son of Abel and his wife, Abigail (Judd,) born March 20th, 1787; he was a farmer and butcher; lived on the old Clark home of his father and grand-father, where now, 1862, Omri North owns and resides, at the foot of "Clark Hill." He established the first "meat market" in the village, and it stood on or near John Stanley's garden, by the railroad. In several respects she is an extraordinary woman, having passed through peculiar vicissitudes in life; was bedrid several years, and helpless; recovered and is healthy now, 1863, and has been

many years; has a great gift of prayer and exhortation, and feels called of God to travel as a missionary. She left our church for the Methodist communion, as being more congenial with her views and emotions. He died Jan. 25th, 1835, aged 48. She was admitted to Farmington church, August, 1808.

THEIR CHILDREN.

1. Jane, born Nov. 14th, 1813, bap. Feb. 13th, 1814, died Feb. 17th, 1818, of canker rash, aged four years.

2. Matilda, born Oct. 24th, 1815, bap. March 10th, 1816, see No. (703.)

3. George, born June 20th, 1817, bap. Aug. 4th, 1817, married Jan. 16th, 1845, Sarah E. Castlon, of Georgia; he died July 15th, 1845, at Macon, Georgia, aged 28.

4. Abel Newel, born June 12th, 1819, bap. Oct. 17th, 1819, married April 27th, 1840, Emily I. Braddock; he died at Hartford, March 25th, 1867, in his 48th year, of cancer; was editor of the Courant.

5. John Woodruff, born July 3d, 1822, bap. Oct. 25th, 1822, married April 7th, 1858, Caroline Beckley.

6. Jane Louisa, born Oct. 2d, 1827, bap. April 6th, 1828, married March 2d, 1845, Deming W. Sexton.

7. Mary Prudence, born Nov. 2d, 1830, died May 21st, 1834, aged three.

8. Ellen, born Dec. 2d, 1833, married April 16th, 1856, Cornelius Everest, of Rev. C. B. Everest.

385. "Minerva Lee," to church April 4th, 1813, daughter of No. (356) and No. (357,) born April 22d, 1798, married Sept. 8th, 1818, No. (954;) she taught school, both day and Sabbath school; was teacher in the first Sabbath school in the town or county, in the spring of 1816; intellectual and energetic, an ornament to her sex and the church.

386. "Betsey, wife of Isaac Lee," to church May 9th, 1813, by letter from the church of Christ in New Hartford; she was daughter of Major Peter Curtiss, of Farmington, of Revolutionary memory, and the widow of David Lusk, of New Britain. She married second, Oct. 29th, 1812, No. (168;) her first husband had died July 6th, 1793; he was son of David, senior, and his wife, Prudence (Hurlburt,) and they lived in the valley back of "Dublin Hill." She died Aug. 1st, 1828, aged 64.

HER CHILDREN BY FIRST HUSBAND.

1. Laura, born , married Eli Wood, of Windsor.

2. Austria, born , married Asahel Crow, of New Hartford.

3. Solomon, born 1790, married Nov. 25th, 1809, No. (880.)

387. "Wife of Allen Francis," to church June 6th, 1813—her maiden name, Esther Judd, daughter of Heman, of Farmington, and his wife Anna (Goodrich,) born Feb. 14th, 1771. She married, first, Timothy Hotchkiss, of Wethersfield, a hatter by trade; was divorced, and married, second, May 12th, 1797, Allen, son of Josiah Francis, of Newington, and his wife Milly (Stoddard,) born Oct. 23d, 1760. They lived in Hart quarter, next house north of "Landlord Hart." She died April 9th, 1836, aged 64. He died Feb. 15th, 1850, aged 89.

HER CHILD BY FIRST HUSBAND.

1. William Frederick Hotchkiss, son of Timothy and Esther, born Jan. 1st, 1793; he died, 1829, at Brooklyn, N. Y.

CHILDREN BY SECOND HUSBAND.

1. Bernard, Josiah, born Oct. 9th, 1798, served a clerkship with William H. Imlay, of Hartford, as a merchant; he died in New Orleans.
2. Edwin Judd, born April 22d, 1808, married Sept. 14th, 1825, No. (709.)
3. Sarah Wells, born , bap. Nov. 28th, 1813, died young. All baptized same date.

388. "CANDACE, wife of Solomon Churchill, jun.," to church April 2d, 1815, by letter from church in Worthington, daughter of Hooker Gilbert, and his wife Candace (Sage,) born July 12th, 1791, married Dec. 1st, 1812; he was son of Solomon, sen., No. (240,) and his wife, No. (241,) born Oct. 20th, 1791; he was a tinman by trade, learned of Enoch Kelsey; lived in various localities. She was dismised by letter June 15th, 1817. She died June 9th, 1835. He died May 11th, 1834, aged 43.

THEIR CHILDREN.

1. Laura, born Dec. 26th, 1813, bap. March 20th, 1814, married Giles Colvin, who died in 1835, in Indiana, see No. (753.)
2. William, born Jan. 6th, 1816, bap June 9th, 1816, married Sarah Ann Sedgwick.
3. Sarah, born May 10th, 1818, married Sylvester Elton.
4. Emeline, born Sept. 16th, 1821, married I. Bradley Elton.
5. Gilbert, born Sept. 10th, 1824, died in Illinois.
6. Cyrus, born Dec. 11th, 1826.

389. "BETSEY PENNFIELD," to church Aug. 6th, 1815, daughter of No. (237,) born April 13th, 1793, married Feb. 6th, 1820, Enos Pennfield, son of Jesse, of Plymouth, Ct.; he died at Clarkson, Dec. 23d, 1833, and she married, second, April, 1835, Deacon Joseph Langdon, of Sugar Grove, Pa., where she lived in 1860, or at Russellburg. Her second husband is also dead. She was dismissed by letter to Camden, N. Y., Feb. 6th, 1820. She died at Warren, Pa., Jan. 3d, 1866, aged 72.

390. "DIADAMA STEELE," to church Aug. 6th, 1815, baptized same time, daughter of No. (852) and No. (853,) born Oct. 6th, 1798, married Feb. 8th, 1821, Abraham W. Neal, of Southington, and she was dismissed by letter to church in Southington, March 3d, 1822, and received there April 21st, 1822. He was an extensive wagon maker, formerly at the "South end.' She died May, 1854, aged 55.

THEIR CHILDREN.

1. Salman, born , bap. Aug. 4th, 1822, at Southington.
2. Henry, born , bap. June 27th, 1824, at Southington.
3. Hiram, born , bap. May 29th, 1831, at Southington.
4. Diadamia Maria, born , bap. Aug. 23d, 1825, at Southington.

391. "URSULA, wife of Newton Skinner," to church Aug. 6th, 1815; her maiden name, Wolcott, daughter of Samuel and Jerusha his wife, born Nov. 17th, 1788, at East Windsor; to this church, as above, by letter from the First church in that town; married May 10th, 1815, Rev. Newton Skinner, son of Roswell, of East Granby, and his wife Mary (Gay,) born Oct. 10th, 1782, graduated at Yale, 1804, settled as colleague with Dr. Smalley, Feb. 14th, 1810. He bought the house, soon after his marriage, on the corner of East and Smalley streets, and it has retained his name to this day. She was a woman of grave deportment, strong mind and great economy. He died March 31st, 1825, aged 42, of malignant fever. She was dismissed and recommended to Centre church, Hartford, in 1832.

THEIR CHILDREN.

1. Mary Gay, born Feb. 14th, 1818, bap. March 29th, 1818, married Livermore.
2. Samuel Wolcott, born June 19th, 1820, bap. Aug. 27th, 1820, a physician at Windsor Locks.
3. Ann Grant, born Aug. 23d, 1823, bap. Oct. 12th, 1823.

392. "LUCY, wife of Ethan A. Andrews," to church Aug. 6th, 1815, by letter from the First church in Farmington, daughter of Col. Isaac Cowles, of Farmington, and his wife Lucina (Hooker,) baptized June 14th, 1795, by Rev. Mr. Washburn, and to church in Farmington, Oct. 4th, 1807, married Dec. 19th, 1810, No. (464,) and were both dismissed, Feb. 5th, 1832, and recommended to the Third church in New Haven; She was received again to our communion Feb. 5th, 1860, by letter from South church, New Britain.

393. "SARAH, wife of Simeon Lincoln," to church Oct. 22d, 1815, by letter from church in Wolcott, daughter of No. (1) and No. (96,) born June 19th, 1773, baptized July 25th, 1773, married Oct. 22d, 1792, Rev. Israel B. Woodard, of Wolcott, son of Israel, of Watertown, and his wife Abigail (Stoddard,) born 1767, graduated at Yale 1789, studied theology with Dr. Smalley, settled at Wolcott, and died October, 1810, aged 43. She married, second, 1814, Simeon Lincoln; was occasionally partially insane. After the death of Mr. Lincoln, she lived at the old house of Dr. Smalley and Deacon Whittlesey. She died Oct. 22d, 1843, aged 70. She left no posterity; was the 3d wife of Mr. Lincoln.

394. "ELISHA S. LEWIS," to church Dec. 3d, 1815, by letter from Farmington church. He was a joiner by trade, and learned of Capt. Selah Porter, of Farmington; married Oct. 16th, 1814, No. (455,) lived on "Horse Plain" next north of the Capt. Hotchkiss place. Both dismissed June 30th, 1822, and recommended to the church in Camden, N. Y. He was a native of Plymouth, Ct., and a man of singular eccentricities; he died near Pittsburg, Pa.

THEIR CHILDREN.

1. Marinda, born , married in Pennsylvania.
2. Mary Ann, born , died near Pittsburg.
3. James Wells, born
4. Jane Eliza, born
5. Lucy Maria, born

395. ELIZABETH, wife of Solomon Clark," to church March 17th, 1816, daughter of Elijah Smith, sen., and his wife Sarah (Grimes,) bap. March 23d, 1760, married June 3d, 1784, No. (434.) She died Oct. 7th, 1823, aged 64.

396. "BETSEY, wife of Seth J. North," to church March 17th, 1816, daughter of No. (115) and No. (125,) born July 17th, 1780, married Sept. 27th, 1801, No. (449;) greatly resembles in mind, form and manners her mother. Still (A. D. 1861) living with her son Frederick, and retaining much of the freshness, vigor and vicacity of forty, while she is over eighty; to South church 1842. After this was written (Aug. 1861,) she was suddenly partially deranged, and was taken to the Retreat at Hartford, where now (Dec. 1861,) she remains. She died there Aug. 28th, 1862, aged 82; the last of Col. Gad Stanley's family.

397. "LUCINA, wife of Jesse Hart," to church March 17th, 1816, daughter of Asa Cowdry, of Hartland, Ct., and his wife Abigail (Ensign,) born Sept. 17th, 1788, married April 5th, 1810. No. (430.)

398. "ESTHER DEWY," to church March 17th, 1816, daughter of No. (179) and No. (157,) born 1788, never married; baptized March 30th, 1788; died March 7th, 1852, aged 64; has a head stone in the old part of the cemetery. She had removed her church connection to Harwinton, and returned Aug. 7th, 1825; to South church 1842.

399. "ANNA CLARK," to church March 17th, 1816, daughter of No. (434) and No. (395,) was baptised on admission to church; born March 20th, 1790; never married, lives much of her time with her sister, No. (724.)

400. BETSEY BURRITT," to church March 17th, 1816, daughter of Elihu, and No. (290,) born July 22d, 1796, bap. Nov. 2d, 1800. Betsey Hinsdale, married Aug. 24th, 1829, Hezekiah Seymour, of Hartford, son of Joseph W., and his wife Lovisa (Warner,) born Oct. 29th, 1788. They lived several years in the Burritt house, on the "Hinsdale Lot," then built a cottage on Elm street. He was an Episcopalian, and she joined that communion with him.

THEIR CHILDREN.

1. Infant, born Feb. 20th, 1831, died without a name.
2. Henry Griswold, born May 5th, 1832, died May 20th, 1853, aged 21; an interesting young man, and their only earthly prop and hope.

401. "CHAUNCEY CORNWALL," to church March 17th, 1816, son of No. (296) and No. (297,) born Sept. 22d, 1795, married July 15th, 1819, No. (404;) built west side South Green, house now (1861) owned and occupied by Charles Warner, and his brass shop was the present dwelling house of Henry Nash, Esq. He carried on the manufacture of brass goods extensively for several years. He was appointed deacon in 1837, and served the First Church in that capacity until July 5th, 1842; then to south church. He was one of the early teachers and laborers in the Sunday school cause, a constant and faithful attendant on the ordinances of the Gospel and the means of grace. He unfortunately lost part of one hand by a circular saw, and he also grew somewhat deaf in later life. He died Sept. 18th, 1863, aged 68, of consumption.

THEIR CHILDREN.

1. Jane Adeline, born July 8th, 1820, bap. Sept. 3d, 1820, married No. (915.)
2. Francis Edwards, born Sept. 29th, 1822, bap. March 9th, 1823, No. (799.)
3. Sarah Gilbert, born Aug. 3d, 1824, bap. Oct. 3d, 1824, see No. (935.)
4. Julia Ann, born Nov. 9th, 1827, married Sept. 4th, 1849, William S. Booth; she died March 31st, 1855.
5. Elizabeth Augusta, born May 19th, 1830, bap. Aug. 22d, 1830, married June, 1850, Henry F. Peck.
6. Ellen Sophia, born Feb. 25th, 1833, bap. June 2d, 1833, married Oct. 20th, 1853, Leverett L. Camp.
7. Charles Henry, born April 10th, 1836, bap. 1836; is, 1862, Captain of Company A, 13th regiment C. V., and was successor of Capt. Bidwell, who was discharged at New Orleans.

402. JOHN EELLS," to church Oct. 6th, 1816, by letter from the church in Stockbridge, born July 20th, 1753, to Rev. Edward, of upper Middletown, and his wife Martha (Pitkin,) married March 3d, 1773, Elizabeth Lord, of Middletown; she bore his children and died, when he married, second, Oct. 12th, 1806, Rachel, daughter of No. (113) and No. (114,) born March 20th, 1761, married March 12th, 1792, Capt. Eleazur Curtiss, son of Daniel, born Sept. 3d, 1754; he died July 19th, 1796, aged 42, when she married, second, as above. Mr. Eells was a weaver by trade and occupation; lived on the "New Highway" leading to Hartford from "Stanley quarter." He was dismissed, Nov. 14th, 1821, by letter to Lenox, Mass., where he died, Nov. 3d, 1840, aged 87. She also died there, Nov. 16th, 1835, aged 74.

HIS CHILDREN.

1. Lydia, born July 19th, 1774, died Sept. 27th, 1791.
2. Martha, born Dec. 6th, 1775, died Dec. 28th, 1791.
3. Elizabeth, born Aug. 6th, 1777.
4. John, jun., born May 11th, 1780, died Oct. 17th, 1826.
5. Patience, born Feb. 14th, 1782, died Feb. 8th, 1807.
6. Hannah, born Oct. 22d, 1784, died Nov. 28th, 1791.
7. Erastus, born July 21st, 1790, died Aug. 16th, 1791.

403. "LUCY, wife of Jesse Stanley," to church Oct. 6th, 1816, by letter from the church of Christ in Farmington, daughter of Joseph White, of Whitestown, N. Y., and his wife Lucy (Buckley,) of Wethersfield, born July 22d, 1785; to church in Farmington, 1807, by letter from Whitesborough, N. Y.; married, first, Ornan Clark, of Farmington, who died, when she married, second, as above, May 1st, 1816. She was dismissed, 1842, by letter of recommendation to Farmington church. Mr. Stanley had a previous wife, viz., Almira, daughter of No. (168) and No. (154,) born July 17th, 1780, married Sept. 27th, 1801, died Sept. 29th, 1815, aged 35. Mr. Stanley's first wife was a most amiable and benevolent woman, but in feeble health, and lost all her children in infancy. He was a very successful farmer, and lived where now, 1862, Thomas Tracy owns and resides, the house built by Thomas Stanley, 4th, (son of Thomas, 3d, and brother of Lot.) This Thomas, 4th, married Anna Fords, of Wethersfield, who died 1787, leaving two children, when he married, second, Mixanda Nott, and had twelve children by her. She died 1851, at Marietta, Ohio, where the family moved to from here, 1787.

CHILDREN OF ORNAN CLARK AND HIS WIFE LUCY (WHITE.)

1. Henry White, born Feb. 23d, 1807, at Farmington, see No. (628.)
2. Sarah, born July 18th, 1809, see No. (712.)

JESSE STANLEY'S CHILDREN BY ALMIRA.

1. Philip, born Nov. 4th, 1802, died Sept. 2d, 1803.
2. Philip, 2d of name, born Nov. 30th, 1804, died May 31st, 1805.
3. George, born Nov. 1st, 1807, died April 2d, 1808.
4. Waldo, born March 8th, 1811, died April 9th, 1811.
5. Son born Jan. 16th, 1814, died without a name.
6. daughter born Sept. 11th, 1815, died without a name.

HIS CHILDREN BY LUCY.

7. } twins, born March 20th, 1818, { son, died, aged three weeks.
8. } twins, born March 20th, 1818, { Almira, bap. June 21st, 1818, see No. (844.)
9. Margaret, born Nov. 26th, 1820, bap. May 13th, 1821, see No. (843.)
10. Oliver Cromwell, born Feb. 23d, 1823, bap. June 15th, 1823, married Oct. 13th, 1847, No. (1027.) The father, Jesse Stanley, died Aug. 19th, 1827, aged 48. Lucy, his widow, died April 13th, 1863, at Brooklyn, N. Y., in her 78th year, but buried in New Britain cemetery.

404. "MARY COSSLETT," to church Jan. 26th, 1817, daughter of Francis, and No. (636,) born Nov. 3d, 1791, baptized (Mary Goodrich) June 28th, 1801, by Rev. J. Belden, at Newington; married July 15th, 1818, No. (401;) a discreet, worthy woman, of great diligence and firm Christian principles; to South church 1842.

405. "ESTHER HART," to church Jan. 26th, 1817, daughter of No. (131) and No. (132,) born March 5th, 1798, married March 16th, 1819, Edwin Gridley, of Southington. She was dismissed by letter and received there Dec. 5th, 1819. He was born June 21st, 1797, to Noah of

Southington, and his wife Luana (Andrus,) of Josiah. He was a farmer, and died October 3d, 1852, aged 55.

THEIR CHILDREN.

1. Levi Andrus, born July 15th, 1820, married April 13th, 1842, Rosanna Dunham; he died June 13th, 1844.

2. Marietta, born June 14th, 1823, died Dec. 19th, 1825.

3. Infant, born April 26th, 1827, died April 26th, 1827.

4. Ellen Eliza, born Jan. 10th, 1830, died Jan. 19th, 1842, aged 12 years 9 days.

5. Sarah Hart, born January 16th, 1836, married Dec. 24th, 1854, Henry, son of Henry Lewis, of Southington; 1st Lieut. Co. K, 20th Reg. C. V.

406. "SALMON STEELE," to church Jan. 26th, 1817, and baptized same time; was son of Ebenezer, jun., and his wife Lucy (Wright,) born April 7th, 1780; was a brass founder by trade, learned of Barton, of Wintonbury; married Nov. 29th, 1803, Nelly Williams, of West Brookfield, Mass., daughter of Samuel, and his wife Nelly (Wright,) born Sept. 12th, 1786. They lived in various localities, raised a large family on small means. He was a soldier in the war of 1812, and was in the battle of Lundy's Lane. He fell under censure of the church, and, April 12th, 1824, they, after much labor and delay, passed sentence of excommunication. He was a skillful mechanic, with an active and inventive mind. He died June 22d, 1836, aged 55. His widow lives now, 1863, in Almont, Lapeer county, Mich., with her son.

THEIR CHILDREN.

1. Samuel Williams, born April 20th, 1805, bap. June 22d, 1817, married Nov. 6th, 1833, Clarissa Andrews; he married, second, Lucina Merrell; married, third, He is an ordained minister of the Baptist denomination, and lives in Romulus, Mich.

2. Mary Darling, born March 10th, 1807, bap. June 22, 1817, married Sept. 1st, 1836, Philip Recor, see No. (742.)

3. Ebenezer, born Oct. 18th, 1808, bap. June 22d, 1817, married Mary Pilgrim; a Methodist preacher.

4. William Moloneaux, born March 7th, 1811, bap. June 22d, 1817, married Elizabeth Bradley; he is a shoe-maker.

5. Salmon, born Nov. 12th, 1812, bap. June 22d, 1817, married Eliza Morgan; married, second, Adelaide Lamberton; he is a Methodist preacher, and presiding elder at North Port, Mich.

6. Marinda, born Feb. 25th, 1816, bap. June 22d, 1817, died unmarried, aged 25, at Hartford.

7. Jason, born Aug. 24th, 1817, bap. Oct. 12th, 1817, married Marinda Rigley, he is a Methodist preacher.

8. Emri, born Sept. 25th, 1819, bap. Sept. 17th, 1820, married Laura Judd, daughter of No. (459.) He was ordained to the work of a Gospel minister March 10th, 1853, and now, 1863, resides at Imlay, Mich.

9. Martha, born May 31st, 1821, bap. Sept. 9th, 1821, married William Wilson, of New York state; lives in Iowa.

10. Amzi Hart, born April 14th, 1823, married Oct 30th, 1843, Laura Ann Miller; she died Dec. 22d, 1862.

11. Albert Lewis, born March 10th, 1826, married Nov. 3d, 1853, Mary F. Hyde; is a cabinet maker and lives in Almont, Lapier county, Michigan.

407. "OZIAS HART, jun.," to church Jan. 26th, 1817, son of No. (281) and No. (282,) born Dec. 9th, 1793, married Nov. 15th, 1816, No. (410,) who died at St. Louis, when he married, second, Jan. 25th, 1831, Triphena Elmer, who died March, 1845, when he married, third, Jan. 11th, 1852, widow Mary Conover; she died May 2d, 1858. He left this place in 1819; was never dismissed, and lives now, 1861, in Buffalo, and has seen much trouble in life.

THEIR CHILDREN.

1. Emily Eliza, born Jan. 8th, 1818, bap. April 12th, 1818, at New Britain.
2. George Henry, born March, 1819, bap. April 25th, 1819 at New Britain.
3. William Otis, born 1821.
4. Charles Augustus, born Oct. 30th, 1837, died April, 1842.
5. Willard Otis, born Feb. 13th, 1838.
6. Sarah Ann, born March 5th, 1845; living in Illinois, 1860.

408. "OTIS HART," to church Jan. 26th, 1817, brother of No. (407,) born February, 1800, died July 1st, 1819, aged 19.

409. Wife of Charles Wright," to church April 6th, 1817, by letter from the Third church in Wethersfield; her maiden name, Abigail Marsh, daughter of John, of Wethersfield, and Abigail (Buckley,) his wife, born Oct. 16th, 1756. They moved into this parish in 1817, and lived on Dr. Smalley's farm on the South Mountain. He died Jan. 23d, 1829, aged 76. He was the son of Justice and Ann (Williams,) his wife, who is said to have been grand-daughter of Eunice Standish, of pilgrim memory. The widow Abigail died, Aug. 11th, 1842, aged 86.

THEIR CHILDREN.

1. Lois, born Dec. 16th, 1777, married Salmon Booth, son of Elisha, jun.
2. Rhoda, born Oct. 16th, 1779, married Aaron Belden, of Rocky Hill.
3. Selden, born March 29th, 1782, married Anna Cole, daughter of Selah, Nov. 25th, 1802.
4. Mehitable, born June 16th, 1784, married Barzillai Dickinson, of Rocky Hill.
5. Abigail, born Sept. 3d, 1786, married Sylvester Belden of Rocky Hill.
6. Miriam, born May 7th, 1789, married Orrin Dickinson, brother of Sylvester.
7. Lucy, born April 22d, 1792, married Amos Flint, of Rome, N. Y.
8. Harvey, born Aug. 23d, 1794, married No. (590.)
9. Maria, born March 29th, 1797, married October 30th, 1817, Ira Steele; she No. (910.)
10. Electa, born 1800, died in infancy.

410. "PAMELA, wife of Ozias Hart, jun.," to church April 6th, 1817, by letter from the church in Durham; her maiden name, Baggs, married Nov. 15th, 1816, No. (407,) and died at St. Louis; took no letter of dismissal and recommendation.

411. "CLARISSA, wife of Alvin North," to church June 1st, 1817, baptized same time, daughter of Oliver Burnham, Esq., of Cornwall, and his wife, Sarah (Rodgers,) born June 7th, 1788, married May 1st, 1816, No. (330;) has a friendly disposition, and much Christian charity; to South church, 1842.

412. "LYDIA HART," to church June 1st, 1817, daughter of No. (293) and No. (294,) born May 13th, 1796, married Nov. 25th, 1818, John C. Root, of Farmington, son of Ezekiel and Cynthia Cole, of Kensington; she was dismissed and recommended to Farmington church, by letter, July 31st, 1819, and from there, 1823, to Harwinton church; they subsequently moved to Ohio; he a shoe-maker; she living, 1865, at Talmadge, Ohio; he died Dec. 10th, 1862, aged 67.

ONLY CHILD OF JOHN C. AND LYDIA ROOT.

George Hart Root, born May 21st, 1833, married Oct. 7th, 1856, P. Marie Upson, of Talmadge, Ohio.

413. "ELIJAH FRANCIS," to church Aug. 3d, 1817, son of No. (91) and No. (92,) born Jan. 6th, 1760, consequently was more than fifty-five years of age at his conversion; his convictions were pungent and distressing, but he was a remarkable instance of the renewing and regenerating grace of God; he was evidently constrained to testify of the great goodness and mercy of God, in his own experience, being extremely diffident naturally. He was a shoe-maker and tanner by trade; learned of Deacon Timothy Stanley; was in the Revolutionary army at sixteen years of age, as a teamster. He lived in the valley east of "Osgood Hill;" was elected deacon of the church July 19th, 1822. He represented the town of Berlin in the legislature several times. He married Dec. 21st, 1785, No. (221,) but left no posterity. He gave thirty dollars towards the cost of our communion service; he loved Zion, and prayed much for her welfare. He was one of the constituents of the South church, 1842. He died Oct. 30th, 1846, aged 87. He seldom spoke in public, but was gifted in prayer; he wept, mourned and sighed over the delinquencies of the church and the sins of the world.

414. "MARY, wife of Ebenezer Gridley," to church Nov. 9th, 1817, daughter of No. (138) and No. (139,) born Dec. 27th, 1778, married April 23d, 1800; he son of Seth, of Plainville, and his wife, Esther (Blakesley,) of East Haven, born July 2d, 1780, occupied the home of her father; was a man of wonderful memory; had an active mind, but abused his faculties. He died at the alms-house, April 26th, 1860, aged 79. She was a pious, good woman, careful to attend upon the means of grace; she died Oct. 16th, 1856, aged 78; she was one of the constituent members of the South church, 1842.

THEIR CHILDREN.

1. Betsey, born March 4th, 1801, bap. Oct. 18th, 1818, never married; lives, 1862, in Hartford.

2. Hannah Dunham, born June 16th, 1802, bap. Oct. 18th, 1818, married Peter McVoy.

3. Infant, born , died Feb. 19th, 1804.

4. Nancy, born , married a Brooks.

5. Julia, born , died Sept., 1809.

6. Delia, born 1810, died Aug. 22d, 1811, aged one year.

7. Walter Blakesley, born June 3d, 1812, bap. Oct. 18th, 1818, married Feb. 14th, 1840, Mary Hunter, daughter of Roswell.

8. David Mather, born Aug. 28th, 1816, bap. Oct. 18th, 1818; went to parts unknown.

9. Edward, } twins. { born Aug. 8th, 1818, bap. Oct. 18th, 1818, drowned in James river, Virginia, near Norfolk, 1834.

10. Edwin, } twins. { b. Aug. 8th, 1818, bap. Oct. 18th, 1818, a brass-worker, No. (808.)

415. "ROSETTA, wife of Salmon Hart," to church April 26th, 1818, by letter from church in Kensington, daughter of Seth North, of Berlin and Eunice (Woodford,) his wife, born Sept. 15th, 1778; she to church in Kensington, June, 1805, as the widow of Elisha Williams, and baptized on admission; she married second, June 2d, 1817, No. (441,) by whom she had two sons; she was married to her first husband, Feb., 1802, before Rev. Benoni Upson, and had two sons; he died March 9th, 1809, aged 36, at Kensington; she has been a woman of much labor and sorrow; to South church, 1842; she died Oct. 6th, 1863, aged 85, at the house of her son, Albert.

HER SONS BY HER FIRST HUSBAND.

1. Albert, born Nov. 14th, 1802, married April 14th, 1824, Thirza Steele, daughter of Selah, see No. (676.)

2. Henry, born Aug. 11th, 1807, bap. Nov. 1st, 1807, at Kensington, married June 30th, 1840, No (759.)

416. "PHEBE, wife of John S. Whittlesey," to church May 3d, 1818, by letter from the church at Southington, daughter of Selah Barnes, of Southington, and his wife, Nancy (Cowles,) born April 3d, 1795, to church in Southington, Feb. 5th, 1815, baptized same time; they lived where Harlowe Eddy (now, 1866,) does, District No. 4, by the school-house; he son of Roger, Esq., of Southington, and his wife, Anna (Smalley,) born July 13th, 1794; had no trade or special occupation; he died July 1st, 1832, aged 38; she dismissed and by letter recommended, 1841, to the first church in New Haven; she was a woman of rare excellence; died June 3d, 1865, aged 75.

THEIR CHILDREN.

1. Sarah Lincoln, born Nov. 7th, 1817, bap. May 10th, 1818, married June 6th, 1847, Rev. Jesse Guernsey, of Dubuque; she died there, May 10th, 1855.

2. Charles Barnes, born Sept. 13th, 1820, bap. June 3d, 1821, married Oct. 21st, 1851, Eliza Antoinette Wilcoxon, of New Haven; he a druggist at New Haven.

417. "GEORGE BURRITT," to church June 7th, 1818, son of Elihu and No. (290,) born Dec. 5th, 1800, died Aug. 22d, 1822, aged 22, in Georgia; a young man of good promise to his friends, and of great hope for himself; his bones lie in that "great charnel house" of young men of the north, where the aspirations, enterprise and high hopes of multitudes of others lie in silence, waiting and listening for the last trumpet to sound.

418. "EMILY BURRITT," to church June 7th, 1818, sister of No. (417,) born Aug. 12th, 1798, married 1838, Capt. Taylor, of Texas, before of New York city, the captain of the vessel that carried a colony from this place to Texas the previous year. She had one child, but the mother and child died, 1839, at Galveston. She was a tailoress by occupation; was industrious and intellectual.

419. "NANCY, wife of Thomas Eddy," to church Oct. 4th, 1818, by letter from the church at Farmington, daughter of Phineas Hamblin, of Farmington, and his wife, Rhoda (Andrus,) born Aug. 3d, 1789, baptized Aug. 16th, 1795, at Farmington, by Rev. Mr. Marsh, of Wethersfield, and to church there, October, 1813. He was son of Charles, senior, and Hannah (Kelsey,) his wife; married Abi Lewis, Nov. 5th, 1802, daughter of No. (88) and No. (111;) she died May 6th, 1814, when he married second, Sept. 18th, 1814, as above; she died Sept., 1852, at Lama, Pennsylvania, and my informant says, with very clear views of her future good estate. He died May 28th, 1830, aged 52.

THEIR CHILDREN.

1. Philip, born March 5th, 1804, married May 7th, 1828, Sarah Pitkin, of East Hartford; he died, 1863.
2. Henry, born Oct. 1st, 1805, see No. (582.)
3. Julia, born June, 1807, see No. (596.)
4. Abi Lewis, born Sept. 1st, 1811, married Oct. 6th, 1831, Charles Parker, of Meriden; she was bap. Nov. 1st, 1818, in New Britain, on her step-mother's account.

SECOND WIFE'S CHILDREN.

5. Thomas Hamblin, born April 2d, 1815, bap. Nov. 1st, 1818, married Sept. 29th, 1833, Sarah M. Moses, of Canton, Conn.
6. Walter Bartholomew, born May, 1818, bap. Nov. 1st, 1818, married Mary A. Judson, 1837.
7. Dolly Jones, born July, 1822, bap. Nov. 3d, 1822, married Jan. 2d, 1836, Charles Blakeslee.
8. Benjamin Franklin, born Sept. 17th, 1826, married Nov. 4th, 1849, Emeline L. Curtiss, of No. (362.)
9. Jeremiah A., born , died at Southington.
10. Anthony, born 1829, died March 14th, 1830, aged nine months.

420. "MOSES D. SEYMOUR," to church April 4th, 1819, son of Aaron, of West Hartford, and Anna (Phelps,) of Litchfield, his wife, born June 3d, 1782; a clothier by trade; learned of the Talcotts, in West Hartford; married Jan. 29th, 1807, No. (421;) he built, and for several years occu-

pied the house at the south end of the village, (now, 1865,) owned and occupied by James Andrews; he had his clothier's shop near the bridge, on the Gilbert river, a branch of the Mattabesset; he also built a house at the foot of "Dublin Hill," where he spent his last days; he could turn his hand usefully to various handicraft; was an athletic man; he died July 7th, 1839, aged 57.

421. "ABIGAIL, wife of Moses D. Seymour," to church June 6th, 1819, daughter of No. (118) and No. (119,) born Oct. 28th, 1786; she died March 16th, 1858, aged 71, at Hartford, but buried in New Britain cemetery, and a neat stone tells where she lies. A discreet and worthy woman.

THEIR CHILDREN.

1. Orson Hart, born Sept. 1st, 1807, bap. June 6th, 1819, married Sept. 17th, 1827, No. (656.)

2. } 3. } Infant twin sons, died March 17th, 1809.

4. Mary Ann, born July 8th, 1811, died March 7th, 1813, aged twenty months.

5. Mary Ann, born Oct. 4th, 1813, bap. June 6th, 1819, married Jan. 8th, 1844, William Palmer, see No. (668.)

6. Henry Phelps, born Aug. 2d, 1818, bap. June 6th, 1819, married Jan. 31st, 1844, Laura A. Pierce; she died, when he married second, May 8th, 1848, Isabel O. Taylor.

7. Oliver De Witt, born Dec. 31st, 1820, bap. June 17th, 1821, married Oct. 18th, 1843, Harriet H. Marsh; he is the popular constable and collector of the town of Hartford, 1862.

422. "ABIGAIL, wife of Cyrus Stanley," to church June 6th, 1819, daughter of No. (168) and No. (154,) born May 14th, 1788, married Sept. 7th, 1806; he son of No. (115) and No. (125,) born July 29th, 1787; he inherited the home of his father, in Stanley quarter; carried on the coopering business, in the days of "corn meal for the West Indies;" also brass business, but failed and came to her father's home in the village, where he died March 25th, 1844, aged 57. He enlisted as an officer into the State troops in the war of 1812; was a farmer and surveyor; of quick, active mind, vigorous body, and versatile genius. She died August 1st, 1867, in her 80th year, in Cleaveland, Ohio, at the residence of her son, No. (628.)

THEIR CHILDREN.

1. Don Alonzo, born June 24th, 1807, bap. June 13th, 1819, see No. (716.)

2. Emily Rowena, born Sept. 11th, 1810, bap. June 13th, 1819, see No. (659.)

3. Charles Norton, born Aug. 18th, 1812, bap. June 13th, 1819, married Feb. 15th, 1821, Eliza S. Moore.

4. Harriet Aurora, born March 25th, 1815, bap. June 13th, 1819, see No. (908.)

5. Isaac Lee, born Dec. 29th, 1817, bap. June 13th, 1819.

6. Gad, born April 17th, 1821, bap. June 17th, 1821, married May 11th, 1846, Fanny Moore; he died Aug. 5th, 1858, aged 39.

7. Amzi, born Nov. 27th, 1823, bap. April 4th, 1824, see No. (848.)

423. "Daniel Smith," to church Oct. 3d, 1819, son of Daniel, of Kensington, and Sabra (Winchel,) his wife, born Dec., 1781, bap. Dec. 24th, 1783, married Nov. 11th, 1804, No. (424;) he a cabinet-maker by trade; owned the house on the corner, near Chester Hart's, on the Shuttle Meadow road; the house burned; he died Aug. 16th, 1821, in Georgia, aged 40.

424. "Wife of Daniel Smith," to church Oct. 3d, 1819, and baptized same time, daughter of Patty Warner, born March 19th, 1781; an energetic woman; went out nursing after she was eighty years of age; she died Aug. 1st, 1864, aged 83.

THEIR CHILDREN.

1. Lorenzo, born April, 1805, bap. Oct. 17th, 1819, married Elenora Hinman; he died March 5th, 1835, aged 30.

2. Susan, born Dec. 7th, 1811, bap. Oct. 17th, 1819, married Albert Boyington, of Southwick, No. (667.)

3. Ann Jane, born Aug. 17th, 1813, bap. Oct. 17th, 1819, married Nov. 29th, 1835, No. (926.)

4. George, born 1816, died Jan. 24th, 1817, aged six months.

5. George, born 1817, bap. Oct. 17th, 1819; killed on the railroad, Oct. 6th, 1843, aged 26.

425. "Joseph H. Flagg," to church Oct. 3d, 1819, son of Solomon and his wife, Olive (Hart,) married Dec. 1st, 1805, Abi, daughter of Ladwick Hotchkiss and No. (278,) born Aug. 15th, 1784; she died July 21st, 1812, aged 28, when he married second, March 17th, 1817, widow of Timothy Percival, of Kensington, (alias) Aurelia Booth, daughter of No. (165) and No. (166;) she married Dec. 8th, 1801, Timothy Percival, son of James and Dorothy (Gates,) his wife; he was uncle to the poet, and died Nov. 6th, 1808; Mr. Flagg was a shoe-maker; he was born Sept. 15th, 1783; was grand-son of No. (263;) lived in various localities; was brother of No. (906,) and died April 22d, 1853, aged 70; had a mild, happy disposition; was honest and conscientious; his birth-place, "Lower Lane," Berlin.

426. "Wife of Joseph H. Flagg," to church Oct. 3d, 1819, see No. (425;) she died Aug. 25th, 1828, aged 48; she was second wife of No. (425,) born 1781.

HER CHILDREN BY TIMOTHY PERCIVAL, HER FIRST HUSBAND.

1. Dorothy, born Jan. 16th, 1803, married Sept. 14th, 1825, Edwin Francis; she No. (709.)

2. Caroline, born 1805, died, aged fourteen months.

HER CHILDREN BY NO. (425,) HER SECOND HUSBAND.

1. Thankful Winchel, born Dec. 23d, 1818, died May 15th, 1819, aged seven mo's.

2. Joseph Beckley, born Feb. 23d, 1820; learned jeweller's trade; died July 11th, 1838, aged 18.

3. William Wallace, born Aug. 11th, 1821, bap. Oct. 14th, 1821; a tinman; married Mary Ann Wilcox, July 25th, 1845; she daughter of Jeremiah and his wife, Dorothy Fitts, of West Hartford.

427. "MEHITABEL, wife of Theodore Riley," to church Oct. 3d, 1819, daughter of Ambrose Fuller, of Burlington, and Rhoda (Williams,) of Berlin, his wife, born Nov. 14th, 1782, married Jan. 18th, 1808; he son of John, of Northampton, and Huldah (Porter,) of Kensington, his wife, born April 7th, 1775; he was in early life a tin-peddler, and traveled south; he sold the Alvin North place for $1,000, A. D. 1800, and bought out Thomas Lee, who then owned the place on West Main street, where Mr. Pettis, now, 1866, owns and occupies; she died Feb. 26th, 1824, aged 52; he was a large, fine looking man, and after early life a farmer; was somewhat deaf, and helpless late in life, with rheumatism; he died March 2d, 1855, aged 80; he was a blacksmith by trade; learned of James North, Esq.

THEIR CHILDREN.

1. Huldah, born Jan. 5th, 1809, died Jan. 19th, 1809, aged fourteen days.
2. Infant, born June 30th, 1800, died Aug. 10th, 1810, aged one month, ten days.
3. Aurora, born May 19th, 1812, died March 5th, 1813, aged ten months.
4. Electa, born April 12th, 1815, bap. May 14th, 1820, married 1838, Lucius T. Cadwell; lives in Ohio.
5. Chloe, born Jan. 25th, 1818, bap. May 14th, 1820, see No. (991.)
6. Theodore, born Oct. 16th, 1820, married first, Hester Taylor; married second, Lydia Sharon; he lives, 1861, in Ohio.

428. "LUCY, wife of Miles C. Winchell," to church Oct. 3d, 1819, daughter of Salmon Hollister, of Berlin, and Sarah (Whaples,) of Newington, his first wife, born May 6th, 1774, married March, 1793; they lived on "Horse Plain," opposite Capt. Hotchkiss; he peddled tin and pewter ware for a living, and raised a large family; he died June 10th, 1844, aged 70; he was son of Dan, of Kensington, and Lois Curtiss, of Jonathan, of Wallingford, his wife, born March 20th, 1774, baptized April 10th, 1774, at Kensington; she to South church, 1842.

THEIR CHILDREN.

1. Willys, born Jan. 25th, 1794, married Nov. 26th, 1818, Sally Osgood, of Deacon John.
2. Chauncey, born Feb. 25th, 1796, married Mary Vibbert, of Vernon.
3. Whiting, born Jan. 6th, 1798, died Jan. 20th, 1798.
4. Albert, born Jan. 24th, 1799, married in Georgia; lives there.
5. Orrin, born May 30th, 1801, married Louisa Bristol, of Cheshire; second, Sophia Carrington.
6. Ira, born Nov. 13th, 1803, bap. Oct. 24th, 1819; never married; lives in New Britain.
7. James H., born June 16th, 1806, bap. Oct. 24th, 1819, No. (543.)
8. Lucy Maria, born Oct. 16th, 1808, bap. Oct. 24th, 1819, No. (535.)
9. Eliza, born Dec. 27th, 1812, bap. Oct. 24th, 1819, married Isaac Sanford, of Vernon.
10. Russel Hollister, born March 6th, 1817, bap. Oct. 24th, 1819, married Jane Stannard; he died Feb. 4th, 1857, aged 39.

429. "THESTA ANDREWS," to church Oct. 3d, 1819, daughter of No. (313) and No. (314,) born Dec. 16th, 1798, married Nov. 27th, 1823, Bryan Porter, of Farmington, son of Samuel and his wife, Abigail (Hamblin;) she was dismissed, and by letter recommended to Farmington, 1824; she died Jan. 25th, 1828, aged 30; she left one daughter, Ann, born Dec. 9th, 1825, and died Dec., 1854, aged 27, unmarried.

430. "JESSE HART," to church Oct. 3d, 1819, son of No. (181) and No. (182,) born April 20th, 1789, married April 5th, 1810, No. (397;) he died Feb. 21st, 1825, aged 36; he a blacksmith by trade; learned in Hartland, of Orrin Lee; his shop where now, 1863, the Baptist church stands, and his residence still standing, next west of the Bank building.

THEIR CHILDREN.

1. Artemas E., born Feb. 11th, 1812, bap. May 5th, 1816, No. (622.)
2. Lucina, born Dec. 3d, 1821, bap. April 21st, 1822, No. (937.)

431. FRANCES, wife of Osmyn Booth," to church June 5th, 1820, by letter from second church, in Hartford, daughter of Josiah Hempsted, of Hartford, and his wife, Polly (Hempsted,) of New London, first cousins, married Dec. 22d, 1819, No. (673;) she died Nov. 3d, 1833, aged 42; to church in Hartford, 1814.

432. "ELIZABETH, wife of John Pennfield," to church Feb. 4th, 1821, baptized same time, daughter of Roger Hart and Sybil (Robinson,) of Middletown, his wife, born Sept. 17th, 1791, married March 12th, 1815, No. (373,) died Oct. 21st, 1849, aged 58; was a zealous, warm-hearted Christian; she joined the Methodist church with her husband, and our watch was withdrawn, Dec. 1st, 1831. The Christian Advocate and Journal of January 3d, 1850, had an article from the pen of Rev. A. Rushmore, her pastor during her last sickness, stating that "she died of cancer, but in the triumphs of faith, and hope of future glory."

433. "ELMINA RUGG," to church Feb. 4th, 1821, baptized same time, daughter of Matthew and Polly (Webb,) of Salem, Conn., his wife, born March 27th, 1803, married April 27th, 1826, Erastus Kilbourn, of Newington; he, 1861, post-master; lives near the church.

REVIVAL OF 1821.

434. "SOLOMON CLARK," to church Aug. 5th, 1821, son of Joseph and Sarah (Curtiss,) his wife, born 1758, baptized April 5th, 1758, by Rev. Ebenezer Booge, of Northington, while supplying our pulpit, (see his record;) this was two weeks previous to the organizing the first church in New Britain parish. He inherited the home of his father, on East street, where now, 1861, Edwin Clark, his grand-son, owns and lives; he was a farmer and successful; was over sixty years of age when converted; his case was marked with great distress, and happy issue. He died March

29th, 1824, aged 66. He married, June 3d, 1784, No. (395.) He had been a constant attendant at public worship, and a conscientious man through all his life, yet his convictions were extremely severe and pungent.

THEIR CHILDREN.

1. Chauncey, born April 15th, 1787, see No. (477.)
2. Anna, born March 20th, 1790, No. (399.)
3. Infant, born , died
4 Betsey, born Dec. 20th, 1794, see No. (724.)

435. "DANIEL JUDD," to church Aug. 5th, 1821, born Aug. 14th, 1761, to No. (38) and his wife, Hannah (Andrews,) married Irene, daughter of Amos Hitchcock, of Southington, and Azuba (Cook,) widow of Samuel Benham, his wife, born 1767, bap. June 7th, 1767, and died June 17th, 1790, aged 23, leaving two children, when he married, second, No. (436.) He was a farmer and inherited the home of his father and grandfather on East street, and this was formerly the extreme north end of the "Great Swamp parish." He was a kind, obliging man, with a large share of genial and social qualities. He, in company with No. (195,) owned the saw-mill near O. B. North's factory, known as "Judd's mill." He died Oct. 17th, 1834, aged 73.

436. "HANNAH, wife of Daniel Judd," to church August 5th, 1821, daughter of Abraham Bartholomew, of Farmington, and Eunice (Orvice,) his wife, born April 19th, 1766, married No. (435,) and was his second wife. She died January 20th, 1838, aged 72. She was tall and good looking, with a kind heart and Christian principles.

THEIR CHILDREN.

1. William, born Dec. 9th, 1787, married April 23d, 1807, Polly Eddy, No. (524.)
2. Daniel, born April 14th, 1790, married Oct. 11th, 1815, Abigail Squire.

CHILDREN BY SECOND WIFE.

3. Irene, born Nov. 13th, 1793, married Dec. 5th, 1819, John Ellis; she No. (956.)
4. Polly, born Dec. 15th, 1795, married April 23d, 1823, No. (376.)
5. Eri, born Jan. 13th, 1798, married Jan. 21st, 1819, Lovisa Bronson of Elijah; he died Feb. 15th, 1862.
6. Amon, born Oct. 27th, 1800, married Aug. 4th, 1824, No. (506.)
7. Betsey, born Aug. 13th, 1804, bap. Nov. 11th, 1821, married Oct. 3d, 1832, Henry Gladden.
8. Richard, born January 23d, 1807, bap. Nov. 11th, 1821, see No. (1119.)
9. Rhoda, born Nov. 4th, 1809, bap. Nov. 11th, 1821, married July 28th, 1830, William Hart, of Stephen; she died Sept. 3d, 1856, when he married, second, May 26th, 1857, No. (663.)

437. "DOLLY, wife of Lemuel Smith," to church August 5th, 1821, daughter of No. (29) and No. (30,) baptized April 29th, 1764, married Oct. 10th, 1790. He was son of No. (8) and No. (9), born March 11th,

1759 ; a tall man, of commanding form and manners, and was many years teacher and leader in church music, and appropriations of some $30 to $50 per year were made by the Ecclesiastical society for his services. He lived, immediately after his marriage, in an old house on the corner, directly opposite the present school house in South-east district, formerly the home of John Kelsey. He built the house where Dr. Smalley and Deacon Whittlesey lived and died. He afterwards built on the corner north of the school-house in Shipman district, where he died, Jan. 17th, 1839; aged 80. She died March 11th, 1836, aged 74.

THEIR CHILDREN.

1. Anson, born 1791 ; traveled south ; died here Oct. 2d, 1825, aged 34.
2. Desdemona, born 1797, see No. (487.)
3. Lester, born , never married, died near Kaskaskia, Ill., aged 23.
4. Bela, born 1800, never married, died near Kaskaskia, October, 1826, aged 26. These two brothers went west together.

438. "ADNA STANLEY," to Church Aug. 5th, 1821, son of No. (14) and Ruth (Norton,) his wife, born Jan. 28th, 1763 ; graduated at Yale in 1787, was a successful physician in this place, and carried on farming ; lived in the Stanley quarter ; house was vacated by his brother Seth and built by him, 1773, as marked on the chimney. Dr. Stanley was a man of few words, dignified appearance and manners, of correct habits, sound and vigorous mind. He left a large estate, and died Dec. 30th, 1825, aged 62. He married April 26th, 1809, No. (1294.) He taught school in 1788, in Stanley district.

THEIR CHILDREN.

1. Julia Ann, born Feb. 12th, 1810, bap. Sept. 23d, 1821, married Dec. 21st, 1830, No. (746.)
2. Augusta, born Nov. 3d, 1811, bap. Sept. 23d, 1821, died October 11th, 1834, aged 22.
3. Sophia, born June 14th, 1813, bap. Sept. 23d, 1821, see No. (1296.)
4. Nancy, born Aug. 18th, 1815, bap. Sept. 23d, 1821, married Nov. 15th, 1838, John H. Goodwin, of Hartford ; she died Jan. 15th, 1849, in her 34th year, when he married, second, No. (937.)
5. Cordelia, born Jan. 23d, 1820, bap. Sept. 23d, 1821, see No. (940.)

439. " SETH LEWIS," to church Aug. 5th, 1821, son of No. (88) and No (111,) born May 3d, 1772, married Feb. 15th, 1795, No. (440 ;) he was a tinman by trade, and lived on East street, near " Landlord Smith." He afterwards bought the farm of " Capt. Belden's." He was dismissed by letter, Dec. 18th, 1843, to Presbyterian church in Philadelphia, where he died, Feb. 2d, 1849, aged 77.

440. " LYDIA, wife of Seth Lewis," to church, Aug. 5th, 1821, daughter of Thomas Wright, of Newington, and Esther (Andrus,) daughter of

Caleb, his wife, born May 14th, 1772, bap. May 24th, 1772, at Newington, by Rev. J. Belden, married Feb. 15th, 1795, No. (439;) dismissed by letter to Presbyterian church in Philadelphia, Dec. 18th, 1843, where she died, Aug. 17th, 1858, aged 86.

THEIR CHILDREN.

1. George W., born Dec. 20th, 1803, died Oct. 12th, 1810.
2. William Goodwin, born March 8th, 1806, see No. (595.)

441. "SALMON HART," to church August 5th, 1821, son of No. (140) and No. (141,) born May 20th, 1775, married May 2d, 1796, No. (347;) she died Aug. 2d, 1815, aged 38, when he married, second, June, 1817, No. (415.) He inherited the home of his father and grandfather, opposite the school house in South-west district; sold his farm to Henry Williams, and spent the last years of his life with his son Frederick, in the village. He was lame for many years with rheumatism; to South church 1842. He died Sept. 18th, 1857, aged 82; a kind and obliging neighbor.

THEIR CHILDREN.

1. Sarah Woodruff, born May 24th, 1798, bap. August 11th, 1811, died Jan. 27th, 1813.
2. Orpha, born April 2d, 1800, bap. Aug. 11th, 1811, married May 2d, 1820, Ira Hart; married, second, No. (465.)
3. Lavinia, born Sept. 1st, 1802, bap. Aug. 11th, 1811, married Dec. 9th, 1824, Samuel A. Hamblin.
4. Sophia, born Nov. 18th, 1806, bap. Aug. 11th, 1811, married July 3d, 1826, Ralph I. Dunham.
5. Salmon North, born June 18th, 1811, bap. Aug. 11th, 1811, married May 3d, 1832, Martha Corning; she died, when he married, second, Dec. 14th, 1846, Joanna F. Gardner. He is a carriage maker and now, 1863, resides in Hartford.

SECOND WIFE'S CHILDREN.

6. Silas Williams, born Sept. 12th, 1818, bap. Nov. 15th, 1818, married Nov. 24th, 1846, Abigail Merwin.
7. Frederick Woodford, born Nov. 19th, 1822, bap. June 29th, 1823, married June 2d, 1857, Jennie Maria Bassett, daughter of William; he was a Captain in the war of the rebellion, 1861.

442. "IRA STANLEY," to church Aug. 5th, 1821, baptised same time, son of Lot, and Rhoda (Wadsworth,) of Farmington, his wife, born Oct. 12th, 1773, married Abi, daughter of No. (107) and No. (108,) baptized July 30th, 1775; she died March 12th, 1807, aged 32, when he married, second, Nov. 25th, 1807, No. (319.) He was a good farmer, regular in support and attendance upon the means of grace, and a peaceable and quiet citizen. He lived next door north of Levi O. Smith, in Hart quarter, until late in life, when he, with his son, built on the corner of Main street and railroad, in the village, where he died Dec. 21st 1854, aged 81.

THEIR CHILDREN.

1. Ira, jun., born July 7th, 1795, bap. April 23d, 1809, on account of step mother, No. (921.)

2. Abi Langdon, born March 12th, 1807, bap. April 23d, 1809, see No. (605.)

SECOND WIFE'S CHILD.

3. John, born Sept. 22d, 1808, bap. April 23d, 1809, see No. (851.)

443. "JAMES NORTH, jun.," to church Aug. 5th, 1821, son of No. (149) and No. (150,) born Dec. 19th, 1777, married May 1st, 1800, Rhoda, daughter of No. (158) and No (159,) born Dec. 22d, 1781. He was one of the three "New Britain boys" who went to Stockbridge, Mass., and learned the brass business of Joseph Barton; they were North, Booth and Shipman, North being one year older than Shipman and six months older than Booth, but Shipman being the largest of the three, and passing for the same age. Facts show that the enterprise and the plan was originated by the father of James, viz., James North, Esq., for he personally applied to the father of Booth and the father of Shipman, and urged them to let the boys go together. James, the subject of this notice, and Shipman, having finished their term of service with Barton, returned, and for a while occupied together, in company, the north room of the Sugden house, which was then owned by Esq. North, and stood just a little north of the present residence of Henry Stanley, and faced west as his house does; the lightning rod of Stanley's house enters the well of the old Sugden house; where they made the first sleigh bells ever manufactured in New Britain. This old house was, however, soon pulled down to give place to a new one for Seth, the brother of James, when each set up for himself as best he could, under the aid of their friends. Booth left for New York and New Jersey, having bought his time; so that the town is indebted to James North, Esq., for the plan, and to James North, jun., and Joseph Shipman, as the effective agents in making this a manufacturing place. After starting brass business here, he removed to Cherry Valley, where he carried on the business extensively, and built largely, but he lost all, and returned in 1818 to his old home, poor. He was converted in 1821, set up business again here, and was an active Christian. He died Sept. 9th, 1825, aged 48. His widow, Rhoda, died July 20th, 1827, aged 45. He was unselfish, liberal and generous (if possible) to a fault. Honest, credulous, and unsuspecting himself, his trade, his skill, and his property became the prey of the scheming and avaricious. It is hoped that the consolations of the Gospel, which he found so rich and sweet in his last days, compensated for the loss of all things else. He had no enemies, consequently left none behind him.

THEIR CHILDREN.

1. Marcia, born Aug. 27th, 1801, bap. Nov. 4th, 1821, married Aug. 7th, 1825, No. (652.)

2. Maria, born Sept. 10th, 1803, died March 6th, 1815, of dropsy, aged 11 years, at New Britain.

3. William, born Sept. 23d, 1805, died Jan. 20th, 1806, at Cherry Valley, New York.

4. Nancy, born Nov. 22d, 1806, bap. Nov. 4th, 1821, see No. (655.)

5. William, born March 13th, 1809, bap. Nov. 4th, 1821, supposed to be lost at sea.

6. Mary, born August 21st, 1811, bap. Nov. 4th, 1821, married May 23d, 1834, Samuel Raymond.

7. Henry, born Oct. 19th, 1813, bap Nov. 4th, 1821 ; traveled south, see No. (624.)

8. Maria, born June 14th, 1816, bap. Nov. 4th, 1821, see No. (805.)

9. Augustus, born March 8th, 1819, bap. Nov. 4th, 1821, married May 12th, 1845, No. (847.)

10. Adeline, born May 26th, 1823, bap. Aug. 24th, 1823, (see No. (832.)

444. "JOSIAH STEELE, jun.," to church Aug. 5th, 1821, baptized same time, son of Josiah, and No. (377,) born Feb. 9th, 1778, married Nov. 5th, 1798, No. (445.) He lived at the south end of the village, directly east of the Hubbard house, and on the corner; was a farmer and worked Aaron Roberts' farm many years. He died Jan. 29th, 1856, in Parishville, N. Y., aged 78.

445. "PRUDENCE, wife of Josiah Steele, jun.," to church Aug. 5th, 1821, and baptized same time, daughter of Timothy Kilbourn, jun., and Mary (Deming,) his wife, born 1775, married Nov. 5th, 1798, No. (444.) She died Nov. 29th, 1852, aged 77.

THEIR CHILDREN.

1. Laura Lewis, born Nov. 25th, 1798, married July 4th, 1815, Truman Hart.

2. Mary Deming, born June 4th, 1810, bap. Nov. 25th, 1821, married April 14th, 1845, No. (965.)

446. "JOHN HAMBLIN, jun.," to church Aug. 5th, 1821, baptized same time, son of Left. John, of "White Oak," Farmington, and Eleanor (Orvice,) his wife, born March 7th, 1778, married April 4th, 1802, at New Britain, before Dr. Smalley, widow Eunice Andrews, No. (447.) He was a farmer, and lived several years in the "State House," and at other localities. He was dismissed by letter to Farmington church, July 15th, 1823. He was dismissed from there, in 1837, to Bristol Church. He died May 20th, 1853, aged 75.

447. "EUNICE, wife of John Hamblin, jun., to church Aug. 5th, 1821, she was daughter of Charles Eddy, sen., and Hannah (Kelsey,) his wife, born Feb. 25th, 1778, married Nov. 14th, 1796, Samuel Andrews, jun., son of No. (124,) and lived on West Main street, two miles from the village, and on the opposite corner from the present residence (1866) of Alfred Andrews. He died June 1st, 1799, of nervous putrid fever, near Boston, aged 27, when she married, second, April 4th 1802, No. (446.) She died 1833, in Farmington, aged 55.

HER CHILDREN BY FIRST HUSBAND, SAMUEL ANDREWS, JUN.

1. Sally, born April 17th, 1797, married June 14th, 1817, Philip Deming, of Berlin.

2. Marinda, born Aug. 30th, 1799, married 1817, Joseph North, of Berlin.

HIS CHILDREN BY WIFE EUNICE.

1. Samuel Andrews, born April 11th, 1803, married Dec. 9th, 1824, Lavinia Hart, of Salmon; she died April, 1866, in her 64th year.

2. John Denison, born Jan. 14, 1805, married Nov. 9th, 1829, Esther Maria Sweet, daughter of James.

3. Ellen Eliza, born July 17th, 1806, married April 8th, 1828, Samuel G. Forbes, see No. (552.)

4. Charles Francis, born June 24th, 1814, bap. Oct. 14th, 1821, died August 15th, 1846, at New Haven.

5. Dolly Maria, born Aug. 5th, 1816, bap. Oct. 14th, 1821, married Norris Slater; married, second, Charles H. Hills.

448. " HANNAH, wife of Joseph Root," to church Aug. 5th, 1821, born July 11th, 1776, sister of No. (447,) married Feb. 15th, 1796. He was son of Joseph, of Farmington, and his wife Martha (Moore,) born 1768, in the " Clark house," opposite Capt. Root's, Farmington street; was a tin maker, and peddler. He died Dec. 7th, 1823, aged 55, of consumption. He was brother of Orrin and Seth. She was a worthy woman, of true Christian fortitude; to South church, 1842. She died Jan. 2d, 1852, aged 76.

THEIR CHILDREN.

1. Sylvester, born , died at Cincinnati, aged 22, in employ of his uncle, Jesse Eddy.

2. Mary, born April 9th, 1802, never married, imbecile, died September 3d, 1864, aged 62.

3. Dennis, born Dec. 3d, 1805, see No. (691.)

449. " SETH J. NORTH," to church Aug. 5th, 1821, son of No. (149) and No. (150,) born August 13th, 1779, married Sept. 27th, 1801, No. (396;) a blacksmith by trade, stout built, and athletic, learned his trade of his father, located at the " Sugden place," or old home of Joshua Mather. He became a large manufacturer, was very successful in business, and liberal in his public benefactions. He was major in the militia, and had the title ever after. His wealth, and business talent, gave him extensive influence in public matters. He was the projector of that movement in the parish which resulted in the organization of the South Congregational church, in 1842, deprecated by many at the time, but since proved beneficial from the rapid growth of the town. He died March 10th, 1851, aged 71.

THEIR CHILDREN.

1. Charlotte, born April 5th, 1804, bap. May 5th, 1816, see No. (592.)

2. Eliza Stanley, born Nov. 27th, 1807, bap. May 5th, 1816, see No. (593.)

3. Walter Judd, born August 3d, 1810, bap. May 5th, 1816, died Aug. 28th, 1828, aged 18.

4. Frederick Henry, born August 10th, 1824, bap. Oct. 24th, 1825, see No. (829.)

450. "SHELDEN UPSON," to church Aug. 5th, 1821, son of Noah, of Plymouth, Ct., and Rachel (Frisbie,) his wife, born March 24th, 1785, married April 26th, 1809, No. (317.) He was a brick and stone mason by trade, and also a butcher; lived near the school house in Stanley quarter, but the house burned down. He died March 4th, 1838, aged 53.

THEIR CHILDREN.

1. Harriet Eliza, born Jan. 10th, 1812, bap. March 1st, 1812, married Nov. 24th, 1833, George H. Stannard.

2. Julia Ann, born March 22d, 1814, bap. June 5th, 1814, see No. (623.)

3. Nancy Jane, born Feb. 9th, 1821, bap. June 10th, 1821, see No. (857.)

451. "WILLIAM EDDY," to church Aug. 5th, 1821, son of Charles and his wife Hannah (Kelsey,) born Oct. 20th, 1781, married Dec. 13th, 1808 Mary Butler, of Farmington, daughter of Richard, of Hartford, and his wife Prudence (Parks,) born Sept. 21st 1778. They lived near the foot of "Osgood Hill." He died Jan. 25th, 1829, aged 46, when she married, second, Oct. 1st, 1835, Theodore Riley. She died, Sept. 26th, 1844, aged 66.

THEIR CHILDREN.

1. Catharine Gridley, born Oct. 25th, 1809, bap. Sept. 9th, 1821, married Feb. 4th, 1827, Silas Wright.

2. William Butler, born Nov. 15th, 1810, bap. Sept. 9th, 1821, died Sept. 10th, 1823, aged 10.

3. Charlotte, born May 25th, 1812, bap. Sept. 9th, 1821, married May 9th, 1836, George Hills, of Plainville.

4. Mary, born March 8th, 1814, bap. Sept. 9th, 1821, married William E. Clark, of Windsor, May, 1840.

5. George Washington, born Feb. 22d, 1817, bap. Sept. 9th, 1821, married Maria Merrill, of New Hartford.

6. Sylvester, born 1818, bap. Sept. 9th, 1821, died Oct. 6th, 1828, aged 10.

7. Charles Butler, born July 2d, 1823, bap. Sept. 21st, 1823, died Nov. 27th, 1843, aged 20.

452. "SOLOMON BUTLER," to church Aug. 5th, 1821, son of Moses, of East Hartford, and Elizabeth (Forbes,) his wife, born Jan. 12th, 1783, married Feb. 3d, 1805, No. (548.) He was a chair maker and house painter; his home was opposite the Deacon Whittlesey place. He died Jan. 21st, 1828, aged 45.

THEIR CHILDREN.

1. Timothy, born Nov. 30th, 1805, bap. Oct. 14th, 1821, married Jan. 7th, 1831, Nancy Belden, and died June 10th, 1858, aged 53.

2. Leonard, born Dec. 24th, 1808, bap. Oct. 14th, 1821, married Sept. 25th, 1831, Sophronia Mack; he died June 5th, 1866, aged 58.

3. Harriet Elizabeth, born March 11th, 1811, bap. Oct. 14th, 1821, see No. (777.)

4. Henry, born Sept. 16th, 1813, bap. Oct. 14th, 1821, married Sept. 16th, 1835, Harriet Cadwell, of Bloomfield.

5. Sarah Ann, born Nov. 21st, 1815, died April 18th, 1816, aged five months.

6. Sarah Ann, born Nov. 23d, 1817, bap. Oct. 14th, 1821, married Dec. 24th, 1840, Henry Benton, M. D.

7. Nancy Brown, born July 19th, 1821, bap. Oct. 14th, 1821, married William Cochran.

8. George H., born July 19th, 1823; went to parts unknown.

9. Julia Maria, born July 15th, 1825, bap. Oct. 2d, 1825, died Nov. 16th, 1847, aged 22, see No. (973.)

453. "SELAH HART," to church Aug. 5th, 1821, son of No. (181) and No. (182,) born Nov., 1784, married Oct. 5th, 1805, No. (454;) he was a cooper by trade, located in Hart quarter, near the spot where his great-grand-father settled, i. e. first Elijah Hart; he became a major in militia; kept a public house; was a large and effective farmer; had a hotel at Saratoga, New York; he died Sept. 7th, 1851, aged 68.

454. "JEMIMA, wife of Selah Hart," to church Aug. 5th, 1821, daughter of David Webster, Esq., of Berlin, and his wife, Anna (Kelsey,) born April 5th, 1783, married Oct. 5th, 1805, No. (453;) a tall woman, of courtly and dignified manners and appearance.

THEIR CHILDREN.

1. Edward, born Sept. 4th, 1806, bap. Sept. 2d, 1821, married March 26th, 1834, Viana Perry, of Egremont.

2. Selah, born Nov. 25th, 1808, bap. Sept. 2d, 1821, married Nov. 11th, 1829, Sarah North.

3. Nelson, born Nov. 25th, 1812, bap. Sept. 2d, 1821, married Oct. 8th, 1834, Lucy Jane Dewy.

4. Lura Ann, born Nov. 15th, 1816, bap. Sept. 2d, 1821, married Anson W. Francis, April 13th, 1837.

5. Harriet, born Dec. 10th, 1821, bap. Sept. 29th, 1822, married Cary B. Moon, Oct., 1835.

455. "KESIAH, wife of Elisha S. Lewis," to church Aug. 5th, 1821, daughter of Ebenezer Steele, jun., and his wife, Lucy (Wright,) married Oct. 16th, 1814, No. (394,) dismissed by letter to Camden, New York, June 30th, 1822.

456. "LUCY SHIPMAN," to church Aug. 5th, 1821, daughter of Samuel and his wife, Sarah (Stanliff,) of Chatham, born Feb. 27th, 1775; a single woman, and lived with her parents until their decease, then several years with her niece, Abigail, No. (608,) then with Newel Shipman, at Springfield, New York, where she died July 11th, 1860, aged 85; notable as one of those females of New Britain, who turned with pliers so many hooks and eyes and clasps, in the early days of manufacturing.

457. "NANCY PENNFIELD," to church Aug. 5th, 1821, daughter of No. (175) and No. (190,) born July 20th, 1783; never married; lives in Faribault, Minnesota, A. D. 1861; had an unblemished character.

458. "ISAAC LEWIS," to church Aug. 5th, 1821, son of No. (88) and No. (111,) baptized Oct. 13th, 1782 ; was a tinner by trade; lived first in the Cadwell house, in Stanley street, next south of the residence of Henry Francis, and near it; (house long since disappeared;) after which he bought the house on West Main street, now owned by Mrs. Tolles ; he married Oct. 28th, 1804, No. (957 ;) he died Oct. 20th, 1837, aged 55 ; he was a conscientious Christian; had a frail constitution, and died of consumption, after lingering years.

THEIR CHILDREN.

1. Caroline, born July 5th, 1805, bap. Oct. 7th, 1827, No. (633.)
2. Norton N., born July 3d, 1808, married Nov., 1830, Julia A. Bird ; he died Dec. 16th, 1833, aged 25.
3. James Francis, born March 11th, 1813, bap. Oct. 7th, 1827, married Aug. 25th, 1845, Emily R. Roberts, who died March 9th, 1849, when he married second, July 15th, 1850, Harriet M. Beckley. He was for many years leader of our church choir.
4. Charles Mason, born June 13th, 1816, bap. Oct. 7th, 1827, No. (916.)
5. Horatio Stanley, born Sept. 25th, 1819, bap. Oct. 7th, 1827, No. (983.)
6. Bernard, born Oct. 19th, 1821, bap. Oct. 7th, 1827, died Aug. 4th, 1841, aged 10; gangrene.

459. "JAMES JUDD, jun." to church Aug. 5th, 1821, son of No. (195) and No. (318,) born March 12th, 1785, married May 7th, 1805, No. (460;) she died, when he married second, Jan. 4th, 1832, No. (574;) he was a farmer; lived next door north of his father, in Shipman District; he to South church, 1842; he died Oct. 13th, 1860, at the house of his son, Cyrus, aged 75.

460. "SALOME, wife of James Judd, jun." to church Aug. 5th, 1821, twin daughter of Solomon Lusk and his wife, No. (226,) born Nov. 20th, 1785; she died April 3d, 1831, aged 45.

THEIR CHILDREN.

1. George, born Oct. 7th, 1805, died Dec. 16th, 1828, aged 23.
2. Cyrus, born July 17th, 1807, died Nov. 11th, 1808, instantly, by fall of a cart body.
3. Nancy M., born July 13th, 1809, died Aug. 27th, 1811, aged two years.
4. Cyrus, born March 8th, 1811, bap. June 29th, 1823, married May 1st, 1833, Elizabeth Hubbard, who died May 22d, 1849, when he married second, Oct. 17th, 1849, Widow Lina E. Pond.
5. Nancy Maria, born Feb. 13th, 1813, bap. June 29th, 1823, see No. (730.)
6. Julia Ann, born May 5th, 1815, bap. Oct. 4th, 1822, married Nov. 9th, 1835, Timothy Stephens, of West Hartford.
7. Loretta, born May 9th, 1817, died Jan. 31st, 1818, aged nine months.
8. Laura Electa, born Feb. 1st, 1819, bap. June 29th, 1823, married Emri Steele.
9. James, born June 7th, 1822, bap. June 29th, 1823, married Julia Hoyt.
10. Walter, born Aug. 26th, 1825, bap. Oct. 13th, 1825, died Oct. 17th, 1825, aged seven weeks.

SECOND WIFE'S CHILDREN.

11. Catharine Emeline, born Feb. 19th, 1836, bap. 1836, married Oct. 15th, 1845, Joseph Rennolds.

12. Henry Bass, born Dec. 9th, 1838, bap. 1841, married May 5th, 1858, Katie O. Conor.

461. "JOSEPH SHIPMAN," to church Aug. 5th, 1821, son of Samuel and his wife, Sarah (Stanliff,) of Chatham, grand-son of Capt. Samuel Shipman, of Saybrook, Conn., born Dec. 23d, 1779; learned his trade of brass-founder, clock-maker, and silver-spoon maker of Joseph Barton, of Stockbridge, Mass.; his apprenticeship with Barton expired in December, 1799, he being but twenty, having served the stipulated time; he in company with his fellow-apprentice, No. (443,) whose term of service expired the same month and year, began business in the north room of the Sugden house, then owned by Esquire North, and stood near the present mansion of Frederic North; this room was vacated for the purpose by the family of Elihu Burritt; thus North and Shipman commenced the making of the first sleigh-bells ever manufactured in the place, in the spring of 1800; they worked together only that summer, for in the fall each of them set up separately, under the patronage of their fathers; Mr. Shipman in part of his father's joiners shop, (which soon after burned down.) The fact of North and Shipman making sleigh-bells together in the Sugden house, is fully established by the testimony of two living witnesses, now, 1862, corroborating the statements of Mr. Shipman himself, while living; the capital stock he employed was fifty dollars he borrowed of Dr. Smalley, and his manufactured goods he transported to Boston on horse-back; at the prices and profits of those days he was able not only to refund his money borrowed, but to supply himself with raw material for further profit, and thus he rose to comparative wealth, respectability and influence. He married July 11th, 1802, No. (349,) and on the 11th of January, 1803, he bought the place on Stanley street, formerly owned by Nathan Booth, jun., where he built extensive shops, took his two sons in process of time, into partnership, bought out the Judd's mill place, erected large works, but failed in 1837, during the great revulsion of business and trade. He learned more young men the trade than any other manufacturer in town. He was public-spirited and patriotic, always ready to bear his full share of public expenses for improvements. Several of the last years of his life were spent with his son, at Yonkers, N. Y, but he died March 9th, 1859, aged 79, at New Hartford, with his daughter, Mrs. Brown.

THEIR CHILDREN.

1. Ralph, born March 4th, 1803, bap. May 5th, 1811, married Nov. 2d, 1825, No. (678.)
2. Mary Lee, born April 14th, 1805, bap. May 5th, 1811, married Sept. 15th, 1824, No. (478.)
3. Eliza, born Feb. 18th, 1807, bap. May 5th, 1811, see No. (607.)
4. Abigail Goodrich, born Oct. 13th, 1809, bap. May 5th, 1811, see No. (608.)

5. Horatio Waldo, born Sept. 10th, 1811, bap. Nov. 18th, 1811, married Nov. 4th, 1835, No. (781.)

6. Orpha, born Dec. 12th, 1813, bap. Feb. 13th, 1814, see No. (734.)

462. "JOSEPH EDDY," to church Aug. 5th, 1821, son of Charles, sen. and his wife, Hannah (Kelsey,) born Feb. 27th, 1786; was both farmer and mechanic; could turn his hand usefully and cheerfully to several employments; had an active mind, with great force of character, but uncultivated. He married May 13th, 1807, No. (320;) he built near his father's, on the road north of "Job's Corner;" he died June 14th, 1836, aged 50.

THEIR CHILDREN.

1. Horace, born April 25th, 1808, bap. June 26th, 1808, married Sept. 22d, 1829, Roxy Ann Wright.

2. Lorenzo, born Oct. 30th, 1810, bap. Jan. 27th, 1811, married Nov. 4th, 1832, No. (730.)

3. Infant, born , died Feb. 27th, 1813.

4. Norman Pennfield, born Feb. 7th, 1813, bap. Aug. 1st, 1813, married March 25th, 1834, Maria W. White.

5. Lucy Ann, born Nov. 15th, 1816, bap. April 13th, 1817, married Isaac Bird, of Hartford, an Englishman; she died April 27th, 1838, aged 21.

6. Martha, born Nov. 6th, 1819, bap. May 14th, 1820, married Oct. 16th, 1839, Daniel B. Fowler, of Meriden,

7. Eunice, born July 15th, 1822, bap. Oct. 6th, 1822, died March 8th, 1837, aged 15.

463. "CYPRIAN MATHER," to church Aug. 5th, 1821, baptized same time, son of Cotton and his wife, No. (375,) born May 30th, 1792, married Jan. 18th, 1814, No. (341;) he was a stone-mason; a heavy, robust man, with good intellectual powers, fond of reading, slow in his movements and conclusions; lived in various localities; he neglected his covenant obligations to God and the church, and was excommunicated, Oct. 11th, 1837, after much labor with him; he died Oct. 1st, 1845, aged 54.

THEIR CHILDREN.

1. Silas Hart, born March 9th, 1814, bap. June 18th, 1815, married Jan. 20th, 1836, Caroline Sperry.

2. Caroline, born , died May 26th, 1823, aged six.

3. George W., born Oct. 5th, 1819, bap. April 30th, 1820, married Aug. 18th, 1844, Jane Hubbard.

4. John Newton, born Feb. 2d, 1824, bap. May 2d, 1824, married May 21st, 1843, Martha Morgan.

5. Henry Franklin, born June 15th, 1831, bap. Aug. 20th, 1831, married July 4th, 1852, Chloe Todd, daughter of Daniel, of Sidney, N. Y. and his wife, Maria Tuttle, of North Haven; he died May 28th, 1867, in his 36th year.

464. "ETHAN A. ANDREWS," to church Aug. 5th, 1821, son of No. (122) and No. (123,) born April 7th, 1787, married Dec. 19th, 1810, No. (392;) he graduated at Yale, 1810; studied law in Farmington; com-

menced practice in this town, 1812; they were both dismissed to the third church in New Haven, Feb. 5th, 1832. He built on Stanley street, near his father, A. D. 1813; taught a select school in it several years, with good success; he was professor of languages in the University of N. C.; had a select school of young ladies at New Haven, and at Boston. While residing in this place he several years represented the town of Berlin, and for the first year the new town of New Britain, A. D. 1851; he was a magistrate and judge of probate; but he gained his eminence and celebrity from his literary taste and labor as a Latin author; in 1848, his "Alma Mater," Yale College, gave him the honorable degree of LL. D. He died March 24th, 1858, aged 71, in the midst of his literary labors. He was gentlemanly in his deportment, and had a peculiar suavity of manner; he to South church by letter, 1843, and died in that connection.

THEIR CHILDREN.

1. Levi, bap. Dec. 7th, 1811, in Farmington, died Sept. 26th, 1830, at New Haven, and buried there.
2. Isaac Cowles, bap. Dec. 12th, 1813, at Farmington, married Sept. 1st, 1859, Jane L. Thomas, of New Haven.
3. Lucy Ann, bap. Aug. 6th, 1815, married Aug. 24th, 1842, E. D. Sims; second, William McKinley.
4. Julia Hooker, bap. June 8th, 1817, married Oct. 9th, 1848, Archelaus Wilson, Esq.; he died Feb. 26th, 1862.
5. Horace, bap. Aug. 29th, 1819, married Julia R. Johnson.
6. Grace, bap. May 27th, 1821, married Professor E. D. Sims; she died Sept. 2d, 1839, aged 18.
7. Charles S., married Elizabeth Alden, of West Hartford.
8. Mary, see No. (932.)
9. Ellen Amelia, bap. Sept. 3d, 1831, see No. (1,281.)
10. Elizabeth Cogswell, see No. (1,280.)

465. "HORACE BUTLER," to church Aug. 5th, 1821, baptized same time, son of Moses, of East Hartford, and his wife, Elizabeth (Forbes,) born Feb. 4th, 1789; was a chair-maker by trade, but became an extensive manufacturer of hard and plated ware; he first built near his brother, opposite the Dr. Smalley house, but subsequently on Stanley street; married May 14th, 1814, No. (466;) she died when he married second, May 2d, 1835, No. (485;) he was the first convert of the "great revival of 1821," in the congregation; was awakened in Farmington, under the preaching of Dr. Nettleton.

466. "BETSEY, wife of Horace Butler," to church Aug. 5th, 1821, baptized same time, daughter of Benjamin Howd, of Branford, Conn., married May 14th, 1814, No. (465,) born Feb. 14th, 1792, died Aug. 18th, 1834, aged 43; was the mother of his children.

THEIR CHILDREN.

1. Ruel Howd, born May 16th, 1816, bap. Oct. 14th, 1821, married 1838, Lucetta Finch.

2. Horace, born Aug. 23d, 1820, bap. Oct. 14th, 1821, died March 13th, 1825.

3. Edwin Benjamin, born Nov. 30th, 1822, bap. May 25th, 1822, married Fanny Stephens.

4. } twins. { Hubert Mills, born Aug. 31st, 1825, bap. Oct. 2d, 1825, married Harriet Whaples.

5. } { Horace Brainard, born Aug. 31st, 1825, bap. Oct. 2d, 1825, died Dec. 8th, 1836, aged 11.

6. Eliphalet Newel, born Feb. 10th, 1829, bap. Aug. 30th, 1829, died Aug. 8th, 1838, aged 9.

7. Mary Elizabeth, born Aug. 21st, 1831, bap. Sept. 10th, 1831, married Dec. 9th, 1863, Edwin Westover.

467. "John Recor," to church Aug. 5th, 1821, baptized same time, son of Michael and his wife, Lydia (Griswold,) born July 25th, 1791, married May 23d, 1810, No. (468;) he a farmer and mechanic; a quiet, inoffensive man; lived on the road to Farmington, back of Dublin Hill; lost his property through the treachery of false friends, and on the 8th of November, 1837, he fell under the censure of the church, by neglecting public worship and the ordinances of the gospel; he died March 11th, 1860, aged 69.

468. "Lucy, wife of John Recor," to church Aug. 5th, 1821, daughter of Stephen Booth and his wife, Lucy (Booth,) his first cousin, born Nov. 10th, 1793, married May 23d, 1810, No. (467;) after her husband fell under the censure of the church she attended occasionally, worship at the Baptist church, and for contempt of the church and its ordinances, was excommunicated March 14th, 1844.

THEIR CHILDREN.

1. Horatio, born Sept. 3d, 1810, bap. Sept. 9th, 1821, married March 24th, 1829, Eliza Kilby; second, Julia Steele; he died Nov. 11th, 1865, aged 55.

2. Marcia, born Sept. 12th, 1812, bap. Sept. 9th, 1821, married Nov. 26th, 1829, No. (691;) second, Oswin Stanley.

3. Henry, born Aug. 26th, 1814, bap. Sept. 9th, 1821, married Calista Sandford; second, Maria Kilby.

4. Philip, born Sept. 1st, 1816, bap. Sept. 9th, 1821, married Sept. 1st, 1836, Mary Darling Steele, No. (742.)

5. Ann Jane, born May 1st, 1820, bap. Sept. 9th, 1821, married Oct. 29th, 1829, Barzillai Deming; he died Feb. 18th, 1863.

6. Charles, born Nov. 10th, 1827, adopted in place of an infant who died without name; this Charles, No. (966,) son of Curtiss Warfield, of Hartford; married Dec. 19th, 1849, Sarah Farnsworth.

7. Caroline, born Nov. 17th, 1835, married May 11th, 1851, Vietta Hille; live in Burlington; he son of Noble and his wife, Marks.

469. "Phineas Pennfield, jun." to church Aug. 5th, 1821, son of No. (175) and No. (190) born Oct. 18th, 1785, married Nov. 25th, 1812, No. (526;) by occupation a farmer; he was illiterate, but nevertheless a prominent convert and missionary in the revival of 1821; of great simplicity of mind and manners, his sincerity and earnestness reached the

hearts of very many; he built near his father, south of "Osgood Hill;" died Aug. 3d, 1845, aged 60.

THEIR CHILDREN.

1. Mary Ann, born Oct. 4th, 1813, bap. Sept. 9th, 1821, see No. (835.)
2. Harvey, born June 7th, 1815, bap. Sept. 9th, 1821, see No. (833.)
3. Martin, born Aug. 23d, 1816, bap. Sept. 9th, 1821, married Charlotte Dix.
4. Lydia, born May 29th, 1819, bap. Sept. 9th, 1821, see No. (834.)
5. Lemuel, born April 17th, 1821, bap. Sept. 9th, 1821, married April 12th, 1846, Caroline Allen, who was drowned Sept. 27th, 1866.
6. Dennis, born Dec. 24th, 1823, bap. March 28th, 1824, see No. (961.)
7. Fidelia, born Sept. 10th, 1826, bap. Oct. 29th, 1826, see No. (977.)
8. Emily, born Sept. 11th, 1829, bap. June 27th, 1830, married April 15th, 1858, William Bradford.
9. Horace, born June 11th, 1831, bap. Oct. 23d, 1831, married Nov. 25th, 1855, Mary C. Spencer.
10. Francis Newel, born Nov. 25th, 1833, bap. April 20th, 1834, married Oct. 31st, 1855, Martha I. Boardman.
11. Harriet Amelia, born Aug. 5th, 1835.

470. "Romeo Francis," to church Aug. 5th, 1821, baptized same time, son of No. (354,) born May 30th, 1790, married Nov. 24th, 1813, No. (471;) he a farmer and school-teacher; lived in an extended part of his uncle Elijah's house, east of "Osgood Hill;" by extreme industry and economy, accumulated quite an estate; to South church, 1842; died March 30th, 1849, aged 59; he was intelligent, and an assistant superintendent of the Sabbath school one or two years.

471. "Catharine, wife of Romeo Francis," to church Aug. 5th, 1821, daughter of No. (191) and No. (192,) born June 8th, 1790, married Nov. 24th, 1813, No. (470;) to South church, 1842; living A. D. 1861, in Brooklyn, N. Y., with her son, Mason; she died there Feb. 26th, 1867, in her 77th year; was buried here.

THEIR CHILDREN.

1. Jane Eliza, born Aug. 24th, 1814, bap. Sept. 16th, 1821, see No. (729.)
2. James Elijah, born April 20th, 1817, bap. Sept. 16th, 1821, died Oct. 11th, 1836.
3. Romeo Benedict, born June 2d, 1818, bap. Sept. 16th, 1821, died April 22d, 1822.
4. Mason Bernard, born Sept. 21st, 1820, bap. Sept. 16th, 1821, see No. (806.)
5. Catharine Amelia, born Sept. 3d, 1825, bap. Nov. 13th, 1825, died Sept. 26th, 1849, No. (947.)

472. "Lucretia, wife of William Smith," to church Aug. 5th, 1821, daughter of Abijah Moore, of New Hartford, and his wife, Abigail (Drake,) born May 20th, 1789, at Windsor, and Feb. 10th, 1812, became the second wife of No. (337;) she to South church, 1842; has for many years been in feeble health; lives A. D. 1862, with her daughter, Mrs. Harriet Brown; she died March 17th, 1866, aged 77.

473. "Lucy, wife of James Francis, jun." to church Aug. 5th, 1821, daughter of Asa Risley, of Hartford, and his wife, Lucy (Dillings,) born

Feb. 2d, 1797, married Feb. 28th, 1820. He was son of No. (354,) was a farmer, and inherited the old home of his father and grandfather, on which his son Henry now dwells. He died Sept. 19th, 1849, aged 63. She died May 22d, 1866, aged 69.

THEIR CHILD.

Henry, born July 13th, 1829, bap. Oct. 1829, married Dec. 5th, 1855, Elizabeth Hubbard, of Wethersfield, daughter of Leonard C., and his wife Nancy (Churchill.)

474. "LYDIA BASS," to church Aug. 5th, 1821, daughter of Samuel, and his wife, No. (153,) born 1792 ; had a child, baptized John Williams, Sept. 16th, 1821. She died October 6th, 1830, aged 37 ; lived and died with her mother.

475. "WAKEMAN N. STANLEY," to church Aug. 5th, 1821, son of Noah, and No. (202,) born March 9th, 1793, married No. (476 ;) lived on Stanley street, next south of his uncle, Dr. Adna Stanley, now Martin Brown. He was a farmer, plain and unpretending, industrious and generous. He died Aug. 19th, 1823, aged 30.

476. "ELIZABETH, wife of Wakeman N. Stanley," to church Aug. 5th, 1821, daughter of No. (174) and No. (224,) married No. (475,) and married, second, Azmon Woodruff, of Avon ; she became a Baptist, and died Jan. 3d, 1852, aged 54, at Richland, N. Y.

THEIR CHILDREN.

1. Charlotte, born May 14th, 1817, bap. Sept. 16th, 1821, married George Hale.
2. Horatio, born June 26th, 1820, bap. Sept. 16th, 1821, married Margaret Brace.

477. "CHAUNCEY CLARK," to church Aug. 5th, 1821, baptized same time, son of No. (434,) born April 15th, 1787; was a farmer, and inherited the home of his father and grandfather, on East street ; married Sept. 15th, 1818, Eunice, daughter of No. (174,) she died Oct. 16, 1819, aged 30. when he married, second, Dec. 22d, 1824, No. (572.) He was quiet and honest, and very successful as a farmer and business man. He died Dec. 22d, 1855, aged 70.

HIS CHILDREN BY SECOND WIFE.

1. Laura Louisa, born June 3d, 1826, bap. Nov. 22d, 1826, married Elizur N. Smith.
2. Lucy Eliza, born June 16th, 1828, married June 22d, 1848, James P. Moore.
3. Edwin Smith, born Dec. 3d, 1830, bap. April 24th, 1831, married May 15th, 1856, No. (1381;) he died suddenly of bilious cholic, April 12th, 1865, in his 35th year.
4. Chauncey D., born May 6th, 1839.

478. "ALFRED ANDREWS," to church Aug. 5th, 1821, son of No. (313) born Oct. 16th, 1797 ; taught school in early life, learned wagon and carriage making, and carried on the business ; married Dec. 16th, 1818, No. (479.) She died, and he married, second, Sept. 15th, 1824, No.

(657;) residence nearly opposite his father, on West Main street, two miles from the village—house built 1820; appointed one of the standing church committee, Dec. 30th, 1823, in place of Ensign Levi Andrews, resigned; was a teacher in Sabbath school, 1816, and superintendent in 1826; deacon, Oct. 23d, 1851; been a teacher or superintendent from November, 1815, either in day or Sabbath school, to 1867; was early in the temperance reform, and anti-slavery agitation; failed in business in 1837, and commenced his genealogical researches in 1855, and this memorial, Feb. 1858. Was appointed secretary of the Sabbath School Union, for Wethersfield, Berlin, and vicinity, Sept. 6th, 1832, and resigned, Sept. 4th, 1866.

479. "CAROLINE B., wife of Alfred Andrews," to church Aug. 5th, 1821, daughter of No. (211,) born April 15th, 1798, in New York city, married Dec. 16th, 1818, No. (478;) taught school before marriage; left two daughters, and died Aug. 22d, 1823, of spotted fever, aged 25. Was intelligent and reflective.

THEIR CHILDREN.

1. Julia Ann, born Nov. 15th, 1819, bap. Aug. 19th, 1821, see No. (785.)
2. Caroline Hart, born Dec. 4th, 1822, bap. Feb. 9th, 1823, see No. (786.)

CHILDREN BY SECOND WIFE.

3. Margarette, born Aug. 30th, 1826, bap. Oct. 29th, 1826, see No. (946.)
4. Eliza Shipman, born April 8th, 1828, bap. 1828, see No. (1051.)
5. Edwin Norton, born Sept. 1st, 1832, bap. Oct. 21st, 1832, see No. (1052.)
6. Cornelius, born Nov. 1st, 1834, bap. May, 1835, see No. (1103.)
7. Alfred Hinsdale, born Dec. 25th, 1836, bap. June 1st, 1837; is extensively engaged at Chicago, Ill., in the manufacture and sale of school furnishing goods.
8. Jane Louisa, born April 22d, 1842, bap. 1842, died Jan. 25th, 1844, aged 21 months.
9. Herbert Lee, born June 6th, 1844, bap. Oct. 6th, 1844.
10. Jane Louisa, born Aug. 10th, 1847, bap. June 1st, 1848, see No. (1366.)

480. "JOSIAH DEWY, jun.," to church Aug. 5th, 1821, son of No. (179,) born Aug. 11th, 1792; was a brass founder; located on East Main street; was a manufacturer; married March 2d, 1814, Betsey Recor, daughter of Michael, and his wife Lydia (Griswold,) born Jan. 26th, 1795, died Nov. 16th, 1822, aged 28, when he married, second, May 8th, 1823, No. (488.) He lived a consistent Christian life, and died March 31st, 1851, aged 58.

THEIR CHILDREN.

1. George, born Sept. 23d, 1814, Bap. Oct. 21st, 1821, see No. (626.)
2. Lucy Jane, born Nov. 8th, 1816, bap. Oct. 21st, 1821, married Oct. 8th, 1834, Nelson Hart.
3. Harriet Eliza, born April 2d, 1822, bap. Oct. 6th, 1822, died Dec. 17th, 1822, aged 9 months.

CHILD BY SECOND WIFE.

4. Arabella, born Feb. 19th, 1824, bap. May 30th, 1824, married Dec. 24th, 1845, William Gaylord.

Yours Truly
Alfred Andrews

481. "CHESTER HART," to church Aug. 5th, 1821, son of No. (247,) born Feb. 7th, 1793, married Sept. 19th, 1821, No. (489;) she died, when he married, second, May 12th, 1824, her sister, No. (490.) He was by trade a shoe-maker and tanner, learned of Abijah Flagg, in West Hartford; lived in Hart quarter, first on the corner of Shuttle Meadow road and West street, with his tannery near by on the west, but on the death of his wife's uncle Lemuel, in Yonkers, New York, she had a patrimony with which he built a fine and substantial residence on the corner east. He died March 20th, 1865, aged 72.

THEIR CHILDREN.

1. Levi Wells, born June 7th, 1825, bap Aug., 1825, see No. (944.)
2. John Henry, born April 13th, 1828, bap. June, 1828, married Jan. 4th, 1853, Jane Griswold, of West Hartford, daughter of Josiah; she died April 7th, 1864.
3. Hannah Jennette, born March 9th, 1835, died March 16th, 1853, aged 18 years and 1 week.

482. "SELAH STEELE, jun.," to church Aug. 5th, 1821, baptized same time, son of No. (852,) born May 25th, 1789, married Oct. 5th, 1825, No. (719.) He was a harness maker by trade, learned of Ira Andrus; lived a few years in Southington; his wife Phebe died, when he married, second, Oct. 29th, 1856, Lavinia C. Merrills, widow of Salmon Merrills, of New Hartford, and daughter of Fithen Case, of Simsbury; she died, when he married, third, the widow of Daniel Humphrey, of Torringford, her maiden name, Eliza Burr. He was dismissed by letter to South church, New Britain, Nov. 17th, 1845; he then had a residence on Pearl street, but sold out and moved to West Winsted.

HIS SON BY FIRST WIFE.

Harvey Baldwin, born Feb. 23d, 1827, bap. June 3d, 1827, at Southington; is a physician, and married at the Humphrey House, New Britain, April 30th, 1861, Mary Mather, of West Winsted.

483. "JONATHAN HART," to church Aug. 5th, 1821, son of No. (181,) born Feb. 20th, 1792; traveled south, was a clothier by trade; was for many years a magistrate in West Troy, N. Y.; has been dissolute; never married. He died March 4th, 1863, aged 71, at West Troy, N. Y. Nature lavished much on both his body and mind.

484. "IRA HART," to church Aug. 5th, 1821, son of No. (181,) born July 22d, 1798; a clothier by trade, lived in north part of his father's house; married May 3d, 1820, No. (485,) died Dec. 1st, 1824, aged 26; left no posterity.

485. "ORPHA, wife of Ira Hart," to church Aug. 5th, 1821, daughter of No. 441, born April 2d, 1800, married May 2d, 1820, No. (484;) he died, when she married, second, May 2d, 1835, No. (465;) a discreet, modest woman; has had no children; to South church, 1842.

486. "CHESTER PENNFIELD," to church Aug. 5th, 1821, son of No. (237,) born January 23d, 1796, married June 4th, 1820, No. (528;) was a farmer, and lived in the west part of his father's house on Horse plain. He died Aug. 6th, 1825, aged 30.

THEIR CHILDREN.

1. Jeremiah, born March 16th, 1821, bap. Aug. 19th, 1821, married May 22d, 1840, Sarah J. Webster; he died July 10th, 1863, aged 42.

2. Julia Ann, born Sept. 26th, 1822, bap. Nov. 3d, 1822, married Nov. 25th, 1841, Samuel M. Knowles,

487. "DESDEMONA SMITH," to church Aug. 5th, 1821, daughter of Lemuel and No. (437;) never married, lived with her parents; baptized on admission to church. She died June 4th, 1835, aged 38.

488. "LYDIA S. COSSLETT," to church Aug. 5th, 1821, daughter of Francis, and his second wife, No. (636,) born January 31st, 1800, married May 8th, 1823, No. (480;) was a dressmaker, efficient in her occupation, and resides on East Main street. Her daughter, Catharine, born March 31st, 1817, baptized Sept. 23d, 1821, married April 17th, 1839, George M. Landers. Mrs. Dewy to South church, 1842. She died Aug. 19th, 1864, aged 64½ years.

489. "HANNAH WELLS," to church Aug. 5th, 1821, daughter of No. (299,) born Aug., 1797, married Sept. 19th, 1821, No. (481,) died Sept. 1st, 1823, when he married, second, May 12th, 1824, No. (490.)

490. "ELVA WELLS," to church August 5th, 1821, daughter of No. (299,) born Sept, 11th, 1800, married May 12th, 1824, No. (481.) She was a good scholar and a godly woman; she had a patrimony by the death of her uncle Lemuel, in Yonkers, New York, who was wealthy, with which they built a good and substantial residence on the corner of the turnpike and Shuttle Meadow road; she to South church, 1842.

491. "MARILLA WELLS," to church Aug. 5th, 1821, daughter of No. (299,) born Sept. 26th, 1805, married Nov. 2d, 1825, No. (678.) She had property left her by her uncle Lemuel, with which they built on a fine site on the banks of the Hudson river, in Yonkers, N. Y. She was dismissed by letter to the church there, April 20th, 1843.

492. "BETSEY W. PRATT," to church Aug. 5th, 1821, daughter of No. (345,) born Feb. 23d, 1797, a twin sister of Henry M., married May 31st, 1826, Amon Richards, of Newington, son of Oliver, and Lydia (Andrews,) his wife, born May 1st, 1798; is a successful farmer. She was dismissed, 1826, and recommended by letter to church in Newington.

THEIR CHILDREN.

1. Lydia, born February 27th, 1828, married Oct. 16th, 1848, Martin, son of John Ellis.

2. Susan Pratt, born July 9th, 1832, married Jan. 14th, 1857, Luther S. Webster, of Jonathan.

3. Infant, born Nov. 30th, 1825, died at three days old.
4. William Mudge, born Nov. 23d, 1837, lives (1864) with his father.

493. "NANCY D. PRATT," to church Aug. 5th, 1821, daughter of No. (345,) born March 25th, 1803, married July 8th, 1827, Cyrus Francis, of Newington, son of Justus, and No. (212;) she was his second wife, his first being Sabra Blinn. His wife Nancy dismissed Oct. 7th, 1827, and recommended by letter to the church in Newington; she died there of cancer.

HIS CHILD BY FIRST WIFE SABRA.

1. Blinn, born March 22d, 1825, married Lucy Hart.

CHILDREN BY SECOND WIFE NANCY.

2. Pratt, born Sept. 22d, 1831, married August 30th, 1855, Adeline H. Hurd, of Avon.
3. Cyrus W. born June, 1838, a graduate of Yale Col., 1867; ordained a minister.
4. Nancy, born Dec. 29th, 1840, educated at Holyoke, Mass.

494. "REBECCA EDDY," to church Aug. 5th, 1821, daughter of Charles, and No. (270,) born Oct. 3d, 1799, bap. Nov. 17th, 1799. Rebecca Bass married June 28th, 1825, Albert Norton, of Kensington, son of Roger, and Hannah (Rice,) of Wallingford, his wife. She was received to Kensington church, Dec., 1826, by letter from New Britain. She died Aug. 31st, 1828, aged 29, at Kensington. She was by trade a tailoress, and learned of Polly Judd, who married Jesse Eddy. She was the second wife of Capt. Albert Norton, his first being, Lucy, daughter of John Lee; she died April 25th, 1824, when he married, second, as above. Mr. Norton married, third, March 25th, 1829, Ruth, daughter of Cyprian Hart and his wife, Lucy (Hooker.)

HIS CHILDREN BY HIS FIRST WIFE, LUCY.

1. William Hart, born Nov. 30th, 1819, died April 16th, 1847.
2 Albert Roger, born June 23d, 1821, married October, 1846, Elizabeth Stocking; he died March 11th, 1848.
3. Lucy Harriet, born Jan. 26th, 1824, died Sept. 2d, 1839.

HIS CHILD BY HIS SECOND WIFE, REBECCA.

4. Frederick Henry, born March 17th, 1828, married May 3d, 1852, Jane S. Carter, of Southington.

HIS CHILDREN FY HIS THIRD WIFE, RUTH.

5. Isabella Hannah, born Oct. 15th, 1831, died Dec. 15th, 1840.
6. Harriet Isabella, born July 5th. 1843.

[Capt. Albert Norton was grandson of Roger, sen., who was son of Serg. John, who was son of John, 2d, of north end of Farmington village, who was son of John the imigrant, born in London, England, 1625, to Richard.]

495. "EMELINE EDDY," to church Aug. 5th, 1821, daughter of Charles, and No. (270,) born Feb. 22d, 1802, married October 12th, 1822, Ralph Stanley Cornwell, son of Stephen, and Abigail (Stanley,) his wife, born

January 28th, 1799, a twin with Richard. He was a brass founder by trade, learned of Cyrus Stanley, in Stanley quarter, at the old home of Colonel Gad. He died July 26th, 1827, aged 29.

THEIR CHILD.

Thomas Stow, born Nov. 19th, 1823, bap. April 10th, 1825, died June 3d, 1845, at New Bedford, Mass., aged 21. She married, second, Nov. 17th, 1831, No. (955.)

496. "SALLY PENNFIELD," to church Aug. 5th, 1821, daughter of No. (237,) born Nov. 8th, 1800, married Aug. 5th, 1821, David Northrop; living, 1861, in Russellsburg, Pa. She was dismissed, Oct. 3d, 1824, to Camden, N. Y., by letter.

497. "PHEBE L. ANDREWS," to church Aug. 5th, 1821, daughter of No. (197,) born Oct. 28th, 1797, married March 18th, 1823, Asa Cowdry, brother of No. (397;) he was born Nov. 9th, 1798, at Hartland, to Asa, and his wife Abigail (Ensign,) and learned the blacksmith trade of No. (430.) She was consumptive, and lost her speech for several months, but had it restored, suddenly, while praying. She died Sept. 17th, 1826, aged 29, at the home of her father; a lovely woman. He married, second, Laura (Farr,) moved to Florida and set up his business, and died there Aug. 8th, 1833, aged 35.

"498. "SALOME HART," to church Aug. 5th, 1821, daughter of No. (183,) born, Aug. 14th, 1801, married Jan. 30th, 1832, Henry Judd, son of No. (195,) born Jan. 15th, 1801, live in the old home of his father; is a farmer. She died Oct. 20th, 1865, of cancer, aged 64.

THEIR CHILD.

Henrietta, born April 26th, 1824, married Nov. 30th, 1843, Justus Morgan, son of Amos, and Mary Wetherel, his wife; has a fine location next door to his father Judd.

499. "HANNAH J. BELDEN," to church Aug. 5th, 1821, daughter of Leonard, jun., and No. (324,) born July 23d, 1800, married April 30th, 1832, Rev. Alfred Gardner, pastor of a church in East Windham, N. Y., to which place she removed her church connection. Her present location, A. D. 1861, Wayauwega, Wawpacca county, Wisconsin. Their children are Sarah, Leonard Belden, Mary, Emma, and Andrew.

500. "ALMIRA JUDD," to church Aug. 5th, 1821, daughter of No. (178.) She was dismissed and recommended by letter to Meredeth, N. Y., Nov. 11th, 1821.

501. "MARY BURRITT," to church Aug. 5th, 1821, daughter of Elihu, and No. (290,) born Feb. 18th, 1803, married May 26th, 1825, William Williams, of Kensington, son of Gideon, and Eunice (Cowles,) his wife. He was a shoe-maker by trade, learned of Ashbel Hooker, in Kensington. After living a few years with his wife, mostly in Southington, to which church she was recommended, went to parts unknown, but subsequently it

was found he had changed his name and married a beautiful woman in Philadelphia, of wealthy and doating parents, whose hearts were broken by knowing the facts in the case. Mary, his lawful wife, obtained a divorce, and plied her needle so successfully as to earn a fine situation on Lafayette street, where she built in 1844, and resides, 1867.

THEIR CHILDREN.

1. Elizabeth, born Feb. 10th, 1827, bap. June 3d, 1827, at Southington, married May, 1843, William Miller.
2. Ann Watson, born Nov. 30th, 1828, bap. June 14th, 1829, at Southington, married spring of 1845, George Waugh, of Torringford, Ct.

502. "RHODA HAMBLIN," to church Aug. 5th, 1821, born April 9th, 1797, at White Oak, in Farmington, to Phineas, and his wife Rhoda (Andrews,) baptized at Farmington, July 31st, 1797, married Jan. 1st, 1832, Reuben Hitchcock, of Cheshire, son of Asa, and his wife Asenath (Doolittle,) born June 17th, 1794. She was dismissed by letter, June 3d, 1832, to church at Southington. She died June 15th, 1846, aged 49. He died Oct. 12th, 1863, aged 70.

THEIR CHILDREN.

1. Henry R., born Dec. 24th, 1832, at Cheshire, died Dec. 27th, 1832, aged 3 days.
2. Harriet, born March 21st, 1834, at Cheshire, married Nov. 5th, 1849, Jacob Day, of Bristol.
3. Martha A., born March 17th, 1836, died Dec. 5th, 1858, aged 22½ years.

503. "EMILY HART," to church Aug. 5th, 1821, baptized same time, daughter of Stephen, jun., and No. (638,) born March 15th, 1804, married Sept. 21st, 1823, Erastus Parker, of Lenox, Mass., a tanner and currier by trade. He was born Jan. 5th, 1800, at Bristol, Ct., to Richard, from East Haddam, and his wife Lydia (Eells.)

THEIR CHILDREN.

1. Sarah Ann, born Nov. 9th, 1825, married March 25th, 1856, J. F. Barrett,
2. Julia Amelia, born Dec. 24th, 1827, died Aug. 13th, 1829.
3. Emily, born May 7th, 1830, died Jan., 1832.
4. Elizabeth, Mary, born March 24th, 1833.
5. William, born Dec. 17th, 1838, graduated at Williams College in 1862.
6. Hattie Amelia, born January 17th, 1847.

504. "THIRZA LEE," to church Aug. 5th, 1821, daughter of No. (356,) born Nov. 19th, 1801, educated at Troy, N. Y., and became a teacher there; erected and established a female seminary in New Britain, on the corner west of the fountain, 1843; married Sept. 20th, 1849, Rev. David Tilton, of Andover, Mass., son of John, and Sally (Bachelder,) his wife, of Gilmantan, N. H. She was dismissed and recommended by letter to Dr. Beeman's church, Troy, Aug. 2d, 1832, and by letter, Aug. 6th, 1843,

returned and received back. A lady of literary and Christian adornments.

505. "ELIZA WINCHELL," to church Aug. 5th, 1821, born 1805, to No. (561,) married Nov. 26th, 1828, No. (741 ;) dismissed by letter, Oct., 1834, to church in North Coventry, with her husband. She died April 27th, 1838, aged 33, at the house of Thomas Tracy. She was lame from childhood. Her grave stone is in New Britain cemetery.

506. "JERUSHA BELDEN," to church Aug. 5th, 1821, baptized same time, daughter of Aziel, and his first wife Azuba (Goodrich,) born July 11th, 1805, married Aug. 4th, 1824, Amon Judd, son of No. (435,) born Oct. 27th, 1800. She died April 13th, 1831, aged 26, when he married, second, Dec. 7th, 1831, No. (898.) They lived on East street, next door south of Richard Judd. He died March 22d, 1840, aged 39.

THEIR CHILDREN.

1. Mary Annette, born April 9th, 1826, bap. July 23d, 1826, see No. (1196.)
2. Frances Maria, born Dec. 11th, 1828, bap. March 29th, 1829, married Carlos Huntley, of Newington.

SECOND WIFE'S CHILDREN.

3. Austin, born April 5th, 1834, bap. 1840, married Sept. 3d, 1856, Julia Miller.
4. Jane Eliza, born July 16th, 1838, bap. 1840, married July 13th, 1857, William G. Loveland.

507. "ELIZA SOUTHWORTH," to church Aug. 5th, 1821, daughter of Samuel, and Hannah (Shipman,) his wife, born June 3d, 1806, at Paris, N. Y., married Nov. 25th, 1830, No. (595 ;) took a general letter, 1842 ; received back, Dec. 5th, 1830, by letter from church in Gaines, N. Y. ; lives now, 1863, in Philadelphia, Pa.

508. "MARY B. ANDREWS," to church August 5th, 1821, daughter of No. (313,) born April 13th, 1807, married April 21st, 1839, No. (761.) She taught school before marriage, was very efficient for some years after marriage, but lost her good health, and was bedrid some five years ; was one year at the insane retreat, Utica, N. Y. She was dismissed, Oct. 2d, 1831, to church in Southington, by letter, was received back, and again dismissed, A. D. 1837, to church in Southington. Resides now, 1867, in Waterloo, Wis.

509. "LYDIA PENNFIELD," to church Aug. 5th, 1821, baptized same time, daughter of Nathaniel, 3d, and No. (549,) born May 1st, 1806, married March 20th, 1825, No. (516 ;) has been most of life in a state of religious despondency, arising from ill health, probably.

510. "SAMUEL RECOR," to church Aug. 5th, 1821, bap. same time, son of Michael, and his wife Lydia (Griswold,) born 1801, married Nov. 25th, 1829, Almira Steele, daughter of Avery, and his wife Polly (Rugg,) he was cut off from the church, Feb. 23d, 1832, for immoralities and neglect of ordinances. He died May 27th, 1835, aged 34.

511. "HORACE WELLS," to church Aug. 5th, 1821, son of No. (299,) born Aug. 11th, 1795, married Dec. 24th, 1823, No. (643.) He was a farmer, and inherited his father's homestead on East street, also a portion of his uncle Lemuel's estate in Yonkers, New York. He has represented the town in the Legislature. He built a new house on the opposith side from the old house of his father; he has become wealthy, and is much interested in the prosperity of the church and society. He died Nov. 2d, 1865, aged 70.

THEIR CHILDREN.

1. Levi Sedgwick, born Feb. 25th, 1825, bap. June 12th, 1825, see No. (942.)
2. Lemuel Russell, born Jan. 2d, 1827, see No. (943.)
3. Lucelia, born Oct. 27th, 1828, see No. (979.)
4. Catharine, born February 15th, 1833, bap. June 9th, 1833, died Feb. 2d, 1850, aged 17.

512. "LEMUEL WELLS," to church Aug. 5th, 1821, son of No. (299,) born July 4th, 1803, married Nov. 15th, 1827, No. (605;) moved to Yonkers, N. Y., and had there a portion of his uncle Lemuel's estate; he removed his connection to the church in that place, April 20th, 1843, with his wife. He died at Yonkers, N. Y., Sept. 11th, 1861, aged 58, of paralysis.

THEIR CHILDREN.

1. Florilla, born July 2d, 1829, at New Britain, and bap.
2. Marietta, born Nov. 15th, 1832, at New Britain, bap. Jan. 17th, 1832, at New Britain, married Jan. 30th, 1850, Ethan Flagg, of Yonkers; she died Feb. 3d, 1851.
3. Lemuel, born Nov. 1st, 1839, at Yonkers, N. Y., bap. 1841, at New Britain; he married, Sept. 16th, 1863, Sarah Jones, daughter of Alfred, of Yonkers, N. Y.

513. "NOAH HAMBLIN," to church Aug. 5th, 1821, son of Lemuel, of "White Oak," in Farmington, and his wife Mary (Hart,) born April 26th, 1801, married Jan. 24th, 1825, Eliza Wright, daughter of Huldah Wright, who married Isaac Jones, of Hartford, after the birth of this daughter. He was a brass founder, learned of Cyrus Booth. His connection with the church was by vote dissolved, Feb. 23d, 1832, for gross neglect of ordinances and intemperate habits. His wife, Eliza, died Nov. 20th, , when he married, second, Elmina Clark, of Burlington, daughter of Capt. Asa; she died, when he married, third, July 30th, 1851, Catharine Riley.

HIS CHILDREN BY SECOND WIFE, ELMINA.

1. Noah Clark, born Jan., 1842, was a soldier in Co. B., 6th Regimint C. V., at Hilton Head.
2. Ellen Eliza, born Feb., 1844, married Oct., 1862, Willard Stedman, of Bristol.

514. "ROSWELL S. STEELE," to church August 5th, 1821, baptized same time, son of No. (852,) born Nov. 25th, 1796, married May 4th, 1826, No. (725.) He was a farmer and inherited the old home of his father on the side of the mountain in Southwest district.

THEIR CHILDREN.

1. Julius Elbridge, born Feb. 16th, 1827, bap. June 3d, 1827, see No. (982.)
2. Ogden L., born March 11th, 1829, bap. June 21st, 1829, married August 28th, 1851, Ann Judd.
3. Amzi, born June 4th, 1832, died Sept. 7th, 1832, aged 3 months.
4. George Brainard, born Dec. 19th, 1833, bap. May 25th, 1834.
5. Charles D., born July 5th, 1837, married April 11th, 1863, Mary E. Farnum.
6. Harriet A., born Jan. 6th, 1840.
7. Matilda, } twins, born July 24th, 1844, { died Jan. 24th, 1844, aged 5 months.
8. Melissa, } twins, born July 24th, 1844, { died Jan. 28th, 1844, aged 5 months.
9. Ransom, born Jan. 29th, 1848.

515. "BENJAMIN SMITH," to church August 5th, 1821, baptized same time, son of Moses, and his wife Sally (Judd,) born July 13th, 1800; traveled south; was a butcher; kept a store, and lived in different localities; married, Dec. 9th, 1824, No. (627.) He was active in the temperance reformation; died Feb. 18th, 1860, aged 60. He was a man of kind feelings, with ready sympathy for those in trouble.

THEIR CHILDREN.

1. Infant, born Dec. 9th, 1826, died same day.
2. Abigail Urania, born Feb. 9th, 1828, married Oct. 11th, 1846, Nelson T. Judd.
3. Julia Ann, born June 19th, 1830, bap. October 31st, 1832, died Dec. 1st, 1855, aged 20.
4. Ellen Sophia, born Feb. 12th, 1837, bap. Aug. 3d, 1837, see No. (1127.)

516. "ADNA HART," to church August 5th, 1821, son of No. (183,) born Jan. 28th, 1804, married March 20th, 1825, No. (509;) a brass founder by occupation; residence on Elm street, the place formerly owned and occupied by George W. Southworth.

THEIR CHILDREN.

1. Antoinette, born Nov. 13th, 1825, bap. April 26th, 1826, see No. (960.)
2. Henry Franklin, born June 1st, 1829, married Eliza Steele, of Jefferson.
3. Jane Melissa, born Feb. 22d, 1833, bap. 1841, married Nov. 28th, 1854, Jonathan Nott.
4. Charles Watson, born Oct. 13th, 1837, bap. 1841.
5. Oliver Dwight, born June 26th, 1840, bap. 1841.
6. George Adna, born Dec. 21st, 1850, bap. Oct. 23d, 1851.

517. "SAMUEL WELDON," to church Aug. 5th, 1821, son of Luther, and his wife Jerusha (Hurlburt,) born Feb. 3d, 1799, at Argyle, N. Y.; a wagon maker by trade; married Oct. 15th, 1823, Sally Bartholomew, daughter of Ursula Andrews; she died Sept. 17th, 1837, aged 35, when he married, second, Sarah M. Keach, of Wethersfield; she died Aug. 3d, 1847, when he married, third, Feb. 3d, 1848, Mary, the widow of Walter Gridley, and daughter of Roswell Hunter, born Sept. 3d, 1802, at Newington. His residence is by the "Black Rock," in Southwest dis-

trict. He was voted out of the church, March 10th, 1831, for neglect of the ordinances and public worship.

THEIR CHILDREN.

1. Caroline, born Nov. 26th, 1824, married Elias Barnes, of Bristol.
2. Eli Everest, born Aug. 8th, , married widow Delia Fuller; he was a soldier in the Reg. Mass. V. Cavalry, Army of the Potomac.
3. George, born Aug. 19th, 1829.
4. Samuel Andrus, born March 22d, 1831, see No. 1258.
5. Sarah E., born April 2d, 1833, married Nov. 22d, 1855, Thomas Franklin Hart, of Alonzo, of Bristol; married second, Henry Wright.
6. Munroe, born Oct. 5th, 1834, married Sept. 29th, 1860, Catharine E. Buckley, of West Hartford.
7. Mary Ann, born June 30th, 1836.

SECOND WIFE'S CHILDREN.

8. Washington, born Jan. 31st, 1841, died March 7th, aged 5 weeks.
9. Oliver H., born April 18th, 1842.
10. Walter Augustus, born June 8th, 1844, died Feb. 21st, 1863, at Newbern, N. C., a soldier in Co. D, 46th Reg. Mass. Vols., of fever, at Camp Stanley Hocs, aged 19 years; buried in New Britain on the 13th day of March, 1863. He was a worthy member of the Methodist church.

518. "SYLVESTER PENNFIELD," to church Aug. 5th, 1821, baptized same time, son of Nathaniel, 3d, and No. (549,) born Nov. 22d, 1803, married Nov. 25th, 1825, Aurora Gilbert, daughter of Jonathan, and his wife Eunice (French,) born Aug. 30th, 1809. He was a cooper by trade, learned of his father, but removed to New York city in 1843, and spent the last of his life in putting up town and church clocks. He joined the Methodist church and the First Congregational church withdrew its watch Dec. 1st, 1831. He died August 7th, 1858, in New York, aged 55, but was brought here for burial.

THEIR CHILDREN.

1. Rosella, born July 18th, 1827.
2. George C. born July 30th, 1830.
3. Sylvester G., born Dec. 8th, 1834.
4. Ellen L., born Oct. 25th, 1838.
5. Washington Y., born Nov. 3, 1846, died Sept. 24th, 1865, at New York; buried at New Britain.

519. "GEORGE BOOTH," to church Aug. 5th, 1821, son of No. (338,) born Jan. 30th, 1806, married Oct. 2d, 1828, No. (615.) He was a brass founder. He and wife were dismissed by letter to church in Portsmouth, N. H., Feb. 23d, 1832. He was for some years paralyzed, and died Aug. 15th, 1860, aged 55, at Oxford, Ohio.

THEIR CHILDREN.

1. George Newton, born Jan. 1st, 1830, married Sarah Thorp, of Ohio.
2. Waldo Cornwell, born May 20th, 1836.

3. Orlando Wilcox, born April 21st, 1838.
4. Louisa, born May 21st, 1842, died March 15th, 1847, aged 3 years.
[These three sons volunteered into the Union army as soldiers.]

520. "CHLOE, wife of Abijah Smith," to church October 7th, 1821, daughter of No. (121,) born April 24th, 1767, married Jan. 18th, 1792, Abijah Smith, son of Samuel, and his wife, No. (89,) born Nov. 14th, 1767. He inherited the home of his father, on Stanley street, a prosperous farmer, quiet and retiring, he died April 6th, 1850, aged 82. She is remarkably strong minded, of good memory, but her sight and hearing have somewhat failed. She is, A. D. 1862, still living, and has aided much in this work, by remembering the connections of families, being born only nine years and five days after the first organization of the church. She died in Hartford, with her grand daughter Louisa, Feb. 22d, 1863, in her 96th year; buried in New Britain.

THEIR CHILDREN.

1. Chester, born Dec. 12th, 1798, died unmarried, March 13th, 1838, aged 39.
2. Nancy, born Jan. 12th, 1801, married May 11th, 1832, Horatio Waldo; she died June 17th, 1858, aged 56. She was for many years a distinguished teacher in this town. He died Nov. 19th, 1863, aged 63.
3. Samuel, born Dec. 27th, 1806; a farmer, and inherited the old homestead; his inventory, $30,000. He died Feb. 22d, 1861, aged 54; never married.

521. "HANNAH, wife of Simeon Harrington," to church Oct. 7th, 1821, baptized same time, daughter of Ashbel Griswold, and his wife Elizabeth (Woodruff,) of Farmington farms, daughter of Noah, born April 15th, 1776, married May 12th, 1808. He was born Aug. 1st, 1782, at Union, Ct. They had no certain dwelling place, but raised a large family on small means. She died April 13th, 1838, aged 52.

THEIR CHILDREN.

1. Ethan Lilly, born Jan. 29th, 1809, married Betsey Fielding.
2. Elizur D., born February 22d, 1811, married Margaret Davenport; married second, Almira Quinly.
3. Elizabeth Woodruff, born May 30th, 1813, unmarried, lives in West Hartford.
4. Cyril Pearl, born Aug. 8th, 1815, died Jan. 25th, 1838.
5. Gideon Griswold, born April 28th, 1818, married Margaret , lives in Iowa.
6. Gardner Simeon, born Oct. 9th, 1820, died May 5th, 1825.
7. Diana Hannah, born June 27th, 1824, died Jan. 13th, 1825.
8. Justin Simeon, born Jan. 2d, 1826, married Maria Dorman, of Burlington.
9. Angeline Louisa, born May 5th, 1828, married Orlando Palmer, of Farmington.
10. Lorin Gardner, born June 30th, 1832.

522. "REUBEN GLADDEN," to church Oct. 7th, 1821, son of Azariah, of Norwich, and his wife Anna (Hudson,) of Saybrook, born July 19th, 1782, married April 15th, 1804, No. (523.) They lived on Main street,

near the "Sand Hill." He was a farmer, of industrious habits and of great economy, and by dint of hard labor raised a large and respectable family. He died Feb. 21st, 1852, aged 70.

523. "SALLY, wife of Reuben Gladden," to church Oct. 7th, 1821, daughter of Ladwick Hotchkiss, and his wife, No. (278,) born Aug. 26th, 1782, married April 15th, 1804, No. (522,) a faithful wife and anxious mother. She died Feb. 9th, 1857, aged 74, having built a commodious house towards the close of life on East Main street.

THEIR CHILDREN.

1. William Henry, born April 15th, 1805, bap. Nov. 24th, 1821, married Betsey Judd; married second, No. (711.)
2. Marcia, born Nov. 12th, 1806, bap. Nov. 24th, 1821, see No. (614.)
3. Laura Jane, born Jan. 7th, 1809, bap. Nov. 24th, 1821, married May 26th, 1857, William Hart.
4. Jesse Hotchkiss, born Dec. 17th, 1810, bap. Nov. 24th, 1821, married Almira Stowe; married second, Jane Blinn.
5. Abi, born Feb. 17th, 1813, bap. Nov. 24th, 1821, see No. (700.)
6. Walter, born April 12th, 1815, bap. Nov. 24th, 1821, married July 30th, 1840, Charlotte Dayton, of Glastenbury. He was a joiner by trade; been captain, representative, post-master, and been active in the temperance reformation and politics; built and lived on Washington street, but in 1861 sold to Widow Dr. Stanley, and built new on West Main street.
7. Minerva, born Aug. 12th, 1818, bap. Nov. 24th, 1821, married No. (1019.)
8. George born Nov. 12th, 1820, bap. Nov. 24th, 1821, died March 2d, 1823, aged two years.
9. Sarah Ann, born June 19th, 1823, bap. Aug. 10th, 1823, see No. (1231.)
10. George Newton, born Aug. 14th, 1826.

524. POLLY, wife of William Judd," to church Oct. 7th, 1821, baptized same time, daughter of Charles Eddy, sen., and his wife Hannah (Kelsey,) born Oct. 11th, 1790, married April 23d, 1807. He was son of No. (435,) and his wife Irene, born Dec. 9th, 1787. He was a farmer, and was sexton many years; house nearly opposite his father. He died June 3d, 1855, aged 67. She died July 31st, 1835, aged 45.

THEIR CHILDREN.

1. William, born Sept. 1st, 1807, bap. August 10th, 1821, married May 6th, 1829, No. (701.)
2. Norton, born Dec. 19th, 1810, bap. August 10th, 1821, died October 22d, 1828, aged 18.
3. Maria, born Oct. 22d, 1812, bap. Aug. 10th, 1821, married Nov. 16th, 1831, Philip Hart, son of Stephen, and Sally (White,) his wife.

525. "SARAH, wife of Hezekiah C. Whipple," to church October 7th, 1821, baptized same time; her maiden name, Capron. They lived next south of Alvin North. He was a jeweler, from Providence, R. I.; born Feb. 22d, 1787, married July 23d, 1808, No. (525.) He died July 23d. 1835, aged 47. She was born Oct. 24th, 1787, at Providence, R. I., died Nov. 24th, 1825, aged 38.

THEIR CHILDREN.

1. Ann Jane, born Nov. 12th, 1808, bap. October 21st, 1821, married March 14th, 1831, Ethiel Sanger, of Ludlow, Mass.

2. Joseph, born Sept. 19th, 1811, bap. Oct. 21st, 1821.

3. William C., born April 5th, 1814, bap. Oct. 21st, 1821, see No. (749.)

4. Charlotte C., born Nov. 28th, 1815, bap. Oct. 21st, 1821.

5. Christopher C., born July 7th, 1818, died March 11th, 1820, aged two years.

6. Frances, born Aug. 26th, 1821, bap. Oct. 21st, 1821, married Nov 26th, 1846, George A. Richards, of North Haven.

526. "RUTH JUDD, wife of Phineas Pennfield," to church Oct. 7th, 1821, daughter of Linus Hart, of Avon, born May 3d, 1793, married Nov. 25th, 1812, No. (469.) She died Dec. 11th, 1848, aged 55.

527. "MINERVA, wife of Jesse Recor," to church Oct. 7th, 1821, daughter of No. (175,) born Oct. 22d, 1798, married Dec. 1st, 1819, Jesse Recor, son of Michael, and his wife Lydia (Griswold,) born March 26th, 1798; he died April 5th, 1842, aged 44. They lived until his decease in the old home of his father; she then lived near the foot of "Osgood Hill," and earned a living by weaving; sold her place and moved to Faribault, Minn., with her son-in-law, Samuel C. Dunham, of Plainville, where she died, March 7th, 1866, aged 67.

THEIR CHILDREN.

1. Nancy Almeda, born Dec. 17th, 1820, bap. Dec. 16th, 1821, see No. (837.)

2. Betsey Adeline, born April 6th, 1822, bap. March 9th, 1823, see No. (968.)

3. Roxy Ann, born Feb. 15th, 1826, bap. June 18th, 1826, married, 1848, Henry D. Vorburgh.

4. Augusta H., born Nov. 12th, 1827, married Aug. 29th, 1847, Samuel C. Dunham, of Faribault, Minn.

5. Cordelia Lydia, born Nov. 23d, 1838, bap. 1842.

6. George Dwight, born March 18th, 1841, bap. 1842.

528. "AURELIA, wife of Chester Pennfield," to church Oct. 7th, 1821, daughter of Nathaniel Carrington, of Plainville, and his wife Sybil (Steele,) born May 12th, 1800, married June 4th, 182,0 No. (486,) he died Aug. 6th 1825, aged 30, when she married, second, Nov. 19th, 1827, Henry Steele, son of William, born April 5th, 1806, died August 19th, 1847, aged 41. She joined the Methodist church, and, Dec. 1st, 1831, our church voted to withdraw its watch. She is a woman of good sense and kind disposition, and much respected.

HER CHILDREN BY HER FIRST HUSBAND.

1. Jeremiah, born March 16th, 1821, bap. Aug. 19th, 1821, married May 22d, 1840, Sarah J. Webster, da. of Ebenezer, of Bloomfield; he died July 10th, 1863, aged 42.

2. Julia Ann, born Sept. 26th, 1822, bap. Nov. 3d, 1822, married Nov. 25th, 1841, Samuel M. Knowles, of West Hartford.

HER CHILDREN BY SECOND HUSBAND.

3. Jane Eliza, born Sept. 12th, 1828.

4. Charles Henry, born Jan. 27th, 1832, married April 12th, 1854, Louisa A. Steele, daughter of Jerome; she died Oct. 20th, 1854, aged 22, when he married, second, Angeline Pennfield, daughter of Nathaniel.

5. Jane Eliza, 2d, born Nov. 15th, 1834.
6. Sophia Winchell, born June 6th, 1838.

529. "Eliza, wife of Ira Stanley, jun." to church Oct. 7th, 1821, daughter of John Riley Lincoln and his wife, No. (319,) born Oct. 19th, 1801, married Oct. 6th, 1819, No. (921 ;) she was dismissed and recommended by letter to Farmington church, Dec. 1st, 1822, and returned, by letter December, 1835 ; residence now, 1862, on Washington street.

530. "Maria Butler," to church Oct. 7th, 1821, daughter of Joseph, of Berlin, and his wife, Roxanna (Cadwell,) born Feb. 7th, 1804, in Berlin, married Jan. 12th, 1832, Walter Beckley, son of Luther, Esq. and his wife, Sarah (Flagg,) born June 22d, 1808, at Beckley quarter; moved to Texas, with his family ; she united with the Universalist church of Berlin, and made a lengthy communication to us, in which she stated that her views of some of the doctrines which we esteemed essential, had changed, upon which, Dec. 1st, 1831, this church withdrew its watch and fellowship; she died July 12th, 1860, at Mount Pleasant, in Texas, aged 56.

THEIR CHILDREN,

(And the mother's birth and death, from the Beckley family records, which her brother thinks, makes her too young.)

1. Frances Laura, born Oct. 15th, 1832, at Berlin, Conn.
2. Henry Augustus, born March 10th, 1834, died Oct. 22d, 1844.
3. Jane Maria, born July 22d, 1836, died Sept. 22d, 1849.
4. Joseph Walter, born Nov. 10th, 1837, died in Texas, Aug. 14th, 1860.
5. George Alfred, born May 13th, 1839.
6. Rosina Maria, born Sept. 13th, 1841.
7. Frank Ludovico, born Sept. 4th, 1845.

531. "Matilda Cogswell," to church Oct. 7th, 1821, born May 23d, 1802, to Salmon, in Southington, and his wife, Sarah (Smith,) baptized there, July 24th, 1803 ; was dismissed and recommended from this to that church, Dec. 1st, 1822; received there Feb. 2d, 1823, and their record says their watch is withdrawn; she married Jan. 31st, 1826, Thomas McMahon, of Canaan, and was divorced, when she married second, Peter Boyd, of Boonville, Oneida county, New York; she was received to this church again Feb. 11th, 1855, by letter from the church in South Windsor, and dismissed by letter back to the same church, Jan. 9th, 1858; she now, fall of 1861, is in the alms-house of her native town, Southington, and her husband, Peter Boyd, lives in Wisconsin.

532. "Abigail Andrews," to church Oct. 7th, 1821, born May 16th, 1806, to No. (197,) married Nov. 27th, 1827, No. (542;) he died, when she married second, May 11th, 1848, Comfort Hewlet, son of Comfort, of Kensington, and his wife, Patty (Pemberton,) of Groton, Conn.; she dismissed and recommended by letter to South church, 1856, and is now, A. D. 1861, living on Arch street.

533. "SOPHIA HART," to church Oct. 7th, 1821, born Nov. 18th, 1806, to No. (441,) married July 3d, 1826, Ralph I. Dunham, son of Elisha, of Berlin; a harness-maker and carriage-trimmer by trade; learned of Moses W. Beckley; was in company with Salmon N. Hart, of Hartford; went to Natchez, La., to sell work and died there, Nov. 9th, 1834. She was dismissed and recommended by letter to church in Hartford; she was a scholar in the Sabbath school, 1816, and could repeat 1,000 verses of Scripture per week; to South church, by letter, 1852; lives now, 1861, on Walnut street.

THEIR CHILDREN.

1. Sarah Elizabeth, born July 8th, 1830, died April 14th, 1836, aged six.
2. Helen Sophia, born July 4th, 1833, died Aug. 2d, 1835, aged three.

534. "SARAH G. WHITTLESEY," to church Oct. 7th, 1821, born Sept. 15th, 1808, to No. (321;) lives with her sisters in Ottawa, Illinois, and Sheboygan, Wisconsin; never married; remarkable for memory and sociability; dismissed Jan. 5th, 1866, by general letter.

535. "LUCY M. WINCHELL, to church Oct. 7th, 1821, born Oct. 16th, 1808, to Miles C. and his wife, No. (428,) married Willys Bronson, of Berlin; married second, Timothy Lewis, of Pennsylvania, but now, 1861, lives in Illinois.

THEIR CHILDREN BY FIRST MARRIAGE.

1. Louisa, born
2. Willys, } twins, born
3. Willard, }

536. "MARY B. BOOTH," to church Oct. 7th, 1821, born April 18th, 1808, to Cyrus and his wife, No. (340,) married June 1st, 1826, Edmund F. Booth, son of Joseph and Charlotte (Bowman,) his wife; she died Nov. 2d, 1830, aged 23. He was born Nov. 15th, 1812, at New York; was a brass-worker.

THEIR CHILDREN.

1. Antoinette, born Jan. 11th, 1827, died Jan. 3d, 1828, aged one.
2. George, born March 13th, 1828, died Nov. 26th, 1828.
3. Joseph, born , bap. Nov., 1830.
4. Cyrus, born Oct. 25th, 1830, bap. Nov., 1830; in the Union army three years.
5. George, born

537. "AMZI W. HART," to church Oct. 7th, 1821, baptized same time, born Nov. 3d, 1801, to Asahel and his second wife, Sarah, daughter of Judah Hart; he learned the cooper's trade of Selah Hart, and died at his house in Hart quarter, of spotted fever, Aug. 10th, 1823, aged 22; was a young man of good parts and habits, and much promise.

538. "CYRENUS BOOTH," to church Oct. 7th, 1821, baptized same time; born June 21st, 1801, to David and his wife, Hannah (Mather;) a wagon-maker by trade; married Oct. 22d, 1826, Almena Hough, of Mer-

iden; dismissed and recommended by letter to the church in Meriden, in 1840; he has a pleasant home in West Meriden.

THEIR CHILDREN.

1. Burdette, born March 27th, 1828, married Sarah Belden; he died Dec. 30th, 1860, aged 32.
2. Cordelia, born March 26th, 1830, died March 3d, 1848, aged 18.
3. Albertus Hough, born Aug. 1st, 1838.

539. "JOHN ANDREWS, jun." to church Oct. 7th, 1821, born Oct. 10th, 1803, to No. (197;) a shoe-maker by trade; married Nov. 8th, 1836, Lucy Foote, of Madrid, N. Y., born Feb. 28th, 1813; he dismissed and recommended by letter to church in Cleaveland, Ohio; died March 22d, 1857.

THEIR CHILDREN.

1. Sarah S., born May 27th, 1839, at Cleaveland; teacher.
2. Mary E., born Dec. 13th, 1840, at Cleaveland; teacher.
3. Charles J., born Oct. 12th, 1845, at Cleaveland; a telegraph operator.
4. Horace F., born July 7th, 1851, at Cleaveland.

540. "HARRY JUDD," to church Oct. 7th, 1821, baptized same time, born Nov. 2d, 1804, to John and his wife, No. (637;) was a brass-worker; lived several years in Southington; married May 8th, 1828, No. (733;) his mother provided a home for him and family, on West Main street, the old house of Sergeant Moses Andrews, near the railroad crossing, where he died May 27th, 1854, aged 50; he had been cut off from the church for neglect of public worship and the ordinances, Jan. 31st, 1838.

THEIR CHILDREN.

1. Franklin, born May 13th, 1829; partially insane in adult years.
2. Ann Eliza, born June 4th, 1834, married Aug. 28th, 1851, Ogden L. Steele, of Roswell; his residence on West Main street, at the railroad crossing.

541. "WILLIAM WHITTLESEY," to church Oct. 7th, 1821, born Sept. 19th, 1805, to No. (321;) graduated at Yale, 1827; ordained to the ministry, 1837; was a Sabbath school missionary at the west; preached in several places, and teacher in several localities; built near his father on the Dr. Smalley farm; married Sept. 9th, 1845, No. (1111,) and for several years has been occupied in agriculture.

THEIR CHILD.

Louisa Hart, born May 23d, 1847, see No. (1,247.)

542. "AARON HART, jun." to church Oct. 7th, 1821, born Nov. 25th, 1805, to No. (247;) was a joiner by trade; learned of Capt. Porter, of Farmington; married Nov. 27th, 1827, No. (532;) built nearly opposite his father; lived in different localities; he died May 20th, 1845, aged 39.

THEIR CHILDREN.

1. Newton Francis, born Jan. 2d, 1829, bap. June 14th, 1829, see No. (972.)

2. John Andrews, born May 2d, 1830, bap. July 25th, 1830; killed by kick of a horse, June 11th, 1843, aged 13.

3. Aaron Adolphus, born Dec. 22d, 1830, bap. June 17th, 1832, died Sept. 12th, 1832.

4. Abigail Jane, born June 2d, 1837, bap. Sept. 24th, 1837, married Dec. 25th, 1860, John G. Lewis, of Hampton, Conn. and of New Haven; she has excelled in teaching.

543. "JAMES H. WINCHELL," to church Oct. 7th, 1821, born June 16th, 1806, to Miles C. and his wife, No. (428;) he was received to church in Farmington by letter from this, July 30th, 1824, and their record says, excommunicated, 1827; he went to Georgia, and married there, Selina Jackson; lived in Cherokee county, and became a slave-holder, and since moved to Arkansas.

544. "JOHN STEDMAN," to church Oct. 7th, 1821, born Oct. 25th, 1804, to Samuel and his wife, No. (333.)

545. "THOMAS G. LEE," to church Oct. 7th, 1821, born Sept. 1st, 1808, to No. (356;) graduated at Yale, 1830; studied medicine with Dr. Todd, of Farmington and Hartford; became superintendent for the McLane Asylum, at Charlestown, Mass.; he married in Vermont, April 21st, 1835, Susan Clark, who since his death has married Rev. Joseph S. Gallagher, now, 1861, of Bloomfield, New Jersey. Dr. Lee felt unwell, and while on his journey to New Britain, for his health, called at Worcester, to see Dr. Woodward, when he was taken with typhus fever, and died Oct. 29th, 1836, aged 28. The trustees passed the highest encomiums on his character and talents; he had a great love for historical facts, and the notes he took while in Farmington and New Britain, have (since the original is lost,) greatly contributed to the early history of this church and society in these pages; he was dismissed and recommended by letter to Winthrop church, Charlestown, Mass., (so says tradition;) he left no posterity.

546. " Widow SARAH HART," to church Dec. 2d, 1821, daughter of No. (140,) born Nov. 7th, 1770, married July 30th, 1793, Asahel Hart, of Jehudi, and was his second wife; died Dec. 19th, 1841, aged 71.

CHILDREN.

1. Amon, born Nov. 18th, 1790, died Aug. 17th, 1798, aged seven, of dysentery.

2. Hannah, born Oct. 7th, 1792, married Sylvester Clark, son of Abel.

SECOND WIFE'S CHILDREN.

3. Amzi, born June 13th, 1795, died Aug. 25th, 1798, aged three, of dysentery.

4. Sarah, born March 20th, 1797, died March 20th, 1797, aged one hour.

5. Eliza, born Oct. 10th, 1799, married April 18th, 1824, Ralph Pearl, of Southington, son of Frederic.

6. Amzi Woodruff, born Nov. 3d, 1801, see No. (537.)

7. Amon, born Dec. 19th, 1802, died Dec. 22d, 1803, aged one year.

547. "OLIVE, wife of Uni Wright," to church Dec. 2d, 1821, baptized same time, born Aug. 18th, 1775, to Leonard Belden and his wife, Rebecca (Dix,) of Wethersfield, married August, 1797; he a farmer, son of Simeon and his wife, Anne (Whaples,) of Newington, 1768; bought and lived on the place built by Moses Andrews, jun. at "Pond River Bridge," so called; he died Oct. 28th, 1843, aged 76; she died June 11th, 1864, aged 89.

THEIR CHILDREN.

1. Silas, born Feb. 1st, 1798, married Feb. 4th, 1827, Catharine G. Eddy, daughter of William.
2. William, born Feb. 12th, 1812, married May 15th, 1836, Lucy Maria Slater, of Benjamin.

548. "SALLY, wife of Solomon Butler," to church Dec. 2d, 1821, born Sept. 6th, 1783, to Isaac Brown, of Glastenbury, and his wife, Hannah (Hills,) married Feb. 3d, 1805, No. (452;) she died Feb. 20th, 1849, aged 65; a pious woman.

549. "POLLY, wife of Nathaniel Pennfield," to church Dec. 2d, 1821, born 1782, to Ebenezer Steele, jun. and his wife, Lucy (Wright;) given in childhood to her grandmother, on whose account she was baptized, May 29th, 1791; she married Nov. 5th, 1798; he son of No. (237;) was a cooper by trade; learned of his father; built house and shop on West street, between Capt. Lemuel Hotchkiss and Josiah Steele, sen.; his shop became the dwelling-house of Miles C. Winchell, and his house disappeared; he subsequently built a small house on the same road, north of Josiah Steeles, where he died March 8th, 1837, aged 56; she died Nov. 17th, 1837, aged 55.

THEIR CHILDREN.

1. Laura, born , married Jan. 1st, 1818, Solomon Sandford.
2. Sylvester, born Nov. 22d, 1803, see No. (518.)
3. Sophrone, born , married Milo Pond, of Camden, New York.
4. Lydia, born May 1st, 1806, see No. (509.)
5. Hiram, born Nov. 20th, 1808, married March 16th, 1829, Rhoda Cogswell, sister of Matilda.
6. Adelia, born , married July 5th, 1840, Edward Andrews, of Rodney, of Farmington.
7. Caroline, born , married Benjamin Hicks; live, 1867, at Jamestown, N. Y.
8. Celestia, born , married Sept. 13th, 1840, Thomas Andrews, of Rodney, of Farmington.
9. Lucy Ann, born June 5th, 1821, married Sept. 1st, 1840, William Curtiss, son of Shubel.
10. Angeline, born July 11th, 1831, married Oct. 3d, 1855, Charles H. Steele, son of Henry.

550. "AMON STANLEY," to church Dec. 2d, 1821, baptized same time, born March 10th, 1778, to Lot and his wife, Rhoda (Wadsworth,) of Farmington; by trade a hatter; learned of his father; but later in life a

successful farmer; inherited the home of his father, on the corner of Stanley street and "New Highway;" modest and retiring, yet interested in every good work and reformation; married Oct. 10th 1802, No. (339;) he was appointed one of the church standing committee, Dec. 30th, 1823, in place of Joseph Mather, resigned; he died Feb. 2d, 1846, aged 68; he was the third of fourteen children of his father's family.

THEIR CHILDREN.

1. Julia, born Dec. 24th, 1803, bap. Jan. 27th, 1811, see No. (603.)
2. Thomas, born Sept. 22d, 1805, bap. Jan. 27th, 1811, see No. (680.)
3. Henry, born Sept. 24th, 1807, bap. Jan. 27th, 1811, see No. (704.)
4. James, born Oct. 22d, 1809, died in infancy.
5. James, 2d, born March 31st, 1812, bap. May 24th, 1812, see No. (1165.)
6. Augustus, born April 11th, 1814, bap. May 29th, 1814, see No. (604.)
7. Timothy Wadsworth, born July 13th, 1817, bap. Aug. 24th, 1817, see No. (915.)
8. Lot, born July 8th, 1820, bap. Sept. 3d, 1820, see No. (846.)
9. Martha, born Aug. 11th, 1822, bap. Oct. 6th, 1822, see No. (847.)
10. Amelia, born Jan. 1st, 1825, bap. May 1st, 1825, see No. (933.)
11. Mary Antoinette, born Sept. 22d, 1828, bap. Nov. 23d, 1828, died May 16th, 1838, aged 10.

551. "Anna Deming," to church Dec. 2d, 1821, born Oct. 19th, 1780, to Elizur Deming, of Newington, and his wife, Lucina (Francis;) lived with her sister, No. (1294,) and died April 28th, 1849, aged 68, in Hartford, at her house; never married; buried in the old Episcopal Church cemetery, Newington; marble slab.

552. "Ellen E. Hamblin," to church Dec. 2d, 1821, baptized same time, born July 17th, 1806, to John, of "White Oak," Farmington, and his wife, No. (447,) married April 8th, 1828, Samuel G. Forbes, son of Daniel and his wife, Belinda (Gridley;) she was dismissed and recommended by letter to Farmington church, and received there Oct. 2d, 1831; they now, A. D. 1861, live in Plainville; no children.

553. "Emeline Franklin," to church Dec. 2d, 1821, baptized same time, born A. D. 1807, to Sarah Wright, daughter of Simeon, and who was an imbecile; she married, 1825, John Riley Jones, son of Benoni and his wife, Sally (Olmsted;) he was a wheelwright; lived in various localities; she died April, 1843, at Deerfield, near Utica, N. Y.; he married second, March 23d, 1845, Elizabeth Couch, daughter of Amos and his wife, Phebe (Barnes,) sister of Blakesley, of Berlin, born July 6th, 1804; he died June 13th, 1859, aged 56.

THEIR CHILDREN.

1. Chester, born 1829, died June 11th, 1835, aged six.
2. Mary, born Aug. 9th, 1831, married Dec. 23d, 1849, Richard Hart; he in the army, 1863.
3. Anna, born 1837, died Sept. 16th, 1838, aged one year and three months.
4. Caroline, , married Edward Callender, of Unionville.

5. John, born at Utica, N. Y.; a three months, and a three years volunteer, at Port Royal, company G., Capt. John Tracy, sixth regiment Connecticut Volunteers; re-enlisted, 1864; he died Sept. 6th, 1864, at Andersonville prison, in Georgia, aged 25.
6. Infant, born , died at Deerfield, New York; no name.

554. "SUSANNA TRYON," to church Feb. 3d, 1822, baptized same time, born June 19th, 1778, at Bolton, Conn., a twin-sister of Simeon Tryon, to Aaron, of that town, and his wife, Sarah (Landfear;) she lived, after six years of age, with Gideon Griswold, and after his death with Michael Recor, during life; she died Sept. 26th, 1826, aged 48; had a brother, Aaron, jun., who died young; had also, a sister, Sally, who was a cripple from childhood; the subject of this notice never married, but had a daughter, called Laura Dunham, who married Aug. 7th, 1825, Andrew Curtiss, and had a family.

555. "KEZIAH L. ANDREWS," to church Feb. 3d, 1822, born Dec. 6th, 1805, to Truman and his wife, No. (265,) married May 5th, 1825, Lyman Wilcox Booth, son of No. (338;) he was by trade a shoe-maker, and soon after marriage went to parts unknown; she married second, Seth Philips, and lived and died in Hartford.

556. "RHODA R. BELDEN," to church April 7th, 1822, born Aug. 24th, 1802, to Leonard, jun. and his wife, No. (324,) married March 28th, 1834, Isaac N. Cornwell, of Windham, Greene county, N. Y.; she removed her church connection to the church in that place, (called) Windham Center.

THEIR CHILDREN.

Peleg, Rufus K., Leonard B., George H.

557. "ABIGAIL, wife of Norman Woodruff," to church Feb. 2d, 1823, by letter from the church of Lenox, Mass., married March 19th, 1813, No. (381;) she was born July 5th, 1792, to No. (194;) to South church, 1842.

558. "JOHN BRAY," to church Aug. 3d, 1823, by letter from the church in West Hartford, born June 7th, 1768; to that church Aug. 3d, 1811, by letter from Burke, Vermont; he came as a miller, to this place, and attended Deacon Hart's mill; was dismissed by letter Oct. 1st, 1826; he probably married Nov. 26th, 1789, at Southington, Mercy or Mary Fields, who with her daughter, Paulina, were members of a Baptist church in Burke, Vermont, and recommended to the church in West Hartford, but not connected with this church; she was a weakly woman, and mostly confined to her room; she died July 26th, 1848, in Ohio, aged 82; he died Oct. 1st, 1854, in Ohio, aged 86.

THEIR CHILDREN.

1. Sarah, born Oct. 1st, 1790, see No. (576)
2. Sylvester, born April 2d, 1792, died here, April 7th, 1824, aged 32 years and five days.

3. John, born , went to Texas, then to Ohio; lived there, 1861.

4. William, born , lives, 1861, in Ohio.

5. Paulina, born , married Chauncey Woodruff, of Farmington; married second,

6. Alfred, born Jan. 20th, 1799, died March 11th, 1835, aged 36, two months and eleven days.

7. Helace, born 1811, died 1817, at West Hartford, aged six years, eight months.

8. Anson, born , died Oct. 10th, 1846, at Albany, New York.

9. James, born , lives in Ohio, A. D. 1861.

559. "DOROTHY, wife of Joseph Wright," to church Oct. 5th, 1823, born Sept. 16th, 1795, to Ebenezer Hart and his wife, No. (307,) married Feb. 3d, 1814, Col. Joseph Wright, son of No. (274,) born Oct. 7th, 1779; lived in the home of his father, now owned and occupied by Almon Goodwin, south end of East street, formerly the home of Lieut. Elisha Booth, who built it, 1761, as indicated by a mark on the barn, still visible. He was Colonel of Militia, Judge of Probate, Representative, and Selectman, many years, and an ardent temperance reformer. A. D. 1850, sold his place and built on Chesnut street, in the village, where he died July 19th, 1855, aged 76. She was dismissed and recommended by letter to South church, 1845.

THEIR CHILDREN.

1. Lucy Hart, born Dec. 11th, 1814, bap. Aug. 6th, 1826, on reception to church, see No. (586.)

2. Benjamin Gailord, born Oct. 26th, 1816, married April 17th, Prudence Hubbard; second, Frances E. Trowbridge.

3. Oliver Cromwell, born Sept. 16th, 1819, married Oct. 6th, 1841, Mary H. Jones, of Vermont; she died 1867.

4. Edwin Culver, born Dec. 4th, 1821, married July 27th, 1852, Louisa C. Jessup, of New York.

5. Emily Elizabeth, born Dec. 11th, 1828, died Aug. 30th, 1838, aged ten.

6. Hercelia Ann, born April 21st, 1833; she died Dec. 24th, 1854, aged 22.

560. "EMMA, wife of Samuel Judd," to church Oct. 5th, 1823, born June 14th, 1799, to Russel Case, of Simsbury, and his wife, Hannah (Gilbert,) of Kensington, married April 23d, 1822, No. (969;) after the decease of her husband, she bought a place back of the "Stone store," where now, 1861, she lives, and cared for her mother, who died July 12th, 1865, aged 77; she has no children.

561. "CALVIN WINCHELL," to church Oct. 5th, 1823, by letter from the church in Kensington, son of Hezekiah, of Kensington, and his wife, Rachel, baptized Sept. 15th, 1765, at Kensington, married No. (562;) he was a joiner by trade, and in Kensington, lived just west of the church; he bought in New Britain, the Ozias Hart, (alias) William North place south of the village; was a devoted Christian; he and wife to Kensington church, 1811, by letter from (Stepney,) Rocky Hill; he died May 25th, 1838, aged 73; grave stone in New Britain cemetery.

562. "CHLOE, wife of Calvin Winchell," to church Oct. 5th, 1823, by letter from Kensington church; her maiden name, Goodrich; she died Aug. 4th, 1843, in Hartford, aged 78.

THEIR CHILDREN.

1. Sabra, born , married Gilbert Chapman,
2. Orrin, born , married Laura Cook; married, second, Mix, of New Haven.
3. Asa, born , never married, died at the South.
4. Lucretia, born , married Jason Peck, of Berlin.
5. Lucy, born 1796, married Oct. 20th, 1819, Seth Hooker, of William, and died, 1823, aged 27.
6. Aurelia, born , married Thompson; married, second, Snow, of Hartford.
7. Calvin, born , married May 5th, 1824, Louisa Pattison, and died Sept. 9th, 1825, aged 23.
8. Eliza, born 1805, married Nov. 26th, 1828, No. (741.)

563. "Widow RHODA HART," to church Dec. 7th, 1823, by letter from Farmington church, daughter of Charles Stedman, and his wife Jemima (Gaines,) of Wethersfield, widow of Stephen Hart, son of Daniel, and Abigail (Thompson,) his wife, born Dec. 8th, 1744; had an impediment in his speech, was a farmer and lived at the foot of "Clark Hill." He inherited his father's estate which was one of the three farms and families excepted in the incorporation of the society. The Farmington town record says they were married Oct. 8th, 1767. He died Nov. 20th, 1816, aged 71. She died March 26th, 1832, aged 81.

THEIR CHILDREN.

1. Ebenezer, born Feb. 8th, 1768, married Oct. 2d, 1791, No. (307.)
2. Mary, born June 25th, 1770, see No. (288.)
3. Chestina, born Oct. 22d, 1773, married Feb. 12th, 1795, Theodore Webster, son of Stephen, of West Hartford, born April 15th, 1769, died Aug. 2d, 1856, aged 83. She died April 26th, 1828, aged 55.
4. Stephen, born Oct. 21st, 1775, married June 25th, 1797, No. (638.)
5. Nancy, born , married Nov. 27th, 1806, Simeon Kilby, of Simeon, of Wethersfield.

564. "MARY, wife of Selah Andrews," to church Dec. 7th, 1823, by letter from church at Westfield, Middlesex county, Ct., daughter of Joel Bacon, and his wife Lydia (Hubbard,) born July 31st, 1788, married Sept. 5th, 1822. He was son of Hezekiah, and his wife, No. (721,) born Sept. 5th, 1789; a farmer, lived on and inherited the home of his father on West Main street, some two miles west of the village. She united, 1843, with the Baptist church. He died May 11th, 1865, aged 76.

THEIR CHILDREN.

1. Levi, } twins, born Sept. 22d, 1823, died next day.
2. Eli, }

3. Rhoda Porter, born March 20th, 1825, bap. June 19th, 1825, died Nov. 2d, 1834, aged 9 years and 7 months,

4. Sylvanus, born Sept. 18th, 1826, bap. June 24th, 1827, died Oct. 12th, 1834, aged 8 years.

5. Maryetta, born March 11th, 1831, bap. July 24th, 1831, married April 14th, 1852, Butler Warren, son of David, and Sally (Boardman) his wife. She died Dec. 12th, 1858, in Hamden, leaving two sons ; 1, Leroy, 2, Wilbur, who died.

565. "Amos Woodruff," to church Feb. 1st, 1824, by letter from the church in Lenox, Mass., son of Robert, and his wife, No. (17,) born 1745, married Oct. 27th, 1768, No. (566 ;) lived at the home of his father, where Horatio A. Pratt owns and resides. He died Jan. 31st, 1828, aged 83.

566. "Wife of Amos Woodruff," to church Feb. 1st, 1824, by letter from Lenox, Mass., maiden name, Sarah Clark, daughter of Joseph, and Sarah (Curtiss,) his wife; she was sister to No. (434.) She died April 24th, 1824, aged 75.

THEIR CHILDREN.

1. Gad, born May 17th, 1769, married, Nov. 4th, 1790, Sarah Loomis, of Harwinton.

2. Alma, born Aug. 19th, 1771, an Albino, No. (863.)

3. Truman, born Nov. 23d, 1773, an Albino, married Sept. 17th, 1804, Ann Hart; he died Feb. 15th, 1854.

4. Elizabeth, born Jan. 3d, 1776, an Albino, died Nov. 20th, 1812.

5. Sarah, born April 7th, 1778, married John Robinson, of Lenox, Mass.

6. Betsey, born June 7th, 1783, married William Ford, of Lenox, Mass., died Feb. 25th, 1818.

7. Robert, born Dec. 28th, 1788, died Oct. 8th, 1818.

567. "Erastus Lewis," to church Oct. 3d, 1824, by letter from church in Waterbury, born June, 1774, to No. (88,) married May 28th, 1801, No. (568.) He was a tinner by trade, learned at his brother's shop on East street, see No. (439.) He lived, after his marriage, in the home of his wife, the old Nathan Booth house, which stood northwest of the South church, some five rods. His tin shop was near the site of George Hart's new house now in building. He left the tin making for the manufacture of clock weights and bells, and moved to Waterbury to carry on the business, where he lived twelve years; his health failed, and he returned and died May 2d, 1826, of consumption. He was a pious, good man.

568. "Wife of Erastus Lewis," to church Oct. 3d, 1824, by letter from church in Waterbury; maiden name, Salome Booth, born March 15th, 1785, to No. (193,) married May 28th, 1801, No. (567 ;) lives on Main street now, 1862, with her son Edward. She died Sept. 3d, 1866, aged 81.

THEIR CHILDREN.

1. Edward, born Jan. 26th, 1802, see No. (569.)

2. Mary, born Aug. 2d, 1803, died Jan. 25th, 1821.

3. Betsey, born March 13th, 1805, died Dec. 9th, 1826, No. (577.)

4. Adeline, born Sept. 15th, 1807, died Aug. 13th, 1857, see No. (617.)
5. Julia Ann, born April 7th, 1810, see No. (578.)
6. Erastus Barton, born April 21st, 1812, see No. (625.)
7. George, born Aug. 6th, 1814, see No. (919.)
8. Eliza S., born May 2d, 1817, died Jan. 8th, 1840.
9. }
10. } Three boys, born Jan. 24th, 1820, all died in infancy.
11. }
12. Thomas Hopkins, born Feb. 8th, 1823, bap. Sept. 9th, 1827, died Sept. 9th, 1852, aged 29.

569. "Edward Lewis," to church Oct. 3d, 1824, son of No. (567,) married April 22d, 1839, No. (739.) He was a brass and iron worker; to church by letter from Waterbury; lives, 1866, with his mother, on Main street; had no children to live. His wife died Aug. 27th, 1864, when he married, second, May 1st, 1866, No. (1327.)

570. "Mary E. Southworth," to church Dec. 5, 1824, from the Fourth church in Saybrook, born Sept. 3d, 1803, to Samuel, and his wife Hannah (Shipman.) She was dismissed and recommended by letter to the church in Gaines, N.Y. She died, Feb., 1846, aged 42, at Cooperstown, N. Y., at her brother Henry's.

571. "Chloe, wife of John Steele," to church Dec. 5th, 1824, by letter from First church in Farmington, born Nov. 28th, 1803, to Nathaniel Carrington of Plainville, and his wife Sibil (Steele,) married Dec. 2d, 1822. He is a brass worker, lives north of the cemetery, son of William, and Beccarena (Pennfield,) his wife, born Feb. 13th, 1801.

THEIR CHILDREN.

1. Samuel John, born Nov. 6th, 1823, gone to parts unknown.
2. Lydia, born Oct. 7th, 1825, died Feb. 8th, 1827, aged 18 months.
3. Henrietta Lydia, born April 5th, 1830, married May 2d, 1847, William A. Thompkins, of Farmington.
4. Cornelia Jannette, born June 21st, 1833, married Gad E. Langdon.

572. "Mary Clark, wife of Chauncey," to church Feb. 6th, 1825, by letter from church in Meriden, born Oct. 11th, 1796, to Solomon Smith and his wife, No (206,) married Dec. 22d, 1824, No. (477,) and was his second wife.

[Here ends the ministry of Rev. Newton Skinner, who died of fever, March 31st, 1825, greatly lamented.]

[Here, Oct. 12th, 1825, begins the ministry of Rev. Henry Jones—ordained and installed—the interim being six months and twelve days.]

573. "CHLOE, the widow of Treat Deming," to church Dec. 4th, 1825, born July 24th, 1793, to No. (168,) married Oct. 8th, 1820, Treat Deming, of Wethersfield, son of Richard, and his wife Milicent (Belden,) born June 19th, 1792; he died August 9th, 1823, in New Rumley, Ohio, aged 31. She returned to her old home and built a small house, but since sold, and now, 1867, lives with her daughter on Prospect Hill, Waterbury, to which place she removed her church relation by letter.

THEIR CHILDREN.

1. Elizabeth, born May 2d, 1821, bap. Dec. 4th, 1825, see No. (939.)
2. Catharine Deming, born Jan. 5th, 1823, bap. Dec. 4th, 1825, married Nov. 17th, 1844, Gordon Spencer Andrews, son of Timothy, of East Haddam, and his wife Rhoda (Spencer,) born June 17th, 1809; is a stone cutter in Waterbury.

574. "GUNILDA BASS," to church Dec. 4th, 1825, by letter from church in Farmington; born Oct. 3d, 1795 to Samuel, and his wife, No. (153,) married Jan. 3d, 1831, No. (459.) She spent several years of her life usefully and pleasantly in Timothy Cowles' family, in Farmington; living, 1861, with her family friends; to South church, 1842.

575. "DANIEL RICHARDS," to church June 4th, 1826, baptized same time, son of Jonathan, of Vermont, and his wife Abigail B. (Knapp,) born July 21st, 1798, at Canaan, married, 1823, No. (591,) at Wolcottville, Conn. He had brothers, Lawrence, Charles and Joshua, sisters, Sally, Polly, Delia, Almira and Abigail, mostly born in Canaan,

THEIR CHILDREN.

1. Frederick Benoni, born March, 1825, bap. June 4th, 1826, married Church, in Ohio; lives in Eaton County, Mich.
2. Daughter, born , bap. Sept. 2d, 1827, died young.
3. Daughter, born , died young.

576. "SALLY BRAY," to church June 4th, 1826, daughter of No. (558,) born Oct. 1st, 1790, married Charles M. Stowe, of Berlin. She was dismissed and recommended to church in Worthington, by letter, Dec. 4th, 1831; she died there Oct. 3d, 1832, aged 42 years and 2 days; grave in Beckley quarter cemetery.

THEIR CHILDREN.

1. Emily, born Jan. 17th, 1829, married Levi Avery; married, second, William Van Derren.
2. Elizabeth, born April 11th, 1830, lives, 1861, in West Hartford.
3. Sarah, born Sept. 23d, 1832, married Sept. 23d, 1851, John Woodruff, son of No. (381.)

577. "BETSEY LUCRETIA LEWIS," to church June 4th, 1826, baptized same time, born March 13th, 1805, to No. (567;) committed suicide from insanity, Dec. 9th, 1826, aged 21, at her father's home in New Britain.

578. "JULIA ANN LEWIS," to church June 4th, 1826, born April 7th, 1810, to No. (567,) married Feb. 11th, 1829, Philo, son of Simeon Rowley, of Farmington, and his wife Elizabeth (Griswold,) of Ashbel, of New Britain. She was dismissed and recommended by letter to Farmington church, Oct. 5th, 1844, and lives, 1862, on the old home of Simeon Rowley, the blacksmith, east part of Farmington Farms.

THEIR CHILDREN.

1. Jane Eliza, born May 21st, 1833, married Horace Woodford, of Avon.
2. Ellen Maria, born June 1st, 1840.

579. "NANCY, the wife of Alvin Belden," to church Aug. 6th, 1826, daughter of William Steele, and his wife, No. (246,) twin with James, married Nov. 4th, 1819, No. (955,) and died April 22d, 1830, aged 31, leaving three children.

580. "MARIA, wife of Alvah Brockway," to church Aug. 6th, 1826, born Dec. 9th, 1801, to Elijah Hull, from Farmington, and his wife No. (821,) married Sept. 2d, 1818. He was a blacksmith, and lived at the south end of the village, at the place now called the "Burrill place." He was son of Leman, and his wife, widow Ester Gillette, maiden name, Bishop. He was born, May 29th, 1795, learned his trade of Adna Hart, of Farmington; lives now, 1861, in Hartford. She was dismissed and recommended to Fourth church, Hartford, 1838; she died April, 1863, aged 62.

THEIR CHILDREN.

1. Julia Maria, born Oct. 16th, 1819, at Farmington, married Sidney Ensign, the great shoe dealer.
2. Almira S., born April 3d, 1822, in New Britain, married Nathan S. Grey, of Stonington.
3. Norman F., born June 29th, 1833, drowned in Connecticut river, 1845.
4. Mary Lucinda, born July 10th, 1837, married Alonzo P. Hills, of Richmond, Mass.

581. "CURTISS ANDREWS," to church Aug. 6th, 1826, born May 16th, 1803, to Truman, and his wife, No. (265,) married Almira Barnes. For neglect of public worship, and intemperance, he was cut off from the church, Jan. 26th, 1832. He died in Farmington alms house, Jan. 4th, 1836, aged 33.

THEIR CHILD.

Chauncey Curtiss, born

582. "HENRY EDDY," to church Aug. 6th, 1826, baptized same time; born Oct. 1st, 1805, to Thomas, and his first wife, Abi (Lewis,) graduated at Yale, 1832, studied theology at Andover and New Haven, settled in the ministry at Granville, Mass.; dismissed and studied medicine; marmied January, 1835, Cornelia Wood, of Clinton, Ct., daughter of Rev. Luke Wood; she died, 1841, when he married, second, Sarah H. Torrey,

of North Bridgewater, Mass., where now, 1861, he resides, engaged in inventions and patent improvements. He was dismissed and recommended to Yale College church, May 31st, 1829. He was aided in acquiring his education, and was in the ministry about fifteen years.

HIS CHILDREN BY FIRST WIFE.

1. Cornelia, born July 13th, 1839.

CHILDREN BY SECOND WIFE.

2. Henry T., born June 9th, 1844.
3. Willard, born Aug. 29th, 1845.
4. Sarah H., born July 8th, 1848.

583. "ELECTA LEE," to church Aug. 6th, 1826; born March 24th, 1806, to No. (356,) married Aug. 20th, 1826, Wells Hubbard, of Middletown, a harness maker, who became deranged. She died Sept. 1st, 1829, aged 23. She was a fine scholar and an accomplished lady, but was very unfortunate in her marriage. He died at the alms house in Middletown.

THEIR CHILD.

Electa Lee, born 1828, at Plainville, married, 1850, Capt. Bee, of Quincy, Florida; she died, 1855, at Savannah, Georgia, leaving two children.

584. "ELIHU BURRITT, jun.," to church Aug. 6th, 1826; born Dec. 8th, 1810, to Elihu, sen., and his wife, No. (290,) is the celebrated learned blacksmith, learned his trade of No. (370;) was the editor of several public journals, author of various works, laborer, and lecturer on peace, ocean penny postage, temperance, and other reforms. He became popular in Europe and America as a general philanthropist, as well as for literary attainments. Was dismissed and recommended by letter to the church of the Puritans, in New York, Nov. 2d, 1857. He has spent much time in England and on the continent, in Canada, and other parts, but is now, 1862, located in his native town. He rose from obscurity to eminence, against every opposing obstacle and untoward circumstance, simply by personal effort, and close, persevering application, to say nothing of native talent. He is now, 1867, United States consul at Birmingham, England.

585. "MARY WHITTLESEY," to church Aug. 6th, 1826; born Sept. 2d, 1809, to No. (321,) married Sept. 4th, 1827, No. (679;) dismissed and recommended by letter, May 13th, 1859, to church in Durant, Iowa.

586. "LUCY H. WRIGHT," to church Aug. 6th, 1826, baptized same time; born Dec. 11th, 1814, to Col. Joseph, and his wife, No. (559.) She lay prostrated by nervous debility for years, shut away from all society but her mother. She died happy in the Lord, April 24th, 1858, aged 43, a rare instance of Christian patience and submission under trying circumstances.

587. "STEPHEN HAZZARD," to church Oct. 1st, 1826, by letter from West Hartford; married Abigail Knowles; she died July 10th, 1826, aged 34, at New Britain. They were both received to church in West Hartford, Feb. 2d, 1817, and baptized same time, but moved into this place and lived in the Lincoln house in Southwest district, but did not remove their church standing. He however did so, after her decease, when he married, second, Sept 3d, 1826, Electa Landers, of Wethersfield. He died in West Hartford, Sept. 16th, 1829, aged 42.

THEIR CHILDREN.

1. John, born March 15th, 1812, married January 13th, 1833, Mary M. Steele, of William.
2. James, born Oct. 3d, 1814, married Emily Loomis, of Suffield.
3. Rowland, born August 19th, 1816, married Sarah ; went to California; died here.
4. Sarah, born , died in Rhode Island.
5. William, born
6. Julius, born , married Isabel Ives, of Suffield.
7. Abigail Francis, born June 7th, 1826, given to James Francis, jun., married Henry Long, see No. (930.)

SECOND WIFE'S CHILD.

8. Child, born , died March 3d, 1828, aged one year.

588. "ELIZA S. W., wife of Henry Jones," to church Oct. 1st, 1826, by letter from the First church in New Haven; she was daughter of Noah Webster, LL. D., of New Haven, and wife of Rev. Henry Jones, the third pastor of this church, and the quotation is from his own record. She was intelligent and accomplished, and was dismissed by letter, Feb. 6th, 1831. She was born Dec. 21st, 1803, married Sept. 5th, 1825. He was son of Maj. Daniel Jones, of Hartford, and his wife Rhoda (Mather,) born Oct. 15th, 1801, graduated 1820, at Yale, and in theology at Andover in 1824; settled in New Britain, 1825; taught high school in Greenfield, Mass., and Bridgeport, Ct.

THEIR CHILDREN.

1. Francis Juliana, born July 15th, 1826, bap. Nov. 2d, 1826, married Jan. 22d, 1857, Rev. Thomas K. Beecher.
2. Emily Ellsworth, born Nov. 8th, 1827, married October 30th, 1850, Daniel J. Day, Esq.
3. Eliza Webster, born Feb. 16th, 1833, at Greenfield, Mass., died there October 17th, 1833.
4. Henry Webster, born March 10th, 1835, at Greenfield, Mass., graduated at Yale in 1855, A. B., and in 1858, M. D.; married June 9th, 1859, Annie Maria Ward, at New Haven. They had a daughter, Eliza Webster, born Feb. 3d, 1861, at Chicago, Illinois.

589. "CHLOE, the widow of Gad Stanley," to church Feb. 4th, 1827, born Aug. 29th, 1777, to No. (122,) married Nov. 3d, 1799, Gad Stanley,

son of No. (115,) born Aug. 13th, 1776; lived in the north part of Stanley quarter; house next door north of his father's, and opposite his cousin, Oliver; he died June 1st, 1820, aged 44, at sea, coming from Martinique; he was gifted by nature; she by nature and grace; she died May 1st, 1851, aged 73; had sold her place in Stanley quarter, and built on Washington street, where her sons, Frederic and William, now, 1867, reside.

THEIR CHILDREN.

1. Levi Andrews, born Dec. 5th, 1800, died March 27th, 1804, aged four.
2. Frederick Trenck, born Aug. 12th, 1802, married July 4th, 1838, No. (948.)
3. William Burnham, born July 18th, 1804, see No. (687.)
4. Hubert Montgomery, born July 21st, 1806, died July 16th, 1822, aged 16.
5. Alfred Hamilton, born Oct. 13th, 1808, died Nov. 13th, 1837, at Galveston, Texas.
6. Catharine Andrews, born May 26th, 1811, see No. (618.)
7. Mary Chloe, born , bap. June 3d, 1827, died Aug. 20th, 1828, aged 14.

590. "Harriet, wife of Harvey Wright," to church Feb. 4th, 1827, daughter of Isaac Peck, of Kensington, and his wife, Theodocia (Gridley,) daughter of Dr. Amos, married Jan. 4th, 1816; he son of Charles, of Rocky Hill, and his wife, No. (409,) born Aug. 23d, 1794; learned of William Kelsey, jun., the trade of wheelwright; lived several years in the Ames house, in Hart quarter; moved to Utica, New York, and died there, 1845; she died Dec. 20th, 1851, at Utica; she had been dismissed by letter to the church in Utica, Oct. 3d, 1830; she baptized Sept. 1st, 1793, in Kensington.

THEIR CHILDREN.

1. Weltha Peck, born , bap. April 6th, 1828.
2. Sheldon, born , bap. April 6th, 1828, died on the way to California.
3. Harriet, born , bap. April 6th, 1828.
4. Calista, born , bap. April 6th, 1828.
5. Persis Rosetta, born , bap. April 6th, 1828.

591. "Experience, wife of Daniel Richards," to church Feb. 4th, 1827, daughter of Benoni and Rhoda Leach, born Dec., 1797, at Torrington, Conn., married April, 1823, No. (575,) at Wolcottville, Conn.;) she was divorced after leaving New Britain; her husband, Mr. Richards, while here, built the corner house, west of the South Green; the house next north, built the same year, by Adna G. Andrews, and the Bingham house, built the same year, by George Hart.

592. "Charlotte, wife of John Stanley," to church Feb. 4th, 1827, daughter of No. (449,) born April 5th, 1804, married Jan. 1st, 1824, No. (675;) he died, when she married second, July 29th, 1844, Rev. Samuel Rockwell, then pastor of the South Congregational Church; she became a constituent member of the South church, 1842; Mr. Rockwell born April 18th, 1803, to Alpha, of Winchester, Conn., and his wife, Rhoda (Ensign,) of Salisbury; he is, on the maternal side, the eighth generation from Gov.

Bradford; he graduated at Yale, 1825; settled at Plainfield, 1833; at New Britain South, Jan. 4th, 1843; he married June 6th, 1833, Julia Plummer, of Glastenbury; she died, when he married second, May 5th, 1840, Elizabeth Eaton, of Plainfield; she died, when he married third, as above.

CHILD BY HIS FIRST WIFE, JULIA.

1. George Plummer, born May 9th, 1834, at Plainfield, married June 18th, 1857, Eliza S. Ames; was a member of company F. 14th regiment Connecticut Volunteers, 1862; was sick and honorably discharged.

CHILD BY SECOND WIFE.

2. Elizabeth Eaton, born April 9th, 1863, at Plainfield, died March 12th, 1866.

593. "ELIZA S. NORTH," to church Feb. 4th, 1827, born Nov. 27th, 1807, to No. (449,) married June 10th, 1829, No. (704;) she died April 18th, 1837, aged 29.

594. "JOHN ROOT," to church Feb. 4th, 1827, son of John, of Worthington, and his wife, Mary (Gilbert,) born Sept. 28th, 1800, married March 31st, 1833, Mary E. Brown, born July 4th, 1814, at Reedsborough, Vermont, to David and his wife, Mary (Woodward,) married at Bristol; he was dismissed by letter, 1840, and is, 1862, living in Hanover, Chetauque county, New York; is a farmer.

THEIR CHILDREN.

1. Mary Helen, born July 17th, 1835, at Berlin.
2. John Henry, born Feb. 3d, 1838, at Berlin.
3. Harriet Amanda, born June 17th, 1843, at Hanover, N. Y.
4. Laura Emeline, born Aug. 12th, 1845, at Hanover, N. Y.
5. George Woodward, born Sept. 5, 1848, at Hanover, N. Y.
6. Adelaide, born

595. "WILLIAM G. LEWIS," to church Feb. 4th, 1827, baptized same time, born March 8th, 1806, to No. (439,) married Nov. 25th, 1830, No. (719;) he was in early manhood a school-teacher; also travelled at the south; lived in Cleaveland, Ohio; now, A. D. 1863, in merchandise at Philadelphia, Pa.; he died Nov. 10th, 1866, in his 61st year.

THEIR CHILDREN.

1. Henry Martin, born Oct. 24th, 1831, bap. June 3d, 1832, married Amelia Smith.
2. Mary Justina, born Nov. 4th, 1833, bap. July 11th, 1834, married William P. Atkinson.
3. William Goodwin, jun., born March 8th, 1840, at Philadelphia; in his father's store, 1861.

596. "JULIA ANN EDDY," to church Feb. 4th, 1827, daughter of Thomas and his first wife, Abi (Lewis;) she was baptized on admission to the church; endowed with peculiar physical and mental energy; was a school-teacher; went south; married there, Abraham Walker, of N. C.;

she died August, 1844, at Lowndesville, S. C., aged 37, being born June, 1807.

597. "MARY DEWY," to church Feb. 4th, 1827, born July 2d, 1804, to No. (179,) married June 20th, 1827, No. (920;) to South church, 1842.

598. "ISAAC BURRITT," to church Feb. 4th, 1827, born May 31st, 1808, to Elihu and his wife, No. (290,) married Oct. 16th, 1832, Nancy, daughter of Selah Barnes, of Southington, and his wife, Nancy (Cowles,) born April, 1808, baptized Oct. 21st, 1821, by Rev. Mr. Hawks, of Peru, Berkshire county, Mass.; they have no children; he was dismissed to Southington church by letter, April 20th, 1834; lives at the south part of that town; makes himself useful to church and society; has been a school-teacher, and is earnest in every good work; has a gift of prayer, exhortation, and off-hand speaking in public; is brother of No. (584.)

599. "EUNICE W. BURRITT," to church Feb. 4th, 1827, born May 2d, 1813, to Elihu and his wife, No. (290,) married April 24th, 1833, Jabez Cornwell, a joiner, from Middletown; he built the house now owned by Walter Stanley, and that owned and occupied by S. L. Strickland; he went to Texas, in 1837, and died there, Nov. 9th, of that year, when she married second, March 17th, 1853, A. J. Sawyer, of Chicago, who is a Professor in Chicago University; she went west as a teacher, under the patronage of Governor Slade; she was among the few saved from the wreck of the Atlantic, when that vessel was run into and sunk on the lake; saved, in the good providence of God, by her coolness and intrepidity, with the loss of all but her night-clothes.

CHILDREN.

1. Alonzo Burritt, born Feb. 11th, 1854.
2. James Hosmer, born Aug. 5th, 1857.
3. Grace, Alice, born June 4th, 1860.

All by second husband and born in Chicago.

600. "MARIA S. KELSEY," to church Feb. 4th, 1827, baptized same time, daughter of William, of Kensington, and his wife, Lucy (Stanley,) daughter of Lot, of this place,) born Dec. 14th, 1807; inherited property which came to her mother, by her uncle, Lot, who was a bachelor, and wealthy; she lives in a pleasant residence on Orchard street; never married; sister to No. (766,) with whom she resides, A. D. 1862; they have a sister, Harriet, who married May 28th, 1837, Ira Foster, of Meriden, and he died there, Nov. 19th, 1862, aged 50; their father, William Kelsey, jun., built, occupied, and once owned the house in Kensington, where the late Norman Warner lived so many years, and where he died.

601. "SUSAN S. BROOKS," to church Feb. 4th, 1827, baptized same time, born Nov. 19th, 1806, to Joshua, at Randolph, Vermont, and his wife, Prudence (Thomas;) she lived in the family of John Clark, and was hopefully converted while there; she was dismissed and recommended by

letter to the North church in Stockbridge, Mass., Sept. 17th, 1837; never married; died June 14th, 1841, at Richmond, Mass.

602. "CAROLINE U. HART," to church Feb. 4th, 1827, born Sept. 16th, 1809, to No. (183,) married July 3d, 1828, No. (912;) to South church, 1842.

603. "JULIA ANN STANLEY," to church Feb. 4th, 1827, born Dec. 24th, 1803, to No. (550;) never married; lives with her mother, on Park street; a pattern of Christian meekness and cheerfulness.

604. "AUGUSTUS STANLEY," to church Feb. 4th, 1827, born April 11th, 1814, to No. (550;) bred a farmer, but in middle life, been a manufacturer; residence, corner of Park and Orchard streets; married Oct. 5th, 1842, No. (984.)

THEIR CHILDREN.

1. Mary Melvina, born Nov. 12th, 1843, bap. Feb. 18th, 1844, see No. (1246.)
2. Martha Elvira, born July 7th, 1846, bap. Nov. 8th, 1846.
3. Louisa Maria, born May 3d, 1849, bap. Sept. 9th, 1849, died May 21st, 1850, aged one.
4. Sarah Augusta, born Feb. 21st, 1851, bap. Nov. 16th, 1851, No. (1409.)
5. Willington North, born July 10th, 1852, died Sept. 12th, 1852, aged two months.
6. Charles Brown, born April 11th, 1854, bap. June 10th, 1855.
7. Clarence Augustus, born July, 1860, died Aug. 9th, 1860, aged five weeks.

605. "ABI STANLEY," to church Feb. 4th, 1827, born March 12th, 1807, to No. (443,) baptized April 23d, 1809, Abi Langdon, after the name of her mother; married Nov. 15th, 1827, No. (512;) was in the Sabbath school, 1816, and could repeat with astonishing accuracy, passages of scripture, to the number of 1,000 or more per week; this was in competition with others of her age, and with a premium offered by the society that established the school; she was dismissed by letter to the church in Yonkers, New York, April 20th, 1848.

606. "JULIA ANN STANLEY, 2d," to church Feb. 4th, 1827, born Feb. 12th, 1810, to No. (438,) married Dec. 21st, 1830, No. (746,) dismissed by letter to the Free Church in Hartford, 1838.

607. "ELIZA SHIPMAN," to church Feb. 4th, 1827, born Feb. 18th, 1807, to No. (461;) was one of the competitors for prize in the Sabbath school of 1816; was a school-teacher; married April 24th, 1827, Dr. Henry A. Hart, son of No. (211,) who possessed brilliant talents, and settled in North Haven, as a physician, but fell a victim to fever, March 24th, 1828, aged 25.

THEIR CHILD.

1. Henry Abijah, born Nov. 13th, 1828, in New Britain, posthumous, baptized March 1st, 1829; became a physician, and then farmer, in New Hartford.

She married second, Feb. 22d, 1837, Dr. David Martin, of Springfield, N. J.; he was born Jan., 1793; was an eminent physician and counselor; he died March 24th, 1838.

THEY HAD ONE DAUGHTER, VIZ.

Ann Eliza, born May 23d, 1838, at Springfield, N. J.; she died June 15th, 1844, at New Hartford, Conn., where she has a monument at her grave.

After the decease of Dr. Martin, his widow married third, March 13th, 1839, Major Sanford Brown, of New Hartford, and was his second wife; he born Dec. 14th, 1792, in Sandisfield, Mass.; he was a farmer, and extensive manufacturer in the "Green Woods" and other companies; he died Sept. 16th, 1857, aged 65; she died July 8th, 1866, of cancer, aged 59; her church relation was transferred.

THEIR CHILDREN.

1. Hubert Sanford, born March 28th, 1840, graduated at Yale College, 1861; is, 1862, studying law at Cambridge, Mass.; was on the staff of Gen. Hazen, in the Union army of 1864, and belongs now, 1866, to the regular army of the United States.
2. Ellen Elvira, born June 10th, 1843, married Nov. 12th, 1866, George D. Colt, of Hartford.

608. "Abigail G. Shipman," to church Feb. 4th, 1827, born Oct. 13th, 1809, to No. (461;) was a school-teacher; married Dec. 22d, 1830, Rev. Spofford D. Jewett, then of Griswold, Conn., grandson of Deacon Jeremiah, of Rowley, Mass., born Sept. 21st, 1801, to Dr. Jeremiah, of Barnstead, New Hampshire, and his wife, Temperance Dodge, all descendants of Edward, of Lancaster, England, Joseph, senior, being the emigrant, 1638, to Rowley, Mass.; he graduated at Dartmouth College, 1826; has been pastor of the church in Griswold, Windsor, Westchester and Middlefield, Conn.; she was dismissed and recommended by letter, June 5th, 1830, to the church of Griswold, Conn.

THEIR CHILDREN.

1. Jane, born Oct. 13th, 1831, died April 10th, 1832.
2. Henry, born June 20th, 1833, died March 10th, 1836.
3. Levi, born Jan. 9th, 1835, married Sept. 10th, 1857, Mary I. Taylor, of Middle Haddam, where he now, 1861, resides; he was educated a physician; graduated in New York; but 1862, accepted the appointment of assistant-surgeon in the 14th regiment of Connecticut Volunteers.
4. Henry Shipman, born Dec. 4th, 1836; graduated at Amherst; has been a teacher in Williston Seminary; now, 1861, in Durham Academy; 1862, in the Academy at Meriden, Conn.; he married July 11th, 1866, Hattie M. Rice, of Poughkeepsie.
5. Mary Lee, born Feb. 28th, 1839, died March 8th, 1857.
6. William, born Jan. 16th, 1841; a merchant-clerk in New York, now, 1862.
7. Martha, born April 12th, 1843, married Sept. 30th, 1862, Henry L. Coe, of Middlefield.
8. Charles Taylor, born Jan. 31st, 1847; was a midshipman in the Navy, at Newport, Rhode Island, but 1867, a medical student in New York.
9. Ann Elizabeth, born Aug. 6th, 1849.

609. "Caroline Lee," to church Feb. 4th, 1827, born Nov. 8th, 1810, to No. (356,) married Oct. 18th, 1840, Rev. Joshua Phelps, son of Joshua

and his wife, Peck, born Nov. 16th, 1812, in Otsego county, New York, ; graduated at Union College, Schenectady; went to Florida, in 1840, as a missionary for the American Board, but took charge of the church in Monticello, which was self-sustaining; he has been honored by different appointments, in different localities, by the Old School Presbyterian Church, and now, 1861, is pastor of a Presbyterian church in Sacramento city, California.

THEIR CHILDREN.

1. Carrie M., born Sept. 11th, 1842, at Monticello, Florida.
2. Willie W., born June 15th, 1846, at Quincy, Florida.
3. Angeline Lee, born May 22d, 1852, in Bond county, Illinois, died Aug. 11th, 1853, at Dubuque, Iowa.

610. "NANCY S. WHITTLESEY," to church Feb. 4th, 1827, born Feb. 19th, 1807, to No. (321,) married Feb. 19th, 1827, No. (680;) she was dismissed by letter to Springfield, Mass., April 1st, 1832; was connected with the church in Ottawa, Illinois, but returned and died April 27th, 1853, aged 46, of consumption; was intellectual, intelligent and devotional.

611. "JOHN S. WHITTLESEY," to church Feb. 4th, 1827, born Oct. 2d, 1812, to No. (321,) married March 19th, 1834, No. (883;) graduated at Yale Theological Seminary, 1844; he was licensed to preach by the Hartford County South Association, June 6th, 1843, at Eastbury; ordained over the church in Trumbull, Conn., 1844; in Bethel, 1849; came to this place in 1852, with his family; moved to Durant, Iowa, in 1857; since a missionary in that State; but in 1861 he became a chaplain of the 11th regiment of Iowa Volunteers; was at the battle of Pittsburg Landing, Tenn; went to St. Louis with the wounded, but died May 11th, 1862, at Durant, aged 49, of fever.

THEIR CHILDREN.

1. John Evarts, born Dec. 21st, 1835, see No. (1083.)
2. David Haskell, born July 21st, 1837, died Dec. 29th, 1837, aged five months; burned in a cradle.
3. David Haskell, born June 28th, 1840, baptized in 1840, died April 19th, 1862; was a volunteer in company A. 13th regiment, at Lawrence.
4. Charles Porter, born Jan. 17th, 1844, died Aug. 1st, 1845, aged eighteen months.
5. Eliza Smalley, born Jan. 17th, 1845, died Dec. 11th, 1859, at Durant, Iowa, aged 15.
6. Charles Porter, born April 1st, 1849, died May 5th, 1848, aged thirteen months, at Trumbull, Conn.
7. Mary Galland, born Aug. 20th, 1850, died Nov. 26th, 1859, aged nine.
8. Charles Camp, born Dec. 6th, 1851, died Dec. 11th, 1859, aged eight.
9. Rebecca Smalley, born Sept. 23d, 1854.

612. "DIANA SISCO," to church Feb. 4th, 1827, a colored girl, baptized same date; lived with the family of No. (321) several years; she from New Haven; has been chamber-maid on the New York boat; has been

nurse at the Water Cure establishment at Northampton; dismissed by letter, Oct. 4th, 1829, to the African church, in New Haven; she married · Peters.

613. "JOHN C. ANDREWS," to church Feb. 4th, 1827, son of Col. Sidney, of New York city, and Montague, Mass., born Dec. 19th, 1809; his mother, Mary (Clark,) daughter of Abel, of this place; he married Jan. 22d, 1832, Tirza Ann Field, of Deerfield, Mass.; he is a trunk and harness-maker by trade; lives, 1861, in Hartford, Conn.; his wife, Tirza, died March 19th, 1856, when he married second, Feb., 1863, Susan Boyden, of Hartford.

THEIR CHILDREN.

1. Alfred Hobart, born Nov. 1st 1832, died at Montague, April 20th, 1859, greatly lamented; he was buried in Hartford.
2. Arthur Wellington, born Sept. 9th, 1835; an officer in the Rebel army.
3. Ann Field, born Nov. 9th, 1837, married Oct. 6th, 1855, Walter Weir, of West Point, N. Y.; live in St. Louis.
4. Mary Jane, born April 20th, 1841, died Sept. 1st, 1842, aged sixteen months.
5. Sidney Wadsworth, born July 25th, 1843, died Aug. 4th, 1855, aged twelve.
6. Delia Jane, born Sept. 2d, 1846; lives at St. Louis.
7. John Augustine, born Nov. 30th, 1850.

614. "MARCIA GLADDEN," to church Feb. 4th, 1827, born Nov. 12th, 1806, to No. (522,) married June 17th, 1829, Enos H. Hun, son of David, of Newington, and grand-son of Enos; his mother, Abigail Higby; he born July 9th, 1807; he is a brass-worker; she died Dec. 19th, 1857, aged 51.

THEIR CHILDREN.

1. Abigail Rowena, born Oct. 14th, 1830, married Benjamin Baker, of New Hartford.
2. George Albert, born July 1st, 1833, bap. 1833, married Margaret Parks, of Middlefield; in company F. 14th regiment, Connecticut Volunteers; was in the battle of Antietam; now, 1863, at the Hospital, in Philadelphia.
3. Sarah Jane, born Dec. 6th, 1835, died Sept. 23d, 1860, aged 25, at Naugatuck.
4. Valentine, born Feb. 9th, 1846.

615. "ABIGAIL S. CORNWELL," to church Feb. 4th, 1827, baptized same time, daughter of Stephen W. Cornwell and his wife, Abigail (Stanley,) born Jan. 14th, 1810, married Oct. 2d, 1828, No. (519;) now, 1861, lives in Ohio; she and her husband were dismissed Feb. 23d, 1832, and by letter recommended to the church in Portsmouth, N. H.; she now, 1863, resides in Brooklyn, N. Y.

616. "EMELINE BARTHOLOMEW," to church Feb. 4th, 1827, daughter of Jonathan, of Plainville, and his wife, Polly (Hotchkiss,) born Oct. 18th, 1807, married first Tuesday of October, 1827, No. (677;) both dismissed and received to Coventryville, Chenango county, N. Y., Dec. 15th, 1831; now, 1862, live in Plainville.

617. "ADELINE LEWIS," to church Feb. 4th, 1827, born Sept. 15th, 1807, to No. (567;) never married; died Aug. 13th, 1857, aged 50.

618. "CATHARINE A. STANLEY," to church Feb. 4th, 1827, baptized same time, married Sept. 5th, 1838, No. (704;) was his second wife; daughter of Gad and his wife, No. (589,) born May 26th, 1811; to South church, 1842.

619. "LUCINA DUNHAM," to church Feb. 4th, 1827, daughter of Samuel, of Southington, and his wife, No. (634,) born March 10th, 1811, married Jan. 26th, 1828, No. (918;) took a letter to the church in Southington, and received there, Aug. 10th, 1834, but in 1838, returned by letter from that church to this; she died March 21st, 1853, aged 42.

620. "MATILDA WRIGHT," to church Feb. 4th, 1827, baptized same time, born June 18th, 1812, to Joseph, jun. and his wife, Esther (Kelsey,) married Nov. 4th, 1832, Elam Slater, son of Capt. Benjamin and his wife, Lucy (Andrews,) born Nov. 26th, 1810; is a farmer; lives on Horse Plain, and is an extensive land-holder; she died April 1st, 1848, aged 36, when he married second, Jan. 31st, 1849, Martha A., daughter of Chauncey Lewis, of Southington; (she had been wife of Horace Booth, son of Nathan, of Granville, but had been divorced;) born Nov. 28th, 1810, at Southington.

THEIR CHILDREN.

1. Emily Matilda, born Aug. 13th, 1834, bap. Oct. 4th, 1835, m. Edward De Wolf, April 14th, 1851.
2. Jane Smith, born Dec. 28th, 1836, bap. Sept. 28th, 1837, married Elbridge Capen.
3. Joseph Benjamin, born May 25th, 1840, married March 27th, 1861, Hattie Andrews; he died Dec. 10th, 1865, aged 25.

SECOND WIFE'S CHILDREN.

4. Elam, born Nov. 19th, 1849.
5. Ella, born July 25th, 1854.

621. "URSULA WOODRUFF," to church Feb. 4th, 1827, daughter of Joseph and his third wife, who was Widow Wright, when married to Mr. Woodruff; her maiden name, Prudence Spellman, of Granville, Mass.

622. "ARTEMAS E. HART," to church Feb. 4th, 1827, born Feb. 11th, 1812, to No. (430;) a jeweller by trade; learned of William B. North; he built on Washington street, the house now owned by Rev. L. Perrin; sold his interest in his father's estate, and now, 1862, living in Hartford; he was a boy of fifteen years only, when he joined the church; soon found he had no relish for religious duties, and so neglected the ordinances, and the church practically withdrew its watch from him; he married Aug. 24th, 1836, Elizabeth Ann Clark, of Litchfield, daughter of Abel and his wife, Catharine (Eckert,) born Dec. 7th, 1816, at Litchfield, South Farms, now Morris; he was some years clerk and treasurer of our Ecclesiastical Society.

THEIR CHILDREN.

1. Virginia Veeder, born Aug. 1st, 1838, married Nov. 4th, 1857, Henry Pember, son of Elisha; he died Dec. 1st, 1866, aged 33.

2. Charles Richmond, born June 17th, 1840, married Ellen M. Woodruff.
3. Artemas Elijah, born June 20th, 1842, married Oct. 13th, 1865, Kate Litchfield.
4. Lucina, born Sept. 27th, 1844, died, aged one year.
5. Elizabeth Ann, born Nov. 10th, 1846, married Oct. 9th, 1866, Charles Mackin.
6. Henry Lockwood, born Nov. 19th, 1848, died Aug. 27th, 1849, aged nine months.
7. Joseph Clark, born June 4th, 1850.

623. "Julia Ann Upson," to church Feb. 4th, 1827, daughter of No. (450,) born March 22d, 1814, married Nov. 26th, 1835, Homer Curtiss, of Meriden; she was dismissed and recommended by letter to Meriden church, in 1837.

THEIR CHILDREN.

1. Elizabeth C., born Sept. 13th, 1836, at Meriden.
2. Augusta L., born June 28th, 1841, at Meriden.
3. Helen M., born Feb. 22d, 1843, at Meriden.
4. Homer A., born June 14th, 1845, at Meriden.

624. "Henry North, 2d," to church Feb. 4th, 1827, born Oct. 19th, 1813, to No. (443;) has been some years in Monte Video, South America, where he accumulated an estate; he returned and bought the building opposite the fountain, on the corner west, called the "Miss Lee Seminary;" also bought the Ozias Hart, alias Rev. Mr. Gihon property, at the south end of the village; carries on farming and manufacturing at the same time; is a single man; he was young when he united with the church; found he had no relish for it; he neglected the church and ordinances, and they, by vote, withdrew their watch from him in 1856.

625. "Barton Lewis," to church Feb. 4th, 1827, born April 21st, 1812, to No. (567,) married Oct. 23d, 1841, Cynthia Maria Church, of Haddam, daughter of James and his wife, Huldah (Barnes,) born Sept. 20th, 1815; he a brass manufacturer; residence on Washington street; he from free choice united with the Baptist church, when, Dec. 1st, 1831, this church withdrew its watch from him.

THEIR CHILDREN.

1. Mary Ella, born July 14th, 1843.
2. Anna Maria, born July 4th, 1845.
3. George William, born March 13th, 1855.

626. "George Dewy," to church Feb. 4th, 1827, born Sept. 23d, 1814, to No. (480,) married June 26th, 1842, Jane Bingham, born Sept. 21st, 1817, at Wethersfield, to Ebenezer, of Windham, and his wife, Huldah (Blinn,) of Wethersfield; he was a brass-worker by trade; went whaling voyages; went to Texas; he neglected the ordinances of the church, and they withdrew their watch; he died Feb. 13th, 1846, aged 31; he had noble and generous impulses.

627. "Elvira, wife of Benjamin Smith," to church April 1st, 1827, born June 18th, 1807, married Dec. 9th, 1824, No. (515,) daughter of Silas Pennfield, and his wife, No. (341.)

628. "HENRY W. CLARK," to church April 1st, 1827, born Feb. 23d, 1807, to Ornan, of Farmington Farms, and his wife, No. (403,) married Oct. 21st, 1832, No. (659;) both dismissed and recommended by letter, June, 1834, to church in Cleaveland, Ohio, where they, 1864, reside; he has been successful and useful; they have no children.

629. "LAURA F. BOOTH," to church April 1st, 1827, born in Granville, Mass., Nov. 28th, 1811, to Nathan, 3d, and his wife, Ruth (Bates;) not married; living, 1861, in Springfield, Mass.; dismissed by letter.

630. "CHLOE ALMIRA COATS," to church June 3d, 1827, born Feb. 1809, at Middlefield, Mass., to John and his wife, Chloe (Bacon;) she was baptized on her admission to church; she never married, but died, April, 1835, at Westfield, Conn., at her grand-father's, Joel Bacon.

631. "JULIA CLARK," to church June 3d, 1827, baptized same time, born Jan. 29th, 1804, to Abner and his wife, No. (639;) had an active mind, but became insane, and died July 20th, 1854, aged 50, at the alms-house.

632. "BETSEY, wife of John Judd," to church Oct. 7th, 1827, born Feb. 26th, 1803, to No. (247,) married April 10th, 1822, No (674;) to South church, 1842.

633. "CAROLINE LEWIS," to church Oct. 7th, 1827, baptized same time, born July 5th, 1805, to No. (458;) was a school teacher; had literary taste; never married; died Oct. 12th, 1841, aged 36.

634. "LUCY, wife of Abijah Hart," to church Oct. 7th, 1827, by letter from the church in Southington, daughter of John Ariail, a Frenchman, of Southington, and Hannah Rich, his wife, born Aug. 27th, 1781, and baptized there, Oct. 14th, 1781, married Feb. 4th, 1798, Samuel Dunham, son of Cornelius and his wife, Jemima (Andrus,) who died Sept. 26th, 1811, when she married second, Oct. 26th, 1826, No. (211;) he died May 3d, 1829, aged 65, when she married third, Sept., 1831, Isaac Stearns, of Lanesboro, Mass.; she dismissed by letter March 24th, 1850, to Oxford, Conn.

HER CHILDREN BY FIRST HUSBAND, SAMUEL DUNHAM.

1. Roxana, born Nov. 10th, 1799, married May, 1826, Elijah Ashley.
2. Diadema, born June 20th, 1801, married Dec. 25th, 1826, George Everet; second, married George Woodruff.
3. Lucy Maria, born Feb. 20th, 1803, married Nov. 29th, 1822, Oliver Lewis; she died April 23d, 1824.
4. Albert, born Aug. 20th, 1804, married Feb. 24th, 1825, Sylvia Cowles, of Plainville.
5. Henry, born May 1st, 1806, married Henrietta Tucker, of Oxford, Conn., daughter of Daniel.
6. Elizabeth, born Feb. 20th, 1808, married April 7th, 1827, George Seymour.
7. Sarah, born March 24th, 1809, married Nov. 9th, 1830, William A. Seymour.
8. Lucina, born March 10th, 1811, married Jan. 26th, 1828, Morton, son of John Judd.

635. "FANNY, wife of Henry L. Parsons," to church Aug. 5th, 1827, by letter from the church in Rocky Hill, born Jan. 26th, 1801, to Elisha Wetherell, of Rocky Hill, and Mary (Buckley,) his wife, married Nov. 24th, 1825, No. (924;) they withdrew from us, to attend the Advent church; our watch withdrawn, Dec. 4th, 1856, by vote of the church.

REVIVAL OF 1828.

636. "SARAH COSSLETT, the widow of Francis Cosslett," to church Jan. 4th, 1829, born April 5th, 1761, to Samuel Smith and his wife, No. (89,) married April 21st, 1791; was his second wife; his first was Rachel (Adkins,) of Benjamin, who owned and lived by "Churchill's Mill;" they were married before Rev. Joshua Belden, Sept. 16th, 1784; he was a British soldier, and taken with John Watson, (in the capture of Burgoyne,) by Gen. Lusk, while they were in the act of firing a cannon at their captors; Mr. Cosslett was a shoe-maker; was to church in Newington, May 3d, 1801, and had his children baptized there; she died Oct. 8th, 1838, aged 77; he died Dec. 31st, 1826, aged 77.

THEIR CHILDREN.

1. Mary Goodrich, born Nov. 3d, 1791, baptized June 28th, 1801, see No. (404.)
2. Sarah, born Nov. 4th, 1792, baptized June 28th, 1801, married Dec. 26th, 1810, No. (743.)
3. Rachel, born Jan. 24th, 1795, baptized June 28th, 1801, married Thomas Smith, lawyer, Vienna, N. Y.
4. Lydia Smith, born Jan. 31st, 1800, baptized June 28th, 1801, see No. (488.)

637. "URSULA, the widow of John Judd," to church Jan. 4th, 1829, baptized same time, born Jan. 24th, 1776, to Lot Stanley and his wife, Rhoda (Wadsworth,) married May, 1792; he was a blacksmith; residence where Deacon Morton Judd has his, and his children are the fifth generation who have lived on the same site; Mr. Judd's shop was opposite the house; he learned his trade of Esquire North, who, the first day of his apprenticeship was set to cut appletree brush; some one inquired of him towards the close of the day how he liked; he replied he was "sorry he learned the trade;" this vein of wit is still extant; he died July 18th, 1822, aged 50; she died Aug. 24th, 1858, aged 83, of cancer.

THEIR CHILDREN.

1. Nancy, born Sept. 17th, 1793, see No. (360.)
2. Aurora, born March 20th, 1795, see No. (369.)
3. John, born March 25th, 1796, see No. (674.)
4. Polly, born Sept. 24th, 1797, see No. (1025.)
5. Marilla, born May 7th, 1799, see No. (1146)
6. Minerva, born July 11th, 1801, died Oct. 1st, 1801.
7. Marinda, born Nov. 11th, 1802, died March 15th, 1804.
8. Harry, born Nov. 2d, 1804, see No. (540.)
9. Anna, born Nov. 4th, 1807, see No. (1016.)

10. Morton, born Nov. 5th, 1808, see No. (918.)
11. Lydia, born Feb. 9th, 1810, died Oct. 16th, 1810, aged nine months.
12. Oliver Stanley, born Nov. 30th, 1816, see No. (823.)

638. "SARAH, widow of Stephen Hart," to church Jan. 4th, 1829, baptized same time, born June 14th, 1775, to Ezra White and his wife, Lucy (Stanliff,) of Chatham, married June 25th, 1797; he was a farmer; lived on the old home of his father, Stephen, senior, and his grand-father, Daniel, at the foot of "Clark Hill," born Oct. 21st, 1775; his mother was No. (563;) he died Dec. 9th, 1816, aged 41; she died Sept. 6th, 1859, aged 84, at her son's, Philip, on East street.

THEIR CHILDREN.

1. Stephen, born Feb. 19th, 1798, see No. (646.)
2. Edmund, born April 23d, 1799, married June 2d, 1824, No. (654)
3. George, born March 16th, 1801, see No. (812.)
4. Emily, born March 15th, 1804, see No. (503.)
5. Philip, born June 25th, 1805, married Nov. 16th, 1831, Mary Judd, daughter of William.
6. William, born Oct. 12th, 1808, married July 28th, Rhoda Judd, of Daniel; married second, Laura J. Gladden.
7. Henry, born , died Sept. 27th, 1814, of dysentery.
8. Ebenezer, born , married Mary Pease, of Warehouse Point.

639. "POLLY, the widow of Abner Clark," to church Jan. 4th, 1829, born April 9th, 1780, to No. (158,) married Feb. 14th, 1802; he was son of Elijah and Hannah , his wife, born Aug. 23d, 1775, in Hartland; he built the house now owned by Charles M. Lewis; carried on harness and saddle-making in the chambers of the house; his barn stood where Rev. Mr. Rockwell's house stands; he died March 27th, 1817, aged 42; she was left destitute, but by great energy and economy she raised a large family to respectability; she died July 29th, 1855, aged 75; to South church, 1842.

THEIR CHILDREN.

1. Fidelia, born Jan. 26th, 1803, died Jan. 26th, 1803.
2. Julia, born Jan. 29th, 1804, see No. (631.)
3. Melvil, born Feb. 11th, 1806, died Oct. 20th, 1809.
4. Erwin, born Jan. 16th, 1808.
5. Melvil, 2d, born Dec. 10th, 1809, married 1832, Weltha A. Pilgrim; he died Dec. 21st, 1844.
6. Abner, born Dec. 9th, 1811.
7. Mary, born Jan. 28th, 1814, died Feb. 10th, 1815.
8. Mary, 2d, born June 17th, 1816, see No. (732.)
9. Marcellus, born June 18th, 1816, married May 31st, 1858, Mary Tolles, daughter of Orris; he studied law with Ira E. Smith, Esq.; has been post-master, and represented the town in the legislature.

640. "ROZINA, wife of George Doolittle," to church Jan. 4th, 1829, baptized same time, born at Poultney, Vermont, April 17th, 1787, to Daniel

Richards and his wife, Huldah (Fellows,) married June, 1806; he was an iron and brass-smelter; distinguished as a temperance reformer in the Washingtonian movement; he died Dec. 3d, 1858, at White Hall, Illinois; she was dismissed April 23d, 1855, with a general letter, and is now, 1861, in White Hall, Illinois; a woman of true Christian fortitude.

THEIR CHILDREN.

1. Lyman L., born Dec. 16th, 1808, died, aged 23.
2. Fitch Edward, born March 26th, 1811, see No. (693.)
3. Emily Eliza, born Aug. 6th, 1813, see No. (702.)
4. Lydia Maria, born Jan. 24th, 1818, see No. (802.)
5. Henry A., born Nov. 7th, 1819, died at sea, aged 18.
6. George L., born Nov. 2d, 1822, see No. (803.)
7. Abigail S., born Aug. 20th, 1825, see No. (929.)

641. "Julia Maria, wife of Lester Osgood," to church Jan 4th, 1829, baptized same time, born Dec. 7th, 1798, to Elias Brown, of Farmington, and his wife, Prudence (Fitch;) was the second wife, and married Nov. 8th, 1821, her sister Harriet, being his first wife; she was born Jan. 30th, 1796, married Nov. 27th, 1815, and died Aug. 28th, 1819, aged 24; he was son of Deacon John Osgood and his wife, Mary (Hall,) born Dec. 3d, 1793; was a farmer; lived in his father's house; was an only son; died Nov. 10th, 1829, aged 36; Julia, his widow, had her children baptized as below; she married second, July 6th, 1830, Harlow Humphrey, from Simsbury.

THEIR CHILDREN.

1. Harriet Eliza, born Oct. 19th, 1819, died Jan. 20th, 1827, aged eight.
2. John Lester, born Feb. 17th, 1823, baptized Dec. 27th, 1829, married June 17th, 1850, Pamela Shields, of New York.
3. Julia Louisa Ann, born Aug. 1st, 1824, baptized Dec. 27th, 1829, married Aug. 7th, 1845, James L. Philips, of Farmington; he died, when she married second,

642. "Amy, the wife of Ira Andrews," to church Jan. 4th, 1829, baptized same time; born July 5th, 1787, to No. (852,) married May 28th, 1807. He was son of No. (245,) born Dec. 8th, 1785; a saddle and harness maker by trade; lived several years in Meriden, where he carried on his business; came back and lived on the Reuben Wright farm, north of "Osgood Hill." She died Feb. 20th, 1842, aged 55. He sold and went to Illinois; living, 1861, in Manchester, had no children.

643. "Pamela, wife of Horace Wells," to church Jan. 4th, 1829, baptized same time; born Feb. 28th, 1798, at West Hartford, to Timothy Sedgwick, and his wife, who was Lucy Sedgwick when he married her. She married, Dec. 24th, 1823, No. (511.)

644. "Maria Catharine, wife of Moses P. Belknap," to church Jan. 4th, 1829; born Nov. 17th, 1799, in the city of New York, to John Burgers, and his wife Catharine B. (Hamn,) married Oct. 24th, 1815. He

went to Buenos Ayres, South America, and has not been heard from since. She was dismissed and recommended, March 17th, 1850, to Brick church, New York, Dr. Spring, pastor. She was sister of No. (651.)

THEIR CHILD.

Theodore A., born June 23d, 1822, at Charleston, S. C., see No. (922.)

645. MATTHEW CLARK," to church January 4th, 1829; born Oct. 2d, 1773, to Dan, and his first wife Lucy (Stanley,) married June 27th, 1793, No. (715;) lived on the home of his father, on "Clark Hill," and was a successful farmer; was a man of strong passions, but noble impulses. His wife Rhoda died, when he married, second, Nov. 8th, 1841, Sarah Giddings, daughter of Solomon, and his wife Ruth (Wright,) born Oct. 24th, 1789, at Preston, Ct. He died Jan. 16th, 1851, aged 77. Sarah, his widow, lives, 1861, in Hartford.

THEIR CHILDREN.

1. James Stanley, born Nov. 3d, 1794, married Oct. 9th, 1817, Amanda Rowe, (issue) Mary Antoinette, born Sept. 26th, 1819; he died Feb. 7th, 1820, aged 25.
2. George, born Aug. 1st, 1796, died young.
3. Lucy, born March 6th, 1799, died young.
4. Abi, born Feb. 5th, 1801, bap. July 2d, 1809, at Farmington, see No. (658.)
5. Dan, born Jan. 15th, 1805, bap. July 2d, 1809, at Farmington, see No. (679.)
6. George, born Aug. 18th, 1807, bap. July 2d, 1809, at Farmington, died young.

646. "STEPHEN HART," to church Jan. 4th, 1829, baptized same time; born Feb. 19th, 1798, to Stephen, sen., and his wife, No. (638,) married Aug. 24th, 1818, No. (647;) was a farmer and butcher, and lived some years on the old home of his ancestors, when he sold and bought in the village, the present house of Deacon Orson Seymour. He neglected public worship and the ordinances, and was cut off from the church Nov. 15th, 1837. He died Sept. 6th, 1846, aged 49.

THEIR CHILDREN.

1. Infant, born , died March 29th, 1822.
2. Fidelia, born June 7th, 1820, bap. June 21st, 1829, married October 22d, 1846, Mansfield Stacy; she died Aug. 6th, 1847, aged 27.
3. Emily P., born May 8th, 1823, bap. June 21st, 1829, married April 13th, 1845, John Proffitt, of Hartford.
4. Nancy, born October 26th, 1822, bap. June 21st, 1829, married July 31st, 1839, Doctor William Allen, son of William, sen.; he died Sept. 6th, 1851, at Meriden, aged 33.
5. Maria, born March 11th, 1827, bap. June 21st, 1829, married Oct. 1st, 1848, Allen Stacy, of Pennsylvania.
6. Sarah E., born Feb. 11th, 1834, married Nov. 14th, 1857, Asa Sheldon Parsons, of Bridgeport.
7. Frederick, born Aug. 20th, 1840, lived some years in Pennsylvania, where he enlisted into the 11th Reg. Penn. Cavalry, Co. E, was a corporal and killed at Black-

water; buried in New Britain, Feb. 13th, 1863, aged 23. He was killed Jan. 30th, 1863, in North Carolina.

647. CYNTHIA, wife of Stephen Hart," to church Jan. 4th, 1829; born April 8th 1796, to William Steele, sen., the fifer, and his wife, No. (246.) married Aug. 24th, 1818, No. (646;) has a home in Bridgeport with her daughter, now, A. D. 1863, an active, energetic woman; she has experienced some joys and many sorrows.

648. "ELISHA S. BOOTH," to church Jan. 4th, 1829; born June 8th, 1794, to Nathan, and his wife, No. (261,) learned his trade of shoe making and tanning of Oliver Stanley, his brother-in-law; has lived in various localities and raised a large and respectable family; he married Dec. 5th, 1822, No. (649.) They were dismissed and recommended by letter, Oct. 6th, 1832, but returned July 22d, 1852, by letter from church in Torrington. He died May 31st, 1865, aged 71.

649. "ALVIRA ABIGAIL, wife of Elisha S. Booth," to church Jan. 4th, 1829; born May 18th, 1801, at Durham, Ct., to Asa Squire, and his wife Charlotte (Weld.)

THEIR CHILDREN.

1. Lucius Saxton, born Dec. 6th, 1823, bap. June 14th, 1829, married Josephine Durkee, of New York.
2. William Squire, born April 28th, 1826, bap. June 14th, 1829, married Julia A. Cornwell, Sept. 4th, 1849; she died and he married, second, Fidelia M., daughter of Jedediah North, of Berlin, Aug. 4th, 1857.
3. Lester Smith, born January 19th, 1828, bap. June 14th, 1829, see No. (1114.)
4. Eliza Anstace, born March 16th, 1830, bap. March 17th, 1830, died March 20th, 1830.
5. Henry Weld, born April 20th, 1831, died August 19th, 1834.
6. Helen Melissa, born July 8th, 1833, see No. (1113.)
7. Henry Bishop, born May 18th, 1835, died July 20th, 1850, aged 15.
8. Elisha Smith, born July 24th, 1837, married Eliza Sandford, see No. (1116.)
9. Edward Munson, born Jan. 26th, 1840, see No. (1165.)
10. Frances Charlotte, born May 12th, 1842, see No. (1180.)
11. George Baldwin, born March 21st, 1844, see No. (1242.)
12. Mary Jane, born March 23d, 1846, died at 3 days.

650. "WILLIAM B. NORTH," to church Jan. 4th, 1829; born Dec. 6th, 1797, to No. (149;) learned the jeweler's trade of Oakes, of Hartford, and set up the business in this place, where now Churchill & Stanley occupy, in the same line. His house, once Abner Clark's, now, 1861, Charles M. Lewis'. He was the first to introduce this business permanently and successfully into the place. He married, Aug. 16th, 1824, No. (651.) He died, 1838, aged 40, greatly lamented as a man of pure mind and morals.

651. "SARAH, the wife of William B. North," to church Jan. 4th, 1829; born Aug. 7th, 1802, in New York, to John Burgers, and his wife Cath-

arine (Hamn;) her residence is next door to their former one, on Main street, and very pleasant; to South church, 1842.

THEIR CHILDREN.

1. Georgiana Maria, born June 4th, 1825, bap. June 7th, 1829, see No. (903.)
2. Louisa Burnham, born Dec. 15th, 1826, bap. June 7th, 1829, see No. (904.)
3. Caroline Augusta, born July 20th, 1828, bap. June 7th, 1829, died October 4th, 1852, aged 24.

652. "WILLIAM H. SMITH," to church Jan. 4th, 1829; born Oct. 22d, 1800, to No. (337,) is a brass manufacturer; married Aug. 7th, 1825, No. (653,) she died June 16th, 1841, aged 40, when he married, second, April 27th, 1842, No. (770.) His residence is on Main street, on South Park. He has represented the town, and held various responsible positions; to South church, 1842.

653. "MARCIA, wife of William H. Smith," to church Jan. 4th, 1829; born Aug. 27th, 1801, to No. (443,) and his wife Rhoda, daughter of No. (158,) married Aug. 7th, 1825, No. (652.) She died June 16th, 1841, aged 40.

THEIR CHILDREN.

1. Thomas Henry, born Apr. 1st, 1826, bap. June 14th, 1829, died March 4th, 1852.
2. Cordelia, born June 7th, 1828, bap. June 14th, 1829, married No. (815.)
3. James North, born Nov. 17th, 1833, bap. June 1st, 1834, died Nov. 26th, 1855.

CHILDREN BY SECOND WIFE.

4. Willie Hart, born June 11th, 1846, died Sept. 16th, 1847.
5. Annie Louisa, born Oct. 19th, 1849.

654. "MEHITABLE, wife of Edmund Hart," to church Jan. 4th, 1829; born Jan. 28th, 1797, to No. (179,) married June 2d, 1824, Edmund, son of Stephen Hart, jun., and his wife, No. (638,) born April 23d, 1799; lived in various localities; he was a brass worker, learned of Cyrus Stanley, in Stanley quarter. He died January 25th, 1853, aged 54. She to South Church, 1842. She died May 26th, 1856, aged 59.

THEIR CHILDREN.

1. Antoinette, born April 11th, 1825, married May 24th, 1846, Andrew Rapelye; she No. (960.)
2. Adeline, born March 21st, 1827, married Nov. 26th, 1845, Levi Wells.
3. Julia Ann, born March 24th, 1832, married April 10th, 1850, Oscar Butler, of Martin.
4. Ellen Maria, born June 12th, 1838, married Jan. 12th, 1860, Wallace Cornish, of Simsbury.

655. "NANCY, wife of Philip Lee," to church Jan. 4th, 1829; born Nov. 22d, 1806, to No. (443,) married Dec. 28th, 1823. He was son of No. (351,) born May 6th, 1802; a shoe maker by trade, been formerly, for some years, engaged in the liquor traffic, partly as agent of the town under the Maine law. His residence was on Main street; has represented

the town, been assessor, and held other public offices. His wife died Dec. 21st, 1838, aged 32, when he married, second, June 4th, 1855, the widow of No. (626.) He died May 22d, 1864, aged 62 years and 16 days, of apoplexy.

THEIR CHILDREN.

1. Charles Henry, born March 2d, 1825, died Oct. 13th, 1825, aged 7 months and 11 days.
2. Charles Henry, 2d, born April 3d, 1826, married March 19th, 1849, Maria B. Massey, of New York; he died Nov. 4th, 1866, at Osborn, Ohio, of cholera, aged 40.
3. Harriet Maria, born Feb. 5th, 1828, married Dec. 3d, 1849, Chester M. Foster.
4. Mary North, born March 27th, 1832, married Dec. 4th, 1854, Ransom R. Foster.
5. Ellen Frances, born May 17th, 1835, married Oct. 1st, 1856, George L. Massey, of New York.

656. "Henrietta Maria, wife of Orson H. Seymour," to church Jan. 4th, 1829, baptized same time; born Jan. 30th, 1807, to Amzi Stanley, and his wife Lucy (Webster,) married Sept. 17th, 1827. He was son of No. (420,) born Sept. 1st, 1807; a shoe maker, learned of Capt. Weldon; 1862, a merchant, residence on Main street,

THEIR CHILDREN.

1. Eliza North, born April 20th, 1828, bap. April 19th, 1829, married, 1847, Frederick Langdon.
2. Lucy Webster, born Sept. 3d, 1829, bap. May 16th, 1830, died June 8th, 1830.
3. Lucy Webster, 2d, born March 12th, 1831, married May 4th, 1852, Ira B. Smith, of Oxford.
4. Frederick Stanley, born Nov. 8th, 1836, married Nov., 1855, Hattie Granger, of Suffield; he enlisted, 1862, into Company F, 14th Regt., as Sergeant, J. E. Blinn, Captain.
5. Hattie A, born Aug. 24th, 1837, married Oct. 1st, 1857, William M. Bird, of Charleston, S. C.

657. "Mary L., wife of Alfred Andrews," to church Jan. 4th, 1829; born April 14th, 1805, to No. (461,) married Sept. 15th, 1824, No. (478,) was his second wife; had been a school teacher; named after her mother, who was grand daughter of Col. Lee.

658. "Abi Clark," to church Jan. 4th, 1829; born to No. (645,) Feb. 5th, 1801, on "Clark Hill," never married, died Jan. 18th, 1840, aged 39, of consumption.

659. "Emily R. Stanley," to church January 4th, 1829; born Sept. 11th, 1810, to Cyrus, and his wife, No. (422.) married Oct. 21st, 1832, No. (628;) dismissed and recommended to church in Cleveland, Ohio, by letter, June, 1834; have no children.

660. "Lucy Tyler," to church Jan. 4th, 1829, baptized same time; born Dec. 23d, 1803, at Hamden, Ct., to Jared, and his wife Octavia (Allen,) of Southington; dismissed and recommended to church in Vernon, Sept., 1834; living, 1861, in Southington; never married.

661. "Lucy Newell," to church Jan. 4th, 1829; born Oct. 11th, 1810, in Southington, to Quartus, and his wife Lucy (Foote,) baptized Dec. 2d 1810, at Southington, married Oct. 10th, 1830, No. (689;) to South church, 1842.

662. "Betsey Hull," to church Jan. 4th, 1829; born Dec. 10th, 1807, at Wallingford, Ct., to Benjamin, and his wife Sarah (Curtiss,) married in this place, Sept. 2d, 1829, No. (682.) She died January 20th, 1846, aged 29; to South church, 1842.

663. "Laura Gladden," to church Jan. 4th, 1829; born Jan. 7th, 1809, to No. (522,) married May 26th, 1857, William Hart, son of Stephen, and his wife, No. (638,) he born Oct. 12th, 1808; is a brass worker and lives at the south end of the village, on Main street. She is his second wife, his first being Rhoda Judd, daughter of No. (435,) married July 28th, 1830, she died Sept. 3d, 1856, aged 46. His second wife Laura joined the Baptist church, of which he is a deacon.

664. "Rachel Maria Perkins," to church Jan. 4th, 1829, baptized same time; born Feb. 7th, 1807, at Wolcott, Ct., to Lyman, and his wife Phebe Hurlbut (Andrews;) dismissed and recommended by letter to Hartford.

665. "Orpha Andrews," to church Jan. 4th, 1829; born May 13th, 1813, to No. (359,) married Sept. 6th, 1830, Thomas Burrill, a brass worker; lives on Main street, opposite the South Park. She joined the Methodist church.

666. "Rachel Spencer," to church Jan. 4th, 1829; born Feb. 17th, 1809, in Worthington Society, Berlin, to James, and his wife Rachel (Hubbard,) baptized on admission to church, married April 8th, 1829, Hiram Jerome, of Bristol, a brass worker, son of Benjamin, and Sarah (Andrews,) his wife, born Jan. 9th, 1802; they lived, 1861, in Bristol. He has been to California. She was received by letter and recommended to Farmington church, 1837, from this church.

THEIR CHILDREN.

1. Augusta, born Feb. 5th, 1830, bap. July 18th, 1830, married Aug. 15th, 1852, Jairus Monroe, of Warren.
2. Abby, born Oct. 14th, 1833.
3. Anna, born July 26th, 1836, married Oct. 12th, 1862, Stephen Tibbals; live in Providence, R. I.

667. "Susan Smith," to church January 4th, 1829; born Dec. 7th, 1811, to No. (423,) married Albert Boyington, of Southwick, Mass. He has gone to parts unknown. She is a tailoress by trade, and lives, 1863, with, and in her mother's house, on Arch street; she is quite deaf; has one son, George L., born July 22d, 1849. She died December 20th, 1863, aged 52.

668. "MARY ANN SEYMOUR," to church January 4th, 1829; born Oct. 4th, 1813, to No. (420,) married Jan. 8th, 1844, William Palmer, son of William, of Haddam, who died March 24th, 1854. She married, second, April 19th, 1860, Bradford Bullock, son of Ezra, of Rehoboth, Mass., and his wife Susan (Horton,) born August 24th, 1810. She to South church, 1842. They are now living in Hartford.

669. "MARY B. CORNWELL," to church Jan. 4th, 1829, baptized same time; born Aug. 1st, 1813, to Stephen W. Cornwell, and his wife Abigail (Stanley,) daughter of No. (115.) She married, 1836, Dennis Reed, son of Starling, of Granby; he died Jan. 9th, 1848, when she married, second, May 23d, 1855, William Booth, son of No. (370.) They lived, 1861, in Illinois. She was dismissed by letter.

670. "SARAH WOODRUFF," to church Jan. 4th, 1829; born Dec. 21st, 1813, to No. (381,) married Oct. 8th, 1838, Horace Clapp, son of Capt. Winthrop, and Clarissa (Rowe,) his wife, born July 21st, 1813, at Montague, Mass. He built on Washington street, place now, 1864, owned by C. B. Erwin. She died June 11th, 1847, aged 34. He died June 3d, 1851, aged 38, at Montague, Mass.; was a carpenter by trade; she was dismissed by letter, to a Presbyterian church, in Columbus, Georgia.

THEIR CHILDREN.

1. Julius Jennings, born Sept., 1839, at Columbus, Georgia.
2. Clara, born August, 1842, at New Britain, died Sept. 9th, 1843, aged eleven months and twenty-two days.
3. Horace Burdette, born Aug. 31st, 1844, at New Britain.

671. "LUCETTA BOOTH," to church Jan. 4th, 1829; born Aug. 6th, 1814, to No. (338,) married Sept. 28th, 1836, Henry B. Phelps, of New Harmony, Indiana, son of Aaron, of Granby, and his wife Elizabeth (Bassett,) born February 14th, 1813, at Granby, Ct. She was dismissed and recommended by letter, 1840, to the free church, Hartford, Rev. Mr. Sprague, pastor. Now, 1863, resides in Brooklyn, N. Y.

THEIR CHILDREN.

1. Ellen Elizabeth, born January 17th, 1839, at Hartford, died Feb. 21st, 1842, at Hartford.
2. George Henry, born January 20th, 1842, at Hartford, died Sept. 28th, 1849, at Brooklyn, N. Y.
3. Emily Wilcox, born Oct. 2d, 1844, at Brooklyn, and died there March 20th, 1849.
4. Edwin Dennis, born Jan. 14th, 1850.

672. "ROXANNA ANDREWS," to church Jan. 4th, 1829; born April 6th, 1815, to No. (313,) married May 20th, 1835, Enos M. Smith, of Lenox, Mass., a merchant, son of Allan, and his wife Amanda (Woodruff.) He built on High street where he lived some few years; the place was sold to, and occupied by, the Flagg family. They moved to the state of New York. She died Sept. 21st, 1854, aged 39, at Lenox, Mass., of

consumption; he married second, July 10th, 1855, Lucy Alvord, of Broadalbin, New York and they live in the city of New York.

THEIR CHILDREN.

1. Jane Elizabeth, born March 29th, 1836, baptized 1837, died April 27th, 1837, at New Haven.

2. Enos Nathan, born May 26th, 1838, died Sept. 24th, 1864, in hospital in New York harbor; a soldier.

3. Edwin A. M., born Jan. 20th, 1841, at Volney, New York.

4. Everett, born Sept. 5th, 1845, died Sept. 29th, 1845, at Batavia, New York.

673. "Osmyn Booth," to church Jan. 4th, 1829, born 1796, to No. (165,) married Dec. 22d, 1819, in Hartford, No. (431;) was a cabinet-maker; learned of Daniel Dewey, of Hartford; lived in his father's house here, which stood where now, 1867, stands the residence of John Stanley; he died Aug. 2d, 1839, aged 43.

THEIR CHILDREN.

1. Frederic Josiah, born Sept. 14th, 1820, baptized Nov. 19th, 1820, married May 1st, 1842, Luannah Blin, daughter of Elias, born Aug. 11th, 1824; live on Main street.

2. George Hemsted, born Aug. 5th, 1823, baptized Nov. 9th, 1823, married No. (960.)

3. Eliza Winchel, born Jan. 2d, 1825, baptized July 3d, 1825, died Sept. 10th, 1825, aged eight months.

674. "John Judd," to church Jan. 4th, 1829, baptized same time, born March 25th, 1796, to John and his wife, No. (637;) a shoe-maker by trade; lived on West Main street, where now, 1861, Dan Capron's house stands, but now in District No. 4, in the house built by Mr. Sharp, in Hart quarter; he married April 10th, 1822, No. (632;) to South church, 1842. They live, 1867, in New Britain village.

THEIR CHILDREN.

1. Luman Stanley, born June 9th, 1824, married Feb., 1844, Martha Hotchkiss, of Boston.

2. Francis Deming, born Feb. 3d, 1827.

3. Sarah Hart, born July 10th, 1829.

4. John Bernard, born Dec. 18th, 1831, married Nov. 30th, 1854, Eliza H. Keeney, of New York.

5. Frederic William, born June 31st, 1834.

6. Ellen Nancy, born Sept. 27th, 1837, married April 10th, 1860, George C. Gridley, son of Solomon D. Gridley, of Southington, but now of New Britain.

675. "John Stanley," to church Jan. 4th, 1829, baptized same time, born Sept. 26th, 1798, to Oliver and his wife, Fanny (Booth,) daughter of Nathan, jun.; he was bred a merchant, in Hartford; married Jan. 1st, 1824, No. (592;) he built in Stanley quarter, on the site of Colonel Gad, but sold to Henry L. Bidwell, and built in the village, where now Rev. Mr. Rockwell occupies; he was a man of few words, and of sterling integrity, of courtly bearing and liberal views; he died Feb. 19th, 1839, aged 40.

THEIR CHILDREN.

1. Frances Louisa, born Dec. 8th, 1824, died Sept. 17th, 1826.
2. Oliver, born March 24th, 1827, baptized July 15th, 1827, married Aug. 29th, 1850, Cordelia U. Peck.
3. Walter North, born Dec. 29th, 1828, baptized May 17th, 1829, died Feb. 15th, 1850.
4. Jane, born June 1st, 1831, baptized Sept. 18th, 1831, died Feb. 3d, 1839, aged 8.
5. Emily Louisa, born Dec. 25th, 1834, baptized May 17th, 1835.
6. Edward, born Jan. 21st, 1837, baptized June 11th, 1837, died July 19th, 1843.

676. "ALBERT WILLIAMS," to church Jan. 4th, 1829, born Nov. 14th, 1802, in Kensington, to Elisha and his wife, No. (415,) married April 14th, 1824, Thirza Steele, daughter of No. (852,) born July 11th, 1804; they live in Hart quarter, near the school-house, District No. 4.

THEIR CHILDREN.

1. Rosetta North, born June 12th, 1827, baptized Nov. 17th, 1829.
2. Orrin Elisha, born Oct. 11th, 1829, baptized Nov. 17th, 1829, died Nov. 17th, 1829, aged five weeks.
3. Henry Elisha, born Nov. 29th, 1831, baptized Sept. 15th, 1833, married No. (1184.)
4. Selah Albert, born April 20th, 1833, baptized Sept. 15th, 1833, died Dec. 23d, 1852, aged 18.
5. Charles Orrin, born June 13th, 1836, died Feb. 25th, 1837, aged eight months.
6. Charles Orrin, 2d, born Nov. 27th, 1839; is, 1863, in company H. first regiment heavy artillery, Connecticut Volunteers; married March 1st, 1864, Rebecca Richards, of Berlin.
7. Amy Andrews, born June 24th, 1842, married Elbridge Hill.
8. John, born Feb. 2d, 1846.

677. "CHARLES LEWIS," to church Jan. 4th, 1829, born June 8th, 1803, in Farmington, to Rice and his wife, Electa (Newel;) was a shoe-maker; learned of Capt. Strong, of Farmington, but is now, 1864, a harness-maker, in Plainville; married first Tuesday in October, 1827, No. (616;) both dismissed by letter and received to Coventryville, Chenango county, New York, Dec. 15th, 1831; they now, 1864, live in Plainville.

THEIR CHILDREN.

1. Henry N., born the summer of 1828, married Julia H. Hoyt, of New York State.
2. Romeo Warren, born spring of 1830, baptized Sept. 19th, 1830, in New Britain; he married Mary Brooks, of Norwich, New York State.
3. Gustavus, born 1833, in the State of New York.
4. Marion, born Oct., 1835, at Coventryville.
5. Cornelia, born Nov., 1841, at Coventryville.
6. Josephine, born Aug. 3d, 1851.

678. "RALPH SHIPMAN," to church Jan. 4th, 1829, born March 4th, 1803, to No. (461,) married Nov. 2d, 1825, No. (491;) brass-founder by trade; in company of J. Shipman & Sons, once extensive manufacturers; he built the house now owned by L. A. Viberts; they were both dismissed

and recommended by letter, April 20th, 1843, to the church in Yonkers, New York, where she inherited property from the estate of her uncle, and on which they built, overlooking from the high ground, the village, and the beautiful Hudson river.

THEIR CHILDREN.

1. Julius Rockwell, born Sept. 25th, 1826, baptized Dec. 17th, 1826, married Mary Clark, of Bristol.
2. Mary Jane, born July 4th, 1829, baptized Nov. 22d, 1829, died May 12th, 1830, at New Britain.
3. Ann, born Nov. 8th, 1831, baptized June 3d, 1832, died March 22d, 1836, at New Britain.
4. Annie, born Oct. 1st, 1841, baptized at Yonkers, by Rev. V. M. Hulbut.
5. Charles Savage, born Aug. 11th, 1845, baptized at Yonkers, by Rev. V. M. Hulbut.

679. "DAN CLARK," to church Jan. 4th, 1829, born Jan. 15th, 1805, on "Clark Hill," to No. (645,) baptized July 2d, 1809, at Farmington, married Sept. 4th, 1827, No. (585;) a farmer, and later in life a mover of buildings; lived on "Clark Hill," in a house vacated by the death of his brother, James; he sold to Elizur N. Smith, and moved to Durant, Iowa, to which church they were both recommended by letter, May 13th, 1859, where he has been a deacon and superintendent of the Sunday school; he was colonel of militia, regiment of cavalry, and held other offices; was chosen one of the standing committee of the church in 1843.

THEIR CHILDREN.

1. James Stanley, born April 20th, 1829, baptized May 31st, 1829, died June 20th, 1839, aged ten.
2. Rebecca Smalley, born Feb. 8th, 1832, baptized July 8th, 1832, see No. (1067.)
3. William Whittlesey, born March 19th, 1834, baptized June 22d, 1834, see No. (1098.)
4. Frances Fedora, born Feb. 28th, 1836, baptized 1836, died April 3d, 1837, aged thirteen months.
5. Elbert Cornelius, born July 30th, 1838, baptized 1838, married Sept. 8th, 1864, Ada T. Hitchcock.
6. Frances Fedora, born March 15th, 1841, baptized in 1841.
7. James Eliphalet, born May 18th, 1843, baptized Nov. 19th, 1843, died Oct. 25th, 1844, aged seventeen months; burned.
8. Matthew Henry, born Aug. 8th, 1846, baptized June 6th, 1847.
9. Adrian Ives, born Sept. 15th, 1849, baptized August, 1850.

680. "THOMAS STANLEY," to church Jan. 4th, 1829, born Sept. 22d, 1805, to No. (550,) married Feb. 19th, 1827, No. (610;) bred a merchant, but followed several other callings; house on East Main street; was dismissed and recommended by letter, April 1st, 1832, to Springfield, Mass., and 1839, to Ottawa, Illinois; his wife, Nancy, died, when he married second, Sept., 1855, the widow of Stephen W. Cornwell, No. (1250.)

THEIR CHILDREN.

1. Arthur W., born Feb. 15th, 1828, died Feb. 19th, 1828, aged three days.
2. Sarah Elizabeth, born April 17th, 1829, baptized May 31st, 1829, see No. (1017.)
3. Julia Calista, born Nov. 20th, 1830, baptized Feb. 13th, 1831, see No. (1018.)
4. Arthur W., born Aug. 19th, 1832, died Oct. 31st, 1849, aged 17, of consumption.
5. Thomas Porter, born Jan. 7th, 1834, died Sept. 10th, 1834, at Springfield, Mass.
6. Thomas Henry, born Aug. 23d, 1835, at Springfield, Mass.
7. James Augustus, born Feb. 1st, 1839, died Aug. 26th, 1834, aged 15, by accidental discharge of a pistol he was loading.
8. Catharine Rebecca, born Nov. 9th, 1840, see No. (1251.)
9. Mary Eliza, born July 9th, 1843, see No. (1252.)
10. Flora, } born July 29th, 1848, baptized Aug. 17th, 1848, died Aug. 18th, 1848.
11. Ella, } born July 29th, 1848, baptized Aug. 17th, 1848, died Aug. 24th, 1848.

681. "SAMUEL S. CARPENTER," to church Jan. 4th, 1829, baptized same time, born Nov. 11th, 1799, to Joshua, of Lenox, and his wife, Elizabeth (Smith,) of Rehoboth, Mass.; a brass-founder; he is unmarried, 1861, and was dismissed and recommended by letter, March 28th, 1858, to Lenox, Mass.

682. "JOSHUA CARPENTER," to church Jan. 4th, 1829, baptized same time, born Nov. 6th, 1805, at Lenox, Mass., to Joshua, senior, and his wife, Elizabeth (Smith,) married in this place, Sept. 2d, 1829, No. (662;) she died, when he married second, May 3d, 1848, Elizabeth Hough, of Hamden, born March, 1825, to Amos B. and his wife, Nancy (Rice,) where he now, 1862, resides; he is a brass-founder, and carried on the business in this place; he and Betsey, his first wife, to South church, 1812.

THEIR CHILDREN.

1. Samuel Walker, born Sept. 3d, 1830, baptized Feb. 27th, 1831, married May, 1855, Emma Sloper, who died at Waterbury, May 29th, 1862, aged 26.
2. Mary Elizabeth, born Jan., 1835, died May 27th, 1827, aged two years and four months.
3. Mary Elizabeth, 2d, born Jan., 1839, died July 18th, 1839, aged six months.
4. Elizabeth Augusta, born Nov. 18th, 1840, baptized 1841; lives, 1862, in Hamden.

SECOND WIFE'S CHILDREN.

5. Nancy Hough, born Jan. 8th, 1851, at Hamden.
6. George S., born Feb. 13th, 1859, at Hamden.

683. "AMOS WESTOVER," to church Jan. 4th, 1829, baptized same time, born Feb. 7th, 1804, at New Marlboro, Mass., to Noah and his wife, Rosanna (Allen,) married May 13th, 1828, No. (698;) he is a brass-worker; lives in Park street; he was, for neglect of public worship and gospel ordinances, cut off from the church, March 14th, 1833; they have both since attended the Methodist church.

THEIR CHILDREN.

1. William Wallace, born March 28th, 1829, baptized May 24th, 1829, married May 3d, 1860, Mary L. Gilbert.

2. Charles Curtiss, born Sept. 22d, 1830, baptized Feb. 27th, 1831.

3. Edwin Elijah, born Sept. 17th, 1833, baptized July 11th, 1834, married Dec. 9th, 1863, Mary E. Butler; he was a three months volunteer; also a three years man in the army; he died March 26th, 1864, of lung fever, at Portsmouth, Va., aged 30.

4. Henry Clay, born Dec. 13th, 1835, died Oct. 10th, 1837.

5. Ann Louisa, born Dec. 12th, 1837.

6. Frederic Henry, born Oct. 10th, 1841, died Oct. 27th, 1858.

7. Ella Mary, born Nov. 19th, 1844, died April 15th, 1849.

8. Jane Eliza, born March 21st, 1847.

9. Ida, born Dec. 8th, 1851.

684. "AARON C. ANDREWS," to church Jan. 4th, 1829, born Feb. 25th, 1804, to No. (359,) married Sept. 6th, 1830, No. 745;) was a brass-founder by trade; he died Oct. 22d, 1847, aged 43; to South church, 1842.

THEIR CHILDREN.

1. Elizabeth R., born Nov. 4th, 1832, baptized June 9th, 1832, married Oct. 30th, 1855, George F. Hamilton.

2. Charles W., born Nov. 18th, 1836, baptized July 16th, 1837; is a jeweller.

3. Frederic B., born July 2d, 1839, baptized 1839.

685. "HENRY N. WOODRUFF," to church Jan. 4th, 1829, born Feb. 3d, 1804, at Southington, to Capt. Philemon and his wife, Mary Ann (Matthews,) of Bristol; he lived several years with Dr. Samuel Hart, of this place; was much respected; lost his health; went south to regain it, but died in 1835, in S. C.; was never married; aged 31.

686. "SAMUEL M. HART," to church Jan. 4th, 1829, born Aug. 30th, 1807, to No. (211;) brass-founder by trade; learned of Deacon Chauncey Cornwell; went to Texas, in 1837; died there in 1838, aged 31; was never married.

687. "WILLIAM B. STANLEY," to church Jan. 4th, 1729, born July 18th, 1804, to Gad and his wife, No. (589;) an extensive manufacturer, in company with his brother, Frederic, and others; never married; to South church, 1842; was baptized on admission to church, in 1829.

688. "STEPHEN W. CORNWELL," to church Jan. 4th, 1829, baptized same time, born June 15th, 1807, to Stephen and his wife, Abigail (Stanley,) married Sept. 5th, 1832, No. (1251;) dismissed and recommended March 4th, 1832, to the church in Granby, by letter; he died there, much respected, Dec. 17th, 1849, aged 42; had been an extensive manufacturer in, and represented that town in the legislature, and held a prominent position in society there.

THEIR CHILDREN.

1. Ellen Stanley, born March 27th, 1836, died Dec. 14, 1854, aged 18.

2. Arthur Temple, born Sept. 11th, 1845, see No. (1243.)

689. "EDMUND STEELE," to church Jan. 4th, 1829, born Oct. 9th, 1804, to Ebenezer, jun. and his second wife, No. (225,) married Oct. 10th,

1830, No. (661;) lived with and labored for Alvin North, many years, in early life; bought the Capt. Belden place, (alias) Seth Lewis place, where he is a farmer now, 1863; to South church, 1842.

THEIR CHILDREN.

1. Dwight Newell, born Aug. 3d, 1832.
2. Frederic Newton, born June 7th, 1837, baptized Sept. 6th, 1837.
3. Walter Pomeroy, born July 24th, 1844.
4. Charles Edmund, born Nov. 29th, 1847.

690. "Ezekiel Andrews, jun." to church Jan. 4th, 1829, born July 19th, 1809, to No. (313;) blacksmith and carriage-maker by trade; in company with his brother, Alfred, under the firm of A. & E. Andrews; lives on West Main street, on the home of his father and grand-father; since 1839, a farmer, and runs the saw-mill, which by renewal has continued more than a century; he has been a magistrate, select-man, and a military officer; has lived two seasons in Texas; he married Aug. 7th, 1833, No. (793;) both to South church, 1842.

THEIR CHILDREN.

1. Infant, born June 27th, 1834, died same day.
2. Angevine, born Sept. 7th, 1835, baptized 1837, married Aug. 24th, 1857, Lester Hills, of Hartford.
3. Nathan Hosmer, born Dec. 28th, 1837, baptized, 1838, died Sept. 9th, 1843, aged six.
4. Franklin Hall, born July 31st, 1839, baptized 1840, died July 27th, 1843, aged 4.
5. Roderic Baldwin, born Oct. 9th, 1841, married June 4th, 1867, Emma R. Fiske, Springfield, Mass.
6. Agnes Hosmer, born Nov. 9th, 1843, married Feb. 1st, 1866, Wilbur D. Fiske, of Boston.
7. Nathan Hall, born March 7th, 1846.
8. Franklin Hinsdale, born Sept. 26th, 1849.

691. "Dennis Root," to church Jan. 4th, 1829, baptized same time, born Dec. 3d, 1805, to Joseph and his wife, No. (448;) learned shoemaking of Seth Dickinson, in Kensington, married Nov. 26th, 1829, Marcia Recor, daughter of No. (467,) born Sept. 12th, 1812; he fell under the censure of the church, Oct. 11th, 1837, for neglect of public worship and gospel ordinances; he died Nov. 18th, 1843, aged 38, by falling under a cart-wheel; she married second, Jan. 30th, 1853, Oswyn Stanley, of Kensington, son of Hezekiah.

THE CHILDREN OF DENNIS AND MARCIA ROOT.

1. Angelina, born Jan. 10th, 1832, married Nov. 23d, 1851, Henry Goodrich, son of Samuel.
2. Waldo D, born Nov. 11th, 1833, married Aug. 14th, 1853, Orpha Andrews, of Thomas; he died Jan. 18th, 1856, aged 23.
3. George, born Nov. 10th, 1835; in company A, eighth regiment Connecticut Volunteers.

4. Dwight, born Jan. 23d, 1839, married Feb. 11th, 1860, Laura A. Spencer, daughter of Silas.

692. "SALMON MERRIMAN," to church Jan. 4th, 1829, born Sept. 13th, 1809, in Southington, to Albert and his wife Roxana (Hart;) he married Myra Mix, of Cheshire; she died, when he married second, Maria Stephens, of Cromwell. I find no record of his dismissal. He lived here a short time only. He united with a Baptist church in Cromwell, but now, 1861, lives in Sag Harbor, Long Island. Their children are, Albert L., Roxana L., and Ada Jansen.

693. "FITCH EDWARD DOOLITTLE," to church Jan. 4th, 1829, baptized same time, born March 26th, 1811, to George and his wife, No. (640;) he died in 1850, in Illinois.

694. "ISAAC NEWTON LEE," to church Jan. 4th, 1829, born Nov. 18th, 1810, to No. (351,) bred a merchant, became a manufacturer; residence on Main st., opposite the home of his father, grandfather, and great-grandfather; married Oct. 20th, 1833, his cousin, No. (734;) she died, when second he married June 13th, 1843, No. (989;) she died, when third he married Oct. 25th, 1855, No. (1152.) He is now, 1862, extensively engaged in the manufacture of shirts.

CHILDREN BY HIS FIRST WIFE.

1. Isaac Newton, born Sept. 26th, 1834, bap. May, 1835, died Nov., 1835.
2. Isaac Shipman, born Jan. 1st, 1837, bap. June 1st, 1837, see No. (1167.)

CHILDREN BY HIS SECOND WIFE.

3. Martin Cowles, born June 16th, 1844, died July 11th, 1844.
4. Thos. Fessenden, born Jan. 23, 1846, bap. June 14th, 1846, died Sept. 17, 1847.
5. Thos. Fessenden, 2d, born June 9th, 1848, bap. Sept. 29th, 1848.
6. Harriet Wells, born Sept. 3d, 1850, bap. Nov. 28th, 1850.
7. Edward Butler, born April 13th, 1853, bap. June 3d, 1860.

CHILD BY HIS THIRD WIFE.

8. Henry Newton, born Oct. 9th, 1859, bap. June 3d, 1860.

695. "WM. CHURCHILL," to church Jan. 4th, 1829, baptized same time, Wm. Allen Churchill; born May 10th, 1810 in the limits of Newington, near "Churchill's Mill;" learned jeweller's trade of William B. North, became a partner in the business, has been successful; residence on Main st., where the house of Wm. Bassett formerly stood, and his shop where Bassett's wagon shop stood; married Sept. 14th, 1835, No. (729;) she died, when second he married, Dec. 4th, 1838, in Wethersfield, No. (885.) He had a leading influence in building the "*Center church*," and gave liberally; he has been assistant superintendent of the S. School for several years, and made one of the "Standing Committee" of the church, Jan. 6th, 1867.

THEIR CHILDREN.

1. Eliza Jane, born Aug. 24th, 1836, see No. (1023.)

SECOND WIFE'S CHILDREN.

2. Sarah Augusta, born July 8th, 1841, bap. 1841, see No. (1181.)
3. Julia Isabella, born Aug. 14th, 1843, bap. Nov. 26th, 1843, see No. (1179.)
4. Wm. Wolcott, born Sept. 22d, 1845, bap. May 3d, 1846, see No. (1239.)
5. Frederic Hosea, born March 27th, 1847, bap. Sept. 29th, 1848, see No. (1240.)
6. Annie Florence, born Feb. 4th, 1853, died March 14th, 1858.

696. "JOHN SHIPMAN," to church Jan. 4th, 1829; baptized same time; born Nov. 23d, 1812, at Berlin, to Chauncey of Berlin and Kentucky, and his wife Maria (Roberts) of Berlin, daughter of Merils. He went to Kentucky and married there June 19th, 1834, Julia A. Hogan, and lives in Bryantsville, Garard Co., Ken. They have four daughters.

697. "SAMUEL R. MORSE," to church Jan. 4th, 1829; born Feb. 15th, 1812, at Southington, to Rice and his wife Lucy (Hitchcock.) He learned the jeweller's trade of Wm. B. North; no record of his dismissal and recommendation. He is now living, 1861, at Napierville, Ill. He married April 29th, 1846, Sarah Jane Bailey, of Westchester Co., N.Y.; has no children living. Has owned and worked a farm in Ill.

698. "MARY ANN, wife of Amos Westover," to church Jan. 4th, 1829, by letter from 1st church in Farmington. She was born May 10th, 1806, at Southington, to Lyman Perkins and his wife Phebe Hurlbert (Andrews.) She to church at Farmington, June 30th, 1824; she has been a cripple for years from rheumatic affection; she left our communion for the Methodist church; she married May 13th, 1828, No. (683.)

699. "ELI CARRINGTON," to church March 1st, 1829, born at Plainville Oct. 21st, 1807, to Nathaniel and his wife Sybil (Steele); baptized at Farmington, Dec. 20th, 1807; married Lucina Graham, of Stockbridge, daughter of Aaron and Deborah Painter his wife, and was divorced after a few years, she being thought insane, when 2d he married Jan. 17th, 1848, Susan S. Downs, daughter of Samuel; lives, 1861, in Ansonia, Ct. He was dismissed and recommended Jan. 5th, 1833, to Kensington church.

THEIR CHILDREN.

1. Maria, born , baptized Sep. 13th, 1834, in Kensington, married Dec. 25th, 1855, James Messenger, at New Jersey.
2. Wm. Henry, born , baptized July, 1837, drowned in Bristol May 9th, 1850.
3. Harriet Mary, born , baptized 1839 at Kensington, died aged 2 years, in Kensington.

700. "ABI GLADDEN," to church March 1st, 1829, born Feb. 17th, 1813, to No. (522,) married Sept. 2d, 1825, No. (914.)

701. "MARY COGSWELL," to church March 1, 1829, born Nov. 9, 1805, at Southington, to Salmon and his wife Sarah (Smith,) baptized April 20th, 1806, married May 6th, 1829, No. (705); he died, when 2d she married Dec. 17th, 1844, Elisha Crosby, and was divorced; she left our communion for the Baptist church, and we withdrew our watch; she died June 14th, 1863, at alms house, at New Britain, (57)

702. "EMILY ELIZA DOOLITTLE," to church March 1st, 1829, baptized same date; born Aug. 6th, 1813, to Geo. and his wife, No. (640,) married , Samuel Warner, son of Salmon, living, 1861, at White Hall, Ill.; she was dismissed and recommended to the Methodist church Sept. 20th, 1829.

703. "MATILDA CLARK," to church March 1st, 1829, born Oct. 24th, 1815, to John and his wife, No. (384,) married Dec. 11th, 1836, No. (913,) before Rev. Dr. Porter; she to south church 1842.

704. "HENRY STANLEY," to church March 1, 1829, born Sept. 24th, 1807, to No. (550); an extensive manufacturer, residence on Main st., near south park; married June 10th, 1829, No. (593,) she died, when 2d he married Sept. 5th, 1838, No. (618); he to south church 1842.

THEIR CHILDREN.

1. Walter Henry, born June 25th, 1830, bap. Sept. 26th, 1830, married Sept. 7th, 1854, Mary Jane Peck.
2. Theodore Augustus, born July 22d, 1833, bap. Nov. 21st, 1833, was 2d Lieut. Co. F, 14th Regt., 1862; he was mortally wounded while as 1st Lieut., in the absence of his Captain, he bravely led his company on in the battle of Fredericksburg, Va.; he died the last day of 1862, at Washington, and was buried in New Britain with military honors the 5th of January, 1863. He died for his country.

SECOND WIFE'S CHILDREN.

3. Mary Louisa, born May 8th, 1840, died Sept. 9th, 1840, aged 4 mo.
4. Louisa Catharine, born April 7th, 1842, died March 26th, 1847, aged 5 years.
5. Frederic North, born March 17th, 1844; C. V., Co. A, 13th Reg't, Capt. Bidwell, made, 1863, a 2d Lieut.; married April 15th, 1866, Mary Welch, of Forestville.
6. Catharine Amelia, born Oct. 10th, 1849.

705. "WM JUDD, JUN.," to church Mar. 1st, 1829, born Sept. 1st, 1807, to Wm. and his wife, No. (524,) married May 6th, 1829, No. (701;) was a brass worker; fell under censure of the church for gross neglect of worship in public, and gospel ordinances, Oct. 18, 1837; he died Oct. 10th, 1840, aged 33.

706. "LUCY WRIGHT," to church March 1st, 1829, baptized same time; born April 9th, 1796, at Wethersfield, to Elizur and Hannah (Wright) his wife; brought up in the family of Capt. Luke Bronson of Kensington; in after life made her home in the family of Sam'l Kelsey; never married; has lived in Iowa; to South church 1842; an exemplary devoted christian.

707. "Sarah Maria Perkins," to church March 1st, 1829, baptized same time; born Feb. 25th, 1812, at Meriden, to Liberty and his wife Sarah (Lyman,) married April 6th, 1836, James Turner, son of John and his wife Amelia (Wilcox;) he is now, 1861, a grocer in Middletown. She was dismissed and recommended by letter to church in Meriden, April 20th, 1834.

THEIR CHILDREN.

1. John A., born March 25th, 1838.
2. Mary P., born July 26th, 1843.

708. "Abigail Bronson, widow," to church August 2d, 1829; she was the widow of Jesse Bronson, son of Aaron, of Kensington, married to him May 7th, 1767; daughter of Ephraim Allen and Hannah his wife. Sister of No. (159) and No. (318;) she spent her last days with her daughter, No. (378,) and died Aug. 20th, 1830, aged 82; he died Nov. 29th, 1816, aged 78.

THEIR CHILDREN.

1. Sally, born 1766, married Nov. 12th, 1801, Marvin Andrews, of Meriden; she died 1810, aged 44.
2. Caroline, born Feb. 1st, 1769, see No. (378.)
3. Phebe, born 1780, never married, died Jan. 20th, 1834, aged 54.
4. Miranda, born June 30th, 1793, married July 27th, 1836, Simeon Rowley, of Farmington, a blacksmith.
5. Ephraim, born , died , aged 6 months.
6. Peter, born , married , Griswold of Meriden, he died 1813, aged 37.
7. John, born , married Huldah Clark of Kensington.
8. Abigail, born , never married, died June 3d, 1812, aged 28.

709. "Dorothy, wife of Edwin Francis," to church Aug. 2d, 1829, baptized same time, born Jan. 16th, 1803, at Kensington, to Timothy Percival and his wife Aurelia (Booth,) daughter of No. (165;) married Sept. 14th, 1825; he son of Allen and his wife No. (387,) born April 22d, 1808; a farmer; inherited his father's home in Hart quarter; she to South church 1842.

THEIR CHILDREN.

1. Bernard, born Sept. 5th, 1826, died Jan. 18th, 1829, aged 2 years, 4 mo.
2. Caroline Percival, born Oct. 11th, 1827, bap. June 27th, 1830, married Nov. 4th, 1855, Henry Ratcliffe.
3. Adelaide, born Jan. 1st, 1830, bap. June 27th, 1830, married Oct. 2d, 1850, Wm. J. M. Fish, of Providence, R. I.
4. Bernard, born Aug. 7th, 1836, bap. 1839, died Feb. 23d, 1839, aged 3 yrs. 7 mo.
5. John Newton, born July 4th, 1838, bap. 1839.
6. Edgar Loomis, born Sept. 2d, 1842, enlisted in 22d Reg't C. V.; married Dec. 7th, 1864, Nellie E. Booth.

710. "Sarah Ann Whiting," to church Aug. 2d, 1829, baptized same time; wife of Henry W. Whiting, married Sept. 5th, 1826; she

was born Sept. 14th, 1805, to Samuel Kelsey and his wife Lydia (Bronson,) who was daughter of Capt. Luke Bronson, of Kensington; Mr. Whiting is a joiner by trade, son of Ephraim of Bridgeport, and his wife Sarah (Youngs;) born Nov. 17th, 1804, came into the place 1822, while an apprentice to work on the North church; he located on Stanley st., near his father Kelsey; he has a fine farm, been successful in business, distinguished himself as an expert collector of public taxes; she to South church 1842.

THEIR CHILDREN.

1. Francina Theresa, born Sept. 3d, 1827, bap. Aug. 22d, 1830, married June 26th, 1848, Philip Corbin.
2. Sarah Elizabeth, born Feb. 11th, 1829, bap. Aug. 22d, 1830, married Oct. 26th, 1847, Levi O. Smith.
3. Henry William, born Jan. 26th, 1831, bap. Sept. 18th, 1831, married Nov. 8th, 1854, Amelia D. Adams.
4. Mary Amelia, born Nov. 22d, 1834, bap. May 31st, 1835.

711. "Elvira Hills," to church Aug. 2d, 1829, born Sept. 9th, 1807, to Elijah and his wife Lucretia (Riley,) of Middletown; she was brought up in the family of Rev. Newton Skinner, and married March 9th, 1836, Henry Gladden, son of No. (522,) born April 15, 1805; a brass worker, learned his trade of Joseph Shipman; lives on Stanley st., near the location of the first meeting house in the place; is an undertaker; his first wife was Betsey Judd, daughter of No. (435,) born Aug. 13th, 1804, married Oct. 3d, 1832, died Jan. 4th, 1835, aged 30.

THEIR CHILDREN.

1. George, born July 7th, 1834.

SECOND WIFE'S CHILDREN.

2. Cordelia, born Oct. 31st, 1838, bap. 1839, married June 21st, 1865, Niles M. Keeney.
3. Charles Riley, born June 25th, 1840, enlisted in Co. A, 13th Reg't, C. V., died July 1st, 1863, of fever, at Sem. Hospital, N. O., his body brought on and funeral attended March 1st, 1864, at Center church; sermon and eulogy.
4. Wm. Henry, born Feb. 10th, 1842, see No. (1253;) enlisted in Co. A, 13th Reg't, C. V.
5. Charlotte Melissa, born June 10th, 1843, see No. (1399.)

712. "Sarah Clark," to church Aug. 2d, 1829, born July 18th, 1809, in Farmington, to Ornan and his wife No. (403,) married Feb. 3d, 1831, Orrin S. North, son of No. (330,) born July 13th, 1805; lives on corner of East Main and Stanley sts., house built by Anthony Judd, and formerly stood on west side of street, moved to opposite corner. He is a manufacturer, have no children; she to South church 1842.

713. "Mary G. Hart, wife of Geo. Hart," to church Aug. 2d, 1829, daughter of No. (359,) and his wife Mary (Griswold,) bap. Dec. 15th,

1811, married March 2d, 1826, No. (812,) she died Aug. 10th, 1831, aged 23.

714. ELIZABETH COGSWELL, wife of Rev. Jonathan Cogswell, fourth pastor of the church, by letter from the church in Saco, Maine, Aug. 2d, 1829, born in Westford, Mass., about 1790, to Joel Abbott and his wife Lydia; she was early left an orphan, and was adopted by her uncle Samuel Abbott, the founder of Andover Theological Seminary and the Abbott Professorship; she was an ornament to her sex, to the church, and to society; she died April 30th, 1837, at East Windsor Hill. An obituary notice of that date passes the highest encomiums upon her life and character. The mound which first marked a spot near the Institute as a resting place for the dead, is that which covers Mrs. Cogswell. He second married Dec., 1837, Miss Jane G. Kirkpatrick, daughter of Chief Justice Andrew Kirkpatrick, of New Jersey, where he resided, 1862, at New Brunswick; he died there Aug. 1st, 1864, in his 82d year.

HIS CHILDREN BY ELIZABETH, HIS FIRST WIFE.

1. Mary, bap. March 12th, 1815, at Saco, Me., married Oct. 16, 1833, Franklin S. Kinney, Esq., N. Y.
2. Elizabeth L., bap. Aug. 8th, 1819, at Saco, Me., married Oct., 1840, Hon. James Dixon.
3. Louisa, bap. July 30th, 1826, at Saco, Me , married , A. R. Wood, Esq., of Va.
4. Anne W., bap. May 11, 1828, at Saco, Me., married Oct., 1848, Edgar Howland, Esq., of N. Y.; she died at Cuba, Jan. 18th, 1849.

HIS CHILDREN BY SECOND WIFE, JANE.

5. Andrew K., born , studying law in N. Y., 1861, one of the famous 7th Regiment of N. Y. who went to the rescue of Washington, April, 1861.
6. Jane E., born

715. "RHODA, wife of Matthew Clark," to church, Oct. 4th, 1829, by letter from Farmington church, received there on profession, June 4th, 1809; born Feb. 10th, 1776, to No. (149,) married June 27th, 1793, No. (645;) she died April 19th, 1840, aged 64.

716. "ALONZO STANLEY," to church April 4th, 1830, born June 24th, 1807, was a deaf mute; learned the tailor's trade, educated at the Asylum in Hartford, and admitted to the church here by Rev. Mr. Gallaudet by signs; he was quick of apprehension, social and intelligent; he was killed in New Britian, near the depot, by a locomotive, Feb. 11th, 1851, aged 44; by industry and economy he had acquired some property; never married; to South church, 1842.

717. "WILLIAM ELLIS," to church Dec. 5th, 1830, by letter from the 3d church in Berlin, born Feb. 16th, 1792, at Berlin, to Abel and his wife Thankful (Dickinson,) married Sept. 16th, 1815, No. (718;) his stone residence stands on the site of Dea. Anthony Judd's of "Great

Swamp" memory; he is a successful farmer, and has one of the oldest and best farms in the place; both to church in Worthington, Dec., 1821.

718. "WIFE OF WM. ELLIS," to church Dec. 5th, 1830, by letter from 3d church in Berlin, born Nov. 29th, 1791, to Amos A. Webster, of Berlin, and his wife Mabel (Andrus,) daughter of Daniel, her maiden name Lydia Webster, married Sept. 16th, 1815, No. (717;) both to church in Berlin, Dec., 1821.

THEIR CHILDREN.

1. Sylvender, born Sept. 18th, 1816, see No. (1079.)
2. Charlotte, born May 5th, 1818, see No. (949.)
3. William, jun., born Feb. 4th, 1821, see No. (804)
4. Edwin C., born Dec. 5th, 1823, see No. (970.)
5. Jerusha, born June 1, 1826, see No. (980.)
6. Jane, born July 2d, 1828, bap. June 28th, 1831, died Aug. 23d, 1837, aged 8.
7. Julia, } born Aug. 22d, 1830, bap. June 28th, 1831, { see No. (1126.)
8. Julius, } born Aug. 22d, 1830, bap. June 28th, 1831, { he d. May 13,'38, by a fall.
9. Henry Julius, born May 2d, 1837, bap. 1838, see No. (1259.)

719. "PHEBE, wife of Selah Steele, jun.," to church by letter from Southington; her name first appears on our record as being dismissed by letter to South church, Sept. 5th, 1845; her maiden name was Baldwin; born June 18th, 1789, at Milford, Ct., to Phineas and his wife Abigail (Woodruff;) married Oct. 5th, 1825, No. (482,) she died April 27th, 1856, aged 67, leaving one son, Harvey, who became a physician, and now, 1862, resides in West Winsted, Ct.; she to church in Southington by letter from North Milford, Dec. 3d, 1826.

720. "JOHN M. HOAR," to church April 3d, 1831, by letter from 2d Presbyterian church in Rochester, N. Y., Rev. William James, pastor, and the record says his name has been changed to Hobart; he lived several years with Alvin North, was an active, zealous christian; moved to Southington by letter, April 20th, 1834; married Oct. 9th, 1833, Vesta Potter, of Southington, daughter of Capt. Martin and Phebe (Barrett,) his wife, born July 18, 1807; he was born July 6th, 1805, at Homer, N. Y.; living now, 1863, in Southington, and is a brass founder.

THEIR CHILDREN.

1. Ellen Augusta, born Aug. 16th, 1835, married May 16th, 1855, Stephen Walkley, jun.
2. Jane Elizabeth, born Dec. 9th, 1836, married May 16th, 1855, John M. Cowles, of Farmington.
3. Vesta Sophia, born Oct. 5th, 1838, bap. June 30th, 1839.
4. Sarah Maria, born July 10th, 1840, bap. June 4th, 1841, died June 4th, 1842.
5. Julia Maria, born Aug. 25th, 1843, bap. Aug. 2d, 1844, died Feb. 7th, 1845.
6. John Potter, born Oct. 19th, 1845, bap. July 31st, 1846, drowned June 1st, 1861, bathing.
7. Rhoda Amelia, born Aug. 6th, 1847, bap. Sept. 29th, 1848.

8. Charles Parsons, born June 1st, 1849, bap. July 5th, 1850.
9. Anna Alida, born Sept. 7th, 1853, bap. June 30th, 1854.
10. Joseph Willie, born Jan. 24th, 1857, bap. July 1st, 1859.

721. "RHODA ANDREWS, widow of Hezekiah," to church Aug. 7th, 1831, born March 10th, 1759, at Worthington, to Dea. Aaron Porter and his wife Rhoda (Sage); married June 25th, 1787; he son of No. (112,) born Jan. 22d, 1758, baptized May 14th, 1758, the first on Dr. Smalley's record of baptisms. He was a farmer, built on West Main st., near his father, and his son Selah owns and occupies now, 1862, the same; he died March 19th, 1818, aged 60, she died July 26th, 1845, aged 87.

THEIR CHILDREN.

1. Selah, born Sept. 5th, 1789, married Sept. 5th, 1822, No. (564.)
2. Rhoda, born April 12th, 1795, married April 23d, 1817, Asahel, son of Oliver Hamblin; they located in White Oak, Farmington, where she still lives, 1863.

722. "ELIJAH HART," to church Aug. 7th, 1831, born Sept. 11th, 1804, to No. (181,) married March 15th, 1826, No. (723); was crippled somewhat in one hip by rheumatism; inherited the old home of his father and grandfather by the mill, south part of the village; he was a magistrate and selectman, had strong passions and force of character; to South church 1842; he died April 5th, 1856, aged 52.

723. "LOUISA, wife of Elijah Hart," to church Aug. 7th, 1831, bap. same time; born Feb. 23d, 1804, in Hamden, to Isaac Warner and his wife Damaris (Wooding); to South church 1842.

THEIR CHILDREN.

1. Henrietta W., born March 25th, 1827, bap. Oct. 16th, 1831, married Darwin Francis, Sept. 14th, 1846.
2. Eliza Ann, born July 12th, 1828, baptized Oct. 16th, 1831, married Hector F. Humphrey, of Bloomfield.
3. Augusta C., born May 12th, 1830, bap. Oct. 16th, 1831; married Henry Humphrey, of Bloomfield.
4. Elijah W., born March 13th, 1832, bap. Aug. 26th, 1832, died Sept. 17th, 1832, aged 6 months.
5. Mary J., born Sept. 5th, 1834, bap. May 31st, 1835, married Feb., 1862, Julius S. Doolittle, of Bethany.
6. Isaac W., born April 22d, 1838, married Feb. 5th, 1865, Emily N. Warner, of Hamden.
7. Emma L., born July 14th, 1844.

724. "ELIZABETH, wife of Cyrus Hart," to church Aug. 7th, 1831, baptized same time; born Dec. 20th, 1794, to No. (434,) married March 31st, 1819, No. (917); she died Feb. 22d, 1862, aged 66.

725. "ABIGAIL, wife of Roswell Steele," to church Aug. 7th, 1831, baptized same time; born Nov. 3d, 1802, at Southington, to Wm. Blakesley and his wife Lucy (Hitchcock); married May 4th, 1826, No. (514.)

726. "HARRIET PERKINS," to church Aug. 7th, 1831, baptized same time; born 1809, at Meriden, to Liberty and his wife Sarah (Lyman); married, 1838, James Cook of East Windsor, an Englishman; they have parted, and she, A. D. 1861, is living in Hartford; no record of dismissal.

727. "EDWIN BELDEN," to church Aug. 7th, 1831, baptized same time, born April 3d, 1812, to Jonathan jun., and his wife Katharine, (Andrews,) of Phineas; married Sept. 7th, 1835, No. (787;) he is a joiner, learned of No. (920,) they went to Texas 1837; he is living there it is supposed now, 1861, or in Mexico; he second married in Texas.

THEIR CHILD.

1. Elizabeth, born Oct. 2nd, 1836, married Francis Dagget of Springfield, Mass., Oct. 27th, 1858, she was baptized July 23d, 1837, at New Britain; living 1861, at Springfield, Mass.

728. "ERASTUS HAMBLIN," to church Aug. 7th, 1831, son of Lemuel, of "White Oak, Farmington," and his wife Mary, (Hart,) of Amos, born Sept. 23d, 1803; he a brass worker, was dismissed and recommended, 1840, by letter to Granby; married Maria Bull of Burlington, Ct., lives now, 1863, in Windsor, has no children; he died Nov. 30th, 1866, aged 63.

729. "JANE ELIZA FRANCIS," to church Aug. 7th, 1831, born Aug. 24th, 1814, to No. (470,) married Sept. 14th, 1835, No. (695,) was his first wife; she died Jan. 23d, 1837, aged 23, leaving one daughter, No. (1023.)

730. "NANCY JUDD," to church Aug. 7th, 1831, born Feb. 13th, 1813, to No. (459,) married Nov. 25th, 1832, Lorenzo Eddy, son of No. (462,) born Oct. 30th, 1810; is a farmer, lives near the home of his father and grandfather, southwest of "Osgood Hill;" she to south church, 1842.

THEIR CHILDREN.

1. George Henry, born Jan. 8th, 1835, baptized Oct. 4th, 1835.
2. Ann Louise, born Jan. 25th, 1837.
3. Royal Charles, born Oct. 21st, 1838, was a soldier of 1861.
4. Martin Van Buren, born Sept. 16th, 1840, served three years in army, honorably discharged.
5. Alphonso Judd, born July 24th, 1842.
6. James Munro, born Sept. 29th, 1844; in first Conn., artillery, 1864.
7. Grace Rosabella, born Nov. 10th, 1846, died March 22d, 1856, aged 9.
8. Lillie Victoria, born June 29th, 1853.
9. Rosabella Grace, born Sept. 25th, 1857.

731. "REBECCA WHITTLESEY," to church Aug. 7th, 1831, born June 26th, 1814, to No. (321,) married Jan. 1st, 1845, Deacon Daniel Fairchild, of Curtissville, Mass., he was born Sept. 19th, 1804, at Stockbridge, Mass., to Daniel and his wife Mary, (Buttlis.)

THEIR CHILDREN.

1. Rebecca Octavia, born Aug. 29th, 1846, died July 10th, 1866, aged 19, at Stockbridge.
2. Emma Louisa, born Sept. 3d, 1848.
3. Arthur Whittlesey, born Aug. 15th, 1851.

732. "MARY CLARK," to church Aug. 7th, 1831, baptized same time, born June 17th, 1816, (a twin sister of Marcellus,) to Abner and his wife No. (639,) married May 18th, 1836, No. (872.)

733. "JULIA ARTENTA JUDD," to church Aug. 7th, 1831, baptized same time, born March 24th, 1805, at Rocky Hill, to Chauncey Lewis and his wife Sybil, (Howel,) of New Haven; married May 8th, 1828, No. (540;) lives now, 1861 with her son in the Moses Andrews' house, near the "Black Rock;" she died April 9th, 1867.

734. "ORPHA SHIPMAN," to church Oct. 2d, 1831, born Dec. 12th, 1813, to No. (461,) married Oct. 20th, 1833, No. (694,) she died July 19th, 1837, aged 24.

735. "LUCY WASHBURN," to church Oct. 2d, 1831, born Feb. 5th, 1813, at Unionville, Farmington, to Erastus and his wife Laura, (Hart,) daughter of Gideon, of Kensington, baptized May 9th, 1813 at Farmington; learned the milliner's trade of No. (488,) set up her trade in Burlington, but her health failing, she returned to Farmington, where she died May 14th, 1832, aged 19, of consumption; she was niece to Rev. Mr. Washburn, of Farmington, and a lovely girl.

736. "BETSAY HOWD," to church Oct. 2d, 1831, baptized same time, born March 30th, 1814, at East Hartford, to James and his wife Martha, (Williams,) married Sept. 30th, 1833, Philip S. Judd, son of Maj. Wm. S. of Farmington, and his wife Esther Stanley; he died May 3d, 1851, aged 50; she united with the Episcopal church.

THEIR CHILDREN.

1. Esther Maria, born April 22d, 1836.
2. Thomas Henry, born Aug. 13th, 1838, died Oct. 4th, 1860, of typhoid fever, aged 22.
3. Wm. Samuel, born July 7th, 1844.
4. Alfred Stanley, born June 18th, 1847.

737. "AMOS E. STRONG," to church Oct. 2d, 1831, son of Noah and his wife, No. (748) born March 23d, 1811, at Southbury; learned trade of North & Smith, brass founders; married Jan. 17th, 1836, Eliza Maria Thomas, of West Haven, daughter of Thadeus and his wife Louise, (Clinton,) born at West Haven, Jan. 26th, 1816; he now, 1861, a farmer located at Muscatine, Iowa.

THEIR CHILDREN.

1. Lonise Maria, born
2. Edwin Burr, born

738. "ORVILL WATSON PARSONS," to church Oct. 2d, 1831, baptized same time, born Jan. 22d, 1813, at Hartland, Conn., to Paul and his wife Phebe, (Coe,) married Feb. 5th, 1834, Ruah Tuller, daughter of Jabes, of Simsbury, his wife Lucy, (Gilbert,) born April 24th, 1809 ; he was a brass worker, he died Aug. 31st, 1836, aged 23, of consumption.

THEIR SON.

1. Orville Franklin, born Oct. 6th, 1834, married Nov. 22d, 1855, Sarah J. Magee, of N. Haven.

739. "MISS ELIZA PARSONS," to church Oct. 2d, 1831, by letter from the church in Lenox, Mass., born Oct, 15th, 1802, at Hartland, Conn., to Paul and his wife Phebe, (Coe,) married April 22d, 1839, No. (569,) have no children ; she died Aug. 27th, 1864, in 62d year.

740. "MRS. LAURA LEE.," to church Oct. 2d, 1831, by letter from Congregational church in Newington, daughter of Martin Kellogg of Newington, born Nov. 1784 ; married Sept. 18th, 1805, Asaph Whittlesey, he died, when second she married, Feb. 2d, 1831, No. (356 ;) she died Feb. 9th, 1837, aged 52 ; her mother's maiden name was Hannah Robbins.

741. "MR. JOHN W. MURPHY," to church Oct. 2d, 1831, by letter from church in South Wilbraham ; was a house painter by trade; married Nov 26th, 1828, No. (505 ;) he was dismissed and recommended to church in North Coventry, Oct. 1834 ; he died at Hartford.

THEIR DAUGHTER.

Cornelia, born

742. "MARY STEELE," to church, 1827, it is supposed she was dismissed from the church in Newington, and recommended to this, (by Rev. J. Brace, Pastor,) May 13th, 1827 ; her full name was Mary Darling Steele, born March 10th, 1807, to No. (406,) and his wife Nelly (Williams,) married Sept. 1st, 1836, Philip Recor, son of No. (467,) and his wife No. (468,) born Sept. 1st, 1816 ; live north east of "Osgood Hill," their house originally the shop of No. (244 ;) her name is not on our record, but the Newington church record shows when she was dismissed and she is now, 1862, living, and says she joined the first church by the letter by Mr. Brace, and left our communion a few years after, for the Baptist church in New Britain.

THEIR CHILDREN.

1. Lucy Jane, born Feb. 20th, 1837, married Marshall Gladden, son of Truman, she died Nov. 23d, 1863, (26.)
2. John, born Feb. 1st, 1838, married Adeline Filbrooks.
3. Martha, born Feb. 8th, 1840, married Goth Sunderland.
4. Philip, born July 30th, 1843, enlisted into Company G, 6th reg. C. V., died April 4th, 1862, of fever, at Hilton Head, S. C.
5. Alfred Hart, born June 19th, 1845.
6. Mary Matilda, born Jan. 19th, 1848.

743. "Henry North," to church Dec. 4th, 1831, born Sept. 24th, 1789, to No. (149,) married Dec. 26th, 1810, Sarah Cosslett, daughter of Francis and his second wife, No. (636,) she died Sept. 11th, 1814, aged 22; when second he married, Jan. 24th, 1821, No. (744,) he inherited his father's homestead; was a wagon maker by trade, but became an extensive manufacturer, and a man of considerable wealth; he was a man remarkably honest and scrupulous in all his dealings, liberal in his benefactions, and died Feb. 1st, 1853, aged 64, without an enemy; to south church 1842.

744. "Wife of Henry North," to church Dec. 4th, 1831, born Sept. 24th, 1802, to No. (337,) married Jan. 24th, 1821, and was his second wife, and lives at the old home; to south church, 1842.

THEIR CHILDREN.

1. Sarah, born Dec. 24th, 1811, married Nov. 11th, 1829, Selah Hart, jun., and they reside in Philadelphia, 1862.
2. Augusta, born Feb. 1st, 1814, died July 5th, 1814, aged 5 months.

SECOND WIFE'S CHILDREN.

3. Son born March 18th, 1822, died next day.
4. Henrietta, born July 10th, 1823, died Dec. 19th, 1829, aged 6.
5. Waldo S. born Nov. 25th, 1826, died April 14th, 1827, aged 5 months.
6. Julia Ann, born Aug. 11th, 1828, bap. July 15th, 1832, married June 11th, 1851, Thos. S. Hall.
7. Augusta Maria, born Jan. 15th, 1831, bap. July 15th, 1832, married Oct. 26th, 1852, Henry C. Bowers.
8. Mary Elizabeth, born Oct. 9th, 1833, bap. June 1st, 1834, married Aug. 28th, 1850, No. (829.)
9. Walter Henry, born March 12th, 1836, bap. 1836, died Jan. 10th, 1837, aged 11 months.
10. Ellen Louisa, born Jan. 21st, 1838, bap. 1838, died Dec. 10th, 1839, aged 2.
11. Georgiana L. born July 19th, 1840, died June 6th, 1846, aged 6.
12. Cordelia B., born March 11th, 1843.

745. "Electa Andrews," wife of Aaron C. Andrews, to church Dec. 4th, 1831, by letter from the church in Southington, born Dec. 8th, 1811, to Capt. Urbam Barrett of Southington and his wife Electa, (Woodruff,) to church there Dec. 2d, 1827; she married Sept. 6th, 1830, No. (684,) to S. church, 1842.

746. "Henry L. Bidwell," to church Dec. 4th, 1831, by letter from church in Farmington, Noah Porter, D. D., Pastor, born Oct. 20th, 1804, at Farmington, to Titus and his wife Nancy, daughter of Joseph Langdon, married Dec. 21st, 1830, No. (606;) he bought the John Stanley place, near the old home of Col. Gad Stanley, Stanley quarter, owned and occupied now, 1863, by No. (1315,) where he manufactured cooking stoves. He became a clerk and cashier of the Exchange Bank, Hartford, and his church connection was removed from this to the Free or 4th in

Hartford; he was chosen Deacon of the South church in Hartford, in 1842, but resigned in 1858 and came under censure of that church for bank defalcations. He built a fine residence in Hartford, South Main St., but went to New York City; he recruited and became Capt. of Company A, 13th Regiment, Conn. Volunteers, in New Britain, and went to Ship Island and New Orleans, after which he recruited a Company in New York, which began under the auspices of the Young Men's Christian Union, of which he became Capt. and went on to New Orleans, Jan. 24th, 1863; he was taken sick with typhoid fever, and died June 15th, 1863, aged 58.

THEIR CHILDREN.

1. Julia Augusta, born Jan. 12th, 1832, bap. July 8th, 1832, married Randolph B. Loomis.

2. Henry Stanley, born June 27th, 1836, bap. 1836, at New Britain, clerk in Nausau Bank, N. Y., was a three months volunteer 1861, to defend Washington, also went a second time and was called a third, but sent a substitute; he married Nov. 8th, 1865, Mary Allen.

747. "Eli Smith," to church Dec. 4th, 1831, by letter from church in Farmington, son of Dr. Aaron, of Bethany, and his wife Olive(Lewis,) alias (Widow Olive Talmage,) born Oct. 3d, 1774, at Bethany; was a farmer by occupation; married Aug. 19th, 1795, Susanna Smith, daughter of Daniel, she died Nov. 16th, 1822, when second he married Oct. 23d, 1835, Widow Betsey Wells, No. (334;) they lived at her father's old home on West Main Street, where he died June 1st, 1854, aged 80.

HIS CHILDREN BY HIS WIFE SUSANNA.

1. Lewis, born Nov. 14th, 1796, died young.
2. Lewis, born Oct. 24th, 1798, married , Cynthia Osborn.
3. Augustus, born Feb. 19th, 1800, died Nov. 27th, 1822, aged 22.
4. Roswell, born April 12th, 1802, married Cina Smith, of Harwinton.
5. Aaron, born March 27th, 1804, married Augusta Fuller, died May 18th, 1843, aged 39.
6. Anna, born May 9th, 1806, married No. (1031.)
7. Eliza, born April 1st, 1808, see No. (758.)
8. Caroline, born July 17th, 1812, see No. (759.)
9. Eli B. born Nov. 25th, 1815, see No. (871.)

748. "Mrs. Sarah Strong," to church about 1829, by letter from church in Torringford; her name was omitted on the record, except as being dismissed and recommended, to a church in Waterbury, Feb. 23d, 1832, her maiden name, Sarah LaVoy, daughter of James, a Frenchman, and his wife Clarissa Foote, born 1779, at Newtown; married Noah Strong, son of Selah, of Southbury, their children all born there; the family came to this place about 1828, lived in the Skinner House, and at the lower Mill of Hart's; she died July 30th, 1860, aged 81, at New Haven; he died July 5th, 1847, aged 78, at New Haven.

THEIR CHILDREN.

1. Obedience, born , married Hazzard Terrel, second Asa Bromford, 3d, Hiram Weed.
2. Ransom, born , married Fanny Barnes, of N. Hartford, second, married Widow Cadwell.
3. Esther, born , married Elihu Osborn, of Woodbridge; live at Wallace St., N. Haven.
4. Sarah, born , married Lucius Hine, of Naugatuck.
5. Amos E. born March 23d, 1811, married Eliza Thomas, see No. (737.)
6. Maria, born Sept. 15th, 1815, married Jarvis Johnson, of Waterbury, lives there A. D. 1861.
7. Burr, born 1819, died , aged 24.

749. "William C. Whipple," to church April 1st, 1832, son of Hezekiah C. and his wife No. (525,) born April 5th, 1814, married Nov. 1st, 1836, Elizabeth Osborn, in New Haven, daughter of Henry F. of that city, and Louise (Sperry, his wife,) born March 3d, 1820; they live in Westville, Conn.

THEIR CHILDREN.

1. Jane Eliza, born Dec. 6th, 1838, married Nov. 22d, 1858, John Willmarth.
2. Charles, born Oct. 6th, 1840, died Oct. 12th, 1840.
3. Everard, born July 18th, 1842, died Feb. 14th, 1844.
4. Edwin, born Sept. 14th, 1844, died Nov. 16th, 1845.
5. Wm. Frederick, born Sept. 15th, 1846.
6. Sarah Elizabeth, born Dec. 21st, 1848, died Nov. 17th, 1860.
7. Cornelia, born May 5th, 1852.
8. Adelaide, born June 17th, 1856.

750. "Enos S. Hurlburt," to church April 1st, 1832, baptized same time; born Jan. 5th, 1814, at Newington, to Charles, and his first wife Julia (Sage,) of Simsbury, married March 19th, 1836, Clarissa Gorham, of North Haven, daughter of Elisha, and Hannah (Bradley,) his wife; she died at New Haven, March 11th, 1844, when he married, second, Jan. 1st, 1845, Eliza, sister of his first wife; they now, 1861, live in Waterbury. I find no record of his dismissal and recommendation.

THEIR CHILDREN.

1. Oscar B., born May 21st, 1837.
2. Franklin, born Oct. 27th, 1839.
3. William Wallace, born Nov. 25th, 1841.

SECOND WIFE'S CHILDREN.

4. George, } twins, born March 4th, 1848, { he died May 4th, 1848, aged 2 mo's.
5. Charles, }

751. "Rene, wife of Moses Gilbert, 2d," to church April 1st, 1832, by letter from the Third church in Berlin; born Feb. 2d, 1794, to William Steele, sen., and his wife, No. (246,) married Sept. 25th, 1814; lived at the James Moore house, at the time of her admission to church. He

was son of Hooker Gilbert, and his wife Sarah (Hooker,) daughter of Samuel, born March 17th, 1793; is a farmer, has traveled much at the south, lives now on the old homestead of his ancestors, in "Christian lane," in the brick house built by his father. She died Feb. 28th, 1862, aged 68.

THEIR CHILDREN.

1. Bathsheba, born Aug. 23d, 1815, died Sept. 5th, 1823, aged 8.
2. Walter, born March 30th, 1818, died July 20th, 1825, aged 7.
3. Caroline, born March 8th, 1820.
4. Moses, jun., born March 28th, 1822, married March 11th, 1850, Lucelia Steele, daughter of Jefferson.
5. William, born Feb. 7th, 1826.
6. Rena, born March 15th, 1834, died Sept. 15th, 1834, aged 6 months.
7. Adeline, born Feb. 14th, 1840.

752. "EVELIN E. WOODFORD," to church Feb. 3d, 1833, by letter from church in Avon: born March 13th, 1814, to Romanta, of Avon, (now, 1862, of Kensington,) married Marcia Churchill, of Newington; she died, when he married, second, in Texas, Mrs. Mary Aiken, a widow. He died in San Francisco, Cal., Nov. 6th.

753. "LAURA CHURCHILL," to church Feb. 3d, 1833, from the church in Kensington, by letter; born Dec. 26th, 1813, to Solomon, jun., and his wife, No. (388,) married Giles Colvin, son of Giles, of Scituate, Mass., and his wife Nancy (Ward,) of Middletown, Ct., born , he died 1835, in Indiana.

754. "ELIJAH H. BURRITT," to church June 2d, 1833, by letter from the church in Simsbury; born April 20th, 1794, to Elihu, sen., and his wife, No. (290.) He learned the trade of blacksmith of No. (370,) hence his connection with the church in Simsbury, where Mr. Booth carried on his business for a few years. He graduated at Williamstown College, Mass., became a distinguished mathematician and astronomer, was an editor of a weekly paper in Georgia some years, and became a teacher of a private school in New Britain. He was author of several works. He was at the head of a small colony that unfortunately went to Texas, A. D. 1837. He married, Oct. 28th, 1819, Ann W. Watson, of Milledgeville, Georgia, No. (754.) He died Jan. 3d, 1838, in Texas. He was a well built, large man, of commanding appearance and dignified address, of more than ordinary talents, but somewhat erratic. He owned and occupied for a time the block in this place called the "Stone store," had his residence and boarding school in the same building. He sold this and bought the Nickerson place on the corner of Park and Orchard streets, where his family lived at the time of his decease in Texas.

755. "ANN, wife of E. H. Burritt," to church June 2d, 1833, from the Presbyterian church in Milledgeville, Ga.; her maiden name, Ann Williams Watson, born Dec. 24th, 1797, to John, and his wife Elizabeth

(Williams,) near Warrenton, Ga. She is distinguished for good sense and force of character; married Oct. 28th, 1819, No. (754,) to South church, 1842. She lived lately at St. Paul, Minn., but in 1863, near Chicago, Ill., now, 1867, in New Britain.

THEIR CHILDREN.

1. Elizabeth, born April 22d, 1822, in Georgia, died Oct. 28th, 1826.

2. George Hinsdale, born Feb. 28th, 1826 in Georgia, married Oct. 20th, 1849, Maria L. Parsons, of Cleveland.

3. Anna Elizabeth, born Nov. 30th, 1829, married April 19th, 1860, Joseph B. Hawkes, of Charlemont, Mass.; he died June, 1865, at Vicksburg.

4. Julia Watson, born March 11th, 1833, bap. June 2d, 1833, married Aug. 16th, 1852, Dr. Warner N. Dunham; she died May 20th, 1865, aged 33, at Bricktown, Ill.

5. Elijah Hinsdale, born July 11th, 1835, bap. Oct. 4th, 1835, married Dec. 20th, 1866, Matred E. Tilden, of Cleveland, Ohio; living in St. Paul, Minn.

756. "David Hough," to church June 2d, 1833, from the church in Meriden; born Aug. 3d, 1777, in Wallingford, to Andrew, and his wife Lois (Hough,) he was a weaver by trade, he married Aug. 3d, 1805, No. (819.) He owned and occupied the Samuel Bass place on West Main street; the house has disappeared, but it stood a few feet east of that of his son Norman. He was a plain, honest man, of great industry and integrity. He died March 27th, 1847, aged 69.

THEIR CHILDREN.

1. Polly Burritt, born May 25th, 1806, died July 27th, 1814, aged 8.

2. William Ogden, born Nov. 25th, 1807, married Jan. 20th, 1831, Isabel G. Thorp; he died at Bristol, June 8th, 1865, in his 58th year.

3. Louisa Thankful, born October 30th, 1809, married March 7th, 1838, Horace Deming.

4. David Norman, born Nov. 4th, 1811, see No. (774.)

5. Phebe Maria, born Dec. 2d, 1813, see No. (757.)

6. Mary Burritt, born Feb. 26th, 1816, see No. (881.)

7. Levi, born June 18th, 1818, married April 23d, 1840, Betsey Tuttle, of Northfield, daughter of Eber.

8. Horatio, born May 25th, 1820, married May 9th, 1841, Maria L. Dickinson; married, second, May 27th, 1858, Augusta A. Hazard; she died, when he married, third, Dec. 2d, 1861, Anna H. Squirrel.

9. Elizabeth Jerusha, born Feb. 29th, 1824, see No. (820.)

757. "Maria Hough," to church June 2d, 1833, from church in Meriden; born Dec. 2d, 1813, at Bristol, to No. (756) and No. (819,) never married, lives with her brothers and sisters.

758. "Eliza Smith," to church Aug. 4th, 1833, by letter from church in Burlington; born April 1st, 1808, at Harwinton, to No. (747,) and his wife Susanna; never married. She died Aug. 11th, 1847, aged 39, at her father's residence on West Main street, in New Britain, now, 1862, the residence of No. (1030.)

759. "CAROLINE SMITH," to church Dec. 1st, 1833, from the church in Farmington, by letter; born July 17th, 1812, at Harwinton, to No. (747,) married June 30th, 1840, Henry Williams, son of Elisha, and his wife No. (415,) born Aug. 11th, 1807, at Kensington, and baptized there Nov. 1st, 1807. He was a farmer in middle life, but learned the shoemaker's trade of Munson, in Southington, made money by his trade at the south, and bought the Salmon Hart farm. He died Aug. 28th, 1855, aged 48.

THEIR CHILDREN.

1. Rodman Church, born August 8th, 1842, bap. Dec. 3d, 1842, died June 17th, 1853, aged 11.
2. Edgar Lewis, born Aug. 4th, 1844, bap. Dec. 29th, 1844; a volunteer in Co. F, 14th Reg., in 1862, and was at the battle of Antietam; he married, Sept. 1st, 1865, Jane, daughter of Thomas Webb, of New Haven.
3. Elisha Henry, born Nov. 5th, 1846, bap. April 25th, 1847.
4. Lyman Smith, born April 9th, 1848, bap. Oct. 15th, 1848.
5. Arthur Watson, born April 5th, 1851, bap. Oct. 12th, 1851.
6. Wilber Augustus, born Oct. 13th, 1852.
7. Rodman Hawley, born Sept. 11th, 1854, bap. June 24th, 1855.

760. "AMY HOUGH," to church Dec. 1st, 1833, from the church in Meriden; daughter of Andrew, of Wallingford, and Lois, his wife, sister of No. (755,) and lived with him; never married; died at the home of Rezin Jones, on Arch street, Sept. 28th, 1848, aged 61.

761. "SAMUEL E. CURTISS," to church Dec. 1st, 1833, from the church in Southington, by letter; born March 8th, 1808, at Southington, to Leverett, and his wife Ruth (Barnes,) a shoe-maker by trade, was located in south part of Southington, but sold out and resided in this place several years, and is now, 1863, at Waterloo, Wis. He married, April 21, 1830, No. (508.) He and wife were dismissed and recommended, 1837, to church in Southington.

THEIR CHILDREN.

1. Frances Marion, born May 30th, 1834, bap. July 11th, 1834, in New Britain, died April 27th, 1860, at Madison, Wis.
2. Edwin Rodney, born May 6th, 1836, married May 11th, 1859, Eva Lingenfalter, of New York state; he was bap. Nov. 6th, 1836, at Southington; is a daguerrian in Madison, Wis.
3. Nathan Selah, born Oct. 19th, 1838.
4. George Frederick, born Oct. 11th, 1849, died June 12th, 1854, at Broadalbin, New York.

762. "HULDAH, wife of Ezekiel Andrews," to church Dec. 1st, 1833, by letter from the church in Simsbury; her maiden name, Goodrich, born Jan. 5th, 1788, at Simsbury, to Stephen, and his wife Lydia (Terry,) married May 2d, 1809, Luther Moses, who died Jan. 20th, 1830, when she married, second, Oct. 20th, 1833, No. (313;) had a dower from his estate, drew his bounty land as his widow, for service in the war of 1812; lives,

A. D. 1867, with her daughter, Mrs. Richardson, in Hartford, was dismissed by this church and received there by letter general, Oct. 13th, 1854.

HER CHILDREN BY HER FIRST HUSBAND, MOSES.

1. Huldah Selina, born Feb. 19th, 1810, at Simsbury, married Merick Richardson, now of Hartford.
2. Celestia, born Nov. 10th, 1811, married Violet H. Pease, of Lee, Mass.
3. Morgan, born Sept. 9th, 1813, at Simsbury, died April 30th, 1815.
4. Luther Morgan, born March 27th, 1816, married Mary Lampson.
5. Stephen Goodrich, born April 27th, 1818, married Mary Atkins.
6. Alfred, born May 4th, 1820.

763. "ISAAC CATLIN," to church April 6th, 1834, by letter from a church in Ohio; son of Isaac, of Harwinton, and Ruth his wife, born Jan. 27th, 1800, married April 21st, 1824, No. (764,) dismissed and recommended, 1838, to a church in Augusta, Ill.; living now, 1861, in Quincy, Ill.

764. "REBECCA, wife of Isaac Catlin," to church April 6th, 1834, by letter from a church in Ohio; born Aug. 26th, 1801, to No. (179,) married April 21st, 1824, No. (763,) dismissed and recommended, 1838, to Augusta, Ill.; now, 1861, living at Quincy, Ill.

THEIR CHILDREN.

1. Homer D., born Feb. 21st, 1826, in Ohio.
2. Sarah B., born June 10th, 1829, in Ohio.
3. Elizabeth H., born Feb. 19th, 1834, in New Britain.
4. Charles F., born Sept. 26th, 1841, in Illinois.

765. "JULIA ANN LEWIS," to church April 5th, 1835, by letter from church in Farmington, admitted there Aug. 9th, 1821; daughter of No. (211,) and his wife, No. (326,) born Sept. 1st, 1795, married Dec. 16th, 1818, Seth Lewis, of Farmington, son of Phineas; he died Dec. 19th, 1833, aged 68, when she married, second, Sept. 27th, 1838, Mr. Oakley, of Pennsylvania, he died, when she married, third, Dec. 27th, 1842, Samuel Hull, of Candor, N. Y. She was dismissed and recommended to church in Pennsylvania. She died Aug. 22d, 1859, at Candor, N. Y., of dropsy, aged 63.

HER CHILDREN BY FIRST HUSBAND.

1. John Sedgwick, born Sept. 27th, 1824, bap. Jan. 9th, 1825, in Farmington, married Dec. 10th, 1851, Harriet Alden, of Michigan.
2. Thomas Norton, born March 27th, 1827, bap. May, 1835, at New Britain, married April 27th, 1853, Mary F. Lake.
3. Henry Hart, born June 13th, 1829, bap. May, 1835, at New Britain, married March 10th, 1852, Mary Chaine.
4. William Hall, born May 22d, 1831, went to California.

766. "JULIA ANN KELSEY," to church December, 1835, by letter from church in Farmington, to church there April 1st, 1827, and baptized same time; born Dec. 10th, 1811, at Kensington, to William, and his wife Lucy (Stanley,) unmarried, A. D. 1862; is sister to No. (600,) and they live together on Orchard street, and have a pleasant residence.

767. "DAVID W. WHITTLESEY," to church December, 1835; born March 31st, 1816, to No. (321,) occupied the home of his father until after his decease, when he bought in East Berlin. He married, Sept. 4th, 1839, No. (892;) he taught school in early manhood, was early interested in Sunday schools, and gave his influence to the cause of temperance and humanity. He and wife were dismissed and recommended by letter to church in Berlin, May 30th, 1852, where he is a successful farmer and greatly useful in church and society; he was chosen a deacon in Berlin church Sept. 5th, 1862, and lived on a fine farm in East Berlin. They moved to Morris, Litchfield county, 1864.

THEIR CHILDREN.

1. Laura Calista, born April 10th, 1842, bap. 1842.
2. Samuel Averill, born Aug. 7th, 1844, bap. Oct. 13th, 1844; a soldier in Co. I, 22d Reg. C. V., nine months' men; married Oct. 9th, 1866, Ada J. Savage of Berlin.
3. Asenath, born Feb. 25th, 1849, bap. Dec. 2d, 1849.
4. Lyman Walter, born April 6th, 1852, at East Berlin.

768. "CALISTA C. WHITTLESEY," to church December, 1835; born Nov. 7th, 1818, to No. (321,) married Oct. 10th, 1843, Amos M. Ebersol, son of Joseph, and his wife Elizabeth (Shuey,) of Ottawa, Ill., where now, 1863, they reside.

THEIR CHILDREN.

1. James Clark, born March 6th, 1845, at Ottawa, Ill.
2. Alice Whittlesey, born July 24th, 1847, at Ottawa, Ill.
3. Ella C., born March 18th, 1849, at Ottawa, Ill.
4. Lela H., born April 30th, 1850, at Ottawa, Ill.
5. Calistus S , born Nov. 20th, 1854, at Ottawa, Ill.
6. Elizabeth L., born Dec. 23d, 1856, at Ottawa, Ill.

769. "HARRIET A. NORTH," to church December, 1835; born Sept. 28th, 1818, to No. (331,) and his second wife, No. (411,) married July 17th, 1839, Roger H. Mills, Esq., of New Hartford, born April 19th, 1813, at New Hartford, to Roger, and his wife Harriet (Merrill,) live, 1862, in Beloit, Wis. She was dismissed and recommended by letter to New Hartford, 1839. He was once Secretary of State of Connecticut, now, 1862, is mayor of Beloit, Wis.

THEIR CHILDREN.

1. Roger Henry, born Oct. 24th, 1852, at New Hartford, Ct.
2. John Hammond, born May 26th, 1854, at New Britain, Ct.
3. Clara Burnham, born July 24th, 1857, at Beloit, Wis.

770. "LUCINDA HART," to church December, 1835; born Aug. 30th, 1820, to No. (311,) and his wife, No. (366,) married April 27th, 1842, No. (652,) and was his second wife, a woman of active mind and quick perceptions; to South church, 1842.

771. "BURDETTE HART," to church December, 1835; born Nov. 16th, 1821, to No. (954;) graduated at Yale College, 1842, settled at Fair Haven, Ct., in the ministry; married, Aug. 21st, 1849, Rebecca W. Fiske, daughter of David, and his wife Laura (Severance,) of Shelburne, Mass., born Feb. 22d, 1823. His voice having partially failed, he traveled in Europe, and visited for a season at St. Paul, Minn., where he gathered a Congregational church and preached to them some twelve months, but not gaining much relief, he was dismissed from Fair Haven, and moved to Philadelphia, Pa., and engaged in mercantile pursuits. He was a good scholar, easy writer, and a popular preacher. He was dismissed and recommended to Yale College church, 1839, is now, 1862, living in Philadelphia.

THEIR CHILDREN.

1. Frederick Burdette, born Aug. 2d, 1850, died Aug. 6th, 1851.
2. Arthur Burdette, born Sept. 5th, 1852.
3. Mary Arabella, born May 30th, 1855.
4. Minerva Lee, born Nov. 9th, 1859.

772. "MRS. SUSAN NICKERSON," to church December, 1835, by letter from Norfolk, Ct.; born Sept. 9th, 1814, at Norfolk, to John Camp, and his wife Esther (Potter,) of New Haven, married Sept. 27th, 1835, Major A. Nickerson, a lawyer by profession, came to this town A. D. 1834, and located on the corner of Park and Orchard streets. She was educated at Troy and Litchfield, attempted to establish a ladies' boarding school here, but failed for lack of means. He left the place and the law and became an Episcopal minister at Havanna and Crossing, N. Y., also at St. John's church, at Stillwater, Saratoga county; he died Dec. 23d, 1848. She, A. D. 1861, is a teacher of French and music, at her boarding school, Albany, N. Y. She was dismissed and recommended to church in Leroy, N. Y.

THEIR CHILDREN.

1. John, born July 25th, 1837, at Leroy, N. Y., is a banker in Albany.
2. Charles Metcalf, born Sept. 11th, 1843, at Catharine, N. Y.; 1861, at Hobart College, Geneva, N. Y.
3. Susan Camp, born Sept. 30th, 1846, at Stillwater, N. Y.

[Here commences the ministry of Rev. Dwight M. Seward, ordained and installed Feb. 3d, 1836.]

773 "REZIN G. JONES," to church February, 1836, by letter from First church in Farmington; born Feb. 3d, 1795, at "White Oak,"

Farmington, to Samuel, and his wife Almira (Gridley,) daughter of Capt. Rezin, married Aug. 15th, 1827, Jerusha Mather, No. (379.) He was a farmer and wagoner, and kept the toll gate at the western extremity of the town several years, then built on Arch street, in the village. She died, when he married, second, April 23d, 1840, No. (881.) He was the only son of his parents; has no posterity.

774. "NORMAN HOUGH," to church, 1836, by letter from Meriden; born Nov. 4th, 1811, at Meriden, to No. (756,) married April 9th, 1834, No. (775,) has his residence on West Main street; is a mechanic, and industrious and economical.

775. "HARRIET, wife of Norman Hough," to church 1836, from First church in Farmington, daughter of Paul Burrows, and his wife Roxanna (Hungerford,) born April 23d, 1807, at "Scott's Swamp," in Farmington; to church there August 1st, 1822.

THEIR CHILDREN.

1. Edward Norman, born May 15th, 1835, married Nov. 7th, 1854, Laura Ann Slater, daughter of Sherman; he enlisted into Co. G, (Capt. Tracy,) 6th Reg. C. V., and went to Port Royal.
2. Henry Martin, born Oct. 23d, 1840.
3. Sarah Burrows, born Oct. 25th, 1842.

776. "SYLVANUS STONE," to church 1836, by letter from Meriden; born May 28th, 1805, at Litchfield, to Elisha, and his wife Mary (North,) daughter of Asher, married Nov. 2d, 1828, No. (777,) she died, when he married, second, Jan. 6th, 1850, No. (1056.) He is a paper box maker, his residence and shop on Elm street. He was appointed one of the "Standing Committee," January, 1861.

777. "HARRIET, wife of Sylvanus Stone," to church, 1836, by letter from Meriden; born March 11th, 1811, to No. (452,) married Nov. 2d, 1828, No. (776,) died March 1st, 1839, aged 48.

THEIR CHILDREN.

1. Levi Butler, born June 19th, 1830, see No. (1029.)
2. George Brown, born May 23d, 1834, died Feb. 15th, 1836.
3. Mary Elizabeth, born Aug. 23d, 1837, see No. (1176.)

CHILD BY SECOND WIFE.

4. Harriet Eliza, born Dec. 17th, 1853.

778. "L. N. TRACY," to church 1836, by letter from ; born Feb. 16th, 1807, at Cornish, New Hampshire, to Lemuel, and his wife Phebe (Parker;) he graduated, 1834, at Dartmouth College, and came to this place as teacher of our academy, in preparing our young men for college. He married Isabella Nutting, daughter of Timothy, and his wife Elizabeth (Quinton.) He was licensed to preach by the Hartford County

South Association, June 5th, 1838, at Kensington, on recommendation of Rev. Dwight M. Seward, of New Britain. He went from here to Hartford, where he engaged in teaching; both joined the South church there, 1846, he by letter from this church, 1839. They had two children, Arthur Quinton and Isabella, but both died at Hartford. He died June 13th, 1846, aged 39, at John H. Goodwin's in Hartford. She died in Hartford, Feb. 9th, 1846, aged 31. His name, Levi Nelson Tracy.

779. "Mrs. PHEBE, wife of Oscar McLean," to church 1836, by letter from Norwich. She was dismissed and recommended, 1840, to South church in Glastenbury, but received back by letter, Aug. 5th, 1855, from South church of New Britain. Her residence, 1861, on Chestnut street, born Jan. 13th, 1811, at Windham, Ct., to Stephen Congdon, of Rhode Island, and his wife Martha (Peckham,) married June 22d, 1835, Silas Oscar McLean, of Glastenbury, son of Silas, and his wife Anna (Pulsifer,) born Jan. 29th, 1812; he died at Glastenbury, Jan. 3d, 1841.

THEIR CHILDREN.

1. Charles Oscar, born March 24th, 1836, bap. 1836, see No. (1175).
2. George Gorham, born Sept. 21st, 1838, see No. (1174.)

780. "MRS. ELIZA ANN, wife of Wm. C. Marshall," to church Nov. 1836, by letter from church in Barkhampsted, daughter of Enoch Gaines and Anna (Warner,) his wife, born April 24th, 1813, at Barkhampsted, to church there, A. D. 1826; came to this place as milliner; married Oct. 12th, 1836, Wm. C. Marshall, son of Shubel and his wife Sarah (Thompson,) born Dec. 21st, 1809, in city of New York; she to south church, 1842; family resides now, 1861, in Hartford. He was a brass manufacturer, and successful, shop on Mill St.

THEIR CHILDREN.

1. Mortimer W, born Dec. 19th, 1837, at New Britain, was a three months' soldier in defence of Washington, and in the battle at Bull Run, married Nov. 20th, 1862, No. (1212.)
2. Wm. E. born April 22d, 1841, at Hartford.
3. Albert G. born Aug. 7th, 1853, at Hartford.

781. "ELIZABETH W. wife of Horatio W. Shipman," to church Aug. 6th, 1837, by letter from Hartford south, daughter of Wm. Wadsworth and his wife Catharine (Bunce,) born June 9th, 1817, at Hartford, Ct., a decendent of Capt. Joseph, of Charter Oak celebrity; married Nov. 4th, 1835; he was son of No. (461,) born Sept. 10th 1811; learned the jewelers trade of Goodwin in Hartford, entered into partnership with his father and brother in the brass business, which they extended until they failed in 1838; he lives now, 1861, in Brooklyn, N. Y. She was dismissed by letter and received to Pres. church N. Y. City, (Dr. Krebs,)

July, 1844. He had a taste for military and obtained the title of Col. in the militia of Conn. She was for years secretary of the Brooklyn Industrial School Association, and a beautiful reporter of their doings. He died Oct. 11th, 1864, aged 53.

THEIR CHILDREN.

1. Wm. Wadsworth, born Oct. 23d, 1836, bap. June 1st, 1837, clerk in Philadelphia. But Aug. 15th, 1861, married Lizzie Buckins, of Philadelphia. He now, 1862, is a soldier in Mansfield's Division, Va., 13th Reg. N. Y. Militia.
2. Catharine, born June 6th, 1843, bap. July, 1844, excels in music; married June 6th, 1866, Henry Whitney, N. Y
3. Mary Lee, born Jan. 7th, 1846, bap. March 14th, 1847, at New Britain; married 1867, Doctor Whitney, N. Y.
4. Elizabeth Wadsworth, born June 15th, 1855.

782. "Dorcas Parsons," to church Aug. 6th, 1837, by letter from Kensington ; her maiden name was Bronson ; born Jan. 1st, 1766, married Jan. 15th, 1795, Aaron Parsons, of Kensington ; they had several children, but none to live long. He died Aug. 1814, aged 53 ; her adopted daughter, Clarissa Cole, married Wm. Burritt, of this place, and Mrs. Parsons lived here with them and died Sept. 15th, 1855, aged 89, at their house having been aided by the church towards the close of her long life, and kindly cared for by Mrs. Burritt.

783. "Sarah, wife of Ezekiel Andrews, jun.," to church Aug. 6th, 1837, born June 26th, 1815, to Hiland Parker and Lydia (Pratt,) his wife, at Coventryville, Chenango County, N. Y., married Aug. 7th, 1833, No. (690,) to south church, 1842, (her name was Sarah Elizabeth.)

784. "Jane Andrews," to church Aug. 6th, 1837, born Feb. 2d, 1818, to No. (313,) baptized April 26th, 1818. Jane Louisa married Sept. 11th, 1837, Wm. Miles second, of Goshen ; she was dismissed and recommended by letter to the church in Goshen, 1838, when she died April 7th, 1842, aged 24, had no children to live long ; her grave and monument are in Goshen Hill Cemetery.

785. "Julia Ann Andrews," to church Aug. 6th, 1837, born Nov. 15th, 1819, to No. (478,) and his first wife No. (479,) baptized Aug. 19th, 1821, at the old church.

786. "Caroline Andrews," to church Aug. 6th, 1837, born Dec. 4th, 1822 to No. (478) and his first wife No. (479,) baptized Feb. 9th, 1823, Caroline Hart, and Rev. Mr. Skinner in his record says the first baptized in the new meeting house. She married Jan. 21st, 1852, Elisha B. Bridgman of Belchertown, Mass., son of Oliver, before Rev. S. D. Jewett, then of Westchester, Conn. She was dismissed and recommended by letter, 1852, to the church in Belchertown, Mass.

THEIR CHILDREN.

1. Elizabeth Cornwell, born March 6th, 1853, died Feb. 22d, 1854, aged 1 year.
2 Oliver Burt, born March 8th, 1855.

3. Anna Julia, born July 9th, 1857.
4. Infant, born Nov. 6th, 1860, died aged 36 hours.

787. "MARY ANN, wife of E. Belden," to church Aug. 6th, 1837, baptized same time; her maiden name was Ellis, daughter of Jediah of West Springfield, Mass., and his wife Betsey (Leonard,) born , at West Springfield; married Sept. 7th, 1835, No. (727.) She died Nov. 1837, at Houston, Texas, leaving daughter Elizabeth, born Oct. 2d, 1836, at New Britain, and baptized here July 23d, 1837; she married Oct. 27th, 1858, Francis Dagget of Springfield, Mass., and now, 1861, lives there.

788. "MARY ANN BISHOP," to church Aug. 6th, 1837, baptized same time; born Aug. 10th, 1816, at North Haven, to Dr. Joy Bishop and his wife Mehitabel (Colver,) married Aug. 14th, 1845, Lucius Sperry, of Avon, son of David and Filena (Potter,) of Burlington, his wife, born Jan. 8th, 1817; she was dismissed and received by letter to Center church, Hartford, Sept. 17th, 1837; they now, 1861, live at West Avon, she, 1861, no church connection.

THEIR CHILDREN.

1. Ellen Maria, born Nov. 8th, 1849.
2. Hercelia Ann, born June 7th, 1852.
3. Lillian Ella, born May 18th, 1857.
4. Cornelius David, born May 5th, 1860, died Nov. 14th, 1860, aged 6 months.

789. "NANCY N. BOOTH," to church Aug. 6th, 1837, born Oct. 26th, 1814, to Cyrus and his first wife, No. (340;) baptized April 16th, 1815, Nancy North, after the name of her mother; married Sept. 17th, 1837, David P. Hughes, of Canton. They went the same year to Baton Rouge, La., where she had two children, both of whom died; the mother died 1839, and the father and husband soon after died, at the same place.

790. "LAURA BOOTH," to church Aug. 6th, 1837, (correctly) Laura Stanley Booth, daughter of Nathan jun., of Granville Mass., and his wife Ruth (Bates,) born July 20th, 1823; married Nov. 26th, 1847, Wm. A. Lee, of West Bloomfield, New York, Ontario Co. She was dismissed and recommended by letter, Dec. 14th, 1848, to church in Galesburg, Ill.; she died there, Sept. 3d, 1850, aged 27, childless.

791. "HUBERT BOOTH," to church Aug. 6th, 1837, born Dec. 12th, 1823, to No. (370,) baptized March 28th, 1824. Hubert Henry, married July 18th, 1846, Rebecca Pretlove, of Troy, New York, daughter of James of New York, and his wife Ann (Mackay,) of Elizabethtown, New Jersey. He is a brass and iron worker, living A. D. 1861, at Greenport, New York. He was dismissed and recommended by letter to West Meriden, Jan. 30th, 1856. Is a leader in church music, but now, 1862, a soldier to defend his country, is in New Orleans. He died July 29th, 1862, and was buried at sea off Hatteras, on his return from the war.

THEIR CHILDREN.

1. Alice Annette, born Aug. 3d, 1847, died Aug. 24th, 1847.
2. Anna Hubertine, born May 24th, 1849.
3. Mary Louise, born May 16th, 1851, died Nov. 22d, 1853.
4. Eva Wells, born April 12th, 1853.
5. Mary Denton, born Dec. 30th, 1855, died Jan. 17th, 1856.
6. Hubert Holmes, born Feb. 14th, 1857.
7. Fannie Angel, born March 21st, 1859.

792. "NANCY BOOTH," to church Aug. 6th, 1837, born Aug. 22d, 1821, to No. (370,) was a teacher at the south; married Sept. 4th, 1851, Samuel Seaver Knox, son of David and Elizabeth (Seaver,) of Brooklyn, New York, his wife, born Jan. 1st, 1822, at Tridelphia, Va. He was a merchant at Wheeling, Va., but died May 29th, 1854, at Ontonagon, Mich., near Lake Superior, of hemorrage of the lungs. She has since visited England. They had one daughter, Anna, born Feb. 21st, 1853, but died same day. Mrs. Knox has adopted the name of Anna, by which she is now known.

793. "HORACE BOOTH," to church Aug. 6th, 1837, born Nov. 6th, 1821, to No. (338;) married May 5th, 1847, No. (1034.) He inherits and occupies the old home of his father, and a portion of the farm of his grandfather; has been a hard laboring farmer, but in 1859, entered a partnership with his brother Ralph, and bought a manufacturing establishment in Winsted, where they make hardware articles. As the war came on he returned to his farm.

THEIR CHILDREN.

1. Horace Wilcox, born Oct. 18th, 1849, bap. June, 1850.
2. Olive Almira, born July 24th, 1856, bap. July 26th, 1857.
3. Mattie Lucetta, born Oct. 25th, 1863, bap. July 3d, 1864.

794. "SARAH BUTLER," to church Aug. 6th, 1837, born Nov. 23d, 1817, to No. (452,) baptized Oct. 14th, 1821. Sarah Ann, married Dec. 24th, 1840, Henry Benton, a dentist, now, A. D. 1861, living in Guilford. She was dismissed and recommended by letter to Meriden, March 14th, 1844.

795. "ELIZABETH CARTER," to church Aug. 6th, 1837, born April 14th, 1821, at New Hartford, to Hermas and his wife Hannah (Booth,) daughter of Joseph, baptized in infancy; dismissed and recommended by letter, Jan. 11th, 1844, to first Congregational church in New Hartford. She married July 3d, 1861, Milo Shepherdson, son of Stephen, of Colerain, Mass., and his wife Laura, born April 10th, 1820, at Colerain, now, 1863, residing on North Main Street, Hartford.

796. "LOIS D. CARTER," to church Aug. 6th, 1837, sister of No. (795,) born Feb. 6th, 1816, at New Hartford, to Hermas and his wife Hannah (Booth,) dismissed and recommended by letter to first Congregational church at New Hartford, Jan. 11th, 1844, A. D. 1862, is unmarried and

lives in Hartford with her brother Newton Carter, at the American House. She was baptized in infancy, at New Hartford, Conn.

797. "MARIA CHURCHILL," to church Aug. 6th, 1837, baptized same time; born Feb. 14th, 1812, to Joseph Churchill of Newington, and Anna (Judd,) his wife, now, 1861, unmarried and living with her brother, No. (695.) She died Sept. 16th, 1864, aged 53 years.

798. "ROBERT CORNWELL," to church Aug. 6th, 1837, born Aug. 16th, 1801, to No. (296,) by trade a brass founder, never married; died March 21st, 1839, of consumption, aged 38, of mild temperament and kind disposition.

799. "FRANCIS CORNWELL," to church Aug. 6th, 1837, born Sept. 29th, 1822, to No. (401;) baptized March 9th, 1823, Francis Edwards, graduate at Yale, 1842, to which church he was dismissed and recommended 1839 or 1840. He studied law, and follows that profession in New York State; married Sept. 23d, 1847, Catharine Livingstone Howe, of Albany, daughter of Hon. Estes and his wife Anna J. (Willard,) born Aug. 18th, 1823. The family now, 1863, residing in Buffalo, N. Y. and he follows his profession there.

THEIR CHILDREN.

1. Edward Livingstone, born June 24th, 1848, at Lyons, N. Y.
2. Wm. Carroll, born Aug. 19th, 1851, at " "
3. Francis Estes, born Aug. 8th, 1856, " "
4. Charles Landers, born Nov. 1st, 1858, at Buffalo, "

800. "JULIA ANN CURTISS," to church Aug. 6th, 1837, and baptized same time; born March 16th, 1824, to Shubel and his wife, No. (362,) married Aug. 24th, 1852, Jarvis Hall, of Millbury, Mass, a brush maker; he died there, March 16th, 1856, aged 25. She was dismissed and recommended to Methodist church, Hartford, in 1837.

801. "MRS MARY ANN DAY, wife of James Day," to church Aug. 6th, 1837, of English origin. He died April 4th, 1838, aged 25. She returned to England. They lived in the Moses Seymour House, at the foot of Dublin Hill.

THEIR CHILD.

Mary Jane, born , bap. Aug. 20th, 1837.

802. "LYDIA M. DOOLITTLE," to church Aug. 6th, 1837, born Jan. 24th, 1818, baptized on admission to church; went south teaching; married Dec. 24th, 1839, Thos. J. Huddleston, of Columbus, Miss., to which place and church she was dismissed and recommended by letter 1838; she died there Jan. 10th, 1844, aged 26. She was daughter of George and his wife, No. (640.)

THEIR CHILDREN.

1. Melissa Lucinda, born Sept. 11th, 1841, at Warsaw, Ill.
2. Caroline Morse, born Feb. 18th, 1843, at " "

803. "GEORGE L. DOOLITTLE," to church Aug. 6th, 1837, baptized same time; born Nov. 2d, 1822, to George and his wife, No. (640,) dismissed and recommended by letter to church, in Hartford, A. D. 1839.

804. "WM. ELLIS, JUN.," to church Aug. 6th, 1837, born Feb. 4th, 1821, to No. (717,) graduate at Yale College, 1842; was dismissed and recommended to the church there, 1839, (returned from there by letter, 1848, April 10th.) Studied medicine and is a practicing physician at Washington Harbor, Dorr County, Wis. He married Feb. 29th, 1852, P. Jane Boyce, of Canton, Onondago County, New York, daughter of Adam and his wife Mary (Weaver,) born Feb. 13th, 1832. He is still a member of this church.

THEIR CHILDREN.

1. Henry E. born March 15th, 1853, at Washington Harbor, Wis.
2. Wm. M. born Sept. 16th, 1855, at " " "
3. Mary W. born May 22d, 1859, at Mackinaw.

805. "MRS. MARIA ERWIN," to church Aug. 6th 1837, born June 14th, 1816 to No. (443,) and his wife Rhoda (Belden,) at Cherry Valley, New York; married May 18th, 1836, Cornelius Buckley Erwin, son of Peter of Boonville, New York, and his wife Lydia (Buckley,) of Rocky Hill, Conn., born June 7th, 1811, at Boonville, New York; learned the trade of shoe making of his father, came to this place 1832, seeking for employment, worked for North & Stanley; became partner with Belden, Lee & Co., brass founders, and in 1836 a partner with Geo. Lewis, under the name of Erwin & Lewis. In Jan. 1839, was engaged at the Lock Factory, and in that establishment has become wealthy. At the incorporation of the "New Britain Bank," he was chosen its President. He is also President of the Russell & Erwin Manufacturing Co., 1867. She to South church, 1842, to which he united 1857. They have no children.

806. "MASON FRANCIS," to church Aug. 6th, 1837, born Sept. 21st, 1820, to No. (470;) baptized Sept. 16th, 1821. Mason Bernard, married Dec. 13th, 1843, No. (842.) He learned the trade of Jeweler at Churchill & Stanley's; inherited the home of his father, but bought the house built by Joshua Carpenter, now occupied and owned by J. A. Picket. he lives now, 1861, in Brooklyn, N. Y. He was dismissed and recommended by letter to Chapel Street Church, New Haven, Aug. 25th, 1852, and also his wife, No. (842.)

THEIR CHILDREN.

1. James Elijah, born Jan. 6th, 1846, baptized May 24th, 1846.
2. Frederick Stanley, born July 1st, 1848, baptized Nov. 30th, 1848, died Oct. 18th, 1855, aged 7.

807. "MINERVA GLADDEN," to church Aug. 6th, 1837, born Aug. 12th, 1818, to No. (522;) married Oct. 7th, 1846, No. (1019,) and was

dismissed and recommended by letter to church in Stratford, Sept. 27th, 1853.

808. "EDWIN GRIDLEY," to church Aug. 6th, 1837, born Aug. 8th, 1818, to Ebenezer and wife, No. (414;) was a brass founder by trade and occupation, went to Bristol to work at his trade; unmarrried, no evidence of being dismissed and recommended to any church; lives now, 1866, at Thomaston, Conn.

809. "ELIZABETH GRIDLEY," to church Aug. 6th, 1837, born July 9th, 1817, to Salmon, of Harwinton, and his wife Cynthia (Bull,) daughter of John; never married, she died May 21st, 1838, aged 21, of consumption, at Burlington; was a sister to Mrs. J. R. King.

810. "NAOMI, wife of Riley Griswold," to church Aug. 6th, 1837, born Sept. 24th, 1791, to Noah Stanley and his wife No. (202;) was a school teacher, intelligent and accomplished; married Nov. 18th, 1818, Riley Griswold, of Torringford, son of Norman and his wife Susannah (Munson,) born Oct. 23d, 1793; resided corner of Park and Stanley sts.; he died Jan. 31st, 1859, aged 64; was in early manhood a school teacher; she died March 29th, 1851, aged 60.

THEIR CHILDREN.

1. Lucy Jane, born Nov. 13th, 1820, bap. on admission to church; see No. (811.)
2. Susan Munson, born Sept. 20th, 1822, married March 29th, 1843, Lucius D. Blake, son of Harry, see No. (1321.)
3. Laura Barber, born Dec. 1st, 1824, bap, Aug. 20th, 1837, married June 10th, 1846, Ransom Hills.
4. Martha Riley, born March 1st, 1827, bap. Aug. 20th, 1837, married No. (994.)
5. Cynthia Stanley, born Feb. 28th, 1829, bap. Aug. 20th, 1837, see No. (974.)
6. Stanley C., born Feb. 27th, 1832, died March 27th, 1833, aged 1.
7. Mary Adelaide, born March 10th, 1834, died July 9th, 1837, aged 3.
8. Sophia Adelaide, born June 18th, 1837, bap. Aug. 20th, 1837, mar. April 17th, 1860, James West, and lives in Petersburg, Va.

811. "LUCY JANE GRISWOLD," to church Aug. 6th, 1837, bap. same time; born Nov. 13th, 1820, to Riley and his wife No. (810,) married May 13th, 1840, Albert A. Mason, a brass manufacturer, now, 1862, in Brooklyn, N. Y.; son of Thomas of Sharon, Ct., and his wife Polly (Sherwood;) born Jan. 9th, 1811.

THEIR CHILDREN.

1. Frederick A., born Sept. 28th, 1841, at Wolcottville, Ct.
2. Charles S., born Nov. 18th, 1843, " " "
3. Stanley G., born Dec. 25th, 1847, " " "
4. Jennie, born Oct. 24th, 1849, " " " died March 6th, 1855, at Brooklyn, N. Y.

812. "GEORGE HART," to church Aug. 6th, 1837, bap. same time, born March 16th, 1801, to Stephen, jun., and his wife No. (638,) married

March 2d, 1826, No. (713;) she died, when second he married Sept. 11, 1832, No. (813.) He was by trade a shoemaker, but was occupied in teaming and staging, in which he has been successful; his residence west side Central Park; he and his second wife to South church, 1842; she died, when third he married, May 6th, 1863, Mrs. Elizabeth, widow of Wm. Perry, of So. Windham, and daughter of Job Ellsworth of East Windsor, and his wife Laura (Osborn,) born Sept. 21st, 1823; Mr. Perry died May 20th, 1853, aged 34.

HER CHILDREN BY FIRST HUSBAND, WM. PERRY.

1. Josephine G., born May 18th, 1844, at East Windsor.
2. Wm. E., born Dec. 22d, 1846, drowned Aug. 6th, 1855, aged 8, at Willimantic.

MR. HART'S CHILD BY FIRST WIFE, MARY.

1. Charles, born , 1827, died Feb. 27th, 1837, aged 10.

MR. HART'S CHILD BY SECOND WIFE, ELIZABETH.

2. Wm. H., born July 25th, 1834, bap. Aug. 20th, 1837, married Sept. 19th, 1855, Martha Peck, daughter of No. (920.)

813. "ELIZABETH, wife of George Hart," to church Aug. 6th, 1837, born Oct. 31st, 1811, to Cyrus Booth and his wife No. (340,) bap. Dec. 22d, 1811, Elizabeth Francis, married Sept. 11th, 1832, No. (812;) she died of slow consumption April 25th, 1862, aged 50.

814. "JONATHAN HART," to church Aug. 6th, 1837, born Dec. 4th, 1818, in Kensington, to Eri B. Hart and his wife Lydia (Gilbert,) and named Jonathan Thomas, bap. May 23d, 1819, at Kensington; he is a brass founder, learned of No. (381,) and married, June 3d, 1842, Maria, his daughter, No. (862;) he carried on business some years in this place, when he located in Kensington, at the place called "Percival's Mills," where he has built largely, and drives business extensively and successfully; they were received to Kensington church from this by letter, Dec. 1854; he second married Sept. 20th, 1864, Alice R. Upson of Kensington.

THEIR CHILDREN.

1. Louisa M., born Aug. 28th, 1845, married Oct. 20th, 1866, Frederic A. Cowles, of Southington.
2. Sarah W., born Aug. 18th, 1847, died May 30th, 1864, aged 16 years, 9 mos.
3. Ella M., born Nov. 11th, 1849, died Nov. 28th, 1860, of consumption, aged 11.
4. Era Thomas, born July 25th, 1852.
5. Francis Gillette, born March 15th, 1855.
6. Leumas Pease, born June 11th, 1858.

815. "SAMUEL W. HART," to church Aug. 6th, 1837, born May 22d, 1825, to No. (311,) graduated at Yale 1855, married Oct. 22d, 1851, Cordelia M. Smith, daughter of No. (652,) is now, 1863, a successful practicing physician in this town; has traveled in Europe; was to South

church 1842; occupies the home of his father on west side Central Park. His wife born June 7th, 1828, bap. June 14th, 1829; to South church 1847; died June 10th, 1857, aged 29; he second married Nov. 10th, 1864, at St. Mark's church, Margaret C. Smyth, daughter of Wm. B. and his wife Annie (Goldsborough.)

THEIR CHILDREN.

1. Mary Louise, born Oct. 8th, 1852.
2. Gerald Waldo, born July 23d, 1856.

816. "JULIAETTE HART," to church Aug. 6th, 1837, born May 20th' 1820, to No. (917) and his wife No. (724;) baptized Nov. 13th, 1831, Juliette Andrews; married June 27th, 1838, Imly Bird Veits, son of John of Granby, and his wife Abigail (Eno) of Simsbury;) born Dec. 19th, 1808; he is a farmer, and lives with his father Hart on Arch st.; she was dismissed and received to Granby, 1841, by letter; she died Feb. 23d, 1842, aged 22, when second he married June 27th, 1843, her sister, No. (936.)

817. "ROYAL S. HALL," to church Aug. 6th, 1837, born Dec. 20th, 1816, at Newington, to Dr. Archibald and his wife Harriet (Deming;) baptized May 5th, 1822, at Newington, Royal Sereno; was clerk to Stanley & Whaples, went south, and died in Milledgeville, Geo., Oct. 1st, 1842, aged 26; his mother, daughter of Robert Deming and Lucy (Blinn,) his wife, both of Newington; he never married; was brother of No. (818.)

818. "CORNELIA HALL," to church Aug. 6th, 1837, sister of No. (817,) born Dec. 28th, 1820, to Dr. Archibald at Newington; baptized May 5th, 1822, "Cornelia Hale;" married Sept. 7th, 1841, George Andrus, son of Anson of Leyden, N. Y.; they lived in Berlin; he died there Jan. 26th, 1848, of small pox, when second she married, March 13th, 1850, Lyman Beckley, son of Orrin and his wife Harriet (Patterson;) he was born July 10th, 1815, at Berlin; he shot himself with a pistol in despondency or derangement, at his own hired house in this place, Sept. 13th, 1860, aged 45; she dismissed and recommended by letter to South church, Nov. 26th, 1858.

HER CHILDREN BY FIRST HUSBAND.

1. Hellen M., born Aug. 6th, 1842; excelled in vocal music; she died Oct 18th, 1866, of yellow fever, at New Orleans, aged 24.
2. George Barton, born Oct. 12th, 1845, lives with his grandfather at Lyden, N. Y., 1863.

CHILDREN BY HER SECOND HUSBAND.

3. Hattie, born Dec. 2d, 1851.
4. Caroleena, born Jan. 13th, 1855.

819. "MRS. PHEBE HOUGH," to church Aug. 6th, 1837, wife of No. (756,) daughter of No. (217,) born July 30th, 1780, married Aug. 31st 1809, No. (756;) she died Nov. 9th, 1843, aged 63.

820. "ELIZABETH HOUGH," to church Aug. 6th, 1837, born Feb. 29th, 1824, at Meriden, to No. (756;) dismissed and recommended by letter, March 29th, 1849, to Missionary Church, Choctaw Nation; her name Elizabeth Jerusha; has been a teacher and missionary at Little Rock, Ark., and also among the Oneidas, N. Y.; now, 1861, unmarried, and is in Michigan.

821. "MRS. LUCY HULL," to church Aug. 6th, 1837, widow of Elijah Hull, from Farmington, son of Isaac, daughter of No. (175,) born Jan. 26th, 1777, married April 7th, 1800; he died May 8th, 1817; they lived at the foot of "Half-way Hill," where now, 1861, Barzillai Deming owns and occupies. She was dismissed and recommended by letter, Aug. 24th, 1845, to church in Sherman, Chatauque Co., N. Y., where she died Nov. 1st, 1850, at the home of her son George.

THEIR CHILDREN.

1. Maria, born Dec. 9th, 1801, see No. (580.)
2. John Pennfield, born Sept. 10th, 1803.
3. Romeo, born , died Aug. 20th, 1814, aged 10.
4. George, born , married widow Sally Spencer, of Killingworth; lives at Sherman, N. Y.
5. Samuel, born , married Abi Adams, in Wis.; lives there.
6. Lucy Jane, born March, 1816, died Dec., 1834, aged 18.

822. "MRS. ELIZA JUDD," to church Aug. 6th, 1837, bap. same time; daughter of James Howd of East Hartford, and his wife Martha (Williams,) born Jan. 6th, 1813, married Jan. 29th, 1836, No. (1119;) she to South church 1842, but returned by letter, March 3d, 1844.

823. "OLIVER S. JUDD," to church Aug. 6th, 1837, baptized same time; born Nov. 30th, 1816, to John and his wife No. (637,) a jeweller by trade, but in 1861 an extensive manufacturer of hardware; residence on corner of west Main and Washington sts.; married April 15th, 1838, No. (959,) who died, when second he married, Jan. 5th, 1860, Evelina Atkins, of Bristol, daughter of Rev. Ireneas and his wife Eunice (Beckwith,) born April 7th, 1825. He has contributed much to church music by playing double bass.

THEIR CHILD.

Rollin D., born June 9th, 1840, see No. (1377.)

824. "HARRIET N. LAMPSON," to church Aug. 6th, 1837, bap. same time, "Harriet Newel" Lampson; daughter of Sylvanus and Martha (Gillett,) his wife, of East Hartford; born June 18th, 1819, at Granby, Ct.; she was dismissed and recommended to South church, by letter, Dec. 25th, 1845, received there 1846; married Nov., 1845, Amon L. Finch, son of Caleb and his wife Lucy (Gilbert, daughter of Seth,) born Feb. 20th, 1817, at Simsbury; she died Feb. 16th, 1853, aged 35; he is a

hame maker, corner of Pearl and Orchard sts., factory back of house, was burned down 1856.

THEIR CHILDREN.

1. Katie, born
2. Ann, born

825. "ALMIRA S. LEE," to church Aug. 6th, 1837, born Aug. 9th, 1812, to No. (356;) educated at Troy, N. Y.; married, Oct. 17th, 1837, Andrew K. Hunt, of Charlestown, Mass., assistant cashier of the Suffolk Bank, Boston; born Aug. 26th, 1811; she dismissed and recommended by letter to Winthrop church, Charlestown, Mass., 1837; a woman of uncommon attractions; she died Dec. 14th, 1841, aged 28, he died July 25th, 1853, aged 42, and both buried at Woodlawn Cemetery, at Malden, Mass.; they left no posterity.

826. "ANGELINE LEE," to church Aug. 6th, 1837, born Jan. 4th, 1824, to No. (356,) educated at Baltimore, married Oct. 13th, 1852, at Burlington, Iowa, Mark Howard, Esq., son of Mark of Devonshire, Eng., and Mary Ann (Bees,) his wife, of Somersetshire, Eng., born May 27th, 1817, in the county of Kent, Eng., came to this country 1830, located in the city of Hartford, and now, 1861, president of the Merchants Insurance Company; Mrs. Angeline Howard was dismissed and recommended by letter, March 9th, 1854, to the North Congregational church, Hartford.

THEIR CHILDREN.

1. Angeline Lee, born Nov. 6th, 1854.
2. Amy Lee, born Jan. 7th, 1857.
3. Wm. Lee, born Nov. 1st, 1860.
4. Myra Lee, born Nov. 23d, 1862.

827. "MARY MILLS," to church Aug. 6th, 1837, baptized same time; born Nov. 29th, 1825, to Alvin and his wife Dorothy (Ford,) of Plymouth; married, Sept. 6th, 1849, Russel Lewis Perkins, son of Lewis and Aurelia (Morse,) his wife; born May 14th, 1827, and is a mechanic; volunteer in the 14th Regt., Co. F., from Aug., 1862 to June, 1865.

THEIR CHILDREN.

1. Eva Mary, born Aug. 15th, 1853.
2. Lewis Elmore, born Oct. 3d, 1855.

828. "ELISHA MIX," to church Aug. 6th, 1837; son of James of West Hartford, and his wife Lucy (Steele,) born Nov. 17th, 1818, at Watertown, Ct.; married, July 10th, 1843, Amelia Edmonds, daughter of James of Bristol, and Eliza, his wife, (English family to America, 1832;) he now, 1861, lives at Manlius, Allegan Co., Mich.; is Col. and surveyor; never dismissed by letter.

THEIR CHILDREN.

1. Rosina, born Sept. 1st, 1846, at New Haven.
2. Elisha, born Jan. 18th, 1850, " "

829. "FREDERIC HENRY NORTH," to church Aug. 6th, 1837, born Aug. 10th, 1824, to No. (449) and his wife No. (396;) graduated at Yale College 1846, dismissed and recommended by letter, 1842, to church there; married, Aug. 28th, 1850, Mary Elizabeth North, daughter of No. (743,) and his wife No. (744;) born Oct. 9th, 1833. He inherits the home and wealth of his father, is engaged in extensive manufacturing, and is liberal in his benefactions.

THEIR CHILDREN.

1. Charles Frederic, born April 24th, 1854.
2. Grace Eugene, born Aug. 4th, 1856, in Paris, France.
3. May Frederica, born Feb. 19th, 1862.

830. "SARAH NORTH," to church Aug. 6th, 1837, born Aug. 28th, 1820, to No. (330) and his second wife No. (411;) baptized Nov. 5th, 1820, Sarah Rogers; married, Aug. 19th, 1847, Samuel Brace, of Newington, son of Rev. Joab, D. D., and his wife Lucy (Collins;) he born Feb. 24th, 1817, at Newington, graduated at Yale College, 1841; been a teacher, but now, 1861, manufacturer in New Britain, and in 1866 in New Haven.

THEIR CHILDREN.

1. Samuel North, born May 14th, 1848, died Aug. 29th, 1849, aged 16 months.
2. Henry Mills, born Nov. 17th, 1849, died Feb. 4th, 1850, aged 3 months.

831. "HUBERT F. NORTH," to church Aug. 6th, 1837, born Nov. 13, 1822, to No. (330) and his 2d wife No. (411;) he graduated at Yale Coll. 1843; was dismissed and recommended by letter to the church of Yale, 1840; he studied law with Ex. Gov. Ellsworth, married, Sept. 1st, 1852, Jane M. Hendrick, born May 11th, 1825, at Milton, Saratoga Co., N. Y., to Abel and his wife Harriet (Upson.) He became a manufacturer, and at first settled with his father; he was for a time sup't of S. School at the South church; his health was poor for several years; he purchased the residence of No. (1190,) 1861, improved and beautified it. If he was facetious and eccentric, yet he possessed a kind and benevolent heart; he died Oct. 27th, 1863, of consumption, aged 41 years, 14 days, sincerely lamented.

THEIR CHILD.

Louisa Cordelia, born May 7th, 1862.

832. "ADELINE NORTH," to church Aug. 6th, 1837, born May 26th, 1823, to No. (443) and his wife Rhoda Belden, daughter of No. (158;) she went south as a teacher, and was a sweet singer; she married, at

Marion, 1847, Robert R. Kimbal, of Eutaw, Ala., eleven days before her death; she died of consumption July, 1847, at Eutaw, Ala., aged 24.

833. "HARVEY PENNFIELD," to church Aug. 6th, 1837, born June 7th, 1815, to No. (469;) a brass worker, lives on Stanley st., near its junction with North st; married, Oct. 21st, 1839, No. (889;) he is very useful as nurse in sickness

THEIR CHILDREN.

1. Lorin Dwight, born June 15th, 1840, bap. 1840, 1862 a private in Co. A, 13th Regt., C. V., and in 1863 a clerk at N. O., in Medical Department; married, June 20th, 1866, Carrie McNary.
2. Mary Angeline, born Feb. 5th, 1842, mar., Oct. 19th, 1864, Edwin E. Hubbard.
3. George Henry, born June 14th, 1843, bap. Nov. 19th, 1843; volunteer in Co. K, 14th Regt., C. V.; he died Dec. 20th, 1862, at Hospital, D. C., of consumption, and buried in New Britain, Dec. 25th, 1862.
4. Catharine Ann, born March 15th, 1845, bap. Aug. 21st, 1845, married, Oct. 12th, 1863, Chas. A. Dorman, son of Allen; he was an army steward at Port Royal, 1863.
5. Chas. Frederic, born Jan. 1st, 1847, bap. June 27th, 1847.

834. "LYDIA PENNFIELD," to church Aug. 6th, 1837, born May 29th, 1819, to No. (469;) married, Sept. 16th, 1844, Charles H. Hills, of Farmington; she was dismissed and recommended to Farmington church by letter, and received there May 4th, 1845; she died there June 8th, 1850 aged 31.

835. "MARY ANN PENNFIELD," to church Aug. 6th, 1837, born Oct. 4th, 1813, to No. (469;) married, Oct. 30th, 1839, Omri L. Hart, son of Zina, of Avon, and his wife Rhoda (Griswold;) she was dismissed and recommended by letter to Sherman, N. Y., 1840; she died Dec. 6th, 1853, aged 40; he married second, and lives in Avon, 1861.

836. "ISABELLA PARKER," to church Aug. 6th, 1837, born Oct. 4th, 1813, at Coventry, N. Y., to Hiland Parker and his wife Lydia (Pratt,) daughter of No. (345,) and his second wife No. (271;) married, Sept. 1st, 1841, Benjamin Blake, born March 3d, 1817, at Winchester, Ct., to Ithuriel and his wife Wealthy (Benedict,) by trade a joiner, but now a farmer, 1862, in Coventryville, N. Y.; she was dismissed and recommended to church in Coventryville, N. Y., Sept., 1841, where she was received April, 1842, and now resides.

THEIR CHILDREN.

1. Franklin J., born Sept. 1st, 1843, died Nov. 18th, 1851, aged 8.
2. Andrew Pratt, born Sept. 16th, 1845.

837. "ALMEDA RECOR," to church Aug. 6th, 1837; born Dec. 17th, 1820, to Jesse, and his wife, No. (527,) baptized Dec. 16th, 1821, "Nancy Almeda," married May 6th, 1845, Sheldon Hills, of Farmington. She was dismissed and recommended by letter to church in Plainville, Feb. 5th, 1846. She died Feb. 17th, 1849, aged 29.

838. "Mrs. PHILENA ROWLEY," to church August 6th, 1837; born Feb. 11th, 1815, to Israel Buck, of Wyalnsing, Pa., and his wife Elizabeth (Webb,) married Oct. 11th, 1832, No. (866,) dismissed and recommended by letter to church in West Avon.

839. "ADALINE, wife of Ephraim Sanders," to church Aug. 6th, 1837; born 1813, to Shubel Curtiss, and his wife, No. (362,) married Ephraim Sanders, son of Timothy, of Granby, he died, when she married, second, Thomas Butler, of Hartford. She died October, 1839, aged 26.

THEIR CHILDREN.

1. Edward, } twins, born August, 1831.
2. Edwin, }
3. Harriet, born , married April 10th, 1853, Elbert Rowe, of Fair Haven.
4. Jane, born , married Allen, of Waterbury.

840. "HARRIET SMITH," to church Aug. 6th, 1837; born Sept. 29th, 1820, to No. (337,) and his wife, No. (472,) baptized June 3d, 1821, "Harriet Strong," married May 14th, 1845, Horace Brown of Newington, son of Zacheus, of Killingly, Ct., and his wife Sarah (Hale,) of Wethersfield, born Dec. 22d, 1810, at Trenton, N. Y.; a joiner by trade, but now, 1861, a farmer, his residence, corner of High and Willow streets, has been successful in business, and has a beautiful home. She to South church, 1842.

THEIR CHILD.

Katie Maria, born Sept. 7th, 1857.

841. "MARIA SMITH," to church Aug. 6th, 1837; born April 11th, 1816, to No. (337,) and his second wife, No. (472,) baptized Oct. 19th, 1817, "Sally Maria," married May 1st, 1832, Grove W. Loomis, son of Abijah, of New Hartford, and his wife Margaret (Barrett,) born Dec. 21st, 1808, at New Hartford; traveled south, engaged in manufacturing in Southwest district, but located in the village and engaged in merchandize; bought the house built by Ebenezer Booth, owned by Samuel Judd, and lately sold to George Hart and moved off. He was standing in his store when he was struck by lightning, and died July 12th, 1856, aged 49, after lingering eleven months. She married, second, July 25th, 1860, No. (1015). She to South church, 1842.

THEIR CHILDREN.

1. Ellen Lucretia, born July 11th, 1840, died Aug. 4th, 1843, aged 3.
2. Louisa Maria, born Dec. 26th, 1842, died Jan. 31st, 1856, aged 14.
3. Harriet Cornelia, born Feb. 14th, 1847.
4. Georgia Augusta, born July 22d, 1851, died Dec. 30th, 1856, aged 5.

842. ELIZABETH STANLEY," to church Aug. 6th, 1837, born March 18th, 1822, to No. (921,) and his wife, No. (529,) baptized Dec. 15th,

1822, at Farmington, "Elizabeth Langdon," married Dec. 12th, 1843, No. (806.) She was a milliner by trade and occupation. She and husband were dismissed and recommended by letter, August 25th, 1852, to Chapel street church, New Haven.

843. "MARGARET STANLEY," to church Aug. 6th, 1837; born Nov. 26th, 1820, to Jesse, and his second wife, No. (403,) married Dec. 31st, 1844, John E. Cowles, of Farmington, son of Martin, and his second wife, Harriet (Wells,) born Nov. 4th, 1819; residence, next door south of his father's home, Farmington street. She to Farmington church, by letter from this church, April 27th, 1845.

THEIR CHILDREN.

1. Henry Martin, born Oct. 1st, 1845.
2. Roswell Wells, born Oct. 17th, 1850, died January 2d, 1851, aged 11 weeks.
3. Gertrude Stanley, born Feb. 16th, 1852, died Nov. 6th, 1854, aged 2 years, 8 months and 18 days.
4. Melanie Stanley, born Dec. 5th, 1854, died March 8th, 1857, aged 2 years, 3 months and 3 days.
5. John Stanley, born April 28th, 1857.
6. Caroline Griffin, born March 1st, 1859, died Sept. 1st, 1863, aged 4 years and 6 months.
7. Sarah North, born Sept. 7th, 1862, died Sept. 6th, 1863, aged 1 year.

844. "ALMIRA STANLEY," to church Aug. 6th, 1837; born March 20th, 1818, a twin daughter to Jesse, and his second wife, No. (403,) married June 15th, 1843, George S. Coe, of Newport, R. I., son of Adam, and his wife Ann (Pease,) born March 27th, 1817. She was dismissed and recommended, Feb. 5th, 1846, to Second Presbyterian church, Cincinnati, Ohio.

THEIR CHILDREN.

1. Lucy Ann, born August 2d, 1843, died October 10th, 1846, aged 3 years and 2 months.
2. George Stanley, born Jan. 1st, 1849, died Sept 19th, 1849, aged 9 months.
3. Edward Prime, born Feb. 2d, 1851.
4. Alice Stanley, born Nov. 17th, 1852.
5. Elizabeth Blake, born Dec. 22d, 1855.

845. "NANCY D. STANLEY," to church Aug. 6th, 1837; born August 18th, 1815, to No. (438,) and his wife, No. (1295,) married Nov. 15th, 1838, John H. Goodwin, of Hartford, born March 2d, 1809, to John, and his wife Anna (Belden.) She was dismissed and recommended by letter to Hartford, 1839. She died Jan. 15th, 1849, aged 33; left no posterity.

846. "LOT STANLEY," to church August 6th, 1837; born July 8th, 1820, to No. (550,) and his wife, No. (339.) He died Nov. 12th, 1839, aged 19.

847. "MARTHA STANLEY," to church Aug. 6th, 1837; born Aug. 11th, 1822, to No. (550,) and his wife, No. (339,) married May 12th, 1845,

Augustus North, son of No. (443,) born March 8th, 1819 ; now, 1861, a merchant in Brooklyn, N. Y. She was dismissed and recommended by letter, April 26th, 1846, to church in Cleveland, Ohio.

THEIR CHILDREN.

1. William Stanley, born April 12th, 1846.
2. Frederick Augustus, born March 21st, 1850.

848. "AMZI STANLEY," to church Aug. 6th, 1837 ; born Nov. 27th, 1823, to Cyrus, and his wife, No. (422,) married Oct. 12th, 1848, at Rensalier, Ind., Esther Hughs, daughter Thomas, and Mary Jones, of Indiana, his wife. She was born Nov. 28th, 1829, her parents were from Derbyshire, England. He was dismissed and recommended by letter, 1841, to church in Indiana, where he engaged in merchandize, but lost his health and returned, and died here Sept. 2d, 1854, aged 31, of consumption.

THEIR CHILDREN.

1. Emily Rowena, born April 18th, 1849, at Indiana, died Feb. 14th, 1850.
2. Isaac Lee, born April 8th, 1851, at Rensalier.
3. Cyrus Thomas, born Feb. 17th, 1853, at Rensalier.

849. "NOAH W. STANLEY," to church Aug. 6th, 1837, born Nov. 19th, 1794, to Noah, and his third wife, No. (202,) married Oct. 26th, 1824, No. (850.) He was a successful farmer and inherited the home of his father in Stanley quarter ; has been a teacher and school visitor many years, and greatly interested in agricultural pursuits and societies ; was one of the standing committee of the church in 1857, been much engaged in public business and reforms.

850. "Mrs. LAURA F., wife of Noah W. Stanley," to church Aug. 6th, 1837, baptized same time ; born March 19th, 1804, to Oliver Stanley, and his wife Fanny (Booth,). She was an only daughter of her parents, and was sister of No. (675,) married Oct. 26th, 1824, No. (849.)

THEIR ONLY CHILD.

Helen Melissa, born Jan. 28th, 1826, bap. August 20th, 1837, died April 29th, 1843, aged 17.

851. JOHN STANLEY, 2d," to church Aug. 6th, 1837 ; born Sept. 22d, 1808, to No. (442,) and his second wife, No. (319,) married May 28th, 1843, Mary Lyman Francis, daughter of Selah, of Candor, N. Y., and his wife Roxy (Buckley,) of Rocky Hill, Ct. ; she died Oct 14th, 1849, aged 34, when he married, second, May, 1855, Martha J. Forbes, daughter of Charles, of East Hartford, and his wife (Ward,) born , died Feb. 26th, 1859, aged 27. He was a brass manufacturer in Hart quarter until , when he bought out the house and former home of James Booth, sen., and moved it to Walnut street, when he built on the

old site. He was dismissed and recommended by letter to South church, April, 1856.

THEIR CHILDREN.

1. Mary Lyman, born July 23d, 1845, bap. Dec. 6th, 1846.
2. John Pembroke, born Oct. 11th, 1849.

SECOND WIFE'S CHILD.

3. Charles Forbes, born Feb. 18th, 1859.

852. "SELAH STEELE," to church Aug. 6th, 1837, born April 19th, 1764, to Ebenezer, and his wife, No. (148;) was in the war of the Revlution; married April 14th, 1786, No. (853,) lived in Southwest district, on the side of the mountain, where now, 1861, his son Roswell owns and occupies; was a plain, honest farmer; converted to Christ late in life; was a fine specimen of plain living, and honest industry of the "olden times." He died Oct. 22d, 1845, aged 82.

853. "Mrs. TRIAL STEELE," to church Aug. 6th, 1837, baptized same time, born May 12th, 1763, to John Stedman, and his wife Mary (Hotchkiss,) married April 14th, 1786, No. (852;) her father was a weaver and learned his trade of Deacon Bull, of Farmington; her mother was daughter of No. (67,) and was a woman of superior mind. Mrs. Trial Steele died, April 16th, 1856, aged 93.

THEIR CHILDREN.

1. Amy, born July 5th, 1787, see No. (642.)
2. Selah, born May 25th, 1789, see No. (482.)
3. Ira, born Aug. 16th, 1792, married Oct. 30th, 1817, No. (910.)
4. Roswell S., born Nov. 25th, 1796, see No. (514.)
5. Diadema, born Oct. 6th, 1798, see No. (390.)
6. Mary, born May 12th, 1802, see No. (1253.)
7. Thirza, born July 11th, 1804, married April 11th, 1824, No. (676.)

854. "ELISHA MASON STODDARD," to church Aug. 6th, 1837, baptized same time, born Jan. 6th, 1811, at Newington, to Elisha, and his wife Bula (Wells,) daughter of Deacon James Wells. He learned the jeweler's trade of North & Churchill, in this place, traveled at the west, and was for several years engaged in Connecticut on railroad; married Oct. 1st, 1850, Julia Merriman, of Southington, daughter of Anson, and his wife Fanny (Hubbard;) located now, 1862, in Dixon, Ill. She was born June 12th, 1829.

THEIR CHILDREN.

1. Willie, born June 22d 1855, died Jan. 21st, 1857, aged 18 months.
2. Fanny, born Jan. 5th, 1857.

855. Mrs. ALMIRA STRICKLAND," to church August 6th, 1837, born July 27th, 1816, to Elihu Burritt, sen., and his wife, No. (290,) married Nov. 24th, 1836, Stephen Lyman Strickland, son of Stephen, of Glasten-

bury, and his wife Nancy (Tryon,) of Middletown, born Sept. 22d, 1813, at Glastenbury, a brick mason by trade, but for several years, and now, 1861, engaged in merchandize; his residence, back from Main street, opposite his block of brick buildings; is warden of the borough, and been active in enlarging and beautifying the village. He died March 24th, 1865, in his 52d year.

THEIR CHILDREN.

1. Ann Cornwell, born Jan. 24th, 1838, bap. 1838, see No. (1128.)
2. Ellen Louisa, born Nov. 16th, 1840, bap. Aug. 3d, 1845, see No. (1183.)

856. "THOMAS TRACY," to church Aug. 6th, 1837, born May 10th, 1809, to Fanning, of Canterbury, and his wife Lucy (Adams,) of Lisbon. He is a machinist of inventive genius; married Nov. 26th, 1835, No. (926,) she died, when he married, second, Sept. 23d, 1847, No. (1035.) His present residence is in Stanley quarter, the house formerly of Jesse Stanley, and after him Nehemiah Peck. Mr. Tracy has gained a great celebrity as a mechanic, in perfecting the hook and eye machines, and especially in the construction of "Isham's bank lock."

THEIR CHILDREN.

1. Elizabeth Adams, born Aug. 17th, 1836, bap. Aug. 20th, 1837, see No. (1173.)
2. Emily, born , bap. 1840, died Aug. 2d, 1843, aged 6.
3. Lucy Augusta, born June 27th, 1840, bap. 1840, see No. (.)
4. (twins.) Thomas Edwin, born Jan. 10th, 1843, bap. Aug. 3d, 1843; a three years volunteer in Co. G, 6th Reg. C. V., and died Jan. 30th, 1862, at Port Royal, S. C.
5. (twins.) William Edgar, born Jan. 10th, 1843, bap. Aug. 3d, 1843, see No. (1325.)
6. George, born June 27th, 1845, died Sept. 20th, 1845, aged 3 months.

SECOND WIFE'S CHILD.

7. Hattie, born Aug. 23d, 1851, bap. Jan. 16th, 1853.

857. "JANE N. UPSON," to church August 6th, 1837, born Feb. 9th, 1821, to No. (450,) and his wife, No. (317,) married Nov. 8th, 1841, William L. Coan, born Dec. 20th, 1822, to Davis, of Guilford, and his wife Catharine (Fowler.) He is, 1862–3, a missionary to ex-slaves at Fortress Monroe. The family formerly lived at Chelsea and Mt. Washington, Mass. She was dismissed and recommended by letter to church in Meriden, 1840.

THEIR CHILDREN.

1. Jane C., born March 2d, 1845, died, aged 17 months.
2. Jennie E., born Sept. 6th, 1849.
3. William N., born Nov. 30th, 1855.
4. Ernest L. born Sept. 7th, 1858, died, aged 14 days.

858. "CURTISS WHAPLES," to church Aug. 6th, 1837, born Nov. 21st, 1804, in Newington, to Elisha, and his wife Nancy (Blinn,) bred a merchant; married June 12th, 1827, Betsey Lee, daughter of No. (351,) and

his wife, No. (348,) born March 27th, 1804 (probably.) She died Dec. 10th, 1836, aged 32, when he married, second, May 2d, 1838, Elizabeth Curtiss Lusk, of New Hartford, daughter of Solomon, and his wife, No. (880.) Mr. Whaples has distinguished himself as a salesman; his residence is on Main street; to South church, 1842.

THEIR CHILDREN.

1. Charles Curtiss, born March 13th, 1828, bap. Aug. 13th, 1837.
2. Elizabeth Lee, born Sept. 10th, 1829, bap. Aug. 13th, 1837, married June 23d, 1851, George R. Post.

CHILDREN BY SECOND WIFE.

3. Infant, born Aug. 11th, 1840, died March 11th, 1841.
4. Amelia Meigs, born Aug. 11th, 1841, bap. 1841, died Sept. 18th, 1842, aged 13 months and 5 days.
5. Meigs Haywood, born July 16th, 1845; clerk in New Britain bank, 1863.
6. Isabella, born Nov. 4th, 1850.

859. "Elizabeth P. Whittlesey," to church Aug. 6th, 1837, born Nov. 1st, 1822, to No. (321,) married Oct. 27th, 1847, Rev. Charles W. Camp, son of Joel, and his wife Comfort (Whittlesey.) He is now, 1863, pastor of a Congregational church at Sheboygan, Wis. She was dismissed and recommended by letter, March 22d, 1846, to the Church of the Puritans, New York.

THEIR CHILDREN.

1. Lilly C., born April 27th, 1849, at Genesee, Wis.
2. Charles E., born April 25th, 1852, in Genesee, Wis.
3. George W., born July 19th, 1854, at Sheboygan, Wis., died Aug. 14th, 1854, aged one month.
4. Mary E., born June 7th, 1857, at Sheboygan, Wis., died Sept. 19th, 1858, aged 15 months.
5. Edgar Whittlesey, born Feb. 27th, 1860, at Sheboygan, Wis.
6. Homer, born April 11th, 1863, at Sheboygan, Wis.

860. "Eliphalet Whittlesey," to church Aug. 6th, 1837, born May 14th, 1821, to No. (321,) graduated at Yale College in 1842; dismissed and recommended there by letter, 1839. Ordained and installed pastor of a church, 1851, in Bath, Maine; married Oct. 31st, 1854, Ann Augusta Patten, born Oct. 5th, 1834, to George F. Patten, and his wife Hannah (Thomas,) at Bath, Me. He was in early manhood a teacher at the south; has traveled, (since his settlement in the ministry,) in Europe for his health. Now, 1862, he is Professor of Rhetoric and Oratory in Bowdoin College, Maine, and chaplain in 19th Reg. Maine Vols., and went to Virginia in Aug. 1862; in Sept., 1862, was promoted to colonel, and was on the staff of General Howard.

THEIR CHILDREN.

1. George Patten, born Feb. 24th, 1856, at Bath, Me.
2. Mary Howard, born Jan. 31st, 1860, at Bath, Me.
3. Frederick William, born July 13th, 1861, at Bath, Me.

861. "BETSEY WOODRUFF," to church August 6th, 1837, born May 19th, 1818, to No. (381,) and his wife, No. (557,) married October 8th, 1838, No. (890 ;) both to South church, 1842. She died Oct. 1st, 1845, at Hamburg, Tenn.

862. "MARIA WOOODRUFF," to church Aug. 6th, 1837, born May 5th, 1820, to No. (381,) and his wife, No. (557,) married June 3d, 1842, No. (814,) dismissed and recommended by letter to church in Kensington, Dec., 1854. She died June 5th, 1862, aged 42, at Kensington.

863. "ALMA WOODRUFF," to church Aug. 6th, 1837, by letter from church in Lenox, Mass., born Aug. 19th, 1771, an Albino, to No. (565,) and his wife, No. (566,) she died July 9th, 1853, aged 82; never married; to South church, 1842.

864. "JULIUS PARKER," to church Sept, 10th, 1837, by letter from church in Meriden, born July 10th, 1805, at Meriden, to Denison, and Lydia (Bradley,) his wife, married Jan. 31st, 1838, No. (891.) His residence and factory, on corner of Arch and Walnut streets; has been a merchant, but now, 1861, is a manufacturer; been successful in business and trade, and liberal in his benefactions.

THEIR CHILDREN.

1. Ellen Warner, born Oct. 18th, 1842, bap. Aug. 6th, 1843, see No. (1179.)
2. Charles Julius, born Oct. 21st, 1849, bap. June, 1850, see No. (1392.)

865. "MRS. ESTHER PINKS," to church Sept. 17th, 1837, by letter from church in East Stafford, Conn ; born Oct. 5th, 1799, to Henry Flint, of Concord, Mass., and his wife Bulah (Wheeler;) married Nov. 7th, 1822, Jonathan Chapin Pinks, (son of John, one of the army of Burgoyne as a tailor;) born Aug. 20th, 1797 ; came to this town soon after marriage and lived in Stanley quarter; he died March 24th, 1841, aged 43. She by industry and economy built a house on Elm Street, where now, 1861, she resides, having returned from Hanover, in Meriden, to which church she was recommended 1857, but returned 1860, by letter from that church.

THEIR CHILDREN.

1. John Henry, born Sept. 13th, 1823, died July 6th, 1837, aged 13.
2. Luther Chapin, born March 10th, 1825, at Boston.
3. Edward Pierson, } twins, born July 6th, 1827, { see No. (986.)
4. Edwin Coweel, } twins, born July 6th, 1827, { see No. (987.)
5. Esther Flint, born July 22d, 1830, see No. (981.)
6. Mary Ballard, born Jan. 16th, 1832; married May 8th, 1853, Rufus Olcott, of Waterbury.

7. Wm. Wisner, born Jan. 12th, 1835, married Abbe E. Hall, of Wallingford.
8. Ellen Tamar, born Nov. 6th, 1836, see No. (1287.)
9. Sarah Elizabeth, born March 3d, 1839, bap. 1840 ; see No. (1122.)
10. Marion Esther, born April 8th, 1840, see No. (1288.)

866. "LEANDER P. ROWLEY," to church Sept. 17th, 1837, by letter from church in Farmington; born Feb. 15th, 1812, in Farmington, to Simeon and his wife Elizabeth (Griswold,) of New Britain, daughter of Ashbel. He married Oct. 11th, 1832, No. (838.) He was admitted to Farmington church, 1829, and baptized same time ; he was a shoe maker; learned of George Hart, of this place; both dismissed and recommended by letter to church in West Avon. He enlisted into the army to put down the great "slave holders' rebellion," of 1861–2, as sergeant drummer in the 8th regiment Conn. Volunteers; was in the battle at Roanoke Island, Newbern and Fort Macon, when his health failed and he returned.

THEIR CHILDREN.

1. Burdette L. born May 22d, 1834, at Farmington ; married May 20th, 1855, Sarah Grant.
2. Mary P. born April 12th, 1836, at Farmington.
3. Perrin W. born April 9th, 1841, at Avon.
4. Burnham C. born Aug. 22d, 1844, at "
5. Edgar Percival, born June 26th, 1850, at Farmington.

867. "ELIZA G. SNATH," to church Sept. 17th, 1837, by letter from Farmington ; daughter of Simeon Rowley, of Farmington, sister of No. (866 ;) born Dec. 25th, 1802 ; to church in Farmington, 1821, and baptized same time ; married Feb. 15th, 1825, Chester Snath, son of Joseph and his wife Jane (Wilcox ;) born April 14th, 1800, at Burlington. She died Aug. 18th, 1854, aged 52, at Hartford.

THEIR CHILDREN.

1. Harriet Eliza, born Oct. 22d, 1826 ; married June, 1848, Geo. Hollister. She died Aug. 12th, 1852.
2. Mary Jenette, born July 22d, 1828 ; bap. Dec. 13th, 1829, at Farmington.
3. Henry Rowley, born Dec. 9th, 1833, at New Britain, and bap. there, Oct. 8th, 1837.

868. "EMILY H. WATROUS," to church Sept. 24th, 1837, by letter from West Springfield, Mass. ; daughter of Leonard Belden and his wife No. (324 ;) born Sept. 12th, 1798 ; married May 16th, 1820, Lee M. Watrous, son of Smith Watrous, of Lyme, Conn., and his wife Eunice (Marven ;) born Oct. 28th, 1796 ; he was a member of Dr. Hawes' church, Hartford, until his death, June 23d, 1838, aged 42. When second she married, June 2d, 1842, Lemuel Hitchcock, of Cheshire, Conn. ; they live now, 1861, in East Windham, New York. (Post office, "Big Hollow.") Mr. Watrous was a blacksmith and machinist. Children, Eliza-

beth L. Watrous, Mary J. Watrous, Hannah B. Watrous; the mother was dismissed and recommended by letter to East Windham church, New York.

869. "Sylvender Ellis," to church Oct. 1st, 1837; born Sept. 18th, 1817, to No. (717;) a joiner by trade, learned of No. (920;) married April 27th, 1842, No. (1080,) residence on Chestnut Street. He was dismissed and recommended by letter to church in Somers, 1842, but returned 1852, by letter.

THEIR CHILDREN.

1. Wm. Henry, born Nov. 10th, 1843, at Somers, see No. (1390.)
2. Marion Roselle, born Aug. 1st, 1848, " " " (1386.)

870. "Marilla Collins," to church Oct. 1st, 1837, by letter from church in New Marlboro, south; born April 14th, 1810, at New Marlboro, Mass., to David and his wife Hannah (Gilbert,) alias Widow Case; married , 1839, Ira Callender, and was his second wife; to south church, 1842. She died May 5th, 1849, aged 39; when third he married Sally Maria (Johnson,) Widow of Benjamin, of New York State. His first wife was Mary (Gridley;) he son of Wm. Callender and his wife Lucy (Dickinson;) born Oct. 14th, 1808, at Rocky Hill, and is a very skillful mechanic. He resides on Elm Street.

HER CHILDREN.

1. Henry Addison, born May 12th, 1840.
2. Dwight Collins, born Aug. 20th, 1842.
3. Frederic Eugene, born July 20th, 1844.
4. Mary Marilla, born April 24th, 1849.

871. "Eli B. Smith," to church Nov. 5th, 1837, by letter from the church in South Cornwell, Conn.; born Nov. 25th, 1815, to No. (747,) at Harwinton; married Nov. 27th, 1838, No. (988.) He is a wagon maker by trade; built the house on horse plain, standing on the site of one built 100 years since, by Capt. Lemuel Hotchkiss. Mr. Smith, now 1861, follows farming; dismissed and recommended to church in Granville, Mass., June 15th, 1866.

THEIR CHILDREN.

1. Infant, born Nov. 3d, 1839; died aged 3 months, buried at Cornwall.
2. Francis M. born March 24th, 1841, at Cornwall; to Plainville church, Sept. 1858; she married 1865, Benj. Page.
3. Infant, born , died aged 3 weeks, buried at New Britain.
4. Infant, born , died aged 3 days, buried " "

872. "Timothy S. Wetmore," to church Dec. 3d, 1837, by letter from church in Litchfield; born July 16th, 1810, to John, of Litchfield, and his wife Anna (Seymour;) he is a joiner by trade and occupation; live on Arch Street; married May 18th, 1836, No. (732;) held civil and military offices.

THEIR CHILDREN.

1. Dwight Erwin born Aug. 12th, 1837, bap Dec. 3d, 1837; died June 30th, 1865, of Hemorrhage.
2. Junius Marcellus, born June 13th, 1839, bap. Aug. 3d, 1845; died April 11th, 1862, of consumption.
3. Mary Seymour, born Nov. 6th, 1850, bap. July 13th, 1851.
4. Frederic Henry, born Nov. 7th, 1853.

873. "LAURA B. GRISWOLD," to church Oct. 1st, 1837; born Dec. 1st, 1824, to Riley and his wife, No. (810;) married June 10th, 1846, Ransom Hills of East Hartford; she was dismissed and recommended by lettêr to Chapel Street church, New Haven, Feb. 11th, 1859; had been dismissed and recommended by letter to East Hartford, and received back, 1854; he is a house painter now, 1863, form the firm of Hills & Butler, New Haven.

THEIR CHILD.

Mattie, born April 7th, 1856, at New Britain.

874. "ELVIRA S. POTTER," to church Oct. 1st, 1837; born Aug. 13th, 1818, at Harwinton, to Isaac and his wife Anna (Scovill;) she spent one year at Holyoke Seminary, Mass.; went west and taught at Rushville, Ill., until 1843; she married 1843, James B. Sweetland, a lawyer from Rochester, New York; he died Aug. 12th, 1845, when second she married, 1847, Alexander Stame, of Griggsville; he a railroad man; she has three sons and one daughter, now, 1861; she was dismissed and recommended by letter to Ill.; is sister of No. (911.)

875. "LUCY P. GAGER," to church Jan. 4th, 1838, by letter from church in Tolland; came to this place as a milliner, a woman of force of character and energy; she married Sept. 6th, 1838, No. (919;) born Feb. 29th, 1816, at Tolland, to Andrew and his wife Lois (Webb,) of Scotland, Windham County, she died Feb. 26th, 1852, aged 36; she had been dismissed and recommended to South church by letter, Nov. 17th, 1845.

876. "OZIAS B. BASSETT," to church Feb. 4th, 1838, by letter from the church in Milton, Conn.; born March 7th, 1806, to Nathan and his wife Mehitable (Buel,) of Litchfield, daughter of Ira, married May 23d, 1833, No. (877;) a farmer by occupation; is a magistrate and has represented the town in the legislature; his residence is south of South Park, on Main Street; owns the farm formerly owned and occupied by No. (198;) has been Superintendent of South church sunday school, selectman, assessor, &c., in town.

877. "MRS. EMELINE BASSETT," to church Feb. 4th, 1838, by letter from the church in Simsbury; born Dec. 11th, 1805, at Simsbury, to Salmon Eno and his wife Polly (Richards;) married May 23d, 1833, No. (876;) to south church by letter, Nov. 1844, with her husband, No (876.)

THEIR CHILDREN.

1. Helen Jane, born Nov. 17th, 1833, bap. 1838; married April 25th, 1855, Edward Doen.

2. Chas. G. born Jan. 1st, 1834 ; died aged 1 month.

3. Aaron Eno, born May 4th, 1835, bap. 1838 ; died May 12th, 1860, aged 25, after long sickness.

4. William, born Feb. 1836 ; died aged 9 months.

5. Mary Ann Humphrey, born Jan. 4th, 1837, bap. 1838.

6. Frederic Henry, born Nov. 4th, 1839, bap. 1840 ; a C. V. in Co. A, 13th reg., 1861-2.

7. Milton Humphrey, born Dec. 15th, 1840, a C. V. in Co. A, 13th, reg., 1861-2.

8. Mary Eno, born May 9th, 1841 ; married May 9th, 1866, Joseph P. Mumford of Philadelphia.

9. Ozias Burdette, born July 5th, 1844.

10. Emeline Julia, born Nov. 24th, 1846.

11. Franklin Nathan, born Feb. 28th, 1849.

12. Rosie Augusta, born April 11th, 1851.

878. "Lemuel Lomady," to church Feb. 11th, 1838, by letter from Farmington, born May 7th, 1815, at Farmington, to Titus and his wife Viletta (Naman,) married Nov. 24th, 1833, Lucinda (Swears,) daughter of John, and his wife Clarissa (Gandy,) born Sept. 15th, 1815, at Poquonnoc. He to church in Farmington, Aug. 2d, 1829. Residence foot of "Burritt Hill," on North Street.

THEIR CHILDREN.

1. Maria, born Nov. 7th, 1834.

2. Sarah, born April 17th, 1839.

879. "Mrs. Elizabeth Meigs," to church Feb. 25th, 1838, by letter from church in New Hartford, North. She was daughter of Benjamin Henshaw, of Middletown, Conn., and his wife Elizabeth (Lord,) born July 3d, 1755, married June 18th, 1781, Major John Meigs, son of Col. Jonathan and his wife Grace (Starr.) He was in the whole war of the Revolution. He was a hatter by trade, learned of his father. After the war he moved to New Hartford, " Town Hill," but about 1800 to North end village. His widow came to this place about the time her daughter Esther married Thomas Lee, Esq., and drew a pension from government of $280.00 per annum. She lived to March 5th, 1847, aged 95 ; buried on the bank of the Conn. river, in Middletown, and a large red stone monument tells where. The whole amount of pension money paid to Major John Meigs and his Widow Elizabeth, was about $6,000. To South church, 1842.

THEIR CHILDREN.

1. Return John, born Aug. 30th, 1782, lived a bachelor, died at Augusta, Ga.

2. Benj. Henshaw, born March 27th, 1784, married Ellen Vandyke, of N. Y.

3. Elizabeth Lord, born Dec. 8th, 1785, died April 28th, 1792.

4. Richard Montgomery, born Aug. 8th, 1787, married Maria Keeler, of Albany.
5. Sally Maria, born March 28th, 1789, married Dr. Erastus Williams, of Knox, New York.
6. Esther Lopez, born Feb. 24th, 1791, married Nov. 25th, 1809, Solomon Lusk, see No. (880.)
7. Joseph Henshaw, born May 18th, 1793, married , lives in Clarksville, Ga.
8. George Lord, born Feb. 23d, 1796, married , died in Knox, aged 50.

880. "Mrs. Esther L. Lee," to church Feb. 25th, 1838, by letter from church in New Hartford, North, born Feb. 24th, 1791, to Maj. John Meigs, at Middletown, married Nov. 25th, 1809, Solomon Lusk, only son of David, of New Britain, and his wife Betsey (Curtiss,) born 1790; they lived in New Hartford, but he died July 19th, 1812, aged 22, under the care of Dr. Todd, of Farmington, when second she married, Jan. 3d, 1838, No. (356.) She to South church, 1842, and died March 18th, 1865, aged 74.

HER CHILDREN BY FIRST HUSBAND.

1. Elizabeth Curtiss, born Sept. 21st, 1810, married May 2d, 1838, No. (858.)
2. Solomon Adna, born May 3d, 1812, died Oct. 22d, 1821, aged 5 months.

881. "Mary B. Hough," to church 1838, by letter from the church in Meriden, born Feb. 26th, 1816, at Bristol, to No. (756,) married April 23d, 1840, No. (773.)

882. "Lois Basset," to church 1838, by letter from church in Southington, to that church, 1831, daughter of Benoni Evans, of Southington, and his wife Lois (Sandford,) of Rocky Hill, born Oct. 29th, 1813, at Southington, baptized there Aug. 4th, 1822, married June 3d, 1838, No. (376,) she died Dec. 3d, 1853, aged 40, at Simsbury.

883. "Eliza, wife of John S. Whittlesey," to church 1838, by letter from church in Petersham, Mass., born Aug. 31st, 1812, to Abraham Haskell and his wife Mary, (Gallond,) married March 19th, 1834, No. (611.) She was dismissed and recommended by letter to church in Durant, Iowa, June 26th, 1857, now, 1863, resides in Janesville, Wis.

884. "Walter Stanley," to church 1838, by letter from Springfield, Mass., born Sept. 1st, 1820, to No. (921,) and his wife, No. (529;) learned the printers' trade in Springfield, of Geo. Merriam, has been a manufacturer, kept a Meat Market for several years, his residence on Lee Street, at the foot of "Dublin Hill;" married April 12th, 1842, No. (997,) has been a constant singer in our church choir for many years. His present residence is on East Main street.

THEIR CHILDREN.

1. Francis Elijah, born Nov. 7th, 1842, was a 3 months soldier on the Potomac, 1861. Also, orderly sergeant in Co. A, 13th reg. C. V., at Ship Island and New Orleans 1862; he fell in the battle of Irish Bend, La., while leading as Orderly Sergeant, his Co., against the rebel forces, April 14th, 1863. He was a fine form, tall and brave, his body was brought on, and his funeral attended March 1st, 1864, at Center church. Sermon and Eulogy.

2. Edward Preston, born June 17th, 1844, bap. July 31st, 1845, died Dec. 8th, 1860, aged 16.
3. Albert Seymour, born Nov. 4th, 1845, bap. June 4th, 1846.
4. George Walter, born Jan. 19th, 1848, bap. Aug. 3d, 1848.
5. Herbert Lyman, born Feb. 1st, 1850, bap. July, 1850.
6. Emma Maria, born March 18th, 1853.

885. " SARAH B. wife of Wm. A. Churchill," to church 1839, by letter from the church in Wethersfield, born, Feb. 24th, 1810, to Capt. Hosea Blinn, of Wethersfield, and his wife Mehitabel (Wolcott,) married Dec. 4th, 1838, No. (695,) was his second wife, and is ready to every good work.

886. " ANNA, wife of James Stanley," to church 1839, by letter from church in (upper Middletown,) now Cromwell. Maiden name, Anna North Stow, daughter of Capt. Thomas and his wife, No. (1021,) born April 18th, 1816, at upper Middletown, married July 5th, 1836, No. (1165;) she died Aug. 10th, 1862, aged 46. She was a woman of uncommon intelligence and spirituality.

887. " LYDIA H. WIFE OF REV. D. M. SEWARD,"to church 1839, by letter from the church in Middletown, born March 26th, 1814, at Middletown, to Col. Simeon North and his wife Lydia (Huntington,) daughter of Rev. Enoch, married March 2d, 1836. He, son of Seth, of Durham and his wife Rhoda (Picket,) born July 31st, 1811, at Durham, graduated at Yale College, 1831. Studied theology at New Haven Seminary. Ordained and Installed over this church, Wednesday, Feb. 3d, 1836, dismissed June 15th, 1842. Settled at West Hartford, and at Yonkers, New York, 1851, had the title D. D. conferred 1862, by Columbia College, New York.

THEIR CHILDREN.

1. Frederick Dwight, born May 29th, 1837, at Middletown, Ct., bap. Jan. 7th, 1838, at New Britain, to Pres. church in Yonkers, July 1858, and July 22d, 1858, graduated at Hamilton College, N. Y. He died May 8th, 1859, at Yonkers.
2. Lydia E. born April 27th, 1846, at West Hartford.
3. Francis Harriet, born June 6th, 1850, at West Hartford, died March 16th, 1862, aged 12, at Yonkers.
4. Wm. Foote, born June 2d, 1853, at Yonkers, N. Y.

888. " CAROLINE S. wife of Oliver P. Olds," to church 1839, by letter from church in Feeding Hills, Mass., her maiden name, *Morley*. She was dismissed and recommended by letter 1842, to church in Westfield, Mass. He was a brass worker.

THEIR CHILDREN.

1. Elizabeth, born
2. Charles, born

889. "MRS. LUCY E. PENNFIELD, wife of Harvey," to church 1840, by letter from church in Berlin; born Oct. 6th, 1818, to Edmund Sand-

ford, of Wethersfield, and his wife Lydia (Beckley,) of John, married Oct. 21st, 1839, No. (833.) Her name was omitted on the record of this church by mistake. She was admitted to church in Berlin, 1835.

890. "EDMUND WARNER," to church 1840, by letter from the church in Wilbraham, Mass., born there Aug. 3d, 1813, to Samuel and his wife Eunice (Jones,) came to this place as a merchant, married Oct. 8th, 1838, No. (861,) to south church, 1842. They moved to Tennessee, where he went into trade, but died at Hamburg, Dec. 8th, 1853, aged 40. He is brother of No. (891.)

THEIR CHILDREN.

1. Hortensia, born July 16th, 1839, bap. 1839, at N. B., died Sept. 29th, 1848, in Tenn.

2. Henry Augustus, born April 19th, 1841, bap. 1841, at N. B., he is supposed to be, 1861, living at Hamburg, Tenn.

891. "LUCINDA, wife of Julius Parker," to church Jan. 5th, 1840, by a letter from the church in Wilbraham, Mass.; her maiden name was Lucinda W. Warner, daughter of Samuel, of Wilbraham, Mass., and his wife Eunice (Jones,) born April 14th, 1811; is sister of No. (890,) married Jan. 31st, 1838, No. (864.).

892. "DOLLY B. wife of David W. Whittlesey," to church Jan. 5th, 1840, by letter from church in New Preston, Conn., daughter of Samuel Averil, of New Preston, and his wife Betsey (Johnson,) born Jan. 23d, 1817, married Sept. 4th, 1839, No. (767.) She with her husband was dismissed and recommended by letter to the church in Berlin, May 30th, 1852.

893. "ROBERT G. WILLIAMS," to church Jan. 5th, 1840, born March 30th, 1816, at New Hartford Conn., to Wm. G. Williams, Esq., and his wife Tryphena King, from Sharon, Conn.; married Nov. 20th, 1837, No. (901,) whe died in New Britain, when 2d he married, May 18th, 1847, Elizabeth M. Smith, of Priaceton, New Jersey, daughter of Rev. D. M. Smith. He studied theology at Princeton, New Jersey, was ordained at Durham, Conn., Oct. 12th, 1853; installed, 1855, over 1st congregational church, at Woodbury, Conn.; left there 1859; preached at Birmingham, Conn., 1861; resided at Brownsville, New Jersey, where his second wife died, May 28th, 1861, when he became Capt. of the Wesleyan Company, raised at Middletown, Conn., for the suppression of the rebellion. He was also in the Mexican War. He was once a hardware manufacturer in New Britain, and was one year a superintendent of the first church sunday school. He and his first wife became consistent members of the south church, 1842. He third married April 2d, 1862, at Saugerties, New York, Miss Mary E. Slater, Principal of Young Ladies' Seminary, and they are both at the head of the Young Ladies' College Institute, at Waterbury, Conn., now 1867. The popularity and success of Miss Slater, (now Mrs. Williams,) as an *educator*, has been remarkable.

HIS CHILD BY FIRST WIFE AMELIA.

Amelia Elizabeth, born May 17th, 1843, at New Britain.

BY SECOND WIFE.

Tryphena King, born July 5th, 1852, at Princeton, N. J.

894. "MRS. SYLVIA, wife of Elisha Crosby," to church Jan. 5th, 1840, baptized same time; daughter of Joel Sperry, of Avon, and his wife Betsey (Kent;) married Feb. 22d, 1833, at Avon; she died May 2d, 1842, aged 27, when second he married, Dec. 17th, 1844, No. (701,) but was soon divorced, when third he married, Sept. 7th, 1851, Lucy, the widow of David Steele, and lives, 1861, on her premises, the former home of Seth Lusk.

HER CHILDREN BY CROSBY.

1. Nancy, born Feb. 26th, 1833, married, April 30th, 1851, Ezekiel R. Meriam, of Meriden, now of Ill.
2. Wm., born Feb. 16th, 1835, gone to Australia, a sailor.
3. Sarah, born Feb. 28th, 1837, married, Edward Yates; she died May 4th, 1861; he was a soldier in Co. G, 6th Regt., C. V., under Capt. Tracy.

895. "ADELINE CORNWELL," to church Jan. 5th, 1840, born July 8th, 1820, to No. (401;) educated at Troy, N. Y.; married Oct. 24th, 1841, No. (915.)

896. "LOUISA HART," to church, January 5th, 1840, born October 5th, 1828, to No (311;) married, Dec. 1st, 1846, Rev. Jared B. Flagg, son of Henry C., of S. C., and his wife Martha (Whiting,) born June 16th, 1820; she to South church 1842; they lived in Brooklyn, N. Y.; she died Jan. 18th, 1867, at New Haven, aged 38.

THEIR CHILDREN.

1. Charles Noel, born Dec. 25th, 1848, at Brooklyn.
2. Jared, born Feb. 26th, 1853, at New Haven.
3. Earnest, born Feb. 6th, 1857, at Brooklyn.
4. Washington Allston, born June 2d, 1860, at Brooklyn.
5. Louisa, born Feb. 15th, 1862, at Brooklyn, N. Y.
6. Rosalie, born Nov. , 1866, at New Haven.

897. "MRS. LUCY B., wife of Nathan R. Cook," to church Jan. 5th, 1840, born Sept. 8th, 1816, to Daniel Judd, jun., and his wife Abigail (Squire;) married Sept. 13th, 1836, No. (909;) to South church 1842; she died Sept. 28th, 1851, aged 35.

898. "MRS. JULIA A., wife of Amon Judd," to church Jan. 5th, 1840, baptized same time; born April 14th, 1815, to Caleb Austin, of Wallingford, and his wife Laura (Neff,) of Wethersfield, married Dec. 7th, 1831; he son of No. (435,) and was his second wife; he died March 22d, 1840, aged 39, when second she married, April 23d, 1843, John Wright, son

of Dan and his wife Roxy (Daniels,) born Aug. 15th, 1809, married Sept. 22d, 1829, Esther Emeline Cameron, who died Aug. 24th, 1838, aged 30, when second he married, April 23d, 1843, No. (898.)

HER CHILDREN BY FIRST HUSBAND, AMON JUDD.

1. Austin, born April 5th, 1834, married Sept. 3d, 1856, Julia Miller, daughter of Caleb; he enlisted at Middletown into Co. B, 14th Regt., C. V., was in the battle of Chancellorville, Va., was wounded in the hand, had a middle finger amputated, and died, June 5, 1863, in consequence; was buried at Middletown, where his family reside, June 11th, 1863.

2. Jane Eliza, born July 16th, 1838, married, July 13th, 1857, Wm. G. Loveland of Middletown, before Rev. John Dudley.

HER CHILDREN BY SECOND HUSBAND, JOHN WRIGHT.

1. Dwight Henry, born Dec. 1st, 1843, enlisted in the 14th Regt.. Co. F, C. V., was in the Sharpsburg battle, was a corporal; died Oct. 23d, 1862, aged 19, of fever, at Bolivar Heights, Md., his body brought home and buried in New Britain, Feb. 24th, 1863; he had been promoted after the battle of Antietam for bravery.

2. Laura Eveline, born Aug. 7th, 1848.

3. Alice Elizabeth, born Oct. 10th, 1855.

899. "JULIA A. NORTH," to church Jan. 5th, 1840, born Aug. 11th, 1828, to No. (743) and his second wife No. (744;) married, June 11th, 1851, Thomas S. Hall, son of George A., of Newbern, N. C., and his wife Emily (Dewey,) born Nov. 6th, 1827; she to South church 1842.

THEIR CHILDREN.

1. Mary Elizabeth, born Jan. 30th, 1855.

2. Emily Lauretta, born March 6th, 1858.

900. "DR. JOHN R. LEE," to church Jan. 5th, 1840, by letter from , born April 22d, 1804, to No. (356) and his wife No. (357;) graduated at Yale College, 1826; bred a physician, spent some years at Worcester, Mass., as physician in the "State Lunatic Hospital," traveled in Europe, Egypt and Palestine; 1861, is living single, retired from business, and is boarding out in New York. He is greatly interested in the reforms of the age, especially on the subject of "human rights" and the cause of temperance.

901. "MRS. AMELIA S., wife of R. G. Williams," to church Jan. 5th, 1840, by letter from Sharon, Ct.; daughter of Maj. David Gould, of Sharon, and his wife Elizabeth; married Nov. 20th, 1837, No. (893;) she with her husband to South church 1842; she died July 30th, 1843, aged 28, in New Britain; was a lovely Christian woman.

902. "HARRIET WOODRUFF," to church Jan. 5th, 1840, born Aug. 4th, 1811, at Simsbury, to Frederic Buel and Lydia (Wright,) his wife; married Jan. 29th, 1837, No. (905;) she with her husband dismissed and recommended by letter March 24th, 1850, to South church.

NOTE.—Our church record in this case is obscure; it ought to read "Mrs. Harriet L., wife of Dr. Lucius Woodruff."

903. "GEORGIANA NORTH," to church Jan. 5th, 1840, born June 4th, 1825, to No. (650) and his wife No. (651;) baptized Georgiana Maria, June 7th, 1829, married, Dec. 27th, 1854, No. (944;) to South church 1842; live now, 1867, in Brooklyn, N. Y.

904. "LOUISA NORTH," to church Jan. 5th, 1840, born Dec. 15th, 1826, to No. (650) and his wife No. (651,) baptized, June 7th, 1829, Louisa Burnham; married, June 4th, 1855, Alexander M. Ward, son of Dr. Josiah of Berlin, and Mary (Peck) his wife, born Aug. 12th, 1816; is manufacturer and Sup't of the American Basket Co., of New Britain; she to South church 1842; they live on Main st., near its junction with Elm.

THEIR CHILDREN.

1. Frederic Meigs, born April 24th, 1856.
2. Mary Louise, born Nov. 5th, 1857.

905. "DR. LUCIUS WOODRUFF," to church Jan. 5th, 1840, by letter from church in Collinsville, born Dec. 1st, 1812, in Farmington, to Simeon and Avis (Bronson,) his wife; graduated, as M. D., at Pittsfield, Mass.; married, Jan. 29th, 1837, No. (902,).came to this place 1840, as a practicing physician, has been successful in business; his residence on Main st.; was dismissed and recommended by letter to South church, with his wife, March 24th, 1850; has been Sup't of that S. School; has represented the town in the State Legislature, and been called to fill other important offices in town; is secretary of the Russell & Erwin Manufacturing Co., 1867; has no posterity.

906. "ABIJAH FLAGG," to church Jan. 5th, 1840, by letter from church in Berlin, to which he was admitted April 5th, 1812; he was born July 18th, 1790, at Berlin, to Solomon and his wife Olive (Hart,) daughter of Zachariah and Sarah his wife; he by trade and occupation a cabinet maker; lived on Main st., in Berlin, but sold and came to this place in 1840, and bought the house built on High st., by Enos M. Smith, where he lived until Oct. 28th, 1842, aged 52. He had been a magistrate in Berlin, and held the same office here; was esteemed for honesty and integrity; he married Feb. 14th, 1813, No. (907;) to South church 1842; he was brother of No. 425.

THEIR CHILDREN.

1. Henry Williams, born March 20th, 1814, mar. May 3d, 1836, Marietta Parker; she died, when 2d he married, Nov. 15th, 1848, Cornelia Esther Cook; he died June 12th, 1857.
2. Norris Robbins, born May 24th, 1820, died Oct. 11th, 1842, aged 22; he was a young man of much promise.

907. "HONOR, wife of Abijah Flagg," to church Jan. 5th, 1840, by letter from church in Berlin, to which she was admitted Feb. 2d, 1812;

daughter of David Beckley, jun., of Beckley quarter, and his wife Eunice (Williams,) of Rocky Hill; born Oct. 11th, 1789; she to south church 1842; died March 7th, 1851, aged 62; she married Feb. 14th, 1813, No. (906.)

908. "HARRIET STANLEY," to church April 4th, 1841, by letter from Cleveland, O.; baptized June 13th, 1819, Harriet Aurora; born March 25th, 1815, to Cyrus and his wife No. (422;) to South church 1842; now, 1861, unmarried, and living in Cleveland, O.; she is sister of No. (716.)

909. "NATHAN R. COOK," to church April 4th, 1841, by letter from church in Meriden, Ct.; born Aug. 10th, 1811, at Wallingford, to Munson and his wife Thankful (Austin;) married, Sept. 13th, 1836, No. (897;) she died, when second he married Oct. 25th, 1852, Abigail Pardee, of Watertown, daughter of Heman and Almira (Nichols,) his wife; born Dec. 20th, 1821, at Watertown; Mr. Cook and his wife Lucy withdrew to South church 1842.

CHILD BY FIRST WIFE.

1. Lewis Rice, born April 9th, 1838; see No. (1218.)

BY SECOND WIFE.

2. Lucy Abigail, born Sept. 2d, 1854.

910. "MARIA, wife of Ira Steele," to church April 4th, 1841, by letter from church in Southington; to church there April 7th, 1822; born Mar. 29th, 1797, to Charles Wright, of (Stepney,) Rocky Hill, and his wife No. (409;) married, Oct. 30th, 1817, Ira Steele, son of No. (852,) and his wife No. (853;) born Aug. 16th, 1792; harness maker by trade, learned of Ira Andrews, son of Elijah; lived several years in Southington; came to this place and bought the old home of Thomas and Abijah Hart, on west Main st., where he carries on farming; she to South church 1842, and died Dec. 14th, 1862, aged 65.

THEIR CHILDREN, ALL BAPTIZED IN SOUTHINGTON.

1. Sherman D., born Jan. 6th, 1820, was, 1861, in California, died there Nov. 28th, 1861, aged 41.
2. Nelson W., born Oct. 20th, 1821; serg't Co. A, 13th Regt. C. V., 1862, at N. O.
3. Nathan, born Nov. 7th, 1826, married widow Robbins, (alias) Harriet Putney, of Ashford, Mass.
4. Caroline, born Feb. 5th, 1830, bap. Oct. 1st, 1830, at Southington; died young.
5. Laura Lentine, } born June 12th, 1833, { mar. Oct. 19th, 1858, H. K. Smith, of Roswell.
6. Caroline Maria, } born June 12th, 1833, { bap. June, 1833.

911. ANDREW P. POTTER," to church April 4th, 1841, by letter from church in Harwinton; born April 25, 1816, at Harwinton to Isaac and his wife Anna (Scovil,) and is brother of No. (874;) while in this town was employed by No. (330;) to South church 1842; mar., Dec. 20, 1847, S. Eliz-

abeth Egbert, of Platteville, Wis., and now, 1861, is living there, engaged in canvassing for books.

912. "DENNIS SWEET," to church April 4th, 1841, baptized same time; born Jan. 13th, 1807, at Farmington; is a shoemaker by trade and occupation, son of James, of Farmington, and his wife Esther (Bidwell;) married, July 3d, 1828, No. (602;) his residence on Elm st.; to South church 1842.

THEIR CHILDREN.

1. Francis James, born June 28th, 1833, bap. Sept. 29th, 1833, married, April, 1855, Mary

2. Charles Hervey, born Aug. 14th, 1835, married Anna Quinn.

3. Helen Augusta, born Jan. 18th, 1848, married, Dec. 7th, 1864, Stephen B. Peck of Winsted.

913. "CHARLES A. WARNER," to church April 4th, 1841, baptized same time; born April 19th, 1811, at Troy, N. Y., to Willard, of Chester, Vt., and his wife Betsey (Burke,) of Coxackie, N. Y.; he is a jeweller by trade and occupation; residence on Main st.; married, Dec. 11th, 1836, No. (703,) both to South church 1842; he has been successful in business.

THEIR CHILD.

William Adolphus, born April 10th, 1838, bap. 1838, died Nov. 1st, 1843, aged 5½.

914. "GEORGE CARPENTER," to church April 4th, 1841, baptized same-time; born Dec. 22d, 1807, at Lenox, Mass., to Joshua and his wife Elizabeth (Smith;) is a brass founder by trade and occupation; his residence on Lafayette st.; he married Sept. 2d, 1835, No. (700.)

THEIR CHILDREN.

1. Walter Gladden, born May 30th, 1837, see No. (1261.)

2. Sarah Elizabeth, born Sept. 25th, 1838, see No. (1170.)

3. Ellen, born Jan. 6th, 1840, bap. 1841, see No. (1171.)

915. "TIMOTHY W. STANLEY," to church April 4th, 1841, born July 13th, 1817, to No. (550) and his wife No. (339;) baptized Aug. 24th, 1817, Timothy Wadsworth; married, Oct. 24th, 1841, No. (895;) learned the trade of printer of Geo. Merriam, at Springfield, Mass.; became a manufacturer, been successful in business; his residence on Park st.; has represented the town in the General Assembly; was chosen one of the standing church committee Jan. 17th, 1856; he was assessor of direct taxes in 1862, is President of the Union Manufacturing Co. of the village, now, 1867.

THEIR CHILDREN.

1. Francis Wadsworth, born June 24th, 1843, bap. Aug. 13th, 1843; corporal Co. A, 13th Regt., C. V., Charles H. Cornwell, Capt.; he was promoted to sergeant, and

was wounded in the battle of Irish Bend, La., April 14th, 1863, and died of his wounds in Brashear City, May 29th, aged 20; a brave soldier, and the only child of his fond parents; he was buried in New Britain, Aug. 5th, 1863.

2. William Cornwell, born Nov. 25th, 1848, died March 10th, 1849, aged 4 mo.
3. Arthur, born June 21st, 1856, died Aug. 17th, 1856, aged 3 months.

916. "CHARLES M. LEWIS," to church April 4th, 1841, born June 13th, 1816, to No. (458,) baptized, Oct. 7th, 1827, Charles Mason; is a jeweller by trade and occupation; married, Nov. 21st, 1860, Tirzah B. Granger, daughter of Hiram, of Suffield, and his wife Harriet (Fuller,) born May 11th, 1839, at Suffield; he to South church 1842; owns the place on Main st. once Abner Clark's, and after him Wm. B. North's; he has been successful in his business; she died May 13th, 1865, aged 26.

THEIR CHILD.

Carrie, born Feb. 20th, 1862, bap. Jan. 2d, 1863, at the South church.

917. "CYRUS HART," to church April 4th, 1841, born July 19th, 1795, to No. (131;) married, March 31st, 1819, No. (724;) his residence on Arch st.; is a farmer.

THEIR CHILDREN.

1. Julietta Andrews, born May 20th, 1820, bap. Nov. 13th, 1831, see No. (816.)
2. Angeline Clark, born July 11th, 1822, bap. Nov. 13th, 1831, see No. (936.)
3. Elizabeth, born Dec. 19th, 1824, died Aug. 24th, 1827, aged 2 years 8 mo.

918. "MORTON JUDD," to church April 4th, 1841, bap. same time; born Nov. 5th, 1808, to John and his wife No. (637;) married, Jan. 26th, 1828, No. (619;) residence on West Main st.; an extensive manufacturer of hardware; was elected deacon Oct. 23d, 1851; his wife Lucina died, when second he married, Feb. 21st, 1855, No. (1102.)

THEIR CHILDREN.

1. Hubert Lewellyn, born April 1st, 1829, bap. June 14th, 1829, see No. (1125.)
2. Albert Dunham, born Dec. 4th, 1832, bap. April 21st, 1833, see No. (1028.)
3. Edward Morton, born Nov. 11th, 1837, bap. 1838, see No. (1236.)
4. Martha Louisa, born July 9th, 1846, bap. Oct. 11th, 1846, see No. (1378.)

SECOND WIFE'S CHILD.

5. Mary Burnham, born April 8th, 1857, bap. June 6th, 1858.

919. "GEORGE LEWIS," to church April 4th, 1841, born Aug. 6th, 1814, to No. (567;) was a brass founder, had his house and shop on Arch st.; married, Sept. 6th, 1838, No. (875;) he was a man of pleasing address, and had a warm, Christian heart; he died Oct. 20th, 1845, aged 31.

THEIR CHILDREN.

1. Martha Gager, born July 6th, 1840, bap. 1840; excels in teaching.
2. George Henry, born Sept. 16th, 1842.

920. "ELNATHAN PECK," to church April 4th, 1841, baptized same time; born Aug. 11th, 1803, at Milford to Michael and his wife Mary (Marshal;) he was a joiner by trade; came to this place in 1822, while an apprentice, to build the "old North church;" he was a builder several years, when he became an extensive manufacturer of hardware; his residence on East Main st.; he married, June 20th, 1827, No. (597;) he and wife became constituent members of the South church 1842; he died Dec. 28th, 1865, aged 62, at New Haven.

THEIR CHILDREN.

1. Henry Franklin, born March 31st, 1829, married, June 4th, 1851, Elizabeth A. Cornwell; he was a corporal in Co. H, 27th Regt., C. V., taken prisoner at the battle of Fredericksburg, Va., was at Richmond only 2 days, when he was paroled.
2. Charles, born March 16th, 1830, bap. June 27th, 1830, married, Sept. 7th, 1853, Mary F. Davis, of Westfield, Mass.
3. Abigail Bryan, born June 8th, 1832, bap. Sept. 9th, 1832, see No. (1152.)
4. Mary Jane, born April 13th, 1835, bap. May 31st, 1835, married, Sept. 7th, 1854, Walter H. Stanley.
5. Martha, born May 12th, 1837, bap. July 23d, 1837, married, Sept. 19th, 1855, Wm. Hart.
6. John Marshal, born Feb. 25th, 1840, bap. 1840.
7. Ann Eliza, born Sept. , 1842, died Aug. 19th, 1843, aged 11 months.
8. Oliver Dewy, born Aug. 15th, 1844; one of the volunteers in Co. E, 6th Regt. a drummer for a Waterbury Co., was promoted to Drum-Major; he served 3 years, and was honorably discharged.
9. Louisa Frances, born July 15th, 1846.

921. "IRA STANLEY, jun.," to church April 4th, 1841, born July 7th, 1795, to No. (442,) and his first wife, Abi Langdon; he was a blacksmith by trade, learned of No. (370;) married, Oct. 6th, 1819, No. (529,) lived several years in Farmington, returned and built where now, 1861, the Center church stands; house owned and occupied by Dr. Comings when moved; he built the house on Washington st., where his widow now, 1862, resides; he led us in prayer and singing in social meetings, and was much in exhortation after his conversion; he died Sept. 23d, 1857, aged 62; he was elected one of the standing church committee Jan. 20th, 1853; he was a zealous Christian, and greatly interested in the cause of "human rights" and in the temperance reformation.

THEIR CHILDREN.

1. Walter, born Sept. 1st, 1820, bap. Nov. 4th, 1821, see No. (884.)
2. Elizabeth Langdon, born May 18th, 1822, bap. Dec. 15th, 1822, at Farmington; see No. (842.)
3. Everett Lincoln, born Jan. 5th, 1825, baptized May 20th, 1826, at Farmington; see No. (971.)
4. Margarett, born Dec. 24th, 1827, bap. Feb. 24th, 1828, at Farmington; see No (931.)
5. Ellen Maria, born April 1st, 1834, bap. July 11th, 1834, see No. (1105.)
6. Abi C., born March 25th, 1836, died in infancy.

922. "THEODORE BELKNAP," to church April 4th, 1841, born June 23d, 1822, at Charleston, S. C., to Moses and his wife Catharine Maria Burghers, No. (644;) baptized Theodore A., in the German Lutheran church of Charleston; came to this place in 1828, spent some years in Cornwall, Ct., returned and learned jeweller's trade of Wm. B. North; married, Nov. 7th, 1846, Frances Olivia Chedister, daughter of J. B. Chedister, and his wife Sarah Guerin; they live, 1861, in Springfield, Mass.; he was to South church 1842.

THEIR CHILDREN.

1. Frederic A., born Aug. 28th, 1847.
2. Byram C., born Aug. 12, 1850.
3. Kate B., born July 6th, 1852.

923. "RICHARD S. SOUTHWORTH," to church April 4th, 1841, born Jan. 20th, 1802, at New Britain, to Samuel and his wife Hannah (Shipman;) baptized May 16th, 1813, the parents being members of a church in Cherry Valley, and on a visit here, where their four eldest children then lived; this was on the principle of "communion of charity," as it was called in the olden time; he was a house-painter by trade and occupation; residence on East Main st.; married, March 9th, 1822, Lucinda Ely, daughter of Elias, of Chester, Conn.; she was born Aug. 29th, 1797, and died March 6th, 1828, aged 31, when second he married, July 25th, 1830, No. (928;) she died, when third he married, Sept. 11th, 1861, Harriet Hamlin, sister of No. (928;) she is represented by No. (1317.)

HIS CHILDREN BY FIRST WIFE.

1. Caroline Elizabeth, born June 24th, 1823, see No. (1106.)
2. Lucinda Ely, born Aug. 20th, 1825, died May 13th, 1829, aged 3.

924. "HENRY L. PARSONS," to church April 4th, 1841, baptized same time, born Aug. 29th, 1800, at Hartland, to Paul, and his wife Phebe (Coe,) married Nov. 24th, 1825, No. (635.) His residence is on Prospect street; been a brass worker, farmer, &c.; left us for the Advent church; our watch withdrawn, 1856.

THEIR CHILDREN.

1. Eliza Jane, born March 4th, 1827, bap. Sept. 9th, 1827, died May 5th, 1828, aged 13 months.
2. Jane Elizabeth, born Dec. 18th, 1828, bap. July 12th, 1829, married June 28th, 1849, Eli Henry Porter; she died Feb. 13th, 1851, aged 23.

925. "GEORGE L. TIBBALS," to church April 4th, 1841, baptized same time, born January 11th, 1818, at Milford, Ct., to Lemuel, and his wife Sarah (Baldwin,) a joiner by trade, learned of Wilson Plumb, Esq., of Milford, and came to this place, Feb., 1839, to work for Elnathan Peck; he built, 1847, the house on Park street now, 1861, occupied by Gilman Hinsdale. He married Oct. 12th, 1842, Mary Ann Hurlburt, of Wethersfield, Ct.; to South church, 1842; lives now, 1861, in Milford, Ct.

THEIR CHILDREN.

1. James Hurlburt, born July 14th, 1847, at New Britain.
2. Sarah Catharine, born Nov. 11th, 1850, at Milford.
3. Fanny Abigail, born Feb. 13th, 1854, at Milford.
4. Frederick Lemuel, born Oct. 25th, 1858, at Milford.

926. "JANE ANN, wife of Thomas Tracy," to church April 4th, 1841, born Aug. 17th, 1813, married Nov. 26th, 1835, No. (856.) She was daughter of No. (423,) and his wife, No. (424.) She died July 4th, 1845, aged 32.

927. "ALMIRA, wife of Alanson Warren," to church April 4th, 1841, born Feb. 2d, 1816, to No. (381,) and his wife, No. (557,) married Jan. 18th, 1837. He was born May 14th, 1808, at Fall River, Mass., to Elnathan, and his wife Ruth (Allen,) a brass founder by trade, and lock maker by occupation; his residence, on West Main street. She was born and baptized at Cherry Valley, N. Y.; to South church, 1842. He died July 20th, 1862, of apoplexy, at New Britain.

THEIR CHILDREN.

1. Mortimer A., born Sept. 21st, 1837, married June 9th, 1865, Lizzie G. Goodwin, of Collinsville.
2. Norman W., born Sept. 13th, 1840; a volunteer in Co. A, 13th Reg.; teacher of freedmen, 1867, at New Orleans.
3. Kate L., born Aug. 19th, 1845.

928. NANCY H., wife of Richard S. Southworth," to church April 4th, 1841, born April 14th, 1797, at Middletown, Ct.; was the widow of Henry Riley, of Charlestown, New Hampshire, daughter of William Hamlin, and Thankful (Knowles,) his wife, married July 25th, 1830, No. (923.) She died Dec 6th, 1860, aged 63, in the triumphs of faith and hope.

HER CHILD BY FIRST HUSBAND.

William Hamlin Riley, born July 24th, 1824, at Charlestown, N. H., was an only child, married Sept. 18th, 1849, No (1160.)

929. "ABIGAIL S. DOOLITTLE," to church April 4th, 1841, baptized same time, born Aug. 20th, 1825, to George, and his wife, No. (640.) She was dismissed and recommended by letter to the Presbyterian church in Columbus, Miss., to which place she went as a teacher, August 13th, 1843. She subsequently went to White Hall, Illinois, where she died, aged 26.

930. "ABIGAIL H. FRANCIS," to church April 4th, 1841, born July 3d, 1826, to No. (587,) and his wife Abigail (Knowles,) was given for the time then passing to James Francis, for his wife, No. (473,) to nurse and bring up, she having lost her mother soon after birth, hence her name "Francis." She married Nov. 30th, 1848, Henry Long, of Windsor

Locks. She having left the communion of this church and united with a different denomination, this church voted to withdraw its watch, Jan. 25th, 1844.

931. "MARGARET STANLEY," to church April 4th, 1841, born Dec. 24th, 1827, at Farmington, to No. (921,) and his wife, No. (529;) for several years a sweet singer in our church choir; married April 5th, 1848, Edwin Christopher Hills, of East Hartford, son of Martin, and Sarah (Bryant,) his wife, born , and is a farmer in his native town. She was dismissed by letter and recommended to church in East Hartford, Oct. 28th, 1852.

THEIR CHILD.

Eliza Stanley, born Jan. 4th, 1849, bap. Dec. 2d, 1849.

932. "MARY ANDREWS," to church April 4th, 1841, born at Chapel Hill, N. C., to No. (464,) and his wife No. (392;) dismissed by letter to South church, March 7th, 1844, and received back by letter, Feb. 5th, 1860; resides, 1863, at Milledgeville, Ga.; 1867, at New Britain.

933. "AMELIA STANLEY," to church April 4th, 1841, born Jan. 1st, 1825, to No. (550,) and his wife, No. (339,) married, Feb. 29th, 1848, No. (1066.) She died May 6th, 1855, aged 30, in hope of a glorious resurrection. She lost one son, and left one to survive her.

934. "CORDELIA M. NORTH," to church April 4th, 1841, born July 1st, 1825, to No. (330,) and his second wife, No. (411,) baptized Oct. 16th, 1825, Mary Cordelia, married Sept. 1st, 1852, Rev. Joseph Emerson, son of Rev. Ralph, D. D., and his wife Eliza (Rockwell,) born May 28th, 1821, at Norfolk, Ct. He graduated at Yale College in 1841, and is a professor of Greek in Beloit College, Wisconsin, now, 1862, in which town the family resides. She to South church, 1842.

THEIR CHILDREN.

1. Ralph Chapin, born March 20th, 1855, at Beloit, died Aug. 31st, 1855, at New Britain.
2. Charles Alvin, born Aug. 29th, 1856, at Beloit, Wis.

935. "SARAH G. CORNWELL," to church April 4th, 1841, born Aug. 3d, 1824, to No. (401,) and his wife, No. (404;) lives with her father now, 1861, unmarried; to South church, 1842.

936. "ANGELINE C. HART," to church April 4th, 1841, born July 11th, 1822, to No. (917,) and his wife, No. (724,) married June 27th, 1843, Imly B. Veits, son of John, of Granby, and Abigail (Eno,) of Simsbury, his wife, born Dec. 19th, 1808, married June 27th, 1838, No. (816;) she died, when he married, second, as above, a sister of his first wife. He is a farmer and lives on Arch street.

THEIR CHILDREN.

1. John Hart, born April 8th, 1844, died Feb. 7th, 1845.
2. Mary Adelia, born March 10th, 1847.
3. Elenora Juliaetta, born July 22d, 1849.
4. Imly Dumont, born March 20th, 1851, died Jan. 22d, 1857.
5. Annie Elizabeth, born Feb. 28th, 1854, died June 23d, 1854.
6. Ida Eugine, born Oct. 29th, 1856, bap. Aug. 2d, 1862.
7. Angie Lilly, born June 30th, 1859, bap. Aug. 2d, 1862, died Aug. 2d, 1862, aged 3 years.
8. Carrie A., born Dec. 29th, 1863, died Aug. 5th, 1864, aged 7 months, 7 days.

937. "Lucina Hart," to church April 4th, 1841, born Dec. 3d, 1821, to No. (430,) and his wife, No. (397,) married Oct. 29th, 1850, John H. Goodwin, of Hartford, son of John, and his wife Anna (Belden,) born March 2d, 1809, and was his second wife, his first being Nancy, daughter of No. (438.) She was dismissed, 1851, by letter, and recommended to South church, Hartford, where she was received, January, 1852.

938. "Elizabeth Smith," to church April 4th, 1841, born Dec. 13th, 1822, (a twin with Elizur Newton Smith,) to No. (337,) and his second wife, No. (472,) baptized June 1st, 1823, Elizabeth Augusta; unmarried, A. D. 1864, and lives with her mother, at the residence of H. H. Brown, her brother-in-law, on High street. She became a constituent of South church, 1842.

939. "Elizabeth L. Deming," to church April 4th, 1841, baptized same time, born May 2d, 1821, at New Hagerstown, Ohio, to Treat, of Wethersfield, son of Richard, and Millicent (Belden,) his wife, and No. (573;) at her own request was rebaptized on admission to church. She died Aug. 2d, 1841, aged 20, at Wethersfield, but interred here, stone at her grave.

940. "Cordelia Stanley," to church 1841, born Jan. 23d, 1820, to No. (438,) and his wife, No. (1294;) was dismissed by letter, May 14th, 1848, and recommended to South church, Hartford, but received back by letter to this church, July 7th, 1861; now, A. D. 1861, unmarried and lives with her mother on Washington street, and has excelled in drawing and painting.

941. "Mary S. Bassett," to church 1841, baptized same time, born Dec. 13th, 1825, to No. (376,) and his first wife Polly (Judd.) She became a constituent member of South church, 1842; took care for her father and his family, in Simsbury, after the death of his second wife; she is now, 1861, unmarried and living with her sister, Mrs. Frederick Hart, in this place.

942. "Levi S. Wells," to church 1841, born Feb. 25th, 1825, to No. (511,) and his wife, No. (643,) married April 24th, 1848, No. (1093.) His residence, built 1849, on North end of East street; is a farmer and

and has good taste and success in raising stock and cultivating his grounds; is often called to public trusts and responsibilities.

THEIR CHILDREN.

1. Herman Francis, born April 29th, 1849, bap. Nov. 10th, 1850, see No. (1357.)
2. Horace Lemuel, born Oct. 5th, 1855, bap. July 6th, 1856.
3. Kate, born Jan. 17th, 1864, bap. June 11th, 1865.

943. "Lemuel R. Wells," to church 1841, born Jan. 2d, 1827, to No. (511,) and is brother of No. (942,) married June 15th, 1853, No. (1033,) residence on East street, opposite his father's. He was chosen deacon for two years, Aug. 12th, 1859, and re-elected indefinitely, Aug. 25th, 1861, and consecrated by prayer and laying on of hands by Rev. L. Perrin, the pastor, and Rev. E. Ripley, assisting, at a preparatory lecture, Aug. 30th, 1861. He was a farmer by occupation. He died Feb. 25th, 1867, aged 40, greatly lamented.

944. "Levi W. Hart," to church 1841, born June 7th, 1825, to No. (481,) and his second wife, No. (490;) graduated at Yale College in 1846, to which church he was dismissed by letter and recommended, Jan. 7th, 1843. He studied theology at Union Theological Seminary, New York city; licensed to preach, 1852, by the South Presbytery of New York, and was one year a missionary to the Germans of the city, and now, 1861, rector of the College Grammar School, Brooklyn, N. Y. He married, Dec. 27th, 1854, at New Britain, No. (903;) distinguished for languages and German literature.

THEIR CHILDREN.

1. Louisa W., born Sept. 8th, 1856, bap. March, 1857.
2. William B. North, born Aug. 11th, 1859.
3. Herbert Winthrop, born August, 1865, died Sept. 2d, 1867.

945. "Norman L. Hart," to church 1841, born Feb. 2d, 1826, to No. (954,) and his wife, No. (385,) married Dec. 6th, 1854, Lavinia M. Kellogg, of Philadelphia, born June 24th, 1834, at Hartford, Ct., to M. A., of Avon, and his wife Marilla (Cooley,) of Hartford. He was dismissed by letter to Tabernacle church, New York, being a clerk in that city. He is engaged in merchandize now, 1862, in Philadelphia. New Britain is indebted to his munificence for the engraving of Dr. Smalley which embellishes this work, and for $500 in paying the church debt.

THEIR CHILDREN.

1. Marilla Mellen, born Jan. 31st, 1858, at Philadelphia.
2. Norman Elwood, born Jan. 21st, 1861, at Philadelphia.

946. "Margaret Andrews," to church, 1841, born Aug. 30th, 1826, to No. (478,) and his second wife, No. (657,) married Oct. 17th, 1850,

by Rev. E. B. Andrews, No. (1065;) dismissed by letter, October 13th, 1854, to First Congregational church in Chicago, Ill.; is now, 1864, residing in Brooklyn, N. Y., but 1867, at St. Louis, Mo.

947. "CATHARINE FRANCIS," to church 1841, born Sept. 3d, 1825, to No. (470,) and his wife, No. (471,) baptized Nov. 13th, 1825, Catharine Amelia. She died Sept. 26th, 1849, aged 24.

948. "MELVINIA, wife of Frederick T. Stanley," to church 1841, born Sept. 5th, 1815, at Sandisfield, Mass., to Samuel C. Chamberlin, and his wife Anna (Conklin,) married July 4th, 1838. He was son of Gad, and his wife, No. (589,) born Aug. 12th, 1802; been a merchant and extensive manufacturer, of hardware; his residence, corner of Washington and Willow streets; has done much in improving and beautifying the village, and extending its business and name. She became one of the constituent members of South church, 1842. She died Aug. 16th, 1843, in her 28th year, of scarlet fever.

THEIR CHILDREN.

1. Alfred Hubert, born Aug. 2d, 1839, bap. 1841, married Dec. 21st, 1863, Sarah J. Lozier, daughter of John Peck Lozier, and Hannah Guess.

2. Frederick Henry, born Feb. 9th, 1841, bap. 1841, died Oct. 10th, 1843, aged 2 years and 8 months.

3. William Chamberlin, born April 14th, 1843, died July 31st, 1844, aged 15 months.

949. "CHARLOTTE ELLIS," to church 1841, by letter from Camden, South Carolina. She first to church in Troy, New York, while receiving her education at that "Female Seminary." She went south as a teacher. She was born May 5th, 1818, to No. (717,) married Sept. 1st, 1846, Thomas J. Huddleston, of Columbus, Miss. She was dismissed by letter, February, 1853, and recommended to church in Warsaw, Ill., where, 1863, they resided on a farm, but now, 1864, they live at Iowa City, in Iowa.

THEIR CHILDREN.

1. Julia Ellis, born June 25th, 1847, at Liberty, Missouri.

2. Thomas Garlick, born Feb. 1st, 1850, died January 14th, 1862, aged 12, at Warsaw, Ill.

3. Katie May, born May 15th, 1853, at Warsaw, Ill.

[Here ends the ministry of Rev. D. M. Seward, June 15th, 1842.]

950. "MARTHA, wife of Nehemiah Peck," to church August, 1842, by letter from church in Middlebury, Ct., born Feb. 10th, 1798, at Plymouth, Ct., to Scovil, married Nov. 6th, 1824, at Plymouth. He was son of Lament, of Bristol, and Rebecca (Tracy,) of Westchester, Ct., his wife, born Sept. 26th, 1793, at Bristol. He bought the Jesse Stanley farm, in Stanley quarter, where she died, May 16th, 1849, aged 51, when he married, second, Jan. 22d, 1851, No. (1075.) He sold his farm here

and lived in East Haven, where his second wife died, when he went to Burlington, Vt., where he died March 30th, 1861, aged 67.

THEIR CHILDREN.

1. James, born Sept. 20th, 1825, at Bristol, died July 19th, 1830, at Marshall, New York.

2. Mary Scovil, born April 20th, 1827, at Bristol, see No. (967.)

3. Nehemiah, jun., born May 2d, 1829, lives in Burlington, Vt., married Jan. 1st, 1862, Minerva Pitkin, of Winchendon, Mass.; they resided, 1862, in New Britain, where he died Feb. 6th, 1863, at the Dr. Smalley house, aged 34, lovely in life, peaceful and happy in death.

4. James Gorham, born May 28th, 1831, see No. (1054.)

5. David Brainard, born March 15th, 1833, lives at Pompey, N. Y., married Frances A. Brainard; is now, 1862, at Ship Island.

6. Susan Rich, born May 11th, 1835, No. (1053.)

7. Sarah Bunnel, born Feb. 7th, 1838.

8. William Henry Harrison, born Feb. 1st, 1841, at Middlebury, Ct., lives at Burlington, Vt., is six feet two inches in height, was captain of Co. I, in the 5th Reg. Vt. Volunteers; is now, April, 1862, before Yorktown, Va.; was shot through the neck but recovered.

951. "TAMAR, wife of Russell Avery," to church August, 1842, by letter from church in Boston, daughter of Henry Flint, of Concord, Mass., and Bulah (Wheeler,) his wife, born Sept. 18th, 1794, at Carlisle, Mass., married Sept. 6th, 1838. He was son of Asa, and his wife Sarah (Green.) She is sister of No. (865,) and was dismissed by letter, June 3d, 1860, to church in Guilford, Ct., where she died Dec. 20th, 1862, aged 68; buried here. She was distinguished for cheerfulness, kindness and charity.

952. "GEORGE THOMPSON," to church October, 1842, by letter from church in New Haven, born Oct. 19th, 1817, at Bristol, Ct., to Benoni, and his wife Mary (Belden,) is a coach lace weaver by trade; married Nov. 27th, 1841, No. (953;) lives now, 1861, at New Haven; dismissed by letter, Sept. 3d, 1843, to church in Plymouth Hollow.

953. "LUCY C., wife of George Thompson," to church October, 1842, by letter from South church in Glastenbury, born March 31st, 1820, at Lebanon, to Jesse Miner, of Glastenbury, and his wife Caroline (Mason,) married Nov. 27th, 1841, No. (952.) She and husband were dismissed by letter, Sept. 3d, 1843, to Plymouth Hollow.

THEIR CHILD.

Ellen C., born Sept. 21st, 1846, at New Haven.

[Here begins the ministry of Rev. C. S. Lyman, Feb. 15th, 1843; he was ordained and installed as pastor of this church and people.]

954. "NORMAN HART," to church April 2d, 1843, born August 5th, 1794, to No. (181;) by trade a woolen manufacturer, residence by

"Hart's Mills," at the south end of the village. He married, Sept. 8th, 1818, No. (385;) was appointed deacon of this church Sept. 21st, 1843; he resigned 1851. He sold his mill and place of residence, and built at the foot of "Dublin Hill," 1851, where he now lives on Main street, 1861. He sold, and in 1867 resides on Walnut street.

THEIR CHILDREN.

1. Burdette, born Nov. 16th, 1821, bap. Jan. 20th, 1822, see No. (771.)
2. Norman Lee, born Feb. 2d, 1826, bap. June 4th, 1826, see No. (945.)
3. Ellen, born Feb. 23d, 1828, bap. , see No. (1033.)

955. "ALVIN BELDEN," to church April 2d, 1843, and baptized same time, born Jan. 25th, 1796, to Aziel, and his first wife Azuba (Goodrich,) daughter of Asahel, married Nov. 4th, 1819, No. (579,) daughter of William Steele, and his wife, No. (246.) She died April 22d, 1830, aged 31, when he married, second, Nov. 17th, 1831, No. (495.) He is a tinner by trade and occupation, as was his father; residence on Washington street.

THEIR CHILDREN.

1. Luana, born Oct. 1st, 1820, married Feb. 9th, 1841, William J. Buckley, the tinner.
2. Sophia, born June 16th, 1823, married August 16th, 1847, Warren J. Hubbard.
3. George Hooker, born Feb. 22d, 1830, bap. Aug. 3d, 1837, married Helen Gridley; he died August 10th, 1866, aged 36; buried in New Britain.

CHILDREN BY SECOND WIFE.

4. Walter, born Jan. 26th, 1833, bap. April 1st, 1833, died July 17th, 1833, aged 6 months.
5. Charles Henry, born Feb. 19th, 1837, bap. Aug. 3d, 1837, see No. (1097.)

956. "IRENE, wife of John Ellis," to church April 2d, 1843, baptized same time, born Nov. 13th, 1793, to No. (435,) and his second wife, No. (436,) married Dec. 5th, 1819. He was son of Abel, of "Great Swamp Society," and Thankful (Dickinson,) his wife, born Oct. 7th, 1793; residence near the south end of East street, formerly the home of Adonijah Lewis. Mr. Ellis was a successful farmer, but formerly was also an extensive manufacturer; his house was built in 1816, and is on a pleasant location. He died July 17th, 1865, aged 72.

THEIR CHILDREN.

1. Abel, born March 2d, 1821, married November 7th, 1847, Matilda Henshaw, of Missouri.
2. Daniel, born June 2d, 1822, a soldier in the Union army at New Mexico, 1863.
3. Martin, born May 22d, 1826, married Oct. 16th, 1848, Lydia Richards, daughter of Amon.
4. Gustavus, born Feb. 15th, 1828, see No. (1220.)

957. "URSULA, widow of Isaac Lewis," to church April 2d, 1843,

baptized same time, born Jan. 18th, 1781, to No. (354,) married Oct. 28th, 1804, No. (458.) She died Sept. 2d, 1850, aged 70.

958. "ABI, wife of David Kelsey," to church April 2d, 1843, baptized same time, born Oct. 23d 1802, to Elisha Vaughn, and his wife Lydia (Steele,) married Oct. 14th, 1824, and was his second wife, his first being Lovisa (Hastings,) who died August 28th, 1823. He was son of Enoch, jun., and his wife Kesiah (Gilbert,) born Oct. 5th, 1779, and married, June, 1810, his first wife. His residence was the old home of his father, just over the line between this town and Wethersfield. He died May 20th, 1858, aged 79.

SOME OF THEIR CHILDREN.

Keziah, born July 21st, 1812, married Daniel Blinn; he died January 10th, 1836, aged 30.

Lorenzo, born Dec. 2d, 1816, married Belinda Kilby, daughter of Simeon.

Enoch, born Dec. 28th, 1818, married Sept. 18th, 1842, No. (1058.)

CHILD BY SECOND WIFE.

David, born July 6th, 1832, married Sept. 7th, 1852, Eliza Ann Deming, daughter of Franklin.

959. "EMILY A., wife of Oliver S. Judd," to church April 2d, 1843, baptized same time, born July 8th, 1818, to Chester Lewis, and his wife Hanna (Beckwith,) married April 15th, 1838, No. (823;) for many years one of the church choir. She died Nov. 5th, 1858, aged 39.

960. "ANTOINETTE HART," to church April 2d, 1843, born Nov. 13th, 1825, to No. (516,) and his wife, No. (509,) married June 4th, 1848, George H. Booth, son of No. (673,) and his wife, No. (431,) born Aug. 5th, 1823; lives on Main street, south part of the village. She was dismissed by letter to Methodist church, Jan. 30th, 1856.

THEIR CHILD.

Jennie Augusta, born July 15th, 1855.

961. "DENNIS PENNFIELD," to church April 2d, 1843; born Dec. 24th, 1823, to No. (469,) and his wife No. (526;) he fell into a state of despondency or insanity and hung himself, Nov. 4th, 1845, aged 22.

962. "DEWITT C. POND," to church April 2d, 1843; baptized same time; born March 29th, 1824, at East Poultney, Vt., to Harvey Curtiss Pond and his wife Marion (Turpen;)married Nov. 15th, 1848, Mary F. Tucker, daughter of Erastus, of Hartford, and Eliza his wife, born Aug. 18th, 1829, at Windham, Conn.; he was a jeweller by trade, learned of Churchill & Stanley; came to New Britain, 1840; was dismissed and received to North church, Hartford, May, 1858; he is in mercantile business in that city, on Main Street, now, 1863.

THEIR CHILD.

Born, April 19th, 1865.

963. "ANNA C. wife of Wm. Morse," to church June 4th, 1843; baptized same time; born Aug. 8th, 1804, at Burlington, to Calvin Hart and his wife Anna (Yale;) married March 27th, 1835; he son of Benoni, of Bristol, and Sarah (Adkins,) his wife, born March 29th, 1793; is a wagon maker by trade; residence on corner of Washington and Myrtle Streets.

THEIR CHILDREN.

1. Anna Rebecca, born Feb. 11th, 1835, died Oct. 2d, 1837, aged 19 months.
2. Lucy, born Jan. 19th, 1837, died March 21st, 1837, aged 2 months.
3. Anna Charlotte, born July 5th, 1838.
4. Justina Rebecca, born Jan. 8th, 1840, died July 16th, 1849, aged 9.
5. Henrietta Alice, born Dec. 2d, 1842.

964. "EDWIN BELDEN," to church June 4th, 1843, baptized same time; born Oct. 14th, 1818, to Aziel and his second wife Nancy (Mitchel;) married Sept. 16th, 1841, No. (968;) built the house next south of the Alms House; now, 1861, lives in Minnesota.

THEIR CHILDREN.

1. Alice, born
2. Ella, born

965. "ABIATHAR HUBBARD," to church June 4th, 1843, baptized same time; born , 1807, at Haddam, to Abraham and his wife Asenath (Wells;) he learned the brass business of No. (480;) married April 14th, 1845, Mary Deming Steele, daughter of No. (444;) born June 4th, 1810; his residence on Main Street, south end; he died March 17th, 1853, aged 45; she died May 11th, 1851, aged 41. She was distinguished for skill in turning hooks and eyes before the machines were invented.

THEIR CHILDREN.

1. Harriet Laura, born Jan. 1st, 1846, at New Britain, lives 1862, at Higganum, Ct., with her Aunt.
2. George Abiathar, born May 2d, 1851, at New Britain, lives in Ponsett Village, with his Aunt, now 1862.

966. "CHARLES C. RECOR," to church June 4th, 1843, baptized same time; born Nov. 10th, 1826, at Hartford, to Curtiss Warfield and his wife Laura (King;) was adopted by No. (467) and his wife No. (468,) in place of an infant they lost without a name. He married Dec. 19th, 1849, Sarah Farnsworth, daughter of Philip, of West Hartford, and his wife Sukey (Cowles;) born Jan. 20th, 1827; he a hame maker, and lives at Plainville, 1862. He never was dismissed from this church.

THEIR CHILD.

Lucy Augusta, born April 4th, 1853, at Bristol, Ct.

967. "MARY S. PECK," to church June 4th, 1843, baptized same time; born at Bristol, April 20th, 1827, to Nehemiah and his wife No. (950;) married Oct. 16th, 1849, Charles N. Shumway, of Milwaukie. She went west as a teacher, under the patronage of Ex-Gov. Slade; she was dismissed by letter May 6th, 1853, to church at Watomas, Wis.; she died Aug. 21st, 1855, aged 28, in Wisconsin, and left one child, now 1861, living in West Haven, Conn.

968. "BETSEY A. BELDEN," to church June 4th, 1843; born April 6th, 1823, to Jesse Recor and his wife No. (527;) married Sept. 16th, 1841, No. (964;) resides 1862, in Faribault, Min.

969. "SAMUEL JUDD," to church June 4th, 1843; born Jan. 25th, 1789, to No. (195;) married April 23d, 1822, No. (560;) was a brass founder by trade, his residence, the house built by Ebenezer Booth and occupied after Mr. Judd's decease by Grove Loomis, now 1861, given place to George Hart's new house. He died May 13th, 1852, aged 63; left no posterity.

970. "EDWIN C. ELLIS," to church June 4th, 1843; born Dec. 5th, 1823, to No. (717;) is a farmer, lives with his father; married Sept. 21st, 1853, Minerva Tuller, daughter of Sylvester, of Simsbury and his wife Hancy (Humphrey;) born May 1st, 1825. He is a member of our church choir.

THEIR CHILDREN.

1. Grace M. born June 21st, 1858.
2. Anna, born July 12th, 1862.

971. "EVERETT L. STANLEY," to church June 4th, 1843; born Jan. 5th, 1825, to No. (921;) married June , 1848, Sarah Flint, of Rocky Hill, daughter of Jared and his wife Sarah (Francis.) He having neglected the ordinances of the Gospel, and resisted all efforts to reclaim him, he was expelled Feb. 19th, 1846. He was divorced from his wife and she second married Augustus Robbins. He second married, Feb. 4th, 1858, Lucy J. daughter of Weston Hopkins, of Vermont, and his wife Laura (Butterfield;) born Dec. 25th, 1833, at Brattleboro, Vt. Mr. Stanley is a large portly man; the family reside, now 1862, at Lawrence, Kansas, and he respects the religion of his fathers.

THEIR CHILDREN.

1. Charles Everett, born July 11th, 1851.

HIS CHILDREN BY SECOND WIFE.

2. Everet Alonzo, born Sept. 26th, 1859, at Lawrence, Kansas.

972. "NEWTON F. HART," to church June 4th, 1843; born Jan. 2d 1829, to No. (542,) and his wife No. (532;) married May 4th, 1852, Nancy Phinney, of Plainville, daughter of Isaac and his wife Dolly

Phelps,) alias Widow of Sherman Carter, born Nov. 13th, 1828, at Plainville. He bred a merchant, served his clerkship with Adna Whiting, of Plainville, and now, 1863, is a druggis tin Meriden. Was not dismissed from this church. They have no children living.

THEIR CHILD.

Ella, born Dec. 9th, 1856, died Jan. 29th, 1857, aged 1 year 1 month.

973. "JULIA M. BUTLER," to church June 4th, 1843 ; born July 15th, 1825, to No. (452,) and his wife No. (548 ;) she died Nov. 16th, 1847, aged 22.

974. "CYNTHIA S. GRISWOLD," to church June 4th, 1843 ; born Feb. 28th, 1829, to Riley and his wife No. (810 ;) married Nov. 15th, 1848, No. (996 ;) she and her husband were dismissed by letter, Feb. 3d, 1860, to Chapel Street church, New Haven.

975. "AUGUSTA H. RECOR," to church June 4th, 1843 ; born Nov. 12th, 1827, to Jesse and his wife No. (527 ;) married Aug. 29th, 1847, Samuel C. Dunham, of Plainville, son of Albert and his wife Sylvia (Cowles ;) she was dismissed by letter to church in Plainville, and received there June 4th, 1845 ; the family live now, 1863, at Faribault, Min.

976. "ELLEN M. ANDREWS," to church June 4th, 1843 ; born Sept. 18th, 1824, to No. (313) and his first wife No. (314 ;) dismissed and recommended to Broadalbin, New York ; living now, 1863, in Warterloo, Wis., with her sister, No. (508.)

977. "FIDELIA PENNFIELD," to church June 4th, 1843 ; born Sept. 10th, 1826, to No. (469 ;) married April 18th, 1852, Wm. R. Bradford, son of Perez and his wife Jerusha (Stannard,) born Sept. 9th, 1831, at Haddam, Conn. ; she died July 18th, 1855, aged 30 ; when second he married, April 15th, 1858, Emily Pennfield, sister of his first wife.

978. "LOIS C. CLARK," to church June 4th, 1843 ; born July 17th, 1825, to Abel, of Litchfield South Farms, now Morris, and his wife Catharine (Eckhert ;) baptized in infancy ; married Feb. 19th, 1845, Edward O. Tuttle ; born Nov. 21st, 1821, at New Haven, to Ansel and his wife Abigail (Short,) of Derby, Conn. She was dismissed and recommended by letter to church in Ridgefield, Conn., Jan. 11th, 1844 ; she is sister to the wife of No. (622,) and now 1861, living in Williamsburg, N. Y.

THEIR CHILDREN BORN AT RIGEFIELD, CONN.

1. George W. born Dec. 5th, 1845.
2. Theron C. born April 8th, 1847.
3. John W. born Aug. 2d, 1849.
4. Wilbur S. born July 1st, 1852.

979. "LUCELIA WELLS," to church June 4th, 1843 ; born Oct. 27th, 1828, to No. (511) and his wife No. (643 ;) married April 25th, 1855,

No. (1028;) she was dismissed Sept. 16th, 1864, to Chapel Street church, New Haven, at her own request.

980. "JERUSHA ELLIS," to church June 4th, 1843; born Jan. 1st, 1826, to No. (717,) and his wife No. (718;) married March 9th, 1857, Josiah Elbert Atwood, son of Josiah of Newington, and his wife Prudence (Kellogg;) born Feb. 20th, 1823; is a farmer and they live, 1861, with his father; she was dismissed to church in Newington, 1861.

THEIR CHILD.

Kate May, born Sept. 10th, 1860.

981. "ESTHER F. PINKS," to church June 4th, 1843; born July 22d, 1830, at Boston, to Jonathan C. and his wife No. (865;) she had a certificate of membership to Baptist church, in this place, New Britain, April 27th, 1848; she subsequently lived in Hanover, and was received back by letter from Congregational church there, June 1st, 1860; unfortunately lost one limb by amputation to save life, when young.

982. "ELBRIDGE STEELE," to church June 4th, 1843; born Feb. 16th, 1827, to No. (514) and his wife No. (725,) learned jeweller's trade of Churchill & Stanley; built a fine residence on Arch Street; married Feb. 22d, 1848, Rebecca Eddy, daughter of Harlowe and his wife Mary (Dobson;) born April 27th, 1829; he joined the Methodist church, and left our communion irregularly and the church withdrew its watch Feb. 5th, 1846; an excellent workman at his trade.

THEIR CHILDREN.

1. Wilbert Elbridge, born Nov. 14th, 1850.
2. Lillian Browning, born Jan. 18th, 1852.
3. Katie Florence, born July 22d, 1856.

983. "HORATIO S. LEWIS," to church June 4th, 1843, by letter from Congregational church in Farmington, Noah Porter, D. D., Pastor; born Sept. 25th, 1819, to No. (458) and wife No. (957;) he served a clerkship with Maj. Timothy Cowles, Farmington, as merchant; married Feb. 19th, 1844, No. (1003,) engaged in merchandise in this village, but died of consumption April 10th, 1848, aged 29; distinguished for christian courtesy and principle.

THEIR CHILD.

Horatio, born Feb., 1845, died Sept. 23d, 1846, aged 19 months.

984. "ELVIRA C. wife of Augustus Stanley," to church June 4th, 1843, by letter from North church, New Hartford, daughter of Thomas Conkling and his wife Chloe (Chamberlin;) born July 24th, 1820; married Oct. 5th, 1842, No. (604;) maiden name Elvira A. Conkling.

985. "NANCY A. HART," to church Aug. 6th, 1843, by letter from

church in Bristol; admitted to that church May 3d, 1840; daughter of Joel, of Burlington, and his wife Sally (Bowers,) of Rocky Hill; born July 17th, 1821; married Dec. 14th, 1845, George Hitchcock, of Southington. Live, 1861, at Harbor Creek, Pa.

THEIR CHILDREN.

1. Mary, born , at New Britain.
2. Jane, born , at Kensington.
3. Andrew, born , at Southington.
4. Charles, born , at Harbor Creek.

986. "EDWARD P. PINKS," to church Aug. 6th, 1843; born July 6th, 1827, at Boston, to Jonathan C. and his wife No. (865;) is twin to No. (987;) the church withdrew its watch from him by vote, Dec. 4th, 1856; he was a three months' volunteer in company G, 1st regiment from Conn., 1861; married Nov. 22d, 1866, Matha E Judd, daughter of No. (1119.)

987. "EDWIN C. PINKS," to church Aug. 6th, 1843; born July 6th, 1827, at Boston, to Jonathan and his wife No. (865,) is twin to No. (986;) married Nov. 25th, 1852, Sophia Lockrow, of Berlin. They live in Hanover, Meriden. This church by vote Dec. 4th, 1856, withdrew their watch and care from him.

Reformed and received back to this church from the Congregational church in Hanover, West Meriden, by letter, Sept. 1st, 1867; Erastus Hubbard, clerk. He labors at the "Cutlery Works," and resides in their new block at this date.

988. "EMELINE, wife of Eli B. Smith," to church Oct. 1st, 1843, by letter from church in South Cornwall; born Feb. 28th, 1819, to Nathan G. Corban, of Danbury, and his wife Abigail (Barnum;) married 27th, 1838, No. (871;) she was dismissed and recommeded to church in Granville, Mass., June 15th, 1866.

989. "CAROLINE A. wife of I. N. Lee," to church Dec. 10th, 1843, by letter from church in Farmington, Noah Porter, D. D., Pastor; born July 15th, 1817, to Martin Cowles, of Farmington, and his wife Harriet (Wells;) married June 13th, 1843, No. (694;) she was distinguished for excellent social qualities; died April 21st, 1853, aged 36.

990. "TIMOTHY W. LOOMIS," to church Feb. 25th, 1844, by letter from church in Torringford; born Sept. 11th, 1813, at Torringford, to Allen and his wife Mary (Read,) of East Windsor; is both joiner and farmer; married Nov. 23d, 1840, No. (991;) his residence the old home of his father Riley, until the fall of 1861, when he sold and moved to the Village; is on High Street.

THEIR SON.

Charles Allen, born Feb. 26th, 1842, married April 15th, 1863, Lydia M. Parker, he died June 24th, 1866, aged 24.

991. "CHLOE, wife of Timothy Loomis," to church Feb. 25th, 1844, by letter from church in Torringford; born Jan. 25th, 1818, to Theodore Riley, of New Britain, and his wife No. (427;) married Nov. 23d, 1840, No. (990.)

992. "ANN E. MURRAY," to church March 3d, 1844, by letter from church in Waterbury; she was dismissed by letter June 4th, 1846, and recommended to the colored Congregational church, New Haven, Rev. Mr. Beman, Pastor.

993. "JULIA S. wife of Dr. Babcock," to church March 3d, 1844, by letter from North Church, Hartford; born Jan. 21st, 1820, in Hartford, to Stephen Spencer and his wife Jerusha (Gilman;) married July 5th, 1843, Edward Denison Babcock, M. D., son of Silas and Therissa (Palmer,) his wife; born June 9th, 1818; graduate at Geneva Medical College, New York; residence on Main Street. He now, 1861, is a surgeon in United States Army; she died July 16th, 1865, aged 45, at Retreat in Hartford.

THEIR CHILDREN.

1. Mary Spencer, born May 30th, 1844, bap. Sept. 6th, 1845, No. (1246.)
2. Geo. G. Spencer, born Nov. 14th, 1846, died Sept. 13th, 1847.
3. Geo. Spencer, } twins, born Aug. 5th, 1848 } died May 14th, 1849.
4. James Gilman, }
5. Louisa, born Jan. 11th, 1852, see No. (1355.)
6. Edward, born June 9th, 1854.
7. Infant son, born Feb. 25th, 1861, died March 8th, 1861, aged 12 days.

994. "HENRY L. CAREY," to church July 31st, 1845, by letter from second Congregational church, Norwich, Conn., Rev. A. Bond, Pastor, son of Elijah of Windham, and his wife Tabitha (Bushnell;) he a jeweller by trade, learned in Norwich; married Jan. 13th, 1848, Martha Riley Griswold, daughter of Riley and his wife No. (810;) born March 1st, 1827; she went to Petersburg, Va., with her husband and died there Nov. 17th, 1855, aged 28, when second he married July 7th, 1859, Eliza Whittington, of Petersburg, Va.; born July 9th, 1837, in Tyrone County, Ireland, to Samuel and his wife Sarah (McMahon;) he was dismissed by letter Jan. 6th, 1854, to Pres. church, Petersburg, Va. He and family now 1863, living in St. Paul, Minn.

HIS DAUGHTER BY FIRST WIFE MARTHA.

1. Martha Virginia, born Nov. 12th, 1855, at Petersburg, Va., died Dec. 11th, 1855.

HIS CHILDREN BY SECOND WIFE ELIZA.

2. George Henry, born March 23d, 1860, at Petersburg, Va., died there, May 7th, 1860.
3. Wm. Henry, born Jan. 19th, 1861, at Petersburg, Va.

995. "MARTHA E. SHERMAN," to church Dec. 7th, 1845, from church in New Haven, by letter, daughter of Cyrus Williams, of New Haven,

and his wife Martha (Wheeler;) married June 11th, 1839, at N. Haven Rev. Charles S. Sherman, former Pastor of this church; she died July 9th, 1846, aged 30, in this place; he second married, July 1st, 1847, No. (1026;) she accompanied her husband to Jerusalem as a Missionary, from 1839 to 1842.

HER CHILDREN.

1. Charles Edwin, born Jan. 10th, 1841, at Jerusalem.
2. Sarah Williams, born April 16th, 1843, at New Britain.
3. Roger Minot, born June 30th, 1846, at New Britain, bap. Aug. 23d, 1846, died Aug. 27th, 1846.

996. "WALTER C. BUTLER," to church Dec. 4th, 1845, by letter from 1st Congregational church, Wethersfield, Dr. Tucker, Pastor; born April 10th, 1823, to Walter, of Wethersfield, and his wife Martha (Curtiss;) he a jeweller, learned of North & Churchill; married Nov. 15th, 1848, No. (974;) he made himself useful among us, was clerk and treasurer of our ecclesiastical society. He and wife were dismissed by letter and recommended to Chapel Street church, New Haven, Feb. 3d, 1860. He is now, 1863, of the firm of Hills & Butler, dealers in paints and oils, New Haven.

THEIR CHILDREN.

1. Ella Stanley, born June 27th, 1856, at New Britain.
2. Henry Carey, born Jan. 20th, 1859, at New Haven.
3. Eddie Walter, born Nov. 14th, 1862, " "

997. "MRS. WALTER STANLEY," to church Jan. 29th, 1846, by letter from 1st church, Springfield, Mass., Dr. Osgood, Pastor; born Jan. 19th, 1823, to Elijah Knox, of Hartford, and his wife Delia (Tryon;) married April 12th, 1842, No. (884;) her maiden name, Maria Knox.

998. "HENRIETTA PARKER," to church Feb. 1st, 1846, by letter from Congregational church in Harwinton, Conn., Rev. Charles Bentley, Pastor; born Oct. 20th, 1816, brought up in the family of Amos Hungerford, of Harwinton, 1861 is unmarried and occupied nursing.

999. "WILLIAM SAGE," to church July 5th, 1846, by letter from church in Derby, Conn., Rev. George Thacher, Pastor; born Oct. 24th, 1818, at Berlin, to Erastus and his wife Elenor (Dickinson;) he a machinist; married Oct. 19th, 1840, No. (1000,) both dismissed by letter April 6th, 1853, to church in Durham, Conn.; they, 1861, live in Berlin.

1000. "LUCY C. wife of Wm. Sage," to church July 5th, 1846, by letter from Congregational church, Derby, Conn.; her maiden name, Lucy Curtiss Farnum, daughter of Isaac, of Stuarttown, New Hampshire, and his wife Lucy (Curtiss;) born Dec. 7th, 1821; married Oct. 19th, 1840, No. (999,) both dismissed by letter April 6th, 1853, and recommended to church in Durham.

THEIR CHILDREN.

1. Wm. Elbridge, born Aug. 13th, 1841, died Sept. 25th, 1841, aged 3 weeks.
2. Walter Finney, born Jan. 25th, 1843.
3. Theodore Andrews, born July 5th, 1845, at New Britain, bap. Oct. 25th, 1846, at New Britain.
4. Ella Catharine, born May 24th, 1849, at Middletown.
5. Frederick Erastus, born July 3d, 1851, at Durham, Ct.
6. Geo. Wilford, born Oct. 26th, 1853, " "
7. Fanny Elenor, born Aug. 25th, 1856, at Durham, died April 6th, 1858, aged 19 months.
8. Chas. Henry, born June 9th, 1859, at Berlin.

1001. "Moses Bachelder," to church July 19th, 1846, by letter from church in Farmington, Noah Porter, D. D., pastor; born March 7th, 1809, baptized on his admission to church there, June 4th, 1843; married, 1835, No. (1002;) he died Feb. 6th, 1857, at New Haven, aged 48.

1002. "Rosana, wife of Moses Bachelder," to church July 19th, 1846, by letter from 1st Congregational church, Farmington, to church there April 1st, 1827; born May 3d, 1807, at New Britain, to No. (183;) she married, 1827, Joseph Yemans, of Farmington; he died, when second she married, 1835, No. 1001.)

THEIR CHILDREN.

1. Victoria, born Sept. 21st, 1839, married, Nov. 10th, 1858, Eli W. Bassett.
2. Burgess, born June , 1842.

1003. "Jane E., wife of Horatio S. Lewis," to church Aug. 9th, 1846, by letter from South church, New Britain, Rev. S. Rockwell, pastor; born June 1st, 1819, at Simsbury, to Salmon Eno and his wife Mary (Richards,) married, Feb. 19th, 1844, No. (983;) he died, when second she married, July , 1850, Paris Barber, of Homer, N. Y., where now, 1862, they reside; he son of Jedediah, of Hebron, Ct., and his wife Matilda (Tuttle.)

HER CHILDREN BY SECOND HUSBAND, PARIS BARBER.

1. Emma Jane, born April 21st, 1851, at Homer, N. Y.
2. Louisa Anna, born Jan. 11th, 1854, at Homer, N. Y.
3. Charles Eno, born Jan. 11th, 1859, at Homer, N. Y.

1004. "Caroline Senior," to church Sept. 13th, 1846, by letter from first church in Stratford, Ct., wife of Edward Senior, son of Wm. and his wife Sarah (Harvey,) born Jan. 15th, 1823; she daughter of Ephraim Beardsley, of Stratford, and his wife Sarah (Bryant,) born March 15th, 1826, married, May 5th, 1846; he a blacksmith and carriage maker by trade; he died June 10th, 1846, in New Britain, when she was dismissed by letter back to the church in Stratford, when second she married, Nov. 22d, 1852, John Perry, son of Albert, of Stratford, and his wife Sarah (Patchen,) where now, 1861, they reside.

HER CHILD BY FIRST HUSBAND.

1. Edward, born March 6th, 1848, died Sept. 10th, 1852, at Plainville, on the way to Stratford.

HER CHILD BY SECOND HUSBAND.

2. Caroline Rebecca, born April 26th, 1858.

1005. "MRS MARY CAPRON," to church Oct. 11th, 1846, by letter from Presbyterian church, Broadalbin, N. Y., Rev. W. J. Monteith, pastor; her maiden name Mary Maria North, daughter of Reuben, of Goshen, and his second wife Amanda (Austin,) of Wallingford, born Dec. 4th, 1816, at Goshen, married, May 14th, 1836, Daniel Beadle Capron, son of Orrin and his wife Rosalinda (Knight,) born Nov. 12th, 1813, at Broadalbin, N. Y.; residence on West Main st.; he has been a mechanic, but in 1862 was in merchandize on Washington st., and now, 1867, in shoe and harness business on Main st.

THEIR CHILDREN.

1. Rosalinda Corinthia, born April 13th, 1840, at Broadalbin; died there, aged 3.
2. Mary Rosella, born Aug. 26th, 1844, see No. (1313.)
3. Cornelius Earl, born Sept. 24th, 1846.

1006. "MISS E. A. CAPRON," to church Oct. 11th, 1846, by letter from Presbyterian church, Broadalbin, N. Y.; her name at this date, Elizabeth Apelonia Capron, daughter of Wm. and his wife Maria N. (Earle,) born Nov. 26th, 1824, at Broadalbin, N. Y.; married, Dec. 7th, 1851, No. (1050;) they united with the Second Advent church, and thus withdrew from our communion, when, Dec. 4th, 1856, this church withdrew its watch.

1007. "ALONZO COLLINS," to church Nov. 1st, 1846, by letter from church in New Marlboro', Mass., Rev. Samuel Utley, pastor; born Dec. 12th, 1813, to David, of New Marlboro', and his wife, whose maiden name was Hannah Gilbert, but became the widow of Russell Case, of Simsbury, when she married David Collins, and became the mother of Alonzo, who married, Feb. 19th, 1844, Lucinda Matilda Downing, daughter of Elisha and his wife Lavinia (Nichols,) born Sept. 7, 1823, at Lincoln, Vt.; their residence at the north end of Stanley street, and in the bounds of Farmington.

THEIR CHILDREN.

1. Ellen Louisa, born Oct. 9th, 1845.
2. Wm. Eugene, born May 28th, 1848.
3. Eda Lucinda, born March 14th, 1854.

1008. "ENOCH FRISBE," to church Nov. 1st, 1846, by letter from the church in Bloomfield, Ct.; born May 4th, 1786, at Barkhamsted, to Lemuel, of Blanford, Mass., and his wife Lucy (Sterling,) of Hadlyme, Ct.; married, Nov. 10th, 1810; No. (1009,) he lived south of the village, on the Kensington road, now, 1861, the residence of James Andrews; he and wife dismissed by letter, March 12th, 1848, to church in West Springfield, Mass.; they both to church in Wintonbury, now Bloomfield, 1808, and he chosen deacon there in 1815, and served in that capacity 30 years.

1009. "MRS. ENOCH FRISBE," to church Nov. 1st, 1846, by letter from church in Bloomfield, Ct.; her maiden name Eliza Taylor, born March 27th, 1791, in Chelmsford, Essex Co., Eng., to Deacon Thomas and his wife Susannah (Theobald;) married, Nov. 10th, 1810, No. (1008,) dismissed by letter with him, March 12th, 1848, to church in West Springfield, where she died March 22d, 1853, aged 62.

THEIR CHILDREN.

1. Isaac E., born Feb. 2d, 1812.
2. Elizabeth, born Sept. 21st, 1815.
3. Jane, born June 29th, 1817.
4. Susannah, born Feb. 28th, 1821, No. (1010.)
5. Lemuel T., born Feb. 7th, 1824.
6. Thomas S., born Dec. 17th, 1827.
7. Sarah M., born March 1st, 1831, No. (1011.)

1010. "SUSANNAH FRISBE," to church Nov. 1st, 1846, by letter from church in Bloomfield, Ct., Rev. Alfred C. Raymond, pastor; born Feb. 28th, 1821, to Enoch, No. (1009;) dismissed by letter, March 12th, 1848, to church in West Springfield; she, 1861, living in Springfield, Mass.

1011. "SARAH M. FRISBE," to church Nov. 1st, 1846, by letter from the church in Bloomfield, Ct.; married, , Franklin Smith, of West Springfield, Mass.; she was dismissed by letter, March 12th, 1848, to the church in that town.

1012. "RICHARD GILLET," to church Dec. 27th, 1846, by letter from the First Presbyterian church, Rome, N.Y., Rev. Selden Haynes, pastor, born 1790, to Aaron and his wife Rachel (Webster,) at Wintonbury, now Bloomfield, Ct.; he was a joiner by trade and occupation; married, , Lucina Hart, of Farmington Farms, daughter of Joel ; she died, when second he married, , Julia Boardman, of Wethersfield, Ct.; she died, when third he married, May 19th, 1841, No. (1013;) he built a house on Maple st., where he died Aug. 19th, 1855, aged 65; they both dismissed by letter to South church May 14th, 1848.

HIS ONLY CHILD BY FIRST WIFE.

Ruby, born , married , James Orton, of Rome, N. Y.

1013. "ELIZABETH, wife of Richard Gillet," to church Dec. 27th, 1846, by letter from Presbyterian church in Rome, N. Y.; her maiden name Frink, daughter of Luke and his wife No. (1014;) born April 24, 1795, at Hoosic, N. Y.; married, May 19th, 1841, No. (1012,) she now 1861, lives in N. Y. city; she was dismissed by letter to South church, with her husband, May 12th, 1848.

1014. "MRS. CATHARINE FRINK," to church Dec. 27th, 1846, by letter from Presbyterian church in Rome, N. Y.; her maiden name Burt, daughter of Benjamin and his wife Elizabeth (Hogle;) she was widow of Luke Frink, and mother of No. (1013;) lived in the family of her daughter, and died there Aug. 8th, 1856, aged 87; she had been dismissed by letter, May 14th, 1848, to South church, New Britain.

1015. "GILMAN HINSDALE," to church Dec. 6th, 1846, born Dec. 25th, 1803, to Dea. Abel, of Torringford, and his wife Mary (Knap;) married, March 25th, 1827, Amanda Ward, born Feb. 2d, 1806; she died Sept. 7th, 1838, when second he married, Sept. 9th, 1840, Anna, widow of Lawrence Richards, and daughter of John Judd and his wife No. (637;) she died, when third he married, Dec. 5th, 1852, No. (1146;) she died, when 4th he married, July 25th, 1860, No. (841;) he has engaged in various employments, now, 1862, an express agent, lives on Park st.; dismissed and recommended to South church Sept. 1st, 1865.

HIS CHILDREN BY HIS FIRST WIFE.

1. Mary Louisa, born Jan. 30th, 1830, see No. (1020.)
2. Luther G., born Aug. 13th, 1832, married Julia Wooden, and was divorced; married, second, Susan Kinney.
3. Edward P., born Aug. 7th, 1836, married

1016. "ANNA, wife of Gilman Hinsdale," to church Dec. 6th, 1846, baptized by immersion previously; born Nov. 4th, 1807, to John Judd and his wife No. (637;) married, March 26th, 1826, to Lawrence Richards, son of Jonathan and his wife Abigail B. (Knapp;) he died at Winsted, June 7th, 1839, aged 35, when second she married, Sept. 9th, 1840, No. (1015;) she died Nov. 25th, 1851, aged 44, of cancer.

HIS CHILDREN BY ANNA, HIS SECOND WIFE.

4. Venelia A., born July 3d, 1843, died Sept. 1st, 1844, aged 1 year, 2 mo.
5. Charles A., born Sept. 17th, 1847.
6. Anna Judd, born Oct. 31st, 1849, died Sept. 15th, 1863, aged 14, at Torrington.

HER CHILDREN BY FIRST HUSBAND, L. RICHARDS.

1. Jonathan, born Nov. 29th, 1826, married June 8th, 1853, Lizzie M. Shaw, of Madison, Iowa; resides, 1863, at Chicago, Ill.
2. George O., born Oct. 1st, 1838, died Feb. 10th, 1839, aged 4 months, 9 days.

1017. "S. Elizabeth Stanley," to church May 16th, 1847, by letter from First Congregational church in Ottawa, Ill., born April 17th, 1829, to No. (680,) is, 1861, a teacher, and has been many years, in different localities; dismissed by letter, Dec. 27th, 1861, back to Ottawa, Ill.; she married, Feb. 21st, 1867, Dr. Taylor.

1018. "Julia C. Stanley," to church May 16th, 1847, by letter from First Congregational church in Ottawa, Ill.; born Nov. 20th, 1830, to No. (680;) married, Aug. 24th, 1853, No. (1096;) 1863, lives in Ottawa, Ill., to which church she was dismissed by letter, Jan. 6th, 1854.

1019. "Amos E. Dudley," to church May 16th, 1847, by letter from Third Congregational church, Guilford, Ct.; born May 11th, 1821, at Guilford, to Amos, jun., and his wife Sarah (Evarts,) married, Oct. 7th, 1846, No. (807;) he has been usefully occupied in various callings; the pedigree of his family is supposed to run thus: Amos, jun., son of Amos, son of Caleb, jun., son of Caleb, sen., who was son of Joseph, son of Wm., the emigrant and first settler of Guilford, 1639, and was a direct descendant of "Lord Guilford Dudley." He and wife dismissed by letter and recommended to church in Stratford, Sept. 27th, 1853, where now, 1861, they reside.

THEIR CHILDREN.

1. Martha Minerva, born Sept. 23d, 1848, at New Britain, bap. here July 15th, 1849.
2. Mary Estelle, born Oct. 13th, 1850, at New Britain, bap. at Stratford.
3. Willie Randolph, born Dec. 7th, 1855, died Feb. 20th, 1856, not bap.
4. Frederic Amos, born Jan. 24th, 1857.

1020. "Mary Louisa Hinsdale," to church June 6th, 1847, born Jan. 30th, 1830, to No. (1015) and Amanda his first wife; married Apr. 11th, 1849, No. (1059;) they live now, 1862, in West Winsted, Conn.; dismissed and recommended there June 13th, 1862.

1021. "Phebe Stow," to church Aug. 5th, 1847, by letter from Second Congregational church in Middletown, Rev. Zebulon Crocker, pastor; her maiden name Phebe Stanley, born Aug. 28th, 1778, to No. (115;) married, Sept. 28th, 1800, Capt. Thomas Stow, of Middletown, son of Zebulon and his wife Rosetta (Riley;) born May 12th, 1777; he died Aug. 14th, 1845, aged 68, when she came to live with her daughter, No. (886,) where she died Sept. 27th, 1857, aged 79.

THEIR CHILDREN.

1. Caroline Rosetta, born June 26th, 1801, married April 26th, 1829, Jonathan R. Paddock.
2. Thomas, born April 14th, 1806, died March 10th, 1807.
3. Jane Stanley, born Dec. 13th, 1810, married, Aug. 26th, 1841, Rev. Israel P. Warren.
4. Anna North, born April 18th, 1816, see No. (886.)

1022. "HANNAH MORSE," to church Dec. 5th, 1847, baptized same time; born Oct. 13th, 1827, at Farmington, to Orson and his wife Amanda (Kellogg;) married, Oct. 19th, 1848, Francis Hart Carter, son of No. (352,) and his wife Mary (Stanley;) born Jan. 20th, 1822, at Leyden, N. Y.; he died Sept. 16th, 1849, aged 27; she is sister of No. (1208.)

1023. "ELIZA J. CHURCHILL," to church Dec. 5th, 1847, born Aug. 24th, 1836, to No. (695) and his first wife No. (729;) married, July 28th, 1858, Emory F. Strong, of Bridgeport, son of Noah, of Bolton, and his wife Grace (Foote;) born Oct. 10th, 1827, at Bolton; is a noted teacher, 1861, in Bridgeport, to which church she was dismissed by letter, Feb. 25th, 1859.

1024. "PLINY SLATER," to church Feb. 10th, 1848, by letter from Black Creek, N. Y.; born Aug. 22d, 1791, at Granby, Ct., to Benjamin Slater, sen., learned shoe making and tanning of Oliver Stanley in Stanley quarter; married, Sept. 2d, 1816, No. (1025;) owned the house where he resided, on corner of West Main and High sts.; she died, when second he married Martha Webster, of Hartland, daughter of Samuel, who died June 25th, 1858; he had one leg broken under an ox sled, and amputated, in 1857; was dismissed by letter, Feb.   1853, to church in Burlington, Ct.; received back by letter from Chapel St. Church, New Haven, July 3d, 1864.

1025. "POLLY, wife of Pliny Slater," to church Feb. 10th, 1848, by letter from Black Creek church, N. Y.; born Sept. 24th, 1797, to John Judd and his wife No. (637;) married, Sept. 2d, 1816, No. (1024;) she died Sept. 20th, 1848, aged 51.

THEIR CHILDREN.

1. Aurora, born March 30th, 1817, married Feb. 28th, 1847, Lorin Hinsdale, of Torringford.
2. Burnham Stephens, born Aug. 27th, 1820, died Aug. 3d, 1848.
3. Lydia Ursula, born April 23d, 1827, married Charles Blakesley, of Southington, April 17th, 1856.

1026. "ESTHER W. SHERMAN," to church Feb. 10th, 1848, by letter from Congregational church in Manchester, Ct., Rev. B. F. Northrop, pastor; daughter of Deacon Horace Pitkin, of Manchester, Ct., and his wife Emily   ; married, July 1st, 1847, Rev. Charles S. Sherman, then of New Britain, and pastor of the first church; she was dismissed by letter, Feb. 10, 1850, and recommended to the Congregational church in Naugatuck, of which her husband was then pastor; she was his second wife, his first was No. (995.)

THEIR CHILDREN.

1. Richard Pitkin, born May 15th, 1849, at New Britain, bap. Aug. 26th, 1849, died June 26th, 1853, at Naugatuck.
2. Edward Crosby, born Dec. 14th, 1851, at Naugatuck.
3. Emily Pitkin, born May 30th, 1856.

1027. "Charlotte Stanley," to church March 17th, 1848, by letter from Congregational church at New Milford, Ct., Rev. J. Greenwood, pastor; daughter of Anan Hine, of New Milford, and his wife Almira (Marsh,) of Vergennes, Vt.; born Feb. 1st, 1823, married, Oct. 13th, 1847, Oliver C. Stanley, son of Jesse and his second wife No. (403;) born Feb. 23d, 1823; he bred a merchant, and went into business with No. (858) very extensively, but failed, and went to Pikes Peak.

THEIR CHILDREN.

1. Jesse, born Aug. 1st, 1848, bap. Nov. 26th, 1848, Geo. White, but name changed.
2. Katie, born Oct. 12th, 1852, bap. , died Oct. 11th, 1856, aged 5.
3. Marvin Clark, born May 6th, 1857, bap. Dec. 6th, 1857.

1028. "Albert D. Judd," to church June 4th, 1848, born Dec. 4th, 1830, to No. (918;) hardware manufacturer, residence on West Main st.; married, April 25th, 1855, No. (979;) chosen deacon for two years, Aug. 12th, 1859, and at the expiration of that time elected by ballot indefinitely, Aug. 25th, 1861, it being Sabbath evening, and was set apart by prayer and imposition of hands, by Rev. L. Perrin, the pastor, and Rev. Erastus Ripley, on the 30th of Aug., 1861, it being preparatory lecture; he was dismissed Sept. 16th, 1864, to Chapel Street Church, New Haven, at his own request.

THEIR CHILDREN.

1. Catharine Wells, born Jan. 5th, 1858, bap. July 3d, 1859.
2. George Morton, born Sept. 27th, 1859, bap. June 3d, 1860.
3. Alice May, born Oct. 5th, 1862, bap. Sept. 6th, 1863, died June 30th, 1864, at New Haven, and buried in New Britain July 1st, 1864, aged 1 year, 8 mo. and 25 days.

1029. "Levi B. Stone," to church June 4th, 1848, born June 19th, 1830, to No. (776,) and his first wife, No. (777,) married March 28th, 1855, No. (1204.) The church withdrew its watch from him for neglect of Christian duties and disorderly walk, Dec. 4th, 1856. He was a three months' volunteer in 1861.

1030. "Arma Jerome," to church June 4th, 1848, by letter from church in Harwinton, Ct., Rev. Charles Bentley, pastor, born Dec. 30th, 1802, at Bristol, to Thomas, and his wife Ruth (Hills;) is a wagon maker by trade; residence, the old place of Joseph Mather, on West Main street, one and one-half miles west of the village, married Oct. 19th, 1825, No. (1031.) They had lived in Cornwall, Ct.

1031. "Anna, wife of Arma Jerome," to church June 4th, 1848, by letter from First church in Harwinton, Ct., born May 9th, 1806, to No. (747,) at Harwinton, married Oct. 19th, 1825, No. (1030.)

THEIR CHILDREN.

1. Augustus Smith, born Oct. 11th, 1827, married Oct. 18th, 1851, Louisa Dickinson; she died Dec. 14th, 1862, at Hartford.

2. Olive Maria, born April 27th, 1829, see No. (1032.)
3. Franklin Minor, born Dec. 13th, 1832, see No. (1238.)
4. Emily Ann, born Dec. 17th, 1834, see No. (1108.)

1032. "OLIVE JEROME," to church June 4th, 1848, by letter from First church in Harwinton, Ct., Rev. Charles Bentley, pastor, born April 27th, 1829, at Burlington, to No. (1030,) died Feb. 24th, 1851, aged 22, at her father's in New Britain, after severe bodily suffering.

1033. "ELLEN HART," to church Dec. 3d, 1848, born Feb. 23d, 1828, to No. (954,) and his wife, No. (385,) educated at Holyoke Seminary; married June 15th, 1853, No. (943.)

1034. "ALMIRA, wife of Horace Booth," to church Dec. 24th, 1848, by letter from the Methodist church in Newington, her maiden name, Beckley, daughter of Solomon, and his wife Lucretia (Evans,) born Jan. 3d, 1834, married May 5th, 1847, No. (793.)

1035. "CHARLOTTE, wife of Thomas Tracy," to church Feb. 11th, 1849, by letter from First Congregational church in Wethersfield, Rev. Mark Tucker, D. D., pastor, born May 15th, 1810, at Wethersfield, to Daniel Russell, and his wife Lucy (Gilbert,) married Sept. 23d, 1847, No. (856,) and was his second wife. She died March 25th, 1867, in her 57th year.

1036. "ASAPH PEASE," to church April 1st, 1849, by letter from church in Winsted, Ct., Rev. J. Pettibone, pastor, born Oct. 18th, 1776, at Enfield, Ct., to Noadiah, and his wife Tirzah (Smith,) of Glastenbury, married Feb. 4th, 1805, No. (1037.) He was by trade a shoe-maker and tanner, as was his father; lived in Sandisfield, Mass., and in Winchester, Ct., and moved to this place in 1848, and bought the farm formerly owned and occupied by Thomas, Lot, and Amon Stanley, in succession, in Stanley quarter. He died Dec. 12th, 1856, aged 80. He was tall and dignified, his locks white, and he had a truly Washingtonian appearance and look, while he lived in this town.

1037. "CLOTILDA H., wife of Asaph Pease, to church April 1st, 1849, by letter from the church in Winsted, Ct., born Jan. 1st, 1777, to Capt. Samuel Hoit, of Madison, Ct., and his wife Clotilda (Wilcox,) married Feb. 4th, 1805, No. (1036.) She is now, 1862, living with her son, No. (1038,) on Stanley street, in Shipman district. She died June 14th, 1864, aged 87.

THEIR CHILDREN.

1. Leumas, born May 9th, 1806, and was drowned, aged 2 years.
2. Mary Clotilda, born Nov. 15th, 1808, at Colebrook, resides with her mother.
3. Leumas Hoyt, born Jan. 20th, 1811, at Colebrook, graduated at Williams College in 1835, ordained minister of the Gospel by the Presbytery of Albany, N. Y.; has visited Palestine and lectured on its history; is still, 1861, preaching as itinerant, and, 1861, was appointed chaplain of the 44th Reg. N. Y. Vols.

4. Julius Walter, born May 19th, 1814, see No. (1038.)
5. Lucy Jemima, born April 10th, 1817, at East Guilford, see No. (1041.)
6. Laura Persis, born April 22d, 1824, see No. (1151.)

1038. "JULIUS W. PEASE," to church April 1st, 1849, by letter from the church in Winsted, Ct., a farmer by occupation; residence on Stanley street, in Shipman district; born May 19th, 1814, to No. (1036,) married Jan. 1st, 1844, No. (1039.)

1039. "MARY H., wife of Julius W. Pease," to church April 1st, 1849, by letter from church in Winsted, Ct., born July 24th, 1817, to Stephen Hotchkiss, of Burlington, and his wife Martha (Wiard,) married Jan. 1st, 1844, No. (1038.)

THEIR CHILDREN.

1. Leumas Hoyt, born Jan. 20th, 1845, No. (1389.)
2. Martha Francis, born Nov. 28th, 1845, see No. (1407.)
3. Julius Hotchkiss, born July 7th, 1847, died Sept. 13th, 1847.
4. Julius Hotchkiss, 2d, born Nov. 22d, 1848, see No. (1414.)
5. William Walter, born Nov. 2d, 1850, bap. May 25th, 1854.
6. Mary Emily, born Feb. 18th, 1853, bap. May 25th, 1854.
7. Edward Clarence, born Dec. 2d, 1854, died Aug. 28th, 1855.
8. Clarence, born Feb. 24th, 1857, bap. July 19th, 1857, died Jan. 6th, 1858.
9. Charles Wiard, born June 18th, 1859, bap. Sept. 3d, 1859, died Sept. 24th, 1859.

1040. "MARY C. PEASE," to church April 1st, 1849, by letter from church in Winsted, Ct., born Nov. 15th, 1808, to No. (1036.)

1041. "LUCY J. PEASE," to church April 1st, 1849, by letter from church in Winsted, born April 10th, 1817, at Guilford, Ct., to No. (1036,) dismissed by letter, Feb. 22d, 1861, to South Congregational church in Springfield.

1042. "FANNY BUTLER," to church April 1st, 1849, by letter from church in Plainville, Rev. William Wright, pastor, born April 15th, 1827, in Plainville, to Chester Hart, and his wife Anna (Lowry,) married Nov. 15th, 1848, Charles Butler, son of Henry G., of Wethersfield, and his wife Mary L. (Woodhouse,) born Aug. 8th, 1823; is a jeweler by trade, learned of Churchill & Stanley; his residence is on Lafayette street.

THEIR CHILDREN.

1. Anna Elizabeth, born Oct. 7th, 1849, bap. June, 1850.
2. William Henry, born July 22d, 1855.
3. Mary Aletta, born Oct. 9th, 1860.
4. Fanny Havens, born Aug. 9th, 1865.

1043. "SOPHRONE M. LORD," to church June 3d, 1849, by letter from church in Hartland, Vt., daughter of Warren, and his wife Matilda (Bugbee,) born Feb. 25th, 1819, at Hartford, Vt., married Jan. 12th, 1852, Israel F. Hale, born July 24th, 1818, at Leyden, Mass., to John, and his wife Chloe (Fox.) He died May 6th, 1856. She was dismissed by letter, Sept. 5th, 1852, to South church, where she was received, Nov. 4th, 1852.

THEIR CHILDREN.

1. Maria E., born March 21st, 1853, died Oct. 2d, 1854.
2. Ellen L., born January 5th, 1855, died April 30th, 1857.

1044. "AZUBA BUCKLAND," to church May 5th, 1850, by letter from church in South Windsor, born June 19th, 1796, at East Windsor, to Oliver Clark, and his wife Azubah (Barber,) married Nov. 28th, 1816, Harvey Buckland, born Aug. 22d, 1792, at Willington, to Capt. Jonathan, and his wife Laura (Sadd.) He died May 1st, 1835, aged 41. She now, 1862, resides with her daughter Emeline, of Wapping, and is partially insane; never dismissed from this church. While here she resided in and owned the brick house on Stanley street, near the pond of O. B. North, house on the hill.

THEIR CHILDREN.

1. Oliver Clark, born Jan. 6th, 1820, at Ellington, married Sarah E. Ellsworth.
2. Harvey H., born Feb. 9th, 1822, married Maryette Foster; married second, Chloe A. Rockwell; she died, when he married third, Mary Snow.
3. Emeline F., born Feb. 7th, 1824, married Sept. 10th, 1845, Eli Webster; married second, Henry S. Nevers.
4. Jonathan, born March 1st, 1827, married M. Maria Snow; he died March 5th, 1854, at Broad Brook.

1045. "BENJAMIN F. PIERCE," to church June 30th, 1850, by letter from church at Middlefield, Mass., born Oct. 10th, 1819, at Peru, Mass., to Isaac, and his wife Polly (Webb,) studied at Oberlin, Ohio; learned the joiner's trade; married Oct. 4th, 1842, No. (1046;) was a deacon at Dalton, Mass.; was dismissed from this church to Peru, Mass., by letter, March 9th, 1854. He became a magistrate in that town, and a nine months' volunteer in Co. C, 49th Mass. Reg., and went to Port Hudson and returned safe.

1046. "SAMANTHA L., wife of B. F. Pierce," to church June 30th, 1850, by letter from church in Middlefield, Mass., born Sept. 5th, 1817, to John Sennet, of Blanford, Mass., and his wife Elizabeth (Mitchell,) married Oct. 4th, 1842, No. (1045;) was dismissed by letter, March 9th, 1854, to the church at Peru, Mass, where they now, 1864, reside. They have no children.

1047. "PHILO A. LOOMIS," to church Oct. 20th, 1850, by letter from church in Torringford, Rev. William H. Moore, pastor, born Aug. 4th, 1809 to Allen, and his wife Mary (Reed,) married Oct. 21st, 1835, No. (1048;) resides in Winsted, Ct., a farmer and tallow chandler.

1048. "Mrs. POLLY ANN, wife of Philo A. Loomis," to church Oct. 20th, 1850, by letter from church in Torringford, Ct., born April 18th, 1807, to David Watson, and his wife Ann (Moore.)

THEIR CHILD.

Luther, born Nov. 15th, 1837, died July 9th, 1843, aged 6.

1049. "SAMUEL BANCROFT," to church Nov. 7th, 1850, by letter from church in Plymouth Hollow, Rev. Joseph D. Hull, pastor, born March 30th, 1777, at East, now South Windsor, to Samuel, and his wife Jerusha (Foote,) married May 14th, 1804, Sally Hosmer, daughter of Joseph, and his wife (Prior,) born, Oct. 18th, 1780, at East, now South Windsor. She died Sept. 19th, 1838, at Windsor. He was dismissed by letter, Nov. 2d, 1855, to Fourth church in Hartford, where, 1861, he resided. He died Jan. 11th, 1864, at Hartford, aged 8

THEIR CHILDREN.

1. Jane Jerusha; born Feb. 18th, 1805, died in infancy.
2. Charlotte Sophia, born July 11th, 1806, married Hiram Pierce, of Plymouth.
3. Theodosia Maria, born April 2d, 1808, married Buckley P. Heath, of East Windsor.
4. Samuel, born June 5th, 1810, married Mary Smith, of Berlin.
5. Joseph Hosmer, born Sept. 22d, 1812, married Emily Adams.
6. Harriet, born Jan. 8th, 1815, died , aged 3 years.
7. Horace, born Dec. 4th, 1817, married Fanny Hunt; married second, Lizzie Root.

1050. "WILLIAM J. PIERCE," to church Nov. 7th, 1850, by letter from church in Plymouth Hollow, Ct., born Sept. 14th, 1830, at Plymouth Hollow, Ct., to Hiram, and his wife Charlotte S. (Bancroft.) His first employment in this town was clerk to Bancroft and Ransom; he was a jeweler by trade, and now, 1861, works silver in Hartford; married Dec. 7th, 1851, No. (1006.) He and his wife joined the Second Advent church, when, Dec. 4th, 1856, this church, by vote, withdrew its watch and care.

1051. "ELIZA S., wife of Sidney Smith," to church Dec. 1st, 1850, born April 8th, 1828, to No. (478,) and his second wife, No. (657,) married Sept. 18th, 1850, Sidney Smith, of Plainville, born July 13th, 1827, at Milford, Ct., to Sidney, and Julia Ann (Smith,) his wife; a joiner by trade, and house builder; to church in Milford, 1843; to South church, New Britain, 1847; to Plainville church, May 2d, 1852, where he now, 1863, resides, and is extensively engaged in manufacturing. She was dismissed by letter, 1852, to Plainville. He is now, 1867, in Leavenworth, Kansas, with his family, engaged in merchandize.

THEIR CHILDREN.

1. Walter Sidney, born Sept. 7th, 1851.
2. Alfred Andrews, born Oct. 16th, 1857.

1052. "EDWIN N. ANDREWS," to church Dec. 1st, 1850, born Sept. 1st, 1832, to No. (478,) and his second wife, No. (657;) graduated at Amherst College, 1861; now, 1862, in "Union Theological Seminary," New York city, and excels in music. He preached his first sermon at New Britain First church, Aug. 9th, 1863, and was ordained to the ministry at New Britain, Jan. 5th, 1864; commissioned as chaplain to 2d

Cavalry Reg. of N. J., Dec. 6th, 1863, by the governor of that state. He did service as chaplain to that regiment, at and near Memphis, Tenn., until Jan. 16th, 1865, when he resigned; 1867, in Kansas.

1053. "SUSAN R. PECK," to church Dec. 1st, 1850, baptized same time, born May 11th, 1835, at Pompey, N. Y., to Nehemiah, and his first wife, No. (950.) She died Oct. 15th, 1853, aged 18, greatly lamented.

1054. "JAMES G. PECK," to church Dec. 1st, 1850, bap. same time, born May 28th, 1831, at Pompey, N. Y., to Nehemiah, and his first wife, No. (950;) is a farmer; married Dec. 14th, 1854, No. (1067;) both were dismissed by letter to church in Ottawa, Ill., June 8th, 1856; they now, 1861, reside in Durant, Cedar county, Iowa, but received back by letter, May 3d, 1863.

THEIR CHILDREN.

1. Charles Scovill, born Oct. 19th, 1855, at Farmington, died Aug. 22d, 1861, at Durant, Iowa.
2. Martha Elizabeth, born March 17th, 1858, at Farmington.
3. James Stanley, born June 6th, 1864, at New Britain, bap. June 11th, 1865.
4. Frederick Whittlesey, born Oct. 28th, 1866, at New Britain, bap. Oct. 27th, 1867.

1055. "EMMA M., wife of Samuel G. Merriman," to church Feb. 7th, 1851, by letter from College Street church, New Haven, Rev. Edward Strong, pastor, born Aug. 18th, 1811, in Southington, to Capt. Anson Mathews, and his wife Lydia (Montague,) of Simsbury, married Sept. 23d, 1833, Frederick Smith, son of Orris, of Meriden, and his wife Azura (Douglas.) He was a carriage maker, and died June 8th, 1846, at New Haven, when she married, second, Feb. 22d, 1849, Samuel Green Merriman, of Southington, son of Olcott, and his wife Sophrone (Hitchcock,) born Dec. 10th, 1809, married Oct. 2d, 1831, Jane Frost, born Aug. 8th, 1809, to Daniel C., of Waterbury, and his wife Lorinda (Johnson;) she died May 10th, 1848, when Mr. Meriman married as above. His residence is on Prospect street, has been state senator for the First district of Connecticut. He is a jeweler by trade.

HIS SONS BY FIRST WIFE, JANE.

1. John Franklin, born Jan. 20th, 1837.
2. Homer Frederick, born Nov. 11th, 1841.

HER CHILDREN BY FIRST HUSBAND, SMITH.

1. Annis, born , died young.
2. Annis Maria, born Jan. 18th, 1839, married May 27th, 1862, Theodore Eugene Welch, of Middletown, Orange county, N. Y., live in Newton, Essex county, N. J.

1056. "ELIZA H.," wife of Sylvanus Stone," to Church April 3d, 1851, by letter from church in Henrietta, N. Y., Rev. S. W. Streeter, pastor, born March 30th, 1810, to Silas Holcomb, of Granby, and Lucy (Gillette,) his wife, married Jan. 6th, 1850, No. (776.)

1057. "Mrs. Nabby A. Woodruff," to church April 3d, 1851, by letter from Congregational church at West Avon, Ct., Rev. Joel Grant, pastor, daughter of Joel Sperry, sen., of Avon, and his wife Abigail (Wheeler,) born Feb. 5th, 1785, married Nov. 1st, 1804, Micah Woodruff, son of Micah, sen., and his wife Betsey (Curtiss.) He died March 29th, 1849, at Avon. She was dismissed by letter to First Congregational church in Waterbury, Aug. 19th, 1859. She died Jan. 18th, 1864, aged 79, at Waterbury, and buried at West Avon.

THEIR CHILDREN.

1. Truman, born Aug. 29th, 1805, married Mary Benton, live in Wisconsin.
2. Elmina, born Sept. 27th, 1809, married Orrin Brainard of Wisconsin.
3. Micah Curtiss, born Sept. 2d, 1813, died, aged two years.
4. Ursula Ann, born Sept. 3d, 1816, lives, 1861, at Cincinnati,
5. Caroline M., } twins, born April 9th, 1819, { see No. (1058.)
6. Catharine, } twins, born April 9th, 1819, { m. Wm. H. Hess, of Waterbury, Ct.

1058. "Mrs. Caroline Kelsey," to church Dec. 1st, 1850, by letter from church in Worthington, Rev. W. W. Woodworth, pastor, born April 9th, 1819, at Avon, to Micah Woodruff, and his wife No. (1057,) married Sept. 18th, 1842, Enoch Kelsey, son of David, and Lovisa (Hastings,) his first wife, born Dec. 28th, 1818; they live at south end of East street, at the ancient home of Robert Booth, and use the same well.

THEIR CHILDREN.

1. Truman Curtiss, born Jan. 29th, 1846.
2. Charles Enoch, born Oct. 8th, 1849.
3. Frank Woodruff, born Nov. 10th, 1852, bap. Jan. 5th, 1862, by Rev. L. Perrin.

1059. "Israel S. Wells," to church June 5th, 1851, by letter from Church in Wethersfield, Dr. Tucker, pastor, born Nov. 14th, 1822, at Wethersfield, to Rositer, and his wife Emily (Butler,) married April 11th, 1849, No. (1020,) his trade, brick mason; residence, on Seymour street, but spring of 1852, exchanged his place for a farm in Winsted, Ct., where they reside; dismissed and recommended there, June 13th, 1862.

THEIR CHILDREN.

1. Ella Louisa, born April 15th, 1852. bap. Oct. 3d, 1852.
2. Herbert Smith, born June 3d, 1856, bap. Oct. 27th, 1856.

1060. "James Glendinning," to church July, 1851, by letter from Berlin, Rev. W. W. Woodworth, pastor; to that church April 5th, 1850, by letter; dismissed by letter, Oct. 31st, 1856, to church in Plymouth; is a tailor by trade.

1061. "Omri M. North," to church July, 1851, by letter from First church in Farmington, Rev. Dr. Porter, pastor, born Feb. 25th, 1802, to Ira, and his wife Viana (Monroe,) married, 1823, Emma Woodruff, daughter of Sylvanus, who died 1826, aged 24; he married second, Feb. 9th, 1829, (No. 1062.) His residence is on Stanley street, north end; grandson of Daniel, of Daniel, of Thomas, of. Samuel, of John, the first settler. He is a farmer; was to Farmington church June 5th, 1829, and baptized same time.

1062. "CYBELIA, wife of Omri M. North," to church July, 1851, by letter from first church in Farmington, to that church June 7th, 1829; born July 11th, 1806, at Farmington, to George Norton and Almira (Gillett,) married Feb. 9th, 1829, No. (1061.)

THEIR CHILDREN.

1. Son, born and died in infancy.
2. Lucius James, born Nov. 28th, 1829, bap. May 2d, 1830, at Farmington; see No. (1063.)
3. John C., born Oct. 10th, 1831, see No. (1064.)
4. Albert, born 1841, died in infancy.

1063. "LUCIUS J. NORTH," to church July, 1851, by letter from the first church in Farmington; born Nov. 28th, 1829, to No. (1061;) married, Oct. 5th, 1853, Lovisa Maria Parsons, daughter of Benjamin P. Parsons and his wife Lovisa (Parker;) born Oct. 14th, 1834, at Enfield, Ct.,; he to church in Farmington Aug. 6th, 1843; he lives, 1863, with his father, north end of Stanley st., at the old home of Abel Clark.

1064. "JOHN C. NORTH," to church July, 1851, by letter from the Congregational church in Farmington, to that church Aug. 6th, 1843; born Oct. 10th, 1831, to No. (1061,) married, Oct. 15th, 1861, Harriet B. Olmsted, daughter of Ashbel, of East Hartford; he spent some years in Wisconsin and Illinois, but in 1861 enlisted as wagoner in the army, and went to Ship Island, New Orleans, and Port Hudson; he re-enlisted in 1864, and went to Va.; 1867, resides in Hartford.

THEIR CHILDREN.

1. Alice Belden, born Aug. 27th, 1864, bap. April 16th, 1865.
2. Frederic Benedict, born Aug. 14th, 1866, bap. Oct. 27th, 1867.

1065. "JAMES B. MERWIN," to church July, 1851, by letter from South church, New Britain, Rev. Samuel Rockwell, pastor; to that church 1847; born May 22d, 1829, at Cairo, Green Co., N. Y., to Joseph Ruggles Merwin, of Milford, Ct., and his wife Emily (Parker,) of Coventryville, N. Y.; he a jeweller by trade, learned of Warner & Lewis, New Britain; married, Oct. 17th, 1850, No. (946,) been for several years editor of various journals, and lecturer on temperance and education, especially in Ill. and Mich.; dismissed by letter to first Congregational church Chicago, Oct. 13th, 1854; his full name James Burtis Merwin; he was appointed, Sept. 12th, 1861, chaplain at large to the U. S. army, by President Lincoln, on condition that he should be ordained; he was ordained at Adrian, Mich., Sept. , 1861; he spent 1861 and 1862 at Washington, and in the Army of the Potomac, but in 1862–3 at City Hospital, Brooklyn, N. Y., and May, 1863, was appointed "visiting chaplain" to all the hospitals in the Department of the East, viz., N. J., N. Y. and New England; he is now, 1867, located at St. Louis, Mo.

1066. "HENRY WALTER," to church Aug. 1851, born June 23d, 1812, at London, Eng., to William and his wife Jane (Thomas;) married, March 1843, Laura Julia Hine, of New Milford, daughter of Anan, and Almira (Marsh,) his wife; born March 1815, and died March 31st, 1845; he second married, Feb. 28th, 1848, No. (933;) she died, when third he married, Dec. 16th, 1856, No. (1266;) he is an extensive manufacturer of hardware; residence on Stanley st., near Smalley street.

HIS CHILD BY FIRST WIFE, LAURA.

1. Anan Hine, born Jan. 18th, 1845, see No. (1241.)

HIS CHILDREN BY SECOND WIFE, AMELIA.

2. Henry Stanley, born Dec. 16th, 1848, bap. April 6th, 1849, see No. (1340.)
3. Edward North, born Feb. 3d, 1852, bap. July 4th, 1852, died Aug. 25th, 1852.

HIS CHILDREN BY THIRD WIFE, ANNA.

4. Anna Clary, born July 5th, 1859, bap. June 3d, 1860.
5. Eliza Farrar, born May 31st, 1861, bap. March 30th, 1862.

1067. "REBECCA CLARK," to church Aug. 1851, born Feb. 8th, 1832, to No. (679) and his wife No. (585;) baptized, July 8th, 1832, Rebecca Smalley; married, Dec. 14th, 1854, No. (1054;) dismissed by letter June 8th, 1856, to church in Ottawa, Ill., residing now, 1861, in Durant, Cedar Co., Iowa, but both received back by letter May 3d, 1863.

1068. "ROSWELL HAWLEY, M. D." to church Oct. 4th, 1851, by letter from the church in South Glastenbury, Rev. F. W. Chapman, pastor; born July 30th, 1813, at Farmington, to Asa and his wife Diademia (Root;) received his degree of M. D. at Medical Department, Yale College, New Haven, in 1842; married, June 8th, 1842, No. (1069;) she died, when second he married, Sept. 13th, 1853, No. (1100;) during his medical practice in Glastenbury, he was appointed deacon of that church, and sup't of their S. School, and likewise in this place he was sup't of the State Reform School, at Meriden, and was dismissed by letter Aug. 10th, 1855, to the church in West Meriden; he subsequently removed to Bristol, where now, 1864, he resides as practicing physician.

HIS CHILDREN BY FIRST WIFE MARY.

1. Gertrude M., born June 5th, 1843, married, May, 1865, O. B. Ives, of Bristol.
2. Emma R. born Sept. 10th, 1844.
3. Bertha A., born March 23d, 1846.
4. Francis R., born Dec. 21st, 1847, died May 31st, 1849.
5. Alice F., born Feb. 14th, 1850.

CHILDREN BY HIS SECOND WIFE, JANE.

6. William R., born Feb. 20th, 1855.
7. Helen E., born June 9th, 1858.
8. Joseph R., born March 29th, 1860.

1069. "MARY, wife of Roswell Hawley, M. D.," to church Oct. 4th, 1851, by letter from church in South Glastenbury, born Jan. 15th, 1820, to Benjamin R. Crane and his wife Bertha (Dunham;) married, June 8th, 1842, No. (1068;) she died July 13th, 1852, aged 32, at New Britain.

1070. "EDWIN WHITNEY," to church Oct. 4th, 1851, born March 8th, 1829, to Ebenezer and his wife No. (1101;) is a teacher; married, Oct. 31st, 1860, Minerva Barrows, daughter of Dea. Salmon and Sally (Dimmick,) his wife; born Sept. 10th, 1830, at Mansfield, Ct.; he graduated at the Connecticut Normal School, Oct. 9th, 1856; dismissed by letter, Dec. 26th, 1856, to church in New London, and in 1862 was Assistant Superintendent and principal teacher of the Reform School at Providence, R. I.; he gave his place in Mansfield worth some $15,000 for the benefit of the "Soldiers' Orphans' Home," and was the Superintendent of the same when he d. Aug. 26th, 1867, in his 39th year, greatly lamented. We are glad to hear that his life was insured for $10,000 for the benefit of his wife and child.

1071. "EDWIN A. WOODFORD," to church March 28th, 1852, by letter from Congregational church in West Avon, Rev. Joel Grant, pastor; born April 22d, 1825, at Avon, to Romanta and his wife Betsey (Hart;) married, 1847, Martha Clemens, of Huntington, daughter of Almon and his wife Huldah; he is a jeweller by trade; dismissed by letter, June 25th, 1858, to Methodist Episcopal church, New Britain; now, 1861, resides in Danbury, Ct.

THEIR CHILDREN.

1. George A. born April 18th, 1851, at New Britain.
2. Nellie M., born Nov. 12th, 1855, at New Britain.

1072. "MRS. AURELIA, wife of Wm. B. Jones," to church April 18th, 1852, by letter from Congregational church in Wolcottville, Rev. S. T. Seeley, pastor; her maiden name was Morse, daughter of Levi, born Oct. 9th, 1806, in Pa.; married, Aug. 6th, 1826, Lewis Perkins, of Litchfield, he died Feb. 10th, 1837, at Harlengen, N. J., when she second married May 6th, 1839, Wm. Bradley Jones, son of Diodate and his wife Mary (Smith;) born Nov. 23d, 1804, at East Haddam; married, Dec. 24th, 1826, Caroline Start; she died Aug. 28th, 1835, when second he married, May 6th, 1839, No. (1072.)

HER CHILDREN BY FIRST HUSBAND, PERKINS.

1. Russell Lewis, born May 14th, 1827, married Sept. 6th, 1849, see No. (827.)
2. Sanford Hervey, born Dec. 10th, 1829, married Adeline M. Barbour, of Wolcottville, Sept. 1851; lives there, but in 1861 was Captain of Co. I, 4th Regt. C. V., since promoted to be Lieut. Col. of the 14th Regt. C. V.

HER CHILDREN BY JONES, HER SECOND HUSBAND.

1. Devereaux, born July 8th, 1841, at Harlengen, N. J., see No. (1217.)
2. Aurelia Melvina, born Nov. 5th, 1844, at Wolcottville.
3. Edgar Bradley, born Nov. 1st, 1846; volunteer in Co. E, 14th Regt.
4. Clarence Olmsted, born April 21st, 1850.

HIS CHILDREN BY FIRST WIFE CAROLINE.

1. Wm. Albert, born June 16th, 1830, married Caroline E. Wilson, lived at Walnut Grove, Ill., 1861.
2. Mary Caroline, born May 19th, 1835, married John Morse, live in Willimantic.

1073. "Mrs. Mary Ann Newel," to church May 30th, 1852, by letter from the Congregational church in East Windsor; born Sept. 14th, 1827, at East Windsor, to John Sadd and his wife Emeline (Clark;) married, April 8th, 1851, John A. Newel, born July 5th, 1825, at Hebron, to Alvah and his wife Laura (Loomis;) is a joiner by trade; she dismissed by letter, June 26th, 1857, to Sun Prairie, Wis.; the family now, 1862, live at Cottage Grove, Wis.

THEIR CHILDREN.

1. James Alvah, born March 7th, 1852, at New Britain, died March 24th, 1852.
2. Ada Henrietta, born Dec. 15th, 1853, bap. March 3d, 1856, at New Britain.
3. Charles Edward, born Sept. 17th, 1855, bap. March 3d, 1856, at "
4. Carrie Elizabeth, born March 24th, 1858, at Sun Prairie, Wis.
5. Albert Frederic, born Oct. 26th, 1859, at Cottage Grove, Wis.
6. Mary Edna, born May 16th, 1861, at Cottage Grove, Wis.

1074. "Mary E., wife of Frederic Knapp," to church May 30th, 1852, by letter from Roxbury, Ct., Rev. Austin Isham, pastor; born July 10th, 1826, at Roxbury, to Daniel F. Burritt and his wife Betsey (Morris;) married, April 22d, 1848, No. (1163.)

1075. "Mrs. Lydia, wife of Nehemiah Peck," to church June 3d, 1852, by letter from the first Congregational church in Plymouth, Rev. I. P. Warren, pastor; born Sept. 16th, 1797, at Burlington, to Abel Frisbie and his wife Ruth (Barnes,) who was sister of Thomas, of Bristol; she was the widow of Willys Roberts, when, Jan. 22d, 1851, she married Nehemiah Peck, and was his second wife; she was dismissed by letter, April 2d, 1858, to church in East Haven, where she died May 16th, 1860, aged 63.

1076. "Mrs. Laura, wife of Henry W. Andrews," to church June 3d, 1852, by letter from church in Berlin, Rev. W. W. Woodworth, pastor;

her maiden name was Rich, daughter of John of Middletown, and his wife Charlotte (Stow,) of Cromwell; born Oct. 10th, 1820, at Westfield Society, Middletown; married, Nov. 29th, 1843, Henry Woodruff Andrews, son of No. (359;) he a jeweller by trade, born April 10th, 1819, baptized Aug. 29th, 1819.

THEIR SON.

Louis LeGrand, born April 29th, 1846.

1077. "Matilda Philips," to church Oct. 3d, 1852, daughter of Richard, and sister of No. (1078;) this family were Protestant Irish; the father died June 5th, 1851, aged 49, also his son, aged 19, May 18th, 1851.

1078. "Eliza Philips," to church Oct. 3d, 1852, daughter of Richard, and sister of No. (1077;) on the death of the father and brother, this family was broken up, and these sisters it is said went to New York, but there is no record of taking letters.

1079. "Sylvender Ellis," to church Oct. 3d, 1852, by letter from Congregational church in Somers, Ct., Rev. Joseph Vaill, pastor; born Sept. 18th, 1817, to No. (717;) married, April 27th, 1842, No. (1080;) is a joiner by trade and occupation, and is a skillful architect; learned of Elnathan Peck; his residence on Chestnut st; he to church in Somers, 1842.

1080. Mrs. Lovisa, wife of Sylvender Ellis," to church Oct. 3, 1852, by letter from Congregational church in Somers, Ct., Rev. Joseph Vaill, pastor; to church there 1845, born June 9th, 1816, at Enfield, to Seth Alden and his wife Peony (Bement;) married, April 27th, 1842, No. (1079.)

THEIR CHILDREN.

1. William Henry, born Nov. 10th, 1843, bap. at Somers.
2. Marion Roselle, born Aug. 1st, 1848, bap. at Somers.

1081. "George L. Smith," to church Feb. 6th, 1853, baptized same time; born Aug. 7th, 1832, at Lisbon, Ct., to Dr. Levi H. and his wife Josephine (Frink;) married, Oct. 4th, 1855, Sophia Burton, daughter of Joseph and his wife Laura (Goodnow;) born Dec. 18th, 1828, at Rome, Mass.; they live now, 1863, at Plainville, Ct.; is brother of No. (1136;) he left our communion for spiritualism, and was excommunicated April 18th, 1865.

THEIR CHILDREN.

1. Burton Frink, born Jan. 7th, 1858.
2. Irving Burleigh, born Oct. 10th, 1860.

1082. "Mrs Phebe McLean," her name first appears on Rev. Mr. Seward's record, 1840, as being dismissed, but his record never tells to what place or church; her name next appears as joining this church by letter from South church Aug. 5th, 1855; she was born Jan. 13th, 1811, at Windham, to Stephen Congdon and his wife Martha (Peckham;) married, June 22d, 1835, Silas Oscar McLean; born Jan. 29th, 1812, to Silas of Glastenbury, and his wife Anna (Pulsifer;) he died Jan. 3d, 1841, at Glastenbury; her residence on Chestnut st., in 1862.

THEIR CHILDREN.

1. Charles Oscar, born March 24th, 1836, bap. 1836, see No. (1175.)
2. George Gorham, born Sept. 21st, 1838, see No. (1174.)

1083. "JOHN E. WHITTLESEY," to church March 1853, by letter from Congregational church in Bethel, Ct.; born Dec. 21st, 1835, to No. (611) and his wife No. (883;) became a teacher, married, March 30th, 1857, Lydia Francis Camp, of Newington, daughter of Col. Joseph and his wife Lydia (Francis;) born March 12th, 1837; he dismissed by letter March 1857, to church in Morris, Ill; was a volunteer in the 13th Reg't of Wisconsin, went to Kansas, was honorably discharged, and is now, 1863, in Janesville, Wis.

THEIR CHILD.

Joseph Camp, born Dec. 24th, 1858, at Durant, Iowa.

1084. "MARY ANN WARD," to church March, 1853, by letter from church in Bethel, Ct.; born July 27th, 1836, at Trumbull, Ct., to Victor and his wife Eliza (Hamlinton;) married, Sept. 23d, 1857, to Isaac B. Smith; born April 7th, 1835, to Wm. C., of Millburn, N. J.; she returned to Bethel, but no record of being dismissed by letter; they are, 1863, residing in Bridgeport.

THEIR CHILD.

Helen A., born Sept. 10th, 1858, at Millburn, N. J.

1085. "ANN R. HOTCHKISS," to church March, 1853, by letter from church in Plainville, Rev. J. L. Dickinson, pastor; born Jan. 16th, 1834, to Alvin, of Kensington, and his second wife No. (1094;) married, Oct., 1856, Harvey Foster, born Sept. 15th, 1828, to Zachariah, of Granby, Ct., and his wife Maria A. (Goddard;) jeweller by trade, learned of Horace Goodwin, of Hartford; lived in 1861 at Meriden; she died July, 1865, at Meriden.

THEIR CHILDREN.

1. Willie, born Sept. 10th, 1858, at New Britain.
2. Frank, born July 17th, 1860, at Meriden.

1086. "MRS. SARAH A., wife of Daniel Sloper," to church Mar., 1853, by letter from church in South Glastenbury, Rev. F. W. Chapin, pastor; born Nov. 27th, 1829, to Daniel Hale and his wife Sarah (Tryon,) of

Glastenbury; married, March 10th, 1851; he son of Daniel, of Southington, and his wife Rebecca (Wilcox,) of Middletown; born May, 1827, was a joiner by trade, residence on Summer st.; he died Jan. 12th, 1856, aged 28, when second she married, June 5th, 1860, Aaron Butrick, son of Samuel and his wife Margaret (Caldwell;) born Feb. 23d, 1825, at Pelham, N. H.; their residence on Summer st.; he works in brass and iron.

CHILD BY SECOND HUSBAND.

Charles Aaron, born July 20th, 1864, at New Haven.

1087. "EBENEZER D. BASSETT," to church April 3d, 1853, born Oct. 16th, 1833, at Litchfield, Ct., to Ebenezer T. and his wife Susan (Gregory;) graduated at Connecticut Normal School, Sept., 1853, and is now, 1863, principal and teacher of the high school for colored youth, in Philadelphia; he married, Oct. 16th, 1855, Eliza Park, of New Haven; he was dismissed by letter, Oct. 27th, 1854, to Temple st. church, at New Haven.

THEIR CHILDREN.

1. Charlotte, born July 21st, 1856.
2. Ebenezer D., jun., born May 21st, 1858.

1088. "MRS. MARY F., wife of Wm. Humphrey," to church April 3d, 1853, by letter from South church, New Britain, Rev. Samuel Rockwell, pastor; daughter of Robert Francis, of Newington, and his wife Mary (Toby;) born Nov. 2d, 1820, at Newington, married, Oct. 18th, 1843, John W. Humphrey, son of John Wells Humphrey, of Wethersfield, and his wife Rebecca (Richardson;) born March 14th, 1820, at Wethersfield, is now, 1862, a hotel keeper at Freeport, Ill.; she was dismissed by letter March 16th, 1858, to Second Presbyterian church, Chicago, Ill.; he built the Humphrey House, of New Britain, A. D. 1850, at a cost of $20,000.

THEIR CHILDREN.

1. Mary Elizabeth, born Oct. 19th, 1844.
2. John William, born Dec. 5th, 1846.
3. Martha Ann, born March 11th, 1849.

1089. "MRS. FANNY PETTIBONE," to church April 3d, 1853, by letter from the First Congregational church, Rockville, Ct.; daughter of Noah A. Phelps, of Simsbury, and his wife Charlotte (Wilcox;) born March 8th, 1795; she became first the wife then the widow of Capt. Jonathan Pettibone, of Simsbury, came to this place with her daughter, Mrs. Winslow, was dismissed by letter, Aug. 13th, 1858, to the church in Great Barrington, Mass.

1090. "MRS. CHARLOTTE H., wife of Rev. Horace Winslow," to church April 3d, 1853, by letter from church in Rockville, Ct.; daughter of Capt. Jonathan Pettibone, of Simsbury, and his wife No. (1089;) born July 23d, 1824, at Simsbury, married May 8th, 1850; he son of John H. Winslow, of Enfield, Mass., and his wife Elizabeth (Mills;) born May 18th, 1814, at Enfield, Mass., graduated at Hamilton College, N. Y., studied theology at Union Seminary, N. Y. city; settled first at Lansingburg, N. Y., second installed at Rockville, Ct., third at New Britain, First church, fourth at Great Barrington, Mass., to which church she was dismissed by letter, Aug. 13th, 1858, and fifth, he was settled at Binghampton, N. Y.

THEIR CHILDREN.

1. Fanny Henrietta, born Oct. 25th, 1851, at Rockville, and bap. there.
2. Lillian, born July 25th, 1854, at New Britain, and bap. June 24th, 1855.
3. Mary, born 1861, at Great Barrington.

1091. "FREDERICK O. ROBBINS," to church June 5th, 1853, born Jan. 14th, 1835, at Rocky Hill, Ct., to Deacon Jehiel and his wife Nancy (Fuller;) he learned jeweller's trade of Churchill & Stanley, and married, April, 1859, Christiana Twiss, of Meriden, daughter of Hiram and his wife (Andrews;) he left our communion for that of the Spiritualists, and has, 1861, received no letter of dismission; has lived in Plainville, with his father, but now, 1861, living at Hamington, Atlantic Co., N. J.; he was excommunicated by vote of the church, April 18th, 1865.

1092. "CATHARINE O. WRIGHT," to church June 5th, 1853, baptized same time; born Feb. 15th, 1830, to Silas Wright and his wife Catharine G. (Eddy,) daughter of William, she married Oct. 19th, 1853, George Tolles, son of Orris, of Plymouth, but now, 1861, of this place and his wife Hannah (Jordon;) born Jan. 30th, 1820, at Waterbury, Conn.; he is a machinist.

THEIR CHILDREN.

1. Estella, born March 20th, 1857.
2. Jennie Alena, born March 2d, 1862.

1093. "MRS. HARRIET, wife of Levi S. Wells," to church June 5th, 1853, and baptized same time; born Nov. 5th, 1824, at Newington, to Robert Francis and his wife Mary (Toby;) married April 27th, 1848, No. (942;) she is sister to No. (1088.)

1094. "MRS. MARY P. HOTCHKISS," to church June 5th, 1853, baptized same time: born July 18th, 1798, at Deerfield, Mass., to George Vincent Roberts; he an English emigrant; she married Aug. 24th, 1825, Alvin Hotchkiss, of Kensington; born May 1st, 1788, son of Ladwick and his wife No. (278,) and was his second wife, his first being Sally (Williams,) of Kensington, whom he married Jan. 31st, 1810, and who died Oct. 5th, 1824. The subject of this notice died Sept. 21st, 1854, aged 56; he died Sept. 11th, 1863, aged 75.

HER CHILDREN BY ALVIN HOTCHKISS.

1. Mary Caroline, born Aug. 12th, 1827.
2. Seth Wm. born Jan. 9th, 1829.
3. Frederick Williams, born Dec, 29th, 1830.
4. Ann Roberts, born Jan. 16th, 1834, see No. (1085.)

1095. "EBENEZER WHITNEY," to church June 5th, 1853, baptized same time; born May 16th, 1818, to Ebenezer, of Worcester, Mass., and No. (1101,) his wife; married Jan. 1st, 1843, Lucinda Brown, of Mansfield, Conn., daughter of Washington and his wife Lovisa (Brown,) being cousins; she died Jan. 25th, 1853. Mr Whitney acted as chorister in our choir, several years with good success; he also led in singing in our State Reform School, at Meriden, but now, 1861, is connected with the Reform School, Providence, R. I. He was dismissed by letter Nov. 25th, 1859, to the Central Congregational church, of Providence, R. I.

THEIR CHILD.

George Henry, born Aug., 1846, died Oct. 9th, 1847, aged 14 months.

1096. "GEORGE F. WARREN," to church Aug. 7th, 1853; born June 1st, 1830, at Bethany, Conn., to Isaac and his wife Leonora (Perkins,) learned the jewellers' trade in New Britain; married Aug. 24th, 1853, No. (1018,) was dismissed and recommended by letter Jan. 6th, 1854, to church in Ottawa, Ill. He follows farming, but 1861, enlisted into 4th regiment Ill., Cavalry, was of the body guard of Gen. Grant, was at the taking of Forts Henry and Donelson, Tenn., but 1864, is 1st Lieut. of 1st Colored Cavalry, of Miss.

THEIR CHILDREN.

1. Arthur Stanley, born June 4th, 1854, in Ill.
2. Wm. Edward, born April 25th, 1856, in Ill., died Oct. 24th, 1863, aged 7½ years.
3. George Frederic, born March 29th, 1858, in Ill., died Nov. 21st, 1863, aged 5½ "
4. Lizzie May, born April 19th, 1860, in Ill.
5. Henry Grant, born Feb. 23d, 1862, " "

1097. "CHARLES H. BELDEN," to church Aug. 7th, 1853; born Feb. 19th, 1837, to No. (955,) and his 2d wife No. (495;) spent one year in California; but 1861 enlisted as volunteer in Capt. Tisdale's company, 13th regiment Conn., Volunteers. He married May 9th, 1867, Paulina M. Carney, of N. Y.

1098. "WM. W. CLARK," to church, Aug. 7th, 1853; born March 19th, 1834, to No. (679;) married March, 19th, 1857, Mary J. Stoddard of Newington; born April 30th, 1834, to Hiram and his wife Fanny, (Filley.) He was dismissed by letter, March 1857, to church in Durant, Iowa, where he is engaged in farming, but 1862, is a Commissary Serg't in 6th regiment of Iowa Cavalry, and gone to fight belligerent Indians, and was at the battle of White Stone Hills.

THEIR CHILDREN.

1. Mary Francis, born Jan. 12th, 1858, at Durant, Iowa.
2. Wm. Hudson, born Aug. 26th, 1860, " "

1099. "MRS. MARY KEENEY," to church Dec. 4th, 1853, by letter from Vernon, Conn.; born Dec. 4th, 1817, to Erastus McCollum and his wife Lydia (Corning;) married Aug. 1840, Hart Keeney, son of Allen and his wife Betsey (Skinner;) born April, 1819, died April 7th, 1852, aged 33, at New Britain, his residence on Washington Street.

THEIR CHILDREN.

1. Fidella, born Nov. 22d, 1842, died Nov. 10th, 1865, at Roxbury, Mass., aged 23, buried at New Britain.
2. Hart J. born Jan. 27th, 1852.

1100. "MRS. JANE, wife of Dr. Roswell Hawley," to church Dec. 4th, 1853, by letter from church in Bristol; born Jan. 24th, 1823, at Bristol, to Wm. Rich and his wife Betsey (Webster;) married Sept. 13th, 1853, No. (1068,) and was his second wife. They were dismissed by letter, Aug. 10th, 1855, to the church in West Meriden; living now, 1861, in her native town, Bristol.

1101. "MRS. ANNIS WHITNEY," to church Dec. 4th, 1853, by letter from church in Stafford, Conn.; born Aug. 22d, 1791, at Webster, Mass., to Elijah Kingsbury and Hannah (Kingsbury,) cousins to his wife; she married March 9th, 1813, Ebenezer Whitney; born May 23d, 1788, died May 15th, 1843, aged 55, son of Ebenezer and Martha (Gates,) his wife. She was dismissed by letter, March 13th, 1860, to church at Independence, Iowa.

THEIR CHILDREN.

1. Martha Gates, born May 22d, 1814, died Sept. 19th, 1835.
2. Henry, born May 23d, 1816.
3. Ebenezer, born May 16th, 1818, see No. (1095.)
4. John Gates, born Aug. 10th, 1820, at Millbury, Mass., married No. (1107.)
5. Prudence Ann, born Jan. 28th, 1824, died July 25th, 1839.
6. Asa Waters, born July 8th, 1826.
7. Edwin, born March 8th, 1829, see No. (1070.)
8. Mary Elizabeth, born Jan. 14th, 1833, died Sept. 5th, 1835.

1102. "MISS JULIA ANN BLIN," to church Jan. 1854, by letter from church in Wethersfield, Dr. Tucker, Pastor; born Feb. 12th, 1817, at Wethersfield, to Capt. Hosea and his wife Mehitabel (Wolcott;) married Feb. 20th, 1855, No. (918,) and was his second wife.

1103. "CORNELIUS ANDREWS," to church April 8th, 1854; born Nov. 1st, 1834, to No. (478,) and his second wife, No. (657;) occupied farming at his father's home on West Main Street, two miles from the village; married June 25th, 1862. No. (1380.)

THEIR CHILD.

Mary Lincoln, born April 14th, 1865, (same night President Lincoln was assasinated,) bap. June 10th, 1866.

1104. "ALDEN A. BAKER," to church April 8th, 1854, baptized same time; born July 26th, 1835, at Montville, to Abishar and his wife Mary G. (Butler;) taught school here, the time he united with the church; has been since in the Map business; was dismissed by letter March, 1859, to church in Colchester, Conn.

1105. "ELLEN M. STANLEY," to church April 8th, 1854; born April 1st, 1834, to No. (921;) married Nov. 3d, 1858, No. (1143;) she is a sweet singer and a member of our church choir, now, 1862, and has been for several years.

1106. "CAROLINE E. SOUTHWORTH," to church April 8th, 1854, baptized same time; born June 24th, 1823, at Chester, Conn., to No. (923,) and his first wife Lucinda (Ely;) has been sorely afflicted with rheumatic affection.

1107. "MRS. ANN E. WHITNEY, wife of John," to church April 8th, 1854; born April 21st, 1826, at Guilford, Conn., to John F. Woodruff and his wife Catharine (Wheaton;) married May, 1847, John Gates Whitney, son of Ebinezer and his wife No. (1101;) born Aug. 10th, 1820, at Milbury, Mass., was a "hardware" manufacturer, in this town; she was dismissed by letter March 13th, 1860, to church at Independence, Iowa, where the family reside, 1861.

THEIR CHILDREN.

1. Mary Eunice, born March 25th, 1849.
2. Edwin North, born Feb. 18th, 1852.
3. Charles E. born Nov. 4th, 1857.
4. George North, born May 13th, 1859.

1108. "EMILY ANN JEROME," to church April 8th, 1854; born Dec. 17th, 1834, at Cornwall, Conn., to No. (1030;) married Sept. 19th, 1854, No. (1236.)

1109. "B. N. COMINGS, M. D." to church April 8th, 1854, by letter from Rockville, Conn., Rev. J. W. Ray, Pastor; his full name Benjamin Newton; born Nov. 2d, 1816, at Cornish, New Hampshire, to Benjamin and his wife Althea (Wellman,) graduate at Dartmouth College, 1842, title, M. D., conferred at Castleton, Vt., 1845; married July 2d, 1847, No. (1110,) is a practicing physician in this town, 1861, residence near the Center church; gives lectures to the State Normal School; has published some works on Physiology, is now, 1862, surgeon to 13th regiment Conn. Volunteers; went to Ship Island and New Orleans, where he is appointed Surgeon General of that department.

1110. "Mrs. Maria, wife of Dr. B. N. Comings," to church April 8th, 1854, by letter from church in Rockville; born April 27th, 1812, in New Jersey, to John Righter and his wife Locky (Stiles;) married July 2d, 1847, No. (1109.)

THEIR CHILDREN.

1. John Righter, born Aug. 5th, 1849, died March 20th, 1855, at New Britain.
2. Willie Righter, } twins, born March 24th, 1852, } see No. (1411.)
3. Emma Shugard, }

1111. "Mrs Louisa, wife of Rev. Wm. Whittlesey," to church April 8th, 1854, by letter from Chapel Street church, New Haven, Rev. Mr. Eustis, Pastor; born Sept. 10th, 1822, at Lyme, Conn., to John Hart and his wife Nancy (Mather;) married Sept. 9th, 1845, No. (541.)

1112. "Esther Henry," to church May 28th, 1854; born Jan. 8th, 1840, at to Edward F. Henry and his wife Eliza A. (Stearns;) she was dismissed by letter, June 6th, 1857, to Pearl Street church, Hartford; she now, 1861, resides in that city.

1113. "Hellen M. Booth," to church May 28th, 1854; born July 8th, 1833, to No. (648) and his wife No. (649,) at Granville, Mass.

1114. "Lester S. Booth," to church May 28th, 1854; born Jan. 19th, 1828, to No. (648;) a shoe maker and dealer, learned of his father, his shop and store on Main Street; married Oct. 6th, 1852, No. (1115.)

1115. "Mrs. Harriet, wife of Lester S. Booth," to church May 28th, 1854; born June 5th, 1832, at Berlin, to Justus Bulkley and his wife Ruth (Savage;) married Oct. 6th, 1852, No. (1114.)

THEIR CHILDREN.

1. Kate Wilcox, born Sept. 14th, 1854, bap. June 24th, 1855.
2. Harriet Bulkley, born July 14th, 1856, bap. April 26th, 1857.
3. Edith Walter, born April 26th, 1865, bap. Nov. 26th, 1865.

1116. "Elisha S. Booth, jun.," to church May 28th, 1854; born at Torringford, July 24th, 1837, to No. (648;) married Nov. 22d, 1858, Eliza Sanford, daughter of Nathan, of Oxford, Conn., and his wife Mary A. (Talmage,) of Cheshire; born Dec. 14th, 1838, at Derby, Conn. He was dismissed Oct. 4th, 1861, to Congregational church in West Winsted, but in 1862, he enlisted as corporal in Company F 14th regiment Conn. Volunteers. He was mortally wounded while caring for the body of his friend Birdsey Beckley, at the battle of Fredericksburg, Va., and died Jan. 5th, 1863, in hospital, at Washington, buried in New Britain, Jan. 10th, 1863. He was a generous and noble hearted man, and fell a martyr to the cause of humanity and his country.

1117. "Sarah A. Cooley," to church May 28th, 1854; born Nov. 22d, 1831, at Southwick, Mass., to Julius and his wife Minerva (Campbell;) married Oct. 27th, 1856, Jared W. Carpenter, of Granby; he born July 1st, 1828. She was dismissed and recommended to the Congregational church in Granby, June 19th, 1863, where they reside.

1118. "CORANCEY CADY," to church May 28th, 1854, baptized same time; born April 8th, 1839, to Asahel, of Manchester, Conn., and his wife Catharine (Hanover,) alias Widow Haskins; married Nov. 26th, 1859, Mary Francis Heath, daughter of Jerome L. Heath and his wife Anne S. (Grant;) born July 26th, 1841, at Rockville, is a member of the church there. He was dismissed by letter to church in Rockville, May 13th, 1859, now 1862, resides in New Britain, and is by trade a wagon maker.

THEIR CHILD.

Emma Lillian, born April 8th, 1861, at Rockville.

1119. "RICHARD JUDD," to church May 28th, 1854; born Jan. 23d, 1807, to No. (435) and his second wife, No. (436;) married Jan. 29th, 1836, No. (822;) he is a farmer on East Street, the old homestead of his ancestors for three generations.

THEIR CHILDREN.

1. Martha Elizabeth, born April 15th, 1840, married Nov. 22d, 1866, Edward P. Pinks, No. (986.)
2. Daniel Bartholomew, born Jan. 29th, 1846, died Sept. 4th, 1848, aged 3.
3. Frank Howard, born May 2d, 1847.

1120. "S. ADALINE CLARK," to church May 28th, 1854; born July 26th, 1833, to Newton and his wife Adaline (Candee;) married Dec. 31st, 1854, Geo. Sherwood, of New Milford, son of Daniel and his wife Fannie (Shove.) They both graduates of the State Normal School, of Conn.; he now, 1863, is a merchant in Chicago, Ill. She was dismissed by letter, Feb. 10th, 1860, to church in Evanston, Ill.

THEIR CHILDREN.

1. Fannie Clark, born Dec. 19th, 1859, at Chicago, died March 10th, 1864, aged 5 years, 3 months.
2. Geo. Northend, born Nov. 21st, 1862, at Chicago, died March 9th, 1864, aged 1 year 3 months.

1121. "HANNAH B. JUDD," to church May 28th, 1854, baptized same time; born Oct. 20th, 1834, to Eri and his wife Lovisa (Bronson,) is a prominent member of the church choir, now, 1867, and for several years past.

1122. "SARAH PINKS," to church May 28th, 1854; born March 3d, 1839, to Jonathan C. and his wife No. (865,) was dismissed by letter June 6th, 1857, to church in Hanover, Meriden, and received back from there July 7th, 1861.

1123. "CORDELIA HOUGH," to church May 28th, 1854, baptized same time; born Feb. 3d, 1837, at Bristol, to Wm. O. of that town, and his wife Isabel G. (Thorp;) she has become a distinguished artistic singer; she married Nov. 21st, 1861, Ralph Guernsey Hibbard, son of Bennet and his wife Laura (Guernsey;) born Sept. 23d, 1837, at Plymouth, Ct., by profession, an Elocutionist.

1124. "CHARLOTTE B. BELDEN," to church May 28th, 1854, baptized same time; born June 11th, 1818, to Ira and his wife Dolly (Bronson.)

1125. "HUBERT L. JUDD," to church May 28th, 1854; born April 1st, 1829, to No. (918) and his wife No. (619,) is a hardware manufacturer; married Aug. 14th, 1851, No. (1126;) dismissed by letter, Oct. 6th, 1856, to church in Davenport, Iowa, but returned and received by letter to this again, Sept. 7th, 1862.

1126. "JULIA, wife of Hubert L. Judd," to church May 28th, 1854; born Aug. 22d, 1830, to No. (717) and his wife No. (718;) married Aug. 14th, 1851, No. (1125;) was dismissed by letter Oct. 6th, 1856, to church in Davenport, Iowa, but returned to this church, Sept. 7th, 1862.

THEIR CHILDREN.

1. Julia Ellis, born May 20th, 1852, died Nov. 19th, 1852, aged 6 months.
2. Morton, born Aug. 8th, 1854, died July 22d, 1855, on steamer Lady Elgin, at Georgiana Bay.
3. Florence Bremer, born Dec. 25th, 1857, bap. Jan. 11th, 1860.
4. Edward Henry, born Aug. 20th, 1859, bap. Jan. 11th, 1860, died Jan. 17th, 1860, aged 5 months.
5. Emma Julia, born Dec. 1st, 1860, bap. July 2d, 1865.
6. Morton Ellis, born March 10th, 1864, bap. July 2d, 1865.

1127. "ELLEN S. SMITH," to church May 28th, 1854; born Feb. 12th, 1837, to No. (515) and his wife No. (627;) married June 1st, 1857, Alonzo McManus, of Forestville, New York State; born Nov. 28th, 1830, to Joseph and his wife Clarissa (Barnum,) of Danbury, Conn. He a member of Methodist church; lives on Myrtle Street.

1128. "ANNA STRICKLAND," to church May 28th, 1854; born Jan. 24th, 1838, to Stephen Lyman Strickland and his wife No. (855,) she went to England with her uncle No. (584,) where she spent a year or more, and is passing A. D. 1861, in Chicago, Ill.

1129. "IRENE ROBERTS," to church May 28th, 1854; born March 25th, 1837, at E. Haddam, to Frederic A. and his wife No. (1134;) married May 2d, 1855, Frederic W. Porter, son of Richard S. and his wife Betsey (Cornwell;) born Feb. 23d, 1829, at Granby, Conn.; she was dismissed by letter Sept. 30th, 1859, to 13th Street Pres. church, New York. She was received back July 1st, 1866, by letter from same church.

THEIR CHILDREN.

1. Isaac Porter, born Aug. 25th, 1858, at Cincinnati.

2. Richard Roberts, born Nov. 24th, 1860, at Cincinnati.
3. Nellie, born Sept. 30th, 1862, at Cincinnati, died April 14th, 1863, buried in New Britain.

1130. "MRS. S. N., wife of J. W. Tuck," to church May 28th, 1854, by letter from Mt. Vernon church, Boston, Rev. E. N. Kirk, Pastor; her maiden name, Sophronia Stephen Norris, daughter of Grafton and his wife Mary (Stephens;) born May 17th, 1828, at Livermore, Me.; married May 27th, 1851, Jeremiah Warren Tuck, son of Jeremiah and his wife Ruth (Woodman;) born Aug. 7th, 1823, at Fayette, Me. He was for several years a popular teacher of our high school. She was dismissed by letter May 7th, 1858, to Elliott church, Roxbury, Mass.

THEIR CHILDREN.

1. Alice Cora, born June 27th, 1857, at New Britain.
2. Marie Louise, born June 11th, 1861, at Roxbury, Mass.

1131. "N. F. EMMONS," to church Aug. 6th, 1854, by letter from church in Guilford, Rev. E. E. Hall, Pastor, name, Noadiah Franklin Emmons, son of Noadiah and his wife Betsey (Cone;) born Feb. 23d, 1807, at East Haddam; married Feb. 13th, 1832, Nancy Carpenter, of Norwich, Conn., daughter of James and his wife Elizabeth, she died Aug. 27th, 1837, when 2d he married, April 10th, 1849, No. (1132;) he is a house painter by trade, residence above High Street.

1132. "MRS. AMELIA S. wife of N. F. Emmons," to church Aug. 6th, 1854, by letter from church in Guilford; born Sept. 14th, 1824, at West Hartford, to Childs Goodman and his wife Sarah (Porter;) married April 10th, 1849, No. (1131.)

HIS CHILDREN BY FIRST WIFE, NANCY.

1. Edward Payson, born Nov. 20th, 1833, at New Haven, O., married June 15th, 1857, Charlotte Miller.
2. Adaline, born May 15th, 1836, at Defiance, died aged 2 years.

HIS CHILDREN BY SECOND WIFE AMELIA.

3. Alexander Franklin, born April 4th, 1850, at Guilford, No. (1415.)
4. Adaline Elizabeth, born July 13th, 1852.
5. Mary Sophia, born March 8th, 1860, died aged 21 days.
6. Harriet Amelia, born July 4th, 1861, bap. Dec. 8th, 1861.

1133. "CLARISSA DARROW," to church Nov. 20th, 1854, by letter from first church in Farmington, Noah Porter, D. D., pastor; born Sept. 16th, 1820, at Farmington, to Asa Darrow and his wife Clarissa (Burchard,) of Norwich, Ct.; she to church in Farmington Feb. 4th, 1838, and has lived in family of Giles Stillman several years.

1134. "MRS. MARY S., wife of Frederic A. Roberts," to church Feb. 11th, 1855, by letter from Congregational church in West Hartford, Rev.

Mr. Morris, pastor; born Sept. 8th, 1813, at East Haddam, to Noadiah Emmons and his wife Betsey (Cone;) married, May 15th, 1834, he son of Asher and his wife Sarah M. (Paddock,) born June 17th, 1815, at East Haddam, by trade a boot maker; she died March 14th, 1856, aged 42, was sister to No. (1131,) when second he married, Nov. 28th, 1857, Julia A. Beckwith, born May 9th, 1831, to Robert and his wife Maria (Anderson.)

THEIR CHILDREN.

1. Mary E., born March 6th, 1835.
2. Irena W., born March 25th, 1837, see No. (1129.)
3. Addie E., born Oct. 6th, 1839.
4. Jennie S., born Dec. 20th, 1842.
5. Freddie E., born June 30th, 1844.
6. Helen L., born Oct. 3d, 1840.

CHILD BY SECOND WIFE.

7. Gracie Tiffany, born Sept. 15th, 1858.

1135. "MRS. MARY ANN, wife of Wm. Stone," to church April 8th, 1855, by letter from the Congregational church in Wolcottville, Rev. Mr. Seeley, pastor; born Oct. 18th, 1820, at Easton, Mass., to Jas. Godfrey, of Norton, Mass., and his wife Martha (Keith;) married Feb. 4th, 1840, he son of Elisha, of Litchfield, Ct., and his wife Mary (North,) of Asher, of New Britain; born Aug. 23d, 1813.

THEIR CHILDREN.

1. Lizzie M., born Aug. 10th, 1841.
2. George Edgar, born Dec. 4th, 1845.
3. Carrie Keith, born Sept. 27th, 1857.

1136. "MISS MARY ANN SMITH," to church June 3d, 1855, by letter from church in Rockville, is sister of No. (1081;) born March 25th, 1830, at Lisbon, Ct., to Dr. Levi H. Smith, of that town and his wife Josephine (Frink,) she went from this town to Plainville, then to Greenfield, Mass., and Brooklyn, N. Y., changed her name to Josephine Burleigh, and been adopted into the family of Wm. H. Burleigh, her uncle; she took no letter from this church; she was, 1863, cashier at Ransom's store in Hartford. She left our communion for spiritualism, and was excommunicated April 18th, 1865.

1137. "MISS JOSEPHINE HIGGINS," to church June 3d, 1855, baptized same time; born Nov. 18th, 1838, at Clinton, to S. Higgins and his wife Susan M. (Turner;) married, July 7th, 1859, John B. Burr, of Durham, born March 20th, 1835, at Durham, to Alfred and his wife Huldah (Brainard;) he a grocer in Norwich; she was dismissed by letter to the church at Clinton, Ct., Dec. 12th, 1856.

1138. "MISS SARAH J. NOYES," to church June 3d, 1855, born May 12th, 1837, at Middletown, to Eben and his wife Fanny (Hunt;) graduated,

1855, at the State Normal School, and is now, Jan., 1862, teaching; dismissed by letter, Dec. 26th, 1856, to church of the Pilgrims, Brooklyn, N. Y., Dr. Storrs, pastor.

1139. "MRS. JANE RODGERS," to church June 3d, 1855, her maiden name was Huston; was the wife of John B. Rodgers, a plater and burnisher from New York; she was dismissed by letter, March, 1856, to church in New York city.

THEIR CHILD.

Martha Huston, born bap. March, 1856.

1140. "AUSTIN BEEBE," to church Feb. 3d, 1856, born Jan. 25th, 1825, at Ellington, to Martin and his wife Anna (Pember;) is a carpenter and joiner, learned of Gager, in Rockville; married, Sept. 23d, 1847, No. (1141;) residence on Arch st.

THEIR CHILDREN.

1. Anna Rozell, born April 25th, 1853, see No. (1413.)
2. Lizzie Maria, born July 5th, 1863, bap. July 3d, 1864.

1141. "MRS. ELIZABETH, wife of Austin Beebe," to church Feb. 3d, 1856, born May 22d, 1828, Schoharie, N. Y., to Philip Buel and his wife Mary (Edgcomb;) married, Sept. 23d, 1847, No. (1140.)

1142. "OLIVE M. LOOMIS," to church Feb. 3d, 1856, by letter from church in New Hartford, Rev. Mr. Hall, pastor; born May 12th, 1833, to Andrew H., of New Hartford, and his wife Laura C. (Merrell;) married, March 16th, 1857, Capt. E. W. Ruggles, son of Rev. Nathaniel and his wife Julia (Hall;) born March 15th, 1821, at Bridgeport; he is sea captain; she dismissed by letter, March 27, 1857, to church in San Francisco, Cal., but returned to Brooklyn, N. Y., where, 1863, they reside.

THEIR CHILD.

Nathaniel, born March 9th, 1859, at San Francisco, Cal.

1143. "JOHN B. MINOR," to church March 23d, 1856, by letter from church in Bridgeport, Ct.; born March 9th, 1821, at Woodbury, to Matthew and his wife Lorena (Bacon;) has been engaged in the lumber trade, his residence on Washington st.; he married, Sept. 24th, 1844, Ursula Allen, of Bethlehem, born Aug. 1823, to Jared and his wife Ruth (Mitchell;) she died July 25th, 1854, when second he married, Nov. 3d, 1858, No. (1105;) he was chosen one of the standing committee of this church Jan. 6th, 1860, in place of N. W. Stanley, whose term expired; he died May 1st, 1865, aged 44, at Porto Rico, (of sun stroke,) where he had gone for his health, buried in New Britain cemetery, May 31st, 1865.

HIS CHILDREN BY FIRST WIFE, URSULA.

1. Willie A., born Sept. 25th, 1851, see No. (1358.)
2. John Bacon, born Sept. 15th, 1853, at Bridgeport, Ct.

1144. "CHARLES NORTHEND," to church April 6th, 1856, by letter from South Danvers, Mass.; born April 1st, 1812, at Newbury, Mass., to John and his wife Anna (Titcomb;) he teacher and author, also editor of Conn. Common School Journal; married, Aug. 18th, 1834, No. (1145;) his residence on Cedar st.; he has been for several years sup't of our S. School; he was chosen one of the standing committee Jan. 3d, 1862; he became President of the American Institute of Instruction in 1863.

1145. "MRS. LUCY ANN, wife of Charles Northend," to church April 6th, 1856, by letter from South Danvers, Mass.; born Sept. 27th, 1808, at Newbury, Mass., to Wm. Moody and his wife Abigail (Titcomb;) married, Aug. 18th, 1834, No. (1144,) her first cousin.

THEIR CHILDREN.

1. John, born Oct. 28th, 1835, see No. (1161.)
2. Charles Augustus, born May 3d, 1841, see No. (1162.)

1146. "MRS. MARILLA, wife of Gilman Hinsdale," to church April 6th, 1856, by letter from Baptist church, New Britain; born May 7th, 1799, to John Judd and his wife No. (637;) married, Dec. 10th, 1820, Rollin Dickinson, son of Daniel, of Southington, and his wife Margaret (Lewis,) born April 15th, 1799, and died June 21st, 1842, at Southington, when second she married, Dec. 5th, 1852, No. (1015;) she was a cheerful and hopeful Christian, and an active woman; they moved to a farm in Barkhamsted, where she died June 8th, 1859, aged 60.

HER CHILDREN BY FIRST HUSBAND, DICKINSON.

1. Margaret, born April 20th, 1823.
2. Charles, born Sept. 18th, 1825, see No. (1157.)
3. Judson, born July 16th, 1830.
4. Jane M., born Aug. 12th, 1835.

1147. "MISS SALLY WOODRUFF," to church June 8th, 1856, by letter from first church in Farmington, Noah Porter, D. D., pastor; born Nov. 30th, 1799, at Farmington, to Solomon and his wife Chestina (Curtis,) sister of Major Peter, of Farmington, of Revolutionary memory; she lives in the family of her brother Ephraim, corner of Elm and Seymour streets.

1148. "HENRY P. STRONG," to church Aug. 3d, 1856, by letter from first church in Bridgeport, Ct., born July 22d, 1822, at Woodbury, Ct., to Anthony C. Strong and his wife Julia (Lambert,) married, Sept. 7th, 1847, No. (1149;) he is in the lumber and coal trade, residence on Elm st.; he was chosen deacon in place of Albert Judd, (resigned,) Jan. 6th, 1865.

1149. "Mrs. Sarah A., wife of Henry P. Strong," to church Aug. 3d, 1856, by letter from the first church in Bridgeport, Ct., born Sept. 17th, 1825, to David C. Bacon, of Woodbury, and his wife Sarah (Wheeler;) married, Sept. 7th, 1847, No. (1148;) she to church in Woodbury first Sabbath in May, 1843.

THEIR CHILD.

Sarah Martha, born March 28th, 1850, bap. July 2d, 1865, see No. (1355.)

1150. "Everett C. Holmes," to church Aug. 3d, 1856, by letter from the North Presbyterian church, N. Y., Dr. Hatfield's; born Aug. 28th, 1821, at Winsted, to Willard, of that town, and his wife Miranda (Frisbe;) he was a school teacher and farmer; married, Nov. 1st, 1848, No. (1151;) dismissed by letter, Oct. 15th, 1858, to church in Winsted.

1151. "Laura P., wife of Everett C. Holmes," to church Aug. 3d, 1856, by letter from the North Presbyterian church, N. Y.; born April 22d, 1824, to No. (1036;) she and her husband dismissed by letter, Oct. 15th, 1858, to church in Winsted, where they now, 1862, reside.

THEIR CHILDREN.

1. Edward Everett, born Dec. 29th, 1849.
2. Laura Isabella, born March 27th, 1852, died July, 1852, aged 4 months.
3. Willard Pease, born Aug. 22d, 1857.

1152. "Mrs. Abbie, wife of I. N. Lee," to church Jan. 18th, 1857, by letter from South church, New Britain; born June 8th, 1832, to No. (920) and his wife No. (597;) was a teacher of day schools in various localities, and became a sup't of the infant department of the S. School; she married, Oct. 26th, 1855, No. (694,) and was his third wife.

1153. "Abiram Chamberlin," to church April 5th, 1857, by letter from church in Colebrook, Ct.; born Oct. 2d, 1797, at Sandisfield, Mass., to Samuel C. and his wife Ann (Conklin;) he lived in Colebrook, and was deacon of that church; married, May 6th, 1829, No. (1154;) his residence on Pearl st.; he is a land surveyor, and engineer of the "New Britain Water Works."

1154. "Mrs. Sophrone, wife of Abiram Chamberlin," to church April 5th, 1857, by letter from Colebrook; born Jan. 17th, 1805, at Tolland, Mass., to Caleb Burt, and his wife Anna (Merry,) of Granville, Mass., married, May 6th, 1829, No. 1153.

THEIR CHILDREN.

1. Eliza Ann, born June 22d, 1831, died March 12th, 1835.
2. Valentine Burt, born April 13th, 1833, was a volunteer in Co. A, 7th Regt., a Captain, located at Port Royal, S. C., was taken prisoner at the assault on Fort Wag-

ner, exchanged in the spring of 1865, and represented the town of New Britain in the Legislature of 1865.

3. John Abiram, born Feb. 22d, 1836, died Feb. 21st, 1837, aged 1 year.
4. Abiram, born Dec. 7th, 1837.
5. Elvira Ann, born Jan. 15th, 1840, died Nov. 17th, 1841, aged 2 years.
6. Cornelia Ann, born Sept. 20th, 1842, see No. (1213.)

1155. "NELSON HIGGINS," to church June 7th, 1857, by letter from church in Hampton, Ct.; born July 6th, 1817, at Glastenbury, to Jared and his wife Harriet (Hurlburt;) married, March 3d, 1844, No. (1156;) residence on Main st., foot of "Dublin Hill."

1156. "MRS. DELIA B., wife of Nelson Higgins," to church June 7th, 1857, by letter from church in Hampton, Ct.; born June 16th, 1814, at Hampton, to Dan Buckley and his wife Phebe (Burnett;) married, Mar. 3d, 1844, No. (1155.)

THEIR CHILDREN.

1. Eugene Buckley, born Jan. 15th, 1846.
2. Vincent P., born March 29th, 1849, died Sept. 6th, 1851.
3. Mary Estelle, born Aug. 20th, 1852, see No. (1410.)

1157. "CHARLES DICKINSON," to church June 7th, 1857, baptized same time; born Sept. 8th, 1825, at Southington, to Rollin and his wife No. (1146;) his residence on West Main st.; is a druggist; married, Jan. 1st, 1850, No. (1396.)

THEIR CHILD.

Fannie Louise, born Sept. 22d, 1850, see No. (1397.)

1158. "ROBERT FRANCIS," to church June 7th, 1857, baptized same time; born Oct. 17th, 1835, at Newington, to Robert and his wife Mary (Toby,) daughter of William, of Nantucket, is brother of No. (1093;) married, Oct. 4th, 1859, Augusta, daughter of John Stannard and his wife Delia (Peck,) of New Marlboro', Mass.; born July 6th, 1834, at New Hartford; married, Dec. 11th, 1856, John Peterson, of Saratoga, N.Y.; he died Oct. 27, 1857, when second she married as above; he is a machinist, and now, 1863, living in Hartford; he was, May 3d, 1867, dismissed and recommended to first Methodist Episcopal church, Hartford

THEIR CHILD.

Grace May, born Nov. 9th, 1863, at Hartford, and died there Dec. 29th, 1863, aged 7 weeks and 1 day; buried in New Britain.

1159. "ELIZA L. STILLMAN," to church June 7th, 1857, baptized same time; born Feb. 18th, 1839, at Farmington, to Giles and his wife Sally (Loveland,) of Wethersfield; resides now, 1862, with her father on Lafayette st.

1160. "MRS. EMILY M., wife of Wm H. Riley," to church June 7th, 1857, baptized same time; born Feb. 19th, 1831, in New Hampshire, to Jacob Warren Wentworth and his wife Louisa Ann (Lee,) of Yelding; married, Sept. 18th, 1849; he a grocer, and deputy sheriff; born July 24th, 1824, at Charlestown, N. H., to Henry and his wife No. (928;) his residence now, 1867, on West Main st., and he is agent of the Union Manufacturing Co.

THEIR CHILD.

Wm. Wentworth, born July 30th, 1859, bap. July 2d, 1865.

1161. "JOHN NORTHEND," to church June 7th, 1857, baptized same time; born Oct. 28th, 1835, at Troy, N. Y., to No. (1144) and his wife No. (1145;) was a volunteer, 1861, in Co. A, 13th Regt., went to New Orleans, but was discharged from ill health, and returned to a clerkship.

1162. "CHARLES A. NORTHEND," to church June 7th, 1857, baptized same time; born May 3d, 1841, at South Danvers, Mass., to No. (1144) and his wife No. (1145;) now, 1867, clerk in the insurance business; he married, Dec. 5th, 1864, No. (1314.)

THEIR CHILD.

Henry Havens, born Nov. 13th, 1866, bap. Nov. 1st, 1867.

1163. "FREDERIC KNAPP," to church June 7th, 1857, baptized same time; born Sept. 26th, 1826, at New Milford, to Levi S. and his wife Eliza (Roberts;) is an accountant and insurance agent; married, April 22d, 1848, No. (1074;) residence now, 1861, on Elm st.

THEIR CHILDREN.

1. Herbert, born April 22d, 1849.
2. Sidney, born Nov. 8th, 1854, died Sept. 1st, 1855.
3. Harry Shepherd, born June 27th, 1856.
4. Eliza Margaret, born Oct. 19th, 1863.

1164. "JAMES STANLEY," to church June 7th, 1857, born March 31st, 1812, to No. (550) and his wife No. (339;) is a jeweller by trade, and manufacturer; married, July 5th, 1836, No. (886;) his residence on Park st.; has been a prominent anti-slavery and temperance reformer, and been successful in business; was active in building the Center church edifice; he second married, Dec. 13th, 1865, No. (1168.)

THEIR CHILDREN.

1. Caroline Eliza, born Nov. 21st, 1827, bap. see No. (1173.)
2. Mortimer Henry, born Nov. 2d, 1839, bap. 1840, see No. (1185.)
3. Alice Louise, born July 3d, 1841, bap. 1841, see No. (1182.)
4. Helen Amelia, born Jan. 30th, 1844, bap. July, 1844, see No. (1245.)
5. Celia Anna, born Oct 22d, 1846, bap. March 14th, 1846.

6. Jane Stow, born Aug. 2d, 1849, bap. Dec. 2d, 1849.
7. Grace, born April 8th, 1852, bap. Oct. 3d, 1852, see No. (1412.)
8. Agnes Warren, born Sept. 30th, 1854, bap. June 10th, 1855.
9. James North, born July 23d, 1862, bap Nov. 2d, 1852.

BY SECOND WIFE.

10. Bessie, born Feb. 6th, 1867, bap. Aug. 30th, 1867.

1165. "EDWARD M. BOOTH," to church June 7th, 1857, born Jan. 26th, 1840, to No. (648;) excels in elocution and music, and is, 1867, in Chicago, Ill.; married, Aug. 23d, 1866, Susan Martin, a successful teacher of the New Britain Grammar School.

1166. "ISAAC S. LEE," to church June 7th, 1857, born Jan. 1st, 1837, to No. (694) and his first wife No. (734;) plays the flute in the church choir; he is one of the firm of I. N. Lee & Co., in the manufacture of shirts.

1167. "SETH E. CASE," to church June 7th, 1857, born Dec. 3, 1825, at Simsbury, to Col. Aurora and his wife Betsey (Case,) of Bloomfield; graduated at Yale College in 1847, began business in New Britain as a lawyer, in 1850 became a Judge of Probate for the District of Berlin; his residence on West Main st.; married, Oct. 15th, 1850, No. (1168;) has been successful in business and useful in the church and town; he died suddenly of heart affection, April 19th, 1864, aged 39 years, 4 mo.

1168. "MRS. MINERVA E., wife of Seth E. Case," to church June 7th, 1857, born Sept. 4th, 1830, to Orville Wilcox, of Canton, and his wife Lydia (Farnum,) married Oct. 15th, 1850, No. (1167.) She married, second, Dec. 13th, 1865, No. (1164.)

THEIR CHILDREN.

1. Charles Averitte, born Sept. 11th, 1853, bap. Aug. 2d, 1857.
2. Robert Edwards, born Feb. 8th, 1859, bap. June 3d, 1860.

1169. "J. A. PICKETT," to church June 7th, 1857, born March 9th, 1829, at New Milford, to Albert, and his wife Mary (Robers;) is a manufacturer of hardware, firm of H. F. North & Co.; residence northern part of Main street, foot of "Dublin Hill," house built by No. (682.) His full name is James Andrew Pickett; he married Sept. 9th, 1857, No. (1173.)

THEIR CHILD.

Anna Mary, born July 9th, 1861, bap. Nov. 2d, 1862.

1170. "S. ELIZABETH CARPENTER," to church June 7th, 1857, born Sept. 25th, 1838, to No. (914,) and his wife, No. (700,) married Feb. 5th, 1861, Frederick L. Ames, of Portland, Ct.

1171. "ELLEN CARPENTER," to church June 7th, 1857, born Jan. 6th, 1840, to No. (914,) and his wife, No. (700,) married Sept. 24th, 1867, before Rev. L. Perrin, George W. Cummings, born Dec. 26th, 1839, to

Abner, then of Salisbury, Ct., and his wife Phebe Curry. He is a mechanic, and works on cutlery in New Britain.

1172. "ELIZABETH A. TRACY," to church June 7th, 1857, born Aug. 17th, 1836, to No. (856,) and his first wife, No. (926.)

1173. "CAROLINE ELIZA STANLEY," to church June 7th, 1857, born Nov. 21st, 1837, to No. (1164,) and his wife, No. (550,) married Sept. 9th, 1857, to No. (1169.)

1174. "GEORGE G. MCLEAN," to church June 7th, 1857, born Sept. 21st, 1838, at New Britain, to Silas O., and his wife, No. (1082;) was a volunteer for three months to put down the rebellion of 1861; married April 6th, 1864, to Bessie Norton, of Portland, Ct.

1175. "CHARLES O. MCLEAN," to church June 7th, 1857, born March 24th, 1836, at Norwich, Ct., to Silas O., of Glastenbury, and his wife, No. (1082,) married Feb. 9th, 1858, No. (1207;) lives with his mother, on Chestnut street.

THEIR CHILDREN.

1. George Oscar, born Dec. 2d, 1859.
2. Howard Case, born Oct. 24th, 1863.
3. Florence E., born Dec. 31st, 1865.

1176. "MARY E. STONE," to church June 7th, 1857, born Aug. 23d, 1837, to No. (776,) and his first wife, No. (777.)

1177. "LUCY A. TRACY," to church Aug. 2d, 1857, born June 27th, 1840, to No. (856,) and his first wife, No. (926,) married October 16th, 1867, Walter W. Roberts, born February, 1830, at Berlin, to John, formerly of that town, now of New Britain, and his wife Lois (Deming.) He is by trade and occupation a jeweller, at Churchill & Co's.

1178. "ELLEN W. PARKER," to church Aug. 2d, 1867, born Oct. 18th, 1842, to No. (864,) and his wife, No. (891.)

1179. "ISABELLA J. CHURCHILL," to church Aug. 2d, 1857, born Aug. 14th, 1843, to No. (695,) and his second wife, No. (885.)

1180. "FANNY C. BOOTH," to church Aug. 2d, 1857, born May 12th, 1842, to No. (648,) and his wife, No. (649,) married July 17th, 1867, Albert Osgood, of Utica, N. Y.

1181. "SARAH A. CHURCHILL," to church Aug. 2d, 1857, born July 8th, 1841, to No. (695,) and his second wife, No. (885.)

1182. "ALICE L. STANLEY," to church Aug. 2d, 1857, born July 3d, 1841, to No. (1164,) and his wife, No. (886.)

1183. "ELLEN L. STRICKLAND," to church Aug. 2d, 1857, born Nov. 16th, 1840, to Stephen L. Strickland, and his wife, No. (855;) now, 1867, is residing in England.

1184. "Mrs. HARRIET M., wife of Henry E. Williams," to church Aug. 2d, 1857, born May 23d, 1834, to John F. Woodruff, of Avon, and his wife Catharine (Wheaton,) married March 16th, 1852. He was son of No. (676,) born Nov. 29th, 1831. They now, 1867, live with his father in district No. 4, or Hart quarter.

THEIR CHILDREN.

1. George Selah, born July 8th, 1853.
2. Catharine Elizabeth, born Oct. 14th, 1855.
3. Mortimer Henry, born Oct. 17th, 1863.

1185. "MORTIMER H. STANLEY," to church Aug. 2d, 1857, born Nov. 2d, 1839, to No. (1164,) and his wife, No. (886;) a volunteer in Co. A, 13th Reg., Capt. Bidwell; went to Ship Island and New Orleans, where he was connected with the medical director's office, but, 1863, was promoted to lieutenant in the engineer corps; was honorably discharged and returned Sept., 1864.

1186. "FRANCIS HARRISON, to church Aug. 2d, 1857, baptized same time, born 1840, to Epaphroditus, of Wolcottville, and his wife Laura (Freeman,) dismissed by letter, Jan. 13th, 1860, to Talcott Street church, Hartford. She was a colored person; died March 8th, 1862, aged 22, at Winsted, Ct.

1187. "MARY ANN SWEARS," to church Aug. 2d, 1857, baptized same time, born Jan. 7th, 1839, to Calvin, and his wife Almira (Loomis.) She is a colored person.

1188. "ELLEN LINASON," to church Aug. 2d, 1857, baptized same time, born April 13th, 1839, to Asa, and his wife Maria (Swears.) Was a colored person; she died June 8th, 1863, aged 24.

1189. "ELIZA A. LINASON," to church Aug. 2d, 1857, baptized same time, born Sept. 23d, 1837, to Asa, and his wife Maria (Swears;) is a colored person, and sister of No. (1188.)

1190, "LORIN F. JUDD," to church Oct. 11th, 1857, born Feb. 3d, 1820, to Eri, and his wife Lovisa (Bronson;) is a hardware manufacturer, firm North & Judd Manufacturing Company; his residence on East Main street; married May 19th, 1842, No. (1191.) He sold his residence, 1861, to No (831,) and built on Main street, 1866, a beautiful French roof house. This firm has been very successful in business.

1191. "JOSEPHINE M., wife of Lorin F. Judd," to church Oct. 11th, 1857, baptized same time, born Nov. 21st, 1826, at Bristol, to James N. Lee, and his wife Abbie (Wightman,) married May 19th, 1842, No. (1190.)

THEIR CHILDREN.

1. Mortimer Nelson, born Nov. 27th, 1845.
2. Grace Ellen, born July 27th, 1849, No. (1387.)

1192. "ELLEN GRIDLEY," to church Oct. 11th, 1857, baptized same time, born April 5th, 1842, to Walter B., and his wife Mary (Hunter,) daughter of Roswell; she is grand daughter to No. (414,) married Nov. 27th, 1861, DeWitt Parkinton, son of Thomas, of England, and his wife Chloe (Offord,) of Southington, born Jan. 9th, 1842, at Hitchcockville.

He is a brass worker, and was a three months volunteer in Co. G, 1st Reg. of Connnecticut. Mrs. Ellen G. Parkinton dismissed by letter to the Methodist Episcopal church, New Britain, Dec. 20th, 1861. His residence, 1864, on West Main street, one-half mile from the village.

1193. "CAROLINE M. BELDEN," to church Oct. 11th, 1857, born May, 30th, 1828, to Aziel, and his second wife, Nancy (Mitchell,) married Feb. 16th, 1858, Charles Read, of Chester, Ct.

1194. "Mrs. SUSAN F., wife of Samuel A. Weldon," to church Oct. 11th, 1857, born March 26th, 1835, to Isaac G. Smith, of Waterbury, and his wife Marilla (Hotchkiss,) of Prospect, married Dec. 27th, 1855, No. (1257.)

1195. "Mrs. MARY ANNETTE, wife of James H. Smith," to church Oct. 11th, 1857, born April 9th, 1826 to Amon Judd, and his first wife, No. (506,) married May 10th, 1846, Burnham H. Pennfield, son of No. 373, and his wife, No. (432,) born April 3d, 1824, was killed Jan. 25th, 1846, by running versus a clothes line, when she married, second, Oct. 8th, 1849, James Henry, son of Peter Smith, and his wife Lucretia (Scott,) born Nov., 1818, at Columbiaville, N. Y.; by occupation a pattern maker; residence on Beaver street. He died June 9th, 1867, in his 49th year.

HER CHILDREN BY SECOND HUSBAND, SMITH.

1. Catharine Annette, born Jan. 21st, 1851; is a teacher.
2. Edgar Huntley, born March 19th, 1854.

1196. "VERNOR CYLER, M. D.," to church Oct. 11th, 1857, by letter from Presbyterian church in Schenectady, son of John, and his wife Mary (Vernor,) born June 19th, 1799, at Albany, N. Y.; took his title at the Medical College, in the city of New York; married May 10th, 1830, No. (1197,) came to this town 1857; he formerly practiced medicine in Albany, but became somewhat deaf, and since practiced dentistry. He was dismissed by letter, July 6th, 1860, to Presbyterian church at Athens, Ga., but, 1864, residing at Schenectady, N. Y.

1197. "Mrs. CAROLINE R. wife of Vernor Cyler, M. D.," to church Oct. 11th, 1857, by letter from Presbyterian church in Schenectady, N. Y., daughter of Isaac Riggs, and his wife Catharine (Seaman,) born May 1st, 1813, at Schenectady, N. Y., and is a music teacher. She died Aug. 28th, 1863, aged 50, at Schenectady, N. Y.

THEIR CHILDREN.

1. John Schyler, born March 3d, 1833, at Schenectady, died July, 1833.
2. Catharine Elizabeth, born July, 1835, at Albany, died August, 1839.
3. Margaret Tillman, born Feb. 22d, 1837.

1198. "CHARLES F. DOWD," to church Nov. 29th, 1857, by letter from church in Waterbury, Ct., born April 25th, 1825, at Madison, Ct., to Willys M., and his wife Rebecca (Graves,) married Oct. 6th, 1852, No. (1199;) he is a teacher by profession, and been successful; is now, 1861, principal of a female seminary in North Granville, N. Y. They were dismissed by letter back to First Congregational church in Waterbury, Ct., May 13th, 1859. He was ordained an Evangelist, Feb., 1864, by the Presbytery of Troy, N. Y.

1199. "Mrs. HARRIET M., wife of Charles F. Dowd," to church Nov. 29th, 1857, by letter from church in Waterbury, Ct., born Feb. 17th, 1830, at Berlin, to Edmund North, and his wife Maria M. (Wilcox;) was dismissed, May, 13th, 1859, by letter to First Congregational church in Waterbury, Ct.; living, 1861, at North Granville, New York; married, October 6th, 1852, No. (1198.)

THEIR CHILDREN.

1. Wyllys Edward, born Feb. 18th, 1855, at Berlin.
2. Charles Field, born April 29th, 1858, at New Britain, bap. Nov. 7th, 1858.
3. Miriam Wilcox, born December 6th, 1860, at North Granville, N. Y.
4. Bertha North, born May 23d, 1862, at North Granville, N. Y.
5. Arthur Dudley, born June 30th, 1864, at North Granville, N. Y.

1200. "Mrs. CORNELIA, widow of Orson Woodford," to church Nov. 29th, 1857, by letter from church in Collinsville, born March 22d, 1822, to Alanson Woodruff, and his wife Eunice (Baldwin,) of Branford, Ct., married May 1st, 1839. He was son of John Woodford of West Avon; he died April 24th, 1855. She first to church in West Avon, then to Collinsville, then here as above.

THEIR CHILDREN.

1. William Orson, born April 13th, 1840.
2. Ellen Eliza, born May 19th, 1844.

[Here ends the ministry of Rev. Horace Winslow, dismissed by a council, Dec. 2d, 1857, to take effect on and after the 20th inst., he having a call to Great Barrington, Mass.]

[Here commences the ministry of Rev. L. Perrin, having been installed by an ecclesiastical council, Feb. 3d, 1858.]

1201. "Mrs. ANN ELIZA, wife of Rev. Lavalette Perrin," to church March 28th, 1858, by letter from church in Goshen, over which church and people he was former pastor some fourteen years. He was born May 15th, 1816, at Vernon, Ct., to Aaron, and his wife Lois (Lee,) graduated at Yale College, 1840, settled at Goshen, Ct., Dec. 1843, married

June 4th, 1844, Miss Ann Eliza Comstock, daughter of William, and his wife Polly (Keeler,) of Ridgefield, born Nov. 29th, 1826, at Peekskill, N. Y. His residence on Washington street, built by No. (622.) He to church in Vernon, Ct., 1832, and dismissed by letter, 1837, to church in Yale College.

THEIR CHILDREN.

1. Bernadotte, born Sept. 15th, 1847, see No. (1324.)
2. Catharine, born Dec. 8th, 1850, see No (1350.)
3. Addison, born Sept. 27th, 1852, see No. (1347.)
4. Giles Griswold, born Jan. 19th, 1856, died March 13th, 1856, aged 2 months, at Goshen.
5. William Aaron, born Dec. 18th, 1858, bap. April 17th, 1859, at New Britain; he died, at New Britain, Friday night, Jan. 30th, 1863, of fever, aged 4 years, 1 month and 12 days.

1202. "JACOB W. BIGLOW," to church June 6th, 1858, baptized same time, born Jan. 10th, 1827, at West Randolph, Vt., to Levi Biglow, of New Hampshire, and his wife Esther W. (French,) of Randolph, Mass. He is a joiner by trade; married, Nov. 20th, 1851, No. (1203;) residence on Park street; is a Sunday school teacher, and otherwise active and useful; he became one of the Standing committee Jan. 1st, 1864. He has sold on Park street and built new on Maple street, 1863.

1203. Mrs. SARAH, wife of Jacob W. Biglow," to church June 6th, 1858, bap. same time, born Oct. 26th, 1833, in New York, to William Kinlock, from Scotland, and his wife Ann (Fram,) married Nov. 20th, 1851, No. (1202;) she is sister of No. (1228;) dismissed, Jan. 5th, 1866, to church in Litchfield, with her husband.

THEIR CHILDREN.

1. Charles Wallace, born Nov. 24th, 1853, bap. June 20th, 1858.
2. Robert Kinlock, born May 25th, 1856, bap. June 20th, 1858.
3. Edward Wales, } twins, born May 31st, 1862, bap. May 3d, 1863.
4. Esther Ann, }

1204. "Mrs. LIZZIE D., wife of Levi B. Stone," to church June 6th, 1858, baptized same time, born Sept. 25th, 1835, at New Hartford, Ct., to Timothy Clapp, and his wife Joanna (Driggs.) Her full maiden name, Elizabeth Driggs Clapp; married March 28th, 1855, No. (1029.)

1205. "Mrs. ELIZABETH H., wife of William Burritt," to church June 6th, 1858, baptized same time, born Oct. 22d, 1832, to Philip Hart, and his wife Maria Mary (Judd,) married Oct. 22d, 1852. He was son of William, and his wife Clarissa (Cole,) born July 16th, 1830; live with his mother on Seymour street. He was 2d Lieut. in Co. G, 6th Reg. Connecticut volunteers, at Hilton Head, 1862.

THEIR CHILDREN.

1. Ella Elizabeth, born Jan. 16th, 1854.
2. Willie Thomas, born Jan. 20th, 1864.

1206. "Mrs. Josaphine, wife of Alva W. Spaulding," to church June 6th, 1858, baptized same time, born Oct. 26th, 1837, at Berlin, to Horace Beckley, and his wife Mary P. (Roberts,) married Sept. 4th, 1854. He was son of Alvah, of Morristown, Vt., and his wife Emma (Cooke,) born March 1st, 1826; is sheriff's deputy, and keeps a livery stable now, 1867; his residence is on West Main street, once owned by S. E. Case, Esq.

1207. "Mrs. Susan J., wife of Charles O. McLean," to church June 6th, 1858, baptized same time, born June 11th, 1836, at Simsbury, to Chester Case, and his wife Sarepta (Case;) her full maiden name, Susan Jane Case, married Feb. 9th, 1858, No. (1175.) They live, 1861, with his mother, on Chestnut street.

1208. "Anna E. Morse," to church June 6th, 1858, baptized same time; born Aug. 5th, 1835, at Burlington, Conn., to Orson and his wife Amanda (Kellogg.) She is sister of No. (1022;) she married May 3d, 1864, No. (1332,) and was dismissed and recommended to church in Sandusky, Ohio, April 27th, 1866, with her husband.

1209. "Frances A. Belden," to church June 6th, 1858, baptized same time; born Oct. 13th, 1832, at New Britain, to George D. and his wife Elizabeth (Sanger,) of Chicopee, Mass.

1210. "Ellen N. Tracy," to church June 6th, 1858, baptized same time; born Feb. 1st, 1838, at Thompsonville, to No. (1269,) and his wife No. (1270.)

1211. "Elizabeth H. Robinson," to church June 6th, 1858, baptized same time; born Oct. 7th, 1839, to Augustus and his wife Mary Hart (Merrill,) alias Widow of John Bunce.

1212. "Julia Andrews," to church June 6th, 1858, baptized same time; born Aug. 28th, 1828, to Joseph W. of New Hartford formerly, now, 1861, of Chestnut Street, in this place, and his wife Ann (Bailey;) married Nov. 20th, 1862, Mortimer Ward Marshall, son of Wm. C. of Hartford. He was a three months' Volunteer for the defence of Washington.

1213. "Cornelia A. Chamberlin," to church June 6th, 1858, baptized same time; born Sept. 20th, 1842, at Colebrook, to No. (1153,) and his wife No. (1154,) she excels in vocal and instrumental music; married Dec. 13th, 1866, Charles E. Mitchell, Esq.

1214. "Lucy A. Rhodes," to church June 6th, 1858, baptized same time; born Aug. 13th, 1842, at Wethersfield, to Henry E. and his wife No. (1248;) she married May 17th, 1865, Frank E. Orcutt, of Cambridgeport, Mass., before Rev. L. Perrin.

1215. "Mary A. Darling," to church June 6th, 1858, baptized same time; born Aug. 6th, 1846, at Cambridgeboro, Vt., to Horace P. and his wife Fanny (Spaulding.)

1216. "NEWTON W. PERKINS," to church June 6th, 1858, baptized same time; born Jan. 31st, 1839, at Harlengen, N. J., to Edwin and his wife Thalia Ann (Morse,) daughter of Levi, of Litchfield. The family live on Franklin Street; a 3 years' volunteer, company A, 13th regiment, promoted to Lieut. and Capt. and is brevetted Major for meritorious conduct.

1217. "DEVEREAUX JONES," to church June 6th, 1858, baptized same time; born July 8th, 1841, at Harlengen, N. J., to Wm. B. and his wife No. (1072;) was a three months' volunteer in 1861; has been a teacher; a volunteer in company A, 13th regiment, was promoted to Capt. July 12th, 1864, in first La. regiment.

1218. "LEWIS R. COOK," to church June 6th, 1858, baptized same time; born April 9th, 1838, to No. (909,) and his first wife No. (897.)

1219. "WILBURT H. BOOTH," to church June 6th, 1858, baptized same time; born Aug. 2d, 1840, to Wm. Belden Booth and his 1st wife Betsey (Blin;) a 3 months' volunteer in company G, 1st regiment; grandson of No. (370;) he died of yellow fever, Aug. 23d, 1863, at Brashear City, near New Orleans, buried there, aged 23.

1220. "GUSTAVUS A. ELLIS," to church June 6th, 1858, baptized same time; born Feb. 15th, 1828, to John and his wife No. (956;) is lame, one leg shorter than the other; married May 21st, 1857, No. (1221;) is, 1861, clerk in "Post office;" lives mostly with his father, has been a merchant.

1221. "MRS. JULIA C. wife of Gustavus A. Ellis," to church June 6th, 1858; had been a member of a Baptist church, in New Haven, came with a certificate, but joined us on profession of faith; born July 31st, 1840, at New Haven, to Eliphalet Cooper, of New Haven, and his wife Julia Ann (Tuttle,) of North Haven; married May 21st, 1857, No. (1220;) her full maiden name was Julia Allis Cooper.

1222. "WM. THORNTON," to church June 6th, 1858, baptized in infancy, in Old England; born there Dec. 21st, 1824, to John and his wife Elizabeth (Iredale,) of Elland, Yorkshire County, England. He is a carriage maker by trade and occupation, came to this place in the spring of 1848; married Sept. 12th, 1847, No. (1223;) both dismissed by letter May 5th, 1860, to some church in Huddersfield, England.

1223. "MRS. SARAH J. wife of Wm. Thornton," to church June 6th, 1858, baptized in England; born Jan. 27th, 1825, in Huddersfield, Yorkshire County, England, to Thomas Johnson and his wife Ann (Dawson;) married Sept. 12th, 1847, No. (1222,) came to this country 1849; both were dismissed by letter May 5th, 1860, to some church, in Huddersfield, England.

THEIR CHILDREN.

1. Wm. Henry, born Oct. 10th, 1851, No. (1417.)
2. Harriet Ann, born Sept. 17th, 1854.
3. Sarah L. , born June 29th, 1867, died Aug. 28th, 1867, aged 2 months.

1224. "LEVERETT HOWELL," to church June 6th, 1858 ; born March 21st, 1828, at New Haven, to Abraham and his wife Francis Elizabeth (Striker ;) married Dec. 9th, 1849, No. (1225 ;) living now, 1861, at N. Haven ; he is a silver plater and works now, Jan. 1862, in Hartford, but enlisted 1862, in 13th regiment, company F. Conn. volunteers, and was at the great battle near Sharpsburg, Md., as a Orderly Sergeant of that company.

1225. "MRS. MARY E. wife of Leverett Howell," to church June 6th, 1858 ; born Aug. 20th, 1830, at New Haven, to Wm. Pennfield and his wife Jane (Beecher;) she is granddaughter to No. (341 ;)married Dec. 9th, 1849, No. (1224.)

THEIR CHILD.

Minnie, born Oct. 10th, 1850, at New Britain.

1226. "HUGH HENRY NORRIS," to church June 6th, 1858 ; born March 28th, 1824, at Articliff, Londonderry County, Ireland, to Wm. and his wife Esther (Rankin ;) married May 5th, 1853, No. (1227 ;) is a brass and iron worker, residence on Winter Street.

1227. "MRS. EMMA G. wife of Hugh H. Norris," to church June 6th, 1858 ; born May 29th, 1831, at Leeds, England, to John Gildard and his wife Sarah (Dixon ;) married May 5th, 1853, No. (1226)

THEIR CHILDREN.

1. Senior Gildard, born April 14th, 1856, bap. Oct. 3d, 1858.
2. Fanny Dixon, born Nov. 2d, 1860, bap. June 23d, 1861.
3. Charles Henry, born April 16th, 1865, bap. July 1st, 1866.

1228. "MRS. JANE K. KENYON, WIDOW," to church June 6th, 1858 ; born April 8th, 1817, near Glasgow, Scotland, to Wm. Kenlock and his wife Ann (Frame ;) married Aug. 21st, 1840, Robert Kenyon, at Amsterdam, New York, who was born at Island Bute, in Scotland, Feb. 22d, 1812 ; he died Nov. 14th, 1854, aged 42, at New Britian ; she sister of No. (1203,) and lives now 1862, at Tariffville, and was dismissed to the church there, Oct. 3d, 1862, but returned and was restored Sept. 6th, 1863.

THEIR CHILDREN.

1. Robert, born Aug. 21st, 1840, at L. I., N. Y.
2. Wm., born Jan. 7th, 1843, is a vol. in Co. G., 6th reg. Conn. Vol., now 1861, at Port Royal.
3. Jennett Turnbull, born March 23d, 1849, bap. June 20th, 1858.

4. John Frame, born Dec. 25th, 1851, bap. June 20th, 1858.
5. Wallace Neil, born Oct. 8th, 1853, bap. June 20th, 1858.

1229. "MRS. MARY E. widow of Homer Lyon," to church June 6th, 1858 ; born May 15th, 1827, at East Windsor, to George D. Belden and his wife Elizabeth (Sanger ;) married May 27th, 1850. He son of Homer and his wife Maria (Taylor ;) born July 29th, 1826, at Ludlow, Mass. He died Nov. 17th, 1856, at Ludlow, aged 30. She was dismissed by letter, April 10th, 1860, to 2d Pres. church in Atlanta, Ga., where she now, fall of 1862, resides, but now, 1867, lives in New York.

THEIR CHILDREN.

1. Charles Henry, born March 24th, 1851, at New Britain.
2. Roxana Maria, born April 24th, 1853, at Chicopee, Mass., died at New Britain, aged 5 months.

1230. "MRS. PRISCILLA H. wife of Julius Hulbert," to church June 6th, 1858 ; born Feb. 8th, 1827, at Granby, Conn., to Joseph Hayes and his wife Clarissa (Gillett ;) married Dec. 27th, 1848 ; he son of Samuel of West Hartford, and his second wife Abigail (Webster ;) born Feb 10th, 1823 ; by occupation a rule maker, lives on Pearl Street.

THEIR CHILDREN.

1. Julia M. born Feb. 25th, 1850.
2. Lewis W. born Oct. 21st, 1855.

1231. "SARAH ANN GLADDEN," to church June 6th, 1858 ; born June 19th, 1823, to No. (522) and his wife No. (523 ;) lives on East Main Street ; house built by her mother.

1232. "GRACE M. WILSON," to church June 6th, 1858 ; born Nov. 21st, 1836, at Paisley, Scotland, to John and his wife Agnes (Gibson ;) married Nov. 16th, 1859, Charles N. Vensel, son of Christian and his wife Catharine (Glover ;) born Oct. 20th, 1835, at New Britain ; is a house painter ; she came to this country, 1855, her father's family located at Middletown, Conn.

1233. "DAVID MAITLAND," to church June 6th, 1858 ; born Sept. 22d, 1837, at Paisley, Scotland, to Alexander and his first wife Ellen (Pinckerton.) He married May, 1859, Susan Taylor, of Middletown. He is now, Jan., 1862, at work at Savage's Arms Company, Middletown.

1234. "SYLVESTER W. NOBLE," to church June 6th, 1858 ; born Jan. 26th, 1827, at Simsbury, to Sylvester of that town, and his wife Margarette (Holcomb ;) is a carriage maker by trade ; is brother of No. (1298.)

1235. "EDWARD M. JUDD," to church June 6th, 1858 ; born Nov. 11th, 1837, to No. (918) and his first wife No. (619 ;) is a hardware manufacturer ; married March 27th, 1860, No. (1299 ;) was dismissed and recommended by letter Dec. 25th, 1863, to Chapel Street church in New Haven, Nov., 1867; makes hardware at Wolcottville.

1236. "EDWARD E. BRADLEY," to church June 6th, 1858; born June 20th, 1830, at Prospect, Conn., to Isaac of that town, and his wife Betsey (Nettleton;) is a brick mason by trade; married Sept. 19th, 1854, No. (1108.)

THEIR CHILD.

Wilber Edward, born July 2d, 1855, bap. June, 1856.

1237. "ELLIOTT BRAINARD ALLEN," to church June 6th, 1858; born July 22d, 1837, at Agawam, Mass., to Aaron P. and his wife Lydia Fox; by trade and occupation a plumber; married Nov. 23d, 1858, No. (1323.) He was dismissed by letter Dec. 7th, 1860, to church in Birmingham, Conn., but was received back by letter from that church, July 6th, 1862. He became superintendent of our Sunday School, Jan., 1867.

THEIR CHILDREN.

1. Geo. Henry, born June 18th, 1862, bap. May 3d, 1863.
2. Willis Burton, born Dec. 24th, 1866.

1238. "FRANKLIN M. JEROME," to church June 6th, 1858; born Dec. 13th, 1832, at Goshen, Conn., to No. (1030,) and his wife No. (1031;) is a brass worker, lives, 1867, with his father on West Main St.; his middle name, Minor.

1239. "WM. W. CHURCHILL," to church June 6th, 1858; born Sept. 22d, 1845, to No. (695) and his 2d wife No. (885;) dismissed and recommended to Dr. Storrs' church, Brooklyn, N. Y., April 27th, 1866.

1240. "FREDERIC H. CHURCHILL," to church June 6th, 1858; born March 27th, 1847, to No. (695) and his 2d wife No. (885.)

1241. "ANAN H. WALTER," to church June 6th, 1858; born Jan. 18th, 1845, to No. (1066) and his first wife Laura J. (Hine,) at New York City.

1242. "GEORGE B. BOOTH," to church June 6th, 1858; born March 21st 1844, at Torrington, to No. (648) and his wife No. (649;) volunteer in company F, 14th regiment, 1862, but 1863 was appointed hospital steward in the U. S. A., and located in N. Y. City.

1243. "ARTHUR T. CORNWELL," to church June 6th, 1858; born Sept. 11th, 1845, at Granby, Conn., to No. (688) and his wife No. (1250.)

1244. "HELEN A. STANLEY," to church June 6th, 1858; born Jan. 30th, 1844, to No. (1164) and his wife No. (886.)

1245. "MARY S. BABCOCK," to church June 6th, 1858; born May 30th, 1844, to Edward D. Babcock, M. D. and his wife No. (993.)

1246. "MARY M. STANLEY," to church June 6th, 1858; born Nov. 12th, 1843, to No. (604) and his wife No. (984;) is a teacher and excels in vocal and instrumental music.

1247. "LOUISE H. WHITTLESEY," to church June 6th, 1858; born May 23d, 1847, to No. (541) and his wife No. (1111,) at New Haven; her middle name Hart.

1248. "MRS. HARRIET B. wife of Henry E. Rhodes," to church June 6th, 1858, by letter from first church in Wethersfield, Rev. Mr. Colton, Pastor; born July 16th, 1816, at Wethersfield, to Levi Blinn and his wife Nancy (Woodruff;) married Nov. 27th, 1839. He son of Selah, of Wethersfield, and his wife Sally (Talcott,) of Glastenbury; he was born Dec. 8th, 1812. He bought the Elnathan Smith place, on East Street, in 1850, for $6,000. He died Aug. 6th, 1860, aged 48, of apoplexy.

THEIR CHILDREN.

1. Franklin E. born May 19th, 1841, married Jan. 1st, 1864, Lucinda Howell.
2. Lucy Ann, born Aug. 13th, 1842, see No. (1214.)
3. Albert W. born Aug. 5th, 1844.
4. Henry E. born July 23d, 1848.
5. Thos. R. born Feb. 2d, 1850, see No. (1398.)
6. Woodruff, born May 24th, 1852.
7. Harriet E. born March 12th, 1855.

1249. "MARCIA L. BALDWIN," to church June 6th, 1858, by letter from church in North Cornwall, Rev. Wm. B. Clark, Pastor; born Jan. 12th, 1828, at South Cornwall, to Ithamar and his wife Electa (Millard.) She married Sept. 29th, 1863, George Leach, of Litchfield, and resides in that town.

1250. "MRS. CORDELIA R. wife of Thomas Stanley," to church June 6th, 1858, by letter from the Congregational church at Plainville, Rev. J. Dickinson, Pastor; born Feb. 20th, 1808, at Granby, Conn., to Martin Reed of that town, and his wife Bernice (Kendal;) married Sept. 5th, 1832, No. (688;) he died when second she married, Sept., 1855, No. (680.)

1251. "CATHARINE R. STANLEY," to church June 6th, 1858, by letter from the Congregational church in Plainville, Rev. J. Dickinson, pastor; born Nov. 9th, 1840, at Ottawa, Ill., to No. (680) and his first wife No. (610;) she is a school teacher, and is successful.

1252. "MARY E. STANLEY," to church June 6th, 1858, from church in Plainville, by letter; born July 9th, 1843, at Ottawa, Ill., to No. (680) and his first wife No. (610;) she died June 3d, 1859, aged 16, of quick consumption; the record says, "literally fell asleep in Jesus; it was a happy death."

1253. "WM. HENRY GLADDEN," to church June 6th, 1858, baptized same time; born Feb. 10th, 1842, to Henry and his wife No. (711;) one of our choir singers; was a 3 years' volunteer in Co. A, 13th Regt., at New Orleans in 1862.

1254. "Mrs. Mary S., wife of Solomon Hamblin," to church Aug. 1st, 1858, baptized same time; born May 12th, 1802, to No. (852) and his wife No. (853,) married Nov. 1st, 1825; he son of Phineas, of Farmington, and his wife Rhoda (Andrus,) of Jacob; born July 7th, 1799, at "White Oak," in Farmington, baptized there Aug. 4th, 1799; residence in district No. 4, in Hart quarter, house the former home of Roger Hart, and was moved from north of "Dublin Hill."

THEIR CHILDREN.

1. Emma, born Sept. 8th, 1826, married, July 4th, 1848, James Wolcott Colt, son of Wolcott, of Harwinton; they had one son James Riley, born May 16th, 1849; she second married, Nov. 22d, 1865, Omri Andrews, son of Elijah.
2. Harriet Eliza, born died July 21st, 1833, aged 18 months.

1255. "Mrs. Caroline M., wife of Meriels Roberts," to church Aug. 1st, 1858, born Jan. 28th, 1822, at Avon, to Adna T. Hart and his wife Lydia (Woodruff;) married, Dec. 1st, 1845; he son of John and his wife Lois (Deming,) born Aug. 9th, 1818; live on Chestnut st.

THEIR CHILDREN.

1. Emily May, born April 18th, 1855, died Oct. 14th, 1855.
2. Grace May, born Sept. 28th, 1856.

1256. "Mrs. Ann Eliza, wife of Charles L. Thompson," to church Aug. 1st, 1858, born July 13th, 1829, at Southington, to Capt. Urban Barrett, and his second wife, widow Freelove (Young,) alias Freelove Smith; married Oct. 3d, 1853; he son of Warren, of South Windsor, and his wife Redoxa (Loomis;) born Oct. 3d, 1853, at South Windsor; living on Washington st.

1257. "Lura Ann Francis," to church Aug. 1st, 1858, baptized same time; born July 14th, 1839, at New Britain, to Anson W., of New Haven, and his wife Lura Ann (Hart,) daughter of No. (453;) been a teacher, lives, 1865, with her grandmother, No. (454,) in Hart quarter.

1258. "Samuel A. Weldon," to church Aug. 1st, 1858, baptized same time; born March 22d, 1831, to No. (517) and his first wife Sally (Bartholomew;) married, Dec. 27th, 1855, No. (1194;) he is a carriage maker, learned of Dickinson & Graham.

THEIR CHILD.

Mortimer Emory, born April 17th, 1858.

1259. "Mahlon J. Woodruff," to church Aug. 1st, 1858, born July 7th, 1836, at Shermon, N. Y., to Robert, of Ohio, and his wife Julia Ann (Fuller;) married, Dec. 16th, 1856, No. (1263;) occupation, accountant, residence on Walnut st., is Secretary of Union Manufacturing Co.; his wife Mary died, when second he married, Jan. 18th, 1865, at Greenport, L. I., No. (1448.)

HIS CHILDREN BY FIRST WIFE MARY.

1. Hattie Eliza, born April 20th, 1859, died June 24th, 1861, aged 2.
2. Grace May, born Jan. 7th, 1863, bap. March 24th, 1863, over the mother's coffin; she died Sept. 19th, 1863, aged 8 months, 12 days.

1260. "HENRY J. ELLIS," to church Aug. 1st, 1858, born May 2d, 1837, to No. (717) and his wife No. (718;) is a grocer, firm of Brown & Ellis, on Main st.; married, Dec. 6th, 1865, No. (1424.)

1261. "WALTER G. CARPENTER," to church Aug. 1st, 1858, born May 30th, 1837, to No. (914) and his wife No. (700;) a corporal in Co. A, 13th Regt., C. V., at New Orleans, 1862; he died there of fever, Nov. 17th, 1862, aged 25, and his body was brought on and buried here, Jan. 22d, 1863; he was a promising young man, and an only son of his parents, greatly beloved.

1262. "SIMEON WOODRUFF," to church Aug. 1st, 1858, by letter from second Congregational church in Berlin, Ct.; born Oct. 1st, 1786, at Farmington, to Elisha and his wife Anna (Griswold,) of Wethersfield; married, Oct. 2d, 1811, Avis Bronson, of Southington, daughter of Joel and his wife Cynthia (Squire,) born Oct. 27th, 1790; she died Jan. 18th, 1855, at Berlin, aged 65; he has been a farmer, and lived mostly near the north west corner of Farmington; moved to Berlin, then to this place; his residence on Walnut st.

THEIR CHILDREN.

1. Lucius, born Dec. 1st, 1812, see No. (905.)
2. Samuel E., born March 15th, 1818, died June 16th, 1842, aged 24.
3. Franklin, born April 25th, 1820, bred a physician.
4. Mary C., } born April 28th, 1825, { died June 2d, 1831, aged 6.
5. Ira, } born April 28th, 1825, { died Feb. 12th, 1835, aged 10.
7. Mary Bronson, born July 3d, 1832, see No. (1263.)

1263. "MRS. MARY B., wife of Mahlon J. Woodruff," to church Aug. 1st, 1858, by letter from second Congregational church in Berlin, Edward Wilcox, clerk; born July 3d, 1832, to No. (1262;) married, Dec. 16th, 1856, No. (1259;) she died at New Britain, March 22d, 1863, aged 31.

1264. "CATHARINE MARIA BUTLER," to church Aug. 1st, 1858, by letter from first Congregational church in Meriden, Rev. Mr. Thacher, pastor; born Oct. 4th, 1837, at Rocky Hill, to Elisha and his wife Catharine B. (Wright;) married, May 1st, 1860, at Meriden, Stephen W. Hazzard, son of John, of New Britain, and his wife Mary Maria (Steele,) daughter of Wm.; born Aug. 19th, 1836, is a brass worker, volunteered in 1861 in the 5th Regt., Co. B, for three years; she dismissed by letter March 27th, 1860, to first church in Meriden, from which she came; she received back from Meriden by letter, Dec. 20th, 1861; the family reside with his father, 1862; she took a certificate of her membership, and joined the Baptist church, Sept. 7th, 1862, by immersion.

THEIR CHILD.

Charles Elmer, born May 9th, 1861.

1565. "WILLIAM W. GIDDINGS," to church Oct. 3d, 1858, by letter from South Congregational church, New Britain, Wm. Hart, clerk; born Aug. 1818, at Norwich, Ct., to Jabez, formerly of Norwich, but in 1861 of Hartford, and his wife Lydia (Alden,) of Stafford; married, Nov. 17th, 1840, No. (1266;) residence on West Main st., now, 1867; is a lumber and coal dealer, firm of Giddings & Strong.

1266. "MRS. CORNELIA A., wife of Wm. W. Giddings," to church Oct. 3d, 1858, by letter from South Congregational church, New Britain; born April 28th, 1822, to Dea. Michael Seymour, of Hartford, and his wife Rebecca (Wooster,) of Litchfield; her full maiden name Cornelia Ann Seymour; married, Nov. 17th, 1840, No. (1265.)

THEIR CHILDREN.

1. Martha Makepeace, born Aug. 27th, 1841, see No. (1314.)
2. Wm. Henry, born Jan. 17th, 1847.
3. Frederic Wooster, born Aug. 27th, 1850, see No. (1418.)
4. George Wight, born May 21st, 1858, bap. July 3d, 1859.

1267. "MRS. ANNA F., wife of Henry Walter," to church Oct. 3d, 1858, by letter from church in New Ipswich, N. H., Rev. Mr. Lee, pastor; born Feb. 6th, 1822, at Dover, N. H., to Rev. Joseph W. Clary and his wife Anna (Farrar;) married, Dec. 16th, 1856, No. (1066.)

1268. "MRS. SARAH T., wife of Nelson P. Woodruff," to church Oct. 3d, 1858, by letter from church in Newington, Rev. Mr. Aiken, pastor; born April 1st, 1832, in Newington, to Unni Robbins and his wife Sally (Dunham;) married, March 16th, 1855; he son of Capt. Urban, of Southington, and his wife Eliza (Bartholomew,) born Feb. 14th, 1825, at Southington; residence on Walnut st., is a paper box manufacturer on Main st.; she dismissed by letter to South church, Oct. 11th, 1861.

THEIR CHILD.

Alice Robbins, born Nov. 26th, 1857.

1269. "SOLOMON F. TRACY," to church Oct. 3d, 1858, by letter from East Woodstock, born Aug. 25th, 1805, at Canterbury, to Fanning and his wife Lucy (Adams,) of Lisbon; married, March 28th, 1833, No. (1270;) is a machinist by trade and occupation, his residence on Winter street.

1270. MRS. ALMIRA N., wife of Solomon F. Tracy," to church Oct. 3d, 1858, by letter from the Methodist Episcopal church, (Fisherville Society,) Thompson, Ct.; born Sept. 28th, 1811, to John Nichols, Thompson, Ct., and his wife Hannah (Robertton,) of Chesterfield, N. H.; married, March 28th, 1833, No. (1269.)

THEIR CHILDREN.

1. Lucy Adams, born May 19th, 1834, married Feb. 28th, 1855, Solomon F. Linsley, see No. (1319.)

2. EllenNichols, born Feb. 1st, 1838, see No. (1210.)

3. John Nichols, born June 18th, 1840, was Capt. of Co. G, 6th Regt. C. V., went to Port Royal.

1271. "THOMAS E. BARRETT," to church Dec. 5th, 1858, by letter from South Congregational church, New Haven, John Nicholl, clerk; born March 28th, 1830, at Brooklyn, Ct., to Joseph P., and his wife Nancy L. (Converse,) is a teacher by profession; married, Oct. 9th, 1854, No. (1272;) both dismissed by letter, Feb. 3d, 1860, to South Congregational church in New Haven, from which they came; he was killed at the battle of Fredericksburg, Va., while as Captain he led his Co., Dec., 1862.

1272. "MRS. JENNIE B., wife of Thomas E. Barrett," to church Dec. 5th, 1858, by letter from South Congregational church, New Haven; born Feb. 12th, 1832, at Milford, Ct., her maiden name Jennie Baldwin; married, Oct. 9th, 1854, at New Haven, to No. (1271;) both dismissed by letter to South Congregational church, New Haven, Feb. 3d, 1860.

THEIR CHILD.

Carrie, born Feb. 8th, 1861, at New Haven.

1273. "BENNETT J. ANDREWS," to church Dec. 5th, 1858, by letter from Congregational church in Southington, Rev. Elisha C. Jones, pastor, born Dec. 5th, 1806, at Southington, to Luman and his wife Lowly (Cowles;) married, March 24th, 1835, Belinda Carter, daughter of Rensalier and his wife Nancy (Averill,) of Branford; she died Sept. 11th, 1837, aged 20, when second he married, March 24th, 1842, Lavinia Frost, of Waterbury, daughter of Daniel C. and his wife Lorinda (Johnson,) born Sept. 4th, 1817, at Stockbridge, Onieda Co., N. Y.; he was a very successful farmer, he died Mar. 18, 1860, aged 53, of cancer, at his farm-house in Southington, where his family reside, 1863; he built a good house in 1851 on Arch st., where his family lived in 1861, but it was sold to Horace Hart in 1862, and occupied by him now, 1867.

HIS CHILDREN BY HIS SECOND WIFE, LAVINIA.

1. Emma Belinda, born Jan. 1st, 1843, married, Oct. 15th, 1866, Arthur Gridley, of Southington.

2. Legrand, born May 3d, 1845, died June 24th, 1846, aged 1 year, 2 mo.

3. Franklin Dewitt, born Aug. 1st, 1847.

1274. "J. EVELYN PIERPONT," to church April 3d, 1859, by letter from the Congregational church in Fair Haven, Rev. Burdett Hart, pastor; born March 27th, 1831, at Canada West, to F. W. Pierpont and his wife Hannah E. (Becker,) all of Canada West; he came to this place as a fish dealer; he was gentlemanly in his deportment, and apparently correct in his habits; he married No. (1275) May 30th, 1854, at Fair Haven; he fell under the censure of the church, Nov. 9th, 1860, by vote of excommunication; he was since a nine months' soldier in the 27th Regt., C. V. and returned safe.

1275. "Mrs. Mary A., wife of J. Evelin Pierpont," to church April 3d, 1859, by letter from church in Fair Haven; daughter of John P. Turner and his wife Almira (Luddington,) born June 20th, 1833, at Fair Haven; she married No. (1274) May 30th, 1854.

THEIR CHILDREN.

1. Evelyn J., born June 25th, 1855.
2. Marion W., born Jan. 18th, 1856.

1276. "Mrs. Jane McElrath," widow of John McElrath, to church April 3d, 1859, by letter from the Congregational church in Newington, Rev. Wm. P. Aiken, pastor; born , 1790, at Leek, Londonderry Co., Ireland, to John Brown and his wife Martha (Pollock;) married, June 5th, 1814; he son of John and his wife Esther (Lemind,) of Buck Mills, county of Antrim, Ireland; he was a school teacher in the north of Ireland, and of Scotch origin, and when required by the Catholics to discontinue the use of the Bible in school, *refused*, and was thrown out of employment; he died March 9th, 1859, in New Britain, aged 72; she had a former husband, John Mcilhare.

THEIR CHILDREN.

1. Sarah, born
2. Matilda, born May 18th, 1829, married, July 23d, 1853, Robert N. Couples.
3. Jane, born Dec. 10th, 1833, see No. (1277.)

1277. "Mrs. Jane, wife of William N. Turner," to church April 3d, 1859, by letter from Congregational church in Newington, Rev. Wm. P. Aiken, pastor; born Dec. 10th, 1833, at Bellemoneye, Ireland, to John McElrath and his wife No. (1276;) married July 23d, 1853; he son of Noah, of Sheffield, Eng.; he died May 9th, 1861, aged 33, when second she married, March 11th, 1864, No. (1337.)

THEIR CHILDREN.

1. Harriet Matilda, born Jan. 5th, 1856, at Newington, bap. July 5th, 1861.
2. Wm. Everet Shaw, born July 28th, 1857, bap. July 5th, 1861.
3. Elizabeth Caroline, born June 28th, 1858, at Hartford, bap. July 5th, 1861.
4. Sarah Louisa, born April 9th, 1861, bap. July 5th, 1861, died Sept. 4th, 1863, aged 3 years.

1278. "MRS. EMELINE G., wife of George H. Smith," to church June 5th, 1859, by letter from church in Wilmington, N. C.; born Aug. 10th, 1825, at Southington, to Augustus Goodsell and his wife Julia (Andrews,) of Beriah; married April 25th, 1848; he son of Asahel P. Smith, of Southington, and his wife Rhoda (Hart;) she dismissed, Jan. 5th, 1866, to second Presbyterian church in Charleston, S. C.

THEIR CHILD.

Julia Emeline, born May 19th, 1850.

1279. "GEORGE S. PECK," to church Oct. 2d, 1859, by letter from first Congregational church, Meriden, Rev. Geo. Thacher, pastor; born May 9th, 1840, at Kensington, to Selden and his wife Lucy H. (Hart;) he was baptized in Kensington in infancy, George Selden; he was here a clerk in Miller's store, until his health failed; he was in 1864, a manufacturer in Meriden, and by his own request was dismissed and recommended to West Meriden church, April 22d, 1864; he died Oct. 11th, 1865, at his father's residence in Kensington, aged 25.

1280. "MRS. ELIZABETH C., wife of Pedro P. Ortez," to church Feb. 5th, 1860, by letter from South church, New Britain, Rev. C. L. Goodale, pastor; born at New Haven to No. (464) and his wife No. (392,) baptized June 9th, 1833, by Rev. J. Cogswell, New Britain; married Dec. 26th, 1855; he from Valparaiso, Chili, S. A.; they reside now, 1862, at the old home of her father, but spend the winter season in New York or Washington.

1281. "ELLEN A. ANDREWS," to church Feb. 5th, 1860, by letter from South church, New Britain, Rev. C. L. Goodale, pastor; born at New Haven, to No. (464) and his wife No. (392;) her full name Ellen Amelia, baptized Sept. 3d, 1831, at New Britain, by Rev. J. Cogswell.

1282. "JOHN N. BARTLETT," to church April 1st, 1860, by letter from church in Collinsville, Rev. Mr. McLean, pastor, born July 3d, 1823, at Bloomfield, Ct., to Rev. John, and his wife Jane (Golden,) married Sept. 7th, 1846, No. (1283;) is a teacher by profession, now, 1863, of New Britain high school, and excels in vocal and instrumental music.

1283. "Mrs. ELLEN S., wife of John N. Bartlett," to church April 1st, 1860, by letter from church in Collinsville, born Nov. 13th, , at Farmington; baptized there March 22d, 1822, married Sept. 7th, 1846, No. (1282.)

THEIR CHILDREN.

1. Ellen Strong, born March 28th, 1848.
2. John Pomroy, born June 4th, 1858.
3. Annie Golden, born Aug. 1st, 1862, at New Britain, bap. April 12th, 1863.

1284. "EDMUND R. SWIFT," to church June 3d, 1860, by letter from the church in Warren, Ct., F. B. Taylor, clerk, born Jan. 22d, 1813, to

Ira, of Cornwall, Ct., and his wife Grace (Rogers,) of Branford, married Sept. 7th, 1841, No. (1285.) He is at the head of the malleable iron works now, 1867; his residence is on West Main street, formerly owned and occupied by No. (1028.)

1285. "Mrs. MARY C., wife of Edmund R. Swift," to church June 3d, 1860, by letter from church in Warren, Ct., born Sept. 7th, 1815, at Warren, to Benjamin Carter, of that town, and his wife Mary (Wadsworth,) of Hartford, married Sept. 7th, 1841, No. (1284;) both to church in Warren the spring of 1851; her full maiden name, Mary Wadsworth Carter.

THEIR CHILDREN.

1. Morton Carter, born Aug. 1st, 1843.
2. Mary Wadsworth, born May 20th, 1845, see No. 1406.

1286. "CHARLES E. OSBORNE," to church June 3d, 1860, by letter from First Congregational church in Middletown, Ct., Rev. Mr. Taylor, pastor, born Oct. 10th, 1836, at Middletown, to Allen, of that city, and his wife Elizabeth (May;) to Mr. Taylor's church, Jan. 3d, 1858, an only child of his parents. He kept a confectionery shop here, but his health failing, he went to Hartford the fall of 1860, where he died Dec. 30th, 1860, aged 24, of quick consumption.

1287. "Mrs. LUCIA H., wife of Lucas M. Wilcox," to church June 3d, 1860, by letter from church in Granby, Ct., Rev. William H. Gilbert, pastor, born June 12th, 1835, at Granby, to Chauncey Holcomb, and his wife Semantha (Goddard,) married Feb. 20th, 1860. He was son of Horace T., and his wife Sarah (Frink,) born May 31st, 1831, at Holyoke, Mass. She was dismissed by letter, Aug. 30th, 1861, to Chapel Street church, New Haven.

1288. "Mrs. ELLEN T. P., widow of Anson S. Bevins," to church June 3d, 1860, by letter from church in Hanover, Ct., Rev. Jacob Eaton, pastor, born Nov. 6th, 1836, to Jonathan Chapin Pinks, of New Britain, and his wife, No. (865,) married June 16th, 1858. He was son of Alvin E., of Meriden, and his wife Vashti (Tyler,) born August, 1828, at Meriden; died Dec. 20th, 1858, aged 30.

1289. "MARION E. PINKS," to church June 3d, 1860, by letter from church in Hanover, born April 8th, 1840, to Jonathan C. Pinks, of New Britain, and his wife, No. (865.)

1290. "ELIZA F. CLARY," to church June 3d, 1860, by letter from church in New Ipswich, N. H., born March 23d, 1827, at Dover, N. H., to Rev. Joseph W. Clary, and his wife Lucy (Farrar;) has been a teacher.

1291. "Mrs. ELIZABETH B., wife of Darius Miller," to church March 3d, 1861, by letter from church in East Windsor, Rev. Frederick E.

Munson, pastor, born Dec. 7th, 1836, at East Windsor, to John Bissell, and his wife Elizabeth (Thompson,) married Aug. 14th, 1860. He was son of Stephen, of Middletown, and his wife Lucretia (Fairchild,) born Oct. 11th, 1830, at Middletown. He is a dry goods merchant at New Britain, on Main street.

1292. "Mrs. Emily F., wife of George F. Hotchkiss," to church March 3d, 1861, by letter from Congregational church in Southington, Rev. E. C. Jones, pastor, born Feb. 4th, 1827, at Southington, to Naaman Finch, of that town, and his wife Sarah (Bishop,) of Cheshire, married Oct. 3d, 1848. He is son of Wooster Hotchkiss, of New Haven, and his wife Mary Loring (Bass,) of Boston, born Jan. 23d, 1822, at New Haven; the family residence is corner of Park and Winter streets.

THEIR CHILDREN.

1. Mary Loring, born Oct. 23d, 1849, at Southington, see No. (1408.)
2. Wooster, born Dec. 21st, 1851, at Southington.
3. Emily Finch, born August 28th, 1854, at Brooklyn, N. Y.

1293. "William C. Bronson," to church May 5th, 1861, by letter from church in Southington, Rev. E. C. Jones, pastor, born Jan. 12th, 1836, to Mary A., daughter of Cyprian Bronson, and his wife Candace (Norton,) of Berlin. He to church in Berlin, May 7th, 1854, then to church in Southington, then as above. He was a volunteer in Co. A, Capt. Bidwell, 13th Reg., but discharged, and lost an arm in H. F. North & Co.'s factory, by machinery, Oct. 21st, 1862.

1294. "Eliza Talcott," to church May 5th, 1861, by letter from church in Rockville, born May 22d, 1836, at Vernon, Ct., to Ralph, and his wife Susan (Bull;) is now, 1861, teacher in the New Britain high school. She married, Feb. 12th, 1866, Rev. Robert C. Learned, formerly of Berlin and Plymouth, Ct.; he died Jan., 1867, at Plymouth.

1295. "Mrs. Nancy Stanley, widow of Dr. Adna Stanley," to church July 7th, 1861, by letter from South church, Hartford, Rev. E. P. Parker, pastor, born April 9th, 1786, at Newington, to Elizur Deming, and his wife Lucina (Francis,) married April 26th, 1809, No. (438;) she first to South church in Hartford, May, 1852, her residence was then near that church edifice, but, 1861, she bought out the place on Washington street, built by Capt. Walter Gladden, where she and her daughters, No. (940) and No. (1296,) now, 1867, reside.

1296. "Sophia Stanley," to church July 7th, 1861, by letter from South church, Hartford, Rev. E. P. Parker, pastor, born June 14th, 1814, to No. (438,) and his wife, No. (1295,) She to South church, Hartford, May, 1852, and from that church to this, as above.

1297. "Mrs. Calista L., wife of Prosper Prior," to church Sept. 1st, 1861, by letter from Congregational church in North Coventry, Rev. G.

A. Calhoun, pastor, born April 10th, 1817, to Samuel Loomis, of North Coventry, and his wife Irene (Tracy,) of Franklin, Ct., married Dec. 3d, 1834. He is son of Roswell, of Windsor, and his wife Phebe (Ladd,) born June 19th, 1807; living now, 1861, on Myrtle street.

THEIR CHILDREN.

1. Harriet Zerlina, born July 13th, 1836, married Jan. 29th, 1854, Willis T. Holbrook; he was a soldier in Company H, 1st Artillery Regiment Connecticut Vols. She died March 12th, 1864, aged 28.
2. Wesley Baldwin, born March 20th, 1838.
3. Roena Willey, born May 15th, 1844, see No. (1405.)

1298. "SARAH NOBLE," to church Nov. 3d, 1861, by letter from church in Cleveland, Ohio, born Dec. 20th, 1825, at Simsbury, Ct., to Sylvester Noble, of that town, and his wife Margarette (Holcomb;) she is an artist and excels in landscape painting; is sister to No. (1234,) mar. Jan. 1st, 1866, Orrin A. North, son of Reuben, of Goshen, Ct.; his residence is on West Main street, and he is of the firm of Dickinson & North, druggists, Main street, New Britain, 1865.

1299. "Mrs. JANE P., wife of Edward M. Judd," to church Nov. 3d, 1861, by letter from First Congregational church in Farmington, Noah Porter, D. D., pastor, born April 16th, 1837, at Farmington, to Joel Peck, of that town, and his wife Charlotte (Scovill,) married March 27th, 1860, No. (1235.) Dismissed and recommended by letter, Dec. 25th, 1863, to Chapel Street church, New Haven, Ct.

THEIR CHILD.

Willie, born March, 1866, died Feb. 20th, 1867, aged 11 months, at West Winsted.

1300. "Mrs. FLORA BRAINARD," to church Jan. 5th, 1862, by letter trom church in Avon, Bev. E. D. Murphy, pastor, widow of Orlando V. Brainard, of Haddam and Bristol, son of Roswell, of Haddam, and his wife Ann (Smith,) born Nov. 3d, 1822, married June 6th, 1853, No. (1300;) her maiden name, Flora L. Thompson, daughter of Uriel, of Avon, and his wife Nabby (Woodruff,) born Dec. 15th, 1826, at Avon. He was a mechanic; he died April 15th, 1854, aged 31, at New Britain.

THEIR CHILD.

Florence Lucelia, born Feb. 21st, 1854.

1301. "LAFAYETTE BOSWORTH," to church March 2d, 1862, by letter from the church in Vernon, Ct., born Oct. 19th, 1825, at Eastford, Ct., to Aaron, and his wife Ruth (Wilcox;) by occupation, in early manhood, a school teacher, now, 1863, a book agent; married Jan. 12th, 1850, No. (1302;) his residence is on Park street. Mary, his wife, died, when he married, second, August 20th, 1862, Miss Susan E. Philbrook, of East

Windsor; she was born May 16th, 1841, at Bristol, Ct., to John Philbrook, then of that town, and his wife Susan (Gillette,) alias widow of Frederick Boardman. She died July 17th, 1863, at New Britain, of consumption, aged 22, when he married, third, April 28th, 1864, No. (1348.)

1302. "Mrs. MARY J., wife of L. Bosworth," to church March 2d, 1862, by letter from church in Vernon, Ct., born Jan. 7th, 1833, at Winsted, to Charles E. Johnson, of Harwinton, and his wife Elizabeth (Smith,) of Winsted. She died May 26th, 1862, aged 29.

THEIR CHILDREN.

1. William Bradley, born June 9th, 1851, at Vernon, died May 30th, 1853, at Salem, N. J.
2. Charles Lafayette, born July 22d, 1855.
3. Ada Caroline, born Oct. 24th, 1857.
4. George McClellan, born Aug. 6th, 1861.

1303. "VICTOR ALVERGNAT," to church March 2d, 1862, and baptized same time, born Dec. 10th, 1824, at Paris, France, to Antoine, and his wife Adelaide Sophie (Tierry,) learned there the trade of cabinet maker; was a volunteer and enlisted, 1844, into the French army, as a marine, where he served seven years, first as a private, then an officer; became an artist, and teaches drawing; arrived in this country February, 1853; married May 8th, 1858, No. (1304.) He was a teacher to the children of the regiment much of the time during his service in the French army.

1304. "JULIA R., wife of Victor Alvergnat," to church March 2d, 1862, by letter from church in Norfolk, Ct., Rev. Joseph Eldridge, pastor, born Jan. 26th, 1826, at Norfolk, Ct., to David Gaylord, of that town, and his wife Phebe (Camp.) She to church in Norfolk, 1843; married May 8th, 1858, No. 1303. She and her husband were dismissed and recommended, Jan. 8th, 1864, to First church, Hartford.

1305. "AMELIA A., wife of Dr. Linus Luddington," to church March 2d, 1862, had been a member of the Fourth Congregational church in Hartford, and after that of the Second Advent church; born May 3d, 1813, at Bloomfield, Ct., to Levi Dudley, and his wife Abigail (Hitchcock,) married Oct. 13th, 1840. He was born Feb. 12th, 1819, at West Springfield, Mass., to Jason Luddington, and his wife (Burr,) of West Hartford. He graduated, 1854, at the Medical College in New York city; he is now, 1862, a member of the 1st Artillery, 4th Reg. Conn. Vols., Capt. R. G. Williams, located at Arlington heights, Va.; family reside, 1862, on Arch street.

THEIR CHILDREN.

1. Luana Amelia, born Dec. 14th, 1841, see No. (1306)
2. Lucilla Maria, born July 20th, 1843, at West Hartford, died Feb. 12th, 1844, aged 1 year.

3. Nathan Burr, born Nov. 24th, 1844, at West Hartford, died Dec. 7th, 1844, aged 14 days.
4. William Linus, born July 6th, 1846, at Chicopee, Mass.
5. John Dow, born July 15th, 1848, at Chicopee, Mass.
6. Charles Franklin, born Feb. 11th, 1852.
7. Henry Parsons, born Dec. 9th, 1853.

1306. "LUANA A. LUDINGTON," to church March 2d, 1862, by letter from the church in Waterbury, Rev. Mr. Bushnell, pastor, to church there 1858, born Dec. 14th, 1841, at Chicopee, Mass., to Dr. Linus, and his wife, No. (1305.) She was a successful teacher, at Waterbury, and now, 1867, in New Britain. She married, May 2d, 1867, Howard C. Fiske, of Springfield, Mass., in Centre church.

1307. "Rev. ERASTUS RIPLEY," to church March 2d, 1862, by letter from Congregational church in Davenport, Iowa, born March 15th, 1815, at South Coventry, Ct., to Elijah Ripley, of that town, and his wife Phebe (Richardson,) graduated at Union College, Schenectady, N. Y., in 1840, licensed to preach, 1843, at Andover, Mass.; ordained and installed, spring of 1845, over the church at Bentonsport, Iowa; married Sept. 26th, 1844, Harriet Rose Riggs, daughter of Silas Riggs, of Drakeville, N. J., and his wife Harriet (Rose.) She died April 4th, 1857, when he married, second, March 30th, 1859, No. (1308.) He is now, 1862, professor of languages and mathematics in the State Normal School of Connecticut, located at New Britain, but, 1865, at Somers, Ct., at the head of a boarding school.

1308. "Mrs. ANNA, wife of Rev. E. Ripley," to church March 2d, 1862, by letter from Second Congregational church, New London, Rev. G. Wilcox, pastor, born July 20th, 1828, at New London, Ct., to Giles Dart, of that town, and his wife Mary (Watrous,) married March 30th, 1859, No. (1307;) her full maiden name, Anna G. Dart.

THEIR CHILDREN.

1. William Bradford, born July 30th, 1845, at Bentonsport, Iowa, died Sept. 2d, 1846, aged 13 months and 3 days.
2. Eugene Bradford, born April 4th, 1848, at Bentonsport, Iowa, see No. (1364.)
3. Charles Edward, born February 19th, 1850, at Davenport, Iowa, died June 13th, 1854, aged $4\frac{1}{4}$ years.
4. Louisa Wheeler, born Nov. 16th, 1852, at Davenport, Iowa.
5. Harriet Elizabeth, born May 8th, 1855, at Davenport, Iowa.

CHILDREN BY SECOND WIFE.

6. Mary Anna, born Jan. 14th, 1860, at Davenport, Iowa.
7. Margaret Matilda, born February 4th, 1862, at New Britain, Ct., bap. July 10th, 1864.
8. Cecil, born Feb. 8th, 1864, at New Britain, died April 12th, 1864, aged 2 months, buried in New London.

1309. "ISAAC POLLY WHITING," to church 1st Sabbath in May, 1862, by letter from church in Norwich, Rev. J. P. Gulliver, pastor, born Sept. 27th, 1825, at Portland, Ct., to Isaac Polly, of that town, and his wife Sarah (Hodge,) married January 9th, 1848, No. (1310;) is a house painter by trade; his surname changed in childhood from Polly to Whiting.

1310. "Mrs AVALINA S., wife of I. P. Whiting," to church 1st Sabbath in May, 1862, by letter from the church in Norwich, Ct., Rev. J. P. Gulliver, pastor, born Jan. 7th, 1829, at Bozrah, Ct., to Champlin Gardner, of that town, and his wife Avalina S. (Abel.)

THEIR CHILDREN.

1. Elizabeth Gardner, born Jan. 17th, 1849, at Chester, died Sept. 1st, 1850.
2. Alice Isabella, born August 8th, 1852, at Deep River, died May 9th, 1854, at Norwich.
3. Evelina Lucretia, born July 24th, 1855, at Montville, died Dec. 6th, 1859.
4. George Champlin, born April 6th, 1857.
5. Alice Jennette, born Oct. 28th, 1860, bap. March 30th, 1862, at New Britain.

1311. "Mrs. EMELINE MEDBURY," to church May 4th, 1862, by letter from church in Rockville, Ct., M. M. Trisselle, clerk, daughter of Samuel Wadsworth, of East Hartford, and his wife Hannah (Roberts,) born May 10th, 1812, at East Hartford, married Dec. 4th, 1837, Chauncey D. Medbury, son of Nathan, of Saratoga county, N. Y., and Abigail (Dunning,) his wife, born March 22d, 1813, at Greenfield, N. Y.; he was by trade a cabinet maker; he died Oct. 27th, 1845, aged 33, at his native place.

THEIR CHILDREN.

1. Frances Emeline, born Sept. 30th, 1838, at Greenfield, N. Y., died March 31st, 1861, at New Britain.
2. James Oscar, born Nov. 18th, 1840, at Greenfield, Saratoga county, N. Y.; a marine in the U. S. navy.

1312. "MRS. JULIA F. wife of John Van Kenren," to church May 4th, 1862, baptized same time; born Oct. 24th, 1832, at Troy, N. Y., to Amasa Kenyon of that city, and his wife Ursula (Haynes;) married June 21st, 1853. He son of Cornelius Van Keurin and Rachel (Miller) his wife; born July 8th, 1830, at Poughkeepsie, N. Y., by trade a jeweller; he is now, 1862, a 2d Lieutenant in the 7th regiment, Conn., volunteers, company A, Capt. Francis, at Tybee Island. After Capt. Chamberlin was taken prisoner, he led the company; had a sword, sash, belt and pistols given him, 1862, by individuals in New Britain.

THEIR CHILDREN.

1. Melissa, born April 27th, 1854, at N. Y., died Aug. 7th, 1854.
2. Walter C. born Nov. 3d, 1855, at N. Y.

3. Lilian, born Jan. 25th, 1857, at New Britain.
4. Eloise Ursula, born Aug. 7th, 1858, "

1313. "MARY ROZELLA CAPRON," to church May 4th, 1862, baptized same time; daughter of Daniel B. and his wife No. (1005;) born Aug. 26th, 1844, at Broadalbin, N. Y.

1314. "MARTHA MAKEPEACE GIDDINGS," to church May 4th, 1862; born Aug. 27th, 1841, in Hartford, Conn., to No. (1265) and his wife No. (1266;) married Dec. 5th, 1814, No. (1162.)

1315. "WM. F. RAYMOND," to church July 6th, 1862, by letter from the South church, New Britain, Rev. C. L. Goodell, Pastor; born Oct. 17th, 1813, at Montville, Conn., to Daniel of that town, and Charlotte (Comstock) his wife; married Nov. 15th, 1852, Lavinia, daughter of Deacon Michael Seymour, of Hartford, and his wife Rebecca (Woster,) of Litchfield. She died Aug. 26th, 1854, aged 30; when second he married Jan. 5th, 1858, No. (1316.) His residence in Stanley quarter; house built by No. (675;) Mr. Raymond is a successful farmer, came to this town, 1839, and represented it 1845 and 1850 in the legislature. His middle name, Fitch.

1316. "MRS. ELIZABETH," wife of Wm. F. Raymond," to church July 6th, 1862, by letter from the Congregational church in Essex, Conn.; born March 1st, 1835, to James J. Llord, of Essex, and his wife Cornelia (Hayden;) married Jan. 5th, 1858, No. (1315.)

HIS CHILD BY HIS FIRST WIFE LAVINIA.

Charlotte Lavinia, born Nov. 30th, 1853, died March 15th, 1866, aged 12.

1317. "MRS. HARRIET, wife of Richard S. Southworth," to church Sept. 7th, 1862, by letter from the church in Albion, N. Y., Rev. H. E. Niles, Pastor. She was born Aug. 21st, 1806, at Middletown, Conn., to Wm. Hamlin, of that town, and his wife Thankful (Knowles,) of Glastenbury. She married Sept. 11th, 1861, No. (923,) and was his third wife, and sister of his second No. (928.)

1318. "MRS. HARRIET L. wife of Stephen R. Lawrence," to church Sept. 7th, 1862, by letter from the church in Swanton, Vt., Rev. C. H. Bullard, Clerk; born June 25th, 1831, at Morristown, Vt., to Alvah Spaulding and his wife Emma (Cooke;) married Feb. 27th, 1851, No. (1447.)

THEIR CHILDREN.

1. Emma Cooke, born Nov. 8th, 1852, at Swanton, Vt., see No. (1356.)
2. Stephen Brainard, born March 20th, 1857, " "
3. Fanny Josaphine, born Jan. 15th, 1860, at New Britain, Ct.

1319. "SOLOMON F. LINSLEY," to church March 1st, 1863, by letter from the Chapel Street church, New Haven, Rev. Wm. T. Eustis, Pastor;

born May 26th, 1830, at Wallingford, to Dea. Marcus of that town, and his wife Clarissa (Fowler ;) a joiner by trade, learned of Lyon Billard, of Meriden; married Feb. 28th, 1855, No. (1320 ;) is now, 1863, 2d, Lieutenant, company K, 15th regiment Conn. volunteers, at Newport News, Va. His family with his father Tracy in New Britain.

1320. "LUCY A. wife of Solomon F. Linsley," to church March 1st, 1863, by letter from the Chapel Street church, New Haven, Rev. Wm. T. Eustis, Pastor; born May 19th, 1834, to No. (1269,) and his wife No. (1270 ;) married Feb. 28th, 1855, No. (1319;) living now, 1863, with her father; both dismissed Feb. 9th, 1866, to church in North Haven.

THEIR CHILDREN.

1. Edward Tracy, born April 15th, 1856, died April 6th, 1860, at New Britain.
2. Louisa Nichols, born June 11th, 1859.

1321. "LUCIUS D. BLAKE," to church May 3d, 1863, by letter from the Congregational church at East Windsor Hill, J. E. Tyler, Clerk; he born Sept. 9th, 1819, at Winchester, to Harry and his wife Hannah (Beach ;) married March 29th, 1843, No. (1322,) they have lived at Agawam, Mass., and at East Windsor Hill, have no children now, 1863; have a residence on Elm Street. His middle name, Dodridge.

1322. "MRS. SUSAN M. wife of Lucius D. Blake," to church May 3d, 1863, by letter from Congregational church, East Windsor Hill, J. E. Tyler, Clerk; born Sept. 20th, 1822, at New Britain, to Riley Griswold and his wife No. (810 ;) married March 29th, 1843, No. (1321 ;) her middle name, Munson.

1323. "MRS. SARAH, wife of E. B. Allen," to church May 3d, 1863; born May 12th, 1836, at Kidderminster, Worcestershire, England, to Joseph Beach and his wife Elizabeth (Price ;) married Nov. 23d, 1858, No. (1237.)

1324. "BERNADOTTE PERRIN," to church July 5th, 1863; born Sept. 15th, 1847, at Goshen, Conn., to Rev. L. Perrin, Pastor of the first church in New Britain, and his wife No. (1201 ;) is now 1867, a member of Yale College. Has good musical taste, and is a very acceptable organist, at the Center church.

1325. "WM. E. TRACY," to church July 5th, 1863; born Jan. 10th, 1843, to No. (856) and his first wife No. (926,) was a twin brother with Thomas E., who died 1862, while a soldier at Port Royal, S. C.

1326. "MRS. MARTHA A. wife of Rollin D. Judd," to church July 5th, 1863, by letter from the Congregational church in Farmington, Rev. L. L. Paine, Jun., Pastor; born April 25th, 1843, at Farmington, to Joel Peck of that town, and his wife Charlotte (Scovill ;) married June 9th, 1862, No. (1377.)

1327. "MRS. MARY ANN BRACE," to church July 5th, 1863, by letter from the church in Torringford, Rev. Mr. Dyer, Acting Pastor; born April 25th, 1811, at Torringford, to Allen Loomis and his wife Mary (Read;) married March 27th, 1833, Hezekiah H. Brace, of West Hartford; born June 7th, 1811, at Bloomfield, to Manning and Lucy Webster of Avon, his wife; he died April 15th, 1863, aged 52, in consequence of a hurt, in Avon, in the machinery of a mill, where he was at work; when second she married May 1st, 1866, No. (569.)

THEIR CHILDREN.

1. Juliaetta M. born July 17th, 1835, married May 20th, 1855, George Kendall, of Geo.
2. Ellen A. born June 28th, 1838, died March 2d, 1839.
3. Infant, born Feb. 28th, 1840, died immediately.
4. Henry Manning, born Aug. 17th, 1842.
5. Ellen A. born Nov. 23d, 1844, married April 2d, 1862, Ralph Foster, of Springfield, Mass.
6. Cornelia E. born Feb. 3d, 1846, married Oct. 19th, 1866, Frank A. Steele, son of Amon.
7. Willie H. born Oct. 28th, 1851, died Jan. 16th, 1852.

1328. "ELAM P. OSBORN," to church Aug., 1863, by letter from Camden, N. Y., Dr. H. J. Torbert, Clerk; born July 10th, 1817, at Camden, N. Y., to David, formerly of Harwinton, and his wife Esther (Potter,) of Plymouth; married May 4th, 1845, No. (1329.) He spent 15 years in merchandise, in Camden, N. Y., came to this place in the spring of 1862, as a farmer, and bought the place formerly Hiram Belden's. He was also a travelling agent for some fire insurance companies. He died Aug. 22d, 1863, of paralysis, a shock of which he had a year previous.

1329. "MRS. MARIA P. wife of Elam P. Osborn," to church Aug. 1863, by letter of recommendation from the Congregational church in Camden, N. Y., Dr. H. J. Torbert, Clerk; born Sept. 21st, 1815, at Middlebury, Conn., to Gideon Platt, of that town, and his wife Lydia (Sperry,) of Waterbury. Her full maiden name, Maria Hannah Platt; married May 4th, 1845, No. (1328.)

THEIR CHILDREN.

1. Lydia Maria, born July 23d, 1847, at Camden, N. Y., see No. (1354.)
2. Platt David, born June 29th, 1851, " " No. (1401.)

1330. "MRS. LOUISA O. MORGAN," to church March 6th, 1864; born Dec. 13th, 1822, at South Windsor, to Warren Thompson of that town and his wife Redexa (Loomis;) married Feb. 21st, 1847, Geo. Morgan, jun.; born Nov. 20th, 1818, at Berlin, to Geo. Morgan, sen., and his wife Esther (Sanford.) He was a blacksmith by trade, learned of Jedediah North; he died Dec. 25th, 1860, aged 42.

THEIR CHILDREN.

1. Alice Eliza, born May 3d, 1848.
2. George, born March 12th, 1852.

1331. "M. ADELIA VIETS," to church March 6th, 1864; born March 10th, 1847, to Imly B. Viets and his wife No. (936.)

1332. "EDWIN S. CHESTER," to church March 6th, 1864, by letter from first Pres. church in Perth Amboy, N. J., Chas. Wallace Mod. of session. He was born Feb. 10th, 1837, at East Haddam, to Elderkin Chester, of that town and his wife Lucy (Morgan;) married July 12th, 1860, Lizzie Walhall, of English origin; born near Liverpool, England. She died March 24th, 1862, in N. J. He has been a 9 months' soldier. He to church in N. J., June, 1862. He second married May 3d, 1864, No. (1208.) He and wife were dismissed and recommended to church in Sandusky, Ohio, April 27th, 1866.)

THEIR CHILD.

Frederick Dixon, born Oct. 8th, 1861, at Port Plate, San Domingo.

1333. "CHARLES BLAKESLEE, to church March 6th, 1864, by letter from Chapel Street Church, New Haven, Rev. Wm. T. Eustis, jun., Pastor; born Feb. 25th, 1816, at Southington, to Laban and his wife Lavinia Thorp; married Jan. 12th, 1836, Dorothy J. Eddy, daughter of Thomas and No. (419,) and was divorced, when second he married, April 17th, 1856, No. (1334.) He is an enterprising manufacturer, in company with No. (823.) His residence on West Main Street, and was formerly owned and occupied by No. (918.)

HIS SON BY FIRST WIFE DOROTHY.

Bernard Franklin, born Sept. 2d, 1843, at Southington, see No. (1452.)

1334. "MRS. LYDIA S. wife of Chas. Blakeslee," to church March 6th, 1864, by letter from Chapel Street church, New Haven, Rev. Wm. T. Eustis, jun., Pastor; born April 23d, 1827, at New Hudson, N. Y., to No. (1024) and his wife No. (1025;) married April 17th, 1856, No. (1333.) Her full maiden name, Lydia Ursula Slater.

THEIR CHILDREN.

2. Charles Burnham, born July 13th, 1857, died June 5th, 1863, at New Haven, aged 6 years, but buried in New Britain.
3. Lillian Ursula, born April 7th, 1864, at New Britain, bap. July 2d, 1865.

1335. "ETHAN JUDD," to church March 6th, 1864, by letter from Congregational church in Rutland, Vt., Rev. Norman Seaver, Pastor; born March 25th, 1798, to No. (195) and his wife No. (318;) married Nov. 18th, 1828, No. 1336; lived many years in Vt.

1336. "MRS. MELISSA C. wife of Ethan Judd," to church March 6th, 1864, by letter from Congregational church in East Rutland, Vt., Rev. Norman Seaver, Pastor; born Jan. 3d, 1808, at New Marlboro, Mass., to David Collins and his wife Hannah Gilbert, who had been Widow of Russell Case, of Simsbury; married Nov. 18th, 1828, No. (1335.)

THEIR CHILDREN.

1. Infant son, born March 28th, 1830, died at 3 hours.
2. Louisa M. born Oct. 26th, 1833, died Aug. 24th, 1852, aged 19.
3. Mary Collins, born June 30th, 1837, died Aug. 16th, 1837.

1337. "SAMUEL MCELRATH," to church March 6th, 1864; born Aug. 1st, 1831, at Boveedy, County of Londonderry, Ireland, to James of that place, and his wife Mary McLean; is a private in company H, 12th regi ment Conn., volunteers; went to Ship Island and New Orleans, has re-enlisted in same company. He is of Scotch origin. He married March 11th, 1864, No. (1277.) He lost an arm Dec. 27th, 1866, in the Knitting Factory.

THEIR CHILD.

James Brown, born Dec. 17th, 1864.

1338. "STANLEY A. CARTER," to church May 1st, 1864, baptized same time; born Nov. 24th, 1840, at Lyden, N. Y., to Loyal W. and his wife Lucy Rose; worked on his fathers' farm until the fall of 1863, when he came to New Britain and labored in the Rule and Level Shop. But June 16th, 1865, was dismissed and recommended to Presbyterian church in Batavia, N. Y.

1339. "GEORGE C. BOOTH," to church May 1st, 1864; born March 5th, 1839, at Farmington, to Alfred of New Britain, and his wife Sophia Williams, of Windsor, Conn. He attended the State Normal School at New Britain, some three terms. He was commissioned a teacher to the Freedmen, at St. Louis, 1864, by the American Mission Association, and went in Sept. to that post. He was dismissed and recommended Oct. 14th, 1864, to Methodist church in St. Louis. He married June 26th, 1865, Sarah Jane Brown, of Quincy, Ill.

1340. "HENRY S. WALTER," to church July 3d, 1864; born Dec. 16th, 1848, to No. (1066) and his second wife No. (933.)

1341. "CHAMPLAIN GARDNER," to church July 3d, 1864, by letter from church in Montville, W. R. Long, Clerk; born Oct. 13th, 1791, at Bozrah, to David of that town, and Sarah Miner his wife; married Oct. 4th, 1812, No. (1342;) a joiner by trade, lives 1865, on Arch Street.

1342. "MRS. AVALINA S. wife of Champlain Gardner," to church July 3d, 1864, by letter from first Congregational church in Montville, W. R. Long, Clerk; born Nov. 18th, 1797, at Bozrah, to Dea. Simeon Abel, of that town, and Lucy H. Leffingwell, of Norwich, his wife; married Oct. 4th, 1812, No. (1341.)

THEIR CHILDREN.

1. Matilda L. born March 11th, 1813, at Bozrah, married June 1st, 1831, Edward Higgins.
2. Lucretia L. born Oct. 18th, 1816, see No. (1343.)
3. Simeon A. born June 24th, 1818, married Sept. 24th, 1843, Matilda Clark.
4. Martin L. born Feb. 9th, 1825, died aged 5 weeks.
5. Martin L. 2d of name, born April 6th, 1826, married Harriet Doane, June, 1850.
6. Avalina S. born Jan. 7th, 1829, see No. (1310.)
7. Revillo C. born Feb. 25th, 1831, died aged 5 months, 16 days.
8. Lucy Ann, born Aug. 24th, 1833, married March 4th, 1855, Frederic F. Parker.

1343. "LUCRETIA L. GARDNER," to church July 3d, 1864, by letter from first Congregational church in Montville; born Oct. 18th, 1816, at Bozrah, to No. (1341) and his wife No. (1342;) united at about 16 with the Congregational church of East Haddam.

1344. "MRS. MARY L. MOORE," to church Jan. 1st, 1865, by letter from the church in Tolland, Mass., Rev. Geo. Ford, Pastor; born Jan. 20th, 1827, at Tolland, Mass., to Joseph C. Potter of that town, and Weltha (Stewart) his wife; married Oct. 2d, 1844, Reynold T. Moore; born June 4th, 1823, at Tolland, Mass., to Deacon Elizur D. Moore, and his wife Harriet (Wadsworth;) 1862 a soldier in 14th regiment Conn. volunteers, was taken prisoner at the battle of Chancellorsville, Va., and paroled.

THEIR CHILDREN.

1. Mary L. born Jan. 25th, 1849, at Tolland Mass., see No. (1346.)
2. Emma L. born Feb. 3d, 1852, " " " see No. (1357.)
3. Mattie E. born July 15th, 1859, " "

1345. "MRS. CHARLOTTE A. BEECHER," wife of Lyman H. Beecher, to church Jan. 1st, 1865, daughter of Rufus Seymour, of Colebrook, and his wife Althea Underwood; born March 25th, 1822, at Colebrook; married Oct. 26th, 1845. He son of Amos Beecher, of Barkhamsted, and his wife Phebe Hart, of Southington. He was born Dec. 20th, 1819, at Barkhamsted.

THEIR CHILD.

Amos Wilbur, Dec. 28th, 1854, at Colebrook, bap. Jan. 1st, 1865, at New Britain.

1346. "MARY L. MOORE," to church Jan. 1st, 1865; born Jan. 25th, 1849, at Tolland Mass., to Reynold T. Moore of that town, and his wife No. (1344.)

1347. "NATHAN SMITH BRONSON," to church March 5th, 1865, by letter from the third church, New Haven, C. L. Cleaveland, pastor; born Nov. 20th, 1837, at Waterbury, to Dr. Henry Bronson, now, 1865, of New Haven, and his wife Sarah Mills (Lathrop,) of Springfield, Mass.; married, May 30th, 1861, No. (1348;) he bought, 1864, the farm formerly called the Skinner farm, but lately the O. B. North farm, on East st.; his residence now, 1867, the Dr. Smalley place, renovated.

1348. "MRS. CHARLOTTE, wife of N. S. Bronson," to church March 5th, 1865, by letter from third church, New Haven, C. L. Cleaveland, pastor; born May 6th, 1840, at Torringford, to Burton Pond, of that town, and his wife Charlotte (Colt;) married, May 30th, 1861, No. (1347.)

THEIR CHILDREN.

1. Alice Pond, born Aug. 23d, 1862, at New Haven.
2. Henry Burton, born Sept. 6th, 1864, at New Britain, died June 7th, 1865, at New Haven.
3. Joseph Lathrop, born Aug. 22d, 1866, bap. April 28th, 1867.

1349. "JESSE STANLEY," to church May 7th, 1865, born Aug. 1st, 1848, to No. (1027) and her husband Oliver C. Stanley.

1350. "ADDISON PERRIN," to church May 7th, 1865, born Sept. 27th, 1852, to Rev. L. Perrin, pastor of the church, and his wife No. (1201.)

1351. "MRS. EMILY A., wife of Lafayette Bosworth," to church July 2d, 1865, by letter from the second church in Rockville; born May 8th, 1830, at North Coventry, to Caleb Fenton and his wife Sabrina (Morley;) married, April 28th, 1864, No. (1301,) and is his third wife.

1352. "MRS. ANGELINE, wife of James Thompson," to church July 2d, 1865, and baptized same time; born May 8th, 1830, to James Blackwell, of Avon, and his wife Dorinda (Alvord;) married, May 10th, 1852, James Thompson, son of John of Farmington, and his wife Nancy (Orvis;) born Feb. 5th, 1822; his residence on Willow st., formerly the residence of Norman Eddy; Mr. Thompson has been very successful in the grocery business, and has a fine store on Main st.

THEIR CHILDREN.

1. Ella B., born June 13th, 1853.
2. Millard B., born May 29th, 1855.
3. Wilbur, born Feb. 18th, 1859.

1353. "CATHARINE PERRIN," to church July 2d, 1865, born Dec. 8th 1850, to Rev. L. Perrin, pastor of the church, and his wife No. (1201.)

1354. "LYDIA M. OSBORNE, to church July 2d, 1865, born July 23d, 1847, to No. (1328) and his wife No. (1329.)

1355. "SARAH M. STRONG," to church July 2d, 1865, baptized same time; born March 28th, 1850, to No. (1148) and his wife No. (1149,) at Woodbury, Ct.

1356. "ELENORA J. VEITS," to church July 2d, 1865, born July 22d, 1849, to Imlay B. Veits and his wife No. (936.)

1357. "EMMA L. MOORE," to church July 2d, 1865, born Feb. 3d, 1852, at Tolland, Mass., to R. T. Moore and his wife No. (1344.)

1358. "LOUISE E. BABCOCK," to church July 2d, 1865, baptized same time; born Jan. 11th, 1852, to Dr. E. D. Babcock, and his wife No. (993.)

1359. "EMMA C. LAWRENCE," to church July 2d, 1865, born Nov. 8th, 1852, at Swanton, Vt., to No. (1447) and his wife No. (1318.)

1360. "HERMAN F. WELLS," to church July 2d, 1865, born April 29th, 1849, to No. (942) and his wife No. (1093.)

1361. "WILLIE A. MINOR," to church July 2d, 1865, baptized same time, born Sept. 25th, 1851, at Derby, Ct., to No. (1143) and his first wife Ursula (Allen.)

1362. "MRS. MATILDA, wife of Robert Couples," to church Sept. 3d, 1865, born May 18th, 1829, to John McElrath and his wife No. (1276;) married July 23d, 1853.

THEIR CHILDREN.

1. Ann Jane, born Dec. 1st, 1847, bap. Nov. 5th, 1865.
2. Robert George, born April 6th, 1860, bap. Nov. 5th, 1865.
3. James Timothy, born Sept. 21st, 1864, bap. Nov. 5th, 1865.

1363. "JOSEPH HANNOE RASCOE," to church Nov. 5th, 1865, baptized same time; born Sept. 25th, 1848, at Windsor, N. C., to Joseph Rascoe, of that town, and Hannah, his hired slave.

1364. "EUGENE B. RIPLEY," to church Nov. 5th, 1865, born April 4th, 1848, at Bentonsport, Iowa, to No. (1307,) and Harriet R. Riggs, his first wife; he is now, 1865, book-keeper for the "Stanley Rule and Level Co."

1365. "MARTHA MARIA BELDEN," to church Jan. 7th, 1866, and baptized same time; born July 29th, 1829, to Geo. D. Belden, and Elizabeth (Sanger,) his wife; successful as a milliner on Main street, New Britain.

1366. "JENNIE L. ANDREWS," to church Jan. 7th, 1866, born Aug. 10th, 1847, to No. (478) and his second wife No. (657;) married, June 6th, 1866, Lyman A. Mills, son of Rev. C. L. Mills and his first wife Rebecca (Lyman;) born Feb. 25th, 1841, at Middlefield, Ct.; she was dismissed and recommended to church in Middlefield, Dec. 20th, 1866.

1367. "AURELIA MELVINA JONES," to church Jan. 7th, 1866, and baptized same time; born Nov. 5th, 1844, to No. (1072) and her second husband, Wm. B. Jones.

1368. "BENJAMIN F. CLOYES," to church Jan. 7th, 1866, by letter from church in Conway, Mass., Rev. E. Cutler, pastor; son of Benjamin, of Framingham, Mass., and his wife Esther Pratt, of Sturbridge, Mass.; born March 27th, 1800, at Charleston, N. H., married, Nov. 24th, 1824,

No. (1369;) he a tinman by trade, and stove dealer, on Main st., opposite the old North church, now Strickland Hall.

1369. "Mrs. Sarah, wife of B. F. Cloyes," to church Jan. 7th, 1866, by letter from church in Conway, Mass., Rev. E. Cutler, pastor; daughter of Benjamin Bird, of Plainville, Ct., and his wife Deborah (Carrington;) born Sept. 17th, 1804, married, Nov. 24th, 1824, No. (1368;) she died Aug. 10th, 1867, in her 63d year, at New Britain.

THEIR CHILDREN.

1. Elizabeth P., born Jan. 27th, 1826, at Esperance, N. Y., married, Aug. 3d, 1847 Wm. M. Foster, of Bloomfield.
2. Joseph H., born Nov. 29th, 1827, married, April, 1852, Eliza D. Wheeler.
3. Julia M., born Nov. 7th, 1831, at New Hartford, Ct., died July 31st, 1833, aged 1 year and 8 months.
4. Sarah J., born Sept. 4th, 1835, at Brooklyn, Ct., married, Jan., 1860, John W. Cleaveland.
5. Fanny M., born Jan. 7th, 1837, at Brooklyn, Ct., married, Dec. 19th, 1856, Stephen W. Deming.
6. Harriet E., born Aug. 2d, 1845, at Springfield, Mass., died Dec. 11th, 1864, at Conway, Mass.

1370. Mrs. Ruth Savage Buckley," to church Jan. 7th, 1866, by letter from church in Berlin, Rev. Wilder Smith, pastor; born July 3d, 1800, at Berlin, to Seth Savage and his wife Esther (DeWolfe;) married, Sept. 15th, 1819, Justus Buckley, son of Justus, of Rocky Hill, and his wife Mabel (Boardman;) he died Jan. 6th, 1844, aged 48; her residence on Franklin st.

THEIR CHILDREN.

1. Maria L., born April 16th, 1821, married; Lyman Wilcox; she died Dec. 1st, 1859.
2. Walter H., born Feb. 25th, 1823, died May 10th, 1862.
3. Edwin L., born Dec. 28th, 1825, died May 15th, 1826.
4. Edwin A., born April 30th, 1827, married Mary Sanford.
5. Mary A., born July 27th, 1830, see No. (1372.)
6. Harriet S., born June 5th, 1832, see No. (1115.)

1371. "Francis Chambers," to church Jan. 7th, 1866, by letter from the church in Berlin, Rev. Wilder Smith, pastor; born May 7th, 1828, at Rocky Hill, to George O., of that town, and his wife Martha (Robbins;) married, Dec. 11th, 1854, No. (1372;) is a lawyer by profession and occupation, and resides on Franklin st.

1372. "Mrs. Mary A. Chambers," to church Jan. 7th, 1866, by letter from church in Berlin, Rev. Wilder Smith, pastor; born July 27th, 1830, at Berlin, to Justus Buckley and his wife Ruth (Savage;) married Dec. 11th, 1854, to No. (1371.)

THEIR CHILDREN.

1. Agnes B., born Dec. 3d, 1855.
2. Mary R., born Oct. 7th, 1861.

1373. "MRS. EUNICE STEBBINS PARKER," to church Jan. 7th, 1866, by letter from church in Meriden, Rev. H. C. Hayden, pastor; born Oct. 8th, 1827, at Springfield, Mass., to Henry Stebbins and his wife Lucy (Atkins;) married, March 15th, 1847, Emery Parker, son of Samuel, of Amherst, and his wife Rebecca (Dickinson;) born June 26th, 1825; his residence on East Main st.

THEIR CHILDREN.

1. Imogene, born Dec. 27th, 1848, died Dec. 27th, 1849.
2. Wm. E., born Feb. 20th, 1851.
3. Franklin H., born June 1st, 1852, died July 18th, 1855.
4. Maria L., born Nov. 4th, 1854.
5. Nellie, born Oct. 5th, 1858.
6. Harriet S., born Aug. 27th, 1860, died April 16th, 1861.
7. Henry S., born Feb. 23d, 1862.
8. Georgiana D., born Nov. 27th, 1864.
9. John Kilbourn, born June 30th, 1866, died Sept. 16th, 1866, aged 11 weeks.

1374. "MRS. LOIS PERRIN," to church Jan. 7th, 1866, by letter from church at East Windsor Hill, E. Ellsworth, clerk; born Jan. 30th, 1793, at South Hadley, Mass., to Elijah Lee, of Vernon, Ct., and his wife Sarah (Higgins;) married April 30th, 1812, to No. (1395.)

THEIR CHILDREN.

1. Mary Ann, born July 26th, 1813, married, Nov. 28th, 1844, Samuel Galpin, of Wethersfield, Ct.
2. Mariette, born July 26th, 1813, married, Nov. 27th, 1839, Edward Brigham, of Coventry, Ct.
3. Lavalette, born May 15th, 1816, married, June 4th, 1844, Ann Eliza Comstock, of Ridgefield.
4. Roselle, born Aug. 31st, 1821, married, Jan. 15th, 1839, Rev. David Bancroft, of Willington.

1375. "JULIA MILLS LYMAN," to church Jan. 7th, 1866, born Aug. 12th, 1849, at New Hartford, Ct., to Rufus Lyman, of that town, and his wife Sarah (Deming;) attending now, 1866, the State Normal School; she was dismissed and recommended by letter, Dec. 21st, 1866, to the Congregational church in Northfield, Ct.

1376. "ALFRED PITKIN WILLIAMS," to church Jan. 7th, 1866, baptized same time; born July 29th, 1841, at Hartford, to Levi Williams, of East Hartford, and his wife Lucy (Roberts;) occupation, a mechanic.

1377. "ROLLIN D. JUDD," to church March 4th, 1866, and baptized same time; born June 9th, 1840, to No, (823) and his first wife No. (959;) married, June 9th, 1862, No. (1326;) he by occupation a mechanic, his residence with his father, corner of West Main and Washington sts.

1378. "MARTHA L. JUDD," to church March 4th, 1866, born July 9, 1846, to No. (918) and his first wife No. (619.)

1379. "JULIA ANN DEWEIR," to church March 4th, 1866, and baptized same time; born March 18th, 1844, at Wolcottville, to John DeWeir, of that town, and his wife Margaret.

1380. "MRS. ANN ELIZA ANDREWS," to church May 6th, 1866, baptized same time; married, June 25th, 1862, No. (1103,) she born Jan. 19th, 1836, at Wethersfield, to Samuel J. Andrews, of that town, and his wife Chloe Ann (Francis.)

1381. "MRS. FANNY M. CLARK," to church May 6th, 1866, baptized same time; born Oct. 20th, 1833, at Middletown, to Leander Hotchkiss and his wife Sarah (Lowe;) married, May 15th, 1856, Edwin S. Clark, son of No. (477;) he lived at the old Clark Homestead, and died there, April 12th, 1865, in the 36th year of his age.

THEIR CHILDREN.

1. Sarah Louise, born Feb. 14th, 1857, bap. Aug. 31st, 1866.
2. Emma Augusta, born Oct. 21st, 1860, bap. Aug. 31st, 1866.
3. Mary Fannie, born Nov. 5th, 1862, bap. Aug. 31st, 1866.
4. Edwin Chauncey, born Nov. 19th, 1864, bap. Aug. 31st, 1866.

1382. "MRS. CLEORA W. WETMORE," to church May 6th, 1866, born May 24th, 1824, at Norwich, Mass., to Artemas Knight and his wife Mary W. (Kingsley;) married, Oct. 18th, 1850, Chas. H. Wetmore, son of John, of Litchfield, and his wife Anna (Seymour;) born Nov. 27th, 1821, at Litchfield; his residence corner of Walnut and Prospect sts.; by trade a joiner.

THEIR CHILDREN.

1. Alice C., born Nov. 18th, 1851.
2. Frank K., born Nov. 17th, 1853.
3. Charles E., born Sept. 30th, 1855.
4. Harry S., born June 5th, 1858.

1383. "MRS. CATHARINE D. HARTMAN," to church May 6th, 1866, born Nov. 12th, 1831, at Bemphlingen, Germany, to Gotleib F. Mack and his wife Catharine M. Kuhefuss; married, Feb. 15th, 1853, Chas. A. Hartman, son of John T., of Germany, and his wife Sophia; born Sept. 19th, 1823.

THEIR CHILDREN.

1. Katie S., born March 27th, 1855.
2. Wm. T., born July 31st, 1857.
3. Frederic A., born March 18th, 1861.

1384. "MARY A. BULKLEY," to church May 6th, 1866, born Nov. 7th, 1841, at Berlin, to Wm. J. Bulkley and his wife Luanna (Belden;) married, June 28th, 1866, Chas. H. Beaton.

1385. "MARTHA E. STANLEY," to church May 6th, 1866, born July 7th, 1846, to No. (604) and his wife No. (984;) married, Sept. 18th, 1866, Charles H. Cornwell; he born April 10th, 1836, to No. (401.)

1386. "MARION R. ELLIS," to church May 6th, 1866, born Aug. 1st, 1848, to No. (1079) and his wife (1080.)

1387. "GRACE ELLEN JUDD," to church May 6th, 1866, and baptized same time; born July 27th, 1849, to No. (1190) and his wife No. (1191.)

1388. "ELLEN S. BARTLETT," to church May 6th, 1866, born March 28th, 1848, to No. (1282) and his wife No. (1283.)

1389. "L. HOYT PEASE," to church May 6th, 1866, born Jan. 20th, 1845, to No. (1038) and his wife No. (1039.)

1390. "WM. H. ELLIS," to church May 6th, 1866, born Nov. 10th, 1843, to No. (1079) and his wife (1080.)

1391. "WM. H. GIDDINGS," to church May 6th, 1866, born Jan. 17, 1847, to No. (1265) and his wife No. (1266.)

1392. "CHARLES J. PARKER," to church May 6th, 1866, born Oct. 21st, 1849, to No. (864) and his wife No. (891.)

1393. "HORACE W. BOOTH," to church May 6th, 1866, born Oct. 18th, 1849 to No. (793) and his wife No. (1094.)

1394. "MRS. EMILY MOORE," to church March 4th, 1866, by letter from church in West Winsted, John Hinsdale, clerk; born Jan. 20th, 1832, at Sheffield, Eng., to Edward Roberts and his wife Mary Lee; married, Nov. 26th, 1854, Thomas W. Moore, of Bantam Falls, and his wife Wealthy (Griswold,) born Jan. 31st, 1830.

1395. "AARON PERRIN," to church July 1st, 1866, born June 26th, 1786, to Solomon Perrin, of Vernon, Ct., and his wife Anna (Kellogg;) married, April 30th, 1812, No. (1374;) resides with his son (our pastor,) on Washington st.

1396. "MRS. ANNA H. DICKINSON," to church July 1st, 1866, baptized same time; born March 10th, 1830 to Lorenzo Hayes, of East Windsor, and his wife Arminda (Robinson;) married, Jan. 1st, 1850, to No. (1157.)

1397. FANNIE LOUISE DICKINSON," to church July 1st, 1866, baptized same time; born Sept. 22d, 1850, to No. (1157) and his wife No. (1396.)

1398. "THOMAS R. RHODES," to church July 1st, 1866, baptized same time, born Feb. 2d, 1850, to Henry E. Rhodes, and his wife, No. (1248.)

1399. "CHARLOTTE M. GLADDEN," to church July 1st, 1866, baptized same time, born June 10th, 1843, to Henry Gladden, and his second wife, No. (711;) choir singer, alto.

1400. "ROXY RECOR," to church July 1st, 1866, baptized same time, born Jan. 21st, 1850, to Philo, and his wife Almira (Morgan,) lives, 1867, with No. (560.)

1401. "PLATT D. OSBORN," to church July 1st, 1866, born June 29th, 1851, at Camden, N. Y., to No. (1328,) and his wife, No. (1329;) remarkably tall, now, 1867, stands six feet four inches in stockings.

1402. "Mrs. SARAH JANE MALLORY," to church July 1st, 1866, baptized by immersion previous week, born March 31st, 1835, at Avon, to Daniel M. Alford, of that town, and his wife Emira (Mills,) of Canton, married Sept. 2d, 1856, No. (1426.)

1403. "JAMES ANDERSON," to church July 1st, 1866, born August 1st, 1821, at Basking Ridge, N. J., to Guion, of New York, and his wife, Mary (Woodward,) married Jan. 30th, 1865, No. (1404;) a tailor by trade.

1404. "Mrs. EUNICE M. ANDERSON," to church July 1st, 1866, born May 26th, 1839, at Old Lyme, to Deacon Charles Comstock, of that town, and his wife.

1405. "ROENA W. PRIOR," to church July 1st, 1866, born May 15th, 1844, to Prosper Prior, and his wife, No. (1297.)

1406. "MARY W. SWIFT," to church July 1st, 1866, born May 20th, 1845, to No. (1284,) and his wife, No. (1285.)

1407. "MATTIE F. PEASE," to church July 1st, 1866, born Nov. 28th, 1845, to No. (1038,) and his wife, No. (1039,) now a teacher.

1408. "MARY L. HOTCHKISS, to church July 1st, 1866, born October 23d, 1849, at Southington, to George F., of New Haven, and his wife, No. (1292.)

1409. "SARAH A. STANLEY," to church July 1st, 1866, born Feb. 21st, 1851, to No. (604,) and his wife, No. (984.)

1410. "MARY ESTELLA HIGGINS," to church July 1st, 1866, born Aug. 20th, 1852, to No. (1155,) and his wife, No. (1156.)

1411, "EMMA S. COMINGS," to church July 1st, 1866, born March 24th, 1852, a twin with Willie, to No. (1109,) and his wife, No. (1110.)

1412. "GRACE STANLEY," to church July 1st, 1866, born April 8th, 1852, to No. (1164,) and his first wife, No. (886.)

1413. "ANNA R. BEEBE," to church July 1st, 1866, born April 25th, 1853, to No. (1140,) and his wife, No. (1141.)

1414. "JULIUS H. PEASE," to church July 1st, 1866, born Nov. 22d, 1848, to No. (1038,) and his wife, No. (1039;) is a book keeper.

1415. "ALEXANDER F. EMMONS," to church July 1st, 1866, born April 4th, 1850, at Guilford, to No. (1131,) and his wife, No. (1132.)

1416. "WILLIAM E. PARKER," to church July 1st, 1866, born Feb. 20th, 1851, to Emory Parker, and his wife, No. (1373.)

1417. "WILLIAM H. THORNTON," to church July 1st, 1866, born Oct. 10th, 1851, to No. (1222,) and his wife, No. (1223.)

1418. "FREDERICK W. GIDDINGS," to church July 1st, 1866, born Aug. 27th, 1850, to No. (1265,) and his wife, No. (1266.)

1419. "William Swift Goodwin," to church July 1st, 1866, born Sept. 30th, 1849, at South Canaan, Ct., to Rev. Harley Goodwin, of that town, and his wife Lydia R. (Swift,) of Cornwall; lives with his uncle, No. (1284.)

1420. "Ernest August Hartman," to church July 1st, 1866, by letter from Ev. Lutheran church, Saxony, married Feb. 15th, 1853, No. (1383.)

1421. "Mrs. Mary E. Robinson," to church July 1st, 1866, by letter from 13th Street Presbyterian church, New York, Rev. S. D. Burchard, pastor, born March 7th, 1835, to Frederick A. Roberts, of Millington, Ct., and his wife Mary (Emmons,) married Oct. 22d, 1856, Gideon Robinson, born Sept. 2d, 1825, in county of Kent, England, to John, and his wife Mary (Chambers,) by trade and occupation a jeweler.

1422. "Adolphus Koehler," to church July 1st, 1866, by letter from Second Congregational church, Holyoke, Mass., Rev. L. R. Eastman, pastor, born June 13th, 1837, to Gotlob, of Germany, and his wife Elizabeth (Fuchs,) married Sept. 20th, 1863, No. (1423;) residence on North street, near Skelley's grove.

1423. "Mrs. Margaret Koehler," to church July 1st, 1866, by letter from Second Congregational church, Holyoke, Mass., born June 15th, 1841, in Germany, to John Bonnett, and his wife Frederick (Wagner,) married Sept. 20th, 1863, No. (1422.)

THEIR CHILD.

Lilly Anna, born July 8th, 1864.

1424. "Mrs. Amelia Ellis," to church Sept. 2d, 1866, baptized same time, born May 20th, 1845, at Huntington, L. I., to John Terry, of that town, and his wife Phebe (Chichester,) married Dec. 6th, 1865, No. (1260.)

1425. "Jennie E. Williams," to church Sept. 2d, 1866, baptized same time, born March 29th, 1844, to George Williams, and his wife Jane M. (Pennfield.)

1426. "Anthony J. Mallory," to church Sept. 2d, 1866, by letter from church in West Avon, Rev. W. W. Atwater, pastor, born Dec. 15th, 1830, at Roxbury, Ct., to Ira, of that town, and his wife Susan (Morris,) married Sept. 2d, 1856, No. (1402.)

THEIR CHILD.

Effie J., born May 31st, 1859, at Avon.

1427. "Mrs. Sally Buel," to church Sept. 2d, 1866, by letter from church in Litchfield, Charles Adams, clerk, born July 29th, 1787, at New Britain, to No. (259,) and his wife, No. (260,) married Oct. 1st, 1809,

Ira Buel, of Litchfield, born Aug. 21st, 1788, to Solomon, and his wife Elizabeth (Mason.)

THEIR CHILDREN.

1. Maria C., born Oct. 24th, 1810, married William Tuttle.
2. Louisa, born March 9th, 1813, married Lewis Downs.
3. Julia A., born Feb. 3d, 1816, married Clark Newcomb.
4. Sarah, born June 3d, 1818, married Henry Merrill.
5. James H., born Aug. 3d, 1820.
6. Elizabeth, born Sept. 3d, 1822, No. (1428.)
7. John Mason, born Oct. 22d, 1825, died Sept. 14th, 1826.
8. Mary J., born Oct. 3d, 1829, married Elijah Abbott.
9. Myron L., born Sept. 26th, 1832.

1428. "Mrs. ELIZABETH POND," to church Sept. 2d, 1866, by letter from church in Litchfield, Charles Adams, clerk, born Sept. 3d, 1832, at Litchfield, to Ira Buel, of that town, and his wife, No. (1427,) married April 12th, 1846, George W. Pond, of Wolcottville, born Sept. 17th, 1818, to Prescott, of that town, and his wife Eliza (Palmer,) he died Feb. 9th, 1856, aged 38, at New Britain.

THEIR CHILDREN.

1. William Buel, born June 14th, 1850.
2. Ella Gertrude, born May 27th, 1856.

1429. "Mrs. MARIA CARTER, wife of Frederick Whittlesey," to church Nov. 4th, 1866, baptized same time, born March 17th, 1837, at Warren, Ct., to Burton Gilbert, of that town, and his wife Maria (Carter,) married Nov. 6th, 1861. He was born Sept. 25th, 1834, at New Preston, Ct., to David Chester Whittlesey, of that town, and his wife Mary (Cogswell.) Mr. Whittlesey is a dry goods merchant, on Main street.

THEIR CHILDREN.

1. Nellie, born Aug. 5th, 1863, died Aug. 25th, 1863, aged 3 weeks.
2. Mary Swift, born May 20th, 1865, bap. Aug. 30th, 1867.

1430. "Mrs. ELIZABETH, wife of Hiram Bigelow," to church Nov. 4th, 1866, baptized same time, born Aug. 11th, 1840, at Natic, Mass., to Moses Layford, of that town, and his wife Olive (Allen,) married Aug. 7th, 1856. He was born Sept. 13th, 1829, at Charlton, Mass., to Hiram Bigelow, sen., of that town, and his wife Betsey (Brown;) he is a sawyer by trade and occupation.

THEIR CHILDREN.

1. Jennie Ida, born Jan. 19th, 1857, at Spencer, Mass.
2. Nellie, born Dec. 28th, 1862, at New Britain.
3. Wilaby, born June 4th, 1865, at New Britain.

1431. "Albina Lyford," to church Nov. 4th, 1866, baptized same time, born Aug. 19th, 1850, at Williamstown, Mass., to Moses Lyford, and his wife Olive (Allen.)

1432. "Rodolphus Lovejoy Webb," to church Nov. 4th, 1866, by letter from church in West Meriden, Deacon Catlin, clerk, born Aug. 12th, 1830, at Rocky Hill, Ct., to Henry Webb, of that town, and his wife Mary (Lovejoy,) married Nov. 26th, 1851, No. (1433,) has a fine residence south side of East Main street.

1433. "Mrs. Harriet Maria, wife of Rodolphus L. Webb," to church Nov. 4th, 1866, by letter from Congregational church in West Meriden, Deacon Catlin, clerk, born May 2d, 1831, at Rocky Hill, to Horace Williams, of that town, and his wife Rachel (Dimock.)

THEIR CHILDREN.

1. James Williams, born June 20th, 1858, died Aug. 22d, 1858.
2. Adele, born Sept. 26th, 1861.

1434. "Peter Gray," to church Nov. 4th, 1866, by letter from South Congregational church, Hartford, Rev. E. P. Parker, pastor, born Nov. 27th, 1828, at Linlithgow, Scotland, to William, and his wife Mary (Carlaw,) married Sept. 11th, 1854, No. (1435,) his residence, the former home of Samuel Smith, in Stanley quarter.

1435. "Mrs. Martha, wife of Peter Gray," to church Nov. 4th, 1866, by letter from South Congregational church, Hartford, Rev. E. P. Parker, pastor, born 1827, at Johnson, Scotland, to William McGee, and his wife Agnes (Potts,) married Sept. 11th, 1854, No. (1434.)

THEIR CHILDREN.

1. Mary Jane, born July 18th, 1855, at Hamaltown, C. W.
2. William David, born July 2d, 1857, at Middletown, Ct.
3. Martha Agnes, born March 3d, 1861, at Hartford, Ct.

1436. "Nelson S. Culver," to church Nov. 4th, 1866, by letter from Congregational church, Unionville, H. Northam, clerk, born Dec. 25th, 1832, at Wethersfield, to James N. Culver, of that town, and his wife Almira (Purple,) married June 10th, 1857, No. (1437.)

1437. "Mrs. Mary M., wife of Nelson S. Culver," to church Nov. 4th, 1866, by letter from Congregational church, Unionville, H. Northam, clerk, born Oct. 19th, 1839, to Daniel Adkins, of Plymouth, and his wife Nancy (Barnes,) of New Hartford, married June 10th, 1857, No. (1436.)

THEIR CHILDREN.

1. Harriet Adella, born Nov. 15th, 1859, died Aug. 1st, 1860, aged 8½ months.
2. Phineas Bird, born Dec. 31st, 1861.

1438. "JANE SMITH BONNEY," to church Jan. 6th, 1867, born May 21st, 1849, at Terryville, to Stephen Bonney, then of that town, and his wife Martha (Smith.) She is now, at this date, a member of the Normal School, and a graduate of 1867.

1439. "CHARLES TOMLINSON," to church Jan. 6th, 1867, by letter from Presbyterian church of Binghampton, N. Y., born Sept. 23d, 1836, at Wales, N. Y., to William, then of that town, and his wife Mary (Burroughs,) married July 13th, 1865, Charlotte E. King, of Saybrook, Ct. She died Sept. 18th, 1866, aged 34. She was distinguished as well for piety as fine taste and great accomplishments. He is a photographic artist, on Main street, New Britain. He married second, Oct. 8th, 1867, Charlotte A. Comstock, of Swanton, Vt.

1440. "WILLIAM N. FELT," to church Jan. 6th, 1867, by letter from Madison Square Presbyterian church, N. Y., born Jan. 12th, 1828, at Wrentham, Mass., to Oliver, of that town, and his wife Almira (Shepherd,) married Sept. 13th, 1864, No. (1441.) He is of the firm of Whittlesey & Felt, dry goods merchants, on Main street, and is a Sabbath school teacher.

1441. "Mrs. FANNIE, wife of William N. Felt," to church Jan. 6th, 1867, by letter from Congregational church of New Preston, Ct., born Oct. 14th, 1836, at New Preston, to D. C. Whittlesey, of that town, and his wife Mary (Cogswell,) married Sept. 13th, 1864, No. (1440.)

THEIR CHILD.

William Pomeroy, born July 31st, 1865, at Richmond, Va., bap. Aug. 30th, 1867.

1442. "ELIJAH F. BLAKE," to church March 3d, 1867, by letter from Congregational church of Winchester, Deacon I. A. Bronson, clerk, born May 22d, 1830, to Harry, of that town, and his wife Hannah (Beach,) married May 1st, 1855, No. (1443 ;) is a farmer by occupation ; residence and farm in Stanley quarter, bought, (1865,) of No. 849. He was a deacon in Winchester church, and elected to the same office here, April 12th, 1867.

1443. "Mrs. JULIA M., wife of E. F. Blake," to church March 3d, 1867, by letter from church in Winchester, Deacon I. A. Bronson, clerk, born June 14th, 1829, to Jared Clark, of Chaplin, Ct., and his wife Julia (Storrs.)

THEIR CHILDREN.

1. Arthur Clark, born July 20th, 1856, bap. at Winchester.
2. Mary, born May 15th, 1860, bap. at Winchester.

1444. "HANNAH BLAKE," to church March 3d, 1867, by letter from Congregational church of Winchester, Deacon I. A. Bronson, clerk, born

May 6th, 1824, at Winchester, to Harry, of that town, and his wife Hannah (Beach.) She was a twin with Harriet, who died young.

1445. "ITHAMAR MEEKER," to church March 3d, 1867, by letter from Congregational church of Terryville, W. T. Goodwin, clerk, born March 1st, 1832, at Walnut Grove, N. J., to Timothy, of that place, and his wife Phebe B. (Wilkinson,) married Dec. 27th, 1854, No. (1446;) by occupation a book-keeper; was appointed, Jan. 4th, 1867, an assistant superintendant in our Sabbath school.

1446. "Mrs. ABBIE F., wife of Ithamar Meeker," to church March 3d, 1867, by letter from church in Terryville, W. T. Goodwin, clerk, born July 17th, 1835, at Clinton, N. J., to Charles Townley, and his wife Margaret (Watkins,) married Dec. 27th, 1854, No. (1445.)

THEIR CHILDREN.

1. Ida, born Oct. 26th, 1855, at Newark, N. J., and bap. there.
2. Phebe Bell, born Oct. 16th, 1861, at Newark, N. J., and bap. there.

1447. "STEPHEN R. LAWRENCE," to church May 5th, 1867, baptized same time, born Aug. 2d, 1828, at St. Albans, Vt., to Stephen, of that town, and his wife Edna (Clark,) married Feb. 27th, 1851, No. (1318;) his residence is on South Main street.

1448. "Mrs. GENEVRA, M., wife of Mahlon J. Woodruff," to church May 5th, 1867, by letter from Methodist Episcopal church, Greenport, L. I., born April 26th, 1840, at Westbrook, Ct., to Cornelius Wright, of Greenport, and his wife Mary (Sitcher,) married Jan. 18th, 1865, No. (1259,) and is his second wife.

1449. "Mrs. HARRIET MARIA NORTHROP," to church May 5th, 1867, by letter from Congregational church in Wallingford, Rev. E. R. Gilbert, pastor, born Jan. 8th, 1819, at Woodbury, Ct., to David C. Bacon, of that town, and his wife Sarah (Wheeler,) of Derby, married April 3d, 1839, Obadiah Preston Northrop, born Jan. 6th, 1809, at Chatham, N. Y., to Job, of that town, and his wife Susan (Cady.) He died, Nov. 9th, 1862, at Wallingford, to which church he was deacon. He had a former wife, married April 2d, 1830, Nancy Maria Judson, born Nov. 11th, 1809, to Truman of Woodbury, and his wife Olive (Stoddard.) She died Nov. 4th, 1837, aged 28.

HIS SON BY HIS FIRST WIFE, NANCY.

George Judson, born April 29th, 1833, died Sept. 12th, 1854, aged 21.

HIS SON BY HIS SECOND WIFE, HARRIET.

John Bacon, born March 27th, 1842, married May 8th, 1867, Bell Morse, of Wallingford.

1450. "Mrs. ELIZA FIDELIA, wife of Henry S. Wellman," to church May 5th, 1867, by letter from Congregational church, Madison, Ct., Rev.

James Gallup, pastor, born March 23d, 1834, at Killingworth, Ct., to Daniel Stevens, of that town, and his wife Mercy (Griffing,) married Nov. 20th, 1859. He was born Sept. 3d, 1834, at Killingworth, to Chauncey, of that town, and his wife Lydia (Clark.) His residence, on Arch street.

THEIR CHILD.

Ellen Eliza, born March 2d, 1861, died March 5th, 1861, aged 3 days.

1451. "MRS. EMILY DREW," to church May 5th, 1867, by letter from 2d Congregational church in Killingly, Conn., Dea. J. Hammond, Clerk; born Aug. 14th, 1821, at Killingly, Conn., to Gurdon Mason of that town, and his wife Sabra Potter, of R. I.; married Nov. 13th, 1842, Benjamin Drew; born July 1st, 1812, in the State of Maine, to Lemuel and his wife Sarah Grierson; he died May 16th, 1866, at Killingly, Conn., in his 54th year. Her residence on Franklin Street.

THEIR CHILDREN.

1. Sarah Sabra, born Feb. 6th, 1844, died Dec. 11th, 1851, in Ill., aged 8.
2. Mary Maria, born Oct. 26th, 1845, married Oct. 29th, 1865, Shubel H. Whaples of Newington.
3. Byron Benjamin, born May 1st, 1851, died same day.
4. Herbert Andrew, born Jan. 6th, 1857, in Ill.

1452. "BERNARD FRANKLIN BLAKESLEE," to church July 7th, 1867; born Sept. 2d, 1843, at Southington, to No. (1333,) and his first wife Dorothy. Was, 1863, in company A, 16th regiment, Conn. volunteers, located at Portsmouth, Va., was promoted to 2d Lieut. of company G, 16th regiment, 1864. At this date in a drug Store at New Haven.

1453. "FREDERIC GOODHUE MEAD," to church July 7th, 1867, by letter from Pres. church at Madison Square, N. Y., Rev. Wm. Adams, Pastor; born March 19th, 1848, at Brattleboro, Vt., to Larking G. of that town, and his wife Mary Noyes, of Putney, Vt. He is at this date book-keeper at the Union Works.

1454. "MRS. LEMINA LUCRETIA CASE," to church July 7th, 1867, by letter from Congregational church of East Avon, Rev. Geo. Curtiss, Pastor; born Nov. 25th, 1822, at Granby, Conn., to Justin Hayes of that town, and his wife Lucretia Case; married Feb. 19th, 1844, Justus Marcus Case, of Simsbury; born Sept. 4th, 1816, to Horatio G. and his wife Hepzibah Cornish. He by occupation a farmer and land surveyor; he died March 23d, 1864, in his 48th year. Her residence is on High Street.

THEIR CHILDREN.

1. Martha Ann, born July 12th, 1845, died April 10th, 1849.
2. Justin Lucius, born Oct. 28th, 1851, at Simsbury.

1455. "MARY LUCY HAYES," to church July 7th, 1867, by letter from Congregational church of East Avon, Rev. Geo. Curtiss, Pastor;

born Oct. 12th, 1844, at Simsbury, to Justin Hayes of that town, and his wife Lucretia Case; she is sister of No. (1454,) and lives at this date with her.

1456. "LUCIUS W. CURTISS," to church Sept. 1st, 1867, by letter from the Congregational church in Hanover, Erastus Hubbard, Clerk; born Oct. 5th, 1830, at Bristol, Conn., to Philo of that town, and his wife Charlotte Curtiss; married May 15th, 1853, Hannah A. Barker, of Chester, Ct.; she died Sept. 11th, 1854, at Meriden, when second he married, Dec. 15th, 1857, No. (1457.) He is by trade and occupation a worker in cutlery, lives now, 1867, on Park Street.

1457. "MRS. OLIVE W. wife of Lucius W. Curtiss," to church Sept. 1st, 1867, by letter from Congregational church in Hanover, Erastus Hubbard, Clerk; born Jan. 21st, 1836, at Meriden, to Lucas C. Hotchkiss of that town, and his wife Rufina (Hall,) of Wolcott, Conn.

THEIR CHILDREN.

1. Nettie Barker, born Aug. 26th, 1860.
2. Bertha Olive, born April 13th, 1863, died Sept. 11th, 1863.

1458. "LYDIA MARIA LOOMIS," to church Aug. 25th, 1867, baptized same time; born April 16th, 1843, at Lenox, Mass., to John E. Parker, of that town, and his wife Sarah H. Sears; married April 15th, 1863, Charles A. Loomis; born Feb. 26th, 1842, to No. (990) and his wife No. (991;) he died June 24th, 1866, in his 25th year. She seemed to be called unexpectedly and suddenly to go to California, and the rule of the church, requiring a candidate to be propounded 2 weeks before admission was by unanimous vote of the church, suspended on her account, and she was admitted to church as above, and sailed the same week to care for an invalid sister, and to live with an aunt of theirs at San Francisco.

1459. "MRS. SOPHIA C. PINKS, wife of Edwin C." to church Sept. 1st, 1867, by letter from Congregational church of Hanover, in West Meriden, Erastus Hubbard, Clerk; born April 23d, 1827, at Albany, N. Y., to Thomas Lockrow of that city, and his wife Harriet Flower, of Wethersfield, Conn.; she married Nov. 25th, 1852, No. (987.)

THEIR CHILDREN.

1. Ida Kate, born Oct. 16th, 1853, at New Britain.
2. Charles Henry, born Dec. 4th, 1858, at Hanover, in West Meriden.

1460. "WM. M. CHURCHILL," to church Nov. 3d, 1867, by letter from Congregational church Southington, Rev. E. C. Jones, Pastor; born Dec. 22d, 1831, at Wolcott, Conn., to Lewis of that town, and his wife Caroline Tuttle, of Bethany, Conn.; married May 8th, 1854, No. (1461;) he by trade a machinist, watch maker and jeweller. Was a 3 years' volunteer in the Union Army, and served his full term. His residence on East Main Street, south side; built 1867.

1461. "Mrs. Julia M. Churchill, wife of Wm. M." to church Nov. 3d, 1867, by letter from Congregational church, Southington, Rev. E. C. Jones, Pastor; born Feb. 10th, 1833, at Cheshire, Conn., to Amasa L. Doolittle, of that town, and his wife Maria Merriman, of Southington; married May 8th, 1854, No. (1460.)

1462. "Almon N. Wood," to church Nov. 3d, 1867, by letter from church in Terryville, W. Goodwin, Clerk; born Dec. 20th, 1827, at Warren, Conn., to David W. of that town, and his wife Beulah Beach, of Litchfield; married Oct. 1st, 1855, No. (1463.) His residence on South Prospect Street, (formerly the "Methodist Parsonage;") he a mechanic by occupation.

1463. "Mrs. Maria, wife of A. N. Wood," to church Nov. 3d, 1867, by letter from Terryville, W. Goodwin, Clerk; born May 16th, 1835, at Harwinton, Conn., to Sheldon Osborn of that town, and his wife Julia Bartholomew.

1464. "Stephen G. Rockwell," to church Nov. 3d, 1867, by letter from Congregational church of Hanover, in Meriden, Conn., E. Hubbard, Clerk; born July 26th, 1832, to Jesse B. of Providence, Saratoga Co., N. Y., and his wife Marilla Ballard; married Nov. 29th, 1855, No. (1465.) He works at the "Etna Works," at cutlery, and lives in their large block at this date.

1465. "Mrs. Abbie F. wife of Stephen G. Rockwell," to church by letter from Congregational church of Hanover, in Meriden, Conn., E. Hubbard, Clerk; born Oct. 8th, 1837, at Wethersfield, to Samuel H. Dix of that town, and his wife Elizabeth Kilbourn; married Nov. 29th, 1855, No. (1464.)

THEIR CHILDREN.

1. Lillie Evadore, born Dec. 12th, 1857, at Meriden.
2. Lula Frances, born Oct. 1st, 1867, at New Britain.

MISCELLANEOUS—A PAGE FOR THE CURIOUS.

Since the organization of the first church of New Britain, is 109 years.

Number of settled Pastors 10, of whom now, 1867, only 3 are dead.

Whole number of members Nov. 1st, 1867, is 1465, of whom 1047 are removed by death or otherwise.

No. admitted on profession, 73 per cent. or 1056. By letter, 27 per cent. or 409.

Members of the church from the most numerous or largest families, are, Hart 97, Stanley 71, Andrews 65, Judd 55, Smith 43, Lee 37, Booth 38, Pennfield 33, North 32, Lewis 29, Clark 25, Steele 23, Woodruff 23, Belden 19, Churchill 21, Whittlesey 17.

The oldest person when admitted, No. (853,) 74¼ years.

The youngest person when admitted, No. (1247,) viz.: 11 years and 13 days.

The eldest person at death, No. (520,) viz.: 96 years nearly.

No. of suicides from insanity, members of the church, 3.

No. of persons members of the church, at Alms-house, and dying there, 6.

No. of members baptized in adult years, 15½ per cent. or 231.

No. of members supposed to have been baptized in infancy, 84½ per cent. or 1234.

Person admitted to church by Dr. Smalley, still living, No. (317,) No. (319,) No. (320) and No. (325,) now Sept. 1st, 1867, and all females.

The average age of the members of this church at death, is 54⅓ years.

The average age of males 58¾, of females 51 years.

Whole number of Communion Seasons, 654, average accessions to the church, $2\frac{22}{100}$ at each communion, or about 13⅓ persons per year.

CLERGYMEN raised in the parish and town of New Britain, Timothy Langdon, Wm. Hart, James Kilborn, Isaac Goodrich, Raphael Gilbert, Wm. Whittlesey, Henry Eddy, Allen Steele, Eliphalet Whittlesey, Burdette Hart, Ebenezer Steele, John S. Whittlesey, Levi W. Hart, Thomas S. Judd, Samuel Steele, Salmon Steele, Jason Steele, Emri Steele, Edwin Norton Andrews.

PHYSICIANS raised in New Britain, Josiah Hart, Thomas Mather, Isaac Lee, Jesse Andrews, Isaac Andrews, John Andrews, Adna Stanley, Samuel Hart, John R. Lee, Henry A. Hart, Thomas G. Lee, Wm Ellis, S. Waldo Hart, Henry A. Hart, jun., Harvey B. Steele.

LAWYERS raised in the town of New Britain, John Patterson, Elnathan Smith, jun., Joseph Smith, Ira E. Smith, Ethan A. Andrews, Horace

Andrews, Francis E. Cornwell, Charles S. Andrews, Sherman C. Belden, Otis Nash.

AUTHORS, natives or residents of this town, John Smalley, D. D., Ethan Allen Andrews, LL D., Elijah Burritt, A. M., Elihu Burritt, Mrs. Almira Phelps, Rev. John S. Whittlesey, Prof. D. N. Camp, Charles Northend, Geo. S. Sherwood, B. N. Comings, M. D., Rev. F. T. Russell, Col. H. B. Sprague, now, 1867, Supt. of the State Normal School, and several of the clergy have published by request single sermons.

During the year 1862 the volunteers from the Sunday School of the first church into the Army to put down the slaveholder's rebellion, was 24, of whom Sept., 1863, 8 had fallen and 4 were discharged and returned, leaving 12 in the field. About the same proportion volunteered from other schools and congregations in the town.

The whole number of soldiers from this town was 640, of whom 80 were killed or died of wounds or disease.

ORGAN.

The first church of New Britain, have worshiped 109 years without the aid of an Organ, until Sept., 1867, when a large and fine one was put into the church by the Baumgarten Organ Co., of New Haven. It was exhibited to the public on the evening of Oct. 2d, by skillful organists to the entire satisfaction of the appreciative audience. The entire wind arrangement is peculiar. The bellows is a double acting force pump, placed in the basement and driven by one of "*Stannard's Motors.*" The wind is conveyed in pipes to the "*receiver,*" in the organ loft, and from there to the various stops of the instrument. Whole expense some $5,000 only. This instrument is esteemed a great acquisition and success.

I quote some just and sensible remarks of editorial, by Mr. Delavan of the New Britain Record.

"Last Wednesday evening, the Center church was well filled by an appreciative audience, assembled to listen to the rich tones of the new organ. The instrument is one of great power, and by good judges is said, in some respects, to equal the world renowned organ at Music Hall, Boston. It was manufactured by the Messrs. Baumgarten, of New Haven, and is an instrument of which the Center church may justly feel proud. We are unable to give a description of it at the present time, but all who listened to it on the occasion of the opening speak warmly in its praise. It was played by Messrs. Eugene Thayer and T. T. Mansfield—the former of Boston and the latter of Meriden—and the applause—greatly subdued by reason of the sacredness of the place—which greeted their efforts, showed how well they were appreciated. A very large number of persons came from adjoining towns, from Hartford and other cities, (extra trains being run for their accommodation) to enjoy the rich repast, and we feel safe in saying that none returned disappointed."

APPENDIX.

SABBATH SCHOOLS.

As the Sabbath School has become a fixed institution, a necessary and blessed appendage to the church, we deem it appropriate to give here a brief history of its establishment and success in this parish. Early in the Spring of 1816, a board of Directors was chosen by the congregation, then under the care of Rev. Newton Skinner, (Colleague Pastor, with Rev. John Smalley, D. D.,) who appointed their junior Pastor President of the board, and Deacon David Whittlesey, Clerk and Superintendent of the Sabbath School. Mr. Whittlesey had been a teacher of a Grammar School in Hartford, previous to his marrying into Dr. Smalley's family, in New Britain, and soon after his coming to this town had been chosen a Deacon in the church. He was therefore the man for the office of Superintendent. A school of some 150 children was soon organized, and very nearly after the present mode, classes of from 6 to 8 with a proper teacher assigned were formed, and occupied the pews of the church. Each teacher was furnished with a card on which was written with the Superintendent's own hand, the names of the teacher and scholars, with blanks for the weekly record of recitations, for scripture, catechism, and hymns, and enough to last through the summer season. The school was opened with prayer every Sabbath, (agreeing with the present custom.) (Mr. Skinner had, previous to this, invited the children of his congregation, once a year in the church, to recite the Assembly's, the Historical and the Doctrinal Catechisms.) The Sunday Schools in Hartford seem to have been organized 1818, two years later than this in New Britain. This first Sunday School in Hartford County, however, had its defects, and in 1826 the present greatly improved system was adopted. We are indebted to Rev. Henry Jones, third Pastor of the church and his intelligent wife, for imparting new life and vigor to this branch of Christian effort. The names of the successive Superintendants were, (after the spring of 1826,) Alfred Andrews, (the compiler of this work,) Chauncey Cornwell, Henry L. Bidwell, Rev. R. G. Williams, Rev. John S. Whittlesey, David W. Whittlesey, Norman Hart, Roswell Hawley, M. D.,

Dan Clark, Charles Northend, and E. B. Allen. Several interesting revivals of religion have had their commencement in the Sabbath School, and from this institution the church has been principally replenished. It is in connection here to note, that this Sunday School, was one of the six formed into a local Union, on the 6th of September, 1832, at Newington, through the agency of Rev. Mr. Grosvenor, of the American Sunday School Union. The original schools were Wethersfield, Worthington, Rocky Hill, Newington, Kensington and New Britain, and Sept. 11th, 1838, the Sunday School of West Hartford, was admitted by vote at their solicitation, and on Sept. 20th, 1842, the South church Sunday School, of New Britain, was admitted by vote of the Union. This local Union at its organization 1832, elected Deacon Israel Williams, of Rocky Hill, President, and Alfred Andrews, of New Britain, Secretary, and it has held its anniversaries in regular succession, from church to church, in rotation ever since, retaining its original secretary to September, 1866. The amount of good these several churches and congregations have derived from their Sunday Schools, is incalcuable. Established on the principle of human equality and christian sympathy, being free, and the labors all gratuitous, bringing the young mind under the very best influences society affords, enjoying the prayerful oversight of the Pastors, and the smiles of our Heavenly Father by his Spirit, how can they fail to bless? A true narrative of Sunday Schools in Connecticut, aye, in the free states, would be the brightest page of history in modern times—even a tithe of the important facts would fill a huge volume. Let them be cherished then, as one of the best boons of Heaven to man; not to supplant the family institution and influence, but to operate as a help from the family to the church and Heaven. We would not forget to mention in this connection, that "Infant Classes" so called, were inaugurated about 1835–6 into several of the Sunday Schools of our local Union, and among others, was one of 85 children commenced in the spring of 1836, and held in the Academy building in this place. The first Superintendent of this department was No. (607.) She left town the next year, and No. (731) was her successor in that department. A school or class of this character has been maintained down to the present period. It has been of high importance as a primary or introductory to the higher school. Several persons have had the care of this department, but no one perhaps has done a greater service than No. (1152.) At the 31st anniversary of the Sunday School Union, for this vicinity, held Sept. 1862, the school connected with the first church in New Britain, reported as the whole number, (teachers and scholars,) 355. Of these 42 per cent. were members of the Church. And of the resident members of the church, it was reported that 48 per cent. were actively engaged in the Sunday School either as officers, teachers or learners.

COMMON SCHOOLS.

That the meeting house and the school honse were early and equally cared for by our ancestors, is evident from what has been said in the introduction to this work, and from incidental votes and remarks scattered through all the records of town and parish doings, from the first settlement of these colonies. It is evident that the Great Swamp society had a common or district school, near their meeting house, for as early as 1717, the parish voted a committee, with instructions to report a plan for "*better accommodations*." And this committtee begin their report (at a subsequent meeting,) by stating, in substance, that the distance is so great, the roads so bad, they advise a division of the parish into five districts, and that the money allowed by the country be divided according to the list, and that the balance of expense in supporting these schools, be paid by the parents and masters of the children taught. Every plantation or settlement was obliged, by law, to maintain a school three months of the year. The colonies provided a little money, yearly, for the encouragement of these schools; it was called country, colony, and excise* money, arising in part from a tax of four pence per gallon on imported distilled spirits. The amount divided to this parish for some years after its organization, was about £12 per annum. This amount did not vary much, even down to the close of the war of the revolution. We are sure that the East street, (or Southeast district of New Britain,) had a common school, located about 1718–19, near the present residence of Leonard Belden. That portion of our present territory, then belonging to Newington parish, and called "Stanley quarter," had a common school located about 1700, perhaps in a room of some private house, as was common in the early settlement of these colonies, as appears from documents still extant. It appears, by inference, that the village or town of Farmington had no public building exclusively for school purposes, until 1688 or 1689.

The Southwest district embraced all Main street, from the foot of Dublin Hill to Kensington line, bounded west by Farmington line; the school house stood on the lot now owned and occupied by Henry E. Russell, and was located on West Main street, opposite the house of Mrs. Tolles; the building was remarkable for a steep roof, and was sold to "Aunt Viah" for a dwelling house.

---

* Be it enacted by the Governor and Council, and Representatives in General Court assembled, and by the authority of the same, That the treasurer of this colony pay out to the several towns the principal sums paid in by them as "Excise Money," together with the interest due at the time of payment, taking a receipt therefor, which monies shall be appropriated to the use of schools, as in said act provided.

Passed 2d Thursday of May, 1773.

The Northwest district is supposed to be the last of the four located. No data is found to fix the date precisely, but supposed to be about 1740; the school house was located on (Half-way Hill) Osgood Hill. The first, or old house, was sold to Ebenezer Steele, and was added to his own house, for a residence for his son William, the fifer. Thus the parish was furnished with four district schools, one at each corner, which remained fixtures, with little variation of progress or location, for half a century. Besides the country or excise money, and the sale of the seven western towns, "so called," the next means of revenue to the schools in Farmington, (to which town the territory under consideration belonged until 1785,) was that derived from the sale of unnecessary highways. Farmington being a large town, with several forty and twenty rod highways, the avails were very considerable. The legality of these sales being questioned, on application of the town, December, 1784, the legislature confirmed the sales already made, since A. D. 1723, and authorized further sales for the same object. When the town of Berlin was set off from Old Farmington, and incorporated A. D. 1785, a due proportion of these funds was secured for Kensington and New Britain, through the influence of Col. Lee and Col. Stanley.

Additions continued to be made to the school fund, down to the year 1813, from the same source. The next and most important means of school revenue, was the sale of the "Western Reserve," so called. This was about 3,000,000 acres located in the present State of Ohio, and owned by Connecticut, and was sold, 1795, for $1,200,000. Through the masterly management of James Hillhouse, Seth P. Beers, and B. Sedgwick, it has a capital of over $2,000,000, which, in 1818, was forever made sure to the benefit of common schools, by the constitution of the state, then adopted. The interest of this fund, previous to 1821, was divided to the several school societies in proportion to their tax lists, but that year the principal of equality was adopted, dividing the avails to each child, between four and sixteen years of age. The same democratic principle was also adopted by our school society and town in the distribution of their private and other funds. The next source of revenue was the "Town Deposit Fund," so called, being that portion of the surplus revenue of the United States divided, 1837, to the several states willing to take it, and by them to the several towns, some of which, and among them Berlin, to which we then belonged, devoted the interest to the support of common schools. This town deposit fund divided to New Britain amounted to $4,700. The consequence is, that New Britain not only enjoys the common dividend from the school fund of the state, but also in addition, the avails of the private highway fund, and the dividend from the town deposit fund, making to each child, of whatever origin, between four and sixteen, a yearly benefit of about $2.50. This in a district numbering seventy children, will pay a female teacher some thirty-six weeks. It should be observed, however, that this large dividend occurs only under the most favorable circumstances. So much concerning the public provisions, for common schools, aside from taxation. Some may ask, what kind of houses were provided for these schools? The author has seen but two of these original houses, one was with as steep a roof as the most exquisite gothic structure of the present day. They were coarse and plain, with small windows, set high, large fire-places, in which was burned in winter, at least a cord, or 128 solid feet of wood per week. The books used were Dilworth's spelling-book, the Psalter, and Bible, until the close of the revolutionary war, 1783–4, when Noah Webster published his American spelling-book, his grammar, and a reading book called the "Third Part." About the same time was introduced "Scott's Lessons," for a reading book, for the first or oldest classes. An abridgment of Morse's geography began to be used by a few of the most advanced scholars, about 1789, when it was first published. To the above reading books succeeded the Columbian Orator, the American Orator, and the American Reader, in rotation.

Some of the early teachers in the parish, previous to 1800, were as follows, viz.: David Mather, John Patterson, Lemuel Hotchkiss, Joel Smith, Timothy Langdon, Elnathan Smith, Elizur Hart, John Andrews, Miles Andrus, Moses Andrews, jun., Salmon Eno, Daniel Ames, Daniel Shipman, from Saybrook, Ashbel Seymour, William Kilbourn, Asahel Hart, Elijah Manross, of Bristol, Bela Judd, Josiah Dewy, Amzi Stanley, Adna Stanley, 1788, Samuel Chapman, 1791, Isaac Lee, jun., Timothy Stanley, jun., Benjamin Hart, jun. Some of the females: Zurviah Bird, Hannah Garnsey, Naomi Burritt, 1788 and 1790, Nancy Smith, of Elnathan, Rachel Stanley, Polly Smalley, Cynthia Stanley, Mrs. Electa Lusk, Elizabeth Gridley, Mehitable Loomis, Sally Churchill, Lydia Belden, Abigail Woods, Polly Crandall, Ismena Hart, Sally White, Asenath Bass, Hope Talbut, Lydia Richards, Sally Hart, Roxy Lincoln, Cina Lewis, of "White Oak," Farmington.

The school visitors for the year 1798, appointed by the school society to "visit and direct the several schools," were Rev. John Smalley, Col. Isaac Lee, Col. Gad Stanley, Capt. Jonathan Belden, Levi Andrews, Dea. Elijah Hart, James North, David Mather, Capt. Nathaniel Churchill. The record of 1800, annual meeting, shows the names of the same men to visit and direct the several schools, as the law directs.

The school visitors, and committee to examine teachers for the year 1824, were Rev. Newton Skinner, Noah W. Stanley, Alfred Andrews, Romeo Francis, Cyrus Stanley, Ira E. Smith. And a quarter of a century later, viz., 1849, they were Rev. Samuel Rockwell, N. W. Stanley, Rev. William P. Pattison, E. A. Andrews, Alfred Andrews, Hubert F.

North, Rev. John M. Guion, Rev. Stephen Rushmore, and Marcellus Clark. The list of School visitors was appointed annually by the school society, and usually, and properly, embraced the clergy of different denominations, and a few others conversant with school matters. It is a singular fact, that the present mode of putting all common schools under the care and patronage of the several towns, is exactly the primitive practice of our fathers in the early settlement of these colonies.* The people have found, after trying the working of ecclesiastical parishes, and special incorporated school societies, that the town is the only proper and legitimate conservator, and patron of common schools. From the year 1754, the ecclesiastical parish had the oversight of the common schools within its limits, down to 1784, when the town of Berlin was incorporated, and when each parish, Kensington, New Britain, and Worthington, were also incorporated into separate and special school societies, having powers and duties conferred, to regulate schools, and protect and improve "burying grounds."

NORMAL SCHOOL.

The Normal school of the state of Connecticut was instituted in the year 1850, and located at New Britain, which happened to be the same year that the town was incorporated. It is an honor and a blessing to the commonwealth. The seventeen years of its existence, as an experiment, and an experience, has proved it worthy of patronage and support, not only by the state as such, but by the community at large.

The whole number who have been benefited by its instructions, is 2,349, a large majority of whom have been females. A large proportion of the whole number have taught more or less, (as was expected,) and many have become permanent "Educators." The effect is apparent upon our common schools, in raising a higher standard of excellence; and this, notwithstanding the great influx of foreigners. As a public institution, capable of much good, it is generally appreciated by the people of the state, and especially by the town of New Britain. Like all other public institutions that ask appropriations annually from the state treasury, for support, it is subject to severe criticisms; but these even have a salutary influence upon its officers, as a stimulus. "If our friends do not tell us our faults, our enemies will." Our mission as a community, is to prevent vice and promote virtue. Hence the importance of educating the "educators."

* Connecticut, by her Legislature, May session, 1856, conferred, by special act, the powers and duties of school societies, with a very few exceptions, upon the several towns of the state.

which principle is well illustrated by the old and homely proverb, that "an ounce of prevention is worth a pound of cure." Our personal experience of more than a half century, in training to some extent, more than 3,000 pupils in various schools, leads us to make these suggestions and remarks.

The hasty act of the Legislature of 1867, on the last day of the session, in suspending this institution, by cutting off its supplies, was unwise in the extreme. The people were not only surprised, but shocked by the reckless blow. Connecticut can ill afford to dispense with this means of advancing its educational interests. If it is not what it might be, and ought to be, then make it so. It is not to be supposed that the people are ready to relinquish to New Britain, the building and grounds, worth some $100,000, without some good reason.

EVANGELICAL AND PROTESTANT CHURCHES

WHICH HAVE GROWN UP IN NEW BRITAIN, OR BEEN OFFSHOOTS FROM THE FIRST CHURCH AND CONGREGATION.

And first the BAPTIST, which has already been alluded to in the history of Dr. Smalley's ministry; several of the constituent members of that church were formerly members of Dr. Smalley's, and nearly all members of his congregation at a previous date. They were early called *separates*, held their first meetings at the house of Samuel Smith in Stanley quarter, but subsequently at the old Hinsdale House on East street, where their church was first organized, June 16th, 1808, the following persons being the original and constituent members, viz.: Jeremiah Hubbard Osgood, Elijah Francis, Gideon Williams, Thomas Booth, John Osgood, Moses Smith, Oliver Weldon, Dan Wright, Sarah Hollister, Lydia Osgood, Mary Booth, Sarah Hinsdale, Anna Daniels, Rebecca R. Steele, Mary Osgood, Sally Weldon, Jerusha Weldon, Lois Booth, Betsey Warner, Roxana Wright. To the above list of constituent members, were added the next year, Asahel Hart, Isaac Goodrich, Lydia Hart, Electa Goodrich, Ruth Hinsdale, Sarah Smith, Allen Steele, and Lucy Steele. They occupied private houses and school houses for public worship until 1828, when they furnished themselves with a small church edifice, and set it at the foot of "Dublin Hill," directly at the head of Main st. In 1842, they built on the corner of Main and West Main streets, one of the best locations in the town. This church numbers now, A. D. 1867, 250 communicants. Their S. School was organized by Rev. Mr. Shaler, in the spring of 1829. From the organization of the church to the spring of

1828, it had no resident pastor. Rev. Enoch Green,* who lived at Middletown, exercised the pastoral supervision until his death, March, 1825. visiting them sometimes monthly, and sometimes semi-monthly. In the spring of 1828, Rev. Seth Higby, the first resident pastor, began his labors with the church, which were continued eighteen months; while he was with them, their first house was built. From autumn, 1829, till autumn, 1831, Rev. N. E. Shaler had the pastoral charge; during this time the first reference to a Sabbath School was made in the report to the Association. The next pastor was Rev. Geo. W. Appleton,* who did not give satisfaction, and ceased to labor as a minister in less than a year; he came in the spring of 1832. For more than a year the church was without a pastor. In the summer or autumn of 1834, Rev. Amos D. Watrous became pastor, and continued till the spring of 1837; after this date there was no resident pastor for two years, Rev. Messrs. O. Allen, G. Robbins, (and for the last year, up to his death,) Rev. Matthew Bolles,* supplying the desk. In April, 1839, Rev. H. S. Haven* became pastor, and continued till the summer of 1841; just before he left the church, began the erection of the present house of worship. From Sept., 1841, until April, 1847, Rev. Levi S. Barney was pastor of the church. Rev. Elisha Cushman regularly supplied the church from June, 1846, until April, 1847, but did not consider himself regularly settled as pastor. From April, 1847, until January, 1851, Rev. Wm. P. Pattison was pastor. For the six months following there was no pastor. In July, 1851, Rev. Robert J. Wilson was called to be pastor, but left in October, 1852, and was succeeded by Rev. E. P. Bond, who was ordained Dec. 2d, 1852. Rev. Mr. Bond left July, 1865, for the "*Connecticut Literary Institution*," at Suffield, Ct., as its principal, and Rev. W. C. Walker was recognized as their pastor the same year. This congregation has so increased as to be straitened for room, and have just now, 1867, voted unanimously to build a new and larger house of worship.

NOTE.—Mr. Bond kindly furnished the above for this work, and says those pastors marked * are deceased.

THE METHODISTS OF NEW BRITAIN.

The first Methodist preaching in this town, of which we have been able to find any account, was by Rev. Henry Bass, in 1815, while on a visit from South Carolina to this his native home. The next we find to have been by Rev. William Jewett, an itinerant, and in 1816, both in the "Osgood Hill" school house. Small meetings were held, often in private houses, in which Capt. Oliver Weldon, (who had moved here from Kensington, as a shoemaker,) took the lead. Rev. David Miller also preached here about 1818, and some have it that he formed the first class. No record of these early transactions, or of the organization of a church or society is found. The compiler, after diligent search in this town and vicinity, has found nothing authentic, except in relation to the purchase of the land upon which their house of worship stands. A private memorandum of Rev. Raphael Gilbert, late deceased, from his family in Brooklyn, N. Y., reveals an item of historic interest, to this respectable and flourishing society, as follows: "The first Methodist class in New Britain was composed of the following persons, viz: Oliver Weldon, Sally Weldon, Cecelia Weldon, Marilla Weldon, Daniel Kilby, John Steele, Rena Steele, Mary Eddy, James Steele, Oliver Newell, Phebe Bronson, Samuel Wilson, John R. Jewett,* Hester Jewett, Clarissa Gilbert, Patty Kilby, Wm. Steele, Esther Steele, Linas Gilbert, and Nancy Tryon, and on the 6th day of May, 1820, Raphael Gilbert† was appointed class leader." The same memorandum states that Raphael Gilbert was appointed an exhorter, Feb. 18th, 1821, and local preacher Oct. 9th, 1823. His family record shows that he died June 6th, 1863, at Whitestone, L. I., and buried at "Cypress Hill Cemetery, L. I." The land records of the town of Berlin, (to which we belonged at that date,) show that Samuel Booth sold for $79.50, to Richard S. Cornwell a piece of land in New Britain, on Main st., 4 × 10 rods, where the present edifice of the Methodist society now (1867) stands, then abutting east on the highway and north on Norman Woodruff's house-lot,‡ and on the same day Richard S. Cornwell deeded for the sum of $79.74, received to his full satisfaction of Raphael Gilbert, to him the said Raphael in trust for the Methodist church, (he being bound to deed the same to the trustees of said church,) the same 40 rods of land, and on the 6th day of May, 1828, Raphael Gilbert and Betsey his wife deeded the same land to Allen Judd,

---

*This is the famous J. R. Jewett of notoriety as a prisoner of the Indians at Nootka Sound for a number of years, a narrative of which was published and made a sensation at the time. Jewett was a noted singer as well as Methodist.

†It is well known by a few persons still living, that Raphael Gilbert, although a *hard* boy, and played truant at school so much as to be unable to read in public at the time of his conversion, yet the grace of God so changed the current of his life that he soon learned to read, and became a man of leading influence in the early development of this society. Probably no one knew its history better, and this memorandum appears conclusive and reliable on sight. It has names and dates, and comes from the class leader himself.

‡When Arch street was laid out, it cut off the east end of this lot a little, and the trustees also sold to Dr. Woodruff some 20 feet from the north side.

Ferdinand Hart, Samuel Richards, Moses Cook, and Linus Burwell, trustees of the Methodist church in New Britain, in trust that they shall erect or build a house or place of worship for the use of the members of the Methodist Episcopal church in the United States of America, according to the rules and discipline which from time to time may be agreed upon and adopted by the ministers and preachers of the said church at their "General Conference." This locality furnished an eligible site for their edifice, which was erected the same summer the deed was procured, and although not finished inside for some years, the first meeting was a quarterly, late in the year 1824; there had been one quarterly meeting in the place previous to this, and held in the chambers of Moses Smith's house, April, 1824. This quarterly in the church was conducted by Rev. Mr. Spicer, of Hartford. This first house of worship was cheap and plain, and gave place* in 1854 to the present commodious and neat one.

According to common usage in this church, those who stood fair and faithful at the end of six months' probation, were admitted to full communion, (if they thus desired,) and in the absence of all evidence to the contrary, we conclude the constituent members of the church were the same persons named above as in the first class, and that their names were sent to the quarterly meeting or conference about the close of the year 1820. To these 21 constituent members were soon added the wife of Raphael Gilbert, Wm. Hart, Mary Dobson, Isaac Dobson, Allen Judd, Huldah Wright, Eliza Wright, Abigail Smith, Allen Steele, Polly Richards, Marinda Bronson, Sally Weldon, Leonard Deming, Mrs. Howd, Chauncey Beckwith, Ebenezer Steele, Ferdinand A. Hart, Linus Burwell, and the wife of Linus Gilbert, and perhaps others. This church and society, so weak at the beginning, and which struggled so bravely many years against poverty and odium, has been a great blessing to the community, has raised† many bright and shining lights, has been favored with frequent revivals, and has had some excellent pastors. The present number of resident members now, (1867) is about 200. Their Sunday School has been flourishing, and was organized A. D. 1829. Their late pastor was Rev. George Lansing Taylor, who left in 1865 for Brooklyn, N. Y., and their pulpit has been since supplied by Prof. Newhall, of Wesleyan University, and by Rev. Dr. Scudder, of Hartford.

Perhaps some special remarks should be made just here, before closing this sketch, in honor and remembrance of the last name on the list of the

---

*The old house was sold and moved to the east side of Arch street, and used as a factory for ax-helves, but now, 1767, is occupied by the "American Fruit Basket Co."

†Ministers raised by this church, and sent out mostly to the west, Raphael Gilbert, Allen Steele, Ebenezer Steele, Salmon Steele, Jason Steele.

first class, Nancy Tryon; her maiden family name was Root, in 1810 was a member of Dr. Porter's church in Farmington; she lived in Berlin, Kensington and New Britain, her family having been broken up, and she having no certain dwelling-place. What "Sister Hollister," No. 79, was to the Baptist society in its forming state, such was "Sister Tryon" to the early history of the Methodist society. They were both remarkable for prayer, piety and zeal. With warm hearts and good conversational powers, they pressed their missionary labors with eminent success. It shows what earnest female workers can do in any good cause. There was a Mrs. Tryon in Berlin, a Methodist, called *Mother* Tryon, whose maiden name was Squire, and the two are sometimes confounded.

The following is copied from the first subscription for building the church; it was drafted by Ira E. Smith, Esq., originally, and then copied for subscriptions.

"We the subscribers, whose names are hereunto annexed, do hereby promise and agree to pay to the Methodist Episcopal church the sums respectively affixed to our names, whenever we shall be thereto hereafter requested, to be applied, laid out and expended in the erection of the Methodist meeting house, the seats of which are to be free to all persons; the said house to be erected upon a certain lot or piece of land situated in the society of New Britain, in the town of Berlin, lying immediately south of Norman Woodruff's house and lot, which said lot has been this day conveyed by Richard S. Cornwell to Raphael Gilbert, in trust for the aforesaid Methodist society. It is understood and provided that our said subscriptions are to be null and void, and in no wise binding upon us, unless the building of the said house shall be commenced within one year from this date. Berlin, July 1st, 1824."

Subscribers' Names.	Money.	Materials.	Work.
Raphael Gilbert,	$30.00		$20.00
Linus Gilbert,	30.00		20.00
Allen Judd,	15.00		10.00
Lorenzo P. Lee,		$50.00	
Ira E. Smith,	15.00	35.00	
Richard S. Cornwell,	10.00	20.00	
Elias Blinn,	10.00		
Philip Lee,		3.00	4.00
Asa Cowdry,	20.00		
Noah Hamblin,	9.00		1.00
Naboth L. Steele,	2.00		1.00
Samuel Judd,	5.00		5.00
Francis Hart,			5.00
Avery Atkins,	3.00		

	Money.	Materials.	Work.
Henry Steele,	$2.00		
Betsey Pennfield,	15.00		
Salmon Steele,	3.00		
Clarissa Gilbert,		$15.00	
Saxa Hooker,		10.00	
Ashbel Hooker,			$6.00
Ira Gilbert,			15.00
Solomon Sanford,			10.00
Dan Wright,			1.50
Amzi Judd,	3.00		
Jeremiah Goodrich,			10.00
Hezekiah Johnson,			5.00
Abigail Smith,		10.00	
Joseph Holmes,	3.00		
Hezekiah Seymour,	1.00		
George Doolittle,	2.00		
Daniel Judd,			4.00
Cyrus Stanley,	1.00		10.00
Cyrus Hart,		5.00	5.00
Leander S. Hart,			1.00
Richard Southmayd,	6.00		3.00
Theodore Riley,	5.00		
Moses W. Beckley,		10.00	
John Parsons,			6.00
Mary Wright,		1.50	
Mary Ann Weldon,		1.00	
Samuel Kelsey,			15.00
Aziel Belden,	2.50		2.50
Oliver Richards,		5.00	
Zacheus Brown,	3.00		
Leonard Deming,	1.50		
Edward White,	1.00		
Charles Hurlbert,	1.00		

NOTE.—The author feels justified in publishing the above, because it reveals the time and origin of the first successful effort towards building the first meeting-house of the Methodists in this town, about which there has been so much speculation and enquiry. The fact that Ira E. Smith, Esq., was elected for the first time representative of the town of Berlin the succeeding spring, shows that his liberality was duly appreciated.

Episcopal Church.

Next in order of time was the origin of St. Mark's Protestant Episcopal Church. The first service according to the usages of the Protestant Episcopal Church was held in New Britain in the old Academy building on the 17th of Jan., 1836, the Rev. Silas Totten, D. D., of Trinity College, Hartford, officiating.

On the 28th of Aug., 1836, the parish was duly organized at a meeting attended by the following named persons:

Ira E. Smith,	Hezekiah Seymour,
Lorenzo P. Lee,	Cyrus Booth,
Emanuel Russell,	John B. Parsons,
George Francis,	Arthur Pendleton,
John Fairbrother,	Henry Baldwin,

Philip S. Judd,

The Rev. Dr. N. S. Wheaton, Chairman.

Lorenzo P. Lee, Secretary.

Their first place of permanent worship was built in 1837, and stood where the present residence of George M. Landers stands. This, however, soon became too strait for the growing congregation, when they sold it for a dwelling-house, and built on West Main st., in the year 1848. It was enlarged in 1859, and a chapel built at the side, and a new and larger organ procured.

At the first meeting of the parish, the following officers were legally elected:

Lorenzo P. Lee, Ira E. Smith, Wardens; and Emanuel Russell, Frederick T. Stanley, Hezekiah Seymour, George Francis, Ralph Dickinson, Cyrus Booth, Vestrymen. Charles N. Stanley, Clerk.

In 1836 there were 8 communicants, in 1862 there were 113, and in 1867 they number 170.

Bishop Brownell held one service April 17th, 1836. The Rev. Dr. Wheaton, President of Trinity College, officiated from June 19th, 1836, to April 16th, 1837. The Rev. Thomas Davis officiated from April 23d, 1837, to June 1st, 1838. The Rev. Z. H. Mansfield and the Rev. John Williams, the Assistant Bishop of the Diocese, officiated from June, 1838, to Nov., 1840.

The Rev. John M. Guion was Rector from Dec. 2d, 1840, to 1845. The Rev. Chas. R. Fisher officiated from Christmas, 1845, to Easter, 1846. The Rev. Abner Jackson, then Prof. of Trinity College, since President of Hobart College, officiated from April 19th, 1846, to Dec. 23d, 1848.

The Rev. Alexander Capron was Rector from Nov. 19th, 1848, to Easter, 1855, and Rev. Francis T. Russell was called to the Rectorship on the fourth Sunday after Easter, 1855. [He kindly furnished the above for this work.—Ed.] He closed his labors in St. Mark's church the last Sabbath of March, 1864, and he was succeeded by Rev. Leonidas Bradley Baldwin as Rector, Oct. 1st, of the same year, who is still Rector July, 1867.

In the absence of all record as to who constituted the original church or communicants, the few still living think the following were the constituent members, viz.: Hezekiah Seymour, Solomon Churchill, Lucy, widow of Nathaniel Dickinson, Betsey, wife of Emanuel Russell, Andrew G. Graham, Emeline Russell, Jennette, wife of L. P. Lee, Mrs. Theresa Bassett, Mrs. George Francis.

The 2d or South Congregational Church.

This offshoot was entirely from the first church and congregation in the town, and has already been noticed in previous pages. Their present Pastor, Rev. C. L. Goodell, was ordained and installed Feb. 2d, 1859, and was successor of Rev. Samuel Rockwell, who was dismissed June 20th, 1858, after a ministry of fifteen and a half years. The number of resident members in this church, 1862—20 years after its organization, was 226, but in Jan. 1867, is 308. It has a flourishing Sunday School, and the church and society are distinguished for large contributions to benevolent objects.

They built during 1865, 66, and 67, a beautiful church edifice, of "Portland free stone," costing some $135,000, which stands on nearly the same ground occupied by the former one, which was moved to the extreme east end of their lot, and used for worship while the new one was being built.

On or about the 13th of June, 1867, the Pastor of this church, Rev. Mr. Goodell, sailed in company with Rev. M. Dudley, of Middletown, and others on a tour of observation in Europe.*

---

*A Joint Stock Company was formed Nov., 1867, of some 15 principal business men of the village, with a capital of some $15,000, and bought a lot of Wm. A. Churchill, adjoining to the new meeting house lot, on the east, and bought the old South Church edifice, and this company are now enlarging and fitting it to move east and south about its size.

The design is to make a convenient "*Public Hall,*" a room for the "Young Mens' Institute," and "Christian Association," and the basement to rent for useful purposes.

This is a laudable enterprise, and these gentlemen will deserve the thanks of the community.

Of Protestant churches in New Britain, it only remains to speak of the "*Second Advent.*" Their first meetings were held in the State House, (so called) in Hart quarter. After about two years, (perhaps more,) the meetings were removed to the school house in the village, by Bassett's corner. Some objections being made to the use of it by the proprietors, the worshipers built a small edifice on Arch Street, A. D. 1850. They delayed adopting a creed, or church order on account of the variety of views and opinions entertained by the worshipers. They are few in number, and only have preaching occasionally. Many of them had formerly belonged to the different Evangelical churches of the town, and some of these returned to their former connections, after a few years had passed, leaving the members that remained few, and feeble as a community or society. The society as such, was organized Aug. 9th, 1850. Charles Burt was appointed Agent, and a piece of land was rented of Mr. Theron Hart; and a small house of worship built the same season.

An uncommon interest has been manifested this summer, 1867, in protracted meetings, in addition to their number on profession, and baptisms by immersion.

St. Mary's or the Catholic church, was built substantially of brick in 1850, and was enlarged in 1863. The building will seat more persons than any other church in town, and the congregation embraces about 1000 persons, 700 of whom are communicants. The church is located on Myrtle Street, and Rev. Luke Daly is the Priest, now 1867, and has been from its first organization.

They have a school house near the church, which will accommodate 300 day school children.

Their Sunday School was organized as soon as their church was finished; and 1866 a large and good toned bell was procured for the church.

Manufacturers, their Progress.

New Britain had a name as an Ecclesiastical Society, 1754, and continued a staid farming community for about half a century, when by the mechanical skill and industry of some two or three individuals, it began a career of progress in the mechanic arts, which at the close of a century has culminated in the title of a manufacturing village. If the reader will peruse the sketches No. (443) and No. (461) in connection with what follows, he will see how the steps of this progress have been developed. The first articles of hardware ever manufactured and offered for sale from this village, were produced by these men and put into market, the summer of 1800, and thus a system of demand and supply was established which has continued from that day to this. Seth J. North, No. (449,) having learned the blacksmith's trade of his father, was received into the brass shop of his brother James for a time, when and where he soon discovered that the brass business afforded profits, with which the common jobbing of the blacksmith could not begin to compare; having become of age in August, 1800, his mind was made up—he would carry on the business himself, and his brother James removed to Cherry Valley, N. Y. The "Sugden place," (so called,) near the present residence of Henry Stanly, having come into possession of Seth J. North, Feb., 1803, by deed of his father, the old house (where the first sleigh bells were made) gave place for his family residence, when he built opposite more extensive shops than had ever before been used in New Britain.

These two brass foundries of Seth J. North and Joseph Shipman, were continued down to 1840 without competition, the markets of Boston and Albany, and New York and Philadelphia being divided between them. They continued the leading business until 1830. The capital on which these two concerns were started was borrowed of the Rev. Dr. Smalley! Lathes were then propelled by *foot* power; as business increased *horse* power used down to 1830, when *steam* power was first introduced by Stanley, Clark & Waters, where the lock business first began in the building now occupied as a Union store, and steam is now in use throughout the village.

In 1807, a company composed of Seth J. North, Isaac and Thomas Lee, Wm. Smith and Joseph Shipman, was formed for making jewelry, and various articles were made, ear drops, breast pins, &c. This commenced in a small building where the barn of O. C. Stanley now stands, and had been the residence of "Old Aunt Viah," so called. In a year or more it was found necessary to build larger, and a new company was formed, a large shop was built a little north of the present residence of Dr. Hart, and when the business was abandoned three or four years afterwards, the building was bought by Isaac and Thomas Lee, and moved on the east side of the road, and occupied as a dwelling. It has been recently known as a hotel kept by J. W. Humphrey, and removed to Cedar street, when the present Humphrey House was built. This jewelry company was the second branch of business attempted until 1812.

In Dec., 1812, Alvin North, Seth J. North, and Hezekiah C. Whipple began what was called the "Plating business," on Alvin North's corner. Silver plated copper wire was drawn and made into hooks and rings for men's overcoats, hooks and eyes for women's use, curb chains for bridles, &c., which business has never been abandoned, terminating at last in plated saddlery hardware, by O. B. North & Co., and H. Butler & Sons, and hooks and eyes by North, Stanley & Co.

During the war a company was formed to make roller buckles, and the buildings stood on ground near the old Post Office. Knives and forks were made by Jesse Hart, on the corner of West Main street, where is now the Baptist church. Wrought iron table butts were made by Chauncey Wright. Bureau locks, bellows pipes, sad irons, &c., were made by Samuel Booth and Norman Woodruff, and *wooden* candlesticks by Theron Hart. The peace of 1815 closed up these different branches, and the brass foundries of Seth J. North and Joseph Shipman, and the plating business of Norths & Whipple were the only manufactories in 1816, at the close of the war.

During this period of fifteen years the agricultural interests of the society of New Britain had been improved and enlarged, and the population of the society had increased. The *store* of Elnathan Smith was the first in the limits of the parish on what is called the "East street." In 1805 and 1806 Isaac and Thomas Lee built the first store within the present limits of the Borough, at the N. W. corner of the green, where is now the residence of Henry North. From 1816 to 1821 little progress was made either in business or population, except in the outskirts of the parish.

The new meeting house, recently known as the "old north church," and at present as "Strickland Hall," was erected in 1822, by the Congregational society, there being no other ecclesiastical society then here occupying any church edifice. A Baptist society was organized in 1805, and a Methodist society in 1818, neither at this time having any place for public worship. The location of this church formed a nucleus for the growth of the village. In the following year, 1823, the Messrs. Lees built the stone store opposite the new church, and soon after the store of O. R. Burnham & Co., was built on ground where now stands the residence of Curtis Whaples, afterwards removed and now known as the "South store." From 1817 to 1823, Messrs. Lees manufactured a few buttons, snaps, hooks and eyes, and glass beads were made into various articles, and the plating business of hooks and rings, hooks and eyes, cloak clasps, &c., had been commenced and continued by L. P. Lee & Co., several years. The brass business had branched off in the hands of Chauncey Cornwell, Josiah Dewey, Norman Woodruff and others; and James North, Jr., had returned from Cherry Valley in 1818, and resumed his former business as brass founder. No great additions of new branches were made until 1830. The business already established had however been much extended from 1823 to 1830, and largely increased in 1836. The financial crash of 1837, paralyzed a large portion of its business, heavy losses were made, and it was not until 1843 that they might be said to have successfully resumed business. From that time to 1857, nearly all branches have been successful, and large additions have been made to the capital and business of the village. The manufacture of hardware has been its leading feature, and the principal exceptions are the shirt factories of Isaac N. Lee & Son, Julius Parker and Wm. Bingham; the hook and eye establishment of North, Stanley & Co., the jewelry business of Churchill, Stanley & Co., and the New Britain Jewelry Company, and the New Britain Knitting Company, the latter one of the largest and most successful corporations in the place. To the above list should be added as hardware manufacturing establishments, "Russell, Erwin & Co.," "The Stanley Works," "F. H. North," "J. B. Sargeant & Co.," "O. B. North & Co.," now "J. Shepherd & Co.," "P. & F. Corbin," "H. F. North & Co.," now "North & Judd Manufacturing Co.," Landers, Smith & Co.," now "*Landers, Frary & Clark*," "Humison & Beckley," "The Maleable Iron Works," "Judd & Blakesley," "E. Doen & Co.," and last but not least, "The Union Manufacturing Co.," built 1866. Some of these companies are said to have indirectly *coined* money during the war, and all with their perfected machinery are able to compete in most articles of "hardware" with the old establishments and cheap labor of England.

This article in substance was prepared some years since by Mr. F. T. Stanley, a native of this place, and a gentleman whose name is identified with the honor and progress of the town, and who has kindly consented that I might use for this work what of it I deemed proper. I add some items which his modesty suppressed. [Ed.]

In workers of other materials is the "Stanley Rule and Level Co.," (doing a large business,) and "The American Basket Co.," and several carriage and other shops and factories; in all of which is supposed to be employed an aggregate amount of capital of over two millions and a half—$2,500,000.

The chief drawback on the business of New Britain has been the expense of transportation. Being inland and about 10 miles from the river this was considerable. This might have been relieved by the Hartford & New Haven Railroad, in 1840, but was not materially, their road passing *too* far east. In 1850, the Hartford, Providence & Fishkill Railroad passed directly through the village, and afforded better facilities, and in 1866 the Middletown extension, and when the Hartford, Providence & Fishkill extension and double track, now called "Boston & Erie," are completed, (the latter running directly to the coal mines of Pennsylvania,) New Britain will enjoy facilities for transportation and commerce equal to any inland town in the state. Through the intelligence, the liberality and enterprise of the villagers, churches and schools have been produced, the streets have been graded, the side walks paved, the dwellings and public buildings furnished with gas, and as a crowning excellence, both of beauty and utility combined, the "Water Works," (devised by the inventive genius of our fellow citizen, Mr. F. T. Stanley, 1857,) have been made a success. *While the "Water Works," *ex*tinguished the devouring flames, they equally *dis*tinguished the projector as a *public benefactor.* While we thus distinguish Mr. Stanley, for introducing the use of steam engines for driving our machinery, and water to supply them, it will not be forgotten that Maj. Seth J. North, was for nearly a half century *the* leading business man of the town. Having far reaching and comprehensive views, while land was $25 per acre, he secured a large tract in the village. Having superior executive power, he always conducted his operations to the most favorable results. Being ambitious to accumulate, a combination of circumstances seemed to conspire to gratify his desire. His tact and talent for business, his wealth, his public benefactions, and private charities, have secured for him a reputation in this direction to which few ever attain.

---

* That it is so, is demonstrated by the fact that owners of property located within the reach of these works, can be, and are insured against loss by fire, at the very lowest possible rates, that like property is insured under the most favorable circumstances any where in the country—thus making New Britain in this respect, a safe place either to invest property or to do business.

INDEX

OF THOSE WHO OWNED THE COVENANT CALLED "HALF-WAY COVENANT," REPRESENTED BY ROMAN NUMBERS, FROM PAGE 125 TO 131.

ALPHABETICAL INDEX

OF THE MEMBERS OF THE FIRST CHURCH IN NEW BRITAIN, IN CHRONOLOGICAL ORDER, AS FOUND ON THE CHURCH RECORD, AND REPRESENTED IN THIS WORK BY CORRESPONDING NUMBERS.

BACHELDER.

Moses, - - - - 1001
Rosanna, wife of Moses, - 1002

BAKER.

Alden A., - - - - 1104

BALDWIN.

Marcia L., - - - - 1249

BANCROFT.

Samuel, - - - - 1049

BARBER.

Hannah, wife of William, - - 84

BARRET.

Thomas E., - - - 1271
Jennie B., wife of Thomas E., - 1272

BARTHOLOMEW.

Widow Eunice, - - - 323
Emeline, - - - - 616

BARTLETT.

John N., - - - - 1282
Ellen S., his wife, - - 1283
Nellie S., - - - - 1388

BASS.

Asenath, - - - - 270
Lydia, - - - - - 474
Gunilda, - - - - 574

BASSETT.

William, - - - 376
Ozias B., - - - - 876
Emeline, wife of - - - 877
Lois, wife of William, - - 882
Mary S., - - - - 941
Ebenezer D., - - - 1087

BATES.

Kilbourn, - - . - 374

BEEBE.

Austin, - - - - 1140
Elizabeth, wife of - - 1141
Anna, - - - - 1413

BEECHER.

Mrs. Charlotte A., - - - 1345

BELDEN.

Jonathan, - - - - 158
Wife of - - - - - 159
Anna, wife of Leonard, - - 233
Roxy, widow of Leonard, - 324
Nancy, - - - - 365
Hannah J., - - - 499
Jerusha, - - - - 506
Rhoda R., - - - 556
Nancy, wife of Alvin, - - 579
Edwin, - - - - - 727
Mary Ann, wife of Edwin, - - 787
Alvin, - - - - - 955
Edwin, - - - - - 964
Betsey A., - - - - 968
Charles H., - - - - 1097
Charlotte B., - - - - 1124
Caroline M., - - - 1193
Francis A., - - - - 1209
Martha Maria, - - - 1365

BELKNAP.

Maria C., wife of Moses P., - 644
Theodore, - - - 922

BEVINS.

Widow Ellen T. P., of Anson, - 1288

BIDWELL.

Henry L., . - - - 746

BIGLOW.

Jacob W., - - - - 1202
Sarah, wife of - - - 1203
Elizabeth, wife of Hiram, - - 1430

BISHOP.

Mary Ann, - - - - 788

BLAKE.

Lucius D., - - - - 1321
Susan M., wife of - - 1322
Elijah F., - - - - 1442
Julia, wife of - - - 1443
Hannah, - - - - 1444

BLAKESLEE.

Charles, - - - - 1333
Lydia, wife of - - - 1334
Bernard F., - - - 1452

BLINN.

Lois, - - - - - 99
Julia Ann, - - - 1102

BONNEY.

Jane Smith, - - - 1438

BOOTH.

Widow Anna, - - - 21
Nathan, - - - - 65
Wife of - - - - - 66
Elizabeth, wife of Joseph, - 155
James, - - - - - 165
Wife of James, - - - 166
Robert, - - - - - 193
Wife of Robert, - - 194
Fanny, wife of Nathan, - - 261
James, jun., - - - 338
Nancy, wife of Cyrus, - - 340
Olive, wife of James, jun., - 358
Samuel, - - - - 370
Frances, wife of Osmyn, - 431
George, - - - - - 519
Mary B., - - - - 536
Cyrenus, - - - - - 538
Leura F., - - - - 629
Elisha S., - - - - - 648
Alvira, wife of Elisha S., - 649
Lucetta, - - - - - 671
Osmyn, - - - - - 673
Nancy N., - - - - 789
Laura, - - - - 790
Hubert, - - - - - 791
Nancy, - - - - - 792
Horace, - - - - - 793
Almira, wife of Horace, - 1034
Helen M., - - - - 1113
Lester S., - - - - 1114
Harriet, wife of Lester S., - - 1115
Elisha S., - - - - 1116
Edward M., - - - - 1165
Fanny C., - - - - 1180

BOOTH.

Wilbert H., - - - 1219
George B., - - - - 1242
George C., - - - - 1339
Horace W., - - - - 1393

BOSWORTH.

Lafayette, - - - - 1301
Mary J., wife of Lafayette, - 1302
Emily A., third wife of Lafayette, - 1351

BRACE.

Mrs. Mary Ann, - - - 1327

BRADLEY.

Edward E., - - - - 1236

BRAINARD.

Mrs. Flora, - - - - 1300

BRAY.

John, - - - - 558
Sally, - - - - - 576

BREWER.

Hannah, - - - - 225

BROCKWAY.

Maria, wife of Alvah, - - 580

BRONSON.

Sibil, wife of Noadiah, - - 160
Jemima, - - - - 218
Widow Phebe, - - - 285
Widow Abigail, - - - 708
William C., - - - 1223
Nathan S., - - - - 1347
Charlotte, wife of Nathan S., - 1348

BROOKS.

Susan S., - - - - 601

BROWN.

Eleazer, - - - - 283
Wife of Eleazer, - - 284
Jesse, - - - - 350

BUCKLAND.

Azuba, - - - - 1044

BUCKLEY.

Ruth S., - - - - 1370
Mary A., - - - - 1384

BUEL.

Mrs. Sally, - - - - 1427

BURRITT.

Naomi, - - - - 202
Wife of Elihu, - - - - 290
Widow Eunice, - - - 301
Betsey, - - - - - 400
George, - - - - 417
Emily, - - - - - 418
Mary, - - - - - 501
Elihu, - - - - - 584
Isaac, - - - - 598
Eunice W., - - - - 599
Elijah H., - - - - 754
Ann, wife of Elijah H., - 755
Elizabeth H., wife of William, - 1205

BUTLER.

Solomon, - - - - 452
Horace, - - - - - 465
Betsey, wife of Horace, - - 466

BUTLER.

Maria, - - - - - 530
Sally, wife of Solomon, - - 548
Sarah, - - - - - 794
Julia M., - - - - - 973
Walter C., - - - - 996
Fanny, wife of Charles, - - 1042
Catharine Maria, - - 1264

CADWELL.

Benjamin, - - - - 382

CADY.

Corancey, - - - - 1118

CAMP.

Joseph E., - - - - 229

CAPRON.

Mary, wife of Daniel, - - 1005
Elizabeth A., - - - - 1006
M. Rozella, - - - 1313

CAREY.

Henry L., - - - - 994

CARPENTER.

Samuel S., - - - - 681
Joshua, - - - - - 682
George, - - - - - 914
S. Elizabeth, - - - - 1170
Ellen, - - - - 1171
Walter G., - - - - 1261

CARRINGTON.

Abijah, - - - - - 303
Eli, - - - - - 699

CARTER.

Lucy, - - - - - 206
Ezra, - - - - - 352
Elizabeth, - - - - 795
Lois D., - - - - 796
Stanley A., - - - - 1338

CASE.

Seth E., - - - - 1167
Minerva E., wife of Seth E., - 1168
Mrs. Lemina L., - - - 1454

CATLIN.

Isaac, - - - - - 763
Rebecca, wife of Isaac, - - 764

CHAMBERLIN.

Abiram, - - - - 1153
Sophrone, wife of Abiram, - 1154
Cornelia A., - - - 1213

CHAMBERS.

Francis, - - - - 1371
Wife of Francis, - - 1372

CHESTER.

Edwin S., - - - - 1332

CHURCHILL.

Janna, - - - - - 97
Wife of Janna, - - 98
Nathaniel, - - - - 104
Wife of Nathaniel, - - 105
Solomon, - - - - - 240
Wife of Solomon, - - 241
Elizabeth, wife of Sage, - - 254
Sage, - - - - - 257

CHURCHILL.

Candace, wife of Solomon, jun., 388
William A., 695
Laura, 753
Maria, 797
Sarah B., Wife of William A., 885
Eliza J., 1023
Isabella J., 1179
Sarah A., 1181
William W., 1239
Frederick H., 1240
William M., 1460
Julia M., wife of William M., 1461

CLARK.

Widow Elizabeth, 185
Jane, 221
David, 255
Mary, 272
Prudence, wife of John, 384
Elizabeth, wife of Solomon, 395
Anna, 399
Solomon, 434
Chauncey, 477
Mary, wife of Chauncey, 572
Henry W., 628
Julia, 631
Widow Polly, of Abner, 639
Matthew, 645
Abi, 658
Dan, 679
Matilda, 703
Sarah, 712
Rhoda, wife of Matthew, 715
Mary, 732
Lois C., 978
Rebecca, 1067
William W., 1098
S. Adeline, 1120
Mrs. Fanny, 1381

CLARY.

Eliza F., 1290

CLOYES.

Benjamin, 1368
Sarah, wife of Benjamin, 1369

COATS.

Chloe Almira, 630

COGSWELL.

Matilda, 531
Mary, 701
Elizabeth, wife of Rev. Jonathan, 714

COLEMAN.

John, 74
Experience, wife of John, 75

COLLINS.

Marilla, 870
Alonzo, 1007

CONE.

Hetty, 363
Erastus, 371

COMINGS.

Dr. B. N., 1109
Maria, wife of Dr. B. N., 1110
Emma S., 1411

COOK.

Oliver D., 227
Lucy B., wife of Nathan R., 897
Nathan R., 909
Lewis R., 1218

COOLEY.

Sarah, 1117

CORNWELL.

Isabel, 215
Robert, 296
Wife of Robert, 297
Chauncey, 401
Abigail S., 615
Mary B., 669
Stephen W., 688
Robert, 798
Francis, 799
Adeline, 895
Sarah G., 935
Arthur T., 1243

COSLETT.

Mary, 404
Lydia S., 488
Sarah, Widow of Francis, 636

COUCH.

Huldah, 201
Ebenezer, 336

COUPLES.

Matilda, wife of Robert, 1362

COWLES.

Pitkin, 304

CRANDALL.

Polly, 291

CROSBY.

Sylvia, wife of Elisha, 894

CULVER.

Nelson S., 1436
Mary M., wife of Nelson S., 1437

CURTISS.

Polly, wife of Shubel, 362
Samuel E., 761
Julia Ann, 800
Lucius W., 1456
Olive W., wife of Lucius W., 1457

CYLER.

Dr. Vernor, 1196
Caroline R., wife of Dr. Vernor, 1197

DARLING.

Mary A., 1215

DARROW.

Clarissa, 1133

DAY.

Mary Ann, wife of J., 801

DEMING.

Anna, 551
Chloe, widow of Treat, 573
Elizabeth L., 939

DEWEIR.

Julia Anna, 1379

HART.

Lydia, - - - - 412
Rosetta, wife of Salmon, - 415
Jesse, - - - - 430
Salmon, - - - - - 441
Selah, - - - - 453
Jemima, wife of Selah, - - 454
Chester, - - - - 481
Jonathan, - - - 483
Ira, - - - - - 484
Orpha, wife of Ira, - - 485
Salome, - - - - 498
Emily, - - - - - 503
Adna, - - - - 516
Sophia, - - - - - 533
Amzi W., - - - - 537
Aaron, jun., - - - 542
Widow Sarah, - - - 546
Widow Rhoda, - - - - 563
Caroline U., - - - 602
Artemas E., - - - - 622
Lucy, wife of Abijah, - - 634
Sarah, widow of Stephen, - 638
Stephen, - - - - 646
Cynthia, wife of Stephen, - 647
Mehitable, wife of Edmund, - 654
Samuel M., - - - 686
Mary G., - - - - 713
Elijah, 4th, - - - 722
Louisa, wife of Elijah, 4th, - 723
Elizabeth, wife of Cyrus, - 724
Lucinda, - - - - 770
Burdette, - - - - 771
George, - - - - 812
Elizabeth, wife of George, - 813
Jonathan T., - - - 814
Samuel W., M. D., - - 815
Juliette, - - - - 816
Louisa, - - - - - 896
Cyrus, - - - - 917
Angeline C., - - - 936
Lucina, - - - - 937
Rev. Levi W., - - - 944
Norman L., - - - 945
Deacon Norman, - - 954
Antoinette, - - - - 960
Newton F., - - - 972
Nancy A., - - - - 985
Ellen, - - - - - 1033

HARTMAN.

Mrs. Catharine D., - - - 1383
Ernest August, - - - 1420

HAWLEY.

Dr. Roswell, - - - 1068
Mary, wife of Dr. Roswell, - 1069
Jane, second wife of Dr. Roswell, - 1100

HAYES.

Mary L., - - - - 1455

HAZZARD.

Stephen, - - - - 587

HENRY.

Esther, - - - - 1112

HIGGINS.

Josephine, - - - - 1137
Nelson, - - - - - 1155
Delia B., wife of Nelson, - - 1156
Mary E., - - - 1410

HILLS.

Elvira, - - - - 711

HINSDALE.

John, - - - - 162
Elizabeth, wife of John, - 163
Gilman, - - - - 1015
Anna, wife of Gilman, - - 1016
Mary Louisa, - - - 1020
Marilla, wife of Gilman, - 1146

HOBART.

John M., - - - - 720

HOLLISTER.

Sarah, wife of Stephen, - - 79
Stephen, - - - 169

HOLMES.

Everett C., - - - - 1150
Laura P., wife of Everett C., - 1151

HOTCHKISS.

Ladwick, - - - - 67
Wife of Ladwick, - - 68
Lemuel, - - - - 121
Wife of Lemuel, - - 188
Martha, wife of Ladwick, jun., - 278
Ann R., - - - - - 1085
Mary P., wife of Alvin, - - 1094
Emily F., wife of George F., - 1292
Mary L., - - - - 1408

HOUGH.

David, - - - - 756
Maria, - - - - - 757
Amy, - - - - 760
Norman, - - - - 774
Harriet, wife of Norman, - - 775
Phebe, wife of David, - - 819
Elizabeth, - - - - 820
Mary B., - - - - 881
Cordelia, - - - - 1123

HOWD.

Betsey, - - - - 736

HOWEL.

Leverett, - - - - 1224
Mary E., wife of Leverett, - 1225

HUBBARD.

Abiathar, - - - - 965

HULL.

Betsey, - - - - 662
Widow Lucy, - - - - 821

HUMPHREY.

Mary F., wife of William, - - 1088

HURLBURT.

Enos S., - - - - 750
Priscilla H., wife of Julius, - 1230

JEROME.

Arma, - - - - 1030
Anna, wife of Arma, - - 1031
Olive, - - - 1032

JEROME.

Emily A., 1108
Franklin M., 1238

JONES.

Eliza S. W., wife of Rev. Henry, 588
Rezin G., 773
Aurelia, wife of William B., 1072
Deveraux, 1217
Aurelia Melvina, 1367

JUDD.

Benjamin, 22
Wife of Benjamin, 23
James, 38
Uriah, 39
Wife of Uriah, 40
Nathan, 41
Wife of Nathan, 42
Phineas, 43
Wife of Phineas, 44
John, sen., 45
Wife of John, sen., 46
John, jun., 134
Wife of John, jun., 135
Wife of Seth, 151
Anthony, 178
James, 195
Selah, 199
Esther, wife of James, 318
Nancy, 360
Aurora, 369
Daniel, 435
Hannah, wife of Daniel, 436
James, jun., 459
Salome, wife of James, jun., 460
Almira, 500
Polly, wife of William, 524
Harry, 540
Emma, wife of Samuel, 560
Betsey, wife of John, 632
Ursula, widow of John, 637
John, 674
William, jun., 705
Nancy, 730
Julia A., wife of Harry, 733
Eliza, wife of Richard, 822
Oliver S., 823
Julia A., wife of Amon, 898
Deacon Morton, 918
Emily A., wife of Oliver, 959
Samuel, 969
Deacon Albert D., 1028
Richard, 1119
Hannah B., 1121
Hubert L., 1125
Julia E., wife of Hubert L., 1126
Lorin F., 1190
Josephine, M., wife of Lorin F., 1191
Edward M., 1235
Jane P., wife of Edward M., 1299
Martha, wife of Rollin, 1326
Ethan, 1335
Melissa, wife of, 1336
Rollin D., 1377
Martha L., 1378
Grace Ellen, 1387

KEENEY.

Widow Mary, of Hart, 1099

KELSEY.

John, 57
Wife of John, 58
Maria S., 600
Julia Ann, 766
Abi, wife of David, 958
Caroline A., wife of Enoch, 1058

KENYON.

Widow Jane K., 1228

KEUREN.

Mrs. Julia F. Van, 1312

KILBOURN.

Ruth, 15
Wife of Daniel, 18
Daniel, 70
Anna, wife of Joseph, 78
John, 86
Mehitable, 157
Josiah, 200

KNAPP.

Mary E., wife of Frederick, 1074
Frederick, 1163

KOEHLER.

Adolphus, 1422
Margaret, wife of, 1423

LAMB.

Jemima, 71

LAMPSON.

Harriet N., 824

LANGDON.

John, 107
Wife of John, 108

LAWRENCE.

Harriet L., wife of Stephen R., 1318
Emma C., 1359
Stephen R., 1447

LEE.

Widow Elizabeth, 24
Deacon Josiah, 33
Wife of Deacon Josiah, 34
Isaac, 35
Wife of Isaac, 36
Stephen, 37
Kata, wife of Stephen, 73
Abigail, wife of Isaac, 3d, 154
Isaac, 3d, 168
Elizabeth, wife of Col. Isaac, 170
Mary, third wife of Col. Isaac, 177
Nancy, wife of Isaac, jun., 348
Isaac, jun., 351
Thomas, 356
Electa, wife of Thomas, 357
Minerva, 385
Betsey, wife of Isaac, 386
Thirza, 504
Dr. Thomas G., 545
Electa, 583
Caroline, 609
Nancy, wife of Philip, 655
I. N., 694

MERWIN.

James B., 1065

MILLER.

Elizabeth B., wife of Darius, 1291

MILLS.

Mary 827

MINOR.

John B., 1143
Willie A., 1361

MIX.

Elisha, 828

MOORE.

Mrs. Mary L., 1344
Mary L., 1346
Emma L., 1357
Mrs. Emily, 1394

MORGAN.

Mrs. Louisa O., 1330

MORSE.

Samuel R., 697
Anna C., wife of William, 963
Hannah, 1022
Ann E., 1208

MURPHY.

John W., 741

MURRAY.

Ann E., 992

NEWELL.

Lucy, 661
Mary Ann, wife of John A., 1073

NICKERSON.

Susan, wife of Rev. Major A., 772

NOBLE.

Sylvester W., 1234
Sarah, 1298

NORRIS.

Hugh Henry, 1226
Emma G., wife of Hugh Henry, 1227

NORTH.

Lydia, 146
James, 149
Wife of James, 150
Mercy, 153
Asher, 259
Wife of Asher, 260
Alvin, 330
Anna, wife of Alvin, 331
Orpha, 366
Betsey, wife of Seth J., 396
Clarissa, wife of Alvin, 411
James, jun., 443
Seth J., 449
Eliza S., 593
Henry, 2d, 624
William B., 650
Sarah, wife of William B., 651
Henry, 743
Lauretta, wife of Henry, 744
Harriet A., 769
Frederick H., 829
Sarah R., 830

NORTH.

Hubert F., 831
Adeline, 832
Julia A., 899
Georgiana, 903
Louisa, 904
Cordelia M., 934
Omri M., 1061
Cybelia, wife of Omri M., 1062
Lucius J., 1063
John C., 1064

NORTHEND.

Charles, 1144
Lucy Ann, wife of Charles, 1145
John, 1161
Charles A., 1162

NORTHROP.

Harriet Maria, 1449

NOYES.

Sarah J., 1138

OLDS.

Caroline S., wife of Oliver P., 888

ORTIZ.

Elizabeth C., wife of Pedro P., 1280

OSBORNE.

Charles E., 1286
Elam P., 1328
Maria, wife of Elam P., 1329
Lydia M., 1354
Platt D., 1401

OSGOOD.

Polly, 262
Julia Maria, wife of Lester, 641

PARKER.

Isabella, 836
Julius, 864
Lucinda, wife of Julius, 891
Henrietta, 998
Ellen W., 1178
Mrs. Eunice S., 1373
Charles J., 1392
William E., 1416

PARSONS.

Isaac, 129
Wife of Isaac, 130
Fanny, wife of Henry L., 635
Orville W., 738
Eliza, 739
Widow Dorcas, 782
Henry L., 924

PATTERSON.

Deacon John, 2
Wife of Dea. John, 3
William, 55
Anna, 80
Ruth, 81
Sarah, wife of William, 82

PEASE.

Asaph, 1036
Clotilda, wife of Asaph, 1037
Julius W., 1038
Mary H., wife of Julius W., 1039

INDEX

ALPHABETICALLY ARRANGED, SHOWING THE PAGE WHERE SUCH NAMES OCCUR IN THIS WORK AS ARE NOT DIRECTLY OR INDIRECTLY REPRESENTED BY NUMBERS.

www.ingramcontent.com/pod-product-compliance
Lightning Source LLC
LaVergne TN
LVHW021257110826
845150LV00003B/409
9781425560744